SELECTED VITAL RECORDS
FROM THE

Jamaican
Daily Gleaner

LIFE ON THE ISLAND OF JAMAICA
AS
SEEN THROUGH NEWSPAPER EXTRACTS

Volume 1: 1865-1915

Compiled by
Madeleine E. Mitchell

HERITAGE BOOKS
2007

HERITAGE BOOKS

AN IMPRINT OF HERITAGE BOOKS, INC.

Books, CDs, and more—Worldwide

For our listing of thousands of titles see our website
at
www.HeritageBooks.com

Published 2007 by
HERITAGE BOOKS, INC.
Publishing Division
65 East Main Street
Westminster, Maryland 21157-5026

The Gleaner Company Limited of Kingston, Jamaica is the source
and copyright holder of the material used in this book. I am grateful
to the Gleaner for permission to use extracts from the newspaper for
the volumes of the book. I acknowledge the help of Leslie Wolfinger
and Debbie Riley of Heritage Books in the publishing of this book.

International Standard Book Number: 978-0-7884-4497-5

For my sisters Nora and Janet

Contents

Selected Vital Records from the Jamaican Daily Gleaner

Contents

Introduction

I started extracting births, deaths and marriages from the Daily Gleaner Newspaper of Jamaica, West Indies in 1984, to find genealogy on my own family. These Vital Records were taken from Microfilms, and in the last two years from on-line sources, (Gleaner Archives) of this newspaper up to 2006. Later I found myself finding items for other families, so although it started out to be a personal family search, it has ended up to be a wider picture of what Jamaican ancestors saw in the paper as they lived it. I also added other items to extract that reflected what my ancestors were involved with in their everyday life. The compilation is biased towards the parish of St Ann and particularly to Brown's Town the place where I was born, but there is a wider spread across the island, in lists of scholars who passed Cambridge Local Examinations and the Royal College of Music exams for example. Names of families I knew at school or by repute were also extracted.

Because of the way it was initiated this is a "Selected" not exhaustive work of the births, deaths and marriages columns of the paper. If you know there was an event, but it is not covered in these pages, there could be several explanations. 1) I was not looking for the family name therefore I have not extracted it. You will recognize that extraction from microfilm takes an instant decision making process to determine if that event is to be saved for the work, and I did not set out initially to do other than my own family names. When I knew that people were interested in a name I added it to my save file, but the earlier films that I had processed were not re-read to find the new names. I did not read the films in strictly chronological order, but skipped about. 2) The event was in a missing issue on the microfilm. There were often notes where the microfilm itself stated that there were missing issues of the paper. Sometimes there were holidays and the paper was not printed. Sometimes the first and second pages were missing. Sometimes there were whole months that were missing e.g. 1903 where July to December were missing on the microfilm I received. (After the 1907 earthquake it was a few weeks before the Gleaner recovered and was printed). It is possible that some other source might have the missing issues. For example the microfilm I read did not have my grandfather's obituary, but some one found it in newsprint form in a library and sent a photocopy to me. 3) The period covered by this volume did not have a Sunday Gleaner issued at all, so the issues covered did not include this day. 4)..Your ancestor might not have had the event sent to the Gleaner. My birth was not entered by my parents, although my older sister's birth was sent in by them. They did not explain to me why this was so. 5) It did cost to have birth, deaths and marriages included in the Gleaner. Some families could not afford to pay the fee even for running it once. To print the event for several days was quite expensive for those times. For example in 1874, it cost 3 shillings to insert a marriage announcement. 6) For births, deaths and marriages the Gleaner from earliest times had that information on the second page of the paper. Occasionally, I noted that a death notice occurred on a page other than page 2. This was more often the case for pre 1900 issues than for later issues. I could have missed some if they were not obvious. Sometimes the column with "Current Items" had an obit but there was no item in the column for vital records and I may have missed it.

Selected Vital Records from the Jamaican Daily Gleaner

The "all name" Index includes not only the names associated with births, deaths and marriages but the names of people attending events, like political meetings, parochial board meetings, agricultural shows, and ministers who married couples, and the sometimes the brothers and sisters and other family members of the deceased. People also wrote notices to thank those who had sent condolence telegrams, notes, cards and letters. The Gleaner was not always consistent in naming people. So in the index you may find the same person listed for example under. Jones, A.B, .Jones, Hon. A.B., Jones, Mr. A.B., Jones, Rev. A.B., Jones, Rev. Ambrose B., Jones, Rev. Dr. Ambrose Bernard (hypothetical name for illustrative purposes) etc. In fact I would recommend that if you are looking for Jones that you check the whole of the listing under "J" in the index. There were sometimes where I knew the person and corrected obvious errors and other times when I was not sure if the same person was intended. Some names in the index could be different families like Isaac and Isaacs but there could have been typographical errors in the Gleaner which I copied. Another example is where the name was written as DePass, or Depass or dePass in the Gleaner. It is not clear if these are the same or different families, so I have left them as indexed and all should be searched. I could also have made typographical errors although I tried not to do so.

When you read a BMD item it may be helpful to take note of where the submitter suggests other countries papers should copy. So for example if at the end a birth notice says "Canadian papers please copy", it is likely that the person had family members in Canada. This may give a lead as to where to find your family. Some foreign papers did pick up the Jamaican items for inclusion in their vital records.

I would recommend that if you find an extract in this volume that you check it yourself in the Gleaner. The paper's archives are now on-line and armed with the date that the extract appeared from this book, you can find the issue. I say this because the Optical reader the site uses has some difficulty with the newsprint and it is hard to determine if you want to read a "hit". So searching by keywords is not as easy as it might appear at first. The site is a pay site at:
 http://gleaner.newspaperarchive.com/DesktopDefault.aspx   The charge is $49.99 for a year or $7.95 for a day (one time payment) in 2007. I have no financial interest in this site. Alternatively you can try to get the microfilm by interlibrary loan through a library, most successfully a university library.

Some World Headlines were included because I wanted to know what my ancestors were reading about the world at that time. There was quite a bit on the Monarchy and authors such as Thomas Hardy. You will find many references to Rudyard Kipling. That is because my sister was writing a book about him and was interested in when he went to Jamaica. Tom Redcam the Poet Laureate of Jamaica was a cousin, his last name being Macdermot (read backwards). I was interested in Vomiting sickness of Jamaica which is now acknowledged to be caused by a toxin in the unripe Ackee fruit. I was keen to learn how this was noted in the press and how the cause was discovered. Most people would overlook the small print headlines of this event that seemed more acute when food was in short supply, but I was looking for it. World War I was featured in the last two years of this volume (the second volume continues from 1916-1939 (in preparation). A list of soldiers who volunteered in the second contingent is on the World Gen Web Jamaica site at: http://www.rootsweb.com/~jamwgw/index.htm

The Daily Gleaner was first published in 1834 as an advertising sheet and had little news. Two issues are available from that year, and one from 1858 on microfilm but the collection really starts at the Morant Bay Rebellion in 1865. The Gleaner became an island wide institution and in fact you will find many Jamaicans today who call any newspaper The Gleaner. In the early days many more events of births, deaths and marriages were of Kingston folk because this was where it was published. Later the telegraph was extensively used by correspondents and more country news was included.

Introduction

I found it fascinating to see how the paper developed over the period and it had its own style of writing of which Microsoft Word does not always approve. (When I was proofreading a year it would often want me to reword the Gleaner's writing). Of course Jamaica being an English Colony, the newspaper used the spelling of British English rather than American English, so I had to instruct Word to ignore this spelling.

My mother enjoyed reading this compilation and she would input names for example on births where the Gleaner only had a daughter or a son was born to Mr. and Mrs. So and So. She really encouraged me to continue this quest, even when it became harder to do because the print was so fine and the on-line newspaper was more time consuming to browse.

Sadly she passed away at 95 years in 2006, so will not see these books finally finished. Still she saw almost all of it, and most of the second volume too. I hope you enjoy it and find it as useful as she did.

Madeleine Mitchell,
Dunnellon, FL 34432-2795
U.S.A.
February, 2007

1865

[In 1865 THE MORANT BAY REBELLION WAS REPORTED IN WHICH JOSEPH WATERHOUSE RUTTY WAS SEVERALLY INJURED AND LEFT FOR DEAD. Rev. W.C. MURRAY WAS ASSIGNED TO BATH, ST THOMAS IN THE EAST AT THE TIME]

Reel #1 NP418 September 13, December 6, 13 1834 and May 1858

No Items

Reel #2 NP418 September 16, October 13-November 30, 1865

November 6, 1865
BROWN'S TOWN

By a private letter received on Saturday last we understand that an outbreak was threatened on Thursday last at the above named place arising out of suits of ejection on Mr Ingram against certain parties. One hundred of the 2nd W.I. Regiment had been ordered to proceed to Brown's Town

November 7, 1865
BROWN'S TOWN

"Rumour with her many tongues" was busy yesterday circulating a report to the effect the Brown's Town in the parish of St Ann's had been destroyed by fire. We have the pleasure in stating that the rumour was false; for a letter dated 8 p.m. on Saturday evening reported that parish exceedingly quiet.

November 20, 1865
DISMISSAL OF VOLUNTEER

Mr George F. Judah, Sergeant Major of the St Thomas ye East Volunteers was publicly dismissed from the service in front of his corps on Friday morning last at 10 o'clock for having written an untrue statement to the Colonial Standard newspaper of this city reflecting on the conduct of Brigadier General Nelson. We feel confident that the measures adopted have been necessary for a more honourable upright and courteous officer than Brigadier General Nelson could not have been found to fulfill duties he has performed. "The tongue of the wise useth knowledge aright"

1

1866

January 26, 1866
ARRIVALS IN THE CITY

Barkly House

Mr and Mrs Isaacs------------Brown's Town
Mr Hopwood-------------------St Elizabeth

January 29, 1866
At Falmouth on 23rd instant at the residence of J.A. Vine Esq of a lingering and painful illness which she bore with patience Mary Isabella Jane aged 14 years the beloved daughter of James Fletcher Esq " Her end was peace, Blessed are the dead which die in the Lord"

February 3, 1866
Wesleyan Services Tomorrow

Spanish Town------------- Rev W. C. Murray

February 17, 1866
ARRIVALS IN THE CITY

Blandal Hall

The most noble the Marquis of Lorne---Southampton
Mr Isaacs----------------------------- Manchester
Mr James-----------------------------St Ann's

February 21, 1866
DIED
At Goshen Estate, St Mary on the 12th February 1866 Mr John Clement aged 48 years and two months leaving a widow an 5 children and a circle of friends to lament their irreparable loss. " Blessed are the dead who die in the Lord"

February 23, 1866
Arrivals in the city

Date Tree Hall

Mr J Duffus-------------Bowden
Mrs Duffus--------------Bowden
DIED
At Battery Place, Rothsay, Scotland, Andrew Scott, Esq late of this City in the 42 year of his age. Leaving a widow and two children to deplore his loss. He was buried on the 2nd inst [February] in the Necropolis, Glasgow, beside the remains of his late father

February 24,1866
DIED
In the City on the 21st inst at her late residence No 27 King Street Miss Elizabeth Petrie. The deceased was sister to the late Mrs Hoyes who died on the 5th inst. "The sisters" were the oldest inhabitants of King Street and have been and have been know as examples of an integrity and harmony during a long and useful lifetime

Monday February 26, 1866
Mr D. D. Depass
We regret to announce the death by drowning of the above named gentleman, who was the son of A. D. Depass Esq formerly merchant of this city and at present resident in London. Mr DePass was on his way to Melbourne from London on board the Steamship "London"

DIED
At Port Antonio, on Monday the 19th inst. Emily Schoults infant daughter of Mr R. C. J.Bacquie aged 4 years

March 6, 1866
ARRIVALS IN THE CITY
Miss Blake

Alexander Escoffery---------------Portland

March 14, 1866
SMALL POX
WE regret to say that Small Pox has again made its appearance in this City. There are we learn two cases in Matthews Lane

March 16, 1866
WOLMERS
A meeting of the trustee of this institution is called on Tuesday the 20th inst at 10 o'clock

March 29, 1866
MARRIED
At Port Antonio Christ Church on Wednesday the 21st inst by the Revd William Smith Rector assisted by the Revd Evan Jones of Manchioneal Mr Alexander Wolcott Escoffery to Miss Ann Eliza Wilkinson

1866

April 9, 1866
BIRTH
AT Malvern Village near this city on 7th inst Mrs Napoleon Alberga of a son

April 10. 1866
W.R.MYERS, Esq

We regret to announce the death of W. R. Myers Esqr Secretary to the Executive Committee at Spanish Town yesterday. Mr Myers was in poor health previous to the late rebellion and grew gradually worse after his onerous duties during that trying period. He has left a widow and many children.

May 17, 1866
Small Pox

We learn by yesterday's Post that a case of Small Pox had occurred at a place called Clarksonville a short distance from Brown's Town. At the last named place Dysentry had appeared and proved fatal in many cases

Reel # 3 May 24, 1866-December 29, 1866

June 8, 1866
Passengers Arrived
In the Steamer Caraibe from
Cape Hayti

Mr P.Gaultier

September 13, 1866
SUBSCRIPTION IN TRELAWNY TO THE EYRE TESTINMINIAL

The following is a statement of the collection made in the Parish in aid of the Testimonial which is to be presented to our late Governor Edward John Eyre Esquire as a mark of general and grateful appreciation for the eminent services rendered by him to the Inhabitants of the Island in suppressing the late Rebellion.

Honourable H Nunes Custos	£10 10 0
William Sewell	£10 10 0
H.M. Purchas	£3 0 0
W. H. Rutty	£1 1 0
J. W. Fisher	£5 5 0
C.J. Moulton Barret	£31 10 0
Rev D.R. Littlejohn	£2 2 0

October 23, 1866
At Lindale Pen, St Ann's, October 10, 1866 Mr E. W. Morris Esq. of Kingston, to Emma Lamar Brough , dau of the late Jos Brough Esq. No Cards

November 12, 1866
Suddenly at his Residence in Moneague, St Ann's on the 1st November instant Soloman DaSilva Lindo aged 61 years, deeply and sincerely mourned by his surviving children relatives and friends.

5

November 23, 1866
LIGHTING THE CITY WITH GAS

1867

January 4, 1867

Advertisement for De Cordova's sheet almanac includes the information that the following were agents:

St Ann's Bay: H.E. Delisser Esq
Falmouth. H. Desousa, Esq
Chapelton: N. Sutherland Esq
Port Antonio: A. Escoffery. Esq

A coloured or uncoloured Map of Jamaica was also available for 1 shilling

January 7, 1867
Passengers arrived in RMC Steamer Seine, from Southampton:

Hon B. Vickers

January 8, 1867
THE MINERALS WATER OF ST. ANN.

A coroners Inquest was held at Cassia Park, in the parish of St. Andrew, on the 3rd instant, before J. R. Brice, Esq, Coroner, on the body of a man named Charles Lindsay, who came to his death by having drank a quantity-nearly half a pint-of the Mineral Water lately discovered at a place named Windsor, in the parish of St Ann. The deceased was attacked with ague and fever, and following, no doubt the popular delusion that the water is capable of curing any and every diseases, procured a bottle of the water, which he repeatedly drank; the water produced violent purging with excruciating pain in the bowels, which never abated till the unfortunate man expired. The jury returned a verdict that the deceased came to his death by drinking immoderately of the Mineral Water of St Ann's.

January 3, 1867
At his Marise, Villa, St Mary's on the morning of thee 15th ult (December), Robert Clemetson, Esq., aged 70 years, Justice of the Peace, Coroner, Harbour Master, and Proprietor of Frenton Estate, leaving a disconsolate widow, and a large family to mourn their irreparable loss.

7

Selected Vital Records from the Jamaican Daily Gleaner

Who dies in Christ, yet lives; who lives in Him,
Dies not, for where Christ is, there is no death.

January 10, 1867
January 6th at Belfast Penn, Morant Bay, the wife of the Revd W. Teall, Baptist Missionary, of a son

January 10, 1867
The Eyre Prosecution

DR Alexander Fiddes, A. H. Lewis, Esq., and Mr A. W. H. Lake, left this city yesterday in the Steamer Seine, for England, it is said, to give information to found a Bill to be presented before the Grand Jury of Middlesex in the prosecution of governor Eyre.

January 11, 1867
VOLUNTEER CORPS DISBANDED

His Excellency the Governor has disbanded the Kingston No 3 Rifles, and the St Ann No. 1 riffles.

January 25, 1867
In this City, on the morning of the 19th inst, Peter Desnoes, Esq., aged 53 years

January 26, 1867
SUNDAY SERVICES TO-MORROW

Providence
Revds. R. M. Parnther, W. C. Murray, and W. Reeves

Presbt. Church East Queen St
Rev J. Watson

February 5, 1867
At Morgon's Valley, Clarendon, on the 30th Ult Jacob B. 8th son of the late Matthew Farquharson, of St Elizabeth aged 34 years

February 8, 1867
On the 10th ult. at the Parish Church of North Stoneham near Southampton by the Revd. George Thornton Mostyn, of St John's Kelburn Park, cousin of the Bridegroom, assisted by the Rev F.F. Beadon, M.A. Robert Thomas Baker, the only son of the late Matthew Baker, Esq. Q. C. of Dublin, to Mary eldest daughter of William Bailey, Esquire, Merchant of this city.

February 7, 1867
Stewart Town
NOTICE

Having Purchased the Stock in Trade, Debts, &c., from Messers Charles S. Cover & co, the subscriber will continue the Business and solicits a continuance of the support hither to bestowed
He requests all parties indebted will at once arrange their account. JOHN ELLIS

1867

The subscribers having sold out their stock in Trade Debts, &c to Mr John Ellis of Dry Harbours, request that partied indebted to the late business will arrange their account with them. all debts due by the business will be sealed at maturity by the Mr. Cover. C. S. Cover & CO

February 26, 1867
A list of Wesleyan Ministers Stations for the Coming year; (abridged by extractor)

Rev. John Corlett (with catechist) Spanish Town.
Rev R. M. Parnther, Morant Bay
Rev W. Hodgson, Watsonville
Rev W. Reeves, Duncans
Rev J.W. Rowbottom, Brown's town
Rev W. C. Murray, Bath
Rev John Duff, Black River

February 28, 1867
On the 23rd inst, at Bath, St Thomas ye East, by the Rev C. F. Douet, Island Curate, Sutton Beierly, fourth son of the late Richard Scolteck Esquire, of the County of Salop, England to Elizabeth Serena second surviving daughter of the lat e, Charles H . McDermott of this Island.

March 18 1867
At the Lodge, St. Thomas ye Vale, on the 5th inst. John Herman Hall, Esq, in the 64th year of his age

March 19, 1867
At Pedro River, in the Parish of St Ann, on Saturday, the 2nd inst., Richard Henry Souch Heming, Esq aged 67 years

April 1, 1867
At her residence in Monk Street, Spanish-Town on the morning of the morning of the 29th March, in the 51st year of her age, Caroline Redware, relict of the late Andrew Graham Dignum, Attorney-at-Law, and daughter of the Rev. Lewis Bowerbank, M. A. for many years a rector of this island,

April 9, 1867
PASSENGER ARRIVED

In the French Str. Carabelle--Mr Joseph Levy from St. Jago-de-Cuba

April 11, 1867
On the 8th inst., at Suttons, in the Parish of Clarendon, Mrs Croskery, of a daughter

At the Orchard, Port Royal Mountains, on Wednesday, the 3rd day of April, instant after a long and painful illness, Edward Ninkell Robinson, M. D., MRCS, England late Practiner in this City. age 35 yrs.

April 18, 1867
On the 12th inst at Yallahs, St David's by the Rev G. Del Rio, Charles Gresham, youngest son of the late Peter Slader, Esq of the county of Devonshire, England to

Juliana Matilda, eldest daughter of George Burrell Snaith, Esq., of Green Wall, St Davids. No Cards

Richard Ross--Information respecting the present address of Richard Ross, who, in July 1865, was in St. Ann's Bay, will be thankfully received at this Office.

May 2, 1867
At Friendship, St Elizabeth, on Friday April 26, 1867, Frances Elizabeth, the wife of the Revd. Robert B. Lynch.

May 8, 1867
The Friends and Acquaintances of Mr Alexr. Burke, are requested to attend his remains this afternoon, at half-past four o'clock from his Residence, No 6, East Queen Street to the place of Burial

May 23, 1867
At Port Antonio on the 19th inst., the wife of Mr. A. W. Escoffery, of a daughter

May 24, 1867
At St. Michaels Church, Kingston, on the 22nd instant, by the Revd Duncan Campbell, Rector of Kingston, assisted by the Revd. C. P. Street, John Fisher, Esq, Surgeon Royal Navy to Susan Elizabeth eldest Daughter of Thomas Heath, Esq, of Worthy Park, Jamaica

July 4, 1867
At Stewart Town, Trelawny, on Sunday 30th ult (June) Mary, the beloved wife of T. P. Kidd, Esq after a protracted illness which she bore with Christian resignation, leaving a large family and a numerous circle of friends to mourn their irreparable loss. "Blessed are the dead which die in the Lord"

July 6, 1867
QUEER NAME-NAME THIS CHILD !

A Lynchburgh paper states, that in Montgomery County, Virginia, a child was christened--"Andrew Jackson Gordon James Buchannan Raise The Flag and Fire the Cannon Dobyns"

July 11, 1867
In the City of Panama, State of Colombia on the morning of the 1st July, after a long and protracted illness which he bore with fortitude and resignation, Mr. J. N. Bonnitto a native of this City, at the age of 34 years and 4 months leaving mother , sister brothers and a large circle of relatives and acquaintance s to deplore their loss. The deceased resided one half his life time in the United States and latterly on the Isthmus of Panama, and during that period, had gained the esteem and respect of all who had the pleasure of knowing him.

July 18, 1867
On the 8th inst, at the Residence of the Revd. Isaac --ehouse, Elletson Road, (Kingston), Emma Alice the beloved daughter of Mr Robert B. Braham, Manchester, aged 11 months and 9 days

1867

August 8, 1867
On the 4th inst, the wife of Henry E. Delisser, Esqr, St Ann's Bay of a son

At Kepp Penn, St Elizabeth on the 20th ult, the wife of S. J. Manley, Esq of a son.

At Kepp Pen, St Elizabeth, on the night of the 20th ult, Samuel John Christian, the beloved and eldest Son of S. J. Manley, Esq after four days illness of Typhoid Fever, aged two years and nine months

At Kepp Pen, St Elizabeth on Saturday 27th July last S. J. Manley Esqr, aged 35 years. The demise of this truly good man is deeply mourned by a young and amiable wife, his relatives, and all who had the pleasure of his acquaintance

St New Savanna, on Tuesday the 30th July last, Samuel John , infant son of the late S. J. Manley, Esq.

August 9, 1867
At Rae's Town on the 30th ult, the Wife of James Dayes, Esq of a Daughter

August 21, 1867
At Glasgow, Scotland, on the 18th ult, Alexander Wallace, Esq, Engineer, formerly of this Island

September 6, 1867
At Gateacre, near Liverpool, on the 11th August, Thomas Roxburgh, Esq late of this city, in the 76th year of his age.

September 11, 1867
THE LATE HON. W.C.McDOUGALL
By the demise of the Hon. W. C. McDougall, late Judge of the Supreme Court of this Island, the Jamaica Treasury has been relieved of the payment of an annuity of £600 (What had he done ?)

September 23, 1867
On Tuesday, the 17th Sept. at Port Royal, by the Revd. Robert Raw, Mr Simeon Hollar, of the Naval Hospital, to Ann, only daughter of Henry Darby, Esq. No Cards

November 4, 1867
At the Parish Church Mandeville, on Thursday, the 31st October, by the Rev. Wm. Forbest, Rector, Henry, youngest son of the late Richard Jackson, Esq of Dunkeid, to Louisa, third daughter of the late Frederick Peart, Esq. of New Ark, all of the Parish of Manchester--No Cards

November 8, 1867
THE C.P.D. AT BROWN'S TOWN

Mr Abraham Harris, the Collector of Petty Debts, for the Brown's Town District of the Parish of St. Ann, has written to us to contradict the report of his suspension in consequence of a charge of extortion. We readily give currency to Mr. Harris' contradiction, and await farther information on the subject

Selected Vital Records from the Jamaican Daily Gleaner

Nothing to end of film

1868

January 6, 1868

At his residence, Sutton Street, on Monday Evening, December 30th, Mr Mark Hendriks a native of Black River in the 52nd year of his age, 30 of which was spent in this city. He was one of the few survivors of the Eight Persons who founded the Christian Union Established Church B Society in this city 21 years ago. He was of meek and quiet spirit, yet naturally cheerful. Depression in his business latterly tended greatly to undermine his health. He had to pass through scenes of great trial, but he bore them with calm submission and pious resignation, having a desire "to depart and be with Christ". He has left a widow and nine children, besides several relatives and friends, to mourn his loss.

January 20, 1868

On Tuesday, the 14th at Sunflower, St Thomas, Caroline, younger sister of Mr Murray, Wesleyan Minister, aged 14 years, 11 months.

January 24, 1868

At Murphy Hill Pen, St Ann's on Saturday night, the 19th inst, Isabel Maud Henriet, the beloved infant daughter of William Michelin, Esquire, aged 12 months. Thy will be done.

February 4, 1868

On Sunday morning, the 2nd instant the wife of Mr Amos Morais, of a daughter

February 8, 1868

On the 7th January 1868, at the Manse Menimail, Fifeshire, Scotland, by the Revd D. S. Maxwell, William Wallace, Esq of Newton, to Alice, third daughter of the late Jas. Maxwell, Esq M. D. of Evandal, Metcalf.

February 10, 1868

The Friends and Acquaintances of the late Colin Campbell, Esqr,. are requested to attend his Remains from his late Residence, corner of Milk and Highholborn Strs to the Place of Interment, at Half-past Four o'clk, this Evening.

On the day following: it says that he was an Inspector of Invoices and Merchant of Kingston, a member of the Society of Arts, of this City

March 12, 1868

In this City on the 9th March, after a short illness, Mrs Elizabeth G. Campbell formerly a Lodging House Keeper in Spanish Town aged 47 years. She has left a daughter and son and other relatives to mourn their loss "Thy will be done"

REPAYMENT OF CHOLERA EXPENSES TO MR COVER.

In consequence of the refusal of the Government, to reimburse Mr Cover in the sum of £38 16s 9d which was expended by him in the month April last to check the progress of Cholera and Dysentery, for sustaining the sick and destitute and for burying the dead at Stewart Town, on the ground that the expenses appeared to have been incurred without any authority whatever from the Government or from the Municipal board. Mr Septimus Barrett has made an appeal to the Public for the purpose of raising the amount by voluntary subscriptions to repay Mr Cover the sum which he has bona fide expended. We are glad in being able to state that the appeal has been readily responded to; the sum of £21 has been subscribed by several gentlemen in this parish; and that the balance will be made up by other subscribers in the course of the present week. Falmouth Post.

March 16, 1868

Letters from Stewards and reply and editorial on letters re departure of Rev W. Clarke Murray from Bath.

March 30, 1868

On the 17th February, of Streatham Church, Surrey, by the Rev. J. R. Nicholl, M. A. Rector, and Rural Dean, the Rev. Ralph Daly Cocking, B. A. Incumbent of St John the Evangelist, Maida Vale, London, W., to Sibylia Elizabeth, eldest daughter of Edward John Lane, Esq, Captain R. N.

April 1, 1868

On Thursday, 26th March at St. Michael's Church by Revd, C. Fyfe, Mr S. R. Fielding, to Miss A. E. Campbell, niece of Wm Campbell, Senr. Esq.

April 9, 1868

On the 7th inst at Water Valley Estate, Metcalf, Wife of William Macdonald, Esq of a daughter

May 9, 1868

It has been notified in the Jamaica Gazette, that His Excellency the Governor has been pleased to make the following appointments under the District Courts Law; Namely Mr John T. Palache to be Asssistant Clerk and Mr Wm Nott Isaacs to be Bailiff, to the Mandeville District Court.

June 8, 1868

On Wednesday last, at the Holy Trinity Church by the Revd. Father Joseph Dupon, S. J. Monsieur Eugene Estavard of Paris, to Madlle. Henriette Clothilde Desnoes, only daughter of the late Peter Desnoes, Esquire.

June 29, 1868

On the 9th May at Nassau, New Providence, Bahamas, Minnie, the youngest child of R. S. Turton, Esq, Lieutenant and Adjutant of the 2nd W. I. Regiment.

1868

July 2, 1868

At Rockfield, St Ann, on the 27th June, 1868 whither she had gone for change of air, Mrs Sarah A. French, wife of Thomas French, St Ann's Bay, aged 41 years. She was for 15 years a consistent member of the Wesleyan Society, and was distinguished for her genuine piety and usefulness as one of the most active and successful Collectors in the Mission cause. Her remains were followed to the grave by a large concourse of friends as a mark of the high esteem in which she was held. "Her record is on high".

July 3, 1868

On the 30th June, from Bad Management "The Sligo Water Company". The remains were interred at Government Quarters . Deeply Lamented By all. May its advent be speedy.

September 14, 1868

Died in the Town of Montego Bay, in this Island, on the 11th instant, Mr DANIEL LEVY at the advanced age of 80 years, leaving a very large circle of Children, Grand Children, and great Grand Children and numerous Relatives, to mourn their loss. The deceased was an Englishman by birth, and his residence in this country extended over Sixty-six years during which period his upright and exemplary character and his urbane and gentlemanly manners, gained for him the esteem and goodwill of all who knew him and by whom his death is greatly deplored.

October 3, 1868

At Port Royal on 30th Ultimo, Elias Wainwright Murray, father of Rev. Wm. Clark Murray, Wesleyan Minister, in the 57th year of his age.

October 27, 1868

At Port Antonio on Friday the 23rd October, after a painful illness of 24 hours, Jesse Eugenie, the only and beloved daughter of Mr Alexander W. Escoffery aged 17 months (verse)

October 28, 1868

On the 24th October, at Trafalgar, Saint Ann's, Mary Rose, the Wife of John W. Gayner, Esquire, and eldest daughter of Robert Robinson, Esquire.

October 30, 1868

On 26th instant at Belmont, St Ann's, John Wilson Davis, Esquire aged 96 years

Nothing to the end of film

1869

January 18, 1869
At Amity Hall, St Thomas, on the 15th inst. The Wife of the Revd Thomas Harty of a Girl

January 25, 1869
Mr Barnard will also be glad of information as to the present representatives of Mr Andrew Johnstone of Annandale, and Mr James Sutherland of Dunrobin, in Jamaica who were two of the Trustees to the settlement of the St Helen's Estate upon Mrs Millward and her children dated June, 1793........

February 2, 1869
At Saint Bay, 28th January, 1869, Edward Charles, infant son of E. C. Tuttie, Esq aged 4 weeks "He is taken from the evil to come".

February 8, 1869
On Thursday the 4th instant, at York Cottage, St Andrew the Wife of Thomas Hendrick, Esq, Solicitor, of a Daughter

February 19, 1869
On the 17th inst at the Mission House, Ridgemount, Mandeville, Elizabeth, the beloved wife of the Revd. W. Alloway of the London Missionary society.

March 3, 1869
THE JAMAICA CHURCH OF ENGLAND HOME AND FOREIGN MISSIONARY SOCIETY

.......They were followed shortly afterwards by Mr J. W. Fisher and Mr. Hogg (a son we understand of Sir John Weir Hogg of London).....

March 22, 1869
At Seaforth, St Thomas, on Wednesday, 10th inst by Revd W. Clark Murray, Wesleyan Minister, Henry Emanuel Lawes, Wesleyan Teacher, to Fanny Eliza Morrison.

March 29, 1869
At Savanna-la-Mar on 25th inst by the Revd Js. Cork, Rector, Frederick A. eldest son of Stephen Touzalin, Junr, to Maria Wainwright, youngest daughter of Mrs J.J. Peynada both of the same Parish

Selected Vital Records from the Jamaican Daily Gleaner

April 16, 1869

Suddenly at the "Moneague New Inn" in the Parish of St Ann, on Thursday night the 8th inst. Mr Joseph Francis Martin, aged about 50 years, leaving an afflicted sorrowing wife, many children, relatives and friends to mourn their loss. Mr Martin conducted the above "Inn" for the last twenty years; he was known throughout the Island (and by many Europeans who have come hither for a change), as a civil, polite, obliging and attentive host. He was esteemed by many and respected by all who knew him. (Verse)

April 28, 1869

At Savanna-la-Mar on the 23rd inst, the wife of Mr. C. S. Farquharson, of a son.

May 17, 1869

In this City, on the 11th instant, the Wife of John C. Nethersole, Esq, of a daughter

July 2, 1869

At Black River, on the 29th instant, at St John's Church, by the Revd. Lynch, Sarah Ann, youngest Daughter of Frederick and Euphemia Hendriks to Thomas E. Wheathe, Esq, Inspector of Constabulary

August 23, 1869

At Clermonnt , Saint Mary, on Thursday 12th August instant, the Wife of the Reverend M. Gregory Constantine, of a son.

September 3, 1869

At the Baptist Mission House, Stewart Town, in the parish of Trelawny, on Wednesday the 25th ultimo, by the Revd W. Webb, Baptist Missionary, Mr James N. Johnston, Baptist School Master, to Miss Margaret Grant, of the same place.

September 6, 1869

At St Mary's Church, St Elizabeth, on the 1st instant by the Rev. J.L. Ramson, Brother-in-Law of the Bride, Ambrose A. Finlayson, Esq. to Mary Louisa Salmon, youngest daughter of the late B.M. Senior, Esq of Compton.

October 6, 1869

On the 4th inst, the Wife of Henry E. Delisser, Mount Olivet, St Ann of a daughter

October 23, 1869

On the 21st September, at Eagle House, Highbury Hill, London, Mr David Henriques D'Souza Jr second son of Mr D. H. D'Souza of Falmouth, Jamaica

November 15, 1869

On the 10th inst, at Claremont Cottage, Savanna-la-Mar, Westmoreland, the wife of Mr E. Wainwright, of a son.

On Wednesday, the 10th November, 1869 at the Cathedral, Spanish Town, by the Rev. Mr Sullivan Mark Cornelius Hendriks, to Matilda McDowell, third daughter of Mr James S. Facey, of Brett's Pen, St Catherine, No Cards

November 19, 1869

At Port Antonio, on Wednesday, the 10th instant of Typhoid Fever, at the early age of 16 years, Letida Emily, the second daughter of Mr George Ffrench.
none to end

1870

January 5, 1870
At Port Antonio, on the 3rd instant, the wife of Mr. A. Walcott Escoffery, of a son.

January 8, 1870
On the 3rd January, 1870 at Monaltrie, St Andrew, Florence Gertrude Augusta, the infant daughter of Dr Cargill, aged 2 months and 25 days.

January 15, 1870
In the Falmouth Church on the 11th instant, by the Rev. Thomas Farrett, B.A. Rector of Trelawny, Mr. John Gordon Chisholm, Surveyor of H.M's Customs of Falmouth, to Mary Ann, daughter of Mr. Wellesley Bourke of Falmouth, Solicitor.

January 31, 1870
At the Kirk, Duke Street, on the 26th January, 1870 by the Revd. John Radcliffe, John Newlands, eldest son of the late Colin Campbell to Marsha Heslop third daughter of the late James Campbell.

April 1, 1870
At Port Antonio, on the 29th ultimo, by the Revd. George Sergeant, General Superintendent of Wesleyan Mission in the Island, the Reverend John Duff, to Emily James, second daughter of J. Malcolm Facey, Esquire.

April 16, 1870
At Brown's Town Church on the 6th inst by the Revd George Hall, Island Curate, Miss Elizabeth Ann Gayner, to William James Nash, Esq of Dry Harbour.

June 6, 1870
ON the 1st instant at St Alban's Church, in the Parish of St Elizabeth by the Rev J. L. Ramson, uncle of the bride, assisted by the Rev. R. B. Lynch, Richard Ramsden, Esq of Camp Hill Nuneaton, Warwickshire and of the Inner Temple, to Elizabeth Frances, eldest daughter of the late John Stokes Salmon, Esq. of Bagdale, St Elizabeth's and granddaughter of the Hon. John Salmon, formerly President of the Council of Jamaica

Selected Vital Records from the Jamaican Daily Gleaner

Advertisement

Falmouth June 14, 1869
Jamaica Quinine Cordial Bitters,
Manufactured by
Mr MICHAEL LAZARUS FOR
DESOUZA, SONS & LAZARUS FALMOUTH

This well-known Cordial Tonic which has now been before the Public of Jamaica for the last three years and which has been so highly spoken of by the numerous customers, and recommended by the Faculty of Trelawny, can be procured at all times of our numerous agents in the Island, viz:

In Montego Bay	of Abm. Hart
	Phillip Hart
	Chas. P Grant
St Ann's Bay	Thomas French
Port Maria	Henry Lindo
	J.B. Goffe & Co
Duncans	DSouza Sons & Lazurus
Alexandria	Geo Lannaman
	William Cover
Stewart Town	C.S. Cover
Chester Castle	J.J. Isaacs
Port Antonio	Edwd Sutherland
Moneague	A.N. Sutherland
St Ann's Bay	Robt Watson
Brown's Town	Joseph Levy

(NOTE this list is abridged)

July 3, 1870
At Bulldead House Mandeville, on the 28th ultimo the Wife of Charles Rampini Esq, Judge of the Mandeville District Court of a daughter

July 4, 1870
At Kingston, on Tuesday the 28th June, 1870, after three days illness which he bore with fortitude and resignation--Willoughby George Levy the beloved Son of Joseph and Mary Levy, of the parish of Manchester. He died in the hope of a glorious resurrection to life eternal, leaving his beloved and grieving parents, his loving and affectionate Brother and Sisters, and a large circle of sincere friends to mourn his death and their loss.

July 6, 1870
At Welchpole Penn, Westmoreland on the 3rd inst the wife of Mr C. S. Farquharson of a daughter

July 8, 1870
On Monday, the 4th July instant, at the Residence of the Bride, by the Revd Josias Cork, Rector, Margaret, only daughter of the late John McKenzie, Esq, of Water Works, Westmoreland, to Robert Tomilinson Loch, Esq of St Elizabeth.

1871

July 23, 1870

At Dumphrey Cottage, Clarendon, on Friday morning at eight o'clock after a lingering and painful illness which she bore with Christian fortitude, Mary Bevecca, the beloved Wife of Mr Jno. Jas. Hall aged 38, leaving a disconsolate husband and three young Children with numerous relatives and friends to mourn her death. The Deceased was justly esteemed for her work of love and charity among the poor as also for her amiability among the better classes. The Lord gave, and the Lord hath taken away. Blessed be the name of the Lord.

July 29, 1870

In this city, on the morning of yesterday, the 28th instant, Mr Frederick A. Judah, in the 28th year of his age. Friends will please take this intimation for the funeral this afternoon, from No 16, Oxford Street, at 5 o'clock.

August 1, 1870

At Lottery Estate in the Parish of Trelawny, on the morning of the 28th ultimo, the wife of Mr W. H. Rutty of a son.

August 3, 1870

At Port Antonio on Saturday the 30th ult, Mrs Anne Eliza, the beloved wife of Mr A. W. Escoffery, after a painful illness of 2 years, which she bore with Christian fortitude, leaving a sorrowing husband and infant and a large circle of Relatives and Friends to mourn their loss [Phrase]

August 17, 1870

In Falmouth on the 12th instant after a few hours illness, Michael Lazarus. The loss of the deceased is deplored by his brothers and friends by whom he was much regarded and esteemed -aged 55 years

August 27, 1870

From Brown's Town, A column's worth of information about an inquest into the death of a Mr Nesbit - an American - who died of wounds to the head by blows inflicted by a Mr Campbell, a shop keeper -- they had been drinking and then fighting. Mentioned in course of the evidence is " Mr Levy's Store" "Mrs Delisser's yard" and the Court House.

September 6, 1870

On the 11th August, at the residence of her son, Dr Franklin, Manchester, G. B. Miriam, the relict of the late Abraham Franklin of that city, and mother of Mr B. A. Franklin of Kingston, in her 81st year.

September 9, 1870

In this City, on the 7th instant, at Stanton Street, Mrs Jas L Verley of a daughter

September 21, 1870

In this city on Thursday the 15th inst at the Parish Church, by the Ven Duncan Campbell, M.A. assisted by the Rev. James Gayleard Oscar Dunscombe Honiball, K. D. to Evelyn Maud, daughter of Augustus Morais, Esq. No Cards.

All during this period Headlines on the Franco-Prussian War.

Selected Vital Records from the Jamaican Daily Gleaner

September 26, 1870

At Brown's Town Church, on Wednesday, the 21st instant by the Rev George Hall, Utten Thomas Todd, Junr, Esq to Louisa, second daughter of William Costa, Esq.

November 11, 1870

At New York on the 13th October last, in his 38th year Colin Campbell, youngest son of the late Colin Campbell, M.D. of Waterhouse, St Andrew.

November 17, 1870

In Panama on the 27th inst. after a few days illness, M. Anthony de Roux late of this City

December 27, 1870

On Tuesday, the 20th December (the day she was 10 months old, Alice Armistead, the beloved infant daughter of the Rev. E. Nuttall. "Our loss is her infinite gain."

December 28, 1870

At Swanswick, Trelawny, on the 5th instant, the wife of H. M. Purchas, Esq of a son.

end of reel

1871

January 4, 1871
At Water Valley Estate, Metcalfe, on 24th ult, Sibyl Emma, youngest daughter of William Macdonald, Esq, aged two years and eight months.
May she rest in peace.

This morning at No. 6. Fort Royal Street, Julia Caroline, the beloved Wife of the Reverend John Leslie Mais, of Walton, Saint Ann.

January 23, 1871
On 19th instant, at Water Valley Estate, Metcalfe, the wife of William McDonald Esq, of a daughter

February 13, 1871
At Clarksonville, Saint Ann, on Saturday, 4th instant, by the Revd James Maxwell, of the Baptist Union, Charles Robinson, Esq., youngest son of George Robinson, Esq., of River Park, Pedroes to Frances Maria, second daughter of William Pasco, Esq of Content Lodge, Dry Harbour Mountains. No Cards.

February 24, 1871
In Spanish Town on the morning of Tuesday, the 21st instant, the Wife of Mr. G. Fortunatus Judah, of a son.

In Kingston, on the morning of Friday last, the 17th instant, Miss Emily Judah, regretted by her relatives and friends.

March 31, 1871
At Dry Harbour, Saint Ann, on the 28th instant, the wife W. J. L. Nash, Esq of a son.

April 5, 1871
At Mahogany Hall, Trelawny, on the 2nd instant, the wife of J. Wanchope Fisher, Esq, of a son.

April 12, 1871
At the Farm, Pedroes, Saint Ann, on Saturday, the 1st April after a lingering illness, which she bore with Christian fortitude and resignation, Susan Frances, Aged 50 years

the dearly beloved Wife of Hamilton Brown, Esq, leaving a disconsolate husband and a large family to mourn their irreparable loss. The deceased had resided in the district during her long life, and was beloved and esteemed by all who knew her.

April 15, 1871
At St Ann's Bay, on the 29th March, by the Revd. Josiah Cork, Rector, Albert J. Hart son of Aaron Hart, Esq of Montego Bay to Isabella, youngest daughter of David Morris Esq, of St Ann's Bay.

May 16, 1871
On Easter Sunday last at No 10, Bloomfield Road, Malda Hill London, the residence of her daughter, Mrs Garrett, Mrs Mary Stewart, relict of the late Rev Samuel Henry Stewart, L.L.D. formerly Rector of Clarendon and Trelawny in this Island, deeply lamented by her relatives and friends.

June 23, 1871
At Black River, on the 21st June inst, at the residence of his parents, William George, youngest son of Frederick and Euphemia Hendriks, aged 26 years much regretted by his family and friends.

July 29, 1871
At Saint Mark's Church, Brown's Town, Saint Ann on the 18th July, by the Rev. George Hall, Abraham Alexander Isaacs, Acting Inspector of the Constabulary Force, to Hannah Elizabeth, eldest daughter of the Rev. E(T). Barry Cahusac of Cookham, England. No Cards.

August 4, 1871
At St Ann's Bay 9 p.m. 1st instant, at his residence, David Morris, 52 years, a native of Epswick, England and resident in the Island for 35 years after a lingering illness of 10 years which he bore with an exampled fortitude, leaving a wife several children and grandchildren to mourn their irreparable sad loss..

September 8, 1871
On the 6th instant at Williamsfield, St Ann, the wife of Sol Isaacs of a son

September 14, 1871
In Kingston, on Tuesday, 12th instant at 2 a.m. the wife of Mark C. Hendriks, of a son.

October 11, 1871
At Orange Valley Estate, on Thursday, the 4th instant after a few days' sickness, the Infant child of Utten Thomas Todd, junr

October 30, 1871
At the Farm, near Brown's Town St Ann's on the 17th October, Mary Elizabeth Arscott, aged 24 years. She left a loving husband and two young children, with a numerous circle of relatives and friends to lament her premature departure.
Farewell ! dear friends, my life is past,
May you and I unite at last;
Mourn not for me nor sorrow take,
But love my children for my sake.

1871

At St Matthew's Church, Claremont, on the 9th November, 1871 by the Revd. W. J. Wood, Mary Malvina eldest daughter of Hamilton Brown, Senr., to Hamilton Brown, Esq., Junr, son of the late Charles Brown, Esq.--No Cards

November 24, 1871

November 15--At Rio Bueno Church, by the Rev E. A. Stewart, Brother-in-law of the bride, assisted by the Revd. R.A. Thomson, Alfred Lovell Simons, Lieutenant in H M's 1st West India Regiment, only Son of the late T.W. Simons, Esq., M. D. of Rugby, Warwickshire, to Amy Louisa, youngest daughter of Utten T. Todd, Esq. The Ridge, Rio Bueno, No Cards.

Nothing to end

1872

January 12, 1872
In this City on the 6th instant after a lingering illness which she bore with resignation Sophia, the beloved wife of Mr Henry J. Hogg leaving a disconsolate husband and two children and a large circle of friends to lament their loss. (poem)

January 29, 1872
On the 24th instant, at Pavillion, Santa Cruz Mountains the wife of Charles E. Isaacs of a Son.

February 13, 1872
Advertisement

MARK C HENDRIKS

Nos 76 and 121 Water Lane, opposite P.J. Ferron's.

Corn Corn Corn

Fifty Bags Fresh Country Corn, (New Crop) on Retail by the Single Bushel .

Lumber Lumber Lumber

A Large Supply of Mahogany Boards, Planks, and Scantling, Also Cedar Boards momentary expected.

February 28, 1872
At Berry Hill, Saint Ann, the wife of R. W. Arscott of a son.

April 26, 1872
On the 22nd instant, at the Official Residence of the Inspector for Westmoreland, Mrs Abraham A. Isaacs,[formerly Cahusac] of a son

May 29, 1872
At the Parish Church St Ann's Bay by the Rev Josiah Cork on the 22nd instant, Hamilton T Brown, to Alice youngest daughter of the late Charles Bayley, Esq, of Manchester.

June 7, 1872
At New Castle, Jamaica on the 3rd June, the wife of Captain R. J. Watson, 29th Regt of a Son

Selected Vital Records from the Jamaican Daily Gleaner

August 12, 1872
On the 8th instant at Cap--Wear---, St Mary, the wife of the Honble William Macdonald of a son.

September 2, 1872
On the 24th August, 1872, at Happy Grove, Portland, the wife of Dr Honiball, Medical Superintendent Coolie Hospitals, St Thomas, of a daughter

September 12, 1872
The friends and acquaintances of Mr Ulysses Lemercier DuQuesnay are invited to attend his remains from No.11 Highholdourn Street to the place of internment at half past four o'clock this evening.

October 5, 1872
At Dry Harbour on the 30th September, the wife of Wm J Nash of a Daughter

AT St Michaels Church on the 25th September, by the Rev Stewart of Falmouth, Charles H. P. Williams to Frances Maria eldest daughter of the late Edward Sharp J. P of Hanover.

October 15, 1872
At Isleworth Parish Church _orden on the 10th September last, William Hogg Esq, Surgeon M _B. only son of Rev A. G. Hogg Jamaica to Lavina F. Newman only daughter of F _. Newman Esq of the Retreat Brentford and Middlesex.

At Fontabelle Estate Westmoreland, on the 8th October after eight days illness of fever, Mr Joshua James Gruber, youngest brother of J. W. Gruber, Esquire,of Saint Ann, aged 24 years, leaving many relatives and friends to whom he was endeared by his amiable manners and estimable character, to mourn long and sincerely his early death

October 18, 1872
At Swanswick, Trelawny, on the 14th inst. the wife of H.M. Purchas of a daughter

October 25, 1872
On the 11th instant, at Orange Valley Estate, in the parish of St Ann, the wife of Utten T. Todd, junr of a son. [Arthur]

November 5, 1872
At Mackfield, on 29th October, Ella Louisa Clare, eldest daughter of Mr William Vickers of Frome, aged 6 years and 11 months

November 19, 1872
At her residence Saint Ann's Bay, on Monday the 4th instant, Miss Mary Ann Morley, aged 79 years and 5 months, leaving many friends and relatives to mourn their loss.

November 22, 1872
At Christ Church, Port Antonio, on Thursday the 14th instant by the Revd William Smith Rector, assisted by the Revd Thomas Bunbury of Hope Bay, the Rev T.C. G. Johnston, of Moore Town to Mary Ann, the eldest daughter of Alexander Escoffery, Esquire, No Cards.

1872

December 30, 1872

At Tweedside Plantation , formerly of the Port Royal Mountains, 20th December, 1872, Maria the beloved wife of William Campbell aged 75 years leaving a large family and circle of friends to mourn her irreparable loss.

1873

January 24, 1873
At Providence Church Manchester on Wednesday 22nd January 1873 by the Rev J. S. Farquharson, Samuel Augustus Shaw Esq., to Isabella Catherine eldest daughter of G. W. Nash, Esq Emporium   No cards.

February 12, 1873
At Annadale, St Ann, on the 5th inst, Mrs Archibald Roxburgh of a son.

March 7, 1873
We regret to hear that by the last post intelligence was received in this city of the death of the Revd James Milne of the London Missionary Society. He died at First-Hill Trelawny, on the 28th ulto at 9.30 p.m.

March 25, 1873
At Williamsfield Pen, St Ann's on the 20th instant, of Remittant Fever, Eliza Palache, the beloved wife of Solomon Isaacs, Esq in the 29th year of her age. Her illness was long and suffering but she bore all with the greatest patience testifying to all around her the strongest evidences of a Heavenly Father's support. Her removal has caused a blank which cannot be filled in the several relationships of life. Four little ones, besides a large family and circle of friends to mourn her loss.

April 12, 1873
On Wednesday last at Spot Valley, St James, after a long and painful illness borne with much Christian resignation, Elizabeth the eldest daughter of Alexander Grant Esq. Blessed are the dead who die in the Lord.

May 26, 1873
At Aboukir on the 21st inst, by the Rev. Geo Hall, Island Curate of Brown's Town, David Falloway Esq, Vale Royal Estate, Trelawny to Ellen Rosalie, only daughter of the late Arthur Lowe Esq Manchester.

June 14, 1873
At Holland Estate in the parish of St Elizabeth on Sunday the 8th June 1973, Sophia Frances wife of John Manderson and daughter of the late Bernard Maria,Senior, Esquire of St Elizabeth.

June 21, 1873
At 12 Lauriston Place, Edinburgh on the 17th May, the Revd James Watson, late of St Andrew Presbyterian Church, Kingston. Aged 74 years

Selected Vital Records from the Jamaican Daily Gleaner

July 2 1873
On June 25th at Brown's Town Wesleyan Chapel, by the Revd H. B. Foster assisted by the father of the bride, Henry B. Foster M. B. to Hephsibah youngest daughter of the Rev John Corlett. No Cards

July 8, 1873
The Friends and Acquaintances of Mrs Precilla E. Oppenheim, are requested to attend the remains of her son Gabriel Oppenheim No 32 Orange Street at 5 o'clock

July 24, 1873
At Brown's Town, St Ann on the 8th July 1873, by the Revd John Corlett, Alfred Nathan Sutherland, Esqr, of Moneague to Ester eldest daughter of the late William Delisser and niece of Charles Isaacs, Esqr. No cards.

August 11, 1873
On the 8th inst at Portland, the wife of Dr O. Dunscombe Honiball of a daughter

September 6, 1873
FOR SALE   The House, Stores and Premises at Mandeville formerly occupied by Messers J. F. Morrish & Co and known as COMPTON HOUSE It is the best stand in the town, and has every convenience for a large family; is well adapted to carry on an extensive business.

Possession will be given on 1st November ensuing. The terms will be cash. For further particulars apply to the subscriber, Joseph Levy, Auctioneer and Land Agent

September 30, 1873
The Friends and Acquaintances are requested to attend the remains of MISS JANE LEVY at the house NO 117 Princess Street, to the place of Interment at 4 o'clock. Please let your Carriage attend.

October 10, 1873
At Scarlett Hall, St Ann's on the 1st inst, the Wife of Mr J. R. Scarlett of a daughter.

December 2, 1873
On the 20th November 1873, at Hopeton in the parish of
St Ann after a lingering and painful illness of 9 weeks, which she bore with sterling Christian fortitude, MILBORGH the dearly beloved wife of Alexander Willis, Esq aged 73 years leaving a sorrowing husband, a large circle of children, grandchildren, relatives and friends to mourn their irreparable loss.

1874

January 20, 1874
On Sunday, the 12th instant, at Arbuthnot Plantation, St Ann's , Mrs Rebecca Gordon Nash, aged 35 years, fifth daughter of Patrick Waugh, Esq., and Widow of the late John E. Nash, Esq., leaving a young family of three children, a large circle of fond and affectionate relations and friends who deeply deplore their loss by her untimely end.

April 4, 1874
At Green Park, St Anns. on the 29th March, in his 78th year, Edward Bond Esq, son of the late Dr Bond, Glastonbury, and grandson of Dr Hodges, Dean of Bath, Somersetshire.

April 21, 1874
At Bland's Delight, Saint Andrew's on the 19th inst, the wife of Mr James Byndloss of a Son

May 15, 1874
At the Cathedral Spanish Town on Tuesday Evening, the 5th instant by the Revd Campbell McKiennon, Mr James C. Bryant, of Spanish Town, Storekeeper, to Alice Ann, youngest daughter of James S. Facey, Esq, of Putt's Penn, St Catherine, No Cards

In Kingston on the 13th instant, by the Revd J. Radcliffe, Capt. Augustus Field, late of the American Army, to Frances Beckridge of Saint James. (Radcliffe was a Methodist)

July 1, 1874
On the morning of Saturday, 27th instant at "The Moneague House" the Wife of Mr A. N. Sutherland of a son.

July 15, 1874
At Epson Downs, Manchester, on Friday the 16th instant, Ralph Segre Esq, in the 87th year of his age. Requiescat in Pace

July 15, 1874
ALBERT MINTZLAFF of Berlin in Germany, Theologist, Fifty years of age arrived in Kingston in August, 1873 And has since not been heard of by his Friends. He had been previously in Jamaica, and then resided in Kingston, or at or near Mandeville. Any information concerning him will be thankfully received by Finke & Co

Selected Vital Records from the Jamaican Daily Gleaner

July 22, 1874

On the 17th ultimo at 4 Cecil Street, Glasgow, by the Revd Joseph Brown, D. D. assisted by the Revd Wm. Gillis, George Henderson Esq, to Mary eldest daughter of the late William Hay of Maryport, Cumberland

July 25, 1874

DUMONT-FOURNIER. In the City of Panama, on Saturday the 11th July 1874, by the Revd Negri, Achille F. Dumont of Kingston, Jamaica to Adrienne, daughter of Adrienne and Honore Fournier, of France

August 11, 1874

THE WESLEYANS AT ULSTER SPRING

A correspondent who visited the above named place on the 26th ultimo sends us the following intelligence which we gladly publish:--

"ON Sunday the 26th ultimo Ulster Spring presented a lively appearance consequent upon a large gathering o new persons to witness the opening of the Wesleyan Chapel there. It was quite a novel and pretty sight to behold the members and adherents of that Church marching in p[recession, from the old to the new building which when completed promises to be one of the finest little Chapels to be met with anywhere throughout the e Island. Great credit is due to the Pastor and members of the Church for the energy and zeal displayed by them in bringing about the erection of this place of worship.

"The services of the day were conducted by the Rev. W. C. Murray of Watsonville, who both morning and evening preached two very eloquent and impressive sermons. The collections which was taken up at the close of each service amounted to £11 odd. It is certainly pleasing to observe the progress our Wesleyan friends are making in the above-named district; and it is a source of pleasure to add that the congregation, which is very much looked after by the worthy minister, bids fair to be a very large one. It is to be hoped that some attention will be paid to the roads leading to Ulster Spring for without this, numbers of persons will be debarred the pleasure of visiting this fine place of worship and worshipping with the congregation assembled there. Falmouth Post

August 12, 1874

The Wife of Mr Edmund M. Hart of San Souci, St Ann's of a son on Monday, the 9th inst.

October 23, 1874

At Retreat Parsonage, St Mary, on the 17th instant, the wife of Revd F.H. Sharpe, Island Curate, of a son.

November 7, 1874

At Pantrepant Estate, Trelawny, the wife of Mr David Archer of a daughter

November 9, 1874

Our Moneague (St Ann's) correspondent under date 4th instant, writes:-

I promised in my last report of the 2nd inst. to give a further account of the hurricane of the night of October, the 31st last past, to near daylight of the 2nd inst.

1874

I think I omitted to mention Walton Free School. The roof of a portion of the building was neatly taken off and landed on another spot. The road also from Walton Town, especially from Rose Hall, on towards the new building of Mr A. N. Sutherland, in course of erection, became a perfect river course, running at rapid rate about five feet deep, but subsided before daylight on Monday, leaving some portions of the road much washed away, was well as about Phoenix Park and Retirement, with the end of trees. (The Moneague Inn also suffered extensive water damage)

November 30, 1874
NOTICE to A.C. WITH MARRIAGE ADVERTISEMENT. A man who begrudges the payment of three shillings for such had better leave marriage alone or at all events not send the Notice to a newspaper

1875

January 5 - December 29, 1875
January 5, 1875

AT Belle Air Pen, St Ann on the 27th December Isabelle Louise second and beloved daughter of E. A. Stephenson aged 2 years

"Beneath the ever peaceful grave,
Thy body findeth rest
Thy life is from all sickness free,
Thy soul with Angels Blest "

In Montego Bay on the 30th December 1874 by the Revd John Thomas, Mr. Joseph Phillps to Miss Catherine Hart

January 7, 1875
On the 6th inst at Rest Pen, St Andrew, Anna Maria Reeva, widow of the late Honble. Mr Justin Cargill

January 9, 1875
At Montego Bay on the 30th ulto at the Residence of Inspector Depass, by the Reverend Adam Thomson, Henry Goodwich Jervis, Esq sub Agent of Immigration, third son the Lieutenant Colonel William Jervis, Chalkyll, Sydenham, England to Rebecca Florence, second daughter of the late Joseph Isaacs Esq of Falmouth. No cards.

January 22, 1875
Yesterday at the Mission House adjoining the Wesleyan Chapel in Tower Street. MRS SPRATT wife of the Revd Edward Spratt. The Funeral will be at five o'clock this afternoon. Friends are requested to regard this as an invitation.

January 26, 1875
In this city at 140 Upper Orange Street, on Saturday the 23rd inst, Mrs Henry De Costa of a son

February 24, 1875
On Wednesday Evening the 17th inst, by the Rev. B. Rittenburg, FLEURETTE, youngest daughter of the late Aaron De Cordova Esq to Mr Fred L. Myers of this city -- No Cards

37

Selected Vital Records from the Jamaican Daily Gleaner

February 23rd 1875
AT the Parish Church, Kingston on the 18th inst by the Revd G.B.Brooks assisted by the Revd Spence, Aubrey Melbourne eldest son the C. A. Robinson Esq to Lilli eldest daughter of Joseph Francis, Esq No cards

March 9, 1875
On the 7th inst, in this city, the wife of J. C. Nethersole, of a son

April 10, 1875
In this City on Wednesday 7th inst, at her Father's residence, No 11 Highholburn Street, MARIE EMILIE, only daughter of J.U. L Duquesnay, Esquire to Mr KENNETT JOHN SPICER No cards.

April 20, 1875
At Castle James, St Andrews on the 5th inst HENRIETTA, the beloved wife of Mr Geo. F. Nethersole aged 63

April 26, 1875
His Excellency the Governor en route To Falmouth was entertained at a dejeune by Mr Justice Roper at Unity Valley, St Anns.

L. F. Stanigar, Esq, son of W. Stanigar, Esq, of Linstead, has been appointed to be Government Medical Officer for the Ulster Spring District of Trelawny

April 29, 1875
On the 23rd instant, at Camperdown Villa, St Andrews, the wife of P.B. Desnoes of a son

May 1, 1875
Tomorrow

Fourth Sunday after Easter

Coke Chapel

| Morning | Rev. W. C. Murray |
| Evening | Rev E. Spratt |

Ebenezer Chapel,

| Morning | Rev A Bourne |
| Evening | Rev W. C. Murray |

Wesley Chapel

| Morning | Rev E. Spratt |
| Evening | Rev. A. Bourne |

May 4, 1875
On the 29th ulte, at St. Ann's Bay by the Revd. Josias Cork, Rector of the Parish, George Cooper Sandes Govt Med. Officer to Jemina Matilda, eldest daughter of Thomas P.Hart, Esq Inspector of Constabulary.

1875

Died on Sunday the 2nd instant at the residence of her Mother, Spanish Town, Ernestine, eldest daughter of the late David Melhade Esq. She was buried at 12 o'clock the same night in the Jewish Cemetery, Mouk Street, followed by a large number of friends. She was a leader among the daughters of Israel-- a fond sister, an affectionate daughter, a sincere friend, a councillor to many, charitable to those in need and a consoler to those in affliction; to sum up her virtues were many her faults few, she died as she lived, firm in her faith and has left an aged mother, an only sister and many friends to mourn their irreparable loss. May her soul rest in peace. Amen !

May 8, 1875
At Woodlands, on the 5th instant, by the Revd. John Reeves Alf. James Johnson, Esq, Manager Farm and Cow Park, St Catherine, to Rosa Mary Carroline, only Daughter of the late Richmond Braham, and grand daughter of Richmond Graham, Esq of Phoenix Park, St Ann's

June 15, 1875
The Reverend W. Clarke Murray, in a sermon on Life and Death, at Coke (Wesleyan) Chapel, on Sunday night last, said:- "In Adam all die, physically. Are we to understand then, from this that there was no death in the world prior to Adam's Transgression? No:we answer "no": the findings of Geology, in its examination of the earth's structure, the discovery of animals buried in the strata of the earth teach us that there were innumerable creatures which moved and had their beings, over which death passed, long before this earth was in existence" The sermon was listened to with marked attention by an appreciative congregation.

June 21, 1875
This morning at four-o'clock at his Residence, No 166 Tower Street, MR JOHN ESCOFFERY, aged 83 years, Friends and Acquaintances are requested to attend his remains at 5 o'clock this evening. Please let your carriage attend.

June 26, 1875
The gentry of Spanish Town we are informed have tendered Mrs Holland a benefit which will take place at Facey's Building, on Monday Evening, the 28th inst, on which occasion the Elfin Star will appear as Belvidera in Venice Preserved , and the Popular Amateur Mr Geo. F. Judah as Pierre, assisted by several Amateurs from the Kingston, and the strength of the Company. The piece promises to be a great success, and the occasion will be sufficient to attract a large audience, Miss Effie Johus has make herself a favorite in Spanish Town, and a number of gentlemen have volunteered to fill the house, we therefore recommend our friends going early to secure seats.

July 15, 1875
At New Orleans on the 8th June ultimo, Mr B. Y. Benjamin, formerly of this City.

July 28, 1875
At St Thomas' Church, Stewart Town on 7th inst by Rev F. L. King, Dr F. L. Stanigar Government Medical Officer to Rosalind Eliza second daughter of C. S. Cover, Enfield, St Ann. No Cards

17 August, 1875
On Sunday Night 15th inst, the wife of Mr Amos Morais of a son.

September 8, 1875

In this City on the morning of the 7th September, EMILIE, the beloved wife of Kenneth T. Spicer, and devoted daughter of J.U. L. and Eugenie Duquesnay. The funeral will take place at 8.30 a.m. from No 87, Hanover Street. Friends will please accept this intimation.

September 22, 1875

Stewart Town, 20th September 1875

Notice

The subscriber having disposed of his business in Brown's Town, carried on under the style of C. S. Cover & Co to Mr JOSEPH HENRY LEVY who had managed the said business for him, intimates that all debts due to the said firm, and all contracts made with unexpired or otherwise, be settled with Mr LEVY who will also liquidate all indebted of the above Firm.

CHARLES SAMUEL COVER,

The Subscriber takes the present opportunity of returning thanks for the generous support afforded to his business in Brown's Town (C. S. Cover & Co)during its existence and solicits a continuance of the same.

CHARLES SAMUEL COVER

Brown's Town, 20th September 1875

NOTICE

The Subscriber having purchased the business of and all the interest belonging thereto of C. S. Cover & Co informs the Public that he will carry on the said business on his own account and hopes the same share of Patronage bestowed on the late Firm as also on his individual business previous to his connection with C. S. Cover & Co will be extended to him in the future; on his part every effort will be directed towards giving satisfaction and gaining the increased confidence of the Public. His Stock will be kept well and full assorted by regular importation from England and every regard paid to quality and prices to suit the times.

J.H.LEVY

No other entries to December 31, 1875

1876

4 January 1876 - December 1876 1 reel

January 15, 1876
On the 14th instant at Kingston, the wife of Fred. L. Meyers of a son.

January 19, 1876
[Advertisement] Now Ready for Delivery
WHO'S WHO
and
WHAT'S WHAT
in which is incorporated
DECORDOVA'S ALMANACK
and
JAMAICA POCKET BOOK
FOR
1876

Among other interesting matter, the BOOK
contains a
business directory
of the city of Kingston

February 5, 1876
Kingston The Friends and Acquaintances of MR DANIEL NETHERSOLE, are requested to attend his remains, at the HOUSE OF Mr. Charles Morrison, NO 26 Georges LANE AT 4 P.M. THIS EVENING. Please let your Carriage attend.

February 8, 1876
DIED Last night at 7.30, at No 37 East Street, HERCULIES FOURNIER, late of Port-au-Prince, Haiti, and native of Charleston, South Carolina. Friends and Acquaintances of the deceased and Mr William McCormack are invited to attend his remains to the place of Interment at 5 p.m. this evening. Please let your Carriage attend.

February 11, 1876
Bridgetown, Barbados, is now lighted with Gas. When will Kingston's turn come?

Selected Vital Records from the Jamaican Daily Gleaner

February 12, 1876

On the 9th instant by the Rev. A. H. Nieto Minister of the Spanish and Portuguese Synagogue Constantia second daughter of the late Nathaniel Brandon of Panama to Mr Daniel Isaac Motta, both of this city

March 14, 1876

In this City on the 2nd March, at the United Presbyterian Church, East Queen Street, by the Rev J. Ballantine, Charles Augustus Smith, to Floretta Agusta Isaacs, youngest daughter of Jacob Isaacs, of this city.

March 29, 1876

ST ANN

Thursday the 2nd inst was a gala day in the Dry Harbour mountains of this parish. At an early hour of that day, the road between Brown's Town and Tabernacle wore a lively appearance from the number of carriages riders on horseback, and persons on foot, all in bright holiday attire, going in the direction of the Wesleyan Station at Tabernacle. The cause for all this manifestation of interest was the expected ceremony of the laying of the Corner-stone of a new Wesleyan Chapel, prevented on the 6th January, by the wet weather. Shortly after 11 o'clock, the old Chapel was crowded with a congregation representing all classes of social life. At the service of the 6th January, the Rev. Geo. Sargeant had delivered a very acceptable address. At this meeting, after the introductory devotions and statement by the resident minister, the veteran John Corlett, and the Revd. W. C. Harty spoke effectively on subjects of practical Christian interest. In the statement referred to, there was the fact that the new chapel was to be on a site at the crossroads at Hopeton, and the reasons for the change. The new site is the gift of Alex. Willis, Esq. After the service in the old Chapel the congregation formed a procession, singing cheerfully as they went. At the new site the scene was very pretty: Rustic Booths flags, gay dresses, animated countenances, lent each their charm. At the ceremony proper, after praise and prayer, Mrs William Cover of Annandale (Armadale) laid the stone in Orthodox style; acquitting herself efficiently in the task. The mallet and silver trowel having been presented, on behalf of the congregation by Miss Ella Johnson, another address from the Rev. J. Corlett, the acknowledgement of kindness and liberality from all classes of the community by the Rev. John Duff, cheers for the Queen, and the Wesleyan Missionary Society, the National Anthem, the Benediction and the interesting service closed. The collections reached the noble sum of £110 and encouraging start in a noble work. The Wesleyan Church at this station is now in a fair way to remove the reproach which has been their's for many years, in the unsightly and delapidated building in which they worship. The opening of the new chapel is pleasingly anticipated, and the event, we trust, will not be long delayed. this report should not close without noticing the pleasing liberality of the laboring class on the occasion; a good many of whom laid bank notes on the stone as their offering. Any sceptic in the matter present at the services, would have had ample proof, that in the way of Christian civilization, "the people" in those mountains are in advance.

May 15, 1876

In this city, on the morning of the 12th instant, the wife of John C. Nethersole Esquire of a son.

June 2, 1876

HENDRICKS- At Kingston, on 1st instant, the wife of Mark C. Hendriks of a daughter

1876

August 14, 1876

By the Revd C.F. Douet, Parish Church 10th August 1876 Leyantee Christiana second daughter of Richard Moor Gordon, Esq deceased to Edward Derbeshire Wright fourth son of Wm Wright Esq of Retreat, Portland

August 24, 1876

AT the Parish Church, Halfway Tree, on Wednesday the 16th instant by the Ven'ble Archdeacon Campbell, assisted by the Revd. G.W. Downer, Rector of Kingston, ROSE BIGHAM ROBINSON, son of George Robinson Esqre., of Grier Park, St Anns, to ANNIE Louisa, second daughter of the late Thomas Gray, Esqre, of Mason Hall, St Mary's and niece of John McLean, Esqre, of Cold Spring St Andrew.

Nothing else to end of roll

1877

February 5, 1877

In Kingston on the 2nd instant, by the Rev J.S.. Roberts, Arthur Parcells, of Luana Pen, St Elizabeth, to Margaret Miller, seventh daughter of the late B. M. Senior, Esq.

February 17, 1877

STEWART TOWN, TRELAWNY

The 27th ulto, will not soon be forgotten by the inhabitants of Stewart Town. The occasion was the laying of the Corner Stone of a projected new Wesleyan Chapel, and certainly every thing in connexion with the service shewed a spirit of earnest interest in the matter which promises entire success. At 11 o'clock on that day a meeting was held in the old chapel and addressed by the Revds. W. C. Harty, H. M. Webb, J. P Russell, R. M. Parnther, John Corlett, and George Sargeant. The Hon J. W. Fisher, Custos, presided, the Revd. John Duff pastor of the congregation, conducted the devotional exercises. At the close of the addresses in the old chapel the congregation proceded to the new site, the generous gift of C. S. Cover, Esq., headed by the Sunday School children, with flags and banners where the Revd. John Duff requested Miss Scholes to present Mrs C. S. Cover with the very elegant silver trowel provided for the ceremony. Mrs Cover then in Happy style performed her task, and declared the stone well and duly laid in the name of the Holy Trinity. The congregation was immensely large, the service deeply interesting and the collection laid on the stone on the day with £5 9s 0d at the sermons on the preceding Sunday amounted to £152 13s. This handsome sum except £20 by Mr Cover and his family, was almost entirely given by the peasant class. This is the second new Wesleyan Chapel started in these regions recently, The other in the Dry Harbour Mountains commenced in May last year, is now nearly completed. We take these facts as indicating not merely an increase of interest and liberality in the Wesleyan Church, but also an increased sense of responsibility on the part of our people.

March 19, 1877

The Friends and Acquaintances of EMILE AND THEODORE Lemercier DUQUESNAY are requested to attend the remains of their mother, MRS CHARLOTTE LEMERCIER DUQUESNAY from her late residence 27, King Street to the place of interment at half past four o'clock this afternoon. Gentlemen will please let their Carriages attend.

April 7, 1877

Died in this City on Thursday, the 5th instant GEORGE ORRETT, Aged 50 years

Selected Vital Records from the Jamaican Daily Gleaner

June 15, 1877

Died At the Villa, Mandeville, on Monday Morning the 11th instant, after a lingering illness which she bore with Christian fortitude and resignation, MARY the beloved wife of Joseph Levy in the 66th year of her age. "Blessed are the dead who die in the Lord"

July 25, 1877

Died. At Spot Valley, on Sunday the 22nd inst, Georgiana, fourth and beloved daughter of the late Alexander Grant, Esq aged 28 years, sincerely regretted by a large circle of relatives and friends.

October 27, 1877

On the 23rd instant at Orange Valley St Ann, The wife of U.T. Todd Jnr of a daughter

1878

January 17, 1878
At Quebec Estate in the Parish of St. Mary, on Friday, the 4th instant, the wife of Rose B. Robinson, Esq., of a son.

January 25, 1878
THE GOVERNOR'S VISIT TO BROWN'S TOWN

Much speechifying at the court House, not many people mentioned. The following: signed the address to the Governor,

John Clark, Baptist Missionary; Geo Hall, Island Curate; Chas Isaacs, J. P.; John Duff, Wesleyan Minister; Jno L. Mawbey, J. P.; U. T. Todd, Jnr., J. P ; &c, &c.

January 19, 1878
For Public Sale.

On Friday, 8th February, 1878, at twelve o'clock, noon, at my Commission Agency, No. 44, Port Royal Street, by Order of the Churchwardens of the Parish Church of Saint Andrew, REST PEN , containing twenty-two Acres, more or less, pleasantly situated near Half-Way-Tree and in Proximity to the Tramway Terminus.

There is a Dwelling House on the Property which, with a small outlay, might be made a comfortable Residence. The Water Works Pipes pass through the Property. JOSEPH STINES, Auct. to H.M. N.C. and O. S. Dept.[Rest Pen is where we lived in Kingston, North Avenue 1953-1968]

March 13, 1878
A Correspondent supplies us with the following:

Trelawny--Estates thrown out of Cultivation, from 1822 to 1877

Biddeford, Manchester, Barnstaple, Stonehenge, Freeman's Hall, Ulster Spring, Sportman's Hall, Lysworney, Hampshire and Berkshire, Kinloss, Forest, Jocks Lodge, Southfield, Acton, Gravesend Garredu, Reserve, Linton Park, Belmont, Colchis, Friendship (Fowler's), Claremont, Windsor, Stewart Castle, Greenfield, Dry Valley, Florence Hall, Grange, Clifton, Roslin Castle, Orange Grove, Merrywood, Potosi, Carickfoyle, Covey, Bunker's Hill, Peru, Friendship (Reids), Dromilly, Retreat, Unity,

Silver Grove, Phoenix, Weston Favell, Wakefield, York, Bounty Hall, George's Valley, Schawfield, Bod Attempt, now "Lichfield" Pen.

Estates in Cultivation in Trelawny. 1877

Hopewell, Arcadia, Brampton, Bryan Castle, Nightingale Grove, Vale Royal, Braco, Lancaster, Harmony Hall, Georgia, Hyde, Long Pond, Swanswick, Etingdon, Hyde Hall, Steelfield, Gibraltar, Oxford, Cambridge, Water Valley, Spring, Lottery, Chester, Hampstead, Lausquinet, Good Hope, Wales, Pantrepant, Fontabelle, Golden Grove, Pembroke, Tilsont, Gales Valley, Dundee, Orange Valley, Kent, Green Park, Holland, Maxfield, Hague,

Thrown up 1822 to 1877	50
In Cultivation	40
	90

March 19, 1878
Our readers will remember the lecture to-night, at the Mico, at 7:30. The Rev. W. Clarke Murray is the lecturer.

April 20, 1878
Government Notice

From the Jamaica Gazette

The Governor has been pleased to appoint Edward Bancroft Lynch, Esquire, to act temporarily as Island Secretary of Jamaica, in the room of the late Honorable Charles Hamilton Jackson.

Edward Bancroft Lynch, Esquire, to act temporarily as Comptroller in Bankruptcy under Law 25 of 1878 in the room of the late Hon Charles Hamilton Jackson.

Edward Bancroft Bancroft Lynch, Esquire, to act temporarily as Administrator-General of Jamaica in the room of the late
Honorable Charles Hamilton Jackson.

April 22, 1878
At Two o'clock on Wednesday morning, the 17th instant, departed this life at her residence No 12, Gold Street, Eliza Miles Watson. the beloved wife of Joseph D. Watson aged 46 years. She was a faithful wife and affectionate mother and daughter, a sincere and hospitable friend and had a kind word and look for every one that she knew. ......She left a husband, an aged mother, five children, and eight grandchildren to mourn their loss--may her children who are now men and women, copy her example and pursue the path of their lamented mother

April 30, 1878
Notice

C. Laloubere & Co, Kingston,

1878

We hereby give notice, to all whom it may concern, that from this day Mr John Z. Herrmann will act during our absence, on behalf of this Firm, and will sign their names by procuration

G.BOETTCHER
C. LALOUBERE & CO.
62, Port Royal Street, Kingston

May 3, 1878
An appeal by W. Clarke Murray for donations towards £300 needed to build a suitable school house on lands connected with Ebenezer Wesleyan Chapel. Address: 81 Hanover Street.

R. W. Arscott was a subagent of the Royal Insurance Company, located in Brown's Town and Levy & Palache, solicitors of Mandeville were also listed as subagents.

Mark C. Hendricks was advertising "Looking Glasses just Received from England".

May 21, 1878
In Lima , Peru on the 10th instant, Horatio Lyon, a native of Kingston, Jamaica at the age of 75

June 3, 1878
A CONFERENCE

The Poverty or wealth of this country depends upon the extent to which its soil is cultivated. Thousands of acres lie in ruinate for want of capital as much as labour. Both things are needed. An effort is being made to secure an addition of labour power: and it seems to me a fitting time to make an effort in the direction of obtaining capital, I believe in co-operation for mutual benefit. The system fosters self-reliance and encourage other manly qualities. An Agricultural Aid Society, &c, on something of the principle of the Kingston Benefit Building Society appears to me sadly wanting in the colony, and I am of the opinion that it would meet with support. Properly organized and worked, I am confident that tin a few years, just as the K. B. B. Society has converted dilapidation and decay into strength and beauty in this city the Agricultural Benefit Society would transform bareness and desolation into fruitfulness and plenty, I may be too sanguine in this matter, but I think the question of attempting the formation of such a Society deserving of consideration; and gentlemen are invited to attend a Conference on the subject to be held at the Rooms of the Commercial Exchange on Friday, the 7th inst at 2 o'clock, p.m.

W. CLARKE MURRAY

June 5, 1878
NOTICE
In reference to my invitation to attend a Conference to consider the question of an Agricultural Aid Association, I beg to say that in consequence of the Celebration of the Feast of Pentecost by my friends of the Hebrew persuasion, the time is deferred to Monday, the 10th inst., at 2 o'clock at the Rooms of Commercial Exchange.
W.CLARKE MURRAY

Selected Vital Records from the Jamaican Daily Gleaner

June 6, 1878

Estate of MARIA LOUISE PIERRE EYNAUD, late of Kingston, Widow (Deceased)Testate

NOTICE

Under Law 19 of 1871

All Creditors of and Claimants against this Estate are required to render in writing the particulars of their claims to the qualified Executor under the Testatrix's Will, Mr Michael Morin, at the office or to the care of the undersigned, at No 8, Church Street and Water Lane, Kingston, on or before the 22nd day of July next, after which the Assets will be distributed accord to Law, regard being only had to such claims of which due notice shall have been given.

Dated this 5th day of June, 1878

Edward A. Bell, solicitor of the Estate

June 7, 1878

In Kingston, on the 6th inst the Wife of Wellesley Bourke, of a daughter.

June 8th 1878

Editorial by the Gleaner on the suggestion by W. Clarke Murray

June 10, 1878

OBITUARY

Brown's Town, St Ann.

Our little town was thrown into a state of the deepest gloom and mourning on Friday, the 31st May, consequent of the death of our much-esteemed fellow-townsman, Charles Isaacs, Esq. The whole place from early morning presented a scene of such sorrow and wretchedness as has never been known even the oldest livers, and which was made doubly deadly by all the places of business being closed, the tolling , at intervals, throughout the day of the Church Bell. No death in this community has ever been attended with so much feeling and regret as this good man's. His amiable and courteous manners, his gentlemanly and refined character, having gained for him the love and respect of all. He was of sons the most devoted, as a brother none more affectionate, as a friend true and unwavering, as a Justice of the Peace impartial and accessible to all. To the poor he was ever ready to extend the hand of charity. That he lived beloved and respected and died regretted and mourned, was fully evinced by the large concourse of friends from far and near who followed, in a procession of twenty-five carriages, his remains to their last resting place. He is gone, leaving behind him a blank, a void which no one can fill. His bereaved mother, sister, and brothers and other family have the sympathy and condolence of a community which will, as long as memory lasts, feel with them that one has passed away who was very dear and very good, and my our great and good God extend to them, in this their hour of sad trouble and bereavement, that consolation and peace which the world and sympathizing friends cannot give.

June 11, 1878

Report on the meeting of W. Clarke Murray

1878

June 14, 1878
By the Rev. Hanburger, Hazan, of the English and German Congregation of the City of Boston Mass:- MARSHALL,DELGADO---Joseph Baertra Marshall, native of London, to Edna Wingred, eldest daughter of the Late Edwin Delgado, of Kingston, Jamaica. No Cards

June 21, 1878
On Thursday morning, 20th instant, the wife of Mr Amos Morais of a daughter

August 2, 1878
At Kingston, on Friday evening, July 26th in the 53rd year of his age, John Cover, Esq,. of Huntly Pen, St Ann. His mortal remains were brought over and interred in the family cemetery at Enfield, St Ann, on Sunday 28th. He leaves a disconsolate widow, several children and other relatives and friends to mourn their irreparable loss. "Thy will be done".

August 8, 1878
On the 8th August, 1878, at 62, Hanover Street, FREDERIC WILLIAM WRIGHT, second son of the late William Wright, Merchant of this City. Friends please notice that the Funeral will take place at five o'clock, this evening.

September 7, 1878
FROM THE GAZETTE

The Governor has been pleased to appoint Commodore the Hon. William John Ward A.D.C., to be a Justice of the Peace of St Andrew and Kingston. Joseph Henry Levy, Esq., to be Justice of the Peace for St Ann.

September 30, 1878
At her residence, Content, St Ann, on Tuesday the 24th September 1878, aged 74 years, Margaret Cox, widow of the late Henry Cox, Esq.

October 17, 1878
The friends and acquaintances of Mr Henry J.F. H. Hogg are requested to attend his remains from his late residence, No 18 Sutton Street, at four o'clock this evening to the place of interment. Please let your carriage attend.

October 18, 1878
On the 13th inst, at "The Bogue", St Ann, Mrs Archibald Roxburgh of a son.

October 21, 1878
At Tannasby, Clarendon. on the 19th inst John Girvan aged 80 years

October 25, 1878
In this city, on Wednesday evening, 16th October after a long and tedious illness, Mr Henry J. Hogg in his 40th year. He has left a widow, two young sons and other relatives and friends to mourn their irreparable loss. Verse
December 12, 1878

At Alverstoke on Saturday, 7th inst. Jane the beloved wife of J. M. Sailman, Esq, aged 73 years. The large and respectable attendance at her funeral, testified to the esteem and affection in which she was held by all classes of the community. She leaves a large family of children and grandchildren to mourn her loss, In life beloved in death lamented.

Nothing to end of Film

1879

February 26, 1879
At 69, Church Street, on the 25th February, Margaret, widow of the late John Duff. Friends and acquaintances are invited to attend the Funeral, which will take place this evening, at half-past four o'clock

February 28, 1979
At Southampton, St Auver's, Dry Harbour Mountains, on the 20th inst. Charles Smart Strachan, the only son of Ann Dodd, aged 57 years. He has suffered for a long time from Rheumatism, which he bore with Christian fortitude. He has left and aged mother, two sisters, widow and children to mourn his irreparable loss. " I know that my Redeemer liveth etc" Job xix 25, 26, 27 vrs

April 18, 1879
The wedding of Mr. Jackson and Miss Stiebel yesterday, at the Half-way-Tree Church was the most brilliant affair of the kind which has occurred here since the wedding of the late Bishop Spencer's daughter to Rev. Mr. Smythe. About forty carriages were in attendance. Two hundred pounds of beef, four bags of rice, one barrel of sugar, were distributed to the poor. Rev Mr. Isaacs performed the ceremony.

May 14, 1879
The Royal Insurance Company. Agents listed:

R. W. Arscott, Esq - Brown's Town
Levy & Palache, solicitors - Sav-la-Mar
Sylvester Cotter, Esq - St Ann's Bay
Solomon Isaacs, Esq - Brown's Town

June 21, 1879
On the 19th June, at the Parish Church, Saint Ann's Bay by the Rev Josias Cork, Philip W. Abbott, Merchant of Kingston, to Emily Smith of St Ann's Bay.

June 23, 1879
LEVY-Henriques. Married in this City, on Wednesday evening, the 18th instant, by the Mr. H.A. Josephs, acting Minister of the English and German Synagogue, Moses Levy, Esq,. Merchant, to Deborah, eldest daughter of A. N. Henriques, Esq. No Cards.

Selected Vital Records from the Jamaican Daily Gleaner

July 5, 1879
In this City, on the morning of the 2nd instant, Emil L'Estrange, infant son of Fleurette and Frederick L. Myers

July 7, 1879
At Tullock, St Thomas ye Vale, on the 28th June, the wife of John McPhail, Esquire, of a son.

On the 3rd instant in Callao, aged 47 years, John Isaac Plunkett, a native of the United States. for many years he was connected with the mechanical department of newspaper offices in Jamaica, Panama and in this country. He possessed many generous qualities and his death is regretted by a large number of friends. His remains were interred on the 4th ult at the British Cemetery with Masonic honors. S. P. Times

August 18. 1879
Delapenha-At Russel Place Pen, Manchester, on Wednesday 13th, the wife of Uriah Delapenha, of a son.

August 25, 1879
Our Friends the Wesleyans, are in treaty for the purchase of thirty acres of Barbican Lands, on which they desire to erect suitable buildings for Girls' Schools, similar in construction and system to the celebrated York College in St. Anns. Such enterprising zeal in behalf of education deserves to be highly commended.`

September 3, 1879
Advertisement

Wanted on October 1st, --a Fourth Mistress for Wolmer's Free School. Salary £36 per annum, rising by increments to £60. Candidates must send in their applications and Testimonials to the Clerk of the Trust not later than noon on Monday, the 15th instant, and must attend at the School Room on Thursday, the 16th instant, at 8 o'clock a.m., to be examined by the Head Master. The Election will take place at the Institution, on Tuesday, the 23rd instant, at 3 o'clock p.m. By order C. Thompson, Clerk to Trustees.

September 19, 1879
Yesterday at noon, at her late Residence No 57, Corner Barry and East Street, Caroline. The Beloved Wife of James Stedman. The funeral will take place at 4.30 p.m. Friends and Acquaintances will please accept this intimation.

October 7, 1879
On the 30th September, 1879, by the Reverend Father Dupont, at the Holy Trinity Church, Kingston. Charles Dacre Lacy, to Alice Marie Louise Nunes, second daughter of the late Joseph N. Cardoza Esq., of this city.

November 1, 1879
At Lucea , on the 26th ultimo, in the 38th year of his age, Mr Thomas W. Johnson. He was a native of that town, but resided for several years in the Parish of Westmoreland.

November 4, 1879
On Saturday, 1st November, instant, at her residence, in Orange Street, Kingston. Mrs Hannah De la Motta aged 83 years and 10 months

1879

November 19, 1879

A Fatal case of Ackie-poisoning is reported in St. Andrew, and we are informed that an investigation is to be instituted at once.

Nothing to end of reel

1880

January 2, 1880
DEMERCADO-DACOSTA--On 31st December 1879 by the Revd. H.H. Isaacs, at Halfway Tree Church, St Andrew, Horatio, youngest son of Joseph DeMercado, Esq to Endora Esther, second daughter of S.M. DaCosta Esq, of this city. No Cards.

January 6, 1880
On the 30th December 1879, at the Parish Church, St Ann's Bay, by the Rev J. Cork, Rector of St Ann, Edward Brown eldest surviving son of the late Thomas Rodgers Esquire, of 43 Fleet Street, Kingston, to Lucy, daughter of the late William Bromley Rose, Esq., M.D. Mount Pleasant, St Ann.

WOLFE-SIMONS--On the 31st December 1879, by Mr. A. H. Joseph, of the E. (English)and G.(German) Synagogue, David, eldest son of Ellis Wolfe, Esq, Hannah, youngest daughter of late Samuel Simons both of this city. At home 10th and 11th inst.

January 9, 1880
At Hopewell Pen, St Ann, on the 2nd January, 1880, Henrietta Moncrieffe, widow of the late Hon Peter Moncrieffe of Friendship Pen, St Ann and eldest daughter of the late Henry Cary, Esq of Highgate, London.

February 29, 1880
On the 28th instant, at 51, High Holborn Street, Helen H. Lillie, Widow of Thomas Fraser, late of Kingston, Jamaica. Funeral will take place at halfpast 4 this afternoon. Friends will please accept this intimation and let their carriages attend.

March 29, 1880
At No 27 East Street, Kingston, on the morning of 25th instant, the wife of Mark C. Hendriks of a daughter

April 17, 1880
At 2 o'clock this morning, at her residence, No 11, Highoborn Street, Marie Eugenie Le Remercier Duquesnay. Friends and acquaintances are requested to attend her remains this evening at 4:30 Please let your carriage attend.

April 28, 1880
Mark C. Hendriks lists himself as Cabinet maker and Undertaker etc. Is also selling corn and market baskets.

Selected Vital Records from the Jamaican Daily Gleaner

June 3, 1880

The friends of the late Alexander Campbell are hereby kindly invited to attend his remains from his late Residence, No 2, Smith Lane to the place of interment, [Scotch Burial Ground] Carriage to remove from the door at 5 p.m. N.B, Please let your carriage attend

July 19, 1880

Walsh-Casserly -July 7th at Charlottenburgh, St Andrew's Elenor Mary, eldest daughter of John Casserly, Esq, J.P. Geo, Patrick Joseph, seventh son of John Galway Walsh, City of Cork, Ireland. Nuptial Mass Celebrated by the Right Revd. Thomas Porter, B.A. assested by the Revds J Ryan, William Spillmann and Joseph Meyers.

August 13, 1880

At Rose Bank House, Kingston, on the 12th inst., the wife of Wellesley Bourke, of a son.

On the 11th instant, at Halfway Tree Church, by the Revd C. H. Hall, grandfather of the bride, assisted by the Revds. Joseph Wildams, H.H. Isaacs, G.W. Downer, and D. H. Lewis, Chaplain R. N. Louis Edward, youngest son the the late Juline Delmege, Esquire, of 36, Fitzwilliam Square, Dublin and Rathkeale House, Co Limerick, Ireland, to Rosalie Annie, daughter of the Revd Hugh Croskery

August 16, 1880

The friends and acquaintances of Mr. Charles Sherlock are requested to attend the remains of his Sister, Mrs Bover Laforest, from her late residence, No 73 Georges's Lane to the place of interment at 4:30 p.m. this evening. Please let your carriage attend.

August 17, 1880

The friends and acquaintance s of Mr. Colin Hogg are requested to attend the remains of his Mother, Mrs. Elizabeth Hogg from his residence No 13 Sutton St to the place of interment at 4 :30 p.m. Please let your carriage attend.

August 23, 1880

Packet edition of the Gleaner containing full and comprehensive account of the frightful Hurricane that passed over this Island on the 18th inst with full details of casualities all over the Island thrilling incidents and loss of life, will be published at this office tomorrow, at 12 o'clock noon. Price 3 d.

September 1, 1880

Storms of the past lists: 1689, 1712 August 28, 1722 August 28th, 1726 October 22,1744 October 20, 1780 October 23,1781 August 1, 1784 July 30, 1785 August 27, 1786 October 20, 1812 October 12,1813 August 1, 1815 October 18,19, 1844 October 5, 1874 November 1

September 10, 1880

Died last night, Abraham R. DaCosta, the funeral will take place from No 161, Orange Street, to the place of interment this evening at 4:30
Friends and acquaintances will please accept this intimation.

September 21, 1880

At Collins Green Park, St Andrews, the residence of S. D. Lindo, Esq, on the 20th instant at noon. Mrs Mary Ann DaCosta (Aged 77) The Widow of Amos DaCosta, late of Kingston, merchant. The funeral will take place this Evening at seven o'clock. Her friends and those of her son, Alex E, DaCosta of Port Maria will please accept this intimation and let their carriages attend.

October 24, 1880
August 6, at Rockforest Co Cork, the Rev George Edward Cotter, M.A. third son of the late Colonel Sir James Laurence Cotter, M.P. of Rockforest aged 86

October 28, 1880
FOR Sale

REST PEN, in the parish of St Andrews, on the main road to Stony Hill and within 10 minutes walk of the Car Terminus; containing 14 acres of land, 6 of which are in well established Guinea Grass. The Dwelling House is new, and contains 4 Bed rooms Drawing and Dining Room, Front Piazza, Side Verandahs, Butlers' Pantry and a large portico in front. The out buildings are also new and are connected to the house by a covered way. There is a splendid Flower and Vegetable garden on the premises and the Water Company's 7 in main pipe passes through the pen and supplies it with water. By permission of the tenant, the premises can be seen at any time. Application to be made to D. M. Polsen, Esq (one door East at Church St on Water Lane) or to Alex Berry L A & C.A.

November 1, 1880
In this city on Monday 1st November, after a long and painful illness, Jane Cleopatra, the eldest and esteemed daughter of Colin Campbell, Amiable, good and kind who was beloved by all who knew her as a devoted and affectionate friend. She leaves a large circle of relatives and friends to deplore their irreparable loss. (Verse)

November 5, 1880
On the 31st October at Wallens the residence of her son-in-law A.C. C. Colthirst, Esquire, Margaret Jane MacKintosh widow of the late Donald MacKintosh Esq of Mammee Bay St Ann--Aged 53 years.

November 11, 1880
In this city, on 8th inst., at No 22 1/2 Mark Lane, after seven hours illness, Eliza Ann Calder, the wife of Serjt. John Beacher, leaving her husband and family to mourn their irreparbale loss, Requiescat in Pace.

November 18, 1880
DELGADO-DECORDOVA- In this city, on the 10th inst, at No 117 Duke Street, the residence of the Brides' Father, Rosalind, eldest daughter of Altamont DeCordova, Esq to Moses eldest son of the late Alfred Delgado, Esq, deceased. At Home at No 17 West Avenue, Kingston Gardens, on Saturday and Sunday eveings, 20th and 21st inst.

November 20, 1880
At Grand Cayman on the 27th Sept, the wife of Rev. John Smith of a son.

November 22, 1880
At the residence of her Nephew, A.D.C. Levy, Esq., Port Maria on Wednesday, the 17th inst, Matilda Lindo aged 74 years, regretted and esteemed by all who knew her.

Selected Vital Records from the Jamaican Daily Gleaner

November 25, 1880

At York Castle, St Ann's on Sunday the 21st inst, John Cooling, B.A. late of Newark, England aged 25 years. Leaving a sorrowing wife and several relatives and freinds by who he was greatly esteemed, to mourn their irreparable loss. (Verse)

December 30, 1880

On the 21st instant at St Michael's Church Kingston, by the Revd. G. W. Downer, Rector of the Parish, assisted by the Revd C. T. Denroche, John Samuel youngest son of the late Revd T. J. Brown to Carrie Louise, youngest daughter of the late S. S. Wortley, Esq

At Lucea on the 22nd instant, George Hall, Rector of that Town and for many years Island Curate of Claremont and Brown's Town Churches, aged 58 years

1881

January 4, 1881
On the 3rd instant the wife of James B. Wolfe of a daughter

January 25, 1881
The friends and acquaintances of Mr R.W. Harty are invited to attend the remains of his wife Georgina Newman, from his residence No 36 King St. to the place of interment at 4.30 sharp.

February 5, 1881
Died. On Friday the 4th intstant, at 140 Orange Street, Kingston. Margaret F.R. Winn, The beloved wife of the Rev. C.A. Winn, (Methodist Free Church) Clarendon. The funeral will take place at 9 o'clock a.m., this day

February 8, 1881
At St. Michael's Church, in this city, on the 29th ult, by the Rev. C. R. Denroche, Samuel Sharpe, eldest son of the late S.S. Wortley, Esq, to Mary Menzies McGregor, third daughter of the late Rev. T. J. Brown. No Cards

February 14, 1881
At 8.45 last evening, at the Mission House, 81 Hanover Street, Herbert James, eldest son of the Revd W. Clarke Murray. The funeral will move at 5 p.m. this evening. Friends are respectfully invited.

February 19, 1881
In this City, on Tuesday morning, the 15th instant, at 3, Parade, Mr. Philip Allwood, aged 53 years. Deeply regretted by all who knew him.

February 22, 1881
Monday 21st inst; Mary Campbell, relict of the late James Campbell, of this city. The funeral will move from her late residence, 47, Hanover Street, for the place of interment at 5 o'clock this evening.

February 24, 1881
The Friends and Acquaintances of Mr David Todd are requested to attend his remains from his late Residence, No 30, Beeston Street, to the Ebenezer Ground at 4.30 this evening. Please let your Carriage attend.

Selected Vital Records from the Jamaican Daily Gleaner

March 1, 1881

The friends and acquaintances of the late Mr Richard Lord are requested to attend the remains of his eldest son Archibald from his residence, No 73 Tower St., to the place of interment at 4.30 this evening. Please let your carriage attend.

March 4, 1881

At Halfway-Tree, on the 3rd instant, Mr James Byndloss. The funeral will take place this afternoon, at 4 o'clock. Friends and acquaintances are requested to accept this intimation.

March 26, 1881

The Friends and acquaintances of William Ross are requested to attend his remains from his late residence, No 6, Bond Street, to the place of interment, at 4 o'clock this evening. Please let your carriage attend.

May 6, 1881

In this city, on the 2nd inst, Caroline, widow of the late Henry Garland Murray, in the 52nd year of her age, deeply regretted by her relative and friends.

May 13, 1881

St Ann's Bay, May 2, 1881

Notice of Copartnership.

Mr Sylvester Cotter has been formally admitted into copartnership with me in the St Ann's Bay business as from the 1st day of January, 1881, and the business will still be conducted under the name and original style of C. S. Cover and Co. C.S. COVER

Mark C. Hendricks

Cabinet MaKer. Upholsterer Undertaker, &c.

121 Water Lane.
Just opened -A fine assortment of

VELVET FRAMES
RUSTIC Ditto
ALSO
Mottoes on perforated Card, Something New.

June 7, 1881

In this city, on the 6th inst, the wife of D. H. DaCosta, of a son.

June 13, 1881

At No 3 John Street, Rae Town, James Douglas,infant son of Mr T. Douglas Dallas, aged 1 month 6 days. Friends and acquaintances are invted to attend the funeral from the above named residence, to the place of interment, at 4.30 this evening.

June 24, 1881

At St Peter's Church, Brooklyn, New York, on 28th April, by the Revd. C.A. Tibbals, Rector, Roger Swire, of Iowa City, Iowa, to Edith Constance, youngest daughter of the late R.L. Foster formerly of H.M. Customs, Kingston, Jamaica.

1881

June 27, 1881
At Mt Plenty, St Anns, on the 22nd inst, Julia C. Mais, the beloved wife of Adam Roxburgh aged 24 years.

July 2, 1881
John Gardiner Died in this City, at No 43, Marks Lane, on the morning of the 26th June, in his 90th year.

July 18, 1881
In this city on the morning of the 16th inst., Ann Elizabeth relict of the late Alexander Evans Todd, Esq, aged 72 years

July 25, 1881
At Mahogney Hall, Trelawny, on the 20th inst., by the Rev. Edward Owen, Lieut Morris H Smyth, R. N. of H.M.S. Sparrowhawk, to Mary Eliza, second daughter of the Hon J Wanchope Fisher. No Cards.

September 19, 1881
At St Paul's Chapelton, on the 14th instant, by the Rev H. W. Whitfield, Blanche, only daughter of the late Col. Strachan, 1st W.I.R. to Wm. Taylor. M.B. C.M. District Medical Officer, Chapelton. No Cards.

September 20, 1881
WOLFE-FRAY. At the United Presbyterian Church, Falmouth on Wednesday, the 14th inst., by the Revd William Murray, L.L. D. assisted by the Rev Edis Fray (uncle of the bride) and the Revd James Martin, Ellis Bollivar Wolfe of Kingston, solicitor, to Edith Teres, eldest daughter of the late Henry Fray, Esq of Georges's Valley in the parish of Trelawny, and grand daughter of the late Andrew M. Cubbin, Esq.

September 27, 1881
POOLE-LEVY. On the 18th August, at the Parish Church Erith, Kent by the Revd R. Curties, Charles B. Poole of Forest Road, Dalston, son of the late Charles P. Poole of the Halton Road, Canonbury Square, to Josephine Sarah, youngest daughter of Joseph Levy, of the Villa, Mandeville.

October 11, 1881
At St George's Kingston on Thursday, the 6th instant by the Rev Joseph Williams, Mr Charles Theophilus Judah to Miss Sarah Spence Peixotto, both of Spanish Town.
November 9, 1881
On the 2nd Novr. 1881 at St George's Church, Kingston, by the Bishop of Jamaica, assisted by the Revd. H.H. Kilburn and Revd. Jos Williams, George Macdougal Duff to Helen Gordon, daughter of the late Alex Jas. Brymer, Esq

November 17, 1881
At NO 15 Tower street on the 6th inst., the wife of Mr S. S. Wortley of a daughter

November 24, 1881
At Collins Green Pen, the residence of S. D. Lindo Eqr, in whose Parents' family she had been a true and faithful servant for over a generation, Mary Ann Taylor at the advanced age of 101 years and three months, deeply beloved and regretted.

Selected Vital Records from the Jamaican Daily Gleaner

November 25, 1881

At Ocho Rios, St Ann, on the 21st inst., the wife of Charles Granville Alberga of a daughter

December 1, 1881

At Minard, St Ann, on the 29th instant, the wife of A. W. Anderson of a son.

Nothing to the end

1882

January 18, 1882
On the 17th January 1882, at the Parish Church, Kingston, by the Right Rev. the Bishop of Jamaica assisted by the Rev J.W. Austin Acting Incumbent, The Rev. Charles F. Douet, M.A. Rector of Spanish Town and Acting Archdeacon of Middlesex to Ellen Mary, youngest daughter of the late Hon. Louis Fullerton Mackinnon, Member of the Legislative Council, of the Whim, Old Harbour.

January 30, 1882
In Spanish Town on the 19th inst. by the Rev John H. Harris, Wesleyan Minister, S.K. Magnus, Esq. to Imogene Catherine, widow of the late Lieutenant Nicholson of the 1st W.I. Regiment.

February 9, 1882
On the evening of the 8th at the Pavillion Hotel, Harbour Street, Charles Fletcher of Mt. Anns

February 10,1882
At 6.30 p.m. yesterday Rebecca Morales, Sister of Abraham Morales, Falmouth. The funeral will take place this evening from the residence 69 Hanover Street at 4 p.m. Friends and acquaintances are invited to attend.

February 21, 1882
At Mount Hermon, St Elizabeth on the 15th inst., by the Revd. John S. Farquharson, assisted by the Revd. Hugh A. Nethercott, JOHN ARTHUR ROBISON Colonial Bank, Kingston, only son of John Robison Esq., Clapham Road, London to ALICE ADELINE, third daughter of J.M. Farquharson, Esq., Long Hill, St Elizabeth.

March 2, 1882
This morning at Rae Town, Edmund Levy, Esq. in the 46th year of his age. Funeral will take place at 4 precisely. Friends will please accept this intimation.

March 8, 1882
Burrell-February 6 at Clifton Terrace, South Norwood, Anne Maria, widow of the late Rev. William Robert Burrell of Jamaica, W.I. and East Woodhay, Hants, aged 52 years.

Selected Vital Records from the Jamaican Daily Gleaner

March 28, 1882

At Greenwood Cottage, Spanish Town, on Saturday morning the 25th inst., Luke Rattigan aged 71 years.

March 29, 1882

Magnus-Branker-At Half-way-Tree Church, on Tuesday the 21st inst., by the Revd. H.H. Isaacs, assisted by the Revd. H. H. Kilburn, Frederick Augustus, second son of Geo. Magnus Esq., to Mary Helen, youngest daughter of Alex. Branker, Esq., merchant of this City. No cards.

At the Parish Church, Kingston, on Tuesday 21st instant, by the Revds. G.W. Downer, and J.D. Hunt, Sub Inspector Herbert T. Thomas, Jamaica Constabulary, to Gertrude, youngest daughter of the late B. Nunes, Esq., of Montego Bay.

May 23, 1882

At his late residence No 45 East Street, John Walker, late Bailiff of the City of Kingston Court, at 11,30 p.m. The friends and acquaintances of the deceased and of his son Mr. Charles A. Walker, are particularly requested to attend his remains from his late residence to the place of interment, at half past four o'clock precisely. Please let your Carriage attend.

June 22, 1882

At No 74 King Street, at 4 p.m. yesterday, Frederick Lindo, aged 61 years. The funeral will move from his late residence at 5 o'clock this afternoon.

July 25, 1882

At the United Presbyterian Church, Falmouth, on Wednesday, the 19th inst., by the Revd. Wm. Murray M.A. assisted by the Revd Dunbar Dey B.A and the Revd. Ellis Fray (uncle of the Bride), Alfred Pawsey of the parish of Kingston, youngest son of the late Robert Pawsey of Bury St Edmunds, England, to Teresa McCubbin second daughter of the late Henry Fray, of the parish of Trelawny, Esquire, and Granddaughter of the late Andrew McCubbin Esquire.

At St Marks Church, Rio Bueno on the 18th instant at 4 p.m. by the Rev J.E. Miller, George Donald Garsia, to Louisa Griffiths Scarlett, youngest daughter of the late John Scarlett, Esquire.

July 27, 1882

In Panama, on the 9th instant, aged 48 years, Alexander Dumont, Compositor, a native of Jamaica. He was for many years, and up to the time of his death which is much regretted, employed in the office of the Star and Herald.

August 8, 1882

Obituary for the Honorable Isaac Levy, Custos of Saint Catherine. (2 columns, page 2)

At York Lodge, at 9 o'clock on Monday night (7th August), Hon Isaac Levy, The funeral will take place from St Jago Park, Spanish Town, at 4.30 this evening. Friends and acquaintances are requested to attend.

August 12, 1882

On the 10th inst. the wife of Revd. H.M.F. MacDermott of a daughter.

1882

August 17, 1882
At Devon House, St Andrew on the 15th instant, the wife of Richard Hill Jackson, Esq. of a daughter.

September 2, 1882
On September 1, at 16 Sutton Street, Kingston Emma, Wife of Dr. Phillippo. The Funeral will leave for May Pen Cemetery, at 4 p.m. this evening.

September 8, 1882
At Logan Castle, Linstead, yesterday morning Alan Huntley, infant son of Albert Delgado Esq., aged 14 months.

September 9, 1882
TURNER-GOUGH-On the 5th September, at Wesley Chapel, by the Rev A.M. Smith, assisted by Revs W. Melville and S. Goodyer, Colin Thompson Turner, to Mary Jane eldest surviving daughter of late Roger Gough-No Cards.

September 11, 1882
The Friends and Acquaintances of Mr. Louis Cuthbert are requested to attend the remains of his wife Ellen, from her late residence, No 78 King Street, to the place of interment at 4.45 o'clock this evening. Please let your carriage attend.

October 16, 1882
On Saturday, 7th October, at St David's after a long and painful illness which she bore with Christian fortitude, Margaret Lamont, widow of the late John C. Lamont, leaving 4 children and a large circle of relatives and friends to mourn their irreparable loss. Verse.

Fishing is good at Rockfort. A sporting medico of this city visited that spot on Friday, and after using up half-a-pound of shrimps bait, succeeded by hard struggling, in landing a fish weighing nearly half an ounce.

October 18, 1882
CORINALDI-DELVANTE-CORINALDI-HENRIQUES. On the 11th inst., by the Revd. A.H. Nieto, at the residence of the bride's mother No 93 King Street, Sydney Anna, eldest daughter of Mrs. E.A and the Late Edwin Cecil Corinaldi of Montego Bay to Mr. Michael Delevante, and Edith Alice, second daughter of the same, to Mr. Jacob C. Henriques. No cards.

November 8, 1882
At Collin's Green, St Andrew, the residence of his uncle, Mr. S.D. Lindo at 9 o'clock last night, Joseph D'Aguilar eldest son of Mr. and Mrs. A.I. Lindo of Friendship, St Mary, aged 20 years. The funeral will leave for the place of interment at 5 p.m.

November 15, 1882
SAMUEL-WOLFE-In this city, on the 8th inst., at the residence of the father of the bride, by the Revd A. Griedhander, Augustus Alexander Samuel, fourth son of the late H.S. Samuel Esq., to Louisa fourth daughter of Ellis Wolfe, Esq. At home on the 18th and 19th instant.

Selected Vital Records from the Jamaican Daily Gleaner

The Friends and acquaintances of the late Miss Catherine J. Jackson, are requested to attend her remains form her residence No 106 East Street, to the place of interment, at 4 o'clock this evening. Please let your carriage attend.

November 20, 1882
At Poslyn, St Andrew, on the 15th instant, the wife of C. J. Ward of a son.

At her late residence, no 77 Water Lane, at 9.15 last night, Rachel beloved wife of Samuel Mordecai. Funeral will leave at 4.30 this evening.

November 27, 1882
On the 15th instant at Rosebank House, Kingston, the wife of Wellesley Bourke, of a son.

November 30, 1882
On the 26th November in Kingston Miss Mary Hannah Morris, the third daughter of the late Cotton Morris, formerly of St. John's Newfoundland and of St Pierre-les-Calais. Aged 76 years Verse.

December 2, 1882
At No. 19 North Street, Jas. Urbain Lemercier DuQuesnay. The funeral will move from the above residence to the place of interment at 4 o'clock this afternoon. Friends and acquaintances are requested to accept this intimation. Please let your carriage attend.

December 5, 1882
At Mandeville, on the 28th ultimo, James Graham Doorly, District Engineer, aged 37

1883

January 26, 1883
On the 24th December last at St Andrews, Columbia of yellow fever, David Charles son of Abraham and Lousia DeSouza of this city, much regretted.

January 27, 1883
On the 24th inst., Geraldine Agusta, youngest daughter of Frederick and Ester DeSouza, aged 7 years.

February 6, 1883
At 20 minutes past 4 o'clock this morning AGNES SUSAN daughter of Geo. P. and Eleanor Walsh, aged 7 months, Funeral at 4 o'clock this p.m.

February 9, 1883
LAY-CODNER On 1st inst., at the Holy Trinity Church by the Revd Joseph Dupont assisted by the very Revd Thomas Porter B.A. Octavio Jose eldest son of Armand Lay of Cuba to Marie Elizabeth eldest daughter of John Strong Codner of this city. No cards.

February 13, 1883
On the night of the 10th inst., at his residence No 63 Orange Street from injuries received at the hand of an assassin, Ellas Halstead a native of Norway in the 30th year of his age, much esteemed by all his friends and acquaintances. Norwegian papers please copy.

February 14, 1883
In this city, on the 9th instant Mrs Aug. A. Lindo of a girl.

February 17, 1883
At Norwood Lodge, St Andrews the wife of F. A. Magnus of a son.

February 24, 1883
At St George's Parsonage, Kingston on Thursday the 22nd instant, the wife of the Rev. H.H. Kilburn of a son.

February 26, 1883
Yesterday afternoon, at 5 o'clock at his residence 16 Bread Lane, Mr. Robert Cole (Cooper) Funeral will take place this after noon at 5 o'clock sharp. Friends and acquaintances are requested to attend.

Selected Vital Records from the Jamaican Daily Gleaner

March 12, 1883

COOPER-MACINTYRE On Wednesday 7th March by the Rev J. Cochrane, assisted by Revd. Dr Robb at 17 North Street, Thomas Cooper of Montego Bay to Julia Nathan second daughter of the late Alexander Macintyre of Edinburgh. No Cards.

April 5, 1883

Last night at his late residence, No 45 Highholborn Street, ROBERT WILLIAM KIRKLAND. The funeral will move at 4.30 p.m.. Friends and acquaintances will please accept this intimation.

At the residence of his father 112 Orange Street, on the 4th instant at 6.30 p.m. Ludlow Arundel Commerford, infant son of Amie and Arundel Cotter. Funeral to take place at 5 p.m. Safe in his Father's arms.

April 10, 1883

At Spanish Town on the 5th instant the wife of S. K. Magnus Esq of a daughter.

May 31, 1883

Died At 20m for 11 last night SOPHIA youngest daughter of the late Edwin Delgado. The funeral will leave from No 19 Fisher's Row, Rae Town at 4 .30 p.m.

June 6, 1883

Died at Port Antonio on Saturday the 2nd inst., Sarah Louise, eldest daughter of J. Malcolm Facey.

June 26, 1883

Died On Monday, 20the instant at St Andrew's Manse, East Queen Street, ISABELLE SOPHIA eldest surviving daughter of the Rev William Gillies. Funeral this afternoon at 4 o'clock. Friends are invited. Please send your carriage.

July 2, 1883

The friends and acquaintances of WILLIAM MORAIS are requested to attend his remains from his residence North Street and Barry Streets to the place of interment at 5 p.m. today. Please let your carriage attend.

July 9, 1883

Died at 11.30 last night at No 113 Orange Street Dr Arundel H. Cotter. The funeral will move at 4.30 this evening. Friends will please accept this notification.

July 13, 1883

Died Last night at 66 Rum Lane, Mrs Jane Elizabeth Wightman. The funeral will leave at 5 o'clock this evening. Please let your carriage attend.

July 30, 1883

Married At the family residence, 39 Duke St, in this city, on the evening of the 25th instant, by the acting Ministers of the Spanish and Portuguese and the German and English Synagogues, Julia Alice to Isaac A. Sasso, Esq of Panama and Rachel Eugenie to Amos D.C. Levy Esq, of St Mary's daughters of A. N. Henriques Esq – No cards.

1883

August 3, 1883
The friends and acquaintances of Mr Collin A. C. Hogg are requested to attend the remains of his beloved sister Jane, from his residence, No 18 Sutton Street to the place of Interment at 4.30 p.m. Please let your carriage attend.

August 8, 1883
MARRIED Charleton-Cocking. July 12 at Holy Trinity, Waltham Cross, Herts by Revd. Ralph D. Cocking, M.A. Incumbant of Holy Trinity, Brighton, uncle of the bride, assisted by the Revd V. F. Hammond, M.A. Vicar of Drightlington, Yorks, uncle of the bridegroom and the Revd.R. Faraker, curate of Waltham Cross, George Thomas only son of Captain George Charleton of Blackheath, late 69the Regiment to Marcella Melvillena Sloan, only daughter of the late James R. Cocking Esq, Jamaica, granddaughter of the late Ralph Cocking Esq., Stipendiary Magistrate, Jamaica.

August 13, 1883
MARRIED- On the 8th instant at Margaretville, St Andrew, the residence of J.J. Wood, Esq, Inspector of Schools, uncle of the Bride, by the Revd. Wm. Griffiths, assisted by the Revd. J.W. Mold, the Revd. R.H. McLaughlin, of Mount Royale, St Mary to Miss Judith Ophelia Wood, third daughter of G. W. Wood, Esq.

IN MEMORIAM of ABRAHAM NOEL CROSSWELL (Eldest son of the late Noel Croswell) who breathed his last at his residence Ivanhoe Cottage Manchester Square, On Sunday morning at 3.30 aged 37 years and 6 months, surrounded by a loving and devoted circle. He had only recently returned from Port-au-Prince Haiti, where, for several years he was engaged in business. Cut off in the spring of life he leaves to mourn a dear and aged mother, an inconsolable wife, six young children brothers and sisters. Through his well known urbanity and strict integrity he had fostered a large circle of friends by who he was held in highest esteem. He was a devoted son, a loving husband, a tender father, a good brother and a true and warm hearted friend. His remains were followed by a large cortege to their last resting place as a tribute to his memory. Verse.

September 1, 1883
At St Michael's Church, Kingston, on the 29th August (by the Revd H.M.F. MacDermot) The Revd Edward Jocelyn, second son of the late S.S Wortley, Esq of Uppingham, Rutland to Bertha Evangeline, fourth daughter of the late Revd. T.J. Brown of Kingston, Jamaica.

At Porus, Manchester on the 22nd August, aged 78 years, Mary McPherson, leaving an only daughter to mourn her irreparable loss. The deceased was well known as a Tavern keeper, and by her amiable qualities endeared herself to a large circle of acquaintances and friends.

September 1883
At Port Maria, St Mary on the 28th utl, the wife of R. Macdonald Cocking of a daughter.

November 9, 1883
At Spanish Town on Sunday Evening the 28th inst (October) Mary Elizabeth Ratigan, daughter of the late Luke Ratigan, Esq., There to rest in hope we laid her, 'Neath the shadow of the cross.

1884

January 12, 1884
MARRIED At 15 Sutton Street, on the 9th instant, by the Rev. Dr. Robb, assisted by the Rev. James Cochrane, the Rev George Davidson, Minister of the Presbyterian Church, Goshen St Mary To Rhoda Groom, fifth daughter of the late Alfred Groom, Esq of this city.

February 8, 1884
The Friends as acquaintances of James Cruchley are requested to attend his remains from his late residence No 21, Water Lane, East to the place of interment at 4.30 this evening. Please let your carriage attend.

February 22, 1884
DIED AT No 23, Hanover Street yesterday. JOSEPH STINES MAGNUS. The funeral will leave at half-past four this afternoon. Friends and acquaintances will please accept this intimation.

March 13, 1884
MARRIED On the 11th inst. at St Andrew's Church by the Right Rev. the Lord Bishop of Jamaica assisted by the Rev. H.H. Isaacs, M.A. Rector of St Andrew's, Vincent John Garland, Lieutenant 1st West India Regiment, son of M. Raven Garland, Esq of King's Lynn, Norfolk, England to Sarah Constance, eldest daughter of Samuel Constantine Burke, Esq Crown Solicitor and assistant Attorney Genl., Jamaica.

April 7, 1884
At Blenheim Manchester the residence of his son, on the 31st March, SOLOMON RODRIQUES DaCOSTA, in the 77th year of his age. He leaves a sorrowing widow, an only son, two daughters and many grandchildren to mourn their irreparable loss. His soul has winged its flight to realms of eternal bliss.

May 3, 1884
BIRTH. AT Devon House, St Andrew on the 29th ultimo, the wife of Richard Hill Jackson, Esq of a son.

May 5, 1884
MARRIED On Tuesday the 29th April at the Parish Church, Savanna-la-Mar by the Rev Henry Clarke, Rector and assisted by his son the Revd Henry Clarke of Petersfield Church, Philip Haughton James, eldest son of John Haughton James Esq of Rooning

River St Anne to Ella Jane, only daughter of Edward John Sadler Esq., Acton House, Westmoreland

May 6, 1884
DIED In this city yesterday evening at No 51 Harbour Street, JONATHAN B BURROWES Snr Friends and Acquaintances are requested to attend his remains at 4.30 p.m. Please let your carriage attend.

May 16, 1884
BIRTH On the 13th instant at Minard Pen, St Ann's the wife of A. W. Anderson, Esq., of a daughter.

May 27, 1884
The Friends and acquaintances of the late JOHN GRAVES are requested to attend his remains from his late residence, No 18 Duke Street to the place of interment at 4.30 p.m. this afternoon. Please let your Carriage attend.

May 30, 1884
DIED On the 10th May instant in the city of New Orleans, U.S.A. Philip Simons aged 31 years. He was a Native of Jamaica and leaves relatives and friends to mourn their loss.

June 18, 1884
DIED At 8 Tower Street, Mrs Catherine Campbell, relict of Duncan Campbell of Falmouth, and mother-in-law of R. T. Clerk, The funeral will take place at 4.30 p.m. this evening. Friends are invited. Please let your carriage attend.

June 20, 1884
In this City on Saturday evening the 16th instant after a few days illness, Elizabeth, the beloved wife of Mr Louis Cunha, aged 65 years. Asleep in death-To wake in God.

June 27, 1884
DIED In this city on the 26th instant, at his late residence, No 3 Laws Street, ROSS JAMISON LIVINGSTON. Friends and acquaintances are requested to attend his funeral which will take place at 5 o'clock this evening.

July 8, 1884
DIED On Wednesday night the 2nd inst., in Spanish Town, ELMA IMOGIN, daughter of DANIEL AND LOUSIA COHEN HENRIQUES JNR., aged 19 years and six months leaving a large circle of relatives and friends to mourn their loss. Verse.

July 10, 1884
Friends and acquaintances of Mr William Delgado are requested to attend his remains from his residence No 34 Rose Lane, to the place of interment at 5 o'clock this afternoon. Please let your carriage attend.

July 16, 1884
DIED at No 31 North Street on the morning of the 10th instant after a long and painful illness, MRS SUSAN HOPWOOD, AGED 96. Her end was peace.

August 6, 1884
DIED In Kingston 5th August, 1884, Daniel Virtue Sutherland, of Manchester.

1884

August 28, 1884
BIRTH In this city on 27th instant, the wife of D. H. DaCosta of a son.

September 3, 1884
At sea, on 4th may in the Bay of Bengal on board the Barque Cape City, the wife of John McMillan master of a daughter.

September 16, 1884
On Saturday, the 13th instant at No 83 Harbour Street from injuries received from a cow, Thomas Calvert Thomason of Portland and Emilyville Pen, St Andrew aged 45 years leaving a wife and two children, with a large number of relatives and friends to mourn his melancholy and premature death.

September 18, 1884
Died yesterday at Holmwood, Rae Town, GEORGE SILVERA, of Crescent, St Mary, aged 77 years. The funeral will take place at 4.30 this afternoon.

September 19, 1884
BIRTH On the 16th instant, at Winchester Park, Kingston, the wife of Alfred Pawsey, of a son.

October 6, 1884
DIED At his late residence No 17 Prince of Wales Street, Allman Town, on Sunday 5th instant, WILLIAM W. McWHINNEY, Aged 58 years, His remains will be conveyed to their last resting place at half past 4 o'clock this afternoon, Friends will please accept this intimation-carriages.

October 8, 1884
DIED At the Rectory Mandeville on Friday 3rd October, RICHARD BROOK MORRISON PANTON, eldest son of the Rev D B. Panton, M.A. Rector.

October 17, 1884
MARRIED On the 8th October 1884, at Stoney Hill, by Revd John Campbell M.A. Cantab assisted by the Revd Acheson Findlay uncle of the bride, George Shannon, only surviving son of the late F. B. Thomason of Aberdeen, Scotland to Marie McCulloch, eldest daughter of the late William Findlay, of Bangor, Ireland and Hamilton, Scotland.

October 21, 1884
MARRIED On the 18th September at St George's Tuffnell Park W., by the Rev. F. M. Harke, assisted by the Rev. G. Sargeant, ALEXANDER McDOWELL NATHAN of Trevennion Lodge, St Andrew, Jamaica to Georgie daughter of the late George Rankin, Esq, Londonderry Ireland.

October 30, 1884
MARRIED KEMP-MACPHIE On the 22nd October, by the Rev James Cochrane, assisted by the Rev J.D. Robertson, at St Andrew's Kirk in this city, Thomas third surviving son of John Kemp, Stirling, Scotland, to JESSIE second daugther of Chas. Macphie, Buchauan, Stirlingshire, Scotland.

November 1, 1884
BIRTH At Friendship Penn, St Elizabeth on the 27th the wife of George R. J. Maxwell of a daughter.

Selected Vital Records from the Jamaican Daily Gleaner

November 14, 1884
The friends and acquaintances of the late George Henriques are requested to attend the remains of his widow, MARTHA, from No 18 ½ Harbour Street, E. to the place of interment at 4.30 this evening. Please let your carriage attend.

November 17, 1884
MARRIED At the residence of the Bride's father, Oct 23, Mr J. Bernard Hart of Boston; formerly of Jamaica West Indies more recently of New York to Miss May E. Clarke, formerly of Roxbury.

November 19, 1884
MARRIED On the 11th instant at the Parish Church, Kingston, by the Revd G. W. Downer, Rector assisted by the Revd H. H. Isaacs, M.A. Rector of St Andrew, Frederick Stephen, second son of the late Frederick Church, Esq of Dawlish, Devonshire, England to Geraldine, eldest daughter of C. A. Robinson, Esq. of this city.

November 25, 1884
DIED At No 16 East Street, VERA infant daughter of Charles and Rosalin Valencia, Funeral at 4 o'clock this evening.

November 20, 1884
At his residence, No 1 North Street, at 4 o'clock yesterday evening, LOUIS PHILLIPPI ALBERGA, aged 44 years. The funeral will leave at 9 o'clock this evening. Friends will please let your Carriage attend.

December 1, 1884
MARRIED On the 25th ultimo at Halfway-Tree Church, St Andrew, by the Revd H. H. Isaacs, M.A. Rector J.B. LUCIE SMITH, eldest son of the late Sir John Lucie Smith, C.M.G. Chief Justice of Jamaica, to KATIE second daughter of S. Constantine Burke, Esq Crown Solicitor and Assistant to the Attorney-General.

Advertizement by Alfred Pawsey 104 Harbour Street. Novelties for Christmas and Christmas cards.

December 9, 1884
On Tuesday November 11th at Teddington, Middlesex, England, Roberta Wilmina Douet, widow of the Rev C.T.P. Douet, Rector of Metcalfe, Jamaica in her 63rd year.

December 16, 1884
DIED In Kingston on Monday the 15th December STERLING FISHER, of Edinburgh, Scotland, aged 50 years.

December 17, 1884
At Heavitree Manchester Jamaica on 3rd December, Mrs Arthur George Ffrench of a son.

December 29, 1884
On the 22nd instant, at No 118 ½ Orange Street Kingston, the wife of John M. Croswell of a daughter.

1884

December 30, 1884

DIED At No 67 Church Street, the residence of his aunt Mrs Prendagast, RICHARD MALVIN LORD, second son of the late R. B. Lord. Friends will please accept this invitation. Funeral at 4.30 this evening.

1885

January 6, 1885
Figueroa-Stines. On 23rd December 1885 at the residence of the brides father, by the Rev. H.H Kilburn, assisted by the Rev, H. Ambrose, Colin Grey eldest son of the late William Gray Figueroa to Viola Ann eldest daughter of Jacob Adelbert Stines of this city, No cards.

January 7, 1885
At Truscotts Villa, Brown's Town, St Ann on the 2nd inst., the wife of James O'Meally, Solicitor, of another son.

January 12, 1885
At his residence Margaret villa, Halfway Tree John Jarrett Wood, Inspector of Schools aged 61 years. Funeral at 4 this evening.

January 26, 1885
At his residence Spanish Town on the 10th instant after a painful and lingering illness, Richard Lindo Morales, aged 39 years, youngest son of the late Dr. Moses Morales, leaving a bereaved wife and numerous relatives and friends to mourn their loss.

January 29, 1885
On the 26th instant at 69 Harbour Street, Mrs Duncan Cotter of a son.

January 30, 1885
On the 22nd instant by the Rev H.H. Kilburn at St Georges Church, Thomas Turner son of the late Walter Murray Turner of St Andrew, to Julia Maria second daughter of David E. Cohen of this city. No cards.

February 25, 1885
In this city on the 18th by Mr Henry Cohen, Reader of the United Israelites, Thaddeus, son of Ainsley Mordicai, Esq., to Julia daughter of Moses Pinto Esq. No Cards.

March 2, 1885
At Coke Chapel on Wednesday the 25th inst., by the Rev. T.M. Geddes, assisted by the Rev. J.A. MacIntosh, John Alexander, eldest son of the late John Lefranc, to Mary Emily second daughter of Mr.J.J. Drew, the grand daughter of the late Stephen Drew, Barrister at Law, St Anne's.

March 9, 1885
On Friday the 6th inst. the wife of Amos Morais of a son.

Selected Vital Records from the Jamaican Daily Gleaner

March 19, 1885
On Wednesday the 18th instant at the Mico Institution, Kingston, the wife of F.G. Gruchy of a daughter.

March 30, 1885
At No 53 George's Lane CHARLES M. NUNES. The funeral will take place at 5 o'clock this evening. Friends will please accept this invitation.

March 31, 1885
On the 18th inst. at St George's Church, Kingston, by His Lordship the Bishop of JAMAICA, assisted by the Revd. J.B. Ellis, the Rev Robert George Ambrose of Plymouth England and Incumbent of Mount Hermon, and Nain, Jamaica, to Sarah Emily Gertrude, eldest daughter of Mr. John C. Nethersole.

April 1, 1885
At the Parish Church, on Wednesday 25th March at 5 p.m. by the Rev. Downer, Estella Constance Morais of this City to Walter George Rackham, eldest son of George Rackham, Tailor and Draper, Saxmundham Suffolk, England.

April 20, 1885
At 10 o'clock last night, at his residence No 14 Elletson Road Samuel R DaCosta in his 60th year. Funeral will leave at 5 p.m. Friends will please accept this invitation.

At Brokenhurst, Manchester, the wife of Walter W. Wynne of a son, on April 15, 1885

April 28, 1885
In this city on Sunday 26th inst. At 48 East Street, the wife of A.M. Alexander of a girl.

May 12, 1885
On the 9th inst. at HalfWay Tree Church, St Andrew, by the Rev. H.H. Isaacs, Henry D.A.Reid, eldest son of G. Lowe Reid, Of Brighton, England to Ianthe, fourth daughter of the late Benjamin NUNES, of Montego Bay.

May 19, 1885
Lord- At 22 Montgomerie Terrace, Mount Floria, Glasgow, on the 19th April, after a brief illness, Mary Jane wife of John Ashley Lord, and second daughter of the late Mary and James Campbell, of Kingston, Jamaica.

June 8, 1885
On the 4th June, at St Andrew's Parish Church by the Right Rev. Bishop of Jamaica, assisted by the Ven. Arch. Douet, MA, Emily Maud eldest daughter of Rev. H.H. Isaacs, M.A. Rector of the Parish, to Frank F.M. Lynch, Esq, Civil Service Ja.

June 10, 1885
At his residence Marshall's Pen, Manchester, on Saturday, the 6th instant Michael Muirhead, Esq,. In his 87th year.

June 27, 1885
High School Calabar College Kingston Jamaica, Founded 1870 Prize and Class List Midsummer, 1885

1885

July 1, 1885
At No. 13 North Street, in this City, on the 6th inst.aged 54 years John Murray Auld, of Steventon, Ayreshire, Scotland, eldest son of the late Rev John M. Auld, Licentiate of the Church of Scotland.

July,1885
The Trial of William Isaacs continues.

July 15, 1885
At Retterings, in the parish of Trelawny, on the 9th July, 1885 by the Revd. Ellis Fray (father of the bride) assisted by the Revds. J. Kingdon, O. Welch and P William, Herbert Leopold Mossman of Ulster Spring, to Emily Fray of Retterings.

July 24, 1885
DIED At 11.20 yesterday at his residence No. 47, Oxford Street James Lindo. The funeral will move at 5 o'clock this evening Friends and acquaintances will please accept this intimation.

July 25, 1885
On the 22nd instant. At the Registrar's Office, Kingston, Victor Emanuel, son of the late Geo Silvera of Crescent Pen, St Mary to Constance Lilla third daughter of the late Septimus Feurtado of Kingston.

July 29, 1885
At Chester Castle, Hanover, on 25th inst, Emma Matilda, relict of the late Joseph H. Isaacs, of Montego Bay in her 76th year.

On the 31st the beloved mother of H.J. Isaacs and widow of the late Joseph H. Isaacs.

August 11, 1885
On the 6th inst. At St George's Church, Kingston, by His Lordship the Bishop assisted by the Revds. H. Kilburn and J.B. Ellis, Revd Odlarne, William Decimus Lane of Clifton Bristol to Clara Antoinette second daughter of Mr. John C. Nethersole of this city. No cards.

August 17, 1885
DIED At 2 o'clock this morning Esther Cohen. Friends and acquaintances will please accept this intimation. The funeral will move from No 17 East Street, at 5 p.m. today. Please let your carriage attend.

Died Last night at No 60 Hanover Street, Charles Cecil infant son of Mark C. Hendriks. Funeral at 4.30 this evening. Friends will please attend.

September 15, 1885
At Margate England on 23rd August, Samuel Morrice, aged 72 years.

October 13, 1885
At Colon, on the 29th September, by the Revd Kerr, by permission of the Government, Joseph Allen Piper to Elizabeth Sachell, both of Spanish Town, Jamaica.

Selected Vital Records from the Jamaican Daily Gleaner

October 16, 1885

This morning at his residence, No 109 Barry Street at 6 o'clock Mr. Alexander Levy. Friends and acquaintances will please accept this intimation and attend his remains to Ebenezer. The funeral will leave tomorrow morning at 7.30. Please let your carriage attend.

October 22, 1885

MARRIED On the 14th inst at St Thomas Church Linstead, by the Revd. Richard Harding, Henry John Mendes to Catherine Nunes, second daughter of Isaac Nunes DaCosta of Newland Park Ewarton. No cards

DIED SUDDENLY

On the 27th Ulto. At 22 Montgomerie Terrace, Mount Florida, Glasgow, in his 70th year John Ashley Lord, late Inspetor of Police, Jamaica. Deeply regretted.

October 28, 1885

At the residence of her brother S.D. Lindo, Esq., 105 East Street, at midday 27th October Rebecca Augusta, widow of Alfred A. Lindo, aged 52 years. The funeral will take place at 5 o'clockof this evening of 28th.

November 5, 1885

West Abbey October 29th the wife of Mr. W.G. Rackham, of a daughter.

In this city on the 3rd of November, Mrs. Elizabeth Maxwell widow of the late James D. Maxwell aged 72 years Verse.

November 27, 1885

At Devon House, St Andrew on the 22nd inst. The wife of R.H. Jackson Esq of a daughter.

December 8, 1885

At St Jago Park, on Sunday morning 6th December, the wife of the Honble.E.G. Levy of a son.

December 9, 1885

Died on the 5th instant in Spanish Town, at the residence of his uncle, Mr. G. Boettcher, Emil Boettcher, aged 18, The only and dearly beloved son of Emil Boettcher, Esq, of Bremen Germany.

December 17, 1885

At Charlemont, son Saturday, 12th December the wife of George McGrath, Esquire, of a son.

MARRIED At Top Hill, Trelawney, by the Revd, J.S. Wollett, S.J. on the 9th instant, Thomas Patrick Madden, M.G. son of Francis E. Madden, Esq., of Ballinasloe, Ireland, to Eugenie Fleurette, second daughter of the Hon Robert Nunes of Trelawney.

December 31, 1885

Died at the Cedars Cottage Highgate, district of St Catherine on the 21st instant, Augustus Field, (late Captain U.S.A) aged 61 years.

1886

January 1, 1886
At Cave Valley, on the 27th December 1885 the wife of David Archer Esq of a son.

January 4, 1886
DIED Yesterday at 2.30 p.m. DANIEL BENNETT. The funeral will leave No 72 Barry street and Mark Lane at 4.30 this evening. Friends and acquaintances will please accept this intimation.

January 5, 1886
On the 2nd January, 1886 at Stroadwick's Lodgings, Kingston, the wife of Sidney Moxey of a daughter.

January 14, 1886
Obituary for Daniel Bennett. aged 69 Died in this city on the 3rd inst. For many years he carried on business at Annatto Bay. etc.

January 15, 1886
On the 14th instant at Marble Hall in this city, the wife of H. Launcelot Edwards of a daughter.

January 16, 1886
At his mother's residence, No 1 Laws St., John Hawkins Figueroa son of the late Joseph Figueroa. Friends and Acquaintances are requested to attend his remains to the place of interment at 4.30 tomorrow evening. Please let your carriage attend.

January 21, 1886
Died on Tuesday 12th January 1886 T.T. Simpson, of the Parish of Trelawny, Aged 42 years.

January 22, 1886
Died Doorley-On the 21st December, 1885 at the Poplars, Sunningfield Road, Hendon, Dorothy Walrond Widow of the late Major Martin Doorly, age 69 years. "Her children arise up and call her blessed".

January 26, 1886
HARRIS-DePASS. On Wednesday evening 13th instant at 1a North Street, the residence of the bride's Father by D. Baruch Esq., reader of the Spanish and Portuguese Synagogue,

Joseph Bravo second son of the late Ralph Harris, to Judith, fourth daughter of Henry John DePass both of this city.

January 27, 1886
ALBERT ISSA, Native of Kingston, Jamaica Died at Colon, on the 19th January in his 21st year leaving a circle of relatives and friends to mourn his loss. R.I.P.

February 3, 1886
On the 31st December 1885 at Funchal Maderia, the Venerable Archdeacon Rowe, M.A. Aged 72 years.

February 10, 1886
MARRIED
On the 1st inst. at the Parish Church Kingston, by the Revd G.W. Downer, John Leslie Cox, L.R.C.P. to Florence Nugent, eldest daughter of the late Robert Oldrey, Esq of Harpole Hall, Northhamptonshire.

February 12, 1886
Died at his residence No 26 Duke Street, Joseph Pelissier, Funeral will take place at 4 30 this evening.

February 20, 1886
At King's Westmoreland in 51st year of her age Charlotte Harkness beloved wife of C.M. MacLeod, Land Surveyor leaving a sorrowing husband and five children. She was deservingly beloved and esteemed by a large circle of relatives and friends and in like is deeply lamented by them. R.I.P.

Auction Sale of Aboukir Plantation.
We will Sell by Public Auction at our Auction Rooms in the City of Kingston on Thursday the 25th inst at 11 o'clock Aboukir Plantation in the Dry Harbour Mountains on the public road leading from Brown's Town to Clarendon and containing 1,000 acres more or less.
The Dwelling House is substantially built, with necessary outbuildings and barbicues, to serve the purposes of curing and housing large crops of pimento or coffee.
There are two large tanks that could be put in order at a moderate outlay and a "Remarkable Spring" that has never been known to be dry.
The Property is well suited for a grazing pen and abounds in young and bearing pimento trees also a lot of coffee in lumps.
Aboukir is situated in a seasonable locality and the salubrity of the climate is equal to the best in the Island. Further particulars will be given on application to us.
Conditions will be given at time of sale! Turnbull, Mudon & Co. Government Auctioneers.

February 22, 1886
Died At Spitzkop, St Andrew on the 19th instant Archibald Spencer, the infant son of John and Georgina Musson, aged 4 months.

February 23, 1886
At Port Royal, 21st instant the wife of W. D. Smedmore of a son.

1886

February 25, 1886
Died Last Night at her residence No 57 Church Street Miss Georgiana Stephenson. Friends and acquaintances will please accept this intimation and attend at half-past four o'clock this evening. Please let your carriage attend.

119 Duke Street, Kingston on the 10th inst. Sainson-The wife of Paul C. Sainson, of Panama of a son.

February 26, 1886
obituary
Died at his residence No 81 East Street, yesterday afternoon Edward G. Tyrrell aged 65. The funeral will take place at 5 o'clock this evening. Friends and acquaintances will place accept this intimation.

March 5, 1886
On the 23rd January at Bath after a long illness, Agnes Eliza, widow of Samuel Rennalls Esq late of Spanish Town Jamaica. Age 82.

March 8, 1886
DIED On Sunday 7th instant at No 93 Kings Street Daniel C. DeSouza, Merchant of Falmouth son of D. H. DeSouza Esq of London. The funeral will take place this afternoon at 5 p.m. His friends are requested to accept this notice and to let their carriage attend.

At No 16 East Street, Vernon, infant son of Charles and Rosalin Valencia. The funeral will move at 4.30 this evening.

March 9, 1886
On the 6th March 1886 at Hagley Park, St Andrew, the wife of C. Colquhown Aitkin, of a son.

March 12, 1886
DIED At his residence Essendene House, East Queen Street, Soloman Nunes DaCosta, late H.M. Customs. His remains will be interred this evening at 4 .30 o'clock. Friends and acquaintances are requested to attend.

March 15, 1886
At Spanish Town, on the 5th inst. William D. Humber, aged 43 years, leaving a large family and numerous friends to mourn their irreparable loss.

March 26, 1886
In this city at North St, Villa, Sigisman DePass. Friends and acquaintances are requested to attend his remains to the place of interment at 4.30 this evening. Please let your carriage attend.

In this city yesterday Isaac H. DeMercado, aged 56. The Funeral will take place from his late residence No 90 Hanover Street at 4 o'clock this afternoon. and ½ column Obituary.

April 2, 1886
March 29th at Sutton's Pasture, Vere the wife of Henry L. Clare, M.B. District Medical Officer of a son.

Selected Vital Records from the Jamaican Daily Gleaner

April 3, 1886
DELGADO-BRANDON
-On the 31st ultimo, by A.B. Josephs, Reader of the Amalgamated Synagogue, Marcus, youngest son of the late Edwin Delgado to Miriam, fourth daughter of the late Nathaniel Brandon. At home Saturday and Sunday 10th and 11th instant. No cards.

April 10, 1886
On Friday evening, 9th April Mrs. Abigail Hicks, the mother of Colonel Hicks and of Mrs. Thomas Oughton. Friends are notified that the funeral will leave Bel Air at 4.30 this afternoon.

April 16, 1886
On 10th march at Sandmere Road, Clapham, London S.W. A.C. Logan, Esq., of Great Valley in the parish of Manchester. Mr. Logan is well known in the island and was a member of the Legislature for a good many years.

April 19, 1886
Married On the 13th instant at St John's Church Ocho Rios by the Rev F. H. Sharpe, Alexander Morrison Lang/Long, M.B. to Wilhelmina Ann (Tiny) Youngest daughter of James Stewart Esq., Shaw Park St Ann's late 22nd Regt.

April 24, 1886
At Galloway Lodge on the 20th inst. Leonard Melroy Radcliffe aged 19 years and ten months, second and dearly loved son of the Revd. John Radcliffe and Isabella his wife.

April 28, 1886
At 69 Water Lane this morning George Henry Bubb, aged 5 years fourth son of J.A.P. and Joseph B. Clarke. The funeral will move at 5 p.m. sharp. Friends and acquaintances will please accept this invitation.

Later on April 30, it says Josefa B. Clarke.

April 29, 1886
At his residence No 108 Princess Street, at 3.15 p.m. yesterday, Edward Duffus, Late of Gordon Town, St Andrew. The funeral will take place this evening at 4.30 o'clock. Friends and acquaintances are requested to attend.

April 30, 1886
List of Students who had passed Local Examinations for Cambridge University. One girl M.Geddes obtained honours
Dayes H.W.W. between 16 and 17 who had passed the examination for Boys.

May 10, 1886
Exhibition in London The Jamaican Court and Plan of the Buildings. Lists of 969 objects in the exhibition. Including spices, botanicals, rum, bamboo, walking sticks.

May 19, 1886
At the Residence of her Son S.D. Lindo, 105 East Street on Tuesday the 18th instant, Rebecca Widow of the late Honbl. A.J. Lindo aged 84 years. Funeral will take place at 5 p.m. on Wednesday 19th instant.

1886

May 20, 1886

On the 17th inst., at Liberty Hill in the Parish of St Ann Georgiana widow of the late George Radcliffe Stennett, M.D. aged 73.

May 21, 1886

On Thursday night at 31 Duke Street, Charles D. Delgado, son of the late Edwin Delgado, aged 32 years. Interment at 4.30 p.m. friends and acquaintances will please accept this intimation.

May 27, 1886

On the 18th of May 1886 at Mizpah in the Parish of Manchester Jamaica by the Reverend Henry Walder (the brother of the bride) George Hicks, Assistant Inspector of Schools to Susette Walder late of the Moravian Jamaica Female Training College.

June 1, 1886

Mark C. Hendriks of Roxburgh House is advertizing as a Cabinet maker, undertaker and Autioneer.

June 3, 1886

At his residence on the Slipe Pen Road (above Torrington Bridge) Horatio Bonitto. Friends and acquaintainces are invited to attend his remains from his residence to the Parish Church at 4 p.m. Please let your carriage attend.

June 10, 1886

At Brighton, England, 13th May, 1886, Brigade Surgeon Iyler Oughton, fourth son of the late Revd. Samuel Oughton. Age 49 years.

June 18, 1886

A SAD STORY-The recent Storm, and the Ruin it has wrought to Life and Property. Men, Women and Children carried away in the Flood.---Graves throw up their dead, and skeletons float on decayed Coffins over the fair plains of the island.

Brown's Town, June 14th- I notice in the Gleaner, the damage done on the South side. I will now give you some idea of the damage done on the Northside. In the Cave Valley districts, a distance of sixteen miles from here. The rain commenced on Saturday the 5th and lasted up to the 10th. On Tuesday it rained in torrents so much so that the overseer, Mr. Archer of Cave Valley, thought it advisable to remove his family to the Great House. He succeeded in carrying one buggy load, returning for a lady, the water became so high he had to get a boy to cross the horses. Himself and the lady was thrown into the water, had it not been for the bookkeeper, who got ropes and put round and dragged them they must have been drowned. By this time the buggy could not be seen, the boy who crossed the horses got drowned. Mr. Surgeons' store was close at hand; they put in there for a short time. The cook who assisted them got drowned. The water then became so high that you could only see the shingles, store and house being submerged, and it is up to this day. I traveled a distance of sixteen miles to see it. It is a fearful sight. Cane fields on Cave valley and Greenock estate, not a cane to be seen up to the present time, there is no signs of its subsiding. It is now amusingly sad to see three large boats, well manned, flying up and down a large body of water, when only a few days ago, it was dry land. Great praise is due to Inspector Black as also Mr. Nash, who went some miles in a boat to see the people. They found them in a state of starvation penned in. On their return, flour, meal and other articles were obtained, and a boat dispatched for the sufferers. Up to the present time, three bodies have been found, it is expected that a large number of cattle will be missing, at present no one can tell the amount of damage done, the water in some places is full 30 to 40 feet deep. Mr. Surgeon will be a very great sufferer; unless the shingles are taken off there is no chance of their being able to get at the goods and when they do, what will they be worth.

June 19, 1886
On the 27th inst. (ultimo) at Halifax N.S. after a very severe illness, Mary E. Widow of the late George Irwin, Druggist.

On Friday Evening Solomon DeCordova aged 51 years, The funeral will move from his late residence Merryfield Pen St Andrew, on Sunday morning at 8 o'clock.

July 1, 1886
On the 29th June at the Hope, St Andrew, the wife of Mr. G. N. Cox of a daughter

July 5, 1886
On the 29th June at 55 Church Street, the wife of V.E. Silvera of Oracabessa St Mary of a son.

July 7, 1886
At her residence No 45 Union Street, Montego Bay on Friday 2nd instant, Florence Alice the beloved wife of Samuel Hart. Aged 25 years.

July 12, 1886
Obituary Raphael DaCosta Lewin-Raphael DaCosta Lewin, Rabbi of the Hebrew Church, died at his residence no 52 East Sixty fifth Street on Friday night. He was born in Jamaica W. I. in 1845. A few years ago he was pastor of a synagogue in Greene Avenue, Brooklyn. This was given up on account of illness and Mr. Lewin has not of late occupied any pulpit. He was editor of the Jewish Advocate. New York Herald, Sunday June 27, 1886

Died At 2.15 p.m. on the 11 instant Florence Leonora the beloved wife of John M. Crosswell (and youngest daughter of the late Juan Hidalgo Esquire). The funeral will move at 5 o'clock this afternoon from the residence no 2 H East Queen Street. Friends and acquaintances will kindly accept this intimation. Please let your carriage attend.

July 15, 1886
Died in this city yesterday Henry Willoughby DaCosta. The funeral will take place from his late residence corner of Charles and Orange Streets at 5 o'clock this evening.

July 16, 1886
In this city on the 13th instant Mrs. Percival C. Cunha of a son.

July 21, 1886
DeCORDOVA-NUNES. On Wednesday 14th July, Joshua eldest son the late Michael DeCordova of Kingston to Viola Ianthe fourth daughter of the late Ralph Nunes of Kingston. At Home At their residence No 129 Upper King Street, on Saturday and Sunday evenings 24th and 25th July. No Cards.

July 23, 1886
Married On the 16th July at Colon, by the Registrar Mr. Leopold Levy to Alice third daughter of the late Jacob Rodriques DaCosta of Kingston.

1886

July 30, 1886
At Falmouth on 26th inst. John Passmore Esquire late Collector of H.M. Customs.

August 2, 1886
At Winchester Park on the 27th ultimo, the wife of Alfred Pawsey of a daughter.

August 5, 1886
Married PINNOCK-LOPEZ. – At St. George's Church on the 29th ulto. By the Revd. H.H. Kilburn, Cynthia Luna, youngest daughter of Edmund Lopez, to Thomas Ricker Pinnock, of Kingston.

August 13, 1886
At 4 p.m. yesterday afternoon, at his residence no 39 Parade, Louis John Desporte, Snr. at the advanced of 86 years. Friends and acquaintances are particularly invited to attend his remains to the place of interment at 4 p.m. this evening. Please let your carriage attend.

August 17, 1886
MELHADO-DOLPHY-At Esterville, Old Harbour on Wednesday 11th inst, by Mr.S. S. Lawton, Hon Lay Reader of the Amalgamated Congregation of Isrealites assisted by Mr. H.A. Josephs, Reginald son of Abraham Melhado to Dinah Irene daughter of Isaac Dolphy. No cards. At home Saturday and Sunday 21st and 22nd inst. No 55 Wildman Street, Kingston.

August 26, 1886
In this city on the 26th instant Edwin Cecil Henriques, the dearly beloved son of Aaron and Matilda Cohen Henriques leaving a bereaved mother, father, sister, brothers many relatives and friends to mourn their sad loss. Aged 17, Gone to Bloom in Heaven.

September 11, 1886
At his residence No 1 Bow Street, yesterday at 11a.m. Donald M. May aged 47 years. Friends and acquaintances are requested to attend his remains to the place of interment at 4 p.m.

At Whitney Estate Clarendon on the 31st ultimo Thomas James Brown, eldest son of the late Revd., Thomas James Brown.

MAGNUS-At No. 63 Duke Street on Wednesday the 8th the wife of Fred A. Magnus of a son.

September 26, 1886
At Port Henderson at 10 o'clock last night Hon Emanuel G. Levy . The funeral will take place from his late residence Spanish Town at 5 o'clock this evening. Friends and acquaintances will please accept this intimation.

It is with deep regret we announce the death at Port Henderson of Hon E.G. Levy. The sad occurrence took place at about ten o'clock last night. Mr. Levy had been ill for the past fortnight but his illness was not of a nature to lead those around him to anticipate an early dissolution. Yesterday however, members of his family were summoned from Kingston to his bedside by the sad intelligence that he was dying. To his disconsolate young widow, his bereaved mother and members of his family we tender our heartfelt sympathies.

Selected Vital Records from the Jamaican Daily Gleaner

September 23, 1886
On the 30th August at 27 Clifton Road Brighton, England the wife of H.D.A. Reid., Esq C.E.of a daughter.

September 24, 1886
On the 22nd instant at no 85 Duke Street, the wife of John E. Lyons, Esq of a son.

September 29, 1886
DePass-Isaacs-On Wednesday 22nd inst by the Revd James Cochrane (marriage officer) Isidore Orlando DePass, eldest son of Henry James DePass of this city to Ada Louise eldest daughter of the late William Nott Isaacs of St Anns.

On the 29th August at 7 Edinburgh Terrace, Kensington, the wife of Sir Adam G. Ellis Chief Justice of Jamaica of a daughter.

October 5, 1886
At his residence Pleasant View, St Andrew on the 28th Sept 1886 age 73 years Thomas Earl a native of Westmoreland England leaving four children to lament their loss. R.I.P.

October 20, 1886
At his residence Spanish Town at 7 o'clock this morning (Tuesday) S.K. Magnus, Age 57 years. The funeral will take place at 9 o'clock tomorrow morning Friends will please accept this intimation.

October 28, 1886
On 22nd October at Erdiston, Barbados, Sarah, beloved wife of Capt. R.H. Macaulay, Supt R.M.S. P. Co. and eldest daughter of the late Richard Munda of Kingston.

October 29, 1886
Golden Grove,29th Oct. 1886
Died At his residence Fair field on the morning of the 26th inst Robert Kirkland Esq in the 66th year of his age leaving a large circle of relatives and friends to mourn their irreparable loss. He was gentle and kind in all the relations of life and his death has caused a void which cannot be easily filled. "Tit tibi Tera levis".

November 3, 1886
MCCaw On the 31st October 1886 at Heathfield Penn, Lindstead, Edward McCaw age 86 years deeply regretted by his relatives and friends.

November 4, 1886
At Spanish Town on the 1st November Dorcas the beloved wife of William Charley. May her soul rest in peace.

November 5, 1886
At Worcester Lodge St Catherine, the residence of her uncle, William Collman, Esq, on Monday 1st November, 1886 Ella Eleanor, youngest daughter of the late Henry Garland Murray in her 21st year, deeply regretted by her relatives and friends.

November 10, 1886
PATTERSON-PASSMORE-At St George's Chruch on the 4th instant by the Rev H. H. Kilburn, assisted by the Revd. Lewis, George Louis, son of Henry Frederick Patterson

Esquire, of Kingston, Jamaica to Edith Elizabeth Gerrard, daughter of James Passmore Jr Esquire of Brown's Town St Ann's Jamaica. No Cards.

November 15, 1886
At Trevennion Lodge St Andrews on the 13th instant the wife of A.M. Nathan of a son.

Died Last night at nine o'clock at the London Tavern, Duke Street, Joseph Rodriquez DaCosta Senr, age 54. Friends and acquaintances are invited to attend the funeral at 4.30 this evening with out further notice. Please let your carriage attend.

November 26, 1886
On Monday 2nd instant at the Wesleyan Mission House, Croydon Lodge, Spanish Town the wife of the Revd J.A. McIntosh of a son.

December 1, 1886
After a long and painful illness (Paralysis) Henry Morris aged 61 years Friends are invited to follow his remains from the residence of Mr. Herbert A Cunha No 77 Duke Street to Coke Chapel and thence to Ebenezer Cemetery at 5 o'clock this evening. Carriages.

December 2, 1886
At 42 Duke Street of Malignant Small-pox Dec. 1st at the residence of his Mother, Mrs. Judith Hart, William Altamont aged 28 third son of the late Andrew Alexander Hart. R.I.P.

December 6, 1886
On the 3rd instant at No 26 Barrett Street, Spanish Town W. Buchan B. French. aged 27 years. May he rest in Peace.

December 7, 1886
At Lillyfield Penn, St Ann on Tuesday 30th November, Richard Moss in the 67th year of his age. Deeply lamented. R.I.P.

December 10, 1886
The Agriculture Show - A fine Day a Goodly number of Exhibits and a large number of spectators.- A list of the awards and a general review of the show.

December 14, 1886
In this city at midnight at Saturday the 11th inst. at the residence of Mrs. A. Lyon No 151 Upper Kingston Street. Maryann the beloved wife of A. J. Lindo Esq of Friendship St Mary age 52 years leaving a disconsolate husband, seven sons, two daughters and a large family to mourn their irreparable loss

December 17, 1886
At St Ann's Bay on Friday the 10th December the wife of James O'Meally, Solicitor of another son.

December 21, 1886
In Spanish Town at his residence, King Street on Thursday 16th inst., Daniel Cohen Henriques age 61 leaving a sorrowing wife,family and a large circle of relatives and friends to mourn their sad bereavement. May his soul rest in peace.

At her residence No 98 Orange Street at 3.30 this morning Miriam relict of the late Jacob Mendes Pereira in her 87th year. The funeral will leave at 4.30 this evening. Friends and acquaintances will please accept this intimation.

December 27, 1886
At No 16 East Street, the residence of her father, William McCormack, Rosalin, wife of Charles T. Valencia. The funeral will move at 4.30 this afternoon.

December 30, 1886
On the 19th inst at 6 p.m. at No 150 East Street residence of F.Lyons Esq., Honble George L. Phillips in the 76th year of his age. Funeral will take place at 4.45 o'clock this afternoon.
[Obituary on the 31st says he was of Montego Bay with a residence in East Street. Was Custos of St James and Member of the Old House of Assembly.]

1887

January 6, 1887
At Belmont, St Ann's on 1st January, 1887 the wife of A.C.C. Colthirst, Esq., of a son.

January 7, 1887
The friends and acquaintances of Mr. J.T. Ritchie are requested to attend the remains of his mother-in-law MRS CHARLOTTE CHANDLER, from his residence No 7 Parade to the place of interment his evening at 4.30 o'clock.

January 8, 1887
Obituary to John McPhail of St Thomas in the Vale.

January 17, 1887
The friends and acquaintances of Hyman Magnus are requested to attend his remains from his late residence, No 54 Duke Street at 8 o'clock tomorrow morning. Please let your carriage attend.

January 18, 1887
At Coke Chapel, Morant Bay, on Wednesday 12th January, 1887 by the Rev. D.J. Reynolds, assisted by the Rev. Wm. Melville ALEXANDER WILLIAM GEDDES, Wesleyan Minister, Bath, to ALICE ELIZABETH WALLACE, daughter of John Wallace, Esq., Lyssons, Morant Bay. No Cards.

January 19, 1887
Local News
The admission of pupils into Wolmer's Grammar School will take place on the 1st prox at eleven o'clock in the forenoon. Applicants are required to attend at eight o'clock in the morning accompanied by their parents or guardians, but no forms for application will be received later than Thursday the 27th instant.

January 28, 1887
On the 24th instant at 46 Barry Street, the wife of Irvin Mr. Colthirst, of a daughter, still-born.

February 2, 1887
Estate of Hon'ble Isaac Levy.
I am instructed to sell by Public Auction on Wednesday, 9th February Next at 11 o'clock forenoon at Mr. John McDonald Store, in this City, the following Sugar Estate and Breeding Pens in the Parish of St Mary belong to the above named estate.

Selected Vital Records from the Jamaican Daily Gleaner
Lot Nonsuch
Lot 2 Orange Hill and Newry
Lot 3 Agualta Vale Sugar estate
Lot 4 Agualta Vale Breeding Pen
Lot 5 Ellis Estates comprising Nutfield and Green or Tullock Castle
Joseph Stine, Auctioneer [Lots more detail].

February 18, 1887
The Hon. Michael Solomon, Custos of the Parish of St Ann, has invited the inhabitants to attend a public meeting at he Court House, in Saint Ann's Bay on Tuesday, the 22nd inst. At eleven o'clock for the consideration of His Excellency he Governor's suggestion for locally marking the important event of the Jubilee of Her Majesty's reign.

February 22, 1887
In this city on Saturday the 19th February, at the Mico Institution, Hanover Street, the wife of L.G. Gruchy of a daughter.

April 16, 1887
At Rosebank House, Kingston on the 8th instant, the wife of the Hon. Wellesley Bourke, of a daughter.

April 26, 1887
Marriage. On the 22nd March 1887 at Saint John the Evangelist, Brownswood? Park, Hortley in the County of Middlesex, by the Rev. G Birket Latreide, George Rochfort Clarke, of Chesteron Lodge, Oxfordshire, and of Swanswick, Hampshire and Barnstable in the Parish of Trelawny, Jamaica, M.A. J.P. Barrister-at-law, to Alice Louisa, youngest daughter of the late James Collins of Norwich.

April 27, 1887
On the 23rd ultimo at Bordeaux, France, the home of her daughters, Madme. Anna Luces and Lucy Vc Contesse Raoul de Joigny, Matilda Susanna in the 69th year, widow of Theophilus Bloomfield Esq., many years resident in Clarendon, Jamaica.

May 23, 1887
At Rae Town in this city on the 17th instant Alexander Douglas, infant son of T. Douglas Dallas, aged three months.

June 1, 1887
The friends and acquaintances of the Revd. Edwin Palmer are invited to attend the remains of his Father–in–law the Rev. Francis Johnson, late of Clarksonville, St Ann's from the Mission House No. 27 Hanover Street, to the place of interment at 4.30 p.m.

A garden party in aid of St. Michael's Church will be held at two o'clock today on the spacious grounds adjoining the residence of J. Stines, Esq. in East Street. The Committee have spared no effort in making the entertainment as attractive as possible, and hope it will be liberally patronized. The band of the 2nd West India Regiment will be in attendance. Among the attractions there will be a Jubilee tree, well stocked with valuable prizes, a maize, a skating rink, a magic well and all kinds of athletic sports.

June 30, 1887
The Jubilee Market—The Governors Levee—Presentation of a score of Loyal addresses—Arm! Arm! Ye Brave! Grand Review of Regulars and Volunteers at Up-Park

1887

Camp—Brilliant Pyrotechnic Display! "Like a Star i'the darkest night stick fiery off indeed"--THE QUEEN IN FLAMING JEWELS-VIVAT REGINA

July 1, 1887
Died. At nine o'clock last night, MAY, the infant child of Mr. and Mrs. Clarence L. Cunha. The funeral will leave from 59 Laws Street at 5 o'clock sharp this evening. Friends and acquaintances are invited to attend. Carriages.

July 6, 1887
On the 30th June, at St Andrew's Church, St Thomas ye East, by the Rev P.D.M. Cornwall, W. Herbert Carter, eldest son of the late Edwin and Anna Maria Carter, and Nephew of the late Robert Kirkland, to Fanny Elizabeth, second daughter of Richard Evans, Esq., of Westmoreland. NO Cards.

July 8, 1887
Died. At No 91 Matthews Lane MARYANN LEVY The funeral will leave her sister's residence at 5.30 this evening. Friends and acquaintances will please accept this intimation. Please let your carriage attend.

In Colon on Friday the 1st instant, JOSEPH MERRICK, eldest son of the late Rev. R.E. Watson of Merrick's Mount. Leaving many relatives and friends to mourn his irreparable loss. "Requiescat in pace".

July 12, 1887
At 3.30 this morning EVELYN VERA LUCILLE, third daughter of Mr. and Mrs. Clarence L. Cunha. The funeral will leave from 59 Laws Street at 5 o'clock this evening. Friends will please accept this invitation to attend. Carriages

July 13, 1887
Trelawny Girls School.
The third annual prize day of this Institution took place on the premises, Manchester Pen near Stewart Town on Wednesday the 22nd June. Several of the friends of the Institution and parents of the pupils were present.
Among the former were Mrs. Clark of Brown's Town, Revd. W.C. Harty of First Hill: Revd, G.S. Collie and Mrs. Collie of Waldensia; Jos. Levy Esq. and Mrs. Levy of Brown's Town Mrs. and Miss Cover of Enfield; Mr. Myers of St Ann's Bay, the Misses Fray of Kettering, Miss L. Knibb of Falmouth, Mrs. Thompson and others. Among those expected but who where unavoidably absent were the Revd O. Welch and Mrs. Welch, of Duncans, Revd S. L. Lindo and Mrs. Lindo of Brown's Town and the Revd. E. Fray, of Kettering. The Revd. G.E.Henderson of Brown's Town an excellent co-worker was also absent, having been compelled to leave for the United States to recruit his health by a season of rest and change. Long column. Mr. Levy distributed the prizes.

July 22, 1887
Jubilee Celebration at Brown's Town

This day being the day fixed upon by the inhabitants of this community for their enjoyment of Her Majesty's Jubilee early gatherings from the surrounding districts made their way into the capital of Dry Harbour Mountains filled with eager expectations and enthusiasm, against the appointed hour; one more to five lively manifestation of the reverence, love and esteem they hold for the Sovereign, under whose benign and peaceful sway they live, safely and comfortably.....

This celebration which has come off decidedly a success, is traceable to the indefatigable efforts of J.H. Levy, Esq., H.J. Bowen, Esq. and the gentlemen in the employ of the former in particular, as well as a few others.

July 29, 1887
At Dirleton, Port Maria, on the 26th inst., the wife of H.L. Mossman, Esq., of a daughter.

At St. George's Parsonage July 27th, the wife of Rev. H.H. Kilburn of a son.

Died At her residence, No 14 Love Lane, on the 22nd July, after a short and painful illness, Cordelia James Hopwood. She sleeps in Jesus.

August 12, 1887
Died last night, WILLIAM aged 20, son of Revd. W.C. Murray, Eureka Pen, Funeral moves to Ebenezer Cemetery at 4.30 this evening. Friends will please accept this intimation.

August 13, 1887
In Panama on the 11th ultimo, by the Rev. S. Kerr, John Edwin Harries of London, to Pathenia Eudora, fourth daughter of David E. Cohen of this city.

August 16, 1887
The marriage of L.F. MacKinnon Esq.
The marriage of L.F. MacKinnon, Esq., Manager of the Jamaica Railway to Miss Lynch took place on Wednesday, the 10th inst. At 1 o'clock in the Cathedral, Spanish Town. The bride was given away by her father E.B. Lynch. The bridesmaids were Miss Dora Lynch, Miss Violet Lynch, Miss Edith Farquharson, Miss Marie Scotland, Miss Mabel Ramsay, the Misses Violet and Gwendoline Martys, Miss Janie Harvey carried the bride's train. Gives a list of guests.

August 24, 1887
On the 23rd inst At No 97 Duke Street, Charles A. Robinson. The funeral will leave at 4.30 this afternoon. Friends please accept this intimation.

Obituary of the above.

August 29, 1887
At St. Ann's Bay on the 25th inst., the wife of Geo. D. Garsia, of H.M. Customs, of a daughter.

August 30, 1887
At No 3. High Holborn St., on Monday the 29th inst. MARIE infant daughter of Theodore and Rosamond Byndloss. Funeral will move for the place of interment at 4.30 p.m. Tuesday (today). Friends will please accept this intimation.

I have been instructed by the executors of the late W. P Todd, Esq., to offer for Public Sale on Thursday the 6th October, 1887 on the property at 12 o'clock Bengal Estate, St Ann's Situate within one mile of Rio Bueno Wharf. More S. Delisser L.A. Falmouth P.O.

1887

December 20, 1887

On the 17th December, 1887, at Roaring River, St Ann's after a residence of 63 years in the Island of Jamaica, John Haughton James, formerly of Farm Hall Huntingdonshire, England in the 89th year of his age. R.I.P.

December 27, 1887

Musgrave House J.H. Levy is advertising his Christmas Supplies.

1888

February 10, 1888
At 91 Hanover Street, Kingston on the evening of the 7th February, 1888, Sarah Guy, the wife of W.W. McGowan, Esq., of Clarendon, widow of the late Charles Brackenridge, M.D. and daughter of Peter Francis Garriques, Esq., late of St Thomas ye Vale, Leaving many friends to mourn their loss. Verse.

February 22, 1888
Married
DELGADO-DaCOSTA—In this city, by the Revd. D. Baruch, of the Spanish and Portuguese Synagogue, on Wednesday 15th inst., at the residence of the bride's mother, Charles Phillips Delgado, of Brown's Town, eldest son of the late Charles Delgado, of Falmouth, to Rachael Naomi, eldest daughter of the late Isaac S. DaCosta of Kingston. No Cards.

April 3, 1888
Resident Magistrates for the Parish of St Ann
Resident Magistrate Isaac Richard Reece, Esq.

April 25, 188
At the Parish Church, Montego Bay, on Wednesday the 18th inst., by the Rev. F.H. Sharpe (father of the bride) assisted by Rev. C. Hendersen Davis, Rector of Lucea, Harold Edward, second son of the late Samuel Nugent Squire to Aimee Isabelle, second daughter of the Rev. F.H. Sharpe, Rector of the Parish Church of St. James.

April 28, 1888
Friends and acquaintances of Mr. John H. Phillipps are requested to attend the remains of his beloved wife ZIPPORAH from his residence No 10 ½ Race Course, Allman Town to the place of interment tomorrow evening at 4.30 pm. She leaves a large circle of relatives and friends to mourn their irreparable loss. Please let your carriage attend.

May 30, 1888
HALL-TODD May 23rd, at St Mark's Church, Brown's Town by   the Revd E.A. M. Stewart, Rector of Trelawny and brother-in law of the bride, James Philip, Rector of Brown's Town to Louisa, relict of Utten T. Todd, Esq., late of Orange Valley Estate, St Ann's.

Selected Vital Records from the Jamaican Daily Gleaner

June 16, 1888

Ayton-Johnson At St. John's Church, Ocho Rios, on 13th June by the Revd J Chandler, Archibald Robinson Ayton to Martha Jane, third daughter of Thomas James and Susan Magdalea Johnson.

June 30, 1888

BIRD-RITCHIE

At St Michael's Church, on the 20th inst., by the Revd. R.G. Ambrose assisted by the Revd. W. Murray, Dr Reginald Wallace, youngest son of the late W.W. Bird, to Ada Beatrice, fifth daughter of J.T. Ritchie.

July 5, 1888

CROSSWELL-HIDALGO-On the 5th instant, by the Revd. Father Spillman, S.J. John M. Crosswell to Juanita, fifth daughter of the late Juan Hidalgo. No Cards.

July 13, 1888

On July 10th, at the Jamaica High School, the wife of the Revd. Wm. Simms. M.A. of a son.

July 30, 1888

At the Parish Church, Mandeville, on the 25th July, 1888 by the Revd. H.H. Isaacs, assisted by the Revd J. S Farquharson, William Powell Clark, of Montego Bay Solicitor, second son of the Honble. J.P. Clark, Custos of Manchester, to Lilian Daughtry Panton, second daughter of the Revd. D.B.Panton, Rector of the parish.

August 1, 1888

MORAIS-MORAIS-on Wednesday evening 25th July 1888 at the Synagogue of the United Congregation of Israelites, by the Rev. S. Jacobs, assisted by Mr. H. A. Josephs, Maurice Mark, seventh son of the late Solomon Morais, to Ada, second daughter of the late Moses M. Morais, both of this city. At home No 79 Orange Street, Sunday evening, 5th August.

August 4, 1888

FROST-ALBERGA- At the residence of the Bride's Parents, Colon, Republic of Columbia, on the 14th July, by the Revd. A.W. Geddes, Frank Frost of Brooklyn, U.S.A. to Heloise Matilda, eldest daughter of Mr. Adolphus P. Alberga, late of Kingston, Jamaica.

August 4, 1888

On the 17th July 1888 at Stratford, Connecticut, U.S.A. Mrs. L. Fraser, for some time a resident in this Island.

August 17, 1888

TYLER-JENOURE July 16, at St. Paul's Clapham, by the Rev G. Forrester, vicar, assisted by the Rev. SF. Williams, rector of Cold Norton, Essex, uncle of the bride, Robert Stephen Tyler, son of Henry John Tyler, of Larghall-rise Clapham, to Constance Ellen, daughter of Alfred Jenoure, and grand-daughter of the Rev. Alfred Jenoure, vicar of Blackpool.

1888

Messrs. Thomas Forbes, of Brown's Town Edward Levatt, of Bamboo, Robert Stewart, of Content, and Robert Waugh of Hammerton, in the parish of St Ann, have been granted licenses as buyers of agricultural produce.

The lovers of the Turf in St Ann's contemplate having their usual yearly meeting towards the end of the year. A meeting of the promoters will be held at the office of Mr. L.L. Fraser, St Ann's Bay at 2 p.m. on Saturday 1st September to which all the gentry of the parish are invited to attend.

The Sunday School children in connection with the United Methodist Free Church in East Street will be entertained at an exhibition of magic lantern on Thursday evening next. The doors will be thrown open to the public at 7 o'clock, the admission fee being only 3d. the proceeds of which will assist in defraying expenses.

August 29, 1888
CALDER AND SINCLAIR-At St Thomas Church, Westmoreland, on the 15th inst., by the Revd. Alan P. Kennedy, Rector of St Andrews, assisted by the Revd. S.G. Shrimpton, Rector of St. Thomas, Wm. Johnson Calder, M.B. M.S. to Emily Isabella, the youngest daughter of the late Daniel Sinclair, Esq., J.P.

September 1, 1888
The Revd. W. Clarke Murray will occupy the pulpit at Wesley Chapel to-morrow, morning and evening.

September 4, 1888
From exchanges of telegrams between Kempshot Observatory Montego Bay and Kingston it appeared that in the morning of 3rd there were indications of a cyclone to the North of Jamaica, and probably North of Cuba. There were also indications in the morning of another depression to the East or Southeast of Jamaica, but these indications were not confirmed during the day; at 8 p.m. it was no lower at Kingston that at Kempshot 77 miles to the Westward. The weather is, however, still disturbed.

September 5, 1888
MAGNUS-At No 58 Hanover Street, on Sunday the 2nd inst. the wife of Fred. A. Magnus of a daughter.

September 6, 1888
Advertizements for Ships Sailing

FOR NEW ORLEANS, DIRECT
The West India and Pacific S.S. Co's
JAMAICAN
Coward-Master
Is due her on or about the 7th Proximate and will have immediate despatch for the above named port, taking freight and passengers. Apply to
James H. McDowell

Royal Mail Steam Packet Co's Office, Kingston 17 Aug, 1888
For Vera Cruz, via Port au Prince and Havana
The Royal Mail Steam Packet Company's Ship
DEE

101

Selected Vital Records from the Jamaican Daily Gleaner
Capt Buckler
will leave on the 13th Prox at 7 am. taking freight and passengers
For further particulars please apply to A. de Montagnac
Actg Superintendent

Royal Mail Steam Packet Company
1st September, 1888
For Southampton, via Jacqel, Barbados, Plymouth and Cherbourg
The Royal Mail Steam Packet Co's Ship
NILE
Capt Woolward
Will leave here on the 12th inst. at 4 p.m. taking freight and passengers.
Through Bills of Lading will be issued for the undermentioned ports:-

Hamburg	Amsterdam	Rottenham
Bremen	Antwerp	Trieste

For further information please apply to A. DeMontagnac, Actg Superintendent

Royal Mail Steam Packet Company
1st September, 1888
FOR COLON AND SAVANILLA
The Royal Mail Steam Packet Co's Ship
ORINOCO
Due here on the 10th inst. will have quick despatch, taking freight and passengers
Through tickets in connection with the Pacific Mail Steamship Company will be issued
by this Company's line via Panama for San Francisco, Hong Kong and Japan, etc. For
further information please apply to
A DeMontagnac, Actg Superintendent.

CARIBBEAN LINE OF STEAMERS
JAMAICA TO LONDON
s.s. CARIB
Capt. Vicary
now in the Island and will be despatched shortly for London. This vessel has excellent
passenger accommodation. For rates of freight or passage, early application must be
made to the Agents at the outports or here to Davidson Colthurst & Co

September 10, 1888
LOCAL NEWS
The W.I. and P.C. steamer "Jamaican" Captain Edwards, arrived her early
yesterday morning from Liverpool, St Thomas and Port-au-Prince last Jeremie, bringing
400 tons of merchandize for this port and following passengers. From Liver pool Mr. A.
Strohm and 3 deckers. The 'Jamaican " leaves shortly for New Orleans.

The public meeting in connection with the Jubilee Emancipation services , held
at the East Queen Street Baptist Chapel yesterday will take place at seven o'clock this
evening, the Hon. J.C. Phillippo in the chair. The Revd. W. Teal;, Revd. C. Berry, Revd.
Leonard Tucker, M.A. Revd. W.C. Murray, Revd. W. Gillies and others will address the
meeting.

September 13, 1888
Bourke, Allan Gray--Died in Melbourne Australia, on the 8th June, 1888. Allan Gray
Bourke age about 65 supposed native of Kingston, Jamaica. Any relatives are requested

1888

to communicate with William Bignell, Old White Hart Hotel, Melbourne, Victoria, Australia.

September 19, 1888
At the Wesleyan Mission House, Croydon Lodge, Spanish Town, on Sunday 16th Sept., the wife of the Revd. J.A. McIntosh of a son.

September 25, 1888
WILLIAMS-9th April 1888. At his Residence 142 John Street, Pyrmont, Sydney New South Wales, Henry Williams, eldest son of the late Henry and Mary Williams, and brother of Elizabeth Williams of Kingston, Jamaica in his 56th year, leaving a widow and six children to mourn their loss.

October 5, 1888
The Friends and acquaintances of Mr. John W. Campbell are requested to attend the remains of his sister Jane, from her residence No 43 Rose Lane to the place of interments at half-past four sharp. Friends will please accept this intimation.

October 8, 1888
At San Pablo, Isthmus of Panama, 18th September 1888, Duncan Donald Daroch Cotter aged 50 years, leaving a widow and three children. R.I.P. Foreign Papers please copy.

October 9, 1888
DIED At Chester Castle, Hanover, Benjamin R. Isaacs, the beloved son of H.I. Isaacs of Kingston in the 38th year of his age.

October 10, 1888
Friends and acquaintances of Mrs. Priscilla E. Oppenheim are invited to attend her remains from her late residence 67 Orange Street, to place of interment this evening at 4 sharp. May her soul rest in peace. American papers please copy.

October 13, 1888
DIED Last night at her residence, No 80 Church Street, Amelia Louisa Lecesne, late head mistress of Wolmer's Free School. The funeral will take place at 4 o'clock this afternoon. Friends will please accept this intimation.

October 23, 1888
THIELE-LEVY. At the Cathedral, Spanish Town, on the 17th inst. by the Revd. W. Bussell, assisted by the Revd. W. G. Downer, Chas. W. Thiele, A M.S. of Bermuda to Mabel Lucille, youngest daughter of the late Hon. Isaac Levy.

October 26, 1888
Alexander Hopwood Esq., has been appointed a Justice of the Peace for the parish of St Ann.

November 1, 1888
On the 27th October ultimo, at Eastwood Park, St Andrew's the residence of her father, Fred. Sullivan, Esq., the wife of Leonard Sutton, of a daughter.

November 13, 1888
At Epsom Penn, Annotto Bay, of the 6th Nov., Ann Grace Montgomery, widow of the late Sigismond DePass deeply mourned by many relatives and friends.

Selected Vital Records from the Jamaican Daily Gleaner

November 20, 1888
At half-past 9 o'clock last night at 11 Parade William Campbell aged 81 years. The friends and acquaintances of him and of his son John Campbell are invited to attend his remains to the place of interment of half-past 4 o'clock p.m. Please let carriage attend.

November 24, 1888
AT 53 Rose Lane, Mrs. Jane Green, The friends and acquaintances of her sons Frederick and Alfred Green and her nephew Nath. Chandler, are requested to attend her remains at 4.30 this evening. Please let your carriage attend.

November 26, 1888
At 75 Orange Street in this city, on Sunday morning 25th inst. Alexander Escoffery Esq., of Port Antonio, age 68. Funeral will take place at 4.30 p.m. today. Friends and acquaintances are hereby notified.

November 27, 1888
In Brooklyn, N.Y. on Nov. 12, the wife of Gustav Boettcher, of Spanish Town of a daughter.

December 3, 1888
At Rosebank House, on Saturday 24th November, 1888 the wife of Wellesley Bourke, of a daughter.

December 4, 1888
On the 9th Novr. 1888 in her 80th year, at her residence 12 Bloomfield Street, Westbourne Terrace, London, Emma widow of the late Samuel Magnus, sometime Custos of the Parish of Trelawny and sister of the late F. L. Phillips of Montego Bay.

December, 1888

The Polytechnic [Picture]
CARRIAGES
Victorias Phaeton
Rumble Buggies, Dog Carts
Very Latest Designs,
Built of A1 Materials
Selected Second Growth Hickory Wheels
Trimmed Best Leather
Call a our Carriage Repository and inspect. Easy terms
Carriage and Buggy Harness, Brass and Plated mountings
Martin & Spicer

December 19, 1888
LORD-DELISSER- At Port Maria on the 6th inst., by the Rev. H. H. Graham, assisted by the Revds. W. Graham and R.J. Winsor, John Leigh second son of the late C. Payne Lord of Isle of Man, England to Florence Louise, second daughter of the late S. J. Delisser of Falmouth, Jamaica. No cards.

December 31, 1888
On the 15 inst., at Colon, U.S.C. Herbert second Son of Alexeis Silvera of White Hall, St Andrew to Sarah Matilda third daughter of the late A.E. Pretto, of St Thomas D.W.I.

1889

January 19, 1889
At his residence, Brown's Town in the Parish of Saint Ann, on Saturday, the 12th instant, at 8.30 p.m. Mr John Williams, in the 86th year of his age, deeply regretted by his children, grand-children, numerous relatives and friends. His loss is irreparable to his children and relatives. Peace: it is I

February 8, 1889
On the 7th instant, at the residence, No. 50, Wildman Street, George Douglas, infant son of Alexander and Caroline Campbell. Funeral will move at 5 o'clock this evening to the place of interment. Friends and acquaintances will please accept this intimation.

April 8, 1889
LEVY-NUNES-On Wednesday evening 3rd April instant, at the Synagogue, Montego Bay, George, eldest son of Maurice Levy of Mandeville, to Lucetta Corinaldi, eldest daughter of Wilford Nunes of Kingston. No Cards.

April 29, 1889
On the morning of the 26th instant, Amy Constance, the infant daughter of Thomas A. and Adela Hogg. Aged 7 months and 17 days.

May 11, 1889
At Spanish Town, on Tuesday the 7th inst, in the 36th year of her age, Jane Ann, the dear wife of J. H. McAnuff Esquire, and eldest daughter of James Samuel Facey Esquire, of St Catherine. "Sweet sweet sleep" Panama Star and Herald please copy.

May 14, 1889
Tax arrears
738 acres Shentamee and Brinamwood, North and part East on Mount Holstein, East on Birnamwood Church Lands and on the Bull Bay river, South on Spring Hill, on Smithfield and on Southfield, and West on Dry River Retreat. Parties entitled or believed to be entitled or last known to be entitled to land: William Wright. Parties in Possession or last known in Possession: William Wright

May 31, 1889
Copper Mining in Jamaica. We understand that what was once known as the Charing Cross Mine in Clarendon has some chance of being reopened........

Selected Vital Records from the Jamaican Daily Gleaner

June 5, 1889

At Greenwich, England, Joseph Bartholomew Kidd, R. S. A., on the 7th May, 1889 in his 82nd year.

June 15, 1889

At 88 Hanover Street at 9 a.m.. yesterday, Annie, the beloved wife of William J. Nash, of Dry Harbour, St Ann. The funeral will move from Hanover Street this morning 15th instant at 9 o'clock. The friends of Mr Nash will please accept this intimation.

June 19, 8189

LYON-DELISSER At Claremont, St Ann's on the 12th instant by the Revd. Smythe, J. Jackson Lyons, of St Ann's Bay, to Marie Alice Louise, eldest daughter of Henry DeLisser, Esq. No Cards.

June 28, 1889

At her residence, "Hagley Park", St Andrew, on the night of the 26th instant, Ann Catherine, relict of the late Revd. Charles Henry Hall, Rector of Clarendon, in her 83rd year.

The Revd. W. Clarke Murray of the Wesleyan Missionary Society, has been appointed a Marriage Officer for the places of worship at Beechamville, Alderton, Epworth, Pedro River, Mount Waddy, York Castle, Golden Spring and Bensonton in the Parish of St Ann.

July 12, 1889

A NEW QUARTERLY.

We are glad to see the first number of the York Castle Quarterly published in connection with the School.

The Venture is commendable in every way, and consists of 20 pages of close letter-press, and the contents consist of an Editorial and seven other papers.

The names of Editor and contributors are withheld, being indicated in the case of the papers by initials or a non de plume.

The Editor in introducing his Magazine says: "This is intended to be a boy's magazine, one written by boys and for boys; a chronicle of our doings upon the top of a Jamaica mountain *** Reports of our Debating Society may be looked for here; details of our scholastic work as well."

An appeal is made to the old York Castle boys for assistance literary and financial, in support of the Magazine and we most cordially hope the appeal will meet with a ready and wide response.

The first paper is called "Jottings about York Castle School," and alludes to Mr Jacques Sicard, the former resident whose memory is still green in the locality in connection with the visit of the Duke of Manchester.

The paper is evidently written for juveniles, it is signed "Acien" and the writer says he is an "old boy" and details a thrilling incident that took place in the "early days" of the school when some of the boys went to look for a bull with a revolver, an adventure which ended in one boy, Cover, being shot by another boy, Richards. The accident did not end fatally however.

The second paper "On Our Debating Society" gives an account of the formation of the Society in question, and of several of the meetings and debates. Among the important topics discussed in this Lilliputian Parliament, we find such subjects as "The advisability of an increase in the number of the Elected Members of the Legislative Council." "Monarchial versus Republican Government" Woman Suffrage," etc.

The next paper purports to give a sketch of the aboriginal inhabitants of Jamaica, the Arawaks, though very little is said about them.

This is followed by a clever little story of an adventure during the siege of Vera Cruz by the United States troops. The tale is remarkably well told and the author has evidently the talent of the raconteur.

The succeeding paper "A Freak of Chance" is the story of the Franco-Prussian War. It has the air of a translation from the German.

A short account of a hurricane at Sav-la-Mar and a little paper, which can hardly be a personal reminiscence, called "Chased by Pirates" brings this interesting and excellent boy's Magazine to a close, and we congratulate the editor on the capital show his youthful contributors make and on the production of so good a number. We sincerely hope the publication will be continued, thus giving the boys of York Castle School, encouragement in composition and literary work which cannot fail to be advantage to them.

July 16, 1889
BROWN-JAQUET- On the 9th July, at St James'Church, Annotto Bay, by the Revd. Fredk. Mercier, B. A., Alexander Alfred Augustus Brown, of Brown's Town, St Ann's to Elizabeth Jaquet, of Epson, Annotto Bay, St Mary's.

July 19, 1889
Sylvester Cotter, Esq., has been recognized temporarily for three months as Acting Consular Agent of the United States at Port Morant.

J.H. Levy was agent for the Clyde line of Steamers to London and Glasgow. and also sold Kaiser Beer, Brewed specially at the Imperial Brewery in Bremen. Kaiser Beer is "the drink of the Great Imperial Chancellor Prince Bismarck."

Mark C. Hendricks was an Auctioneer of property

September 14, 1889
At No 89 Lower King Street, at 7.45 last evening, T.L. Barber. Funeral will leave for the place of interment at 5 o'clock this evening. T.L. Barber was the grandson of a maroon who was sent to Sierra Leone (of Maroon Town, Trelawny). He worked for the Jamaica Railway as an accountant and later was secretary of the Jamaica Street Car Company. (See Obit September 16, 1889)

September 19, 1889
Jack the Ripper was in the news from London

Selected Vital Records from the Jamaican Daily Gleaner

September 20, 1889
Fisher-DaCosta-September 18th at the Parish Church, by the Revd. J.B. Ellis, assisted by the Revd G. W. Downer, Hugh Seymour Charles Scott, eldest son of J. W. Fisher, of Trelawny, to Elsie Geraldine, second daughter of the late Sml. R. DaCosta, Esq of Kingston.

September 25, 1889
On Monday, 16th September, at the Wesleyan Minister's House, Croyden Lodge, Spanish Town, the wife of the Rev. John A. McIntosh of a son.

October 29, 1889
At Colonel's Bridge in Clarendon, on the 22nd October, 1889 Frederick P. Hogarth in the 31st year of his age

November 4, 1889
At Mount Plenty, St. Ann, on the 27th ultimo, the wife of Adam Roxburgh of a daughter

November 8, 1889
At Rockville, Brown's Town, St Ann's on the 31st October, the wife of Charles P. Delgado, of a son.

December 16, 1889
At her residence No. 6 Oxford Street, on Sunday the 15th instant, Anna Naar, the beloved wife of John S. Facey, and sister of the late Alexander Naar de Graffe.   Friends and acquaintances are requested to attend her remains to the place of interment. Funeral at 4.30 this evening --Carriages

1890

January 4, 1890
Died: At her residence, No 11 Heywood Street, at 1.30 p.m. yesterday, Roseta Emily Jessica aged 18 years, the beloved wife of R.F. Haughten and the only daughter of Mrs. Susan Facey. Friends and acquaintances will please accept this intimation. Funeral will move at 4 p.m. Please let your carriage attend.

January 7, 1890
Last night at her residence, No 127 King Street, Sarah Tait, relict of the late Charles Tait of Woodlands in St. Andrew, in the 83rd year of her age. Friends and acquaintances of Mr. C. W. Tait will please accept this intimation. The funeral will leave the house at 4.30 this afternoon. Carriages.

January 8, 1890
On the 6th inst., in Kingston, Marie Winifred aged 13 months, daughter of Wellesley and Resina Bourke.

At Belle Castle Mission House on 3rd instant, Rev. H. B. Harris, Baptist Minister, aged 69 years.

January 10, 1890
On the morning of the 9th, Ivy Blanche infant daughter of James and Ida Campbell.

January 18, 1890
The Right Revd. Enos Nuttall, D.D. the Bishop of Jamaica will hold an Ordination at the Kingston Parish Church at 7.30 am tomorrow, when the Revds. Messrs. Cole, Swaby, Cass, Ormsby and W.S. Taylor will be advanced to the Priesthood. There will be a celebration of the Holy communion at 6 a.m.

(Also an account of the Costume Ball with a list of the participants and their costumes, mostly Jewish names).

January 20, 1890
On the 17th inst. at Devon Lodge, St Andrew, the wife of Phillip Haughton James of a son.

January 21, 1890
Manly-Shearer-On 15th inst., at Kings' Church, Westmoreland, by the Revd. S.G. Shrimpton, Taxs. Albert Samuels of Porus, to Margaret Ann, Daughter of Alexander Shearer, Esq. of Blenheim, Parish of Hanover. No cards.

Selected Vital Records from the Jamaican Daily Gleaner

January 31, 1890
LORD-FULFORD At St Dorothy's Parish Church, on Tuesday 28th inst., by the Revd. C. MacCxxxx, Charles George, eldest son of the late Charles Payne Lord, Clifton, Gloucestershire, to Sissy, eldest daughter of Charles Fulford, Esq., of May Hill, Manchester.

A running article entitled " NOTES OF A TOUR ROUND THE ISLAND gives insight into several communities.

February 5, 1890
DELAPENHA-LINDO At the Synagogue of the Amalgamated Congregation of Israelites on the 29th January 1890 Rodolph Uriah, second son the Uriah Delapenha, to Emma, youngest daughter of Henry Lindo. At home at 56 Duke Street, Sunday and Monday evenings 9th and 10th inst., from 5 p.m. No cards.

February 6, 1890
On the 31st January at Content Cottage, Muirton Manchioneal, Annie Louise, the beloved wife of the Rev. Nathan A. Baquie of Bath, after an illness of 11 hours. Deeply regretted by her relatives and numerous friends.

February 12, 1890
At 90 East Street on Saturday 8th Feby., 1890, Lilia Louise, the beloved wife of Charles Gadpaille of this city aged 66 years.

February 13, 1890
At Denbeigh Estate on the 8th inst., Lislie Isabel, infant daughter of Jone ? and Jessie Orgil, aged 9.

February 19, 1890
At 148 1/2 East Street on Sunday the 16th inst., the wife of John E. Crosswell
of a son.

February 21, 1890
Drawing and map of Exhibition of 1891 in Jamaica

March 7, 1890
In this city, at 135 Orange St., on the morning of the 4th instant, the wife of Eustace G. A. Garsia of a son.

March 10, 1890
Reid and Company Real Estate and Business Agents, Auctioneers, 141 Harbour St.
Kingston
Among the properties we are commission to see are:-
Bridge Water Pen in the parish of St Anns, a very fine cattle rearing property.
Kinloss Pen in Trelawny.
Retreat Pen near Brown's Town very extensive freehold, charming Residence and
invaluable Cattle property.
etc.

1890

March 18, 1890

MARRIED On the 12th inst. at 153 Manchester Square, Kingston Jamaica by the Revd. James Cochrane, James, Alfred son of James A. Vine, Esq., of Falmouth to Susannah, Daughter of the late Alfred Groom.

April 5, 1890

DIED. On Saturday the 15th ultimo, at Sherbrooke, Canada, in his 28th year, Hansford Elliott Lindsay late of Putnam, Connecticut, United States and son-in-law of Mr. John Murray, of this city, deeply regretted.

April 8, 1890

At Mt Pleasant, Bethel Town, at the age of 90, Mrs. Ellen Stephenson, relict of the late Henry Stephenson, Esq., and beloved mother of T.B. Stephenson, of Calabar Model School. "Her end was peace"

April 11, 1890

At Sav-la-Mar at 3 p.m. yesterday at he age of x0 years, Myer, third son of the late Jonas Polack Esq. merchant of that town, and brother of Mr. Jonas Polack of the city.

April 17, 1890

At 1 a.m. at his residence No 87 Orange Street, John W. Escoffery, aged 50 years The friends of his brothers A. C. and C. S. Escoffery are requested to attend. Funeral will move at 5 p.m. Carriages.

April 22, 1890

At his residence No 3 Rae St., Rae Town, James Hally Reid. Friends and acquaintances will please accept this intimation, and attend the funeral which will take place at 4 o'clock this evening. Carriages.

April 28, 1890

We regret to announce the death on Saturday last (April 26) at 1 o'clock of Mr. Hyman Cohen, late a merchant of this city, a man well known in the community and respected by all. His remains were interred yesterday afternoon followed by a large number of friends. To his wife and 4 children we tender our condolence.

April 29, 1890

On the 26th inst., at his residence, 34 King Street, Hyman Cohen in his 70th year, deeply lamented by his sorrowing wife and children. May his soul rest in peace.

May 8, 1890

On Wednesday May 7th 1890 at Ruthven Lodge, St Andrew, the wife of the Right Revd. C.F. Douet, Assistant Bishop of Jamaica of a son.

May 12, 1890

THE GOVERNOR VISITS BROWN'S TOWN

On Thursday 8th inst., at 9 a.m. Sir Henry A. Blake, K.C.M.G., F.R.G.S, accompanied by Lady Blake, Lord George Fitzgerald, and the Hon, M. Solomon, C.M.G. left Seville for Brown's Town via Dry Harbour. On arriving at Runaway Bay they were met by J. H. Levy, Esq., J.P. and Miss Levy who conducted them to the Dry Harbour cave, and there found waiting W. Cover, Jun Esq., J.P and after exploring the cave they proceeded to Dry Harbour, visiting the lagoon en route where His Excellency and Party took the opportunity of looking at the beautiful harbour. All the inhabitants here assembled to do honor to Her Majesty's representative, and it speaks well for the village that they were able to make such a grand display of banners and flags with suitable mottos. Leaving Dry Harbour, crowds gathered the whole way to Brown' s Town to see the Governor: and everybody appeared determined to do their part to make His Excellency's journal as pleasant and agreeable as possible. The party journeyed through Minard, the property of the Hon Geo. Stiebel and arrived at Brown's Town about 1.15 p.m.

In describing the appearance of the town words sufficiently expressive can hardly be found. It is a long established fact that when ever a Governor visits our little town his reception is of the highest class, and on this occasion it was not inferior to previous occasions. From early morning gentlemen and others were to be seen busily engaged in fixing banners and decorating arches: The Norman Market, where the Governor was to be received was tastily and prettily got up. At an early hour the town assumed a thoroughly holiday appearance and presented an unparalleled scene of gaiety and merriment. By this time visitors from the country districts began to arrive and it was then well known that the gathering to greet His Excellency would be very large. The Temperance organizations of the Wesleyan and Baptist Societies united in one large procession numbering several hundreds, and carrying suitable banners and mottos, headed by the band belonging to the 'Band Of Hope" formed on both sides of the main street waiting the arrival of the Governor. On his arrival the Band struck up the National Anthem. The party then proceeded to the Norman market, where the Hon. M. Solomon, C.M. G. present three addresses to His Excellency, one from the people, another from the Brown's Town Philharmonic Society and the other from the Temperance Societies. In a long speech His Excellency thanked the people on behalf of himself and Lady Blake for their enthusiastic reception, and congratulated the people on the appearance of the town. He very particularly touched one by one all the matters brought to his notice in the addresses. His Excellency in going through the island was not merely to become acquainted with the physical character but to know the people and learn their respective wants. His Excellency then referred to the Exhibition and endeavoured to correct some false statements that had been made regarding it. He urged the people to do their best to make it a success. The market building then rang with cheers for the Governor and Lady Blake. This was followed by a presentation of some gentlemen of the town, after which the party proceeded to Windsor House (residence of J.H. Levy Esq.) where they were entertained with some other gentlemen to luncheon. His Excellency, Lady Blake and Lord George Fitzgerald then visited the several chapels and schools and the Constabulary Station. At the Baptist School, the Governor was presented with an Address. It is estimated that there were over 3000 people in the town. The Governor remarked that it was the largest gathering he had seen since his arrival in the island. The following were inscriptions on banners put up at different parts of the town "Welcome to Brown's Town". "Loyal greetings to Sir Henry and Lady Blake" " Success to your Administration" and over the market gate " God Save the Queen" and "Success to the Exhibition". The Temperance procession carried one with the words "Welcome Sir Henry Blake to Brown's Town" and "God Save the Queen". The greatest credit and the thanks of the community are due to one fellow townsman, J. H. Levy Esq. for the success that has attended his efforts to render the Governor's Visit alike memorable and creditable to the town. Follows the Addresses.

The People of Brown's Town asked for "1st In this town a new or improved Court House the present building being dilapidated, it is moreover small and unsuitable, inconvenient alike to Judges, Magistrates and Suitors,2nd a water supply, 3rd A Hotel under the Hotels' Law 1890, 4th The erection of a more suitable Clock Tower for the clock presented to the town by Sir Henry Norman". The Philharmonic Society did not ask for anything but just said what they were about. The Temperance Society asked for the following: " 1st. The number of licenses should be limited in number by the population of the district and should not exceed one to every one thousand persons. 2nd That the shop licensed for the sale of liquors should be separate from any residence, so as to enable Sunday trading to be strictly prohibited. 3rd That licensed shops should be as far as possible, at a distance from Schools and Churches". and was signed by: Geo E. Henderson, President Baptist Temperance Society, Saml. L. Lindo President Wesleyan Band of Hope Temperance Society to Wesleyan Conference, Robr A. Mormon Secretary Baptist Temperance Society and Ellen Cover Secretary Wesleyan Band of Hope.

May 13, 1890
The anniversary missionary services in connection with Coke Chapel came off very successfully on Sunday (May 11). The preachers were the Rev W. Clark Murray of York Castle in the morning at eleven o'clock; the Rev. William Pratt M.A. of the East Queen Street Baptist Chapel in the afternoon at three o'clock and the Rev W. Melville of Clarendon in the evening at seven o'clock. The sermons delivered were all very interesting as well as instructive.

May 15, 1890
George Thomas, the driver of an omnibus, was yesterday taken before the Stipendiary Magistrate an fined 2/- for smoking a cigarette in his bus while he was driving a passenger.

At the Kirk in Duke Street on Sunday next the Rev. John Radcliffe will deliver a sermon on the death of Mrs. John Campbell who had for over thirty years filled the office of Organist at the Church.

May 19, 1890
An entertainment was given by the Brown's Town Philharmonic Society at Brown's Town on Wednesday evening the 14th inst. J. H. Levy Esq. J.P. addressed the audience on the subject of the Exhibition.

May 26, 1890
About 578 time expired Coolies arrived in Kingston by the early morning train on Saturday from Spanish Town, for the purpose of proceeding in the British ship Foyle for Calcutta, They were dispatched to Port Royal in the Steamer Arden and afterwards transhipped to the Foyle which sailed yesterday. They took away a large sum of money, as also over £1000 in jewelry.

May 27, 1890
At Savoy Estate, Clarendon, of typhomalaria fever, William Francis Evans aged 38 years eldest and beloved son of Richard and Rebecca Evans of Duckenfield Hall, St Thomas, deeply regretted by a large circle of relatives and friends.

June 23, 1890
At Rose Bank House, Kingston on Wednesday 18th instant, the wife of Welesley Bourke, of a daughter.

June 27, 1890
On Thursday the 19th inst. at Tobolski Villa, Brown's Town St Ann's Mrs. Wm. Cover Snr after a long and lingering illness which she bore with that patience as only a true Christian can, deeply mourned by her many sorrowing relatives and friends.

"She is gone before to await their coming"

To my dead Sister

Alas! she is dead, so pure! so true!
So good to all around
She lived and died as Christians do,
And now her joy is found.
She is now at rest her pains are o'er
Her soul is gone to Heaven.

We all must meet her on that Shore
When sins are all forgiven,
Good bye ! Sweet soul a long adieu
'Tis hard for me to tell.
The general grief on leaving you
the tender long farewell.

G.

June 30, 1890
JENOURE- On the 27th June, at Boston, Portland, the wife of Frederick A. Jenoure, J.P.
of a daughter

July 7, 1890
Kingston 2nd July, 1890, George William second son of Isaac Abrahams to Clementine
Josphine, daughter of Marguerite Adele Young and of the late Philip Auguste Young, of
Louisiana, No cards.

July 8, 1890
At Mandeville on Saturday 5th SAMUEL infant son of George and Lucetta Levy

July 9, 1890
On 5th inst., at Brooklyn, May Pen, the wife of C.E. Scudamore, of a son.

July 14, 1890
RELEIF FUND in aid of the Sufferers at Martinque
        His Excellency the Governor, appeals to the Community at large, to contribute
to the Fund for the relief of the Sufferers from the Calamitous Fire at Fort la France.
Jamaicans remember your recent trouble from the same dreadful cause! Remember also
the liberal aid extended to you in your troubles! "Contribute your mite." No matter how
small your Donations will be received at the office of this paper and publicly
acknowledged in these Columns.
Send in your Subscriptions
Collections by the Hon. Michael Solomon, St Ann's:-
F.L. Rodon 2.2. 0
T.F. Roxburgh 3.3.0
E.J. Wessels 1.0.0
John Wilson 0.5.0
John Cameron 1.0.0
Ricd. Rigg 0.5.0

Mrs. E. N. Hart 2.0.6
Edwd Pratt 1.1.0
Revd G. House 0 13.0
Wm Cover Jr 1.1.0
Richd. Hemming 0 10.0
F. Ewen 0.5.0
Hamilton Brown 0.10.6
Hon. Michael Solomon 10.10.0
L. T. Bullock 0.4.0
J.S. Trench 0.10.6
Richard Watson 0.6.0
L.L. Fraser 2.2.0
John Garcia 0.1.0
W.F. Morris 0 2.0
Colin Campbell 0.2.0
(others)
Total £58.8.4
Total subscribed £484. 12 .7
C. Arnold Malabre, Hon Secty.

July 16, 1890
HALL- At Kensington, Ulster Spring, Trelawny;, on the 4th inst., the wife of John Herman Hall of a son.

July 22, 1890
Lyon At the Den St Ann's Bay, on the 18th inst., the wife of J.J. Lyon, of a son.

July 30, 1890
VALENCIA On Sunday morning the 27th July 1890 at his residence, 60 Duke Street, Joseph Emanuel Valencia, late Clerk Island Medical Department.

August 4, 1890
DELISSER-ANSELL-On Wednesday evening 30th ultimo at No 13 North Street, Andrew Delisser to Rachel M Ansell. of London. At Home Cleveland Villa, No 5 Windward Road, Saturday and Sunday evening 9th and 10th inst. No Cards.

August 5, 1890
At the Mico Institution on Sunday 3rd August, 1890, the wife of L.G. Gruchy of a daughter.

September 20, 1890(Saturday)
The following passengers were booked to leave Southampton in the R.M.C. Steamer which was set down to leave there on Wednesday last. For this island-Revd G.B. Bay, Revd. W. Maund, Rev F. Godson, Mr. C. F. Dunn, Major Johnson, Lieut. W Dudds, and wife, Mr. W. H. Mitchell, Dr. Care wife and 4 children and Mr. R.M. Turnbull.

September 27, 1890 (Saturday)
The R.M.C. Str. Don, Captain Woolword which was to have left Southampton on the 3rd inst., with the mails and passengers for the West Indies was detained until the following day on account of strikes. The Don however, according to contract time is expected to arrive at Barbados early on Monday morning. Among her passengers for this island are the Revd., G. B. Bay, Revd. W. Maund, Revd F. Godson, Mr. F.F. Dunn, Major Johnson,

Lieut. W. B. Sudds and wife. Mr. W. H. Mitchell, Dr Clare, wife and 4 children and Mr. Richard A. Turnbull.

October 1, 1890
Barbados 30th The R.M.S. [Royal Mail Steamer) Don from Southampton arrived at 12.10 p.m. with the following passengers for Jamaica-- Lieut. and Mrs. Sudds, Captain Barret, Corporal Rowbotham, Revds Hay and Maund, Dr Clare wife and 4 children, Major Johnson, Major Knollys, Revd Mann, Mrs. Narr and child, Mrs. Davis and child, Mrs. Nethercott and 2 children, Mrs. Wingate and 3 children, Messrs Mitchel, Dunn, Turnbull, Kinkead, Erskine, Brandon, Fitzgerald, Taylor, and Schoreid.

At Lookout , on the 27th inst., the wife of A Shamrock Byles of a son.

October 3, 1890
At the Cathedral, Spanish Town, on the Wednesday 1st October, 1890 by the Right Revd. the assistant Bishop, assisted by the Revd. E. J. Wortley, William Maxwell, youngest son of late Revd C. J. P Douet, Rector of Metcalfe, to Elizabeth, Marion Vickers of Swift River, Westmoreland.
(I think Grandfather Mitchell arrived October 4 from Southampton, Barbados and Jacmel)
October 7, 1890
The R.M.C. steamer Don, Captain Woolward left here at 1p.m. on Sunday for Colon taking away the following passengers Mrs. Skerret and two children. Mr.B. B. Bryan and Miss Alvarez and 17 deckers.

October 16, 1890
At 84 Duke Street on the 12th inst., the wife of John J Orgill, H.M. Customs, Kingston of a daughter.

November 10, 1890
LORD At Lodge Estate, on the 6th inst., the wife of C.G. Lord of a son.

December 8 , 1890
St Ann's Local Exhibition-Full Account From Our Own reporter. By Telegraph. St Annes Bay, Thursday Dec 2nd, 1890
3 Columns
Men mentioned:
          Foremost among this band of workers have been Mr. Edmound Hart who shouldered the heaviest part o f the work and to whom principally the credit of the success of the Exhibition is due. He has been ably assisted by Mr. J.C. Lewis, the Hon Secretary the following members of the local committee:- Rev Griffin, Rev Geo House, John Cameron, A. J. Webb, A. N. Dixon J. D. Ormsby, Sol. Isaacs, JS. Trench, A.B. Rerrie, W.F Nunes, F.L Rodon J.J. Lyon, John Boyd, R. Watson Wm Saunders.
Ladies Mentioned:
          Mrs. Cameron, Mrs. Rerrie, Mrs. House, Mrs. Nunes, Mrs. Maunsell, Mrs. Ormsby, the Miss Stennett, Mrs. E. N. Hart, Mrs. Rodon, Mrs. Trench, Mrs. Reece, Mrs. Douet, Mrs. Myers, Mrs. Isaacs, Mrs. Levy, Mrs. J. Duff, Mrs. Hall, Miss Cork, Mrs. Archer, Mrs. Middleton, Mrs. Chandler, Mrs. Pratt, Mrs. Lyon , Mrs. Lewis.

December 15, 1890
deCordova-Silvera- 10th December, 1890 at the Amalgamated Synagogue, by the Revd. S. Jacobs, Charles, third son of the late Michael deCordova to Ruth Edith, eldest daughter

of Alexis Silvera. At home at No 27 North Street, on Saturday and Sunday Evenings 20th and 21st Decr. No cards.

December 27, 1890
At his residence No 48 Hanover Street, on the night of the 24th inst. at 11.40 Jacob Rodriques DaCosta Eldest son of the late Isaac S. DaCosta of this city

At London, December 25th Edith Robinson, second daughter of the late Charles A. Robinson of this city.

1891

January 5, 1891
Current Items
The Rev. W. Clarke Murray the Governor of Barbican High School who left here some weeks ago for Southampton for the purpose of representing the Churches in the West Indies at the Wesleyan Conference in England, is expected to arrive in the R.M.C steamer Orinoco on Friday next.

January 6, 1891
Latest Telegrams
Barbados, Jan 5th Orinoco from Southhampton arrived 6.10 p.m.
Orinoco passengers for Jamaica: Four petty officers, seventeen sailors, sixteen marines. Messrs. Allport, Trench, Norris, Andrews, Bourke, Mason, Stenning, Seaton, Craven, Fraenckel and Benson. Mrs. Spalding, Mr. and Mrs. Abell, Mr. and Mrs. Isaacs, Miss Isaacs, Misses E. and H. Farquharson, Mr. and Mrs. Pussingham and child, Revds. Crawshaw, Murray and Simms and Miss Hammond.

January 7, 1891
Latest Telegrams
Barbados, Jan 5th Orinoco, goes Jamaica about 5.30 p.m.

January 8 , 1891
Description by an American of a trip to Kingston and then to Bog Walk and Porus on the train.

January 10, 1891
Among the passengers by the R.M. steamer Orinoco was the Rev. W. C. Murray, the Governor of York Castle High School. He has brought with him a teacher for the school, and when in England engaged the services of a lady teacher for Barbican who will arrive here by the next mail.

The R.M.C steamer Orinoco which arrived here yesterday morning from Southampton brought 95 passengers most of whom are visiting the island for the purpose of being present at the opening of the Exhibition.

Arrival of the Packet
The R.M.C. steamer Orinoco, captain Andrew Gillis, with the fortnights' European and West Indian Mails arrived early yesterday morning, after experiencing a fine voyage.

Selected Vital Records from the Jamaican Daily Gleaner

The following is her passenger list. From Southampton Rev Wm. Simms, M.A., Mr. S. Bensyn, Mrs. Spalding, Mr. M.L, French, Mr. J.P. Morris, Mr. P. Andrews, Mr. and Mrs. Abell, Mr. and Mrs. Isaacs, Miss Isaacs; Misses Farquharson, Mr. Charles Bourke, Mr. and Mrs. Passingham and child, Rev Crawshaw, Mr. Murray, Mr. John Mason, Mr. W. Stenning. Mr. G. Seaton, Miss Hammond, Mr. E.J. Craven, Mr. R. Fraenckel,. From Barbados--Miss E Cotes, Mr. E.A Smith 1 Officer Mr. C. J. Lawrence, Mr. C. Ripke, Mr. J. W. Toone, Mr. C.H. Parsons and Three deckers. From Trinidad Mr. Sanguinetti. From Demerara 1 recruit. From Jacmel Mrs. Laubere and family, Mr. Massa and child. Mr. Garrand, Mr. Henriques Rev St Thourens 9 deckers and 134 in transit. The Orinoco brought 2614 packages for this port and 379 for outports. She leaves for Colon at 4 p.m. today.

January 13, 1891

INTERNATIONAL EXHIBITION,
Jamaica 1891
Patron:
H.R.H. THE PRINCE OF WALES
President:
H.E. Sir H.A. Blake, K.C.M.G.
GRAND OPENING
BY
HIS ROYAL HIGHNESS
PRINCE GEORGE OF WALES

Tuesday 27th Jany. 1891

Doors open at 10.30 but here will be no admittance by the Main entrance, (South) from 11.30 until after the departure of the Royal Party except for those taking part in the ceremony. The East Entrance will be open continuously.

Admission until 4 p.m. 7s 6d Season Ticket holders 4 s. After 4 p.m. 1s each. No admission after 9.45 p.m. Exhibition closes at 10 p.m.

A limited number of Reserved Seats to witness the Ceremony will be available at the price of 10s 6d each in addition to the charge for admission. They will be allotted according to priority of application.

All tickets are now on Sale at the Secretary's Office 24 Church Street. It is requested that in order to prevent disappointment all those intending to be present will provide themselves with tickets in advance.

S.Lee Bapty
General Manager

January 28, 1891

Picture of the opening of the 1891 Jamaica Exhibition. H.R.H. The Prince of Wales opened the exhibition.

January 30, 1891

In this city, on the 23rd inst. the wife of R. J. Isaacs of a son

Mr Mark C. Hendriks will offer for sale by public auction this morning at 11 o'clock in front of Roxburgh House, some very fine Mules and Horses also 2 very good vehicles.

January 31, 1891

At the Castle, Savanna-la-Mar on the 27th January, the wife of W. A. Milne, of a son.

1891

Advertisement. History of the Church of England in Jamaica, by Rev. J.B. Ellis, M. A., Aston W. Gardner & Co 127 Harbour Street.

April 1, 1891

At his residence, "The Villa" Mandeville, on the 26th March, 1891 Joseph Levy in the 87th Year of his age.

April 11, 1891

Advertisement

A GOOD OPPORTUNITY: NOW IS YOUR TIME

The subscriber in making arrangements for his usual visit to the Foreign Markets. will before his departure in May, and for one Month after dispose of a large portion of his present extensive stock at greatly reduced prices.
Room must be made to receive New Supplies. Goods in many instances will be reduced 25 percent.
5000 Pairs of Boots and Shoes from 1s to 5+
500 Dozens Hats at a sacrifice
1000 Dozen Shirts from 9d each to 4s
Great Reduction in Tweed and Broad Clothes. The Stock in these is especially large and varied- many of them direct from Canadian Manufactures at
MUSGRAVE HOUSE,
£10,000 of Goods select from J.H. Levy
Musgrave House
Brown's Town
April 11, 1891

The Orinoco and Medway brought 50 packages Staple and Fancy Goods now being opened. J.H. Levy

May 5, 1891
Jack the Ripper now in New York

May 14, 1891
Mr J.H. Levy and family (8) left on the Atlas company's steamer Adirondack, Captain Low at 8 o'clock

May 23, 1891
On the 24th inst, at Spanish Town, Julia, aged 85, the widow of the late Robert Russell, Registrar in Chancery and mother of Dr. Logan Russell. (Storer)

May 25, 1891
Jenoure May 20th, at Boston, Portland, the wife of Frederick A. Jenoure, J.P. of a daughter

Selected Vital Records from the Jamaican Daily Gleaner

June 18, 1891

At the Parish Church, Kingston, on Saturday 13th June 1891, Rev. G. Bathurst Hall, eldest son of the late Rev Geo Hall, to Annie Gertrude, fourth daughter of J. Jackman, Esq of Barbadoes.

June 26, 1891
Advertisement

A.N. SUTHERLAND
Musgrove House.
Moneague, P. O
General Importer
Fancy and Dry Goods, Boots and Shoes, Liquors, American Stuffs &c

LIVERY STABLES
Good Buggies, Civil, Clean & Careful Drivers
Reliable Stock,
Moderate Prices.

Letters and telegrams receive Prompt
attention
Private waiting and Refreshment Room on Premises
Your Patronage Solicited.
A. N. Sutherland

Editorial on the Intermediate Examination in Arts by the London University   The complaint is made by the authorities at York Castle High School. Messers Murray and Mitchell were mentioned Letter in the Paper lists W. Clarke Murray, Gov. York Castle, W. H. Mitchell B.A. Acting Head Master. The candidate who was of concern was Mr Cover (which one?Probably C.A.).

July 8, 1891
Last night at No. 18 Wildman Street, Frank Seymour, Infant son of Thomas A. and Adela Hogg. Aged 7 months. Funeral at 5 p.m. Friends and acquaintances will please accept this intimation.

July 13, 1891
McCrea-Macdoneld-On the 9th inst at the Parish Church, Port Maria, by the Revd. J.H. Graham, assisted by the Revd S.S.Swabey, Harry McCrea, Jamaica Constabulary, third son of the late Rear Admiral F. D. McCrea, to Olive, youngest daughter of the late Hon. William MacDonald, Custos of St Mary. More detail on the wedding p 6

July 17, 1891
A pretty wedding took place in the old Cathedral at St Jago de la Vega on Wednesday last when Dr. Turton of Knapdale, St Ann was married to Nina Morales, eldest daughter of the late Mr. Morales of Spanish Town.
August 1, 1891

Ellis-Hendriks-On Sunday 26th July at the Parish Church by Rev. G. W. Downer, Rector Eddley Ernest Ellis, youngest son of the late Edward K. Ellis Esq. to Stella Matilda eldest daughter of Mark C. Hendriks Esq.

1891

Lecesne-Gordon- On the 9th August 1891, at St Mary's Church, Above Rocks, by the Revd. Father J. McCormack S. J.. James Celestic Lecesne, of "Harker's Hall". St Thomas ye Vale, to Adeline Selina youngest daughter of the late Frances Gordon, Esq of Golden River and grand-daughter of the late Sir John Gordon, Bart, of Ulster and Scotland (earlier of Earlston House, Parish of Borgne, Scotland, N.B.[North Britain])

August 19, 1891
St Ann's Bay
Education Conference

An Educational Conference was held in the Church School room, St Ann's Bay on Wednesday August 13 at noon.

Amongst those present were Revs. D.J. East and W. Clarke Murray, the deputation from the Kingston Conference, Rev. J.M. Denniston, J. Duff, J. Chandler, G. House, W. R. Griffin, J. Duffis, and F. Edmond. Mr Mitchell of York Castle, Messers Rodon and Miller and about 15 Teachers.

The Rev J. Cork was called to the chair, and in a few opening remarks spoke of the necessity of following closely the resolutions indicated by the Kingston Conference. After prayer by Rev. W. C. Murray, the Rev. D. J. East gave a clear resume of the resolutions proposed by the Kingston conference. He then spoke of the usefulness of the present system and of the most important benefits we had derived from it, but at the same time thought that the time had come for a change.

The first resolution, affirming the need for legislation was read by Rev. W. Clarke Murray. He spoke of the present educational arrangements as no system at all. We must have a system based on law and well defined legal enactments, in connection with the new system the control Board should be not merely an advisory Board but should have well defined functions, though it should not supersede Mr. Cappers's work or make his position unnecessary. Denominational rights should be recognized; but money must not be spent in denominational interests.

Rev J. Chandler did not agree with what had been said of the satisfactory character of the Chief Inspector's style of working and while others spoke of the gentlemanly qualities he knew him only as an official. The first resolution was unanimously carried.

The second resolution viz:-

2. "That for the due supervision of any educational system that may be created by law a Central Education Board and Local or parochial Boards are indispensable necessary" was moved by F. L. Rodon and seconded by Rev. J. Duff.

Rev. J Duff spoke of his experiences in connection with the present system. Neither managers nor teachers could understand the requirements of the departments and it would take a Philadelphia lawyer to explain them.

Rev George House spoke of the department having no sympathy with managers and teachers, making impossible rules, and stopping portions of the school grants if these impossible rules are found to be not strictly kept by the teachers.

The third resolution defining the constitution of the Central Board was moved by Revd. W. C. Murray and seconded by Revd. Geo House.

Revd J. Duff, spoke of this resolution as having the sting in its tail.

After explanations given by the deputations from Kingston, as to the meaning of "other members representing various interest and sections of the people" the resolution was passed.

Revd. W. C. Murray, moved and Revd D. J. East seconded and amendment in connection with the fourth resolution, so that it reads as follows:-

Selected Vital Records from the Jamaican Daily Gleaner

"That there should be on Education Board for each parish; and that the Parochial Education Board should consist of the school managers of the parish, with say two members appointed by the Parochial Boards from their own number, and a sufficient together with the two, that shall not exceed the number of managers in the parish, appointed by the Governor as representing the different classes of the rate-payers; and these boards to have powers to watch over the interest of education, in their respective parishes, and to make representations thereon to the Central Board"

This amendment was carried unanimously.

The fifth resolution was moved by Revd. J. Chandler, and seconded by Revd. W. C. Murray.

The general feeling of the Conference was that religious teaching should on no account be discontinued. Rev. W. Clarke Murray thought that no Minister of the Gospel would be so dishonourable as to take advantage of his position as school manager, to teach denominational views.

Revd. G. House, thought that the denominational element in connection with education was to a very great extent, a hindrance to progress. Thus we had in some districts two or three low third class denominational schools, in some cases in the care of men, utterly unfit to teach, instead of one good school with a good staff of teachers.

The sixth resolution demanding Secondary Schools in every parish was moved by Mr. Mitchell, Acting Head Master of York Castle High School and seconded by Rev. D. J. East.

Rev J. Cork and Rev W. C. Murray very strongly advocated the establishment of Schools for Secondary Education in all important centres.

F. L. Roden, Esq, objected because he thought the question of primary education should first be settled.

The several resolutions anent (sic) the abolition of fees was moved by the Rev. W. C. Murray, seconded by Rev. G. House, and unanimously carried.

Rev. D. J. East thought it would be impossible to collect a direct tax for education and recommended indirect taxation.

Rev. W. C. Murray spoke very warmly in favour of direct taxation.

Rev. J. Chandler spoke of the wicked injustice done to Teachers through the School fee system.

Rev. J. Duff recommended a poll tax on every male above 21 years of age.

In moving the resolution that dealt with the question of compulsion the Rev D. J. East expressed his opinion that compulsory attendance should be applied in all large towns and thickly populated villages.

Rev. J. Chandler combated the idea that compulsory attendance interfered with the liberty of the subject.

Rev. W. C. Murray strongly opposed compulsory education on the ground that it could not be generally applied, that a man this side of the line would go free. He also thought that the effect of such a measure would lesson the respect of our people for the law.

Another ground on which Mr. Murray opposed compulsory education was that the fathers of many of the children were neither registered nor known, so that in many cases the whole responsibility rested upon the mother. Let us have a law to register the fathers of children then we shall know against who to enforce the law.

F. L. Roden Esq strongly opposed compulsory education on the ground of the evil effects of associating waifs and strays form the streets with respectable children.

Rec. D. J. East did not see why we should be troubled by the fears entertained by Messers Murray and Roden.

The resolution passed by a majority of two.

1891

The eighth and ninth resolutions limiting the age in the 6th Standard Elementary Schools and asking for 7th Standard Elementary Schools, were taken together and carried.

The following resolution was moved by Rev. G. House: "That steps should be taken for obtaining information on the subject of Kindergarten schools and if possible commencing a local effort in St Anne, and with a view to this a small committee be now appointed".

This was seconded by Rev. W. C. Murray and carried.

After a vote of thanks to the chairman the conference was brought to a close at 5.50 p.m.

August 21, 1891
Additional comments on the educational conference by the Rev J. Duff.

September 16, 1891
We regret to learn of the death on Monday night in Mandeville of Rev. David Brooks Panton. He has been ailing for several years being a constant sufferer from gout. (Much more) Memorial on September 19

September 21, 1891
List of Grantees paid into credit of the Jamaica Exhibition Fund

Mr W. Cover, Jnr £20

September 22, 1891
Another piece on Rev D. B. Panton.

Rate payers in St Andrews are reminded that if the rates due for water supplied be not paid by Thursday next the same will be locked off.

September 23, 1891
At Arco Sud Tyrol (Upper Italy) on the 16th ult, "Emily" relict of the late D. S. Ritchie, M. D. For many years a practitioner in this Island) deeply regretted.

September 24, 1891
Pm 23rd instant at Milk River, Herbert Joseph Wilson, aged 30 years, fifth son of the late Nathaniel Wilson, Island Botanist.

It is rumoured that the Rev. H.H. Isaacs of St Andrews has been offered the Incumbency of the church in Manchester to fill the place of the late lamented Mr. Panton.

September 29, 1891
At Devon Lodge, Saint Andrew, on the 24th September, the wife of Philip Haughton James, Esquire of a son.

The Revd. Mr Hall preached in the Parish Church on Sunday night last.

October 5, 1891
At Mandeville on Wed 30th September by His Lordship the Bishop of Jamaica uncle of the bride assisted by Rev. A. Brown. John Henry Clarke eldest son of the Honble. John

Powell Clarke of Kendal Manchester, to Ella Panton eldest daughter of the late Rev. David Brooke Panton, Rector of Mandeville.

October 6, 1891
From an Advertisement

Jamaica Permanent Building Society Office 8 Duke Street, Kingston Directors George Henderson, Esq, Chairman. Alex Berry Esq Honble Geo Stiebel, Louis F. Verley, Esq C.C.A. Hogg, Esq Thomas Hogg Secretary.

October 6, 1891
From an obituary, I learned that in 1891 the Spanish and Portuguese synagogue was located in East St and the English and German Synagogue in Orange street (Mrs Rebecca Nunes Rebeiro contributed to both

October 9, 1891
Obituary

A telegram was received in this city yesterday advising the death of the much respected and esteemed resident of St Ann's Bay, Mr Edmund Nathan Hart. Mr Hart had been suffering for some time and recently had an operation performed by Dr. Armsley. The operation was deemed successful and his friends anticipated his early recovery. Advices by post received the day previous announced that he was rapidly recovering and would soon be in the enjoyment of good health. Following this came the telegram yesterday announcing his sudden and unexpected demise. Mr Hart is about 53 years of age. He is a native of Jamaica (born in Montego Bay) where he spent all his life. He started business in Falmouth where he was a clerk to Fred Lindo and won the esteem of his employer to such an extent that on the closing of the business by Mr. Lindo he recommended his then young clerk to Mr Michael Solomons of St Anns Bay in which business has been passed 20 years of his life. He, during this period rose to be managing partner of the business. We know that he was held in high esteem by Mr. Solomons and all with whom he came in contact both socially and commercially. He married Annie the third daughter of Michael Angelo Nunes and leaves behind him his sorrowing wife and nine children. To his family and friends we tender our sincere condolences in their sudden bereavement.

October 13, 1891
Cooke-Livingston - At the Parish Church, Halfway Tree, on the 7th October, 1891, by the Revds. H. H. Isaacs, M. A. Rector and Revd J. B. Ellis, M. A., Maximillian Henry Stoddard Cooke, eldest son of the late Stephen Cooke, Solicitor , to Edith Blanche Corbett Livingston, eldest daughter of H. W. Livingston, Island Treasurer of Jamaica

October 14, 1891
Estate of David Motta, late of the City and Parish of Kingston, in the Island of Jamaica, Storekeeper, deceased: Letters of administration granted to Emily Motta, the widow of the said intestate. Signed William Andrews, Solicitor for the Administratrix Dated this 5th day of October 1891 (more)

October 19, 1891
Daniel Motta is advertising Tweeds and Gent's Shirts at 106 Harbour Street and 19« Port Royal Street.

1891

October 20, 1891

Breakspear-At Great Valley, Hanover, on the 12th instant, Mary Ann, relict of the late William Breakspear, Esq in her 67th year leaving a sorrowing family to mourn their loss.

Swaby-At Porus, on the 15th October, 1891, Rev Frederick Swaby aged 70 years, after a long and useful career in the Master's service. "Be thou faithful unto death and I will give thee a crown of life"

October 21, 1891

ORMSBY-ISAACS At No 21 North St on Thursday 15th inst., Dr. C. M. Ormsby, of St Ann, to Esther Naomi third daughter of H. I. Isaacs of Chester Castle Hanover. No Cards.

October 26, 1891

On Saturday, October 17th at Richmond Vale, Ann Eliza, eldest daughter of Francis Ross, Esq., of Hull, England and sister of Mrs Pearn of Richmond Vale, St Thomas-in-the East.

At Breezy Castle, Kingston, on the 24th inst, C. W. H. Hall, eldest son of the late Rev. C.H. Hall, Rector of Clarendon and brother of C. S. Hall, of the Colonial Bank.

October 27, 1891

Lord - At Bodles Penn, Old Harbour on Friday 23rd inst, Charles Raymond Leigh infant son of C. George and Sarah Ann Lord Aged 11 months 17 days. "Thy will be done"

November 6, 1891

On Wednesday 28th October, at the Synagogue of the United Congregation of Israelites by the Revd. Solomon Jacobs, Ella third daughter of A.H. Morales, to Clifford C. Henriques, second son of the late Isaac C. Henriques, Snr., both of this city.. At home 45a East Queen Street, on Sunday and Monday evenings 8th and 9th inst. No cards.

At 72 Harbour Street, Ethel Myra, Only daughter of Geo Fisher Jnr, deceased. Friends and Acquaintances of Geo and Chas. Fisher will please accept this intimation. Funeral at 4 o'clock

November 10, 1891

Roberts-Magnus. At the Kingston Parish Church on Wednesday 4th inst. by the Rev. G. W. Downer(Rector) assisted by the Revd. Clair. Allan Davidson Roberts of Linn, Mass; U. S. A. to Evangeline Esther second daughter of Alexander Magnus. No Cards.

November 13, 1891

At 61 Gold St. yesterday a 10.30 a.m. Rev Samuel Smythe, late Rev of Stuart Town. The funeral will take place at 5 o'clock this evening.

November 18, 1891

A Matron is required for Milk River, Bath at a salary of £60 per year.

November 27, 1891

At Annandale Elletson Road at noon on Thursday 26th instant Elsie, only child of Robert and Lena Johnstone aged three years and two mouth. The Funeral will take place at 8.30 a.m. on Friday (today)

Selected Vital Records from the Jamaican Daily Gleaner

November 28, 1891
Earle-Isaacs- On the 18th instant, at St Albins Church, Santa Cruz Mountains, by the Revd. J.D. Ellis Edward R. C. Earle M.B.LB.C.P London M.R.C. A England eldest son of Edward Earle Esq to Lydia Isabel second daughter of Charles Earle Isaacs Esq of Mount Olivet, St Elizabeth's.

December 14, 1891
LATEST GENERAL NEWS

Mr. Rudyard Kipling left Sydney for Colombo, on his way to India. It is not stated whether he called in at Samoa to see Mr Stevenson during his Antipodean Visit.

December 16, 1891
At Elim, St Elizabeth, on 14th Dec, the wife of F. H. Farquharson, Esq., of a daughter.

1892

January 1, 1892

The Retirement of the Hon. M. Solomon from Business

The Retirement of the hon. Michael Solomon from the business which he has so long carried on in St. Ann's Bay creates a blank in the local commercial world which will not be quickly filled. In this extended career Mr. Solomon succeeded in obtaining what is not given to all, the unquestioned confidence and respect of his fellow merchants and traders. This he secured by his personal integrity and the purity of his business transactions. For some time failing in health he now retires into semi-private life to enjoy the rest and relaxation which he has earned so well. Our best wishes go with him, we hope that his usefulness will not cease although he is no longer actively engaged in business, for there is no truer hearted lover of Jamaica and all its varied interests than Mr. Solomon, and none more capable of advising regarding its continued welfare. We trust his health will improve under the influences of quiet and freedom from business cares, and that he will "renew his youth like the eagle". The business at St. Ann's Bay will be taken over by Mr. J.H. Levy who has also leased the wharves belonging to Messers. Bravo Bros. and Coy. and taken over the business of Isaacs & Co and will carry on the whole under the name of Levy, Isaacs and Coy. Mr. Solomon Isaacs being a member of the firm. We wish this new arrangement every success, and have not the slightest doubt that the firm will receive the same support which was accorded to its predecessors.

January 6, 1892
DIED
At Philadelphia Pa. U.S.A on the 20th December 1891 DAVID Son of the late David Rodriques DaCosta formerly of Kingston Jamaica

At Spanish Town, 30th December 1891, PRISCILLA FACEY, wife of James Samuel Facey, leaving a large number of relatives and friends to mourn their loss.

On Tuesday, the 5th instant, at 7 a.m., at his residence, Drominagh, Halfway Tree, FREDERIC SULLIVAN, Esq., late Postmaster for Jamaica, in his 57th year.

THE LATE MR FRED SULLIVAN
Although an event not unlooked for by the few, the announcement of the death of Mr. Frederick Sullivan late Postmaster General for Jamaica will come as a painful surprise to the people of his Island. Mr. Sullivan was rapidly failing in health in October last when he retired from the position he had held for so long a period, and since then he

has gradually been sinking in spite of the assiduous attention of Dr Saunders. Last week it was seen that the end was near, and yesterday morning at seven o'clock the patient expired.

[Picture, The late Mr. Fred Sullivan]

Mr. Sullivan was born, we believe, in England. His mother was before marriage a Miss Bruce, an English lady, and his father was Irish, both being of honourable ancestry. The boy was educated in England, and when still quite a lad, came with his parents to Jamaica, where he entered on a career in the public service. The life of such officials are, as a rule destitute of any striking features of general interest and Mr. Sullivan's was as uneventful as the majority.

The chief circumstances of his life can be briefly told. At the age of 18 he entered the then Governor's Secretary's office. This was at Christmas 1852 and from February of the following year he was employed as clerk in various degrees until May 1859 when being chief clerk he acted as Private Secretary to Governor Darling until November. He was confirmed in this appointment in May of the succeeding year, and continued to hold the office until March 1861 when he was transferred to the Post Office Department as chief clerk. Finally on 1st May 1870 he was appointed Postmaster General for Jamaica, in succession to Mr. Kemble an office which he held until he retired in October of the last year, on a well earned pension.

It is only by looking back and reviewing in detail the improvements which have been effected in the Post Office system of the colony that we can realize how much we owe to the zeal and enterprise of Mr. Sullivan. Previous to his appointment as the head of the department the facilities granted to the public were few and expensive. The rates of Inland postage were high, being for a letter not exceeding half an ounce 4d if conveyed a distance not exceeding 60 miles; 6d if not conveyed over 60 miles but not exceeding 100 miles; and 8d if conveyed over 100 miles. From the time that Mr. Sullivan entered office these rates were gradually reduced until on 1st January 1890 the penny postage system was introduced into the Island. The overseas letters were also high. In 1863 the rate of postage from and to the United Kingdom was 1s per half ounce; subsequently it was reduced to 6d and then to 4d, and in January 1891 it was fixed at 2 ½d at which it remains. In 1891 the rate to the United States and Canada had been reduced to a like figure.

On the 1st January 1872 Mr. Sullivan inaugurated a general house delivery of correspondence in Kingston simultaneously with the introduction of the prepaid system. The issue of post cards for use within the island took place in 1877. The commencement of another great boon to the public occurred in 1879 when a mail coach was established between Kingston and Mandeville for the conveyance of mails, passengers, and parcels. The system of mail coaches gradually extended under the fostering care of Mr. Sullivan until at the present time every village of importance is connected by this useful means of communication. During the year 1879 Mr. Sullivan imported a set of American "lock-boxes" and erected them in the Post Office for the convenience of businessmen who desired their letters as soon after their arrival as possible, and who were willing to pay a small sum for the privilege. These boxes have now become indispensable to merchants and others and their use has extended to other towns throughout the island.

The last decade witnessed many improvements in the Post Office. An extension of the foreign Money Order system was effected; a parcel Post Exchange with the United Kingdom and other countries was established; and last but not the least important, the Postal Order system was introduced. The benefits of the Department were also gradually extended through out the island, until at the present time there are 106 district Post Offices, where there were only 49 in 1860. The establishment of a system of inland posts telegraphs was one of the most important improvements effected under the supervision of Mr. Sullivan, and was effected directly at his insistence. The matter had been mooted so long back as 1859 but it was Sir Anthony Musgrave who acted on the suggestion of the Postmaster general and conferred the boon on the public. An Act was passed in 1879 and immediately after a School of Telegraphy was opened in Kingston where the operators were trained for the work. Telegraphic communication was first established between Kingston and St. Ann's on the 10th October 1879 and the circuit of the island was completed on the 4th March 1881. Telegraph Offices are now in existence in every principal village and town in the island.

One of the last undertakings in connection with his department in which Mr. Sullivan took a deep interest and devoted a great deal of his time and attention was the laying out of the Post Office Court in the Exhibition. The miniature Post and Telegraph Office here exhibited was imported under his own supervision and in the perfecting of all the arrangements – so ably carried out by Mr. Pearce and Mr. Wilson-he evinced the liveliest interest. He was one of those who regarded the Exhibition with great satisfaction and so far as lay in his power, endeavoured to bring the claims of the undertaking before the people of other countries.

Thus briefly and imperfectly have we endeavoured to indicate the useful nature of Mr. Sullivan's official career, It was his fortune to enter on his office when the department was still in its infancy, and he had therefore opportunities ready to his hand to prove his powers of creation and organization. The present institution so admirably managed in all its ramifications, is the visible result. But none can estimate the amount of pains which must have gone to produce this result; we see the complete structure but cannot tell the infinite labor that has been bestowed on every part before it reached the final stage. Browning expresses the idea in stronger language:-
" There's none care's like a fellow of the craft
For the all unestimated sum of pains
That go to a success the world can see,
They praise him, but the best they never know."

The Post Office Department, as it exists today, will be Mr. Sullivan's best monument. No fitter could be raised to him, and none will better serve to perpetuate his memory. As a public officer he was faithful, painstaking and courteous-he was always, emphatically, the gentleman. After so long a service it is a mournful circumstance that he did not live long enough to enjoy his well earned respite from daily labour and thought. To those who are left bereft we tender our sincere sympathy and condolence. The funeral took place last evening at Half-Way Tree Church yard.

January 12, 1892
DIED
On the 9th inst., at the Villa South Camp Road, the residence of the Rev. Wm. Priestnal, JOHN P. FEGAN, Halifax, Nova Scotia
Halifax and New Brunswick papers please copy.

January 13, 1892
Supposed death from Akee poisoning
On Friday afternoon last a cooper named Daley, employed at Messrs. Davidson & Colthirst's wharf, was taken suddenly ill, after having partaken of akee for his breakfast. He commenced to vomit and several pieces of akee came up. Death occurred early on Saturday morning and the body of the unfortunate man was consigned to its last resting place the same evening. It is believed that death was caused from akee poisoning.

January 14, 1892
At Roxborough, Manchester, on the 10th inst., the wife of T.A.S. Manley, of a son.

Selected Vital Records from the Jamaican Daily Gleaner

CURRENT ITEMS

Five dozen akees were offered in the street yesterday for a quattie but could not find a purchaser.

We regret to learn of the death from consumption of Mr. John P. Fegan, B.L. at the youthful age of 26. He was a promising Barrister of Halifax, N.S. and was persuaded by a friend who derived much benefit from a trip, to try the effect of our salubrious climate. He arrived here a few weeks since, unfortunately, however, too late for our warm climate or the skill of Dr. Phillipo to arrest the progress of the full disease. He died on the 9th inst. at the residence of the Rev. Wm. Priestnal and was buried with all the honours of the Roman Catholic Church. To his bereaved parents we offer our sincere condolence.

January 18, 1892
St Ann
FROM OUR CORRESPONDENT

St Ann's Bay, 14 January. Our Xmas and New Year season passed off quietly, the Xmas trade was very dull, not like in the Coffee districts such as Brown's Town, Bethany and Clarksonville. Trade is dead here. It can't be worse and if it continues some of our stores and shops must be closed in fact some are closing already. The poor merchants here must pass very restless nights. Their stores are largely stocked and there is little sale.

BUSINESS CHANGES.

There are some changes here, trade being so dull. Messrs. ORMESBY and Son are removing from here to Clarks Town, they have commenced removing. They tried to dispose of their stock, by selling out in lot, but could find very few, or no purchasers.
A.L. Sweetland is offering to sell out his extensive stock and if he does not get a purchaser will sell out in small lots at reduced rates, or remove the stock. Mr. Sweetland's store is one of the best in the town, and it is a great pity, trade being so dull that he has to close his branch. J.H. Levy, Esq. has bought out the old established business of Messrs M. Solomon & Co and taking over the business that traded by the name of Isaacs & Co. although belonging to Mr. J.H. Levy. Many people always called it Mr. Levy's and could not remember Isaacs and Co. The new firm now is called Levy, Isaacs & Co. Mr. Cooper of Brown's Town is said to be the Co. and no doubt before long the Co will be added openly then it will read, Levy, Isaacs, and Cooper. Mr. Cooper is quite deserving of the promotion he has received. He has made Mr. Levy's business in Brown's Town very extensive and well assorted. We wish the enterprising Mr. Levy every prosperity and trust the business will improve and that before long we shall see Mr. Levy filling Mr. Solomon's place as Custos. It is said that Mr. John Lewis is entitled to it and will get it, but our dear Mr. Levy is the man for it. We love Mas Joe he is so kind and worthy of any honor.

FRUIT TRADE

The Fruit Trade is very quiet. We hope the Boston Fruit Company and Messrs J.E. Kerr & Co will soon commence to buy. The poor people can't sell their fruit and how can they supply their wants?

A NEW PARK

We are getting a Park to be called Solomon Park. A petition is being prepared to go up to His Excellency the Governor. The site selected at Windsor is one well suited and would prove a great addition to the Town. It is said the Hon M. Solomon has offered to pay the £1000 for it so as to give a lasting present to the community. The Custos Hon. M. Solomon is anxious to do all he can now to improve St Ann's Bay.

1892

Poor old Thomas Bartlett who has been 29 years Head Clerk of Bravo Bros and Co. He is out of a berth and is allowed £100 for one year as a gift. The poor old gentleman is to be pitied having a large family and great expenses.

We need a few more Magistrates in the Town.

January 27, 1892
Current Items
York Castle School will be opened on Friday 29th inst.

Miss Maxwell and Miss Hay arrived in the packet yesterday from Southampton to join the tutorial staff at Barbican.

January 28, 1892
Current Items
It was rumored last night that a telegram has been received in this city, announcing the death in England from influenza of Ernest Murray, son of the Governor of York Castle school and a very successful scholar.

February 3, 1892
THE FUNERAL OF THE LATE PRINCE
Full Details of the Ceremony

London Jan 20- The Duke of Clarence was buried today with military honors with the British nation as mourners. The funeral service began at ten in the morning and lasted till five in the evening.

For a whole day politics was sunk, and conservatives, liberals radicals and socialists wore black. The day was fine for England. There was no sun, but there was no rain. The air was raw and chilly, but millions stood for hours without complaint for the heir to the British throne was dead and royalty was weeping.

London though it saw little of the funeral was funereal. So far as business was concerned it was almost dies non.

MEMORIAL SERVICES EVERYWHERE

Memorial services were held in nearly all the churches. St Paul's and Westminster Abbey were packed to the doors. Multitudes were unable to gain admittance. For hours the mournful sound of the slowly tolled bell filled the air. The millions that throng London's streets were in funereal garb. It was truly a day of national mourning.

All roads led to Windsor today, and all roads were crowded. Windsor was the end as Sandringham was the beginning of the greatest funeral England has seen since that of the Prince Consort. At ten o'clock a short service was held in the Church of St Mary Magdalene at Sandringham. It was attended by the royal family. The service was simple consisting of prayers and psalms, with two short, lessons, concluding with the singing of the hymn "My God, My Master, while I stray".

FROM THE CHURCH TO THE GUN CARRIAGE

At the conclusion of the service the coffin was carried by the servants of the Prince of Wales to the gun carriage which the Royal Artillary furnished for the purpose. The gun carriage was drawn by six horses and was covered with a silken Union Jack and two lovely white wreaths and a floral cross placed by the Princess of Wales. In the wake of the coffin walked the Prince of Wales supported by the Duke of Fife (his son-in-law) and Sir Digton Probyn. They walked to Wolverton, a distance of three miles. Prince George followed in a carriage with the Princess of Wales and the Duchess of Fife. Other carriages contained the Duchess of Teck, Princess May, Princess Victoria Princess Maud and Miss Knollys. The principal tenants and members of the household acted a pall bearers.

PEOPLE LINE THE ROUTE.

The entire route was lined by people all bareheaded. The procession was met at Wolverton by a guard of honor, composed of the Thirty volunteer battalion of the Norfolk regiment, a deputation of Freemasons and the corporation of Lynn. The coffin was transferred to the mortuary carriage which was draped with purple velvet and adorned with a large wreath of silver laurel leaves bearing the letter "C and A". The members of the royal family entered the train at noon the populace standing bareheaded until the train was out of sight. Great throngs were at every station en route, all silent, all bareheaded all in somber attire.

All English men and English women, rich or poor, on an occasion of this kind wear black from head to foot and not even the poorest is ungloved.

Gathering at Windsor
ONE OF THE GRANDEST OF FUNERAL PROCESSSIONS.

Windsor Jan 20.—Windsor was reached at three o'clock. For Windsor in one sense, it was fete day. Thames street reaches almost from the railway station to the castle. It is the principal throughfare, and it is a stiff gradient the castle being at the summit. Every pane of glass in Thames Street was worth a guinea today-only the footways costing nothing-and it was packed at one o'clock. Until two o'clock the populace and visitors monopolized the footways and roadway.

UNDER A LEADEN SKY

The bulk of the multitude tried to get a close as possible to the gate of Henry VIII. The castle loomed gray and gloomy under the leaden sky. In every window were heads in every embrasure were heads. From the battlements hundreds looked down upon thousands. The front of every building was shingled with faces. Train after train had discharged its freight, until there was no space from which a glimpse of the great function could be seen. More.

February 5, 1892
A telegram was received yesterday stating that Ernest Murray, the distinguished young scholar, is in perfect health in England.

Referring to the recent death in this city of Mr. JP. Fegan, the Halifax Evening Mail says:- Some months ago J.P. Fegan, barrister, of Morrison & Fegan went to Jamaica, seeking restoration to health in that mild climate. On Saturday his parents received a long letter from him, stating that he was considerably improved, hopefully looked forward to complete restoration to health and expected to be home in Halifax early in the spring. About two hours after the parents received the cheering letter from their son, a cablegram was received announcing his death. The despatch was received by a gentleman in the city, who had a very delicate and painful duty to perform in breaking to them the sad news. Mr. Fegan studied law with McCoy, Fearson & Forbes was an active member of the young men's literary society and of No 1 steamer of the U.E.C. and was a general favourite with numerous friends and acquaintances, who sincerely regret the cutting down in his prime of such a promising young man. The body will it is understood, be brought home for burial".

February 10, 1892
E.T. Forrest Esq. has been appointed a J.P. for St Elizabeth.

February 25, 1892
On the 20th inst. At No 84 Duke Street, the wife of John J. Orgill of a son.

1892

Wesleyan Conference
The conference opened yesterday by a public devotional service in Wesley Chapel, at 7 a.m. The ministers assembled at 10 a.m. for business. The Rev. W. Clarke Murray was elected Vice-President, and the Rev. John Duff was re-elected Secretary of the Conference.

March 1, 1892
Mr. Charles M. Sherlock who has for the past eight or ten years acted as clerk in the store of Nathan & Co. has been admitted into partnership in the firm. We congratulate Mr. Sherlock on his success.

March 3, 1892
Western Annual Conference
STATIONS FOR 1892
Kingston District
Kingston—(Coke) Thomas M. Geddes, William J. Williams, G.H. Baron Hay
Kingston-(Wesley)Thomas P. Russell, James O. Mann
Kingston- (Port Royal) William H.F. Bleby (Chaplain: Army and Work)
Barbican High School W.H.F. Bleby, Governor
Clarendon- William Melville
Manchester-George Lockett, Harvey Swithenback
Mount Fletcher-Alexander M. Smith
Grateful Hill-George M. Ashby, who shall act under the direction of the Chairman of the District
Thomas M. Geddes, Chairman of the District
George Lockett, Financial Secretary.

Montego Bay District
Montego Bay- John A. McIntosh, Albert L. Johnson
Lucea-Samuel Spratt
Falmouth-William H. Atkin
Duncans-Robert M. Parnther, Charles F. Hardwick
Mount Ward-Frederick O. Miller
Sav-la-Mar- Arthur F. Lightbourne, Theodore Glasspole
Black River-Albert H. Aguilar, George S. Lanibb
Robert M. Parnther, Chairman of the District
William H. Atkin, Financial Secretary.

St Ann District
Spanish Town- Stephen Satton, William J. Maund
St Ann's Bay-William R. Griffin. One to be sent
Watsonville-Samuel L Lindo
Ocho Rios-Caleb Reynolds, James G.A. Smith
Bechamville-John Duff
York Castle-W. Clarke Murray
Theological Institution and High School-W. Clarke Murray, Governor and Theological Tutor
Brown's Town-Jonathan Grant
Edmondson- Samuel T. Brown.
Mount Hume-Archibald J. Andrews. The Mount Hume Circuit is under the Superintendent of Edmondson

Selected Vital Records from the Jamaican Daily Gleaner

Guy's Hill and Hampstead-Nathan A. Bacquie

W. Clarke Murray Vice-President of the Conference, Chairman of the District

John Duff (Secretary of the Conference) Financial Secretary

Morant Bay District
(not copied)

March 4, 1892
MARRIED
At Coke Chapel Kingston, on the 2nd March, by the Revd. Thos. M. Geddes, assisted by the Revds. S. T. Brown and A. W. Geddes, ADRIAN BUNTING GEDDES of Eden Bower, Ocho Rios, St Ann's Bay to MARGARITA, only daughter of the late FREDERICK HENRIQUES of Panama, U.S.C.

DIED
At Jersey (Channel Islands), on Tuesday 1st instant, MATILDA relict of the late Theodore de Pass of this city.

At his residence Clifton Lodge, Old Harbour, yesterday morning NAPHTOLI MAGNUS. Funeral will move from the residence of his sister, No 36 Hanover Street, at 8 o'clock this morning. Friends will accept this intimation.

March 19, 1892
DIED
At the Mico Institution on the 18th inst. After a protracted illness, LEILA, the beloved wife of the Revd. William Gilles and second daughter of the late Revd. D.R. Littlejohn, Rector of Trelawny. The funeral will move from the Mico Intuition this afternoon at half past four o'clock.

April 2, 1892
An account of the akee poisoning case taken from the "Gleaner" was cabled by Daisial's New York Agency to the London newspapers and appeared towards the end of last month.

The Art Exhibition in the Jamaica Institute is now daily open to the public, and is well worthy of a visit from those who take an interest in the subject of local art.

The band of the 2nd Batt. W.I. Reg. Played to a very large assembly in the Park on Thursday night. Among the selections were the "Comical Contest" (rendered at the Operatic Festival in the Exhibition and Reminiscences of Scotland).

April 6, 1892
DIED
On the 1st inst. At Shaw Park, Ocho Rios, James Stewart (formerly 22nd Regt. and member of the late House of Assembly) son of the late James L. Stuart of Blenheim House, Cheltenham, and Tudor House, Tenby, aged 78.

April 14, 1892
At Rose Bank House, Kingston, on Wednesday 13th inst. The wife of the Hon'ble Wellesley Bourke of a daughter.

1892

April 20, 1892

On the 19th April 1892 at his Father's Residence No 69 Church Street, ALFRED W. DAYES, son of James Dayes of Kingston, Solicitor. Friends and acquaintances are invited to attend his funeral which will take place at 4 o'clock on the afternoon of the 20th April 1892 from his late residence.

April 27, 1892

A new Wesleyan Church is in progress in the Pedro River district of Clarendon. Corner stones were placed on the basement walls on
Wednesday the 20th inst. by Miss Duff, Miss Atkinson, and Miss Murray. Addresses were delivered by the Rev. John Duff and W. Clarke Murray. Heavy showers of rain fell, during the service, but the contributions we understand were fairly good.

Mark C. Hendriks Stock in Trade of Furniture, Glassware, Electro-Plate and Miscellaneous articles at Roxburgh House will be sold by Auction on the premises at 11 a.m. today in one lot by Turnbull, Mudon & Co.

Advertizement

Institute of Jamaica
LIBRARY AND MUSEUM
Open daily from 11 a.m. to 9 p.m. Admission free
The Curator attends every Monday evening from 8 to 9 to explain
objects in the Museum to visitors
The ART EXHIBITION of Oil and Water Colour Paintings and Drawings, and
Photography, will be closed on Saturday April 30th
BOOKS WANTED TO PURCHASE
Jamaica Almanacs for the years 1783, 1792, 1804, 1809, 1810
1830, 1834, 1835, 1836, 1837, 1840, 1843, 1846, 1848, 1852, 1853, 1854, 1855, 1856,
1858, 1859, 1861, 1862, 1864, 1865, 1866, 1867, 1870, 1872, 1873, 1874, 1863, 1877.

May 4, 1892
DIED
At 168 Orange Street, yesterday at 10 a.m. HERBERT GEORGE DELISSER, aged 42 years. Funeral this morning at 9 a.m.

May 6, 1892
DEATH OF MR. MICHAEL SOLOMON.

Intelligence was received in this city yesterday of the death of the hon. Michael Solomon C.M.G. at his residence in St. Ann's Bay. The event was not unexpected as for some time he had been in failing health, and latterly was seriously ill, although he seemed to be recovering. The sad tiding was received with deep regret by the citizens of Kingston as they will be by all the inhabitants of the colony, when they become known.

We have elsewhere referred to the character of Mr. Solomon and here desire to speak only of the events of his uneventful life. He was born in London in 1818, and arrived in this island when quite a lad, being in fact about twelve years of age only. He came out to his brother Mr. A. J. Solomon, who was an auctioneer and occupied premises where the GLEANER printing office is now situated. We find him next at Spanish Town, as clerk in the business house of Messrs A. N. Henriques and Coy. He married the daughter of Mr. Henriques and when she died he became clerk to the late Mr. S. D. Lindo at Moneague. While stationed here he was offered an appointment by Messrs. Bravo Bros. & Coy. of St Ann's Bay which he accepted. Through their influence he obtained the position of clerk to the Magistrate of the District Courts in 1868, this office was abolished he was given a pension which he was drawing up to the time of his death. He married again, this time the sister of Mr. Bravo, and was eventually taken into partnership, and continued in the business up to the last. He was for a long period Deputy Clerk of the Peace for St. Ann, and although not a member of the legal profession performed the duties with credit to himself and satisfaction to the public.

Mr. Solomon was nominated member of the Legislature under Crown Government, and was an actor in the famous Florence case: The Florence was a schooner with a cargo of arms and ammunition for Venezuela which had been detained by Sir Anthony Musgrave. The damages were assessed at £6,700 and the unofficial members, among whom was Mr. Michael Solomon refused to sanction the vote for the purpose on the ground that the damages were incurred in pursuance of imperial policy and objects. This led to a Royal Commission being sent to Jamaica, and ultimately to the present form of Representative Government. At the election of members in 1883 to the new Legislative Council, Mr. Solomon was returned unopposed.

In 1884 we find him in the Council putting forward a motion having for its object the political and commercial federation of Jamaica and Canada. After a debate the motion was lost, Mr. Solomon being the only one of the elected members voting for it. In the following year, however he brought the subject forward again in another form and was this time more successful. It was in the shape of a resolution that the paralysed condition of the sugar interest of the colony called for relief and that five gentlemen be appointed as Commissioners to proceed to Canada with the object of ascertaining what arrangements could be made with the Dominion Government on a basis either of confederation or reciprocity. This commission was subsequently appointed with a result familiar to our reader. During the recent session of the Legislative Council, Mr. Solomon though in failing health looked actively after the interests of his constituents. His fearless attitude on the Wharfage question will be remembered while he consistently opposed the Pension's Bill from start to finish. On the third reading of the latter bill he was the only member then present who dissented. His attitude on that occasion was referred in our yesterday's issue but here can be no doubt that he was actuated only from motive of the purest patriotism.

Mr. Solomon was magistrate for many years and also Custos of St Ann. For his services to Jamaica he obtained the honor of C.M.G. from Her Majesty. He was a large landed proprietor, possessed numerous estates and penns, and always evinced a keen interest in agricultural pursuits. He was highly esteemed not only in his own parish but throughout the country.

May 16, 1892
JAMAICA AT THE BIG FAIR
The New York Times of the 5th inst. Says:- "The Legislative Council of Jamaica, British West Indies, has voted £5,000 (25,000 dollars) for an island exhibit at the World's Fair.

The Government and people of Jamaica realize the beauty and fertility of their island and will make a full exhibit of its many productions. The large and successful exhibition in Kingston last year has stimulated industry, bettered agricultural methods, and awakened a desire for extended trade and connection. A direct outcome of the exhibition has been an increase in trade between Jamaica and the United States and Canada.

Acting under the advice of the Governor Sir Henry Arthur Blake, K.C.M.G. the Government of this island has under consideration a scheme for first class hotels and for making the island a popular Winter resort for Americans. The whole will have the influence and financial backing of the Government. The island has a perfect Winter climate.

May 30, 1892
HENDRIKS-On the 29th instant at her late residence No 7 Sutton Street, corner of Smith Lane MARIA HENDRIKS, relict of the late Mark J. Hendriks. Funeral leaves at 4.30 p.m. today. Friends and acquaintances will kindly accept this intimation.

Current Items
The pupils of Mr. Lewis, School are deeply interested in the physiological lecture being delivered to them by Mr. John Stuart, M.A. Mr. Stuart gives practical demonstrations every Saturday, and the girl students seem to enjoy the dissections of rabbits, sheep's hearts and so forth.

June 3, 1892
Rudyard Kipling on New York

Current Items
An interesting and solemn service was held in Wesley Chapel on the 25th ulto. when M.C.M. Clarke was ordained as a Missionary to the Isthmus of Panama, in connection with the Mission there of the Wesleyan Church. The candidate for ordination was presented by the Rev. John Duff, Secretary of the conference, the Rev. W. Clarke Murray, Vice President, delivered the charge, the Rev. T.M. Geddes, Geo. Lockett (missy Secretary) and T.P. Russell took part in the service, and all the ministers named joined in the "laying on of the hands of the presbytery". Mr. Clarke has since left for the scene of his labours, where he will be associated with the Rev. A.W. Geddes, the Superintendent of the Mission.

June 6, 1892
REPRESENTATION OF ST MARY AND ST ANN
Full Report of the St Ann's Bay Meeting
At a public meeting held on Thursday at the Court House St Ann's Bay, in accordance with a requisition to Thomas Beecher Scott, Esq., Senior Resident Magistrate for St Ann the following were present. T. B. Scott, C.W. Steer, A.N. Dixon, John Cameron, J.H. Levy, A.J. Hart, (senior) F.L Rodon, A.S. Byles, Thomas Bartlett, Rev. S.D. Lindo, (Weslayan) J.Duff, (Do) G.A. House,(Baptist) Dnl Hart, (Solicitor) A.B. Rerrie, Mrs. Amy Pringle, J. A. Miller, Jas. O'Meally, (Solicitor) J.H. Allwood (Do) Victor Pratt, E.N. Harrison, F.B. Sturridge, J.D. Ormsby, C.S. Campbell, Edwd. Pratt, G. Pratt, W. A. Gaynor, Dr. H.E. Maunsell, Richd. Watson, Saml. Dobson, A.C.C. Colthirst, Henry Steer, Wm Shaw, George Coombs, A.C. Mesquita, H. Mesquita, T.C. Dixon, Wm. Saunders, L.L. Fraser, J.O Clarke, F.A. Morris, A. Tullock, H. Hamilton, Wm. Brown, O.L.M. Sanguinette, C. Sanguinette, Walter Bravo, J.L. Lannaman, E.N. Steele, W.G. Nunes, A.J. Webb, V. Hart, R. Steer, S.D. Cunningham, and many others (of every class and interest represented.)
On motion, A.N. Dixon, Mr. R.B. Scott, senior, was unanimously called upon to occupy the Chair.
Mr. Scott on assuming the chair requested J.O O'Meally, Esq., Solicitor, to act as Secretary.
The Requisition calling the meeting was read by Mr. O'Meally, and the Chairman then explained the object of the meeting and quoted paragraphs 1 and 2 thereof, reading same with full approval.

Chas. Wm Steer then addressed the meeting and thereafter moved the following resolution which was seconded by Mr. J.H. Levy.

Moved by C. W. Steer seconded by J.H. Levy.

That this meeting is of opinion that the want of separate representation for each parish in the Island has to a very large extent deprived the inhabitants of the advantages which it was reasonable to expect from the Constitution of 1884.

That humble petition be prepared for presentation to Her Majesty, praying for an Amendment of the order in Council in this direction.

That any candidate for the approaching election should be requested to give his pledge in support of this object.

Carried unanimously.

Signed by Thos B. Scott, J.P., Senior Magistrate, Chairman.

Mr. J.H. Levy then addressed the meeting in a straight forward manner saying that the Honourable M. Solomon's mantle could fall on no better man under the exigencies of this case than that on the shoulders of the Hon Geo. Solomon, that when the parishes were divided plenty of local men would be found able to go up, and that Mr. Solomons would pave the way for what they now desired.

That he took the opportunity of returning thanks to these gentlemen who asked him (Mr. Levy) to stand but situated as they were no man could conscientiously serve two parishes so diverse in their requirements and although they clamoured for representative government still they had to seek an outsider because in him being disinterested he could serve both parishes. He also said it gave him great pleasure to see the wife of Mr. Pringle present and accorded her with every one present a hearty welcome (loud cheers).

Mr. F. L. Rodon followed in a complimentary manner at the presence of Mrs. Pringle amongst the body present and also asked a fair welcome to be accorded her today. The chairman then named a Committee to prepare the necessary petition for presentation as follows-C.W. Steer, A.N. Dixon, J.H. Levy.

Mr. J.H. Levy rose and proposed Honble. George Solomon of Kingston as candidate to supply vacancy in the Legislative council occasioned by the death of Hon. M. Solomon. He then moved the following resolution. That whilst under ordinary conditions, it is most desirable that each electoral district should be represented by a member resident among his constituents, yet looking to the existing union of two parishes which comprised one sixth, of the area of the country. The conflicting interests which such conditions give and to the possibility that injustice or neglect however unintentional might be done to one parish by the member being specially identified with the other comprising the district, this meeting invites George Solomon Esq. to come forward for election to fill the vacancy in the representation of St Mary and St. Ann.
Signed by T.B. Scott, J.P. Chairman

This was seconded by A.N. Dixon amid applause. Mr. Dixon then showed the position of the two parishes and in a very able speech advocated the Honble. G. Solomon's return.

Mrs. Amy Pringle then addressed the meeting from Judge's Bench. She spoke well, advocating her husband's claim whom she put forward as being an independent man of means and a member of the Agricultural body and that in seeking Mr. Solomon from outside they were stultifying the very desire to obtain representatives from every parish when they had to go outside.

Dr. W.H. Miller then proposed Mr. Pringle of St Mary.

Mr. Danl. Hart stated he seconded it (not to create discussion) but that he intended to vote for George Solomon.

Mr. J.H. Allwood then proposed Dr. Miller of Brown's Town.

Mr. A.S. Byles seconded for purpose of discussion but said that he did not intend to vote for him but to let the people see before them what sort of a representative they would have for the Council. At this juncture questions were put to Dr. Miller by Mr. Levy if he was returned to Council how would he vote for pensions! The reply was "ask me something new".

Question by Mr. Byles-"How about the lands in the hands of men who won't rent, sell or lease, what would you do if in the House, would you continue to tax them 1d? Reply-"Oh that would depend"- At this stage hisses etc. were going on and at the suggestion of friends the Doctor was asked to step down which he did.

Mr. Daniel Hart asked who sold the Railway-if it was not the agricultural interested members?

Mr. A.N. Dixon reviewed the state the area of the several parishes, also the number of voters in each, and pointed out that although St Ann was larger in area than St. Mary yet the latter had more votes than St Ann. Now was it possible for a local resident like Dr. Pringle to be able to act for St Ann for if he did he would offend where he had the major voting power and for this reason alone he should not desire to see Dr. Pringle, but one cause more, that Dr. Pringle before the Royal Commission of Baden Powell and Col. Crossman nine years ago spoke most disparagingly of the people-vide Blue Book-which he had in his hand and read from-also the sweeping condemnation of any medical man holding any land, as vide Commissioners report. At this one or two hissed. Mr. Dixon stated clearly that to elect Dr Pringle was to add one more official vote in Council as for 20 years he had been a Government man and always voted with official element when acting and had only within past few weeks, aye days, severed the connection to come forward (deafening applause).

The question was then put by the Chairman what decision the meeting arrived at—whether to nominate the first named candidate, Honble G. Solomon or the other named gentlemen when by a show of hands the majority decided for Solomon (unanimously)

Moved by A.N. Dixon seconded by Mr. J.H. Levy and unanimously agreed to "That the Secretary do cause a copy of the minutes of the proceedings of this meeting, together with the resolution passed thereat be transmitted, by earliest post to Geo. Solomon Esq.

A vote of thanks was accorded the chairman and the meeting separated.

We have been requested to state that Dr. Miller will contest the seat in the Legislative Council made vacant by the recent death of the Hon M. Solomon. A correspondent at Brown's Town telegraphs us "that Dr Miller's candidature is bona fide as will be shown when the ballot boxes are counted".

June 7, 1892
MR SOLOMON'S REPLY TO THE ELECORS OF SAINT ANN'S
Gentlemen:-

Before proceeding with questions of the present period I think it is due to you and to myself, that I should afford you some explanation of my conduct as your representative which terminated with the abolition of the House of Assembly in 1865. In that year I was in London and owing to my having been in the executive committee under the previous administration of Governor Darling, Mr. Cardwell afterwards Lord Cardwell the new Secretary of State for the Colonies sent for me to meet him in Downing Street. I prepared myself for the interview in belief that information and advise were required for the preparation of new constitution for this Island, and I recommended that single Legislative Chamber should be substituted for the House of Assembly and Legislative Council which were then both in existence. This new single Chamber should embody the elected members from Twenty-two Parishes with the nominated ones from the Legislative Council.

I pointed out that Forty-seven members in the House of Assembly apart from those composing the Legislative Council proved too great a strain upon the Representative element and the Country gentlemen complained of the hardship imposed upon them. I expressed the opinion that this alteration in the constitution would be received by the Island with satisfaction and it would get rid of the power of the legislative Council to disallow the legislation of the House of Assembly. A dispatch was sent from the British Government to the Jamaica Government, urging these views and I understood for a time they were accepted by the House of Assembly, but later on to my great astonishment reports were circulated that local jealousies interposed, and that the House of Assembly actually declined to have any elected members, and that it handed over to the Imperial Authorities a clean sheet for Crown Government pure and simple. This ignoble act of self immolation on the part of the House of Assembly, without the consent of the constituencies, severed my connection with your Parish and on my return to the Island I could not address you again as I was no longer your representative and you were no longer Electors.

It is marvelously strange that I have to tell you 27 years subsequently my hope your wishes may be granted for a representation of fourteen parishes after refusing it for twenty –two, suggested by your representative of the period adopted by the Mother country, but declined by the majority of the members of the House of Assembly for all these years that have expired since that time, both a member inside and outside of the Council I have endeavoured to serve the best interest of the country. It would overburden this address were I to enter into details, but briefly stated I have been the supporter of nearly all the works of progress that have been started in the island in many cases. I have had the honor of being the originator and satisfaction has followed in the wake of these undertakings.

My reply to the requisition from St Mary will occasion you no surprise, for I particularly stipulated a month ago when in your parish that I would not be foisted on St Mary, nor would "I oppose a Resident Candidate" and I understand from a deservedly popular gentleman in your parish, that in case of an unpopular Resident candidate coming forward, he would himself be induced to oppose him. I have however modified this understanding agreeing to stand a nomination upon two conditions.

1st That you approve of my programme.

2nd That in case the resident candidate refuse to adopt it.

It should be remembered that agriculture in this island has been sadly neglected and this has been a great injustice all round. The new lesson to be learned is that the prosperity of the masses, will be the prosperity of the classes.

The island is not half cultivated, and under energetic action, putting our shoulders to the wheel to unite the entire Island in a bond of union to carry out a policy that will give hope and reward to every industry now established, and also what is likely to be successfully established I shall have no fears in the future for this wonderfully prolific Island of Jamaica.

Awaiting the issue which must be determined upon within the next few days and with my heartiest thanks for the confidence reposed in me. I have the honor to be your obedient,

GEO. SOLOMON.

June 8, 1892

THE REPRESENTATION OF ST. MARY AND ST ANN'S

Much disappointment was expressed in the city yesterday when it became known that the Hon. George Solomon had intimated his decision not to accept the invitation of the electors of St Ann's and St Mary to represent them in the legislative Council. It will be remembered that when appealed to in the first instance Mr. Solomon said that he would stand if no local man came forward and when subsequently two did so he laid down a platform which if not accepted by the others he would seek their suffrages.

That platform he had been informed, has been accepted by one at least of the candidates and he consequently he has withdrawn from the field.

The feeling is running very high in St Ann's that that parish should be represented and the electors are determined to induce some one to put himself forward to represent their interests. The gentlemen came up to Kingston to see Mr. Solomon personally on the matter sent a telegram to Mr. J.H. Levy yesterday intimating the position of affairs to him, and requesting him to oppose Dr. Pringle.

We think it would be a wise step in the interests of the parishes for Mr. Levy to accept the invitation. Only one man would be elected, and the other parish would then be able to say that it was not represented in the Council, a position which would be one of the strongest arguments in favor of extended representation.

June 10, 1892
REPRESENTATION OF ST MARY AND ST ANN
Dr. J. Ogilvie

We understand that Dr. Ogilvie has received a requisition from some of the electors of St Ann's asking him to stand as the representative of the Parishes of St Ann and St Mary in the Legislative Council. The Doctor, we are informed, will be willing to serve the parish if the invitation is backed up by the majority of the electors.
MR J.H. LEVY WILL STAND

One or two gentlemen of prominence in the parish of St Mary called at this office and expressed their great regret at the withdrawal of the hon. George Solomon from the election field. They said they would have supported him, and many would have done the same.

These and others will be glad to hear that Mr. J.H. Levy of Brown's Town has consented to contest the election under great pressure from the electors of St Ann. We have received a telegram announcing his decision to acquiesce in the strong wishes of the constituency. For the reason expressed in our yesterday's issue, we are glad that Mr. J.H. Levy has allowed himself to stand, and we may now look to see a warm contest in the parishes.

June 15, 1892
BIRTH
On 12th inst. At Chapelton, the wife of Harry McCrea, of a son.

REPRESENTATION OF ST MARY AND ST ANN
Dr. Pringle retires from the contest

Agualta Vale Penn
Annatto Bay P.O.
June 13th 1892
The following letter has been sent out by Dr Pringle to C. L.
Walker Esq., J.P. and 69 Requisitionists and other my supporters:-

Gentlemen,- It has been credibly announced that Mr. George Solomon has (as might be expected from his past political history) retired at this juncture, on its being shown that there are several local candidates willing to represent the vacant constituency of St Ann and St Mary.

Selected Vital Records from the Jamaican Daily Gleaner

As one who believed that it was necessary at this time, with a view to increased representation that the constituency should be represented from within itself, I consented to become a candidate to indicate a principle though not, as I then wrote desirous or ambitious for legislative honors.

My main object therefore having been accomplished and other local candidates being now in the field, I take the earliest opportunity of intimating that while sincerely thanking my supporters, I have determined to be no longer a candidate for the vacant seat.—I have, the honor to be, your obedient servant

John Pringle

MEETING AT GAYLE

An enthusiastic and highly successful Electoral Meeting was held at Gayle on Saturday the 11th inst.

Among those present we noticed Hon. Dr John and Mrs. Pringle, Dr. L.M. Clerk, Inspector Ponsonby, R.M. Cocking, D.M. Kelly, C.H.C. Goffe, D. R. Clemetson, Allan Evelyn, A.E. Silvera, Osborne G. Fletcher Esqrs. There was a very large attendance of the working classes.

A.E Silvera Esq., J.P. was voted into the chair and after expressing himself in favour of Hon Dr. Pringle and referring in very high terms of the action of Mrs. Pringle he called upon Mr. Kelly to address the meeting which that gentleman did in his usual good and original style. C.H. Goffe Esq., Solicitor was next called upon and gave a powerful address in the Dr's behalf. The event of the day followed in a noble speech from the wife of the Hon. Doctor which was listened to attentively and frequently applauded.

Dr Pringle followed stating his platform and expressed himself ready to answer any question put. After further addresses by Mr. Evelyn, Mr. Williams and others and the vote of thanks to the Chairman the meeting dispersed, hearty cheers being given for Mrs. Pringle.

Feeling is strongly in favour of the Doctor and it is expected he will be returned by a great majority.

Daily Gleaner Editorial
St Mary vs. St Ann

It is with great regret that we learn of the retirement of Dr. Pringle from the contest on the Northside. The reasons given for this act are stated in the letter which is printed elsewhere in our columns and they are perfectly in accordance with what Dr. Pringle avowed at the outset. We certainly did not anticipate his withdrawal, and as we have stated, we regret that he has seen any necessity to take the step. We have been anxious that two good men should go forward, each well backed up by the electors of the separate parishes in order that the parish which was 'left' could say with perfect truth that it was unrepresented in the Legislative Council, a state of things which would demand on the face of it a more rational and extended distribution of representatives. Our hope was gratified when Dr. Pringle and Mr. Levy were finally seen to be the candidates, for scarcely two better men to seek the suffrages of the electors could have been found. Both are popular with the constituency, both possess moral and intellectual qualities of a high order and both are shrewd business men, well versed in the affairs of their respective parishes. The result of the poll it would have been difficult to surmise and while we felt called upon as a public journal to declare on which side our sympathies lay we were actuated mainly by the desire to see a warm contest which would leave warm feelings behind in the mind of the electors of the defeated parish in the hope that these feelings would find vent in a strong demand for equitable representation. By the action of the Doctor in withdrawing from the contest the cause of extended representation has lost the prospect of acquiring a first rate weapon to aid in the struggle. The election seems now to have resolved itself into very simple elements. The result will practically be a 'walkover" for Mr. Levy and Dr. Miller, like St Mary, will probably be left lamenting. Both will have our sympathy and at the next general election we hope St Mary will be able to send up her own local man as in all justice she ought to be able to do at present.

REPRESENTATION OF ST MARY AND ST ANN
St Ann's Bay
10th June, 1892
> To J.H. Levy Esqr. Brown's Town
> Sir- We the undersigned Electors and Taxpayers of the several districts of the Parish of St Ann having heard that the Honble George Solomon, for reasons which have been made public, has withdrawn as a candidate to fill the vacancy in the representation of the Parishes of St Ann and St Mary in the Legislative council, consequent on the demise of the Honble Michael Solomon, and believing as we do that the interests of St Ann and those of the sister parish, agricultural and otherwise will not receive uniform and unbiased protection by either of the candidates whose names are now before the Electors appeal to you, to come forward and contest the election, and we herby pledge ourselves to secure your return.

> The fact that you have all your life been identified with the people, your successful career both commercially and as a landed proprietor has been marked by a zealous and conscientious discharge of the duties which are incumbent on every good citizen, and that both privately and in your public capacity you have invariably striven for the best ends, point to you as a "Representative man" in the fullest sense of the expression.

> We trust that the appeal will be sufficient to induce you to overcome your known reluctance and to place your services at the disposal of the Electors,

We remain,
Yours truly,
(Sgnd.)

A.N.Dixon	Philip H. Grant
Jas O'Meally,	James Delgado
John Ellis,	C.L. DePass
F.L. Rodon,	P. Reginald Smith
Robert J. Steer	Chas. S.Campbell
W.A. Gaynor,	F. Roper, J.P.
S.D. Cunningham	Rev. S.L. Lindo
Richard Watson	A.N. Sutherland
F.A. Morris,	C.A. Brown
D.G. McConnell	James Russell
H.W.H. James	G.T.Scott
Wm. Brown Jnr.	G.L.Mais
Adrian Tulloch,	John Durrant
Thomas Bartlett,	Geo. H. Cooper
Henry Hamilton,	A.C. Dunkley
Colin Campbell,	A.A. Isaacs
Geo. A. Dougall,	J.H. Mawbey
Rev. W.M. Webb	T.W. Miller, J.P.
Wm. Cover, jnr. J.P. David Archer, J.P.	
A.S. Byles	J. L Tapper

St Ann' Bay, June 11th 1892

To F. Roper, J.P., A.N. Dixon J.P., T.W. Miller, J.P., D. Archer J.P., F. L Rodon Esq.,
Revs Lindo and Webb and others,
Gentlemen:

It is very flattering to me to feel that after my repeated refusal to come forward to contest the vacant seat in the Legislative Council, that you, and so many of my parishioners, as also those of the sister parish should be so persistent in your endeavour as to present me with this urgent appeal and requisition. I had hoped that my efforts combined with yours would have removed the necessity, and that Mr. George Solomon, a man in whom we had all confidence as being so eminently fitted to represent us at this particular juncture, would have seen his way to come forward. Mr. Solomon's reasons for withdrawing from the contest have been publicly made known and I may here say that though we all regret it, his conduct is perfectly consistent with his utterances on the occasion when he was first approached on the subject, i.e. that he would not be foisted on St Mary, nor would he contest the seat against a resident of either parish.

You are all aware, gentlemen, that from the very outset, and by my many public expressions since, I have repeated the one thing, that I would prefer waiting until we got extended representation, when if the people of my own parish, desired and though that I was worthy and fitted to be their representative, I would in all probability not be unwilling to come forward, for like Mr. Solomon, I had no desire to be foisted on St Mary, and I saw how difficult it would be for a man of either parish to represent the combined, but varying and unequal interests of both with anything like satisfaction and success. You have however made it so manifest that my services are needed at the present moment when you fear that the election of another may not tend to the welfare of the parishes, that I have no alternative but to place myself at your disposal. It is satisfactory to find that whatever motives my opponents may seem fit to attribute to me for contesting the seat in the Council, the unworthy one of speculating in Legislative honors cannot be justly laid to my charge.

From the deep interest I have always taken in the affairs of the parish, and indeed in every movement brought forward for the benefit of the Island generally which interest I venture to say is not unknown to you, I may be excused from giving the detail of my political platform, especially as it is not an uncommon thing for the platform of political aspirants to be made up of stereotyped phrases which in many instance neither represent the candidates intentions nor convictions. I will, however, say this that if elected, every interest, whether it be Agricultural, Commercial, Educational or Social, will receive at my hands fair, honest, and impartial attention. The Agricultural and Educational interests are certainly the burning questions of the day, and it is satisfactory to find that the public mind is so much exercised over them and as they are the most important and the forerunner of commerce and other successful issues, they will receive my special consideration.

I have now to thank you again for you kindness, and the honour you do me in repeating your invitation for me to come forward and contest the vacant seat for these important parishes and to assure you that if elected, I will, aided by Divine Wisdom and guidance, do my duty faithfully and honestly- Gentlemen
Your obedient servant
J.H. Levy

June 16, 1892
WOLFE-LOPEZ-On 7th June, by the Rev. S. Jacobs, Ellis, youngest son of Ellis Wolfe, to Adela, third daughter of the late Charles C. Lopez. No cards. At Home (Hollis Villa, East Queen St) on Wednesday 22nd and Thursday 23rd June.

1892

Current Items
Messrs. J.H. Levy, F.L Roden and A. Dixon are at present on an election tour in the electorate district of St Ann and St Mary.

St Mary wants her own Representative
To the Editor of the Gleaner.

Sir, Mr. J.H. Levy in his reply to the request of Saint Ann's Electors and Taxpayers that he would come forward and contest the Election says "it is very flattering &c. that so many of my parishioners as also those of the sister parish should be so persistent in your endeavour as to present me with this urgent appeal &c". I have read over the names appended to the requisition and I fail to find one single name of a Saint Mary man on the list. Nay not even the names of certain demagogues who did their worst to inflame the illiterate portion of our voters into their way of thinking; perhaps Mr. J.H. Levy will say who from Saint Mary requested much less persisted in asking him to represent this parish.

'Tis an ill wind that blows nobody good. And this foisting upon Saint Mary such a representative as she will have, will go far-very far- to wards the much desired severance of the parish of St Ann from Saint Mary.
17th June, 1892

Notes from St Ann
To the Editor of the Gleaner

Sir,-Much satisfaction is felt in the parish since our much expected and beloved friend J.H. Levy Esq., has agreed to represent us. Mr. Levy came to us in 1859 and we have known him from a boy of 15, and watched him and all seem to think from his enterprise as a merchant he is quite fitted to represent this parish. Had Mr. Levy agreed to stand when first asked there would have been no occasion for any other candidate to come forward. It is said and generally believed that Mr. Levy is a most liberal man. He is truly a man of noble principle. May he ever follow this course and never change, still be the humble and kind hearted man. He is called the man of the people. We hope yet to see Mr. Levy Custos of this parish. No appointment would give greater satisfaction. If he does not get it we trust Mr. J.C. Lewis will. Mr. Lewis is one who has served the parish faithfully and strange he is not more used more. He should be on the Parochial Board and many other important offices he should occupy at one time. It was thought he would have stood for this parish as legislator but I am told he does not wish to occupy such a sphere just now. He may in time.

We need a few more local magistrates Mr. Isaacs is away in America and if Mr. Lewis does not come in town we are placed to great inconvenience for the want of a J.P. We have a few young men in the town who might hold such an appointment. Why not appoint two or three of these young men? Our much esteemed Governor might do this for us. We would bring the following names to his notice, Messrs A. B. Rerrie, J.J. Lannamann, R. W. Harris. These three gentlemen would fill the position to the satisfaction of all.

Rains have set in again- fine seasons this year-Can't complain.

Trade is very dull, I have never known such for 20 years. I have been in this town all my days and am now getting old and can't remember such dull times. The store and shopkeepers are to be pitied and need great indulgences.

Pimento crop will soon be in when we shall expect to see a great change. Fruit Trade is at a low ebb, am afraid very few people will plant fruit again, they are getting troubled about it, a bad sign. The churches are doing very badly, subscriptions are low. The Ministers find it hard to live. We had a fine Concert here a week ago; it did well only lasted too long, the half would have been enough. The programme was 50 per cent too much. The great teacher of Music at York Castle (Mr. Sibthorpe) was present; he is quite an attraction and draws crowds where ever he goes.

The cry is for a new town clock, one that can strike, Parochial Board see to this. Our new Post Master, Mr. P. Smith is much liked he is so obliging, he has filled his post to great satisfaction. The Clerk of the Court, Mr. A.G. Kingdon is much beloved and from all quarters he is highly spoken of, only regret he was not sent here long ago and not a few months ago. Miss Cameron was made a Mrs. Mais on Wednesday, the marriage was pleasant. Mr. Cameron and Miss Mais are highly respected—Your obd. Svt
Thomas Day

June 21, 1892
REPRESENTATION OF ST MARY AND ST ANN
Nominations
Special Telegram to the Gleaner

The nomination for a member of the Legislative Council was made at the Court House, St Ann's Bay, yesterday at one o'clock. Mr. J.H. Levy was not present being on an electioneering visit to St. Mary. Among those present were—Dr. W.H. Miller, John Cameron, A.N. Dixon, F. L. Rhodon, J O'Meally, A Hart, S. Bartlett, W. G. Nunes, J. R. Reece, J.A. Miller, Inspector Alexander, etc, etc.

The nomination paper for J.H. Levy, of Brown's Town was presented by Mr. O'Meally, Solicitor, and was signed by A.N. Dixon, R.Henriques, John Ellis, G. Barlett, Reginald Smith, F. A. Morris, J.J. Lyon and others.

Dr. W.H. Miller presented his own nomination paper which was signed by W. Costa, J. L. Morris, Chas Costa, J.P., D. Archer J.P. C. Orrett J.P, T. Miller J.P. C.P. Delgado and others.

Dr. Miller before nomination papers were presented addressed the Electors at some length giving his platform and pledging himself to carry out the principle he had advocated in his reply to the request sent him asking him to represent the Constituency.
Mr. F.L. Rhodon spoke on behalf of Mr. J.H. Levy and referred rather pointedly to Dr. Miller who was the opposing Candidate.

The proceedings were conducted with proper order and decorum.

June 22, 1892
Current Items
A Correspondent at St. Ann's Bay writes that Mr. J. Levy has just returned from an electoral tour in St.Mary He was well received throughout the parish, and there was a great demonstration in his favor at Port Maria.

June 27, 1892
Current Items
The polling at the several stations in electoral district of St Ann and St Mary takes place today. It is a foregone conclusion that Mr. J.H. Levy will be returned but the result will probably not be known for a day or two as the ballot boxes have to be returned to St Ann's Bay for the counting after 5 o'clock this evening. The total number of voters is 5,460 being 2,743 in St Mary and 2,717 in St. Anns. The population of the electoral district is 97,442 and the percentage of voters is therefore one to eighteen.

June 28, 1892

ELECTION IN ST. MARY AND ST. ANN
The Polling of Yesterday

1892

LEVY WILL BE RETURNED
Special Telegrams to the Gleaner

Port Maria, 27th June—The election caused little or no excitement here though the masses who take every opportunity to gain a holiday made this an excuse for one. Up to 4 p.m. only 150 votes had been polled at his station. As far as could be gathered the majority were in favor of Mr. J.H. Levy. The voters contrary to the general expectation themselves seemed to take very little interest in the election. The returning officer Mr. Calder took sick and had to leave the polling station, and the election was supervised by his clerk in Mr. Calders office. Many contend that this will upset the election.

Brown's Town, Monday—The polling passed off very orderly here but there was much hilarity and general mild excitement. Hundreds of people thronged the town from morning until the poll closed. The result, of course, is not known but it is supposed that more than 95 percent of the votes have been polled for Mr. J. Levy. Mr. Levy is to address the electors in the market to-night. He is the popular hero to-day.

Moneague Monday—No one would imagine that here anything unusual here to-day. There is not the least excitement, and as far as can be ascertained Mr. J.H. Levy is at the head of the poll. Dr. Miller is simply nowhere. About 40 votes have been polled out of a total of 594 on the voter's list. The people seem to be quite dead to their privileges as voters and unaware that they possess a voice in the affairs of the country.

July 1, 1892
ELECTION IN ST. MARY AND ST. ANN
RETURN OF MR. LEVY
Details of the polling
Special Telegram to the Gleaner

ST.ANN'S BAY, 28th –The poll was closed on Monday evening, and counting commenced early this morning, closing at about 9 o'clock when the result was made known. In the parish of St Ann J.H. Levy gained 543 cotes, while Dr. Miller polled only 21. In St. Mary J.H. Levy gained 481 against 10 for Miller. The voting was conducted quietly and amicably at all the stations. The result in detail is as follows:-

Analysis of Voting
St. Mary

	Mr. J.H. Levy	Dr. Miller
Lucky Hill	35	0
Retreat	70	0
Port Maria	130	5
Richmond	78	3
Annotto Bay	168	2
Total	481	10

Spoilt votes   29

St Ann

	Mr. J.H. Levy	Dr. Miller
St. Ann's Bay	127	1
Moneague	37	1
Dry Harbour	22	0
Ocho Rios	90	1
Brown's Town	220	16
Alexandria	47	2
Total	543	21

Spoilt votes   69

Totals

Mr. J.H. Levy	St Ann 543	
	St Mary 481	1024

Dr. Miller	St Ann 21	
	St Mary 10	31

Majority for Levy--- 995
Total spoilt votes-- 98 .
Total votes recorded- 1,153

July 4, 1892
Current Items
In a dignified address Mr. J.H. Levy, of Brown's Town, has thanked the electors of St Ann and St. Mary for electing him as their representative to the Legislative Council. He states that he does not expect to lie on a bed of roses; he will do his best under all circumstances, his desire only being to forward measures for the good of the country and oppose those brought forward from any quarter which he conceives to lead in the contrary direction; and he pledges himself to try and get separate representation for all the parishes.

July 7, 1892
DIED
At his residence "Hugbenden" Lodge, at 8 o'clock yesterday evening, at the age of 68 years. OSMOND DELGADO. Funeral will move at 5 o'clock this afternoon.

July 8, 1892
Current Items
Mr. Levy's election has been confirmed by the Governor. The country has been fortunate in adding to the names of her legislators that of the Hon J.H. Levy.

Freemasonry
The installation of the Worthy Master and Officers for the Phoenix Lodge, No 4. Port Royal took place on Tuesday 5th instant. The installing officer was Worthy J. Barned. The officers for the ensuing year are:-
Worthy Brother W. C. Cox Master
"   J. MacNish S. Warden
"   Panter   J. Warden
"   G.F. Myers Treasurer
"   J.H. Cox   Secretary
"   J. Debridge S.D.
"   Quint   J.D.
"   C. Gornell J.D.
"   R. Patten Tyler
Visitors were conveyed to and from Port Royal by Steamer Launch, and spent a very happy evening returning to Kingston at 1.30 p.m.

July 11, 1892
DIED
At Port Antonio, on 7th July, 1892, Nancy Barbara, youngest child of John and Georgina Musson aged 1 year and 7 months.

1892

July 13, 1892
DIED
At No 134 East Street, at 11 o'clock a.m., on Tuesday 12th inst., AMOS LINDO, son of Henry and Augustus Rebecca Lindo, aged 27. Funeral will leave the above address at 8 o'clock this morning (13th). Friends and acquaintances please accept this intimation. Please let your carriage attend.

July 13, 1892
The R.M.S. Atrato left this port yesterday for Southampton via Jacmel, and Barbados. She took the following passengers. For Southampton—Mrs. Levy, 5 children and two sisters, Miss C. Levy, Mr. C.H. Ward, Mr. E.H. Jones, Miss Gertrude Levy, Mr. John Ward, Mr. F.C. Dewdney, Mr. George Hurcomb and wife, Mr. William Schiller, Capt. Gugan, Mr. W. Nelson, Mr. A. Clark, For Demerara Mr. Wingying Kee. For Jacmel Mr. D.N. Henriques and 16 Deckers for the Islands.

July 14, 1892
DIED
At Seacole Cottage, 111 Duke St., on the 13th inst. LUCETTA CORINALDI, wife of George Levy and daughter of Wilfred Nunes, after a short illness. Funeral will leave Seacole Cottage at 5 p.m. to-day.

July 21, 1892
DIED
At his residence, "Devereaux Park" at 3 o'clock this morning, GABRIEL JOSHUA deCORDOVA in his 54th year.
The funeral will move from "Devereux Park" at 5 o'clock this evening.
It is with feelings of intense grief that we record the death of Mr. G.J. deCordova who was for the past twenty years Editor-in-chief of this newspaper. It was his own request that this journal should contain no obituary notice of himself when he died—a request repeatedly expressed during the last sad days of his life. In compliance with that desire we remain silent regarding the career of our relative, friend, and co-worker, and can only give but faint expression here to a sorrow which we are sure will find an echo in many hearts.

July 22, 1892
At Mico Institution, on the 21st July the wife of L.G. Gruchy of a daughter.

July 22, 1892
Died
Yesterday afternoon, at No 19 North St. GEORGE ANTHONY, eldest son of T. L. Duquesnay. Funeral will move at 5 p.m. today. Friends and acquaintances will please accept this intimation. Carriages.

The late G.J. DeCordova
A Special Service in memoriam will be held at the Jewish Alms House, Duke Street, on Sunday afternoon at 5 o'clock.

August 4, 1892
At May Hill, Manchester, Monday 1st August the wife of C. George Lord of a son.

Selected Vital Records from the Jamaican Daily Gleaner

August 16, 1892

MARRIED

On the 29th July, at the Parish Church, Halfway Tree, by His Lordship the Bishop of Jamaica, assisted by the Revd. H.H. Isaacs, M. A., Rector, Jasper Farmier Cargill, B.A., C.L.B of Gonville and Caius Coll., Cantab and the Inner Temple, Barrister-at-Law, eldest son of Jasper Cargill, M.D. to Clara Isabel, second daughter of the Hon. John Orrett of Kingston, Merchant.

August 22, 1892

Current Items

MR LEVY TO VISIT HIS CONSTITUENTS

The Hon. J.H. Levy will shortly visit St. Mary and will hold public meetings at Richmond on the 30th and at Annotto Bay on the 31st inst. This is an example set by a young member of the Council which his older colleagues might do well to imitate. We are not aware that this desire on the part of a representative of the people to make himself acquainted with the needs of his constituents by meeting them and discussing their affairs has been manifested on former occasions by members, but it is well worthy of being followed, and great credit is due to the new member for giving such an object lesson in local politics. If each member of the Council were coming into close relations with the electors in this manner there would probably be less dissatisfaction with the results of their legislation.

September 2, 1892

Current Items

Hon. J.H. Levy at Richmond

Richmond 30th Aug—The Hon. J.H. Levy addressed a large and enthusiastic meeting of his constituents here today. His speech touched on many important questions and the large numbers of the electors taking part in the meeting added to its interest.

All present felt they had enjoyed a most profitable day and a vote of thanks to, and confidence in, the hon. member for Saint Ann and Saint Mary was heartily given.

September 6, 1892

MARRIED

On the 1st inst., at the Cathedral Spanish Town by the Rev. E.J. Wortley Rector, assisted by the Rev. W. Kemp Bussell and the Rev J.H.H. Graham, Rector of Port Maria and brother in law of the bride, CHARLES ARBOUIN BICKNELL, Solicitor, eldest surviving Son of the late Henry John Bicknell late Resident Magistrate for St. Catherine, to LILY H. QUINTIN, sixth daughter of the late Benjamin Henry Stamer, M.D. L.R.C.S. Edin. No Cards.

September 7, 1892

PASSENGERS

Sailed in "Medway" yesterday for Southampton:- Miss Simms, Mr. A.C. Haigle, Mr. Arthur Levy, Mrs. Parker, 2 children, and Mrs. A.S. Verley: for Demerara: Miss Isabel Geddes: For Trinidad Mr. Carnegie and three friends; for Barbados: Mr. C.V. Clarke. Also 14 deckers for the various Islands.

September 23, 1892

LEVY-MORALES-At the Synagogue of the United Congregation of Israelites on Wednesday, 14th inst., by the Revd. Solomon Jacobs, Ellis, son of the late Wilfred Levy, to Rose Ethel, second daughter of A.H. Morales, Esq. At home at their residence Elrose, 11, Blake Road, on Sunday and Monday evenings, 2nd and 3rd October. No cards.

September 27, 1892
Isaacs-On Sunday the 18th inst., at Victoria Town, JOHN ISAACS, aged 71 years.

September 29, 1892
BOLTON-At Daysee Villa No 13 Arnold road, on the 23rd inst. the wife of Harold E. Bolton of a daughter

CORK-At his residence St Ann's Bay, on the 26th inst., the Rev. JOSIAH CORK, late Rector, in the 80th year of his age.

October 8, 1892
JENOURE—At Eden Villa, Malvern, on Friday 30th September the wife of F.B. Jenoure of Boston, Portland, of a daughter.

DIED
KIRKLAND-Last night at No 24 Fleet St., JOHN A KIRKLAND. The funeral at 4.30 p.m. this afternoon. Internment at Half-Way Tree Cemetery. Friends and acquaintances are hereby notified. Carriages.

THE LATE REV. JOSIAS CORK OF ST. ANN'S BAY
(By a Correspondent)
After fifty-five years of faithful service in Jamaica the Rev. Josias Cork, late Rector of St Ann's Bay passed away to his rest at noon on Sunday the 26th September in his 80th year.

In sorrowful tones many were heard to say "our good old Rector is gone, he was a good useful man". For twenty two years the deceased clergyman laboured in St Ann's Bay not only in connection with the Episcopal Church of which he was Rector but also as the people's friend.
"We see marks of Mr. Cork's usefulness in many places in St Ann's Bay" people were heard to say on the day he passed away.

His skill as an Engineer and his knowledge of surveying were always at the command of the public, and some of our most useful country roads were gratuitously laid out by Mr. Cork. The lower parts of the town of St. Ann's Bay, although still in a most imperfect sanitary condition, have been wonderfully improved and cleansed through the untiring energy and skill of Mr. Cork. As a mathematician and financier Mr. Cork's equal could not be found in the parish of St Ann.

The deceased Rector with the late Custos the Hon. M. Solomon commenced the St Ann's Benefit Building Society in the year 1873 on purely "Benefit" lines, and although lately it has appeared to be drifting into a sort of financial or banking system, yet with the deceased Rector as its secretary it has been a great benefit to many who are living in their own homes on their own freeholds, and it has assisted in improving to a large extent the town of St Ann's Bay.

The deceased Rector was by no means a Zealot. He has been very frequently seen on other platforms besides his own in connection with missionary, Bible society and temperance meetings.

Although Tuesday the 27th was very rainy, and the streets and cemetery muddy and wet, yet a large number connected with each religious denomination followed the body to the grave.
More.

Selected Vital Records from the Jamaican Daily Gleaner

October 8, 1892
Len Sue Phang-Leahong-On the 6th inst., at the Kingston Parish Church, by the Revd. G.W. Downer, Rector, CHARLES ADOLPHUS, only son of the late Lee Sue Phang of Demerara, to MARY FRANCES, only daughter of the late Henry Lehong of Kingston.

October 13, 1892
DIED
Yesterday at Devon House, St. Andrew, MAGDELENE, the beloved wife of the Hon. George Stiebel, C.M.G. The funeral will move at 5 o'clock this afternoon for the Half-way Tree Cemetery. Friends and acquaintances will please accept this intimation.

October 17, 1892
PORT MARIA
CONSECRATION OF A METHODIST CHAPEL

The above ceremony took place in this town, on Thursday last, before a very large congregation. The chapel, (the foundation stones of which were laid on 7th July last and duly reported in your columns), is a fine building very substantially built of wood. The dimensions are 40 x 25, and it is estimated to seat about 250 people.

In spite of the inclement state of the weather, there was quite a large crowd of members of the Body of Friends and well wishers-from Hampstead, Oracabessa, Ocho Rios, and Port Maria. The following ministers took part, Revs. Caleb Reynolds, I.C.A. Smith, co-ministers for the circuit, Rev. Nathan Baquie of Hampstead, Rev. John Duff of Beechamville, and Rev. Griffin, and Rev. W. Clarke Murray of York Castle of St Ann's. Rev Griffin read first lesson from 2nd Chronicles, 6th and part of 7th chapters; Rev. N. Bacquie read 2nd lesson, 10th Chapter Hebrews, 19th to 26th verse, after the ceremony of consecration was got through. The Rev. Wm. Clarke Murray of York Castle, preached the dedicatory sermon, which was taken from 2nd Kings, 6th Chapter and 17th verse, the sermon was listened to very attentively by the congregation.

Great praise is due to Mr. George Roe of Oracabessa for the decorations which added much to the beauty of the building.

The choir too rendered very good singing under the care and teaching of Miss Stuart the organist.

The opening services are to continue for 3 Sundays—Revd. Griffin from St Ann's Bay, the Revd, G. Baron Hay of Kingston and the Revd. Melville of Clarendon will occupy the pulpit respectively. Judging from the amount of sympathy that has been extended to the body since the start of the mission here, there is no reason to doubt, that his station will become very important in process of time. We wish them further success.—From our Correspondent.

October 22, 1892
ORRETT-On the 21st inst., at No 20 Harbour Street, THOMAS HOOD ORRETT. Funeral will leave the house at 4 o'clock this (Saturday) afternoon. Friends and acquaintances will please accept this intimation.

CURRENT ITEMS
Mr. Frank Cundall has obtained for the Jamaica Institute some magnificent engravings (by the best engravers) of pictures by the most eminent painters, such as Landseer, Constable and Turner to adorn the walls of the Institute. Mr. Cundall evidently intends to provoke Jamaicans to take an interest in Art, whether they like it or not.

1892

October 26, 1892
Death of Mr. Espeut
New York, Oct. 25th—The death is announced in London of the Hon. W. Bancroft Espeut, member of the Legislative council of Jamaica.

November 17, 1892
COCKING-MORRIS-At Coke Chapel, on Tuesday 15th inst., by Revd. T.M. Geddes assisted by the Revd. J. W. Williams and Revd G.H. Baron Hay, HAROLD fifth son of William Cocking Esq., of Market, Rasen, Lincolnshire, to GERTIE youngest daughter of the late Henry Morris, of Kingston, Jamaica. At home at No 2K East Queen Street, from Sunday 27th inst.

November 18, 1892
Current Items
We regret to announce the death of Mrs. Fray, relict of the late Reverend Ellis Fray, Baptist Minister of Kettering and Refuge in Trelawny and daughter of the late Reverend William Knibb, the Apostle of Freedom in this Island. The sad occurrence took place at Duncans on the night of Monday last. Falmouth Gazette.

November 24, 1892
DIED
CAMPBELL-On Tuesday 23rd November at No 68 Hanover Street, residence of Mr. Thomas Gunter, JOHN NEWLANDS CAMPBELL. Funeral will move this afternoon at 4.30. Friends please accept this intimation.

The Weather
        The bad weather continued yesterday all over the country and the roads in many parts were impassable on account of land slips and water. Many of the rivers are still down. No accident was reported up to last evening. Kingston was exempted the greater part of the day from rain, which fell heavily in the uplands. Mr. Johnstone stated to our reporter that he had nothing to communicate regarding the meteorological conditions, and he had heard nothing beyond what had been reported in the GLEANER. Mr. Richmond on being interrogated gave a similar negative reply.
        The Rio Cobre is so swollen that trains passing the bridges near Cumberland Pen have to do so slowly and cautiously. Hundreds of acres of the surrounding land are inundated and it will take some time before the water runs off.
        The rainfall at Cherry Garden, St Andrew in the 30 hours to 4 p.m. on the 22nd was 7 inches and 13 parts.

December 1, 1892
Advertizement

1 lb Tins of the following Meats and Soups varying in prices from 1s to 1s 6d tin
Boiled Beef, Round corned Beef, Mince Chops
Roast Beef, Ox Cheek and vegetables, Stewed and Roast Veal, Boiled Roast and Harricot
Mutton, Spiced Beef, Irish Stew
Mulligatawny, Ox Tail, Julienne, Mutton Broth, Giblet, Ox Cheek
Mock Turtle, Cockle Leekie, etc. etc
½lb tins Potted Ham; Devilled Ham, Tongue, Beef etc., etc.
1000 1 lb tins Loch Fyne Fresh Herrings, 1 lb and ½lb tins Cod Roes
1 lb Tins Royal Kippers, tins Ham, cured Red Herring
1 lb Tins Maconochi's real Yarmouth Bloaters
1 lb Tins and Pots Assorted Jams, Strawberries in Syrup, Bologne Sausages, Oxford and
Cambridge Sausages, Custard and Baking Powders etc
E.A. KINKEAD holds A LARGE STOCK OF DRUGS, TINCTURES AND
PHARMACEUTICAL PREPRATIONS and can give very low quotations to the
MEDICAL PROFESSSION
And
COUNTRY DRUGGISTS
E.D.KINKEAD
20 King Street

December 5, 1892
CASSERLEY-BRANDAY-At Holy Trinity Church, Duke Street, on 23rd November, by
the Rev. F. McCormack, S.J., JAMES MICHAEL CASSERLEY to LOUISE
ISABELLE, fourth daughter of Mr. Louis P. Branday-No cards-N.P. At Home No 3,
East Avenue, Kingston Gardens, on Wednesday's and Thursday's from 28th December.

December 17, 1892
LASCELLES-In New York-On the 15th Dec., Herbert youngest son of Alfred S.
Lascelles of that city.

Current Items
We learn that several changes will take place in the Jamaica High School at the
beginning of next term. Mr. A.E. Harrison, B.A. London leaves his position there as
Assistant master, and becomes Second master in Potsdam School, St Elizabeth. Mr. J.L.
Ramson of University College, and B. A. London will fill Mr. Harrison's place. The
place vacated by Mr. John Stuart M.A. will be filled by Mr. W. Cowper, M.A. Pembroke
College, Cambridge, while Mr. Cowper's place will be filled by Mr. Briggs, M. A.
Cambridge who is expected to arrive in Jamaica on the 2nd January. We understand that
Mr. Briggs possesses qualifications fitting him to sustain the high character of the school,
to win the respect of the pupils and the parents, and to work amicably with the other
members of the staff.

December 22, 1892
MARRIED-
STREADWICK–NEWMAN-On the 15th inst. at St Michael's Church by His Lordship
the Bishop, assisted by the Rev. R. G. Ambrose, JAMES ENOS, eldest son of S.J.
Streadwick of Marine Gardens, to LILLIAN BLANCHE, eldest daughter of the late
William Newman of Manchester.

BALL AT MYRTLE BANK
A public subscription Ball was given at Myrtle Bank Hotel on Tuesday
evening. The affair was a brilliant one, and was enjoyed by all who engaged in it. The

1892

guests began to arrive at 9 p.m. and dancing commenced at 9.30 in the magnificent drawing room of the establishment. The band of the 2nd W.I. Regiment was present and satisfactorily played the various dances. As the march for supper it gave Ta-ra-ra boom de ay. The refection was spread out in the two dining rooms on the ground floor and there was a grand display of delicious viands and niceties of the season. Dancing was kept up until about 4 a.m.

The following is the dance programme and a list of the guests who were present.

Waltz...	...Pleasant Hours
Waltz...	...Phantome
Lancers	...Bragansa
Waltz...	...Mayflower
Waltz...	...Yours sincerely
Waltz...	...Love's old sweet song
Polka...	...Hannah
Waltz...	...Bitter Sweet
Waltz...	...El Dorade
10. Waltz	...Her Majesty's
11. Waltz	...La Gitana
12. Waltz	...Folie Ivresse
13. Polka	...Holly Bush
14. Waltz	...Cloister
15. Waltz	...Love's Dreamland
16. Lancers	...Gondoliers
17. Waltz	...Dolores
18. Waltz	...Chantilly
19. Waltz	...Memories
20. Waltz	...Torcado

Mr. and Mrs. Egerton, Col C.J. Ward, Mrs. Ward, Major Norton, Mr. and Mrs. Innies, (Urgent); Mr. and Mrs. Robinson, Mr. and Mrs. Cole, Mr. and Mrs. C.A. Chevolleau, Miss Chevolleau, Chevolleau Bros., Mr. and Mrs. Dron, Miss Kilburn, Mr. and Mrs. Jose Maynier, 2 Misses Mayniers, Mr. and Mrs. C.L Vendryes, Misses Vendryes, Mr. and Mrs. Herman Stern, Mr. and Mrs. Lionel Finsi, Mr. G. Finzi, Mr. and Mrs. and Miss Alexander, Mr. and Mrs. Moses Levy, Mr. Charles Hope Levy, the Misses Levy, Mr. H. Levy, Mr. Beneckendorf, Mrs. and Miss Beneckendorf, Mr. and Mrs. Liddel, the Misses Harrison, Revd. and Mrs. Jacobs, Mr. and Mrs. Jno. MacDonald, Mr. and Mrs. Ashenheim, the Misses Ashenheim, Mr. Butler, Mr. O'Connor de Cordova, Mrs. Lopes, Miss Lopes, Mr. and Mrs. Ellis Wolfe, Mr. and Mrs. E Samuels, Mrs. Winter, Mr. Puttner, Mr. F. Solomon, Mrs. George Solomon, Miss Solomon, Mr. Ernest Astwood, Mr. Doorly, The Misses Austin, Drs E & A. L. Sturridge, Mrs. Sturridge, Dr Mayner, Mr. and Mrs. Delapenha, The Delapenhas, Mr. Delapenha, Mr. Nethersole, Rev. and Mrs. Ambrose, Miss Ambrose, Messrs. Squire, Mr. and Mrs. Jno. Branday, The Misses Branday, Mr. and Mrs. Arthur George, Mr. and Mrs. A. B. Hart, Mr. Bollvar Wolfe, Inspector Maunsell, Mr. Chadwick, Mr. P. W. Martin, Mr. C. Vidal Hall, Lieut. Neale, Lieut. Coffin, Mr. H. B. Edwards, Mr. Toone, Mr. and Mrs. H. C. Wilson, Mr. and Mrs. Lyons, Misses Lyons, H. A. Walcott, Mr. Lewis, Mr. Alberger, Mr. and Mrs. Corinaldi, Mr. and Mrs. Gerald Morais, Mr. J. W. Kerr, Mr. Jno. Milholland, Miss Milholland, Mr. Geo. Douglas, Mr. Willie Douglas, Mr. Pearce, Mr. and Mrs. Morales and daughter, Miss Layette, Mr. M. C. Solomons, Mr. D. Solomons, Mr. Charles Verley, Mr. Orrett, Mr. and Mrs. Robinson, several Officers from Camp, New Castle and Port Royal, &c, &c.

1893

January 4, 1893
Burke On Saturday the 31st December, 1892 at "Fairlands" Clovelly Road the wife of Alexander A. Burke of a son and daughter

Campbell-On Jan 1st at Stony Hill, Rev. John Campbell, B.A. Rector of St Elizabeth. Age 83 years. (Buried at Half-Way Tree Church).

January 6, 1893
STEPHENSON-At Dry Harbour on the night of the 31st Dec, 1892 at 1 o'clock after a short illness, ADA ELIZABETH second and Beloved daughter of E.B. and ELLA STEPHENSON of Hermon Hill in her 19th year.

January 7, 1893
Dr James Johnston of Brown's Town arrived yesterday from Africa, via Scotland and America.

An absolute order of bankruptcy was yesterday made against J.J. Lanaman of St Ann's Bay.

Oracabessa, St Mary.
      On Sunday 1st January, the Rev. Caleb Reynolds, of the Ocho Rios Circuit was made the recipient of a very handsome silk gown by the members and worshippers of Morley Wesleyan chapel. The Revd. gentleman since his appointment to the Ocho Rios circuit has endeared himself to all with whom he has been brought into contact.
      It is feared however, that our beloved pastor will be removed shortly by the Conference. To this we can but add, we love him, let him stay. It would indeed be an unfortunate thing for the Ocho Rios circuit to lose such an able and painstaking clergyman at a time when various schemes are being formulated by him for the benefit of the circuit. It is to be hoped the Rev. gentleman will be permitted to remain for the carrying out of the good work he has in hand.
      Our esteemed fellow citizen Mr. John Sinclair was deputed by the congregation to read the address which he did in a somewhat pathetic manner.
The members of the circuit view Mr. Reynold's intended removal as nothing short of a calamity.
      The following is the address and reply:-
Oracabessa Wesleyan Church,
1st January, 1893

Selected Vital Records from the Jamaican Daily Gleaner

Revd. and dear Sir,-It is now a period of nearly four years since your Conferential appointment to the Ocho Rios Circuit of which the Morley Church is a part, and during this time it has been to us both a pleasure and profit to have been associated with you not only in Church relationship but also in the wider sphere of social life. It is but just that we should acknowledge our indebtedness as a church and congregation of the many excellent teachings in and of the pulpit. We here also to acknowledge the growth of our Society here, which is an indication of your excellent work among us. We beg to assure your that there exists towards you in this church and community the very kindest feelings of respect and esteem. Such feelings are sometimes manifested in a practical manner, and actuated by these kindly feelings we desire practically to show our deep regard for you by asking your acceptance of the accompanying gown as a New Year gift from the officers, members and other worshippers at Morley Church.. We have but to add the hope that you may be permitted by the Conference to remain for some time as our pastor, counseller, and friend, and that your life may be long spared to carry on the work which the Master has given you to do,

Wishing for yourself and family a happy and prosperous New Year.

We remain dear sir

Yours in Christ.

On behalf of the Morley Church and Congregation

John Sinclair

Oracabessa Wesleyan Church,

1st January.

Mr. Sinclair and officers, and Members of the Morley Wesleyan Church and congregation.

My. Dear Friends, I am exceedingly grateful for the kindly feelings, to which you have given expression in the address just presented to me, and I beg to assure you that the sentiments of respect and esteem therein conveyed are heartily reciprocated.

During the period of my association with the Morley church as its Pastor, I have ever found delight in going in and our among you, not only in the discharge of my ministerial duties, but equally so in that fellowship which as friends we have so frequently been permitted to enjoy. The reference to my work during the four years of my pastorate are very gratifying for next to the approval of my Heavenly Father I value the appreciation of my efforts by the people among whom I live and labour.

Any measure of success, however which my have attended my efforts for the church's extension and consolidation and for the promotion of God's Glory, I feel must not be written exclusively to my credit, for had I not found in you, ready co-operation, and cheerful assistance in every department of my work, we should not be allowed to speak so thankfully of our present condition. I accept, with much pleasure, the handsome pulpit gown, by which your address is accompanied, and it will constantly remind me of the affectionate regard of the Morley friends. Thanking you for your kind wishes for me and my family in the new year, and praying for every temporal and spiritual blessing upon you and your loved ones-Believe me, your affectionately.

Caleb Reynolds.

January 14, 1893

Dr Johnston

All who are aware of the splendid work accomplished by Dr. James Johnston in travelling through Africa from the West Coast will regret to learn that he is suffering from the effects of fever, malaria and cold, and other results of exposures in the hitherto, unexplored regions of that country. From the accounts that we have seen from time to time of the difficulties and privations he has endured and overcome his present condition is not to be wondered at, but we trust that with the rest and the care he will now receive in his own home at Brown's Town he will soon recover his wonted vigourous health.

February 1, 1893
McCrea On January 28th, at Chapelton, John Dobree, infant son of Olive and Harry McCrea, aged 7 ½ months.

February 2, 1893
Poem by Tom Redcam
REJECTED
See also the next few days.

February 13, 1893
Mr. A.J. Hart of St. Ann's Bay put a good deal of property in that parish up to auction the other day and most of the lots fetched good prices.

February 14, 1893
The Gypsy Trail by Rudyard Kipling

April 1, 1893
GARDENER-HAMMOND-At St Michael's Church, Kingston, on March 20th, by the Revd. G.W.Downer, Rector of Kingston, WILLIAM URRIDGE GARNER, son of Revd W. T. Gardner, to EMILY HAMMOND daughter of William Hammond, Esq., London

April 4, 1893
HON. LEGISLATIVE COUNCIL
Thursday 30th March, 1893
The Hon. Legislative Council met at Headquarter House at 11 a.m. Present:
PRESIDENT:
Hon James Cecil Phillippo, M.D.
OFFICIAL MEMBERS:
Hon. N. Porter, C.M.G. colonial Secretary
Hon. H.H. Hocking, Attorney General
Hon V. G. Bell, C.E. Director of Public Works.
Hon. R. Batten, Collector General
NOMINATED MEMBERS
Hon. R. Capper, B. A., Inspector of Schools
Hon J. Pringle, M.D. Acting Superintending Medical Officer.
ELECTED MEMBERS
Hon. J.P. Clarke, Manchester
Hon. C. S. Farquharson, Westmoreland and Hanover
Hon. W Bourke, St James and Trelawny
Hon. J.H. Levy, St Mary and St Ann
Hon W. Andrews, Portland and St Thomas
Hon. G. Solomon, Clarendon

DIED
At New Orleans, La. On 22nd February, PROF NATHANIEL MELHADO, Aged 76 years. Late of Kingston, Jamaica and brother of the late Solomon Melhado.

April 6, 1893
CRICKET MATCH AT YORK CASTLE

Selected Vital Records from the Jamaican Daily Gleaner

The third annual cricket match between a team of Old Boys vs. the present School was played at York Castle on Easter Monday, resulting in a victory for the School by one innings to two.

Although the weather unfortunately, was most unfavourable (it having rained almost the whole day), there was a good attendance and judging from the vociferous cheers, everyone seemed to take the liveliest interest in the game.

The batting of Mr. Meikle, Captain of the School Team, and of Myers was excellent. Messrs Smallpage and Meikle sharing the honors in the bowling line. Dr. Lockett and Mr. Brass doing most of the batting on the Old Boys side.

It would be impossible to speak too highly of the hearty welcome afforded the Old Boys and of the most hospitable treatment extended to them by Mr. and Mrs. Murray, the tutors and the entire school.

The day's proceedings were brought to a close with a Concert in which both teams and the masters took part. Supper then followed and the happy party broke up near midnight as the last strains of Auld Lang Syne were borne through the open windows out upon the moonlit air.

This has been, if possible the merriest reunion that has yet taken place and it is sincerely hoped on both sides that it may not be the last.

April 10, 1893
The Hons. C.S. Farquharson, J.P. Clarke and J.H. Levy left by last train on Friday for their respective homes. They return by first train this morning to attend the Legislative Council at 2 p.m. today.

April 11, 1893
BREAKSPEAR-On the 2nd inst., at his residence 'Avondale' Arnold Road, Kingston, THOMAS BREAKSPEAR, in his fifty second year.

April 15, 1893
BISHOP'S COLLEGE, MONTREAL
The following are the results of the examinations in the Faculty of Medicine, Bishop's College, Montreal.

JAMAICA STUDENTS
Primary Subjects
Passed in Chemistry 1st Class Honors C.H.B. Armstrong, J. A. Holmes, A. Harry.
Passed in Physiology 1st Class Honors, J. A. Holmes, A Harry, C.H.B. Armstrong.
Materia Medica 1st Class Honors: C.H.B. Armstrong, J. Holmes, A Harry.
Anatomy 1st Class Honors: C.H. B. Armstrong, A Harry.
Practical Chemistry, 2nd Class Honors A Harry, J. A. Holmes, C.H. B. Armstrong.
Passed all the Primary Subjects: C.H.B. Armstrong and A. Harry.
Finale Subjects
Passed in Pathology 1st Class Honors, C.H.B. Armstrong, and A. Harry
Medical Jurisprudence, 1st Class Honors, A. Harry and C.H.B. Armstrong
Ophthalmology, 2nd Class Honors, C.H.B. Armstrong and A. Harry.
DEGREE OF C.M., M.D.
Mr. W. E. Wilson of this island has passed all the subjects entitling him to the degree.

CAMBRIDGE LOCAL
Students under 19 years of age who have obtained honors
Class 1. A.W. Levy School, Jamaica High Master Rev. W. Simms. M.A. Distinguished in Religious knowledge, Latin and Greek

1893

Class 3. T.A. Rosado, School Kingston Collegiate. Master, W. Morrison, M.A.
Under 19 who have satisfied the Examiners

	School	Master
K.O. Depass	York Castle	J. Smallpage, B.A.
J. Duff	do	do
A.C. Lockett	do	do
C.J.McGregor	Rusea's Sch	A.E. Tomlinson,do
V.E.Manton	York Castle	J.Smallpage,do

Under 16 who have obtained honors
Class 1. 1st Division- J.D. Stubbs, School Jamaica High Master, Rev. W. Simms, Distinguished in Religious Knowledge, Latin, French, Mathematics
Class 1. 2nd Division S. Lockett, School, York Castle J. Smallpage, B.A. W. Simms, School, Jamaica High, Master, Rev. W. Simms, Distinguished in Religious Knowledge Latin.
Class 2. N. Bowrey, School, Jamaica High. Master, W. Simms, G.S. Husband. School Jamaica High, Master Rev. W. Simms Distinguished in Latin.
D. and T.D. Kennedy, School York Castle, Master J. Smallpage, B.A.
L.D. King, School Potsdam, Rev. W. D. Pearman, M.A. Distinguished in Latin.
F.G. Sharp, School, Jamaica High, Master Rev. W. Simms, distinguished in Mathematics.
Class 3.
A.R. Dignum, School, Jamaica High, Master, Rev. W. Simms
A.H.L. Hart, School, York Castle, Master, J. Smallpage
A.A. Myers, School, Potsdam, Master, Rev. W.D. Pearman.
T.H. Smith, School, Jamaica High, Master, Rev. W. Simms. Distinguished in Latin.
Students under 16 who have satisfied the examiners
W.D. Arscott, School, Jamaica High, Master Rev. W. Simms
J Charley, School, Jamaica High, Master, Rev. W. Simms
J. A. Dickenson, School, Jamaica High. Master, Rev. W. Simms.
C.J. Escoffery, School, Kingston Collegiate, Master, W. Morrison
G.C. Evans, School, Postsdam, Master, Rev. W.D. Pearman
J.H.M. Doorly, School, Jamaica High, Master Rev. W. Simms
J. R. Johnson, School, Jamaica High; Master, Rev. W. Simms
A.Myers, School, Kingston Collegiate, Master, W. Morrison
A.D Melhado, School, Jamaica High, Master, W. Simms
W. Morrison, School, Kingston Collegiate Master, W.Morrison
F. Myers, School, Kingston Collegiate, Master, W. Morrison
B.E. Rodon, School, Kingston Collegiate, Master, W. Morrison
W.A.Webb, School Potsdam, Master, Rev. W.D.Pearman
Students between 16 and 18 who have passed the examination as Juniors,
C.J. Arrowsmith, School, Kingston Collegiate, Master,
W. Morrison
L. D.H. Baugh, School, Kingston Collegiate, Master, W. Morrison
D.J. Casseres School, Ridgemount, Master, Rev. C. A Wookey
A.J.W. Harty, School, Jamaica High, Master Rev. W. Simms
J.A. Mullings School, Potsdam, Master Rev. W. Pearman, distinguished in Latin and Mathematics
Between 16 and 18 who have passed as juniors in preliminary, Religious and English subjects only.
A.M. Desnoes, School, Kingston Collegiate, Master, Morrison

GIRLS

Under 19 who have satisfied the Examiners,

S.L. DePass, School Barbican, Mistress, Miss Bond

Under 16 obtained Honours-Class 3

A.C.J. Hollar School, Barbican, Mistress, Miss Bond

Under 16, who have satisfied the Examiners

A.J.R. Cox, School, Barbican, Mistress, Miss Bond

L.V.Delgado School, Kingston Academy, Mistress, Mrs. Lewis

L.L McDougall, School, Kingston Academy, Mistress, Mrs. Lewis

E. Roberts, School, Kingston High for Girls, Mistress, Miss Long

Between 16 and 18 who have passed the Examination as Juniors

A.J.A. Ashby, Ladies College, Half-way Tree, Misses A.J. Ashby and T. Small

S.D'Costa Kingston Academy, Mrs. H. J. Lewis

A.C. Hill Barbican, Miss Long

F.E. Regg, do   do

Between 16 and 18 who have passed as Juniors in Preliminary Religious Knowledge and English subjects also

M.J. B. Small, Ladies College Half-way Tree, Misses A.J. Ashby and T.M. Small.

April 17, 1893

The Revd. W. Clarke Murray, York Castle School, writes correcting an error in his letter on the Scholarship question viz. by the omission of the word "not" he was made to say that the change from the London Matriculation to the Cambridge Senior with distinction had lowered the standard, whereas his letter was written to show that it had not: Mr. Murray adds: "I see that Mr. J.M. Farquharson has proposed a Resolution in the Council to the effect that the Scholarship should be abolished if the standard has been lowered. I cannot help thinking that the better form would be, not to abolish the Scholarship, but to place it on its former basis, if indeed the standard has been lowered. I suppose the Council, if the Resolution is adopted, will seek evidence on the subject and I for one, have no fear of the results."

April 21, 1893

BROWN'S TOWN NOTES

(From our correspondent)

WATER

During the past fortnight, Brown's Town and the surrounding districts have been blessed with some refreshing showers of rain; some of which lasted for a considerable time. To a place, such as this, where the people depend solely on the rainfall for their supply of water, a copious shower is often considered a real blessing, the absence of which causes considerable hardships. The people are very thankful for the showers which have fallen, and like "Peck's greedy boy" are asking for more whilst upon the subject of water, we would desire to remark; that frequent droughts, and the inconveniences and hardships suffered by the people should make them anxious to secure a permanent supply of water, provided it can be secured on reasonable terms. There are two large tanks in the market, capable of supplying the half of Brown's town with water, if they would hold, but unfortunately the tanks leak and are consequently useless, and the money that was spent in building them is thrown away.

The people here hail with joy that at last the arrangements are concluded with Mr. Edward Eastin, so that the gentleman can come out and report on the possibility of giving a proper water supply to this, and the parishes of Trelawny and Manchester.

NATURE

1893

The rain which has fallen lately, has made its effects seen on vegetation. Nature which had doffed is usual tint of green and had donned a yellowish colour on account of the drought, has now resumed its verdant coat, so very pleasing to the eye. As one walks in the fields, and feasts his eyes on the beauties of nature, he cannot but be struck by the pleasant change.

THE CLIMATE OF BROWN'S TOWN

The climate of Brown's Town is one of the healthiest in Jamaica. It's situation is pleasant. It stands 1,149 feet above the level of the sea; there are no fogs here; no dampness. The air is pure and dry. In the hottest months (July and August) the thermometer rarely goes higher that 80 degrees in the shade. During the other months the average is about 70 degrees in the shade. The climate is particularly beneficial to invalids and especially sufferers from lung disease or any other disease. We venture to assert that as a health resort, this place is second to none, and it only requires to become known to be duly appreciated. Several American gentlemen who were lately here, have expressed them selves to the effect.

RESIDENT MAGISTRATE'S COURT

A Resident Magistrate's Court for the disposal of criminal cases was held here on Friday the 14th instant before His honor Mr. Justice Reece, Resident Magistrate. Mr. Fred Davis, acting Deputy Clerk of Courts prosecuting. There were 81 cases listed, 8 indictments and 28 summary cases.

The first case on the list was Regina v. Ann E. Reid for abandoning a child.

Dr. Hargreaves, Medical Officer at Cave Valley, stated that he examined child and found that it had not sustained any injury by the exposure to which for a short time it had been exposed.

After a careful review of the evidence His Honor came to the conclusion, that there was no case of an abandonment, and the accused was dismissed.

The other indictable cases were for wounding and praedial larceny. His Honor stated that he was determined to put down these offences; and the sentences which he inflicted on the defendants were heavy, and we trust that they will act as a deterrent for other in the like cases offending.

The remaining summary cases were for breaches of the Agricultural Produce Buyers Law, and for opening shops on Good Friday. The cases having been clearly proved, the Resident Magistrate stated that it was a hard case for honest men to take out a license, and others to buy fruit, &c without doing likewise; he then fined these offenders in the sum of £2 10s and remarked that if they came before him again he would fine them the full extent of the law. With regard to the latter cases, (opening places of business on Good Friday) His Honor having regard to the fact that many persons are not acquainted with the law, he admonished and discharged them. We cannot but congratulate Mr. Reece, the respected R.M. of Saint Ann, for the manner in which he is stamping out crime from this parish. Cases of praedial and other larcenies are fast disappearing here; and the cause is not far to seek.

April 21, 1893
GAZETTE NOTICES
The Jamaica Scholarship
The Governor directs the publication for general information, of the following extract from a letter from the Registrar of the University of London, and from a Pass List in connection with the Matriculation Examination of that University, held in January last.
This examination being the Standard of the award of the Jamaica Scholarship, Mr. Henry Isaac Close Brown of York Castle High School, who obtained the highest number of marks among the Candidates from Jamaica who passed the Examination has been awarded the Scholarship in accordance with the Regulations in the matter.

Selected Vital Records from the Jamaican Daily Gleaner

Extract from a Letter to the Colonial Office From the University of London, March 25th 1893

At Kingston, Jamaica, two candidates have passed, one in the First Division and one in the second.

The subjects in which the unsuccessful Candidates at the several centers have failed are given in the enclosed tabulation.

I enclose a few Pass-Lists for distribution to the various centers.

UNIVERSITY OF LONDON, 1893

Colonial Examinations

Matriculation Examination, January

Pass List Jamaica

First Division- 2051 Brown, Hy, Isaac Close, York Castle High School

Second Division-2054 Pearce, Percival Leslie, Jamaica High School

April 26, 1893

WEARIED

Oh life of labour, on whose days
I see the evening shadows fall,
Worn am I by your voiceful ways
And mighty Nature's ceaseless call
To toil, and, wearied by the shock
Where Oceans in wild thunders rock,
I welcome, in the waving light,
The deepening shadows of the night.

On my labour and my frailty,
Soothing hands will be,
Closing vision, hushing hearing;
I shall neither hear nor see;
Death will come as rest to me

TOM REDCAM
Jamaica

April 29, 1893

Current Items

The Hon J.H. Levy visited Mandeville this week; he was present at the Flower Show and ball, and left on Friday morning for St Ann's Bay.

May 12, 1893

The following guests have been staying at Moneague Hotel:- His Excellency Sir Henry Blake, Lady Blake, Miss Olive Blake, Lord George Fitzgerald, (Private Secretary) 4 servants, Hon. Neal Porter, Colonial Secretary, Mrs. Norman and child. Mr. C. Hope Levy, Hon.J.H. Levy, Mrs. Levy, Miss Levy.

May 15, 1893

STURRIDGE-CLARK-On the 10th May, 1893 at St James' Church, (Mt Hermon) FLORENCE MAY, elder daughter of Dr. James H. Clark of Long Hill, Santa Cruz, Jamaica, to A. PERCY STURRIDGE, D.D.S. Surgeon Dentist, of Kingston.

1893

News from the Parishes
Brown's Town
Benefit Society

The Brown's Town Benefit Building Society has now been established and already 20 paid up and 300 subscription shares have been taken. This Society will be a great boon to the inhabitants of the district and will materially assist in improving the town and neighbourhood.

The officers are J. A. Thomason, C.P. Delgado and R. A Norman, Esqrs, Trustees; Dr. W. H. Miller, Chairman, and J. A. Thompson, CP. Delgado, R. A. Norman, R.L. Young, Wm. Kennedy, Esqrs, and Rev. Wm. Webb, Directors; J.H. Allwood, Solicitor, and acting Secretary, and Messrs. Dunckley and Corbett, Auditors.

CLERK OF THE COURT

Mr. D. A Tucker the new Deputy Clerk of the Courts took charge on the 12th instant. This gentleman will no doubt soon become popular as he is very polite and unassuming, and has a thorough knowledge of his work. A properly qualified clerk has been greatly needed since the promotion of Mr. Thomas to the clerkship and the Townspeople are pleased that his excellency has provided for the necessity.

The hot weather has set in, broken now and then in the afternoon by refreshing showers of rain.

May 23, 1893

167

Indies

Visitors Remarks:

I have been at this Hotel four weeks
and have found everything exceedingly
clean and the table the best I have found so far in Jamaica, and therefore recommend it
most cheerfully to tourists, but specially to invalids.
My stay here has been a very pleasant
one and I have been treated most kindly
by both Mr. and Mrs. Merritt.
T.H. Taylor, U.S.A.

Leaving Waverly Hotel with much regret, after a very pleasant stay of five weeks, I have
pleasure in stating that I have been very comfortable and satisfactorily cared for. The
climate is cool and beneficial to invalids.
HUMPHREY E. CRUM-EWING

I have spent seven weeks in picturesque Mandeville, being recommended her by my
physician. Through its invigorating air and the kind and courteous treatment of Mr. and
Mrs.Merritt, I leave here greatly improved in health
JAMES J. HASSETT,
New York City, U.S.A

And other recommendation from Hon. J.H. Levy, Jos. DeCordova, The American
Engineers, Percival C. Cunha.

MONEAGUE HOTEL
Moneague Hotel P.O. St Ann
900 feet above Sea Level, Nine Miles from Ewarton
Railway station and within easy access of the famous Fern Gully and Roaring River Falls
The Rates are:-

For 1 in 1 Room per day	£ 0 12 0	
1 do 1 do per week	3 10 0	
2 do 1 do do do	6 0 0	
Single beds 4s Double	0 6 0	

Special arrangements for families
Conveyances meet any Train ordered.
For further particulars apply to
A.N. Sutherland

June 1, 1893
TO MY FIRST ORCHID
(April 14th 1893)
Now light rains flash from sunny skies,
Like sudden tears,
That sudden fears
Call sparkling to a maiden's eyes;
Mixed smiles and tears,
Bent hopes and fears;
Unrests that swiftly pass;
Light shadows on the grass.

The scorching days are gone,

1893

Another world is born;
The skies are sunny clear,
In leaf and blossom; here
Most beautiful is seen
The birch tree's tender green,
From the mist of green you see,
Where it struggles to be free,
The tangled zephyr showers
A wealth of falling flowers.

The April rains arise,
Bright tears suffuse the skies,
And sunshine thro' the rain
Dawns like a smile thro'pain,
Welcome, exquisite flower,
The April world shall be,
With all its beauty, rendered
More beautiful by thee.
TOM REDCAM
Jamaica

June 16, 1893
DeMERCADO-Yesterday at his residence 12 Love Lane, GEORGE DEMERCADO.
Funeral will take place at 4 p.m. today.

June 19, 1893
A FLIGHT
I stooped from cloudy battlements
To inverse fields of blue,
Where light in cataracts is hurried,
Unwearied on I flew,
Up, by stupendous height I rose,
By mounts of passing cloud,
Where lightnings trace their way with fire,
And thunders echo loud,
Where far in caverns cast and grim,
The mighty tempests roar,
And where, thro'valleys widely dim,
The cloudy surges pour,
Untiring on my flight I winged,
And reached from height to height,
From gloom to gloom and on and on,
O'er fields of open light.
I saw the sunbeams blossom out
Below on fields of blue,
The light ran wreathing cloudy walls,
As swiftly by I flew,
Till, at the very gates of day
My soul her pinions furied,
Then, far below, a spec of dust,
I saw our distant world.
TOM REDCAM

Jamaica

June 20, 1893
ABRAHAMS-MORALES-On the 14th inst., at her residence No 94 East St. by the Revd. Solomon Jacobs, BLANCHE E. MORALES daughter of A.H. Morales to CHARLES VICTOR ABRAHAMS, both of this city. No cards.

Advertizement

June 26, 1893
YOUNG-At Tobolski, Brown's Town, on the 23rd instant, the wife of Robt. L. Young of a son. (Leycester Barclay)

JUNE 27, 1893
MORALES-On Saturday evening, the 24th inst., at her residence, No 94 East Street, PHOEBE ANNA, the beloved wife of A. H Morales, aged 49 years,
New Orleans and Savannah Ga. Papers please copy.

June 28, 1893
Cambridge Local Examination
Distribution of Prizes
        A meeting was held yesterday afternoon in the Collegiate Hall, Church Street, when His Honor Justice Lamb L.L.D., distributed the prizes and certificates gained in connection with the last Cambridge Local Examination, held in Kingston in December last. Amongst those present were Bishop Nuttall, Revd. Wm. Gillies, Rev. M. Simms, W. Simms Esq., Rev. H. H. Isaacs, Wm. Morrison, Esq., Thos. Hendricks, Esq., Rev. J. B . Ellis, Rev. Thompson, Rev. Geddes, Hon. Dr Phillippo, Rev. Spratt and E. Nuttall Esq.
Secretary's Statement
        Revd. Mr. Spratt, the Secretary said:- I have first of all on behalf of the members of the Committee, to acknowledge with thankfulness the favour and honour you have done them by so readily consenting to preside on the occasion of the distribution of the certificates and prizes gained at last December's examination. Such a public function as this is no uncommon occurrence in England in connection with the Cambridge Local Examination but never till now has taken place in this Island. For this reason the Committee has thought that some statement should be presented by its Secretary on this occasion concerning the history, results and prospects of the Cambridge Local Examination in Jamaica.
        The University of Cambridge Local Examination were commenced in England in the year 1858. That year some 370 boys only entered for the examinations; but last year the total number of entries at all centres in Britain and the British Colonies including both girls and boys, amounted to 9,564.

1893

In this colony the examination were not held till December 1882, though they had previously been held in New Zealand, Demarara and Barbados. Early in that year correspondence was opened with the Cambridge University Syndicate by the Hon Dr. Phillippo and result was that the Governors of the Institute of Jamaica of whom he was one, undertook the responsibility of holding the examination in Jamaica. In their annual report the Governors of the Institute expressed their conviction that these examinations would both test the merit of the secondary schools of the island and act as a stimulus to the cause of higher education. Looking back over the years that time it must be admitted that his two fold end has been gained, for here as elsewhere schools have been tested the fittest have survived, whilst the stimulus given to education has been most marked. For six years the holding of the examination was part of the work of the institute of Jamaica; but at the close of 1887 an independent Local Committee was formed which has since that time made all necessary arrangements for the yearly examination. The Hon. Dr. Phillippo has most deservedly continued to be from year to year the Chairman of that Committee; while H. Priest, Esq, rendered most valuable service in the secretariat till the present secretary was appointed at the beginning of last year.

In the year 1888, in accordance with the University Regulations a Ladies Committee (of which from its commencements Miss Johnson the Lady Principal of Shortwood College has been president) was formed to assist in the examination of the girls.

During the same year as the Governors of the Institute have withdrawn all pecuniary aid an application was made by the committee to the Inspector of Schools for an annual grant of £10 and was acceded to. This grant together with the amount realised from the local fees of two shillings and six pence each paid by the candidates has constituted the revenue of the committee. All needful local expanses have been met by this income and in 1891 the committee decided out of its surplus, to give a prize of books to the senior girl and value of £2 to the senior boy and to the value of £1 to the junior boy and the junior girl who should stand highest in the list of successful candidates, provided that the they obtained honors or a mark of distinction. This year these prizes are awarded to A.W. Levy of the senior and J. D. Stubbs of the junior boys and Miss Hollar of the junior girls.

Last year the Committee applied to the Cambridge Syndicate for permission to hold the Higher Local Examinations, and, though they have never up to the present time been hold at any Colonial Centre and as a rule every new centre must guarantee the payment of 20 fees of £2 each the Syndicate made a great concession by permitting the Higher Local Examination to be held in Jamaica in June, only of each year provided that application for forms of entry is specially made not later that the 1st of January of the year in which the examination is desired and fees amounting to not less than £10 are paid in each year. No examination can be held under this concession before June next year; and it is hoped that for that date and from year to year, candidates especially from the ranks of teachers in Secondary Schools will enter for the Higher Local Examinations.

The ordinary Local Examinations have been held regularly in Kingston every December from 1882 to 1892. They have not been devoid of incident. The great Kingston fire occurred on the first day of the examinations in 1882, and as was recorded in the Hand Book, "naturally upset the candidates, especially those of them living in Kingston". In 1885 an error made in sending the examination papers by the Crown Agents put off the examinations some three weeks into the midst of the Christmas holidays and so prevented more that half of those who had entered from competing. With the exception of this latter year, the number of entries has gradually increased from 15 in 1882 to 75 in 1892. And what have been the successes gained? Taking an average from the last five years, Jamaica compares most favourably with the other Colonial centres, which now include Antigua, Bermuda, British Guiana, Ceylon, Mauritius Straits

Selected Vital Records from the Jamaican Daily Gleaner

Settlements and Trinidad. In the Colonial Centres as a whole out of the number examined, 12.7 percent have passed in honours whereas in Jamaica alone 18 per cent have so passed and the Colonial Centres a whole 47.5 per cent have passed not in Honours, and in Jamaica 44.3 per cent, 60.2 percent has been the total of passes for the Colonies as a whole and 62.2 per cent for Jamaica alone; and 39.8 the total of failures for all the Colonial Centres and 37.8 for the Jamaica Centre.

Last December 73 presented themselves for examination: two boys who had entered for were absent from examination account of accident and sickness. Of these 73, 50 (including 38 boys out of a total of 58 and 12 girls out of a total of 17) passed 15 of them in honours (14 boys and 1 girl). Under the Secondary Education Law of 1892 two Senior Boys viz.: A. W. Levy of the Jamaica High School, and F. A. Rosada of the Kingston Collegiate School and one senior girl viz.; G.L. Depass of the Barbican High School, have won scholarships of £15 each; and 8 junior boys viz.: J.D. Stubbs, W. Simms, J. M. Bowrey. G.S. Husband, F. G. Sharp of the Jamaica High School, S. Lockett and T. D. Kennedy of York Castle High School and L. D. C. King of Potsdam School and 2 junior girls, viz.: A. C. J.Hollar of the Barbican High School and E. Roberts of the Kingston High School for Girls, have won scholarships of £10 each.

On the basis of the results of the examination for senior students to be held in Kingston next December, in accordance with the Amended Rules for the Jamaica Scholarship, and regulations of the Amended Secondary Education Law, in addition to all other Scholarships the Jamaica Scholarship of £200 per annum tenable for three years and two scholarships of £60 per annum tenable for the same period, may be awarded. The Cambridge local Examination will in future be the one test recognised by the Government for the Secondary Schools of the Island.

In view of the increased importance thus attaching to the Cambridge Local Examinations, the Committee is firmly convinced that the future will witness a greater development that the past has shown, not only in respect of the numbers who enter for these examination but also in respect of the standard of attainment reached in them.

His Honour Judge Lumb in addressing the audience said that before distributing the certificates it was his duty to address a few remarks pertinent to what brought them there, and also by ways of advice to those young boys and girls who had been in the examination either as successful or unsuccessful candidates. The secretary, had said and it was a fact of financial history that it was as far back as the year 1858 since these examination commenced. He believed he was one of the first of these 280 or 380 candidates in the first examination that was held in England, (applause) and he certainly did not think it was so long ago. He saw before him, on the certificate, a name he knew very well that of John Peel Vice Chancellor of the University of Cambridge. All those facts brought back to him reminiscences of years long gone by and of years that could never return. They had heard what have been done and what was being done in this colony on behalf of secondary education and it certainly did seem as if a great work was being carried on and as if a great awakening was taking place on the question of education. He was glad to see that such high and valuable inducements were held out to those who were in school at the present time to work hard and succeed in their studies. It was a very great method of inducing boys and girls to work by giving them scholarships, because it represented so much money and it was the first proof to them that knowledge meant money and that knowledge meant success. There were valuable scholarships not merely to be held in the island but to those wished to go to the Universities in England. He though, altho' he did not know the terms under which those scholarships were held, that they would be the means of some young men living in this colony going to England and acquiring a knowledge of Agricultural Chemistry and scientific formula and they might come back and be useful in the Colony and do some good in return for the money that had been received from the island.

1893

ELEMENTARY EDUCATION

There was another subject. Although they were there for the purpose of secondary education he could not resist the temptation to say some words about elementary education because it was one that he had taken a very deep interest in and in which he had had some experience. One of the first things which struck a new resident in the island was the black pall of ignorance that enshrouded the minds of the working classes-domestic servants, artisans and agricultural labourers, all alike were unable to read or write. But he was glad to say that by liberal and by generous legislation that had recently been passed this sad condition of affairs would soon pass away and that there would be a system of free and compulsory education. He was sure that the enlightened men who had brought about such a state of affairs deserved the thanks and the credit of the colony for their efforts was spending large sums of money on Elementary Education and he was sure money could not be expended by the state in a better way that by education of the people, provided that the education was of the right sort. To his mind no system of Elementary Education could be complete which did not comprise in it industrial and technical education of boys and girls (hear, Hear). They must remember that the vast majority of those for whom that popular education was provided were children who would be dependent for the subsistence on the labor of their hands and therefore they should educate their hands as well as their heads and so make them better labourers more intelligent and more useful citizens. Of course it would be a difficult matter in Jamaica because there were peculiar disadvantages and complexities to be deal with but he felt sure that with willing hearts and strong efforts those difficulties would be over come.

THRIFT

Another subject in connection with Elementary education was the encouragement of thrift which ought to be taught to the children by their establishment of penny savings banks. It had been found a most successful move to reach habits of thrift. He believed there was a gentleman in the colony at the present time Mr. H. W. Livingstone who was taking up the subject (hear, hear) and -they would pardon him for saying it for of course he did not wish to appear to be in any way patronising that that gentlemen was doing a very important and valuable work. He was sure every person would wish Mr. Livingston success in his efforts and he hoped the time was not far distant when every school in the colony would have its penny savings Bank (hear, hear). He was readying the other day an address by Sir John Lubbock, who treated of that very subject. At the beginning of last year there were 2,600 penny savings banks in the whole of England. Last year all fees were abolished in schools in England. As the result of the abolition of fees and of the increased interest in the subject of thrift, at the end of last year the number which had been 2,600 had increased to 6,400. He hoped the banks would be established here because he had taken part in and founded them himself and had seen the very great good they had done more especially amongst the poorest of the poor in the large towns in England.

TO THE STUDENTS

He wished to say a few words to those boys and young ladies who were before him expecting their certificates and prizes. The examination in which they had taken part was a competitive one throughout because the best was placed first. They heard a great deal said about competition and competitive examinations in these schools leading to cramming. That might be true in a few cases. It was what they had heard for many years but in his opinion competition in education was like competition in trade, the more of it the better for trade and the better for education. After all, what was life itself but one prolonged competitive examination. It had always been so and it had always been every man's duty to make the most and the best of himself. The proverb said "Life is short, Art is long, Opportunity fleeting, experiment uncertain and Judgement difficult." But remember that while study required labour, that the reward was great and they must leave no stone unturned to educate and better themselves. It was said that the Queen of England was once speaking and remarked 'never mention the word trouble until you tell me how the thing is to be done, to be done rightly, and I will do it if I can.' They must take to themselves the words of their beloved Queen and try to do some good both for themselves and their fellowmen. They could be engaged in no nobler work, they could have no higher goal before them that to do what lay in their power to better the fellowmen. (Applause). What was common to all great men was that they served their fellowmen. The really great men such as Shakespeare or Milton or the Duke of Wellington who had left their mark on the world's history had always performed great services to the generations in which they lived. Let each one of them resolve to do what they could, all they could, and even if the result of their life's work was but one humble scarcely noticed deed of good, remember that an infinitesimal number of such good deeds make up in the end and gave a sum total which in the eyes of the world was of exceeding value. What ever situation they might be in, whatever position they might attain, on what ever rung of the ladder of life they may be resting, remember to do all they could for the good of their fellowmen and make the world better for their having been in it. To those who had been successful he would say "Let your success urge you to still greater efforts" and to those who had been unsuccessful, "Take heart and try again," and to all of them he would say "Do not spare time or effort or labour to do what you can, not because it will be of no benefit to you or bring you any material reward but because it is good and right of itself and being so will most assuredly bring its own reward".

After the prizes and certificates had been handed to the various winners, the hon. J. C. Phillippo addressed the meeting.

After congratulating Justice Lumb on his presence there that evening, Mr. Phillippo said he saw before him those who were making their reputation and those whose reputations were already made. He was glad to see the ladies had come so well to the front. A few years ago they had no opportunity of distinguishing themselves, but now they were taking honors not only in love but in learning. He expected the young ladies of Jamaica to yet further distinguish them selves and for one of them to rise and write the wrongs of the people of this island (cheers)

Bishop Nuttall then delivered an address on the subject of education in Jamaica. He spoke of the various landmarks which showed the progress of education in the past, and of the need for legislation in the present. An extended report of his lordship's remarks will appear in our tomorrow's issue.

Mr. Wm. Morrison, principal of the Kingston Collegiate school moved a vote of thanks to his Honor Justice Lumb for presiding.

Mr. SmallPage, M.A. seconded, and the motion was cordially received. The proceedings then terminated.

The full prize list of winners of prizes and testimonials has already appeared in the GLEANER.

July 3, 1893
The next term of York Castle High School commences on 28th inst.

July 6, 1893
Manly at Roxburgh, the wife of Jas. Manly of a son

Bailey-At his residence Allandale, Retirement Road, St Andrew, Jamaica WILLIAM MEW BAILEY, Aged 41 years.

1893

The Royal Wedding between H.R.H. the Duke of York and Princess May takes place today at the Royal Chapel Windsor.

Dr. W.H.Miller of Brown's Town leaves this morning on the Atlas str Alene for Chicago for the benefit of his health.

July 12, 1893
STEWART-July 3rd at Cedar Valley, St Ann's the wife of A.A. Stewart, of a daughter.

July 17, 1893
The sale of Retreat Pen in St Ann, the property of Mr. C.J.Moulton Barrett, will take place at the Court house on the 16th August before Mr. Thomas Hendrick, Registrar.

July 18, 1893
Hart-At Eastbourne," East Queen St. on the 16th inst., the wife of A.B. Hart of a son.

July 20, 1893

The Hon J.H. Levy leaves this morning on a visit to New York. His stay will not be a prolonged one, but he may find time to visit the World's Fair at Chicago.

July 21, 1893
Leave of absence has been granted to Hon J.H. Levy, and to Hon. Dr. J.C. Phillippo, the latter in all his public capacities.

July 22, 1893
RAMSAY-On July 21st, 1893 in Spanish Town, WALTER GRAVENOR RAMSAY, aged 60 years.

August 8, 1893
We are glad to notice that Rev. Horace Scotland who has been ill with influenza is able to be out again. He was in the city on Saturday.

August 9, 1893
Advertizement

Selected Vital Records from the Jamaican Daily Gleaner

August 11, 1893
GENERAL VIEW OF JAMICA COURT -FROM A PHOTOGRAPH (Chicago Exhibition)

August 12, 1893
The Cost of Visiting the Fair--An estimate for Jamaicans
Kingston to New York and Back....$90
New York to Chicago and back..... $18
Sleeping fare for Journeys............$7
12 Admissions to Exposition.........$6
Board and Lodging in Chicago.......$36
at $3 for 12 days
Street cars,Shows, Theatres, etc.....$12
Express and steamer charges
on luggage and other minor details....$6
Total $175
                                   £35
It will be seen that for the sum of £40 the great Fair at Chicago can been seen, and a fortnight spent within the precincts. More

August 16, 1893
The auction sale of that splendid pen in St Ann's "Retreat" belonging to the estate of C.J.Moulton-Barrett, Esqr takes place at the Court House Harbour Street, Kingston today at 1 p.m. before Thomas Hendrick, Esqr., Registrar by Turnbull, Madox and Co.

September 9, 1893
An examination was held at St. Ann's Bay before Mr. Reece on Monday last as to the cause of the recent fire at the Baptist Chapel there. The cause of the fire still remains a mystery and the efforts of Mr. House in that direction have been up to the present successful.

September 11, 1893
Death of Mr. Jenoure
A cablegram was received in Port Antonio on the evening of the 6th inst. announcing the death of Colorado Springs U.S.A. of Mr. P.A. Jenoure the proprietor of Boston in Portland. Mr. Jenoure leaves a widow and three young children to whom we tender our sympathy.

September 12, 1893
MURRAY At No 17 Laws Street, yesterday forenoon, ANN HILL MURRAY sister of Mr. John Murray of this city. Funeral will leave at 4.30 this afternoon. Friends will please accept this intimation.

September 13, 1893
Dr W.E. Wilson to whom we have previously referred arrived on Saturday on the s.s. Andes from England via New York.

October 9,1 893
Clemetson-At Pondside House, Port Maria, on Sunday 1st October, 1893, the wife of D.R. Clemetson, of a son

Lord, At "Ainslie" Old Harbour on Monday 2nd inst., the wife of C.George Lord, of a son.

October 14, 1893
Obituary
We regret to record the death of Mr. R. A. Mornan, the confidential Clerk of the Hon J.H. Levy, Brown's Town. He caught fever, which developed into typhoid and succumbed on the night of the 10th. Mr. Mornan was well known in the district, and was highly esteemed. He lately made a visit to the United States and saw the World's Fair. On his return he communicated some of his impressions through the columns of the Gleaner.

Prize Distribution at Barbican
Speech by the Hon T Capper, B.A.

Prize Distribution
The prizes were then distributed as follows:--
Form 2 Miss Edith Smith
Form 2 Miss Zilla Marshalleck
Form 3 Miss Ethel Smith
Form 4 Miss Frederica Rigg
Miss Anna Hollar
Music Prize-Miss Maud Marshalleck
Shady drawing Miss Edna Murray
Freehand Miss Kathleen Powell
Conduct prize (a silver watch) Miss Isabel James

The Rev. F.O. Miller in giving a short history of the school said it was established in October, 1881 and they had therefore just completed their twelfth year of existence...........More

October 16, 1893
Mornan On the 10th October, 1893 at Clifton, Brown's Town, Mr. R.A. Mornan, second son of Mr. James Wray and Mrs. Mornan and the confidential Clerk of the Hon. J.H. Levy in the 27th year of his age.

We have received further particulars of the death of Mr. Mornan Brown's Town. He was only 27 years of age and had been for 13 years in the employ of the Hon. J. H. Levy, and during all this period manifested an intelligence and aptitude for business, rarely met with. His high sense of honour, his integrity, his many amiable qualities, with his consistent Christian character, gained for him many admirers and friends. He was beside all this a good son, an affectionate brother and a faithful friend. The tribute paid to his memory by the inhabitants of Brown's Town and the surrounding districts was very touching. The bells of the four churches toiled at his funeral, while an immense concourse of people with over 60 carriages, followed his remains to their last resting place. Mr. Mornan in addition to his being the confidential clerk of the Hon. J.H. Levy acted as one of his Attornies whenever he left the Island, and to him his loss will be irreparable, as there was between them a stronger bond than employer, and employee.

November 1, 1893
MCGRATH At London on the 27th inst., of diphtheria, "NELLIE" the dearly beloved wife of George McGrath, Esq. of Charlemont, aged 35 years, R.I.P. (By telegram)

Selected Vital Records from the Jamaican Daily Gleaner

November 6, 1893

Our correspondent at Brown's Town states that the weather there is still against commerce and very much against the curing of coffee which is unfortunately already being brought to market.

November 13, 1893

HOPWOOD - At Lilyfield, St Ann, on the 9th inst., the wife of ALEXANDER HOPWOOD, of a son.

November 14, 1893

MACNISH at 80 ½ Church St Kingston the wife of JAMES HUNTER MACNISH of a daughter.

November 15, 1893

PHILLIPPO-Suddenly at Saxthrope, St Andrews, the HON J.C. Phillippo. Funeral will leave Saxthorpe for Kingston at 3 p.m. today.

November 24, 1893

WHITING At Nightengale Grove, on the 17th inst., ANNIE OUTRIDGE, eldest daughter of the late Revd. Edward Spratt, Wesleyan Minister the beloved wife of Smeethe Whiting of Garredu, leaving a husband and infant son, several brothers and sisters and numerous relatives and friends to mourn their irreparable loss. Age 27. "Thy will be done".

December 2, 1893

LOUIS CUNHA-His friends and those of his sons' are asked to attend the funeral from the residence 136 Church Street to the Ebenezer Cemetery. Funeral 4.45 this afternoon. Carriages.

December 4, 1893

We regret to announce the death of Mr. Louis Cunha, at the advanced age of 82. Mr. Cunha has been connected all his life time with shipping matters and his is a familiar in shipping circles, and has been manager of the Commercial Exchange for several years. He was recently of the Merchants Exchange, but retired some time ago on a pension, on account of old age. He leaves four sons and two daughters, to who we tender our condolence. As a mark of respect for the deceased the flag of the Exchange was placed at half mast all Saturday.

December 18, 1893

Lecesne-At Harker's Hall on Thursday the 14th December, 1893, the wife of James C. Lecesne, of a son.

December 20, 1893

ROBINSON- At Cleveden, St Andrews, on the 17th inst. the wife of John Arthur Robinson of a daughter.

December 21, 1893

ROBISON-At Cleveden, St Andrews, on the 17th inst. the wife of John Arthur Robison of a daughter

1893

MUSSON At Southsea, England on the 25th November, ELIZA C.H. MUSSON daughter of the late Revd. S.P. Musson. D.D.

December 22, 1893
The bankrupt stock of P.B. Desnoes was put at auction yesterday by Messrs. Turnbull and Madon.. The stock was first offered in a lot, but in consequence of some misunderstanding as to fixtures, it was put up in lots to suit purchasers. Fair prices were realized.

December 27, 1893
Montego Bay
It is with feeling of deep regret that we have to chronicle the death on Wednesday the 20th inst. of Mrs. Hall, wife of the Revd. G. Bathurst Hall, Rector of Holy Trinity Church after a few weeks' illness. Three doctors were in attendance. She leaves a husband and one daughter here and other relatives in Barbados to mourn her loss. Her remains were conveyed from the Rectory yesterday evening, Thursday to Holy Trinity Church followed by a very large concourse of persons in all situations of life.

At the church the body was met by the Revds. F.A. Sharpe and C.G. McGregor who performed the service there and at the grave a very impressive one. We tender to the Revd. gentleman and the family our sincere condolence.

December 28, 1893
Cricket
Match at Brown's Town
A very interesting match took place at Brown's Town on the Huntly Commons on Thursday, the 21st December between the Brown's Town C.C. and a team got up by Mr. F. Eaves. On account of the heavy rains the shortness of time in getting up the match, Mr. Eaves could not place a representative team on the grounds and eventually play shorthanded.

Having won the toss the Brown's Town C.C. decided to bat, and at 2 o'clock the game was started under great inconvenience to the bowlers of the visitors. (Messrs Dunn and Eaves the latter being changed after a couple of overs) owing to the downpour of rain at intervals of about ten minutes. For the Brown's Town C.C. Messrs. Turton, Corlett and Young rendered good service by their good batting, whilst for the visitors Dunn proved himself equal to the occasion having made 25 runs and not out. Wickets were down at a very late hour, on account of the darkness. The total scores were, Brown's Town C.C.69, Mr. Eaves' team 53.

Brown's Town Benefit Building Society
At a meeting of the Directors of this Society held on the 2nd December, Dr. W.H. Miller was appointed a Trustee of the Society in place of Mr. R.H. Mornan, deceased. Mr. A.S. Byles was also elected a director in place of Mr. Wm.Kennedy, resigned.

The Society which was established in March of this year, is now in a very flourishing condition, the shares having been promptly taken up, and the funds accruing therefrom as promptly put out again at 7½ per cent interest on security of landed property in the district. Upwards of 500 subscription and 40 aid up shares have been issued, and under the present cheap and efficient management, the shareholders may confidently expect to receive good bonus additions to their shares.

Selected Vital Records from the Jamaican Daily Gleaner

December 28, 1893

LINDO-LINDO-On the evening of the 20th inst. ARTHUR LINDO son of the late Alfred Alexander Lindo to Rebecca L. Lindo, eldest daughter of Henry Lindo of Orange Grove, St Catherine, at Home, Jocelyn Cottage, Musgrave Avenue, Saturday and Sunday 30th and 31st int.

1894

January 4, 1894

CASSERLY-On the 1st January, 1894, the wife of J.M. Casserly, of a son.

January 6, 1894

YORK CASTLE HIGH SCHOOL

This School will be re-opened after the Christmas holidays on Thursday the 25th January. The Staff of Tutors will be strengthened by an Expert in Classics and English from one of the English Universities.

The Tuition, Climate, Care &c make the School a very desirable one for boys.

Applications should be made to

Rev. W. CLARKE MURRAY, York Castle

January 9, 1894

St Ann Parochial Board

Ordinary Meeting

A meeting of the Parochial Board of St Ann was held at St Ann's Bay on the 4th instant, present: The Honourable C.W. Stern in the chair, the Honourable J.H. Levy, Messrs, Dixon, Miller, Brown, and The Reverend J.Duff.

Mr. Perkins

It was resolved that the Superintendent of Parochial Roads and Works Mr. R. F. Perkins had performed his duties during the past year to the entire satisfaction of the Board and that he was entitled to an increment to his salary.

ATTENDANCES

The Clerk placed upon the table the annual statement of attendances of members of the Parochial Board as follow: The Honourable C.W. Stern (Chairman) 11, Mr. Sturridge 4, Mr. Sutherland 1 (elected in March) Mr. Brown 6, Mr. Scott 3, Mr. Harrison 4, Mr. Dixon (Vice Chairman) 7, Mr. Miller 8, the Rev. G. House 10, the Rev J. Duff 9, the Honourable J.H. Levy 7, Mr. Boyles 8, Mr. Delgado 3, Dr Miller 4, the Rev. S. Lindo 7.

More Business

January 10, 1894

We have received the first number of the Fortnightly Review a journal to be published at Brown's Town in the interests of "Good works". It is a vivacious readable paper; is independent in tone and well printed and edited. It proposes to undertake the formation of a teacher's union. The editor says the only "love" about the writings of Dr. Love is his name. We wish the Fortnightly every success.

January 11, 1894
ISAACS-At 45A East Queen St., CELIA MIRIAM, youngest daughter of Henry and Rebecca Isaacs, late of Chester Castle, Hanover. Funeral will move at 11 this morning.

January 12, 1894
FRENCH- At Sevens Plantation, Clarendon on the 5th instant, in her 33rd year MINNIE EMILY, the beloved wife of D. A. French of Demerara. "He giveth his beloved sleep"

January 18, 1894 (Thursday)
Connor January 16th at Musgrave Avenue the wife of Charles Connor of a son.

Current Items
Mr. James Facey, son of Mr. James Samuel Facey, and a well-known Spanishtonian, died at Spanish Town on Tuesday night at 11 o'clock. Deceased had for some time carried on his father's business at the corner of Manchester St. He had been suffering for some time past from a brain disease. He was buried yesterday fore Spanish Town (sic).

Representation of St Ann and St Mary
HON J.H. LEVY TO STAND
We are glad to state the Hon. J.H. Levy after serious deliberation and much anxious thought has decided to accede to the universal wish of his late constituents and has accepted nomination at their hands for the electoral district of St. Mary and St Ann. We congratulate the electors of these two parishes on again obtaining the services of one who has given such great promise of becoming a thoroughly efficient legislator, and who has already proved himself to be of independent and disinterested character.

January 22, 1894
George Fortunatus Judah has a piece on the Livingston Family heritage. H.W. Livingston, Esq. is the Island Treasurer p 2.

January 23, 1894
Jan, 19th. Since the Christmas holidays, things have been very quiet with us. barely any enjoyment, but on the 17th and 18th instant we were most agreeably roused by the advent of the renowned Company the "Fisk's University Jubilee Singers" who certainly maintained their reputation. As the crowded houses on each occasion testified by their vociferous "encores" we can only add our mite to the continuous flow of well merited praise to this talented company and they carry away from Brown's Town heartiest good wishes for prosperity in their noble Work.
After experiencing again the great need of a Public Hall, we would take this opportunity of bringing to the notice of our future member of the Legislative Council the absolute necessity for a suitable Court House in this rapidly growing town and we must have what we have long been promised.
We are truly glad to find that our esteemed fellow townsman has again consented to represent us at and in the Legislative Council. As a parish, we have unbounded confidence in him, and as long as he will do us the honour and favour of representing us we want no other.
Just at this juncture Mr. Levy's business has assumed prodigious magnitude, and for him to give up an inch of his time, shows that he has the interest, not only of his fellow and sister parishioners at heart, but the Island generally.

1894

We earnestly hope and firmly expect that the mark he made last session was only the bud of the blossom of the full blown rose, not only of Legislative honors, but of that integrity for which he stands identified amongst us.

The prefix of Honourable to his name has not in anyway changed his manner nor is it likely to nor will it ever make him suspected of being dishonourable.

January 24, 1894
LINDO-LINDO-On Tuesday 9th January, by the Revd. Solomon Jacobs, at Lincoln Hall, the residence of her uncle, Mr. S.D. Lindo, ALFREDA ALEXANDRA, only daughter of the late Alfred Lindo, Esq., of Moneague, St Ann's to WILFRED AGUSTUS, seventh son of Henry Lindo, Esq., of Orange Grove, St Catherine. At Home at Saithou, Lissant Road on Tuesday and Wednesday 30th and 31st inst. from 5 p.m.

The Late Moses Levy. The friends of the late Mr. MOSES LEVY desirous of paying a tribute of respect to his memory are informed that a short service in memoriam will be held by the Revd. S. Jacobs at the residence of MR.GEORGE LYON, 151 King St) at 6 o'clock every evening during the week of mourning.

January 26, 1894
SHOCKING TRAGEDY AT UP-PARK CAMP--A NON-COMMISSIONED OFFICER POISONS HIS WIFE AND SHOOTS HIMSELF. A ¼ column on this event. The sergeant was a 30 year old Englishman T.J.Grant and his wife Caroline Grant age 25 was a nurse. It was suggested in the piece that he had committed bigamy with a first wife in Halifax who was threatening to come to Jamaica and reveal all to the present wife who he married the year before in Jamaica.

Current Items
The Governor has appointed James A. Dougall and William James Cathcart, Esqs. to be Justices of the peace for the parish of St Thomas.

January 27, 1894
St Ann's Bay, Jamaica B.W.I.
LODGINGS, &c
The subscriber in returning thanks for the past favours, begs to inform the General Public that she still carries on the business of a Lodging House Keeper, at those Commodious Premises in St Ann's Bay, Jamaica British West Indies, known as WATSON'S LODGING HOUSE, under the patronage of His Excellency Sir Henry Blake. The climate is excellent; the accommodations unsurpassable; and the cuisine is all that can be desired. The Establishment is patronized by all the leading men of the Island, as well as notable strangers from abroad. A continuance of patronage is solicited. Letters and Telegrams, will receive prompt attention.
MARY JANE WATSON
For reference, the Subscriber asks permission to submit the name of several Ladies and Gentlemen who have patronized the Establishment--His excellency Sir Henry A. Blake, K.C.M.G. &c, the Duke of St Albans, Mr. and Mrs. Crum Ewing, Hon J.M. Farquharson, Sav-la-Mar, J.T Vipond, (Canada)Capt. Watson (Duke of Wellington Regiment), Sir W. B. and Lady Gorgon, Commander and Mrs. Hall,(England), Benjamin A Watson and wife, Lowell, Mass, U.S.A.) and numerous other whose names will be found in the Visitors Book of the Lodgings. M.J. Watson.

Selected Vital Records from the Jamaican Daily Gleaner

February 12, 1894

DENNISON- At her residence 18 Oxford St., yesterday morning MAYBEL PRICE DENNISON, the eldest and much beloved daughter of Napthali and Ada Dennison, aged 9 years and 7 months. Funeral at 4 o'clock this evening. Please let your carriage attend.

February 13, 1894

SANGUINETTI-VERLEY-On the 6th February at the Kingston Parish Church, by His Lordship the Bishop of Jamaica assisted by the Revds. G.W. Downer, Rector of Kingston, J.B. Ellis, M. A. and H. Seymour Isaacs, M.A. EDMUND HAUGHTON, eldest son of Edmund Shedour Sanguinetti, Esq., of Kingston to JESSIE LOUISE, eldest daughter of James Louis Verley, Esq., of Abbey Court, St Andrew.

February 16, 1894

Hon J.H. Levy and his Constituents.

The Hon. J.H. Levy is again setting a good example to the elected members. He is resolved that the electors will have a fair change of knowing his views and of expressing their opinions. He is visiting St Mary on Thursday 22nd instant, and will speak to the taxpayers and electors at the Court House on same evening. He is also speaking to the people in the Brown's Town Court House today (Friday).

February 20, 1894

McCutchin-Yesterday at 6.10 p.m. at Marine Gardens, No 1, Robert Beatty McCutchin, youngest son of Adam McCutchin of St Croix, DWI, in his 56th year. Funeral will move at 4 p.m. sharp. Please accept this intimation. American papers please copy.

A short paragraph by Fortunatus Judah entitled William Beckford Historian No 2. Siting the will of Edward Beckford declaring that he was the first of that name to come to Jamaica. His will of 1666 is given. His wife is Margaret, but he does not name children. He had a ship and whether he was a trader or privateer is not clear. First deed of Peter Beckford is 1674

February 21, 1894

Hon J.H. Levy and His Constituents--Meeting at Brown's Town

In keeping with announcement, a public meeting was held in this town on Friday evening the 16th inst., to hear the views of the newly elected member to the Legislative Council previous to its assembling, which is expected to be on an early date. The meeting was well attended with classes being fully represented. Among those present were noticed. Dr. Phillippo, Dr Miller, Mr. Chas. Orrett, Mr. Thos. Kemp, Mr. Abm, Isaacs, Mr. A.S. Byles, Mr. O. I. Sanguinetti, Mr. S. Lawrence, Mr. A.B.H. Isaacs, Mr. S.G. L. Sutherland, Mr. H.Q. Levy, Mr. John Collins, Mr. T.W. Doutlwaite, Mr. Jones, Mr. G. L. Mais, Dr. Turton, Mr. J. Passmore, Mr. H. Bloomfield, Mr. Dickenson, Mr. Corbett, Mr. A. Noah, Mr. C. L. Sanguinetti and a great many others.

Much more

February 26, 1894

Saturday being the Feast of St Matthias the Most Reverend the Lord Bishop of Jamaica, held an ordination at the Parish Church at 8 o'clock, when the following gentlemen were ordained; Deacon: Mr. H.S. Sharp; Priests: Rev. G. H. Thompson, Rev. H.A. Cover, Rev. W. Graham. The ordination sermon was preached by the Right Revd. Bishop Douet, and

1894

the Oath of the Queen's Supremacy was administered by Mr. Thomas Hendrick, Registrar for the Diocese.

February 27, 1894
LEVY-At Elrose, on the Blake Road, the wife of Ellis Levy of a Daughter.

Surridge On the 23rd inst., at Lissant Road, the wife of Dr. A.P. Sturridge of a daughter.

March 1, 1894
Hon J.H. Levy on the Cost of the Railway.--He bears Out the Estimate of the "Gleaner". Columns

March 2, 1894
The farther examination of the bankrupt Peter Blaize Desnoes, will be resumed in Chambers today before Mr. Justice Jones.

The Governor has appointed Mr. E.G. Orrett, to be a Second Lieutenant in the Kingston Infantry Militia.

Falmouth
The Churches
Feby 28 The Rev. E.A. Stewart, Rector of this parish is very sick at his country residence "Armagh" The services at 11 and 7 o'clock in the evening were conducted by the Revd Thomas, his assistant. At the Wesleyan Chapel in the forenoon Rev. C.J. Bacquie Esq. Collector of Taxes conducted the service and at 7 in the evening Mr. Hardiman the schoolmaster conducted service, the Rev. J.K. Braham, the pastor being in attendance at the outstation.

March 3, 1894
BAQUIE-Last night at Primrose Cottage, at 7.45, Mr. EDWARD BAQUIE in the 60th year of his age. Funeral will move off at half past four o'clock this evening. Friends and acquaintance are kindly invited. Please let your carriage attend.

The examination of Mr. Peter Blaize Desnoes in regard to his discharge in Bankruptcy was continued yesterday in Chambers. The hearing was not concluded when the Court adjourned until today.

Eleven Wesleyan Methodist Ministers, whose names appear in the passenger list, arrived in the Packet yesterday from the several West Indian Islands, to attend the conference now sitting. They were met at the wharf by Revs. T.M. Geddes, W.C. Murray, John Duff, and several others.

Among the passengers who arrived by the "Medway" from England was Mr. Gerald Waddington of Rio Magno, St Catherine. We are glad to learn that Mr. Waddington has returned to the island after an absence of six months with renewed health, after his recent sad bereavement. He has brought out with him a fine pure bred Suffolk Ram from the celebrated breed of the Marquis of Bristol.

Passenger List "Medway" from Southampton via Barbados and Jacmel.
Among others: Revs. Geo Sykes, Taylor, Wright, Irvine, Tull, Jones, Halliday, Payne Johnson, Bridgewater and Reynolds.

Selected Vital Records from the Jamaican Daily Gleaner

March 5, 1894

The further examination of the bankrupt Peter Blaize Desnoes has been adjourned until this morning at 10 o'clock, before Mr. Justice Hyndman Jones.

A correspondent writes: At Brown's Town on the morning of 1st March, Mary Ann Corlett, widow of the late John Corlett, Wesleyan Minister, died in her 91st year. Her remains after being churched in the Methodist Church there, by the Rev. G. Henderson were removed to Duncans and there interred by Revds. Hardwick and Henderson. The latter minister showed his good feeling and perfect sympathy and headed the procession from Brown's Town to Duncan's where it was met by the Hon J.H. Levy who was telegraphed for while at St Ann's Bay.

March 6, 1894

The examination of the bankrupt, Mr. Peter Blaize Desnoes, was continued in Chambers yesterday. The case lasted up to until about 11.30 a.m. when the examination was formally declared closed.

On Sunday evening last the Revd. W.C. Murray paid a visit for the purpose of hearing a lecture delivered by Mr. Blenman, disproving the Immortality of the Soul. When the lecturer had finished Mr. Murray challenged him to an open debate which he accepted.

March 10, 1894

The preachers at Coke Church tomorrow are: Rev. Geo. Sykes, 11 a.m. and Rev. T. Halliday 6.30 p.m. The latter gentleman was one of the late York Castle pupils, who gained the Jamaica Scholarship.

March 12, 1894

GRUCHY- At the Mico Institution on March 10th, the wife of L.G. Gruchy of a daughter

March 13, 1894

News has been received of the death in England of the Rev. Mr. Nuttall, brother of Dr. Nuttall, the Lord Primate of the West Indies. The rev. Gentleman was here two years ago on a visit. We beg to offer our condolence to His Lordship on his bereavement.

Ladies College and Preparatory School, Half-Way Tree

Of the 7 pupils of the above College, Principals" Misses A.J. Ashby and F.M. Small who sat for the College of preceptors examination in December last, 6 have passed successfully in the following subjects:-

Dorrit King, 1st div-Scripture, Grammar, History, Geography Algebra, French, Music

Daisy Schiller, 1st div-Scrip. Gram.His, Geog. Arith. Alg. Mus

Clarine Small, 2nd div Scrip Gram His. Geo. Arith. Alg

Kathleen Ashby, end div-Scrip, Gram. His, Geog, Arith, Alg Mus

Ethel Solomon, 2nd div Scrip. Gram. Hiss. Geo Arith. Mus

Maud Schiller, 2nd div Scrp Gram. His Geo. Arith. Alg

Of the 13 pupils of the above Preparatory School who sat for the Kinsington Local Examination held in December last all have passed successfully in the following subjects

Jane Miller 2nd class-S,Gr,H,Go,Ar, Al, Mu, drawing

Ellen Taylor, 2nd class

Leopoldina Quesada 2nd class (part)

Amy Ewbank, 2nd class

Gertrude Taylor, 3rd class

Muriel Grant, 3rd class

Maud Grant, 3rd class
Effie Ashby, 3rd class
Florence Roxburgh, 3rd class
Mary Small, 3rd class
Kathleen Robinson, 3rd class
Mabel Schiller, 3rd class
Minnie Solomon, 3rd class
{Note I have not included all the subjects from this list)

March 14, 1894
MOSS On the 9th March at Harmony Portland, drowned while bathing LILLIAN MAUD youngest and dearly beloved child of Mrs. Richard Moss of Southfield, St Ann

SKELTON On the 9th March, at Harmony Portland, drowned while bathing, WILLIAM WALSTON HERBERT SKELTON of Yorkshire England. (Gleaner earlier said they were engaged)

March 16, 1894 (Friday)
The Bathing Fatality in Portland
St Ann's Bay Thursday- The bodies of Miss Moss and Mr. Skelton have arrived here and have been buried. The funerals took place this morning at 6 o'clock and 7 o'clock
Miss Moss was interred in the Jewish cemetery and Mr. Skelton in the Protestant cemetery.
The bodies came from Portland in a cutter and were enclosed in a lead coffin.

March 17, 1894
More on the funerals of Moss and Skelton

March 21, 1894
The session of the Wesleyan Conference having closed, the following clergymen left yesterday in the Medway for their respective destinations: Rev. Wright, Rev. Johnson, Rev Taylor, Rev Tull, Rev. Irving, Rev Jones, Rev Bridgewater, Rev Sykes, Rev Reynolds, and Rev. Paynes. Mr. Halliday, of Demerara remains until next mail. At the wharf, there was a large gathering of the Wesleyan body present.

March 27, 1894
The Western Wesleyan Methodist Annual Conference
Allegations against William Clarke Murray including nepotism for his daughter Edith who married W.H. Mitchell.

March 31, 1894
Captain Woolword's Book "Nigh on Fifty Years at Sea" is out of the publishers hands, and the first installment arrived yesterday by the Don, and can be had from Aston W. Gardner and Company.

April to June not on the shelf at this time, Missing from on-line Gleaner

July 6, 1894
DAYES-On Wednesday the 4th inst. at 3.20 a.m. at his residence No 69 Church Street in his 72nd year, JAMES DAYES Solicitor leaving a widow and large family to mourn their irreparable loss.

Selected Vital Records from the Jamaican Daily Gleaner

July 11, 1894
St Ann's Bay
Business

Levy, Isaacs & Co have been busily engaged taking stock during the past week at their wholesale store, preparatory to their removing from the present place (Bravo's Store) to more spacious premises in Main Street, know as "Market Store" where they intend increasing their business to a large extent. Mr. Cooper, the Musgrave House General is acting for the present as First Lieutenant. The Hon. J.H. Levy visited the town twice this week to see how matters are progressing. Mr. Clarke, the St Ann's Bay Andrew Scott, is having a heavy run of work upon him of late.

July 12, 1894
The boys' and girls' schools at Potsdam and Hampton, in connection with the Munro and Dickenson's schools, will be reopened on the 30th inst. after the midsummer holiday.

It is expected that the 2nd West Indian Regiment will embark about the commencement of October for Sierra Leone to relieve the 1st Battalion now stationed there.

The Intermediate Examination in Arts University of London will commence on Monday at 10 a.m. and will last four days. It will be held in one of the rooms attached to Head Quarter House.

July 19, 1894
The marriage will take place this morning between Mr. Eustace A. Hall second son of the late Rev. B.B. Hall and Miss Agnes Surridge fourth daughter of the late Mr. Surridge.

July 21, 1894
The marriage of Mr. Hall with Miss Surridge was duly solemnized on Thursday morning at Peckover Church. Revd. M. Priestnal officiated, assisted by the Revd. H. Peckover. A large crowd gathered both in the Church and outside to catch a glimpse of the happy couple. The honey moon will be spent at Shortwood.

Advertizement

Richmond Villa School,
Brown's Town
High Class School for Young Ladies
Principal-Miss C.E. Morales
Assisted by Miss Mill-Muldary. A.A. Oxon., Certificated in Honours for Drawing, Painting etc., etc.
Superior Home School. Thorough
Modern Education in English Subjects, French Latin Science Music Piano and Violin, Drawing Painting etc.
Discipline and Moral Training Refinement of Manners are special policies combined with home comforts.
Very best climate in Jamaica
School reopen D.V. on Monday 30th July, 1894

July 26, 1894
Current Items
Why is it almost certain that Shakespeare was a broker? Because no man has furnished so many stock quotations.

1894

July 30, 1894

MILNE-On July 25th 1894 at 1 Manchester Square, Kingston, EMILY ANN widow of the late Reverend James Milne of First Hill, Trelawny.

July 31, 1894

SPRATT-On Saturday the 28th instant, at No 12 Manchester Street, Spanish Town, the wife of EDWD. SPRATT of a son.

August 1, 1894

PASSENGERS BOOKED

To leave Southampton today in the Atrato for this island; Miss E.M. Stuart, Miss F.A. Stuart, Mr. and Mrs. W.H. Mitchell.

August 10,1894

A concert will be given at Aboukir, St Anns on the 13th prox. The hon J.H. Levy will preside. The programme will consist of solos, duets, tableaux, &c. Dr. Hargreaves will be in attendance with his phonograph.

August 11, 1894 (Saturday)

The R.M.S. Atrato is due at Barbados on Monday morning from Southampton. She is due here on Friday morning next.

August 18, 1894

In the Atrato yesterday morning. From Southampton Miss E.M. Stewart, Miss F.A. Stewart. Mr. and Mrs. W.H. Mitchell, Mr. J.H. Vincent, Mr. and Mrs. A. Delisser and infant, Mr. T.N. Aguilar, Mr. A. W. Aguilar, Master Kennett Pringle His Honour Justice Lumb, Dr. L Crane, C.M.G. Master L. Crane. Master L Sisson; From Barbados; Captain H.L Crocket, Miss Priestman, Miss Arnold, Miss Johnstone, and 6 deckers from Jacmel; 2 deckers and 48 in transit also 7 to be landed her to await the arrival of the Larne to proceed to Savanilla.

August 22, 1894

St Ann's Bay

August 18

     We have been quiet this week and there is no news of much importance to communicate. The Wesleyans had their Missionary services on Sunday and Monday last. Sermons were preached by the Rev. W. C. Murray of York Castle in the morning and afternoon and by the Rev. Mr. Jacobs in the evening. Mr. Murray's ability as a preacher is too well known to need any comment and all we can say is that his sermon on Sunday morning was a "masterpiece". Mr. Jacobs made a favourable impression on the congregation on his first appearance in the St. Ann's Bay pulpit, which is a ticklish pulpit to preach in. The Missionary Meeting was rather tame; not so nice as in former years. There were no decorations and no platform and only two strange ministers as speakers. These facts made the meeting rather cold and there was a murmur of disappointment throughout. More.

     The Hon J.H. Levy our popular member visited this town on Thursday and was in such demand by his many friends and admirers that he could pay very little attention to his own business.

August 25, 1894

A pneumatic typewriter has just been invented in England.

Selected Vital Records from the Jamaican Daily Gleaner

August 27, 1894

A correspondent states that York Castle School was struck by lightning on Wednesday last, three servants being injured, though not seriously, by the electric fluid.

August 29, 1894

Mr. Vanderbilt's intention to introduce the mongoose into the United States has caused considerable newspaper and other comment, and the experience of Jamaica and Haiti are cited as an argument against its introduction.

August 31, 1894

Current Items

Hon J.H. Levy of St Anns came to town yesterday.

September 3, 1894

SILVERA-At 55 Church Street on the 29th inst. the wife of V. Silvera of Oracabessa of a son.

September 17, 1894

DELEON-At his residence No 23 Potters Row, Rae Town, CHARLES (CARLOS) M. DELEON, aged 73. Friends and acquaintances please accept this only intimation. The funeral will move at 4.30 this evening to Holy Trinity Church. Please let your carriage attend.

St Ann Interest in the Election

No 1 District Ocho Rios
Frank Ewen, Planter
Caleb Reynolds, Wesleyan Minister
E.N. Harrison, Shopkeeper

No2 Brown's Town, Dry Harbour District
J.H. Levy, Merchant
W.H. Miller, Medical Practitioner
L. Tapper, Planter
Victor Peat, Planter
John Allwood, Solicitor
A.S. Byles, Land Surveyor

No 3 St Ann's Bay Division
George House, Baptist Minster
John Duff, Wesleyan Minister
J.A. Miller, Jeweller
A.N. Dixon, Planter
F.L. Rodon, Chemist and Druggist
A.J. Hart, Auctioneer

No4 Pedro Claremont, Moneague Division
C.W. Steer
A.N. Sutherland, Shopkeeper
H. Brown, Shopkeeper
L. Lindo Wesleyan Minister.

1894

September 22, 1894
THE ELECTIONS
ST ANN
Ocho Rios
Friday There was great excitement at the election yesterday, but no fights occurred. The voting was the heaviest since the new departure. Result:-

E.H. Harrison	177
Frank Ewen	134
Rev. Caleb Reynolds	111

Special Gleaner Telegram
Brown's Town Sept 21st The election was orderly and satisfactory. Results

Byles	183
Levy	171
Tapper	155
Miller	87
Allwood	70
Peat	59

Peat was shut out. The Poll closed while National Anthem being played

Moneague, Sept 21st The election for 4 members for Moneague and Pedro division of St. Ann's closed at 7.30 p.m. yesterday
Following returned

Hamilton Brown	101
Rev. S.L. Lindo	84
A.N. Sutherland	69
Hon, C.W. Steer	44

Number of Votes polled far in excess of any previous election. Utmost good order prevailed all through.

September 28, 1894
Application has been made to the registrar for letters of administration on the estates of Frederick William Con Moltke Hart, late of St. Ann, deceased, by Ella Louise Hart, sister of the deceased. The personality is sworn at
£500

September 29, 1894
Mr. Edgar C. Motta, son of Mr. D. I. Motta of this city, has passed the senior examination in the first division of the Oxford Local Examination, and has gained the degree of "Associate of Arts". Mr. Motta was a pupil of Great Ealing? School.

St Ann's Bay Election
To the Editor of the Gleaner
     Sir I have not observed in the "Gleaner ' any report from your St Ann's Bay Correspondent, on the Parochial Election in the St Ann's Bay Division of the Parish of St Ann. This silence is easily accounted for
     The public will learn with interest and gratification that the "four old members' the happy family" as they have been so aptly and deservedly styled, were elected by overwhelming majorities to the utter annihilation and discomfiture of the representatives of democracy.
The following is the result of the voting:-
Elected

A.N. Dixon	275
J.A. Miller	275
Rev. J. Duff	271
Rev. G. House	243
Rejected	
F. L. Rodon	123
A.J. Hart	72

October 2, 1894
Advertizement

LEVY, Isaacs & Co.,
St Ann's Bay
Beg to call the attention of the Public to the fact that they have removed their Wholesale business from No 2 Bravo Street to the large and commodious premises know as the Market Store. No 35 Main Street. The business is now under the management of Mr. A.C. DUNKLEY. Courtesy and attention are guaranteed to every customer. A large assortment of Fancy and Staple Goods will always be kept on had. Lowest prices quoted. Regular cargoes of Flour Stuffs, Provisions, etc., etc., received from America We offer special inducements to Cash Customers and only ask for a trial to convince.
Received ex s.s. Louissianian and other recent arrivals
Cases Men's and Boy's caps in Tie over and Varsity
Cases Men's and Boys White Shirts from 24s to 60s
etc List not completely copied.

October 15, 1894
The Rev. Caleb Reynolds left here in the Don on Saturday for Colon, to proceed to Panama in order to report on the Mission work at that place.

October 17, 1894
ROPER 14th October at his residence Unity Valley, Moneague, St Ann's FINDLATER ROPER, L.L.B. Trin Coll.: Dublin, Barrister-at-Law. Aged 76

October 18, 1894
PRIZE DISTRIBUTION AT BARBICAN--Addresses by Rev. F.O.Miller and Rev. W. Simms
The annual prize distribution in connection with Barbican High School, St Andrew, took place on Tuesday evening before a good audience, chiefly composed of parents of the young ladies and friends. Column
The Rev Simms then distributed the prizes as follows:
1st Form Prize- Lucinda Cox
2nd " " - Ella Burke
3rd " " - Maud Cunha
3rd " improvement- L. Escoffery
4th " " - Anna Hollar
Shaded Drawing Kathleen Powell
Freehand Drawing -D. Kinkead
Music Prize-Kathleen Powell
Conduct Prize- L. Escoffery

October 25, 1894
Lindo- At Joslen Cottage, Musgrave Avenue on Tuesday 23rd inst., the wife of Arthur Lindo of a daughter

1894

Death of Dr A.G. McCatty Montego Bay died suddenly at his residence at 3 o'clock yesterday morning at the age of 60.
His remains were interred in the cemetery attach to the church this morning and were followed by a very large concourse of people. All classes were represented.

An address with a crayon portrait and pocket copy of the communion service, will be presented to the Rev. Clarke Murray at Edmondson Hall, on the 2nd prox. by admirers of his attitude in the recent Murray-Blemman controversy.

November 1, 1894
YORK CASTLE HIGH SCHOOL
Situation healthy. Record successful. Care homelike. Charges moderate. Education on the lines of the Cambridge Junior and Senior Examinations. Shorthand writing. Book-keeping and Typewriting taught by an expert without extra charge.
Type writing to begin after Christmas.
Apply to
REV. W. CLARKE MURRAY, D.D. York Castle P.O.

November 3, 1894
Latest Telegrams
The death of the Czar
New York, Nov 2 Official information from St Petersburg was wired yesterday afternoon through [out] the world announcing that the Czar had died peacefully. 1/4 column.

Ecclesiastical Echoes
The Rev. H.H. Isaacs would be pleased to know if there is extant any older inscription on Mural Slab or Tablet that the following, which is to be found in the old church yard, Half-way Tree:-
"Here lyeth inter'd the body of Mr. George Bennett, who came here a soldier under General Venables, the 10th day of May 1665, and one of the first settlers. He was of a Dorsetshire family. Here also lyeth inter'd the body of Mrs. Sarah Bennett, the wife of his grandson, the Hon. George Bennett, Esqre. who departed this life the 8th day of October, 1733 aged 58 years."

November 5, 1894
PRESENTATION TO THE REV.W. CLARKE MURRAY
On Friday night last the presentation of an address and testimonial to the Rev. W. Clarke Murray for his services during the recent Murray-Blenman controversy took place at Emondson Hall. About 250 persons were present among them being Revds. T.M. Geddes (President)Revd. T.A. Glasspool and D.D. Parnther, Dr. Love, Messrs Lunan, Cassis, H. A. Cunha, Thompson &c.
After preliminary devotional exercises the Revd. Mr. Geddes said he was sure that every one present would not object to some music, prior to the presentation. Selections &c were rendered on the piano by Mr. Cunha and Miss Clark and two songs were rendered by the Misses Geddes.
Mr. Geddes then said that the meeting would make a memorable page in the history of Kingston. It was in recognition of services rendered by Mr. Murray. In March the building was besieged by a large crowd. Kingston never witnessed such a gathering to hear such a subject. It was a great surprise to the people. A man had come to this island with a strange doctrine, declaring that man's life was no better than a dog's. Mr.

Murray came forward to combat that doctrine and did so fearlessly, for the stranger struck at the foundation of his life's convictions. He was not speaking now as a Wesleyan but as a Christian. The meeting was representative in as much as there were members of all denominations present. He was proud that a Wesleyan minister had the courage to do that work, which he was so fitted to do from his experience. He had known Mr. Murray for 40 years and he knew it was not from the mere desire to debate that he had taken up the work. He must also compliment Dr. Love for the efficient manner he filled the chair and conducted the debates.

Dr Love, Messrs Cunha, Cassis, Patterson, Lunan, Stewart, the gentlemen deputed by the subscribers came forward and Dr. Love present M. Murray with a silver pocket Communion Service and a large crayon portrait of that gentleman and in doing so made a lengthy address to which Mr. Murray replied suitably.

The Rev. D.D. Parnther gave a song and the proceedings were brought to a close by the singing of "God save the Queen".

November 10, 1894
COOPER-At Twickenham Park, St Ann, WILLIAM COOPER in his 75th year, leaving a wife and eight children to mourn their irreparable loss. Requiescat in pace.

November 16, 1894
SUTTON-On November 11th at Mandeville the wife of Leonard Sutton of a daughter.

November 19, 1894
McCREA on 16th inst., at Chapelton the wife of Harry McCrea, of a son.

December 4, 1894
It is stated by the Brown's Town Fortnightly Review that Mr. J.H. Allwood of Brown's Town intends to become a candidate for Trelawny in case of an election in that parish for a representative in the Legislative Council.

In this island says the Fornightly Review (Brown's Town) one solitary teacher, with perhaps a boy or two to assist him as pupil teachers has to keep order among and teach over a hundred children. If some of the amateur writers on the subject would try their hand at teaching such a school they would probably soon begin to write on the subject of cruelty to teachers".

December 11, 1894
Reliable Investment
For sale
Milford in the parish of Saint Ann's situate 1½ miles from Brown's Town containing 60 acres more or less, the property abounds in Pimento, there is fine residence, Drawing room, Dining Hall, four Bed Rooms, Kitchen, Pantry Pimento House, &c, &c Elevation 700 feet above the level of the sea, splendid sea view, and healthy locality. Pastures being planted in grass, the land is adapted for Coffee. Price £400, for permission to view apply to Mr. A. NOATT. Brown's Town or the undersigned prepaid.
JOHN COVER
Lime Tree Garden
Brown's Town

1894

December 19, 1894
Tom Redcam's Poem

A London publisher, probably Messrs. Spottiswoode, will bring out during 1895 a volume of poems by our local author "Tom Redcam". In the first division of the book, "Songs of Jamaica" pieces specially West Indian will be placed. The second part will be poems of "Reverie and Revealment" The pages will probably number 160 and there will be some 60 poems altogether. The price of the volume is not to exceed five shillings. In Jamaica Mr. Justin McCarthy 8 King Street is the gentleman to whom orders should be sent. The volume is to be dedicated to well known and popular West Indian Governor.

December 28, 1894
Brown's Town

Dec 26.-This little place and its surroundings have been the scene of much enjoyment among all classes of persons. The churches have been at work with harvest festivals and although not as successful as might have been on account of the rains that fell, yet on the whole we are grateful

We are pleased to be able to report a fair business on Xmas. There were two markets, Saturday and Monday, and we are sure from the smiles on the storekeepers faces that plenty of money has been taken.

Today at "Lawrence Park" is to be seen races by those who like that sort of sport, and tomorrow at St Ann's Bay will be a concert. On the 2nd January 1895 there will be a concert at our Court House here, in assistance to the Methodist Church for repairs to school house. We expect good success and shall be very disappointed if we do not get a full house.

So far as we have gone and this is the 26th the greatest quiet and good order has prevailed, not even the usual drumming. All our stores and shops have been closed and everybody is enjoying his and her holiday without gluttony or drunkenness

"Lynche's" Artillery has been well engaged at the Court yard throwing up blocks of stone for the new court house, and we expect as result a pretty building, however small the accommodations may be.

1895

January 15, 1895
DELGADO-At Rockville, Brown's Town, St Ann's on Sunday 13th January, EMMA PHOEBE DELGADO, daughter of the late Charles and Harriette Delgado of Falmouth, and beloved sister of Charles Phillips, and Alfred Leopolda Delgado and grand daughter F S. Levien.
"Hear O Israel the Lord our God the Lord is one.
Blessed are they who die in His names."

January 16, 1895
LORD-At Ainslie, Old Harbour, on the 14th inst. the wife of C.G. Lord of a son.

January 17, 1895
SNAITH-At No 6 Tower Street, in this city on the 14th instant, LAURA, relict of the late George B. Snaith, of Greenwall Pen, in the parish of St Thomas, aged 68 years.

January 28, 1895
DEATH FROM EATING AKEES
BULL BAY, Jan 21, A Case of akee poisoning occurred here on Thursday last, 17th instant.
The victim was a boy of six years, the son of a labourer residing at Claremont pen in this district.
It appears that his mother put away some akee (apparently unripe) which the boy contrived to reach and eat. The result of course, was that between 9 and 10 o'clock that night he died. The body however was not buried until Saturday afternoon, as there was no Justice of the Peace to give the necessary order-this district not being blessed with the presence of that very rare "article".

January 25, 1895
WALKER-Yesterday evening at 7 Highholborn Street, CHARLES ARUNDEL WALKER. Funeral will take place this afternoon at 4.30. Friends will please let their carriages attend.

February 1, 1895
Hon J.H. Levy
The Honourable J.H. Levy intends paying a visit to St Mary, and will meet the Electors at the Port Maria Court House on Thursday 7th Feby., his chief object being to hear their views on the recent despatch from the Secretary of State in reference to extend representation on the terms proposed.

Selected Vital Records from the Jamaican Daily Gleaner

February 15, 1895

A fancy costume ball is to come off in St Ann's Bay on the 21st inst. at the Court House. Nearly 400 invitations have been issued. It is expected that all who have the opportunity will go in costume and not in ordinary evening dress. The Committee of Management are Messrs. T. Alexander, C.F. Duff, W.G. Nunes, A.B. Rerrie, D. Hart, Dr. J. L. Cox and C.M. Ormsby.

February 20, 1895

GRAHAM-AT the Rectory Moore Town, on Friday, February 15th, the wife, of the Revd. J.W. Graham of a son.

February 21, 1895

Barbican High School Examination Successes.

Barbican High School entered 10 pupils for the College of Preceptor's examination in December last. Everyone passed in the class for which she was entered, and this is especially gratifying as it is the first time the school has entered pupils for this examination. Miss Powell gained a special certificate for drawing. The following is a list in order of merit of the successful candidates:-

K.H. Powell Class II, Division 1
V.M. Cunha Class II, Division 1
S.L. Escoffery Class II, Division 1
D.T. Kinkead Class II, Division 1
Z. Marchelleck, Class II, Division 3
L.E. Nicholas Class III, Division 1
E.M. Porter Class III, Division 1
M.A. James Class III, Division 2
L. Ermandez Class III, Division 2
M.J. Athias, Class III, Division 2

The subjects passed in were, besides English, Mathematics, French, Music, Drawing and Political Economy.

February 22, 1895

MERRICK-WATSON-On the 18th inst. at "Llielworth Cottage," the wife of R. Merrick-Watson of a son.

March 2, 1895

PHILLIPPO-On the 1st March, at Fair View, St Andrew, the wife of E.C. PHILLIPPO, of a son.

March 8, 1895

The Wesleyan Conference

The Wesleyan Conference was opened at Montego Bay on Wednesday this week.

At 7 a.m. a public prayer meeting was held, at which there was a crowded congregation. At 10 a.m. after the Conference was constituted, the Rev. W. Clarke Murray, D.D., was selected Vice President. The Rev. John Duff was re-elected Secretary for the year; on whose selection the Revs. S.L. Lindo and T.W. Peeling were appointed Assistant Secretaries.

Trelawny Girl's School.

Information was received by last mail from Mrs. Trafford, Hon. Secretary of the Ladies Committee of the Trelawny Girls School in England, that they had appointed Miss Alice M. Townsend of Romford to the post of Lady Principal of the School. More.

1895

March 11, 1895
BUSULTIL-WARD At Holy Trinity Church, on the 21st ultimo, by the Revd. Father MacCormick, MICHAEL BUSTIL, Leicestershire Regt., eldest son of B. Busultil, Esq., Malta, to CONSTANCE, eldest, daughter of Lieut. Col, the Honble. C.J. Ward, C.M.G., Custos of Kingston.

March 28, 1895
On the 17th inst. Mr. A.J. Hart of St Ann's Bay will sell a lot of thorough bred horses which belonged to the late Mr. Findlater Roper. The mares &c are first class stock and names and pedigrees can be seen in the catalogue which can be got at the places mentioned in the advertisement. Mr. Hart will also sell at the same place, Frankfort wharf 5 miles from Ocho Rios a good centre for buying and shipping produce.

April 3, 1895
Current Items
We are pleased to learn that the hon. J.T. Orrett is improving rapidly.

April 5, 1895
Advertizement

F.W. Couch,
Art Tailor
21 King Street, Kingston
The only Establishment from which gentlemen can obtain a good fitting garment of any design.
[Picture of a lady on a horse with "Couch Specialty"]
Ladies Riding Habits
and Jackets
A Specialty
N.B. I the original F.W. Couch, begs to notify the public in general that I have so connection whatever with any other firm in the Parade{?}

April 10, 1895
The thorough-bred horses owned by the late Hon. Findlater Roper of Unity Valley Pen, St Ann will be sold by Public Auction on April 17th.

April 17, 1895
GILLIES at Beith,(Keith?) Renfrewshire, Scotland, on the 15th March, ROBERT GILLIES, Esq., J.P., brother of the Rev. William Gillies, Kingston.

April 18, 1895
Dry Harbour is to have an artesian well, and it is also likely that one will be sunk at Brown's Town.

April 23, 1895
St Aubyn-On the 19th April at Black River, the Hon'ble Mrs. Arthur St Aubyn of a son.

BOURKE-At 18 Sutton St. on the 21st ELIZA ANN, relict of the late Charles N.E. Bourke and second daughter of the late Henry Lord Garriques. Peace perfect peace. English papers please copy.

Selected Vital Records from the Jamaican Daily Gleaner

April 24, 1895

The town clock in the Tower of the Falmouth parish Church was placed there in the year 1796 and repaired for the first time by Mr. Rudolph Forster of Montego Bay on the 18th April 1895

April 27, 1895

The Family of Franklin or Franklyn

The secretary of the Institute of Jamaica has recently received a letter from Mr. W.H. Dickinson, 5 Wesley Terrace, Hyde Park Road, Plymouth, England asking for information about the family of Franklin or Franklyn in Jamaica. Mr. Dickinson writes "I am assisting a friend to draw up a pedigree of the old family of Franklin or Franklyn of Jamaica and I enclose you a copy of what we have got so far"...............Includes a pedigree. Asks about Mr. Henry Franklin of Lignum Vitae Grove a solicitor.

May 3, 1895

COLTHIRST-At Fairview, Saint Andrew, on Thursday the 2nd May, THERESA MARIA, widow of the late Honble Henry Forbes Colthirst. The funeral will leave at 4.30 p.m. today for Saint Andrew's Church.

St Ann's Bay
Burial of Paupers

We have read of late in the papers, letters on the subject of the burial of paupers, more particularly in respect to the absence of any religious ceremony at the grave side.

Here in St. Ann's Bay things appear to be better managed. In the Lodge at the Cemetery fate, is a slope on which is a ruled up book, in which the minister conducting a service over the dead inserts all particulars.

[paragraph]

I have seen myself, the Reverend George House (our respected Baptist Minister) waiting over an hour for a funeral, in wet weather, and when he was apparently drenched to the skin, yet he declined to leave for home until he had performed the late solemn rites over the departed pauper.

Our worthy Rector, Mr. Ripley is also most assiduous in his attention in the respect and never fails to attend when called upon.

May 7, 1895

A meeting of the Jamaica Church Theological College Debating Society will be held at the College this evening at 7 o'clock. Mr. J. L. Ramson, of the Jamaica High School, will read a paper on the "Chautauqua movement" and the Rev. C.H. Coles will give an account of "University Extension movement in England".

Yesterday Bedward was conveyed to the Lunatic Asylum under a strong police escort.

May 9, 1895

Lewis-At Enfield, Manchester, on the 2nd May, 1895 after a few hours suffering, JULIA VICTORIA widow of the late Henry Cerf Lewis, Esq., J.P. Aged 57 years and 6 months.

May 15, 1895

HALL-At Ulster Spring in the parish of Trelawny, on Sunday the 12th inst. the wife of John H. HALL of a daughter.

1895

Among the passengers expected with the W.I.P.S.S. Co Costa Rican to arrive her on the 16th inst. is Miss Alice Townsend, who has come to fill the post of Lady Principal of the Trelawny Girls' School under the management of the Rev. W. M. Webb of Stewart Town. Miss Townsend is accompanied by Mrs. Townsend her mother who will find useful engagement in the institution.

May 16, 1895
BYLES-At his residence "The Lawn" Spanish Town on the 15th inst., after a short illness THEOPHILUS LYNCH BYLES. Funeral will move at 4.30 p.m. today. Friends and acquaintances will please accept this intimation.

May 23, 1895
Panton-At Waliham House, Mandeville Sunday morning, May the 19th CHARLOTTE widow of the late Archdeacon Panton. The family take this opportunity of thanking friends for their affectionate sympathy. "Till He Comes".

May 31, 1895
COVER-At Inglewood Villa, Brown's Town, the wife of Rev. H.A. Cover of a daughter.

June 4, 1895
The Crops in St Ann's
A Correspondent writing from Brown's Town says:- Our pimento crop may not be a large one, for the heavy winds which have passed over the groves have blown off a lot of the berries, and there being a worm that has taken to boring the trees, whereby the trees wither and die, it is reasonable to expect that the crop will be small. The coffee crop bids fair, and we hope with earnestness that the growers will see that it is cured, and not as heretofore bring to market a spurious article. More.

June 6, 1895
MAGNUS After a short illness at Montego Bay, between the hours of eight and nine o'clock on Sunday morning 2nd June, 1895 aged 50 years, JANE ANNA Second daughter of the late Simon and Esther Magnus. "May her Soul be bound in the Bundle of Life".

June 7, 1895
The AKEE QUESTION
What the Commission has not Done
The season for akees which is now over has not passed away without its cases of poisoning through eating the fruit. Many people now decline to eat the fruit at all preferring to run no risks. So far as can be found out there is no danger in eating the fruit provided care is taken to cook only that which is properly fresh and ripe. The unfit akee can always be distinguished by the imperfect formation of the stones and the extreme paleness of the red substance that adheres to the fruit. More.

June 10, 1895
Mr. T. Ellis Bawton, Chemist replies to The Akee Question. He thinks the analysis is not difficult.

June 17, 1895
MOSSMAN-At Linstead, St Thomas Ye Vale on the 9th inst., R.G. Mossman Aged 46 years

Wortley Yesterday at Henbury Cottage, Norman Road, Mrs. HELEN MARY WORTLEY, aged 66. Funeral at 5 p.m. today.

NEW YORK June 6th A very nice little wedding took place last night at St Paul's Episcopal Church, Brooklyn N.Y. and as the bride and groom are both native Jamaicans, a few details might interest readers of the GLEANER.
Christiana Mary, youngest daughter of the late Dr. Alex Geo. McCatty of Montego Bay was married to Dr. Oswald D. F. Robertson, son of Henry Robertson, Esq. of Burnt Ground.

June 29, 1895
Mr. S.S. Wortley has applied to the Governor for a telephone license for Montego Bay.

July 2, 1895
Kingston High School for Girls
Annual Prize Distribution
The fourth annual school gathering of the Kingston High School for girls and Kindergarten was held at 14 Elletson Road Yesterday at noon. There was a large number of parents, and friends of the institution, present, and the Right Revd. C.F. Douet, D.D., presided and distributed the prizes.
Column and a half
Prizes
His Lordship then distributed the prizes:-
Certificates
Second place in term marks, Form IV, Amy Tilley
Second place in term marks, Form III, May Wortley
Second place in term marks, Form II, Clarisse Lewis
Second place in term marks, Form I May Francis
Highest place in German marks, May Thompson
Highs place in French marks, May Wortley
Prizes
Highest percentage in term marks Form IV, Lois Roberts
Highest percentage in term marks, Form III, Blanche Nethersole
Highest percentage in term marks, Form II Helen Brown
Highest percentage in term marks, Form I Norah Brown
Scripture prize, awarded by the Lord Bishop of Jamaica, Senior Division, May Thompson, Junior Division, Helen Brown
Needlework prize, Senior Division, Lois Roberts; Junior Division, Amy Phillips
Good conduct prize, awarded by the vote of teachers and pupils to Helen Brown.

July 10, 1895
We are sorry to observe that the Brown's Town Fortnightly Review has ceased publication. It was edited by Mr. S.H. Wheeldon and was a bright, well written journal with a literary touch about it. Its publication in an inland town was against its success. Mr. Wheeldon has been in ill health recently.

July 15, 1895
Obit for Mr. K.J. Spicer of St Ann's Bay.

July 16, 1895
Stockhausen At Clarice Ville, Upper Orange Street, on the 14th inst. the wife of J.H. Stockhausen of a son

DaCosta-Crosswell On the 10th inst. at the Kingston Parish Church, by the Revd. G.W. Downer, Rector, assisted by Revd. G. Thompson; WILLOUGHBY EUSTACE, youngest son of the late Albert DaCosta, to MARIE LOUISE second daughter of the late Abraham N. Crosswell.

July 23, 1895
GAUNTLETT-SMITH-At Mt. Fletcher, on the 11th instant, by the Revd. A. McNeil Smith, father of the bride, assisted by the Revd. G.S. Lamb, WALTER CHARLES, eldest son of the late Edward G. Gauntlett, of Spanish Town to JULIA ALEXANDRIA eldest daughter of the Revd. A. McNeil Smith.

July 27, 1895
Brown's Town
     July 24 If the old couplet "Satan finds some mischief still For idle hands to do" is really a true saying, there should be a great deal of devilry going off in Brown's Town just now, for very little business is stirring. Stores that should employ one or two active men, have got trade enough to occupy one lazy woman, and tradesmen are more occupied in dunning for old debts that in working to earn fresh money.
     Honest men will soon give over going to church if the condition of our churches does not improve for no honest man like to get into bad company. more
     The new Anglican Church is now approaching completion and it is expected that it will be opened about the middle of September, though the date is not definitely fixed. It is a handsome building and is a decided ornament to the town... Its rector will we feel sure agree with us in hoping that the new church will become not merely a fashionable pleasure resort for Sundays, but that it will become a real power for good in the district-a place where men who have been in the habit of telling lies will learn to speak the truth, and where thieves will learn to steal no more.
     The squabbling about the water supply still continues. Mr. Allwood, backed up by influential friend is doing his best to prevent the tanks from being made.

July 30, 1895
FACEY-At his residence, South Musgrave Avenue, Kingston Jamaica on Saturday 27 July 1895, JAMES MALCOLM FACEY late Clerk of the Eastern District Court, Port Antonio.

July 31, 1895
YORK CASTLE HIGH SCHOOL,
This school will resume work after the Midsummer Vacation on Friday the 26th July. Applications for admission should be made early and to
Rev. W. Clarke Murray, D. D. York Castle P.O.

August 2, 1895
The examination of Messrs. Judah, Lynch and Clarke, prior to their being admitted to practice as Solicitors, will take place on the 6th inst.

August 5, 189 5
DUFFUS-BRANCH-ON THE 15TH July, 1895 at Barruallie, St Vincent, by the Revd Canon Branch (father of the bride) BERTIE this third daughter, to the Revd. DAVID A.M. DUFFUS, B.A. S.T.H. (Durham), Rector of St Andrews, Grenada and youngest son of the late James Duffus, Esq., of Aberdeen.

LYALL-SPRATT-On the 23rd April, at Oodnadatta, South Australia, JAMES CHARLES HAROLD LYALL, eldest son of James Charles Lyall, of Woodlands, Islington, England, to ALICE MARIA, fourth daughter of the late Revd, Edward Spratt, of Duncans Jamaica, Wesleyan minister.

August 6, 1895
St Ann's Bay Baptist Chapel
The Re-opening
Mentions Rev. George House and other Baptist ministers. 3/4 page column.

August 8, 1895
PURCHAS-TODD-On the 1st August at St George's Church, Kingston, by the Rev.J.P. Hall assisted by the Revs H.H. Kilburn, and Lund, FREDK. ARTHUR GORDON PURCHAS, M.B. C.M. EDIN, son of the late H.M. Purchas of Swanswick Trelawny, to ELIZA (CISSIE) only daughter of the late U. T. Todd, Jr., of Orange Valley, St Ann.

August 9, 1895
The Rev H.A. Cover, Church of England minister, has resigned his appointment as a Marriage Officer for the parish of St Catherine.

August 14, 1895
Mrs. McCrea and family would ask their friends in England, San Francisco New York, and Panama, to accept sincere thanks for kingly proffered sympathy in their affliction and condolence in their recent sorrow.

August 16, 1895
WALDER-At Mizpah Mission House, Walderston Parish of Manchester, Jamaica August 10th, 1895, in the 59th year of his life, Rev. Heinrick Walder, Minister of the Moravian Churches at Mizpah, Moravia and Ritchies.

August 17, 1895
The TRINITY COLLEGE MUSICAL EXAMINATION
Senior Honours Marks 100
Beatrice Mary Burger, passed, 83
INTERMEDIATE DIVISION , passed section
Irene Beatrice Lindo passed, 98
Ada Mary Lindo, passed, 98
Junior Division, (pass section)
Henry Alexander Lindo, passed 98
May Thornton Jeffrey Smith passed, 98
Mabel Gertrude Delisser passed, 95
Isabel Emily McBauee passed 92
Una Adeline Jeffrey-Smith passed, 90
Jessie Isabell Harrison passed, 90

Miss Burger who took senior honours was prepared by Mr. Ernest Sibthorpe and the other candidate by Mrs. Danvers, Miss Lindo of Holmwood, and Miss Jeffrey-Smith.

Ecclesiastical Echoes
We are sorry to state that the Rev. G. Bathurst Hall, Rector of Holy Trinity Church, Montego Bay is still very ill.

1895

August 19, 1895

W.Cover Esq., Jr gave 10/6d to Westwood High School for Girls Building Fund.

August 20, 1895

ANOTHER SUCCESFUL JAMAICAN

Among the passengers by the R.M.S. Atrato arrived on Friday was Dr. Ernest Murray, son the of the Revd,. W. Clarke Murray, D.D. Governor of the York Castle High School. Dr. Murray won the Jamaica Scholarship 7 years ago and has now returned to his native land where he intends to follow his profession, preferring Jamaica, notwithstanding many inducements to remain in London. The diplomas of Dr. Murray are M.B. and B.Sc. London . We welcome the Doctor, and wish him a prosperous career in his native land.

August 26, 1895

We are glad to state that the Rev. G. Bathurst Hall, Rector of Holy Trinity Church who was very seriously ill is now very much better.

September 3, 1895

Mary Jane Watson is still using the same advertizement.

September 7, 1895

HOW KIPLING TREATED AN IMPOSTER

A Letter from Kipling June 14, 1895

September 9, 1895

A JAMAICAN ABROAD

We take from the Pinang Gazetteer of the 9th July an account of the presentation of a Jubilee Testimonial to the Hon. J.M. Vermont. That gentleman is a Jamaican, having been born in Falmouth. He is a brother of the late H.S. Vermont, Esq., of Cascades in the Parish of St Mary and as he has many relatives and friends in Jamaica the article will prove interesting:- 3/4 column.

Brown's Town

Sept 6.

Missionary sermons will be preached in the Wesleyan Church on Sunday the 8th inst. by the Rev Caleb Reynolds.

The usual meeting will be held on Tuesday following when addresses are to be delivered by the Revds. Brown, Harty Henderson, Duff, Reynolds and others.

Mr. Cooper, manager of Musgrave House has just returned from a visit to the U.S.A. He looks well.

September 14, 1895

Mr. A.J. Hart auctioneer of St Ann's Bay, has succeeded in disposing of "Chester Pen", the property of F.A. Morris, Esq., to C. L. Reece, Esq., brother to (J)I?.R. Reece, R.M. of St Ann's late of Barbados. Mr. Reece takes possession on September 15th.

September 19, 1895

SOWLEY At Leicester Ville, St Andrews, on the 15th inst. the wife of A.E. Sowley of a daughter.

Selected Vital Records from the Jamaican Daily Gleaner

September 27, 1895
LEVIEN At the residence of C.M. Sherlock 68 Harbour St. Kingston, SIDNEY LINDO
LEVIEN in his 87th year. Funeral will move at 3.30 p.m. Friends will please accept this
intimation and kingly attend.

October 10, 1895
St George's College
The monthly reading of marks took place on Monday October 7 at 1.30 p.m. in St
George's' College Hall in presence of His Lordship Bishop Gordon etc. Gives names of
Roman Catholic pupils.

October 15, 1895
Brown's Town
Oct 6, ACCIDENT
Mr. A. Isaacs of the wholesale department, Musgrave House, met with what might have
proved a very serious accident a few days ago. Whilst examining a loaded revolver, by
some mistake it went off, the bullet piercing one of his fingers. What's most
extraordinary the bullet passed though the finger without injuring the bone.
More about the water supply.

October 18, 1895
BRANDON On the 17th inst. at Maud Villa, Rae Street, Rae Town, the wife of C.A.
Brandon of a daughter.

October 29, 1895
CASSERLY ON 26TH October, at Kingston, the wife of JAMES M. CASSERLY of a
son

November 1, 1895
The abstract of birth and deaths registered in the Island during the quarter ended 30th
September was published in yesterday's gazette.

November 8, 1895
ARSCOTT-At Berry Hill, St Ann, on the 3rd inst. after great suffering, MARY ANN
aged 46 years; only daughter of the late Dr. David Mahony, and beloved wife of Charles
D. Arscott, Leaving a large family to mourn their sad loss
Farewell, dear friends my life is past
May we, in Heaven, unite at last,
Mourn not for me nor sorrow take,
but love my children for my sake.

November 15, 1895
DELISSER-At Ballatter Cottage, South Camp Road on 29th October, the wife of
STANLEY DELISSER of a son.

November 20, 1895
NOAH-At Brown's Town on Sunday the 10th inst. a 3.30 a.m. after a brief illness,
ABRAHAM NOAH OF 'The Ark' Chapelton. English papers will please copy.

1895

December 5,1895

Mr. George Orrett of the Atlas Company was married yesterday to Miss Croskery an account of the wedding will appear in Saturday's issue.

December 16, 1895

Cambridge Locals

The Cambridge Local Examinations begins today in Jamaica at three centres-Kingston, Sav-la-Mar and the High School. The number of students who have gone up is greatly over that in previous years 250 in all. In Kingston, the increase has caused the examination of the boys to be conducted in the Collegiate Hall and the girls in the Mico. The former number 107 the latter 42. The presiding examiners in Kingston are the Revs H.S. Isaacs, L. Tucker, and W. Pratt; in Sav la Mar Mr. W. Cowper, of the High School and at the High School, Mr. W.H. Mitchell of York Castle.

December 18, 1895

VICKERS At Fontabelle Estate, Westmoreland, on 11th December, HUGH ANTHONY VICKERS Esquire, in his 50th year.

December 23, 1895

Death of Mr. James L. Verley

The deceased was the son of Mr. Louis Verley by his first wife and was about 47 years of age. 1/4 column

December 31, 1895

Lindo At Woodlawn, South Camp Road on Monday 23rd inst. the wife of W. A. Lindo of a daughter.

1896

January 2, 1896
HOPWOOD-At Lilyfield, St Ann, on the night of Saturday 28th Decr, the wife of ALEX HOPWOOD of a daughter.

January 7, 1896
Died. SCARLETT-At Mandeville, on 3rd inst. GRACE, infant daughter of C.L. and M.E. Scarlett.

January 20, 1896
THE NEW LEGISLATIVE COUNCIL
President:
Sir Henry A. Blake, K.C.M.G., Governor
Ex-Officio Members:
Hon Major General H.J .Hallowes, C.B. Commander of the Forces
Hon Fred. Evans, C.M.G. Colonial Secretary
Hon Henry R. Pipon Schooles, Attorney General.
Hon V.G. Bell, C.E. Director of Public Works.
Hon Robert Batten, Collector General
NOMINATED MEMBERS
(at present)
Hon Thomas Capper, B.A. Superintending Inspector of Schools,
Hon C.B. Moose, C.B. Superintending Medical Officer
Hon Col C.J. Ward, C.M.G. Member of the Privy Council.
Hon Dr. John Pringle Member of the Privy Council
ELECTED MEMBERS
Hon Philip Stern, Kingston.
Hon Rev. Carey B. Berry, St Andrew
Hon S.C. Burke, St Thomas.
Hon D.S. Gideon, Portland.
Hon A.D.C. Levy, St Mary
Hon A.N. Dixon, St Ann,
Hon. D. Campbell, St Catherine.
Hon R.B. Braham, Clarendon.
Hon J. T. Palache, Manchester.
Hon R.P. Leyden, St Elizabeth.
Hon Rev. Henry Clarke, Westmoreland.
Hon. De B. Spenser-Heaven, Hanover.
Hon D.A. Corinaldi, St James.
Hon C. Whiting, Trelawny.

Selected Vital Records from the Jamaican Daily Gleaner

THE ELECTIONS

We have received a number of communications relative to the recent elections; many from persons dissatisfied with the result in their respective parishes. We think the more gracious way would be to accept the decision of the electorate with out demur. We do not see how the complaints can do any good, and they are better left unpublished. The subjoined article from a correspondent in St Ann seems to possess more than ordinary interest in view of the fact of which we have been informed, that Dr. Johnston and his committee are determined to have a fresh election.

THE SCENE AT BROWN'S TOWN
[From a Correspondent]

Brown's Town in St Ann, has had many memorable days in his history. When the market was opened by the Governor, and when the new church was opened by Bishop Nuttall crowds of people came down into Brown's Town to witness these events. But long as these occasions will live in the memory of the inhabitants, they shrink into utter insignificance compared with the election day on Thursday last.

From valley and mountain vast throngs of excited people came pouring into Brown's Town, till its main street was packed with the enthusiastic multitude. Across the street, mottoes, were stretched some in favour of Mr. Dixon, others for Dr. Johnston. In front of Mr. Levy's store placards were posted on behalf of Mr. Dixon, while the two other leading merchants of the town, Mr. Delgado and Mr. Thomson, were working hard for Dr. Johnston.

A brass band, hired here for the occasion by Mr. Dixon's side, promenaded the town. It is not often that a brass band is an object of dislike among the musical loving people of Brown's Town, but on this occasion its melody was at a discount for the people of Brown's Town were wild in their enthusiastic support, of Dr. Johnston. A crowd of the Doctors supporters formed themselves into a band, and marched through the town singing their election song, a doggerel rhyme written for the occasion by Mr. Wheeldon and set to a popular tune.

But the chief interest of the day centered round the polling station at the Court House. Here Mr. Harry Levy stood exhorting the people through an immense speaking trumpet to vote for Mr. Dixon, while his younger brother, Mr. Willie Levy practised his unfledged speaking ability at intervals on the same theme. The two young gentlemen had to take some rather abrupt back answers from the crowd.

"You talk to us about Missa Dixon" said one "We know Docta Johnston, but we know nothing 'tall 'bout Missa Dixon. Where Missa Dixon now?"

"Oh he's ill in bed," replied Mr. Willie

"You bet Doctor aint in bed today" was the reply. "We wants a man to represent us dat wont stay in bed. What your father ever done for us while him in de Council. Him just go an' come back an' don't have noting fe shew dat he done fe us."

And so the talking went on, the young Levy's and Mr. Byles the surveyor being especially active in trying to stem the current of opinion which was running so strongly in favour of Doctor Johnston. Meanwhile an excited throng of voters were struggling to get through the door into the polling place to record their votes. Some elbows were pushed out and shoulders used in pushing, while great beads of perspiration stood on the faces of the men as they struggled for a little breathing space. The door of the polling place stood at the top of a low flight of steps and when these movements of the would be voters took place half a dozen men would be tumbled in a heap off the platform.

The writer turned away his eyes for a moment from the voters to survey the vast throng of people who had gathered to watch the exciting scene. There must have been a thousand or so of these spectators, most of them standing on the road which led up the hill to the new Court House. In the balcony of the new Court House I could see Dr. Turton, who is a friend of Dr. Johnston looking down on the crowd and watching for a chance to vote. He never saw the chance, for he, like hundreds of others, had to go away without voting.

Suddenly the crowd on the road broke out into a huge shriek of merriment, I turned to look for the cause, and could hardly believe my eyes when I say an old man with a grey beard struggling on all fours on the heads of the voters near the door. How on earth he got there I don't know; but there he was struggling as best he could looking very angry and displeased, while those below him were shoving him away with their hands. The sight of this old grey heading man in such a ludicrous position was inexpressibly comical; and they crowd yelled again and again with laughter until a last the old fellow was safely deposited on the outside of the troop of voters.

Its goes without saying that many a self-respecting man who wished to vote refused to adventure his body in this tumultuous crowd. The Rev. Webb of Stewart Town, one of Dr. Johnston's leading supporters, came up to record his vote, but had to go back without doing so. One respectable old man told me that he had come up three times at intervals to vote but could not get in. It is said that one enthusiastic supporter of Dr. Johnston finding he could not vote at Brown's Town, traveled all the way to the Bethany polling station some seven or eight miles away and voted there. It is commonly reported that Dr. Johnston's committee has stated that some two hundred supporters of his who went to vote for him were unable to do so.

While this strange scene was being enacted outside the polling station another scene equally strange was for a part of the time enacted inside. There were only two voting tables one, of them presided over by Mr. O'Meally the Returning Officer, and the other by Mr. Bennett. Mr. O'Meally suddenly fell down in a fit and remained unconscious.

The door was shut, the voting totally stopped for half an hour or so, and medical gentlemen called to attend to the prostrate gentleman. As he continued unconscious, a telegram was sent to Mr. Thomas, the chief Returning Officer at St Ann's Bay asking for instructions. He wired back instructions that Mr. Dignum must be asked to act for Mr. O'Meally, or failing Dr. Dignum, Mr. W. Brown Jr. Mr. Dignum was sent for, Mr. Mornan, the agent of Mr. Dixon, handed in a written protest against his acting on the ground that he was a minor. Mr. Brown was then sent for twice and at last he arrived and went on with Mr. O'Meally's work. Mr. Bennett's table had been stopped about half an hour, and Mr. O'Meally's three hours and a quarter. During the day 206 votes were taken at Mr. Bennett's table, against only 117 at Mr. O'Meally's.

The people of Brown's Town are very much dissatisfied at the way the election was conducted. It is confidently asserted that if all the voters who had applied to Dr. Johnston's agent to have their numbers on the list found had be able to record their votes, there would have been a total majority in favour of Dr. Johnston. The best way out of the difficulty is for Mr. Dixon and Dr. Johnston to make a mutual application to have the election held over again. It is an open secret that Mr. Dixon is not anxious to go the Council, and whatever may be said for or against his ability, even his opponents believe that he will refuse to accept a seat which has not been fairly won.

January 24, 1896

Public opinion in Brown's Town still continues in a very angry state about the recent polling there. Dr. Johnston fearing that a fresh election would lead to scenes of violence, is understood to have given up his intention of petitioning against the return of Mr. Dixon.

Selected Vital Records from the Jamaican Daily Gleaner

February 6, 1896

SCOTT-At Mango Grove, St Ann on 27th January, Benjamin M. Scott, late of Brown's Town, St Ann leaving a bereaved wife to mourn his irreparable loss; "May he rest in peace,"

February 8, 1896

Mary Jane Watson has the same ad as in the previous 2 years, viz:

LODGINGS, &c

The subscriber in returning thanks for the past favours, begs to inform the General Public that she still carries on the business of a Lodging House Keeper, at those Commodious Premises in St Ann's Bay, Jamaica British West Indies, known as WATSON'S LODGING HOUSE, under the patronage of His Excellency Sir Henry Blake. The climate is excellent; the accommodations unsurpassable; and the cuisine is all that can be desired. The Establishment is patronized by all the leading men of the Island, as well as notable strangers from abroad. A continuance of patronage is solicited. Letters and Telegrams, will receive prompt attention.

MARY JANE WATSON

For reference, the Subscriber asks permission to submit the name of several Ladies and Gentlemen who have patronized the Establishment--His excellency Sir Henry A. Blake, K.C.M.G. &c, the Duke of St Albans, Mr. and Mrs. Crum Ewing, Hon J.M. Farquharson, Sav-la-Mar, J.T Vipond, (Canada) Capt. Watson (Duke of Wellington Regiment), Sir W. B. and Lady Gorgon, Commander and Mrs. Hall, (England), Benjamin A Watson and wife, Lowell, Mass, U.S.A.) And numerous others whose names will be found in the Visitors Book of the Lodgings. M.J. Watson.

February 17, 1896

CHILDREN'S COSTUME BALL AT BROWN'S TOWN

On Wednesday evening the 12th inst. At children's Costume Ball was given by Mr. and Mrs. Delgado at their residence in Brown's Town. It was an event of considerable social importance, children with their guardians being present from places as wide apart as St Ann's Bay and Cave Valley. Fully a hundred people children and adults, were present as guests, and as no pains or expense had been spared by the host and hostess to make the evening's enjoyment thorough and complete, the party was most decidedly a success.

At 5.30 p.m. a contingent of four players from the Falmouth Band, who had been brought over for the occasion, opened the ball by playing a selection of music, and by that hour most of the guests had arrived. The entrance hall was tastefully decorated with palm leaves &c, and in the reception room beyond was a fairy grotto, tastefully constructed of shells and rocks, with a canopy the supports of which were decked with flowers and plants. Under the canopy stood two girls dressed as fairies, with little gauze wings projecting behind their shoulders. During the evening each child in the party received a fairy present from this grotto as a memento of the occasion.

But pretty and attractive as was the fairy grotto, it was eclipsed by a unique and most amusing representation of the "Coat of Arms of Jamaica". Two little children nearly black, stood on two boxes, and were dressed to represent the Indian figures in the well known device. A tin alligator was fixed over the heads of the children, and the motto in card board below them, the other parts of the design being faithfully reproduced in some way. The "Indians" stood as still as statues and as solemn almost as real Indians. They could not be induced to speak, laugh or move, although only little mites of about six years old.

The little guests of the evening looked charmingly pretty in their fancy costumes, and as they walked in procession from the drawing room to the dining room

212

where refreshments such as children delight in were provided, they were duly admired by the adult visitors present.

In the drawing room, some of the children favoured the company with a delightful little entertainment. Master Alfred Delgado first give a speech of welcome composed for the occasion a duet by Master Kemp, aged 2 and Miss Kemp aged 4, entitled "Where are you going to my pretty maid" created great amusement on account of the wonderful way in which the wee things sang their parts. The Misses Harts sang "Di Di" and "Japanese Dolls" in operatic style in a most charming and perfect manner, and other contributions to the evening's amusement was a recitation "The little dog under the wagon", by Miss Trixy Archer, a duet "Pretty pretty maiden will your marry me" by Miss Kemp and Master Cooper, and a song "Two little girls in blue" by Master Harold Cooper. Dancing was then commenced to the excellent music of the band (which by the way had attracted quite a large crowd of people outside the entrance door, for the working people of Brown's Town dearly love good music). Little mites of seven or eight years stepped out gaily in what was perhaps their first dance, helped in the movement by such like adults as Miss Levy, Dr. Turton and Mr. Hart and others, who seemed to enjoy the fun every whit as much as the little ones. After the dancing the children withdrew, and the adult guests were entertained to supper, after which a very pleasant evening's enjoyment terminated.

The following is a list of the guests and their costumes:-

Miss Vi Fraser, Fairy
Miss Edna Fraser, Queen of Hearts
Miss F. Miller, Fairy
Miss Aggie Miller, Flower Girl
Master C. Miller, Sailor
Miss Lena Hart, Music
Miss Gladys Hart, Sea Nymph
Miss Beryl Hart, Bride of the Nineteenth Century
Master Harold Cooper, Troubadour
Master Willie Cooper, Gentleman of the Nineteenth Century
Master Ivan Cooper, Jockey
Master Cooper, Sailor
Miss Kathleen Kemp, Milkmaid
Master Harold Kemp, Man of war sailor
Miss Nettie House, Red Riding Hood
Miss Lena House, Greek Girl
Miss Lucy House, Queen of Hearts
Master Hugo Nash, Fighting Cock
Miss Daisy Delgado, Good Luck
Miss Ruby Delgado, Normandy Bride
Miss Inez Mornan, Red Riding Hood
Miss Marjory Albury, Flower Girl
Miss Ethel Delgado, Cupid,
Master Alfred Delgado, King of Hearts
Miss Rita Delgado, Buy a Broom
Miss Ethel Delisser, Ivy
Miss Sybil Ingram Gipsy
Miss Trixy Archer, Bo-peep
Master Cyril Archer, Little boy Blue
Master Laurie Archer, Jockey
Master Norman Spratt, Sailor
Master W. Costa, Italian Gondolier

Miss Alice Costa, Spring 1896
Miss Winnie Costa, Titania
Master Reginald Hall, Lord Fautleroy
Miss Mary Cover, Daisy
Master Bertie Cover Gentleman of the Thirteenth Century
Miss May Cover, Cossack
Miss Winnie Isaacs
Master Clarence Isaacs
Miss Issie Isaacs
Master Reggie Isaacs
Master Sam Spratt
Miss Vera Isaacs
Master Dudley Isaacs
Miss B. Isaacs
Master Karl Isaacs
Miss Isaacs
Master Jones
Miss Jones

February 22, 1896
DUQUESNAY-SORAPURE-At Holy Trinity Church on February 12th, by Rev. Fr. Collins, S.J. PHILLIP LEMERCIER third son of T. L DuQuesnay to Emma Corrine, eldest daughter of V. B. Sorapure.

February 25, 1896
Barbican High School
The following are the results of the College of Preceptors' examination held in December, 1895. The names are arranged in order of merit: -
FIRST CLASS: Miss V.O.M. Cunha, (Special Certificate for Scripture); Miss K.H. Powell, (Special Certificate for Drawing and Music; Miss D.J.Kinkead.
SECOND CLASS: First Division-Miss L.E. Nicholas, Miss M.A. James, Miss M. A. Athias, (second division)
THIRD CLASS: First Division-Misses L.C. Holler, L.J. Ernandey, J.B.C. Picot, J.E. Campbell, A.M.E. Predergast, Y.O . Facey, E. E. Brown.
Thirteen entered for this examination and all passed. In addition to the ordinary English subjects, several of the candidates were successful in French, Mathematics, Physiology, Theory of Music, Drawing and Political Economy. It will be noticed that Miss Powell obtained Special Certificates for Music and Drawing, and Miss Cunha a Special Certificate for Scripture.

March 5, 1896
The Wesleyan Conference opened in Edmondson Hall in this city, yesterday at 10 a.m. The Rev. W. Clarke Murray D.D. was elected as vice President, and the Rev. John Duff was re-elected as Secretary of the Conference.

March 6, 1896
DELEON-At 55 Duke Street, CHARLES DELEON (eldest on of the late Alexander Deleon, of Spanish Town), aged 46 years.
Funeral will move at 4:20 this evening to the place of interment.
Friends and acquaintances will please accept this intimation and let your carriage attend.

1896

March 7, 1896

The twelfth annual Western Conference was opened at Edmondson Hall on Wednesday 4th at 10 o'clock. Rev. Dr. Murray, vice-President, in the chair. Hymn 433 "Give me the faith which can remove," was sung and Rev. Westmore-Smith led in prayer. The secretary, Rev. Mr. Duff called the roll of members. There were present: Revs. W. Clarke Murray, D.D., T.M. Geddes, J. Duff, R.M. Parnther, M. Barker, T. Picot, Westmore Smith, F.O. Miller, Geo Lockett, Jonathan Grant, A.H. Aguilar, W. Baillie, W. Williams, W.R. Griffin, J.A. McIntosh, J. Kissock Braham. B.D. A.F. Lightbourne, Henry T. Page, and others.

The vice-President stated he had received a communication from the President, Rev. George Sykes, in which he regretted his inability to attend the Conference. The election of vice-President was taken, when Dr. Murray was re-elected. The Rev. John Duff was reelected Secretary; Messrs Grant and Braham were appointed Assistant Secretaries, Rev. F.O Miller Corresponding Secretary. The hours of session were fixed from 10 to 12.30 and from 1 to 3.30.

The vice President read correspondence between himself as vice-President and Missionary Committee, London, on the question of Allowances to Supernumeraries and Widows of ministers who were in connection with the yearly Conference in 1884 when the West Indian Connexion was established. The correspondence was directed to be entered on the journal of the Conference, and Dr. Murray was thanked for his services in the matter.

On motion of the Secretary it was agreed to send a letter to the President, acknowledging his greeting and conveying cordial wishes for his health.

The following were appointed Memorials Committee: Revds Aguliar, Miller, Baillie, Lightbourne, Hay; Mr. Miller, Convener

Revds T.A. Glasspole and J.A. Johnson were on motion, received into full connection with the West Indian Conference, having completed satisfactorily four years service.

Examination of ministerial character occupied the larger part of the day.

The first draft of stations was issued and shews many propped changes. The Conference rose at 3.45.

FIRST DRAFT OF STATIONS FOR 1896

Kingston District

1. Kingston; (Coke) Thomas M. Geddes, George Lockett, Charles G.   Hardwicke, David D. Parnther, B.A.

Kingston (Wesley) George H.B. Hay. One to be sent.

Kingston (Port Royal) Harvey, Swithenbank

Clarendon, Samuel T. Brown

Manchester, Frederick O. Miller

Mount Fletcher, William J. Maund

Grateful Hill Arthur F. Lightbourne, One to be sent.

Montego Bay District

Montego, John Duff, Achilles Lambert

Lucea, Terence M. Sherlock. One requested

Falmouth H. Gilles Clerk

Duncans John A. McIntosh, Alexander M. Smith

Mount Ward William R. Griffin

Sav-la-Mar, William Baillie, George Lamb

Black River, Charles C. Wallace

Mountainside, James C.A. Smith,

St Ann District

16. Spanish Town, Albert H. Aguilar, Nathan A. Baquie
17. St Ann's Bay, William H. Atkin
18. Watsonville, Samuel L. Lindo
19. Ocho Rios, Caleb Reynolds, M.C. Surgeon.
20. Beechamville, Robert M. Parnther,
21. Bensonton, W. Clarke Murray D.D., Walter J. Jacobs
22. Brown's Town, Jonathan Grant.
23. Edmondson, Mannasseh Barker.
24. Mount Hulne, Albert L. Johnson.
25. Guys Hill and Hamstead J.Kissock Braham B.D.

Morant Bay District

26. Morant Bay, Thomas P. Russell
27. Port Morant, Theophilus A. Glasspole
28. Bath. Henry T. Page
29. Manchioneal, Archibald J. Andrews
30. Port Antonio, William J. Williams, Reginald W. McLarty.
31. Yallahs, Hilton, C. Quinlan

Hayti and Santo Domingo

32. Port-au-Prince, Westmore S. Smith
33. Petit Goave An Evangelist
34. Gonaives, Vacant
35. Jeremie, Henri Belloncle
36. Les Cayes Auguste Albert

Cape Hayti and Monte Christo, Thomas R. Picot, an Evangelist

Puerto Plata, An Evangelist

Samana and Sanches, Elijah Mair, Wm. E. Mears: Jacob James, Supernumerary

San Domingo, An Evangelist

Turks Island, James O. Mann

Central America

Panama, Alexander W. Geddes, Clifford M. Clark.

March 20, 1896

Obituary (torn)

We regret to learn of the death of Mrs. Fisher, wife of Hon J. Wanchope Fisher, Custos of the parish of Trelawny and mother of Mr. H.S. Fisher, Acting Assistant Resident Magistrate -------which sad event------Saturday night-----was highly----of friends. We -----sympathy to the relatives------.

March 25, 1896

OCHO RIOS

Mar. 20 We note with pleasure that the Wesleyan Conference has decided to send back the Rev. Caleb Reynolds to this circuit; we again welcome him as he has done good work in the past, and we trust he will at an early date start active work on the new chapel. We hear that the Rev. Scurfield has been appointed curate of the St John's Church here, and that he will next Sunday preach his first sermon. We trust the newly appointed curate will possess the necessary energy required in furthering the welfare of this church which of late has been labouring under great disadvantages.

Last Sunday the service was conducted by a Mr. Jones, lay reader from Clarks' Town who performed the duty in a satisfactory manner.

We are pleased to report that our resident Doctor is getting up a good practice and creating a favourable impression on the community by making some good cures, as

1896

was instanced in a recent case of "Akee Poisoning" the unfortunate victim although being in an almost helpless condition (from the violent vomiting produced) eventually rallied under his skilful treatment.

Although a few barrels of oranges are being bought, trade seems not to improve as the shopkeepers are all crying out for dull times.

The H.M.S. Magiciene dropped anchor in this port on Saturday last but left next evening without giving "general leave" which might have been done had not our harbour master advised the landing as being dangerous.

March 26, 1896
LEFRANC-CAMPBELL-On the 11th inst. At Saint Matthew's Church, Allman Town, by Revd. C.H. Coles. M.A. GEORGE BOLIVAR, fifth son of the late John Lefranc, to ELSA (or ELBA) Ann, daughter of the late Rev. John Campbell, B.A.

March 30, 1896
CAMBRIDGE UNIVERSITY LOCAL EXAMINATION
(Not transcribed in its entirety)

The following are the results of the examinations held in this Island last December, arranged in classes but not otherwise in order of merit:-
BOYS
Students under 19 years of age who have obtained honours.
Class I. G.S. Husband, F.G. Sharpe, (distinguished in Latin and French) I.D. Stubbs, (distinguished in Latin French and Arithmetic) W. Simms, (distinguished in Religious knowledge) A.J. Wookey, (distinguished in French) Jamaica High School.
G.C. Evans (Mathematics) L.C.D. King, (Arithmetic, Latin, Greek and French) Potsdam School
A.H. L Hart, (French), York Castle High School
Class II-S Lockett (Religious Knowledge and English) York Castle High School.
J.M. Bowrey, (Physical Geography) Jamaica High School
Class III S.G. Allwood, C.C. Monton York Castle High School
Students under 19 years of age who have satisfied the examiners.
A.F.C. Findlay, T.J.R. Philips Jamaica High School
T.H. Donaldson, C.J. Levy-York Castle High School
A.A. Myers Potsdam
Students under 16 years of age who obtained honours
Class I. 1st Division H.H.R.Bayley (distinguished in Religious knowledge, Latin, French and Mathematics York Castle High School
Class II- C.A. Escoffery (Latin and French). W.W. Stubbs (Latin) H.C. Husband, Jamaica High School
W.R. Bayley, A.A. Moreno, York castle do
Class III-L.O. Arbouin-Kingston Church of England Grammar School
P.C. Grant York Castle High School
J.L. Archer E.E. Binns, R.G. Roberts-Jamaica High School
Students under 16 years of age who have satisfied the examiners;
W.L.Desnoes, D.E. Fogarty-St Georges College
H.W.R. Scott York Castle High School
J.H. MacDermot-Ropley School Gordon Town
S.C. Dickson, J.A.E. Levy-Rusea's School
L.A. Henry-Manning's Free
Students between 16 and 18 who have passed the examination as juniors:
D.E.Crooks, Arithmetic, York Castle High School

Selected Vital Records from the Jamaican Daily Gleaner

Students under 14 years of age who have obtained honours

Class II F.A. Foster (distinguished in Latin) Jamaica High School

Students under 14 years of age who have satisfied the examiners.

L.S. Gruchy, Wolmer's Upper School

Students above 14 years of age who have satisfied the examiners.

F.H. Arscott, G.W. Edwards, A.S. Linton, W.G.D. Macpherson, T.C. Predergast, W.O. Reid, H. Simms, D.B. Stennet, Jamaica High School

P.A. Harry Wolmer's Upper school

GIRLS

Students under 19 years age who have satisfied the examiners

V.O.M. Cunha, K.H. Powell, Distinguished in Drawing, Barbican High School

G. Simms Kingston High School for girls

Students under 16 years of age who have obtained houours.

Class II M. Willky, Mandeville High School

Class III D.W. Capper, Private Tuition

L.V. Delgado Kingston Academy

Students under 16 years of age who have satisfied the Examiners

M.H. Athias, Barbican High School

E.B. Hendricks, Hampton High

M.C, Lofthouse Kingston Church of England Girl's School

Students above 14 years of age who have satisfied the Examiners

B.A. Nethersole Kingston High School for Girls

M. Wortley, Kingston High School for Girls

B.F. Paine, Girls High School, East St, Kingston.

March 30, 1896

Walker-At Nightengale Grove Pen last evening JOSEPH DILEON WALKER.

Funeral at 4 p.m. today

Friends and acquaintances are invited to attend. Carriages.

April 10, 1896

BROWN'S TOWN WATER SUPPLY

Good News

Our Brown's Town Correspondent writes: A party of gentlemen consisting of the Messrs. J.H. Levy, Allwood, Byles, Dunkley, Mornan, Perking, Peat, and H.Q. Levy took advantage of the holiday on Easter Monday to visit the Bamboo district for the purpose of exploring and testing the various springs which had been reported to abound there, and their labours have been attended with the greatest success.

The party after spending a most enjoyable day amid the hills and rural scenery, having had a real picnic out, returned to town all jubilant over their find; they report having seen no less than 5 springs, all of which can without difficulty be turned into one course, and without detriment to the water supply of the district, yield for the Brown's Town water supply 25,000 gallons per day. The most important thing demonstrated by the visit of the party is, that what has always been regarded as a Lagoon, after being drained by means of a trench cut for about 6 chain is the discovery of a large spring in the centre, sending up the most beautiful pure water, this also if stored, (and there is a natural basin on the spot,) is considered sufficient for Brown's Town. The question now comes, how is it to be paid for! I understand that only £6,000 was granted by the Government for the Brown's Town Water Scheme, as the population could only be taxed to the extent of what is sufficient for the interest and sinking fund on that sum, and the present scheme, if carried out would cost £10,000, it is however to be hoped that Mr. Levy who has always taken so much interest in the water supply for Brown's Town with the co-operation of others will devise some means of meeting the difficulty, as undoubtedly a water supply will add immensely to the growing importance and charms of this already much admired spot.

April 22, 1896
EDUCATIONAL

Mr. Charles Arscott Cover, who, in addition to his recent B.A. Pass at the London University, has just been gazetted as having passed a special B.A. Examination with honours in English, has spent all his school life in the York Castle High School. Entering in the first form he passed up to the sixth, on to matriculation. The intermediate B.A. and then the final B.A. with its supplemental honours in English. He has now a place in the Tutorial Staff, which he fills with honour and efficiency.

April 29, 1896
GAUNTLETT-SEGRE-On Wednesday the 15th April at the Parish Church, Savanna la Mar by the Rev. C. Henderson Davis, A.K.C. (Rector) Oscar Greenwood, second son of the late Edmund Greewood Gauntlett of Spanish Town, to MARY LAURA, seventh daughter of John Swaby Segre, Esq. J.P of Chantilly, Savanna-la-Mar. No cards.

April 30, 1896
ABOUKIR: ST ANNS

You may talk of your concerts your picnics and the like, but let me tell you that for a long while I have not been to an entertainment more calculated to educate and give pleasure then the "Kindespiel" which came off in Aboukir Hall, Aboukir, on Thursday night the 23rd April, 1896

This intellectual treat, taken in hand and brought to a successful issue by a lady was performed by some twenty children from three years old and upwards to lassies and lads of thirteen, all trained and taught by her for whom its was plain they held in the highest respect and love and to whom they looked for every movement.

The chicks behaved well; the principal characters being "Sister Ann" who conducted the performance on the stage. "Mistress Mary" a bright golden haired child who did well and acted her role. Then came "Humpty Dumpty" a character well sustained by Miss Kathleen Kemp aged between three and four years. She shows beyond doubt original talent and a keen sense of the ridiculous. "Jack and Gill" next came on and Miss Kathleen again distinguishing herself. Of course they both fell down the hill but 'Gill most artfully put all the blame on "Jack" who quietly submitted. Poor Little Bo-Peep came on crying because she had lost her sheep and hoped they would soon turn up and bring their tails behind them. "Little Boy Blue" kept the room lively and blew his horn vigorously in the hope of calling back the lost sheep of "little Bo-Peep" Whilst Little Jack Horner" sat in his Corner eating Christmas Pie. Old Mother Hubbard went as usual, to her cupboard to look for a bone which she wished to send "little Red Riding Hood" to her poor old Grannie. Miss Red Riding Hood found a wicked wolf had eaten poor Grannie and so ate the bone herself.

This closed, the first part of the Program was well worth going to see.

The second part consisted of songs, Recitations, &c by ladies gentlemen, Children and the Members of the Aboukir Tonic sofa Union.

There was a good attendance Mr. J.H. Levy kindly consented to take the chair, among the audience we noticed Honorable Henry Sewell, Revd. and Mrs. Austin from Chapelton, The Brown's Town contingent was in full force and effect. When the time arrived for us to return home we were sorry however, we had to go and aided by a lovely moon got back safely. We highly appreciated the performance and wish good luck to Mrs. Kemp and her co-workers in the noble work they have undertaken.

Selected Vital Records from the Jamaican Daily Gleaner

May 15, 1896
FOURNIER-LEVETT-In Kingston on the 11th inst. By the Rev. P. Mulry, S.J., ALEXANDER, eldest son of Achille Fournier, Rimouski, Canada to Viola, youngest daughter of D.L. Levett of this city.

May 19, 1896
BOURKE-At Rose Bank House, Kingston on Saturday 16th inst. The wife of Wellesley Bourke of a daughter

May 29, 1896
BROWN'S TOWN
The 20th was right merrily celebrated in Brown's Town. There were sports at Huntley, and it was pleasing to see how the staid and dignified elders of the town for once threw off their dignity and took the lead. To see Mr. Thompson, Mr. Levy, Mr. Tucker, Dr. Miller and others running foot races was an amazingly good joke and caused no end of merriment. The donkey race, in which others of the dignified elders took part, the one coming in last being the winner, was also great fun. There is a time for all things saith the preacher, and surely the day chosen to celebrate the birthday of our Gracious Queen is of all others the day to be merry. Long live the Queen, and may Jamaica seek worthily to uphold the honour of being subject of Her Majesty. In addition to the races, the national game of cricket formed a part of the day's amusement, the bachelors being ranged against the married men. Of course the bachelors won, seeing that they have no wives to henpeck them and disturb the serenity of their nerves.

Turning to another subject your correspondent has been asked to call the attention of the powers that be to the condition of the main road between Cave Valley and Aboukir. Within the short space of about seven days two accidents have recently happened here for want of parapet walls at dangerous places. One week a team of mules went over a bank and one was killed, and a week after another went over and a mule broke its foot. This road is far too important a one, and has too much traffic for it to be left in this condition.

Turning to matters religious a new church has been organized in Brown's Town. In January last two strange Englishmen put up a tent at Brown's Town pasture, and began to describe in graphic language the tortures of hell and the bliss of heaven in the usual way. By and by these two Plymouth Brethren, as they are called went away, and two more arrived to take their place; all are now gone except one who remains to hold the fort. They have now pulled down the tent and the services are held in a mission room rented for the purpose. The other parsons in town are very mad at them, for several of their best and most useful members have left and joined the tent people. It was at first understood that the creed of the Brethren prevented them from getting married, but this is now seen to be an error for two fair lassies in Brown's Town are rejoicing in the expectation of taking two of the Englishmen "for better or for worse". They are good earnest Christian men, honestly believing that the greater part of mankind are rushing straight into hell and conscientiously bent on saving a few of them from so terrible a fate. They may be right or they may be wrong. "The chances are we go where most men go".

Parson Grant has gone to England for a little change. The Wesleyan society seems in rather a peculiar condition, all the fruits of the spirit as described by a certain apostle seeming to be conspicuous by their absence. By the way, what has been done with that parson who rumour alleged, was guilty of committing perjury in the old Brown's Town Court House several months ago, about a water squabble? For the credit of the connection and for the reputation of the minister in question the matter ought to be

220

investigated, so that if innocent, the minister's innocence may be demonstrated and his reputation not suffer as at present.

June 3, 1896
The premises known as "William Brown Emporium" St Ann's Bay advertised for sale by Mr. A. J. Hart auctioneer, have been sold by private treaty to Messrs J.H. Levy & Co.

June 19, 1896
CAMBRIDGE LOCAL EXAMINATION
Distribution of Certificates
      The formal presentation of certificates won by Students who sat last December in Jamaica for the local examination of Cambridge University took place yesterday at the Collegiate Hall. In addition to those who expected to receive certificates there was a large attendance of ladies and gentlemen interested in the subject of education nearly all the leading schools of the country being represented. Bishop Nuttall presided and there were on the platform Revs. W. Pratt, M.A. (Secretary) W. Gilles, W. Simms, McDermott, Dr. Murray, Wookey, Hon T. Capper, Messrs. W. Morrison, M.A. Dews, &c.
      The Secretary announced that the prizes were not yet to hand and proceeded to read the report on the examinations. Bishop Nuttall then distributed the certificates and afterwards delivered an important address with a special reference to secondary education and its bearing towards agriculture.
      Dr. Murray and Rev. W. Gillies also spoke and a vote of thanks to the Chairman closed the proceedings, a full report of which will appear in to-morrow's issue.

June 30, 1896
STIEBEL-Yesterday at his late residence Devon House, the Hon. George Stiebel, C.M.G., Custos of St Andrew.
Funeral will move at 5 o'clock this evening for Half-way Tree Church
Friends and acquaintances will please accept this intimation.

July 10, 1896
DEPRESSION IN ST ANNS BAY
A correspondent in a position to know writes that things are terribly depressed in St Ann's Bay. Never during all his residence in the town has he seen trade at so low an ebb. No cash is in circulation. All classes are feeling the effect of the depression.

Our Falmouth Correspondent also writes that trade is stagnant in that town.

LECTURE BY DR JOHNSON
Dr. Johnson, of Brown's Town the well known traveler and lecturer will repeat the lecture he delivered before His Excellency the Governor and party at Kings House in the Conversorium on Thursday of next week. A large number of curiosities will be exhibited. The subject of the lecturer will be his tour through Central Africa so that the audience will be "personally conducted " through the Dark Continent. Something will be said about the "reality" and the "Romance" of Africa. Major General Hallowes will be in the chair. The lecture is got up in connection with the Parish Church.

July 17, 1896
HOGG-At 11 a.m. yesterday, at No 13 Sutton Street, CATHERINE HOGG.
Friends and acquaintances of Colin A.C. Hogg, are requested to accept this intimation.
Funeral moves at 4.30 p.m.

Selected Vital Records from the Jamaican Daily Gleaner

July 20, 1896
OBITUARY
We regret to announce the death of Major L. Barrett, R.A. at Malta of typhoid fever. The deceased officer was formerly stationed here, was Inspector of Ordnance and warlike stores. He was a cousin of Mr. Gerald Waddington of Rio Magno.

August 1, 1896
KILBURN-PURCHAS-At St Ann's Bay on the 29th day of July, by the Rev. H.H. Kilburn; father of the bridegroom, assisted by the Rev. R.I. Ripley and the Rev. G.S. Grange, HARRY LINTON KILBURN to MARION LOUSIA GUYON, daughter of the late H.M. Purchas Esq. Of Swanswick, Trelawny.

August 8, 1896
COVER-At Heathfield near Linstead on 30th July, SARAH, the beloved wife of Samuel M. Cover. "Thy will be done as in Heaven so on earth".

August 12, 1890
WORTLEY-On the 10th instant, the wife of Mr. G.M. Wortley, of a daughter.

Mr. J.W. Mennell, the indefatigable Vice Chairman of the parochial Board was not in his usual place on Thursday being engaged with Mr. Douet at the Model Farm at Chilton. Mr. Mennell who is keenly alive to our agricultural requirements is doing all he can to stimulate a healthy feeling that way among the people of the Darliston Mountains. The well known fertility of that neighbourhood, he thinks, would be questioned if its inhabitants did not embrace every opportunity to learn the proper methods of cultivating the soil-Cornwall Herald.

August 14, 1896
The Rev. W.H. Rutty has ceased to be a Marriage Officer for the Cayman Islands.

The Hon. A.N. Dixon having failed to attend a meeting of the Parochial Board of St Ann for a period of six months his seat has been declared vacant and a nomination to fill the vacancy will take place on Tuesday the 18th inst. at the Court House St Ann's Bay. If the seat is contested the Poll will be opened at 8 a.m. on the 25th inst.

August 24, 1896
YORK CASTLE HIGH SCHOOL
Mr. A.K. Boyd, B.A., who was among the passengers by the s.s. Atrato on the 14th inst., came to join the staff of York Castle High School. Mr. Boyd has had several years experience in school work in England; possesses general qualifications of High School work, and special aptitudes in modern languages and science. We welcome him to the educational staff of the country and wish him every success.

31 August 1896 Titles
[First column]John Beecham Goffe of Port Maria in the Parish of Saint Mary, Merchant, Margaret Goffe of Port Maria aforesaid widow of John Beecham Goffe the elder, the said John Beecham Goffe the younger, Cecil Herbert Clemetson Goffe of Port Maria in the Parish of Saint Mary, Solicitor, at present at Derwent House Hotel, Howard Street, Strand, London England, Robert Horatio Goffe, Alfred Constantine Goffe, both of Port Maria aforesaid, Laura Emmeline Goffe of Port Maria in the Parish of Saint Mary at present at Derwent House Hotel aforesaid, Alexander Davidson Goffe of Port Maria aforesaid, Ernest George Leopold Goffe aforesaid at present at No 8 Union Road Gufnell

1896

Park London, England, Clarence Charles Ferdinand McParish Goffe and Rowland Parkinson Goffe of Port Maria aforesaid, to have the Certificate of title of the land herein described issued in the name of the Honorable Amos DaCosta Levy of Port Maria in the parish of Saint Mary merchants.

[Second column] 13th July 1896

[Third column] 23rd July 1896

1stly All that piece or parcel of land situate in Port Maria in the parish of St Mary in this Island, now in the occupation of I.I. Lyon & son. Formerly known by the name of "The Bridge Store" but now Known as No 6 Main Street butting and bounding north by premises secondly herein described south by Port Maria Street, known as Bridge Street, east by Port Maria Street now known as Main Street and west on premises belonging to one William Francis, or howsoever, otherwise the same may be butted, bounded, known, distinguished or described.

2ndly. All that piece or parcel of land with the hereditaments and premises situate in the town of Port Maria in the parish of Saint Mary butting north on land formerly of Sarah Clarke, but now of Harriette Delisser Simmonds south partly on land of William Francis and partly on land firstly herein described, east by the Main Street and west by the Outram River or howsoever otherwise the same may be butted, bounded, known, distinguished or described.

[Fourth Column] 8

[Fifth Column] 2 insertions per week for 2 months (one in the town and once in the country edition in the Gleaner Newpaper)

[Sixth Column] 2 months

September 1, 1896
RADCLIFFE-At Galloway Lodge, on Friday the 28th August, GUY DAVIDSON youngest and dearly loved son of the late Rev. John Radcliffe and Isabelle his wife.

September 19, 1896
LEVY-COVER-On Thursday the 10th inst. at St Mark's Church Brown's Town by the Revd. J.P. Hall, MARIAN LOUISE, youngest daughter of Wm Cover, Senr, Esq., to HARRY QUEENSBOROUGH eldest son of J.H. Levy Esq., of Brown's Town. No cards.

September 22, 1896
Country News
Brown's Town Notes
"An Evening with the Muses"

"What music, and dancing, and diversions, and songs are to many in the world that prayers, and devotions, and psalms are to you". LAW.

It is not very often that the inhabitants of towns and villages in the country are treated with good music, and when such a treat is offered, the people ought to avail themselves of it. Such an opportunity occurred on Thursday last, the 17th inst., when the hymnal oratorio "The Life and writings of St Paul" illustrated by hymns, Ancient and Modern and Golden bells was rendered by the members of the Saint Mark's Church Choir, assisted by some friends at the St. Mark's Church, Brown's Town; of which the energetic Rev. J. Philip Hall is worthy Rector. We may mention en passant that the proceeds of the Oratorio will be devoted to the purchasing of a pipe organ, to replace the small organ which is now in use, but which with the improvements that have taken place in the Church is now inadequate for use.

Mr. Hall is not a Minister who allows the grass to grow under his feet. He believes in the Poet Longfellow's Psalm of Life

"Lives of great men all remind us
We must make our lives sublime
And departing leave behind us
Footprints in the sand of time".

He is determined—and rightly so to leave behind his mark. The word idleness is not to be found in his dictionary, and he is not happy unless he obeys the command of scripture:

"Whatsoever thy hand findeth to do, do it with thy might."

He is devoted to his Church and people, winning the affection of each and everyone, his members love him, and when anything is to be done, they co-operated cheerfully with him, so that his object may be successfully attained.

Very many of our ministers can do no better than take a leaf out of Mr. Hall's book, and we have no doubt, but that greater blessing would result.

We have not space at our disposal to dwell on the different achievements of Mr. Hall. His works are there to be seen; we can only say

"Toil on and in thy toil rejoice,
For after toil comes rest".

Brown's Town, as our readers are aware, is an inland town in the parish of St Ann, about 18 miles from the principal town of St Ann's Bay, and containing about 2,000 inhabitants. The majority are peasant proprietors, who rely on the soil for their living, knowing that it is to agriculture, and to that alone, which will make them independent, and give their sons and daughters thorough education, so as to fit them for the proper place in society.

Brown's Town is a pretty little place-picturesque, the climate is second to none in Jamaica, and travelers who come to the Pearl of the Antilles, would never think of leaving Jamaica without coming here to pay their tribute of praise.

There are four churches here-a Wesleyan, Baptist, the Evangelistic Mission, and last but not the least, St. Marks (Episcopalian). It is to this latter that we must confine our remarks. Up to two years ago the members and visitors worship in the old St Mark's Church. This edifice could not contain more than three to four hundred persons. It could not aspire to architectural pretensions. It was old and shabby. Mr. Hall had often in his mind the pulling down of the old church and the building of a new one in its place; but he was met with this greatest difficulty "the lack of funds" – a difficulty which all of us more or less experience, but the Rector is not one to be discouraged, and with an energy worthy of such a good cause he set about to acquire the necessary funds and in this he was heartily backed up by the members of his congregation and friends, who in a short space of time, raised by contributions, a large portion of the necessary amount,-we are subject to correction but we believe that the new church, cost about two thousand five hundred pounds. The work was entrusted to Messrs. Mais and Sant the well known contractors who have already made a name.

The foundation stones were laid on the seventh day of August 1894 by Major General Bengough, the then officer administering the Government, assisted by Mr. J.H. Levy Merchant, and others and the work of superintending the Building was entrusted to Mr. G.A.S. Pengelly who did the principal part and to whom great credit is due. The work went on speedily, and on the 19th September 1895 it was opened and dedicated by the most Revd. The Lord Primate of the West Indies E. Jamaica.

Large congregations were present on both occasions. The proceedings were duly reported in the GLEANER so a recapitulation here is not necessary.

The New Church

The new Saint Mark's is a very substantial clerestory stone building in Tudor Gothic style of architecture. It is capable of seating about 700 persons. The length of the church is 150 feet, and its width 54 feet and the height from the floor to apex of roof 42 feet. We will here describe the interior of the church, which we are sure will be of general interest to the readers of the GLEANER.

The spacious interior is well ventilated and lighted and is very cool.

The chancel is very richly furnished with carved mahogany choir seats, (for 36) reading desks and encaustic tiles. Under the east window is a very handsome reredos in sculptured work, measuring 10 ft long by 9 ft high. The three panels depict the scene of Christ feeding the 5,000, the centre panel showing Him in the act of blessing the bread, whilst the outer panels show the distribution of food to the multitudes.

The pulpit is another very handsome structure, it was designed and built by Mr. Hall. It is octagonal in shape, standing on a shaft of your heavy columns, it is beautifully mounted.

The indefatigable Rector has just added a Brass Eagle Lectern. It is very massive one costing we believe about £50 odd. We hear that Mr. Hall intends to further improve the sacred edifice.

The Oratorio

We must now describe the oratorio. Words fail us to give an adequate report of the proceeding-but we will to the best of our ability do so.

We confidently say that more persons at times, are attracted to a Church on account of the music than the sermon; and a lot of good results are attained, consequently if the music be bad instead of persons being attracted they are repelled. Music plays a prominent part in the Churches and meetings, and instance of which is to be found in the successes of the Salvation Army in England and elsewhere.

Poets of all ages sing of music and it has rightly been said:-

"That the man that hath not music in himself and is not moved with concord of sweet sounds ..... Let not that man be trusted"

So then good music go hand in hand with good sermons; and the ministers of the Churches realize this, and they strive to get up a good choir to discourse sweet music. 'Music is love, it springs from religion and leads to religion"

Mr. Hall has realized this and his object has been to get up a good choir and in this he has realized marked success.

His efforts have been ably seconded by Mr. William Brown (junior) of Brown's Town. This gentleman-like many of us-has his hobby and his is "music and good singing" and he is never so happy as when he is speaking of his beloved music. He agrees with Sidney Smith who says "All Musical people seem to be happy-it is the engrossing pursuit- almost the only innocent and unpunished passion".

Those of us who knew the choir of St Mark's Church prior to Mr. Brown's taking charge of same, cannot but own that it was not in the same condition as it is now, but we may say this for them, that they hadn't a choir master. Now all is changed, a master has taken charge of the choir, a master who as we have said before, loves music, and whose aim is to see his choir, one of the best in Jamaica. How he has succeeded was best seen on Thursday evening. We confidently say that were it not for Mr. Brown's careful training of the choir, success would not have crowned the efforts of Mr. Hall in this Oratorio. Mr. Brown is blest with a large stock of patience, and his energy is unbounded. He we hear, is punctual in his attendance at the practices, in spite of rain he is always in his place.

Mr. Brown has a rich deep bass voice; and when once he is heard, a desire springs up for hearing him again. We may mention that he performed on the violin, cornet, flute and several other instruments.

To return to the Oratorio. The Life and writings of Saint Paul were read by the Rev. Mr. Grange, B.A. London, Curate of the Parish Church, Saint Ann's Bay. His enunciations were distinct and added greatly to the success.

Selected Vital Records from the Jamaican Daily Gleaner

The Oratorio opened with that grand old hymn "Guard the Bible well" after which prayers were offered and then the Oratorio proper begun.

About thirty to thirty-six members of the choir and friends took part under the direction of the choir master, Mr. Brown. The following instruments also took part:-

The Organ.....................................Miss Clara Mais
Three violins.............................Messrs Samuel, Dobson, Murray and Ingram
Violincello.................................Mr. R. Dobson
Flute and Piccolo...........................Mr. Hamilton
Clarionet......................................Mr. Matthew Edwards
Bombardon..................................Mr. Anderson

Violin Cornet Flute &Organ Mr. Brown at different times

These different instruments blended grandly with the voices and the different pieces were listened to with marked attention by the audience.

Special praise must be given to Mrs. Purchas for her solo, "For ever with the Lord." We detected a little nervousness at the first which she soon overcame; she enthralled her audience until the end of her song. They being breathless on her word. Although Mrs. Purchas has a rich mezzo-soprano voice she took all her notes with ease. We do hope that Mrs. Purchas will allow herself to be more often heard, we promise her that she will always have an appreciative audience.

Great praise must also be given to Mrs. Solomon Isaacs, "There's a green hill far away" Miss Maude Levy's selection from Mendelssohn oratorio of Saint Paul," But the Lord is mindful of his own," and to those ladies who sung were solos.

The Quartette, "Nearer my Good to Thee" by Mrs. Isaacs, Miss Nethersole, Mr. Mais and Mr. Brown was greatly admired, Miss Nethersole' contralto was a success. Mr. Brown as usual took the bass and did well.

The quartette: the King of Love my Shepherd is" by Miss Levy and the other members of the choir, was also a success. The soft instruments adding greatly to the harmony.

Full mede of praise must be awarded to Mr. Brown for the singing of his solos "Just as I am without one plea" and "I heard the voice of Jesus say". To praise Mr. Brown would be like painting the Lily to alter it. His enunciations were most distinct, every word he sung could be heard and understood, and when he was singing you could have heard the dropping of the proverbial pin.

Last but not the least is the young lady who presided at the organ. (Miss Clara Mais). Her task was not an easy one, in fact on her depended in a great measure, the success of the Oratorio, and she was quite equal to the task assigned her, she acquitted herself successfully.

As regards the visitors who took part Messrs. Samuel and R. Dobson, Chas. Murray, Henry Hamilton and Anderson performed on the violin, flute, piccolo, cello and bombardon deserve mention.

The audience behaved well thus showing how much they esteemed the entertainment.

If a professional were present, he could perhaps have detected points which your correspondent could not, but he would have had to take into consideration that the performers were all amateur.

October 1, 1896
FACEY-At "Hill Drop View", St Andrew, LARCHIM M. FACEY, Land Surveyor. Funeral at 4.30 p.m. Friends and acquaintances please accept this intimation.

1896

October 3, 1896
SCARLETT-At 11 Elletson Road, Kingston, on Thursday 24th ultimo, the wife of C. L. Scarlett of a daughter.

October 26, 1896
MUSICAL ENTERTAINMENT AT STEWART TOWN
The dull monotony of Stewart Town was relieved on Wednesday evening the 21st int., by a highly successful musical entertainment which took place in the Church of England school-room in the interest of the "Stewart Town Endeavour C.C." The audience was large representative, and appreciative. Among those present we noticed the following ladies and gentlemen:-Mrs. Noble, Mrs. Arnett, Mrs. Corbett, Miss Townsend, Lady Principal of Westwood school, with her staff of teachers, and pupils, Misses A.M. and T. Barrett, E. Webb, D. Lane, I and I Thomason, Baynes, Ruttys, Kennedys, Lothian, Weirs, Mrs. Greaves, Haughton and others; Revs W.M. Webb, and J.S. Linton, Dr. Miller, Messrs. L. Roper, and Barrister Roper, W. Levy, Sutherland, Ruttys, L.G. Nash, Todd, Dewar, Cusack, F. and T. Kennedy, I. Stockhausen, Saurlincer, C. McFarland, H. Crosdaile, J. Tullock, P. Haughton, Teachers Cunningham, Bailey, Waiters Etc, Etc. More.

October 28, 1896
RESIGNATION OF THE HON. A.N. DIXON
The Hon. A.N. Dixon, member for St Ann in the Legislative Council has resigned his seat. The action is caused, we regret to say, through ill health.
There are now two vacancies in the Legislative Council-St Catherine and St Ann. It is probable that the electors of St Ann will seek to re-elect Mr. Levy who is a favourite in the parish. Dr Johnston, of Brown's Town may also probably stand.

November 4, 1896
THE REPRESENTATION OF ST ANN
Our St Ann's Bay correspondent writes that the nomination for the election is fixed to take place on the 3rd of December and the election on the 10th. One candidate has come forward viz: Mr. J Allwood, Solicitor of Brown's Town. It is reported that the Rev. Dr. Johnston will also stand. Mr. A.J. Hart, M.P.B. has also been asked by several gentlemen to contest the vacant seat but up to the time of writing no decisive answer had been got from him.

November 7, 1896
LEVY-At London on the 5th inst. CHAS LEVY, Esq. in the 74th year of his age. By Cablegram.

Obituary of the above
[part] Mr. Charles Levy was born in the year 1822 and when about seven or eight years of age was sent to England where he was educated at Highgate. He remained in England until he was a young man and then returned to Jamaica to embark in business.

November 26, 1896
PARSONS-From the effects of a Buggy accident at about 5.30 p.m. on the 25th inst., CONSTANCE EYRE, the beloved wife of Lieutenant Dudley Parsons of Hazeldeen, Norman Road Kingston. The funeral will move from Hazeldeen at 5 p.m. today. Friends and acquaintances are requested to accept this intimation. [[Nee Isaacs, Aunt Gertie's Friend]

Selected Vital Records from the Jamaican Daily Gleaner
FATAL CARRIAGE ACCIDENT AT ROCKFORT—The Wife of Lieut. Parsons Killed.

An extremely distressing accident which terminated unfortunately with fatal results, occurred yesterday afternoon on the Rockfort Road, when Mrs. Parsons, the wife of Lieut. Parsons of the General Post Office, Kingston, was thrown from a buggy and killed almost instantaneously. According to the reports which reached us last night, Mrs. Parsons had arranged with a party of friends including the Misses Douglas, and Mr. And Mrs. R.A.Walcott, to drive out to the Rockfort Road and picnic there in the afternoon, returning to town in the evening. Everything was prepared for the excursion, and at about four o'clock two buggies with Lieut. and Mrs. Parsons, and the Misses Douglas drove along to Rockfort which was reached about 5 o'clock in the afternoon. The buggies were stopped near the fort, and Lieut. Parsons jumped to the ground, to lead his wife out of the buggy. Meanwhile the coachman, for some reason which has not yet become apparent, withdrew the blinds from the eyes of the horse attached to Mr. Parsons' buggy. Mrs. Parsons was on the step of the machine in the act of descending to the ground, when the horse, startled by the glare of the sun and frightened by the withdrawal of the blinds, dashed off from the spot where it had been standing and galloped along the road. Mrs. Parsons was immediately thrown to the ground, and the suddenness of the shock and the violence of the fall evidently stunned. In a moment the party was in confusion; Lieut. Parsons raised his wife from the ground but there was no sign of animation about the form, and recognizing the serious aspect of the situation a messenger was dispatched to Dr. Thomas D.M.O who resides at Harbour Head. When Dr. Thomas hurriedly arrived on the scene Mrs. Parsons was still in the comatose condition which had alarmed her husband and friends. Dr. Thomas recommended that she be taken to Kingston without delay. Accordingly a buggy was procured; Dr. Thomas and Mr. Parsons carrying Mrs.Parsons, entered the machine and were driven towards Kingston. On the road they met Mr. And Mrs. R.A. Walcott who was driving to meet the party of picnickers, but on being hastily informed of the accident they turned their buggy and returned to Kingston. At Brown's Town Mr. Walcott telephoned Dr. Saunders to come to Hazeldeen, Norman Road, the residence of Lieut. Parsons. When the party arrived at Hazeldeen Dr. Saunders was on the scene and in examining the body pronounced that life was extinct.

ANOTHER ACCOUNT

Another account states: A carriage accident occurred yesterday evening on the Rockfort Road resulting in the death under terribly sad and tragic circumstance of Mrs. Parsons, wife of Mr. Dudley Parsons, chief of the Registered Letter branch at the Post Office and a Lieutenant in the K.I.M. It appears that from the information gathered yesterday evening Mr. and Mrs. Parsons accompanied by Miss Levy of Brown's Town and a little girl relative went out for a drive in the direction of Rockfort. The reached the grass plot near the bath when the driver was told to pull up. Mr. Parsons and the driver got out whereupon the animal became restive and, it is said with the idea of quieting it, the driver removed the blinkers, bridle and bit. This only had the effect of making the horse plunge the more. Miss Levy and the little girl succeeded in jumping out. The horse made a dash forward and before Mrs. Parsons could leave the vehicle it rushed off. The driver hung on to its head, but failed to check its mad career. In passing through the archway of the old fort the man stumbled or stuck against something causing him to fall and the wheels it was stated passed over him. He received injuries including a fractured arm which prevented him from rendering any further assistance in checking the speed of the animal. Some 20 or 30 yards further on Mrs. Parson tried to jump from the rapidly moving vehicle but unfortunately alighted with great force on her head.

Mr. Dron who was coming up in a buggy when the horse ran away drove as quickly as possible after it and Mr. Parsons himself also ran on in the same direction.

1896

When Mr. Dron came to where Mrs. Parsons was lying he, of course, pulled up at once. She was lying prostrate on the left side of the road, about a yard from the bank. Blood was flowing from her nostrils and ears showing that she had sustained serious injury to the base of the skull. She was quite unconscious and breathing heavily. As expeditiously and carefully as possible she was placed in Mr. Dron's buggy and a messenger was dispatched for Dr. Thomas of Harbour Head who was soon on the spot. Restoratives were administered, but no improvement was visible and it was decided to drive on the unfortunate lady to Kingston. Dr. Thomas and Mr. Parsons supported her in the conveyance, but they had only proceeded a few hundred yards when she breathed her last. This was about half and hour after the accident which occurred about 5 o'clock.

The body was conveyed to Mr. Parsons' residence Hazeldene, Norman Road, where Dr. Saunders was summoned, but Mrs. Parsons had long been beyond human aid. The greatest sympathy is felt for Mr. Parsons in the irreparable loss which he has sustained and we desire to express our sincere condolence with him and the other relatives of the deceased.

November 30, 1896
The St Ann's Election
(From our Correspondent)

St Ann's Bay Saturday. The latest move in the political field is that Dr. Johnston has intimated his willingness to contest the seat in the Council. Mrs. Johnston is here and is acting for her husband. A strong canvass has already begun and interesting developments are looked for. The contest is bound to be a lively one. It will be between the Dr. and Mr. Allwood as Dr. Miller and Mr. Pratt have withdrawn, although placards are being stuck up as follow: vote for J. Alexander Miller the people's Joe or any man whom he may recommend. This is not understood and is causing some surprise. It is the general belief, however that only Johnston and Allwood will go to the poll. Allwood is popular and has good supporters. He is now in town. A big meeting is expected tonight. By Telegraph.

We understand the Dr. Miller intended to stand simply to make a contest. This was the idea he gives his friends. Dr. Johnston was written to sometime ago but we believe he refused to stand. He then partly consented and now he has determined to contest the seat. A nomination paper was going the rounds the other day for signatures in order to be ready if the Doctor wired his consent.

Mr. H.E. Cox of Ramble pen was asked to stand but refused.

Mr. E. Pratt of Melvile Park was also waited on and seemed inclined to consent but he evidently disliked the idea of a contest.

Mr. Allwood is said to be very popular with the yeomanry class. He is actively canvassing, but the rain has prevented him holding some of his meetings.

The fact, however that there is a wish to have a contest shows that there is a party opposed to his candidature.

December 4, 1896
St Ann Election
A Triangular Contest

The following is Dr. Johnston's address to the electors: " Mr. A.N. Dixon having resigned his seat as a member of the Legislative Council, I have been requested to allow myself to be nominated as the representative of this parish.
All my interests are in the island, and especially in the parish which I now seek to represent in the Legislature.

Selected Vital Records from the Jamaican Daily Gleaner

Should you do me the honour of electing me, I shall put forth all my powers for your advancements for, I need hardly say, your interests are mine, and in your retrogression I have to bear an equal share.

You will see, therefore, that I am bound-should I seek my own interests to advocate yours.

The election will take place on the 10th December, and I shall be glad to secure your vote early on that day.

Our St Ann's Bay correspondent writes that Dr. Miller was serious in his intention to try for the seat but now that Dr. Johnston has come forward he has withdrawn in his favour and is canvassing for him. He has struck up above his placard "Dr. Johnston is the man I recommend -vote for him".

Mrs. Johnston who is acting on behalf of her husband will address the electors at Ocho Rios on Friday night. It is said that Dr. Johnston has sailed from New York and that he will be in the island next week, although I cannot vouch for the truth of this statement.

The contest is promising to be a very lively one. As far as I can make out the electors of St Ann's Bay and Ocho Rios are in favour of Mr. Allwood. In the latter place two good men Mr. Edward Harrison and Mr. Frank Ewen both members of the parochial Board are working for him.

At Brown's Town he has also several good men working for him

Dr. Johnston, of course, will naturally stand strong in Brown's Town the Baptist people are said to be solid against him.

Dr. Miller has gone off to Moneague to canvass for Johnston. The general opinion is that Mr. Allwood will win.

THE NOMINATIONS

St Ann's Bay, Thursday, 3rd. At 12 o'clock the returning officer, Mr. J.S. Thomas, read the declaration of vacancy in the Legislative Council caused by the resignation of Mr. A.N. Dixon. Immediately after, nominations were made as follow: Dr Wm Henry Miller, paper handed in by himself, signed by Messrs A. Fullerton, J. Riley Bennett, G. Brown, Charles Orrett, J. Collins, G. Mais. Mr. John Humber Allwood was nominated by Mr. Frank Ewen paper was signed by Messrs. S.A. Norman. W. Peat, H. Morris, C. Murray, J.H.Levy, J. L. Tapper, V. Peat, F. Morales, Frank Ewen, A.B. Rerrie, A.J. Hart, R. Hemming, E.H. Harrison, E. Cresser. Dr. James Johnston's nomination paper handed in by C.P. Delgado was signed by Messrs. R. L. Young, Chas Costa, Wm Cover, Jnr. Alex Hopwood, T. Miller, W.H. Atkin, I.I. Lyon, Colin Campbell, Wm Gaynor, J. A. Miller, Adrian Tulloch, J.C. Ormsby, J. Collins, A. Brown, O. Leo. Matherson, John Fray, J. C. Lewis, Arthur Corbett, C.P. Delgado and eleven others. Dr Miller states that he has put himself up as a compromise candidate. His decision has caused great surprise-By Telegraph.

December 10, 1896

Brown's Town- The following is a specimen of the election literature that is floating around here.

"ALLWOOD IS OUR MAN"

Have you heard that Dixon has resigned;
And chucked his people all behind,
We want a man who surely will
Stand by his people through good & ill
Ta.ra.ra Boom.de.ay-

Now there is Allwood, the people's man
Come and deny it all who can;

And we will clearly show to you,
That he is both upright and true.
Ta.ra.ra Boom.de.ay-

Just look at his prolonged stay
At the Board at St Ann's Bay,
And you 'ill then not fail to see;
That he is the man for you and me.
Ta.ra.ra Boom.de.ay-

In legal matters he is well versed,
And procedure of Council knowest,
So we will him to the Council send,
And he will our rotten laws amend.
Ta.ra.ra Boom.de.ay-

Come one, come all, for Allwood vote,
He will your interests promote,
You 'ill rue it, if you another send,
So stick to Allwood to the end.
Ta.ra.ra Boom.de.ay-

December 16, 1896
Bacquie-At Lindstead, on the morning of the 11th instant, at 12.45 CHARLES BACQUIE of the internal Revenue Service, aged 59 years, leaving a large family to mourn their loss. He lived in the affectionate esteem of an entire community and his death is sincerely deplored.

December 17, 1896
YORK CASTLE
The Breaking up Concert.
"The hand of the diligent Secretary maketh rich the programme." Such was the programme for the night of the 11th arranged by the experienced hand of Mr. C.A. Cover, Secretary of the Debating Society.
The Chairman having humorously protested against a programme which did not include a song from himself, said "unaccustomed as he was to public speaking, at least at concerts," he was sure they expected no Chairmen's address from him. Disappoint them in this particular he would not. Addresses at concerts, he felt were commodities misplaced, blessings very much in disguise. Dr. Murray then called upon Masters Aguilar and Quesada to perform a pianoforte duet, " Les Sylphes" Both young gentlemen appeared again; the latter to give a pianoforte solo, "The Meadow;" Master Aguilar, who holds the Music Prize for 1895-96 to perform with considerable finish, "King of the Camp".
"Rocked in the Cradle of the Deep" was contributed by Master Darrell, a singer well known and always welcome at our school concerts. Master C.J. Levy, who gave "A Little Peach" is to be specially commended for the distinctness, with which he sent home to the audience every word recounted the trouble of "John Jones and his sister Sue," through "the little peach of emerald hue". This young gentleman sang again in the quartette "Come where the lilies bloom" The other singers were Miss Lallie Parnther, Messrs. Mitchell, and Cover. The piece evoked vigorous calls for an encore; but the Chairman, amid concert sparkle and brilliance, as in the fiercest heat of the Society's debates, inflexibly attached to the Institutions rule "lights out at 10 o'clock," was

smilingly implacable. Youth is, however, hopeful' and, when Mr. Cover sang his sorrows as a "Not too plain" and Rather susceptible Chancellor," calls for an encore were, again heard mingling with the applause. They came in a perfect thunder after "Garge's Jubilee" had been delightfully sung by Messrs. Mitchell and Cover; but the Chairman never flinched. "Absolutely impossible, gentlemen;" and the program proceeded to unfold its treasures.

We have high authority for saying "no compound on this earthly ball like another all in all" but certainly "The Twin," Mr. J. Duff sang of, seemed to approach that state of absolute identity. "The captain Flag" one of those sea songs Mr. Mitchell sings so effectively, was very much appreciated.

A selection from Jerome's "Three men in a Boat" was capitally read by Mr. Boyd who greatly amused the audience by the account of "Uncle Rodger's Picture-Hanging."

But now as Browning says about a different subject, "The best is yet to be". We have still to mention the ladies, and express our appreciation of the part they took. Miss Lallie Parnther and Miss Susie executed the Pianoforte Duet "Martha" in a brilliant style. Mrs. Mitchell rendered a pianoforte solo of that very fine piece "Jessie's Dream," a musical description of the "The Siege of Lucknow's". Particularly effective is that part where as Havelock and Outram are "breaking their way through the fell mutineers" and the music of the Highlanders is heard disentangling itself from the roar of battle. It was a sincere pleasure to listen to Mrs. Mitchell's rendering of this piece.
"God Save the Queen" closed the evening's entertainment.

December 22, 1896
CASSERLY-At No 78 Hanover Street, Kingston Yesterday the 21st inst. John Casserly of Charlottenburg, St Andrews in his 82nd year. Funeral at 4 this evening. Requiescat in Pace.

1896

Decorated Chairs
Spring Rockers covers with Velvet, Etc.
Hand Painted Lamps for the
Table, 12 to 36
Hanging Lamps with prisms, very pretty
Glass and China Ware
J.H. Levy & Co
Musgrave House
Brown's Town
Our Drug and Grocery Establishment
Is no replete with every description of
Groceries
And Fancy Sweets, Wines,
Etc., also a general
Assortment of
Drugs
Chemicals,
Patent Medicines
Perfumery & Soaps
J H. Levy & Co

December 30, 1896
The Representation of St Ann.

The address of the Hon Dr. Johnston to his constituents will be found in the advertising columns of to-day's issue. He states in it that he was leaving immediately for Jamaica. He adds that his political opinions have changed very little since the last election and expresses his resolve to support and promote in every way all measures likely to prove of benefit to the greatest possible number of people in St Ann irrespective of class, colour, or creed.

1897

January 4, 1897
HON. DR. JOHNSTON'S WELCOME HOME
Brown's Town, Saturday, Jan 2
Hon. Dr. Johnston arrived at 3.20 yesterday. Amid great enthusiasm was presented with an address at the Court House to which he responded in a suitable an eloquent speech. At the close he was welcomed by Mr. J.H. Levy, by whom an address was made. This brought the meeting to a close; the people then took out the horses and drew Dr. Johnston's carriage to his residence escorted by a band of music.- [By Telegraph]

January 6, 1897
COUNTRY NEWS
Brown's Town
The Xmas passed off very quietly. None of the old residents of the Town can remember such a wet season. Business was therefore suspended; even on the 24th not much was done, people being unable to cure their coffee. The market was however overstocked with fresh beef. Upwards of 9 cows were slaughtered and about 3 in the neighbourhood for the benefit of the people. We are safe in saying 12 in the vicinity of Brown's Town. Naturally all in the market could not find ready sale and many on the evening of the 24th went home sadder, but wiser men. This is the fault with our people even; if an enterprise pays at first it is soon over traded and then no one makes money. We fear butchery has seen its best days in Brown's Town, too many are going in for it and these new Butchers are generally men who have nothing to lose so someone else must be paying the piper.

January 8, 1897
WRIGHT-Boston Villa, 9 Kent Street. Spanish Town, on the 3rd January, 1897 ANNA MARIA, aged 42 years, the beloved wife of Alexander Wright, leaving seven children and her mother to mourn their irreparable loss. She sleeps in Jesus

January 11, 1897
SHARP-PHILLIPS-At the Parish Church, Montego Bay by the father of the Bridegroom, assisted by the Rev. C. Henderson Davis, Rector of Westmoreland, the Rev. Herbert F.R. SHARPE, eldest son the Rev. F.H. Sharpe, Rector of St James, to EMMA LESLIE, younger daughter of Dr. Charles M. Phillips. No Cards.

January 12, 1897
Country News
Brown's Town
        NEW YEAR-The Norman market at Brown's Town presented quite a difference scene on Saturday the 2nd January to Xmas eve. In the beef stalls only a

235

couple of the regular butchers slaughtered cows and this was not sufficient, quite unlike Xmas eve. I suppose the idea of carrying home a lot of beef was not enjoyed and the new butchers did not care to run the risk again.

The Weather. The rainy weather has set in again and from all appearances it mean to continue, "after a storm comes a calm". On Saturday last the town was all in an excitement over the reception of the Hon. Dr. Johnston and lively again on Monday when a band of music was leaving for St Jean D'Acre. Now it is still again and everyone crying out "dull times" and there's no doubt the wet weather will not improve matters. The cold weather has set in too.

ILL-TREATING HIS WIFE. There is a current report that a man beat his wife to such an extent on Monday near Bethany, that she died a few days afterwards. This must however, be accepted with reserve.

January 23, 1897
ORMSBY-RAMSON-At the Parish Church, Sav-la-Mar, STEPHEN OLIVER ORMSBY to CHRISSIE, third daughter of Ven. Archdeacon Ramson. The ceremony was performed by the bride's father assisted by the Rev C.H. Davis.

January 25, 1897
ORGILL-At Southsea, England, on the 23rd ultimo in her 83rd year, HARRIET, relict of the late Rev. T.T. Orgill, B.A., Oxon, late Incumbent of Saint Mark's Church, Portland, and youngest daughter of the late Rev. John Chuston, M.A. Oxon, and late Vicar of Tenbury, Shropshire. She was distinguished in life for her unexceptionable amiability, Christian character and maternal devotion. Requiescat in Pace.

February 11, 1897
BROWN'S TOWN
Two Pleasant Functions. On Thursday the 28th of January, a number of Magistrates and other gentlemen assembled at the court-house of this town to say goodbye to Mr. D.A. Tucker who has been promoted to the Clerkship of the Court in St. Mary and to present him with an address. We noticed J.H. Levy, Esq., senior J.P., C.P. Delgado Esq., J.P., C. Orrett Esq., J.P., Wm Cover, jnr., Esq., J.P. C. Costa, Esq., J.P., Rev. J.P. Hall, Drs. Turton and Todd, A.C. McIntosh, Esq., R.E. Fonseca, Esq. and several others.

Mr. Levy having been called to the chair read the address and in suitable terms spoke of the loss the community and the courts will sustain in the removal of Mr. Tucker who has since his residence here rendered himself beloved and respected by all classes by the manner in which he has conducted the business of the courts. Mr. Delgado and Mr. Hall followed in suitable addresses after which Mr. Tucker replied who seemed much moved by the touching way in which his conduct as a public officer and a member of community had been referred to. The following is the address and the reply:-

Brown's Town January 1897
D.A.Tucker Esq.
Clerk of the Courts, St Mary
Dear Sir-, We the undersigned inhabitants of Brown's Town having heard of your advancement cannot allow you to leave us without congratulating you on your well merited promotion and at the same time expressing our deep regret at your removal from among us.

During the time you have occupied the position of Deputy Clerk of the Courts in this district we have observed with pleasure the unfailing courtesy, attention and impartiality with which you have discharged your duties to the public and we desire to place on record our sincere esteem and respect for you.

Our regret at your departure is lightened by the thought that your removal will mean increased emolument and other advantages to you.

Wishing you long life and prosperity in your own sphere.

We are, yours sincerely,

(Sgd) Jas. Johnston, M.D.

J.H. Levy, &c

REPLY

Brown's Town

28th Jany, 1897

To the Hon James Johnston, M.D., M.L.C. and to J.H. Levy, J.P., C.P. Delgado, J.P., Sol. Isaacs, J.P., J.H. Allwood, J.A. Thomason, Esquires, Dr. R.S.Turton and the Rev. J.P. Hall and others;

Dear Sirs-It is impossible for me to say in words how heartily I thank you for this your very kind address to me on the eve of my departure from this district.

I have occupied the position as Deputy Clerk for this parish stationed here for nearly four years and it gives me infinite pleasure to know that I have performed my duties to your satisfaction.

I have always tried to help the poorer classes in their domestic misunderstandings they have always appreciated it and so very often a miserable law suit is prevented.

Even though I go on promotion it is with deep regret that I leave you all- it is no easy matter to tear one's self away from old acquaintances and friends, for I must confess, with ineffable pleasure that I have many here who I look upon as true and loyal friends.

Thanking you again for all your good wishes-I can but pray that the Creator may bless you and give you all health long to live in this your delightful district.

I am, dear Sirs,

Yours very sincerely

(Sgd) D.A. Tucker

In the evening the Gentry entertained Mr. Tucker at dinner at the well-arranged hotel kept by Mrs. Delisser, 17 gentlemen sat down. Mr. Levy again presiding after the good things provided had been partaken of and duly washed down the following toasts were proposed and responded to: "The Queen" by the Chairman, "The Governor and Legislative Council" by Mr. Delgado, "The Guest" Mr. D.A. Tucker by the Chairman. "The Judicial Department" by Mr. Isaacs, responded to by Mr. McIntosh. "The Civil service" by Mr. H.Q. Levy, responded to by Mr. Gifford. "The Planting Interest: by Mr. J.H. Allwood, responded to by Mr. C. Costa. "The Ladies by Mr. Crum Ewen, responded to by Mr. W. L Levy. 'Education by Mr. McIntosh, responded to by Mr. Hall. "The Chairman by Revd. Mr. Hall" "The Revd Hall" by the Chairman. "The Legal Profession by the Chairman, responded to by Mr. Allwood. Mr. Fonseca proposed 'the continued prosperity of Brown's Town Responded to by Mr. Isaacs. Mr. H.Q. Levy, "the health and improvement of the labouring and peasant class". All the speeches were rendered in fine style- the evening was a most enjoyable one and everything went off with harmony and good will-the entertainment was kept up until 12 o'clock when the signing of "He is a jolly good fellow' and God save the Queen" brought it to a close.

February 18, 1897

GRANT- At Joppa, Scotland, ALEXANDER, in his 13th year, eldest son of D.C. Grant, Spot Valley Penn, St James. (By Cablegram)

Selected Vital Records from the Jamaican Daily Gleaner

February 22, 1897

OBEAH IN BROWN'S TOWN

Our correspondent at Brown's Town writes:- On Wednesday night there was a case of "duppy catching" going on at the Top Road, Brown's Town, and very near to a respectable dwelling. A young woman who is in ill health was declared by her people to be troubled with "duppy" (ghost). Accordingly they secured the services of a man from Runaway Bay and he undertook to catch the ghost, and on Wednesday night he performed his work, but not to the satisfaction of his employer or employers as the young woman up to time of writing is still raving. It was however, explained by one of the believers that a corkscrew had penetrated the cork of the bottle in which the "duppy" was put in, and therefore the "duppy" came though the hole. Unfortunately a constable was not present to catch the man and put him into a much larger bottle with ventilations that he wouldn't get through. It is believed that the sum of ten shilling was paid to the man. On Friday the woman had to be taken to Dr. Johnston. Why wasn't this done at first? We cannot tell. It is remarkable to know the firm belief that prevails in Brown's Town in the black art, yet monies are being sent away to enlighten the heathens. We trust a law will be soon be framed when the purchasers of the art will be punished was well as the obeah men themselves.

February 24, 1897

McCREA- At Chapelton on 22nd inst. the wife of Harry McCrea, of a daughter

A fire occurred at Musgrave House, Brown's Town on Friday the 19th inst. which might have terminated seriously. It appeared that a young man was engaged in the work of bottling turpentine in the oil room. Whilst doing this he lighted a cigarette and threw the match into the tin can that was being used. It immediately blazed up and in the excitement of the moment he threw the can into the larger tin containing the turpentine in order to extinguish it. This naturally took fire also. Some one with good intensions threw water upon the mass of blazing stuff which spread the fire rather than extinguished it. Leather was next used to stop the flames but not until dirt was employed were the efforts successful in quenching the flames. With the exception of a few pounds of leather nothing was destroyed. A couple of the clerks were burnt, but the injuries were not of serious nature.

March 4, 1897

HOPWOOD-At Lillyfield, St Ann, on Sunday the 28th ultimo, after 14 days illness, EUID(sic, ENID) LYNETTE, aged 14 months the beloved daughter of Celeste and Alex. Hopwood.

March 8, 1897

NASH-At Montego Bay on the 27th ultimo the wife of James Nash, Solicitor of a son.

March 11, 1897

FOURNIER-At Sudbury Ontario on the 16th ultimo the wife of Alexander Fournier of a son.

March 20, 1897

FOR SALE

Milch Cows in lots of 15 and 10 or 20 heads

Apply to

ROBT. L. YOUNG

Tobolski, Brown's Town

March 27, 1897
Country News
BROWN'S TOWN

Stagnation- Business continue very dull every body crying out for "hard times". The coffee crop has been very small therefore the people are out of pocket and can scarcely get enough to keep up the necessaries of life. Some of the stores have had to reduce their staff of clerks.

ORANGE SHIPMENTS-We are sorry to see already shipments are being made of oranges which should have remained for a few weeks more at least. We hope the Government will as early as possible institute a law for the protection of the fruit of our Island from being shipped in an immature state, at any rate let those who will persist in putting up young fruit suffer, by having a registered trade-mark so that they may be identified.

ATHLETICS-On almost every evening may be seen the young men of the town practicing cricket and football at the Brown's Town pasture kindly allowed by Mr. J.H. Levy. This being so the Merchant of the town can well afford to give their clerks a half day every Thursday especially at present when very little is being done in the shape of business.

CONFIRMATION SERVICE-At confirmation Service was held at St Marks Church Brown's Town, when about 16 were confirmed. The Assistant Bishop preached from the passages St Luke 9 ch. 57 to 61 verses. His discourse was edifying and so plain that a child could have understood. The church was full and the service on the whole was very much appreciated.

April 1, 1897
The Tri-Weekly Gleaner
Brown's Town

The water diviner has arrived and commenced work. He has traced water in several places in Brown's Town and we have no doubt that at a near future Brown's Town will be supplied with water. Quite a number of people turned out to witness the process of finding water.

We still have to report fine weather but trade is at a perfect standstill. We are safe in saying such a dullness never existed at this time of the year in Brown's Town.
Now that America intends to raise oranges it is to be hoped our people will see that nothing but good well handled fruit leaves our shore. It is a waste of money to pay duty on some of the stuffs we see put up already.

Nothing doing here in the banana trade.

A musical entertainment is at hand to come off some time in April in aid of the St Mark's organ fund. An attractive programme is being arranged.

April 6, 1897
St Ann

April 1.- A very large and influential public meeting was held in the Court House today in re the matter of "How best to celebrate the Diamond Reign of Our Most Gracious Majesty Queen Victoria". Among the audience we noticed the following gentlemen: Revd. Hall, Revd. Atkin, Rev. House, Rev. Ripley, W.G. Nunes, Esq., Messrs. Perkins, Ewen, J. Miller, T. Miller, Dr. Cox, Dr. Ormsby, Rev. Lindo, Hon Revd Dr. Johnston, M.L.C. A.J. Webb, Esq., J.H. Allwood, Esq., J.E. Myers, Esq., Messrs. Harrisson, R.W. Harris, A.J. Hart, Burke, Bennett, Tapper, C. Phillips, J.O Clarke, C.G.

Selected Vital Records from the Jamaican Daily Gleaner

Hay, T.A. Alexander, Esq., Mr. Stears (Water Divina) E.G. Watson, Esq., C.A. Sloley, W.T. Morris, and a host of others.

Rev. S. L. Lindo moved that Jos. H. Levy Esq., the gentleman who called meeting be asked to preside. Mr. Levy on taking the chair gave a very stirring address the gist of which was that he thought the best course to adopt was to follow the lines laid down by her Majesty's ministers to show our loyalty by works of Charity and his opinion was that whatever was done should be entirely distinctive, and should stand forth as a land mark of the loyalty of Jamaica for ages to come, and now that the Water Diviner was here in their midst they should make use of his skill and he would propose to have wells, or tanks in the dry districts and give the poor people free water, and mark such wells or tanks, "Victorian Diamond Jubilee, 1897" (hear, hear). Mr. Levy said he was now giving water to 500 and odd people from one of his properties and some or those people came from about 6 or 10 miles from Brown's Town and he was told by the attorney (his son) in charge that the tanks were getting dry and he would have to stop giving water, but he said common humanity could not allow him to refuse and if it was the last gallon of water he had he would let them have half. (loud cheers and applause). Half the time of the labouring classes was occupied in going up and down the country to get water. He said he considered it the duty of the state to supply the whole Island with water. He would now ask the gentlemen present to give their views on the subject.

The Rev. House then spoke; he said the Council deserved criticism. They were facing a large deficit, depression etc, and £900 was voted to send volunteers to England, £700 for demonstrations and £80 for a statue, and most of them were more caricatures than likenesses. He would therefore beg to move the following resolution viz: "That the most fitting way of commemorating the Diamond Reign of Queen Victoria in St Ann would be the establishment of a Scholarship to be called the "The St Ann's Diamond Jubilee Scholarship". Such scholarships to be open to competition by children of parents in indigent circumstances of any class in the community. That the amount required be raised by voluntary contributions and be vested in the names of Trustees as a Parochial Committee, to be appointed by the Jubilee Committee.

Rev. Lindo thought the idea a very good one, as one or two hundred pounds could be taken out of the amount raised and invested at say 6 percent which would give a perpetual Scholarship of £6 or £12 per annum.

Mr. J.E. Myers made a most eloquent and touching speech on behalf of the Water Scheme, he was against the Scholarship (as a mark of our loyalty) the people were dying from the want of water, and he advocated to give the dry districts water (Hear, Hear).

Rev. Hall of Brown's Town said that he would move as the best way to celebrate the 60th reign of our Most Gracious Queen would be to raise funds in the parish for an additional Ward in the Hospital for children as it was often the case that children were in the same Wards with adults when operations are made. £300 would build such a ward and it could be called "The Victoria 60th Jubilee ward".

Mr. J.H. Allwood, thought the suggestions were all very good in their way but facts must be faced. He did not think £100 would be raised, and the small amount that would be raised should be used to make "a day" of it providing a good dinner for the poor, a treat for the school children, etc.

Mr. Burke said that it was quite true the necessity for water existed, but he agreed with Mr. Allwood that the money would be there and so reluctantly he must throw cold water on the Chairman's Scheme. The suggestion about scholarships had many good points to recommend it, but he money wouldn't be enough. If a small amount was raised let it be devoted to some charitable purpose, poor relief to paupers, etc all the paupers received a grant that would last them a week or two.

1897

The Chairman then put his views in the shape of a resolution: viz: "That the best manner in which to commemorate the Queen's Diamond Jubilee would be to give a water supply to the dry districts of the parish, or in the erections of fountains, tanks and water troughs, and that a fund be raised throughout the parish for the purpose.

Contributions of not more than 16? to go towards local celebrations in the way of school children's treat, feeding the poor, and fireworks for one day and that the members of the Parochial Board, the ministers of religion of the various denominations and the magistrates be asked to be on the committee and to collect funds for the objects.

Mr. R.W. Harris said he would like to hear the views of the hon. Member for the parish.

The Hon Revd. Dr. Johnston then rose and said he endorsed all that the Chairman said and had great pleasure in seconding the resolution. Every commemoration is done by having a fountain. He cited England, Scotland, etc. and he was quite in favour of a water supply scheme and nothing could stand in the face of Mr. Levy's suggestion.

Mr. A.J. Hart said he was quite in accord with the chairman's scheme and he would like to record his idea that fountains should be in each town.

Rev. Ripley agreed with the Water Scheme, but he would suggest that Local Courts be appointed in each district to decide how best to devote the funds, Brown's town might like a fountain, St Ann's Bay something else and so on.

Mr. Burke move an amendment: "That the money colleted by devoted to the erections of fountains in St Ann's Bay, Brown's Town, Moneague and Ocho Rios-this was seconded by Mr. Ewen"

Mr. J. A. Miller said, "That he was astonished to hear gentlemen say that the money would not be raised to do anything tangible. He was of the opinion that a large amount would be raised."

Mr. Allwood was of opinion that if Mr. Burke's amendment was carried it would kill the whole scheme as people from Cave Valley, Bethany, etc, would not subscribe.

Mr. T. Miller of Brown's Town was quite in accord with the Chairman's ideas and would suggest that the ladies of the parish be also asked to solicit subscriptions. The amendment was put and only a few voted.

The resolution was then put to the meeting and carried by a large majority, a subscription list was then taken around by W. G Nunes, Esq., and several gentlemen put down their names for different sums.

Mr. Levy as also Dr. Johnston promised that if the resolution was adopted they would double their subscriptions.

April 10, 1897
The Water Diviner

The St Ann authorities, have commenced the trial boring on one of the spots indicated by the Water Diviner. They have already gone 40 feet, which the Diviner says is excellent work for three days. The boring implements imported are working beautifully. Great interest is still shown in the Diviner. Vast crowds visit the scene where the boring is going on every day. Very valuable and voluntary help has been obtained from the two Engineers in the quarter, viz: Messrs. H.Q. Levy and John Cover, and also from other members of the community.

April 14, 1897
LINDO-ALLWOOD-At Falmouth, Trelawny, on April 4th, by the Revd. E.J. Thomas, ROBERT second son of the late Frederick Lindo of Trelawny, to CONSTANCE

LOUISE, youngest daughter of the late R.W. Allwood, (Collector of Taxes, Hanover) and grand daughter of the late Revd. A.J. Davidson.

April 21, 1897
WATSON- At St. Ann's Bay on 16th April 1897, RICHARD WATSON, aged 65 years, leaving a sorrowing wife and many relatives and friends to mourn his loss.

April, 23, 1897
CHANDLER On Friday 16th inst. the wife of W.C.R. Chandler Esq. Of Clomes, Manchester of a daughter.

April 24, 1897
The Rev. H.A. Cover, the lately appointed Curate of Falmouth Parish Church, took up his duties on Sunday the 11th inst. The young clergyman bids fair to be a favourite among the church people of the town. More.

April 26, 1897
Dallas-At her residence Budgate House Norman Crescent, MARIE ELISE, wife of Frank P. McD. Dallas. Funeral at 4 p.m. Friends and acquaintances please accept this the only intimation.

April 30, 1897
MUIR-KIRKLAND-On Wednesday 21st April 1897 at St Luke's Church, Cross Roads, St Andrews by the Rev. H.S. Isaacs assisted by the Rev. R. Ambrose, CHARLES MACKENZIE MUIR, Jamaica Civil Service, Buff Bay, to KATHRINA ADELAIDE, only daughter of the late John Ambrose Kirkland Esq., of this city. No cards.

SOLEY-On the 24th instant at his residence in Sandy Bay ROBERT SOLEY (teacher Of the Wesleyan School) aged 54 years after a short but painful illness. Requiescat in pace.

May 1, 1897
Depass-In London on Thursday, April 29th ABRAHAM D. DEPASS, Esq. By Cable.

SUCCESSES OF A JAMAICA LADY STUDENT
Miss Maud A. Cover, daughter of W. Cover jr., Esq., Hopewell Dry Harbour, has greatly distinguished herself in music. She is a pupil at Princess Helena College, Ealing, London. In December 1896 at the age of 15, Miss Cover passed first in the Local Examinations for Seniors held by the Royal Academy of Music: by this she won the "Blue Ribbon" of the College, which is the annual prize for music offered by Princess Helena, the prize is usually a gold bracelet, but in this instance we learn that H.R.H. Princess Helena procured Chopin's works, beautifully bound in three volumes, and presented the prize herself.
Three months later, 2nd April 1897, Miss Cover was examined at the Royal Academy, with a view of obtaining honours in a similar examination to the previous one, and we now learn that she has passed a very brilliant examination. The greatest number of marks when lost in any one subject was 4 off the maximum: this for Scales; in other branches only 1 or 2 marks off the maximum. Very few in England have passed with honours. Besides the above successes Miss Cover now hold 15 or 16 prizes for languages and music.
We congratulate Miss Cover on her success.

1897

May 10, 1897

TUCKER-LEVY-At St Marks Church, Brown's Town, on Thursday, May 6th, at 4 p.m. by the Rev. J.P. Hall, Rector DAVID ALEXANDER TUCKER, Clerk of the Courts for the parish of Saint Mary, to SARAH GERTRUDE, the eldest daughter of the Hon. J.H. Levy of Windsor House, Brown's Town. No Cards.

THE DEATH OF MR. A.D. DEPASS

It was very much regret that we reported the news of the death of Mr. Abram D. dePass, of London, which news was received by cable in the city. He died suddenly in London. Mr. DePass was the father of Mr. E.A. dePass of the firm of Messrs. E.A. dePass & Co., London. Mr. dePass came to Jamaica when quite a boy and started business and eventually went into the provision business. He left the island many years ago and his business was bought out by Messrs. Saul Moss & Co which business eventually became Chas Levy & Co. The late Mr. I.H. deMercado, was clerk at the time in the business of Mr. DePass and he went over to the new firm. Although Mr. DePass had been for years absent from Jamaica, he always took a keen and lively interest in everything connected with the island and strange to say his son eventually founded the important commission house of E.A. dePass & Co, and thus the relationship with the island was kept up. On leaving the island Mr. DePass went into business with Australia and dePass Bros was at one time one of the largest shipping houses from London to Australia. Mr. DePass was one of the leaders of the Spanish and Portuguese Jews in England and was highly respected. It was only last year that Mr. DePass celebrated his golden wedding.

May 12, 1897

Mrs. Watson and family beg, through this medium, to return thanks to the many friends from whom letters of condolence have been received on the occasion of their recent sad bereavement.

May 31, 1897

THE DIAMOND JUBLILEE

St Ann's Bay

A meeting was held at the Court House, St Ann's Bay, on Thursday, the 20th inst. to make arrangements for the celebration of the Queen's Diamond Jubilee. The following gentlemen were present: Revs. R.H. Ripley, G. House, Grange and Scurfield, Messrs. A. B. Rerrie,J.P., A.N. Dixon, J.P. D. Hart, solicitor, Dr. Ormsby, and Messrs. Collin Campbell, C. DePass, R. Heming, M.P.B. C.B.H. Phillips, C. Gordon Hay, A.J. Hart, M.P.B. J. Addison, E.P. Pullar, A Townend, J.P. W.G. Nunes, CP.B. C.F. Matherson, H. Hamilton, S. Dobson, and a host of others too numerous to mention.

On the motion of A. N. Dixon, Esq., seconded by Rev. R.J.Ripley, the Rev. G. Houses was called to the chair.

The Rev. Gentleman explained that J.H. Levy, Esq., had called a meeting for 2 p.m. and that Rev. R.J. Ripley, Rector and also called a local meeting for 4 p.m.

The Rector stated that he was willing to postpone his meeting until later.

The Chairman then read a letter from Mr. Levy expressing his inability to attend on account of an accident he had met with. Mr. Levy also expressed his willingness that local arrangements would be made for celebrating the Diamond Jubilee by the local committees.

A circular was read from the central committee suggesting that contributions should be sent from each parish towards adding a wing to the Kingston Public Hospital.

It was then moved by Mr. A.J. Hart, M.P.B., seconded by Mr. A.J. Webb, J.P., "that the suggestion made by the central committee be not adopted and that subscriptions be raised in the district of St Ann's Bay to be spent for some local object. This was carried nem con.

The Rev. R.J. Ripley proposed "That to assist in raising funds for the local celebrations of the Diamond Jubilee, and entertainment be held on the 10th June (say a grand garden party) for that purpose and that the amount so raised together with the share of the £50 from the Central Committee which falls to St Ann's Bay be placed in the hands of the Local Committee for the purpose of providing a treat for the school children and a dinner or dole for the poor."

This was seconded by Dr. Ormsby and carried.

Proposed by A.J. Webb, Esq., seconded by A.H. Hart, Esq., "That ¾ of the amount raised by subscriptions from private and other sources (excepting the amount from the Garden Party arranged by Rev. Ripley and that from the Central Committee) be devoted to acquiring land for the erection of a fountain therein in St Ann's Bay to commemorate the Diamond Jubilee of Her Majesty and that ¼ be placed in the hands of the Committee for their disposal".

The motion carried.

Mr. A.J.Hart proposed and Mr. J.D. Ormsby seconded the motion, "That the Parochial Board of St Ann be asked to grant a sum of money to purchase the site of land in front of the Parish Church on the Main Street for the erection of a fountain to commemorate the Diamond Jubilee of her Majesty. Carried.

June 2, 1897

The Rev. W. Clarke Murray says that when quite a lad an old fisherman, whom he, in common with many of his school fellows, regarded as the embodiment of all practical wisdom told him that crabs were apt to prove poisonous if eaten in the months of May, June, July and August; but not in the other months of the year. "And," he added by way of helping our memories "eat crabs if you can get them properly cooked in every month which has the letter R in it. I have known many persons to follow this rule eating crabs in September, October, November, December, January, February, March, and April, and have had nothing to justify the complaint. I do not enter here upon an explanation, I only state a fact."

June 9, 1897

BROWN'S TOWN NEWS

There was a meeting held in the Court house on Friday night among the merchants of this town to consider the celebration of Her Majesty's Diamond Jubilee. The day fixed for the celebration is Monday 21st of June,1897. The town here is very bright with music. There are two bands now in this town and are practicing every night for that purpose. The gentlemen who are taking part to carry on the celebration are the Hon.J.H. Levy, Mr. Cooper, Dr. Miller, Mr. Isaacs, the Hon Dr. Johnston's band is also in practice to attend that day. There will be a cow killed on that day here for distribution to the poor of this town.

June 12, 1897

Miss Hollar will open a High class Day School for Girls at Vauxhall, Brown's Town in Kingston. The school will begin its first term on 26 July. Miss Hollar is competent to fill the position, and will have associated with her competent assistants of high merit. She won the Cambridge higher local certificate for 1896 and owns four Cambridge certificates for previous work. The curriculum will include English Language, Composition, Arithmetic, Geography, History, Religious Knowledge, French, Algebra, Euclid, Botany, Calisthenics, and needlework. For further particulars reference can be made to our advertising columns.

1897

June 19, 1897
Jubilee
St Ann's Bay Programme
On Sunday the 20th June the 60th anniversary of the Queen's accession to the throne special thanks giving services will be held in each place of worship in the town.
Tuesday, June the 22nd:-
5 a.m. The band will serenade the town
6 a.m. Firing salute of 21 guns from Roselle
6.30 a.m. Ringing of Bells.
7 a.m. Bugle sound for children to assemble in their respective Schoolyards.
At the 3rd Bugle call the procession headed by the band, starts from the Church School in the following order for Drax Hall Common.
1st in order Church of England School,
2nd in order Wesleyan School
3rd in order Baptist School
10 a.m. Singing of special Jubilee songs by School Children and addresses by ministers of religion.
10.30 a.m. 1st distribution of refreshments 12 o'clock to 3.30 p.m. Amusements for the School Children
3.30 p.m. 2nd Distribution of Refreshments
1 p.m. Athletic Sports (open to all comers)
                    EVENTS
100 Yards (open) 1st prize 6 s value, Do do 2nd do 3s do
100 Yards (boys under 16) 1st prize 3 s value
100 yards (girls) 2nd prize 2s value
Tug of War (open) prizes given to winning team.
Long jump (open) 1st prize 6s value; 2nd prize 3 s value
Hurdle Race (open) 1st prize 6s value; 2nd prize 3 s value
Human Wheel Barrow Race, prize 9 s value
3 Legged Race, prize 9 s value
Greasy pole prize Ham 10s
10.Egg and Spoon Race, prize 6s value
11.Sack race, prize 6 s value
12.Veterans Race (open to men born before the Queeen's Accession in 1837) prize Box of Cigars 5s6d
XXX Entrance fees 3d for each event
5 p.m. procession return to St Ann's Bay after singing Jubilee songs.
Children will be dismissed at their respective schools.
In the evening the streets and houses of the town will be illuminated, a bon fire will be lighted at 8 p.m. on Cameron's Peak and another on the reef at St Ann's Bay at the same hour.

July 5, 1897
FOR SALE
BELMONT PEN
        In the parish of St Ann, containing about 647 acres, 46 acres of which are in guinea grass, 389 acres in pimento and common pasture, and 212 acres in wood and ruinate. The residence on this property is on one of the most charming spots in the Island commanding excellent sea and mountain views.
        The property is situate within three miles of Ocho Rios and five miles of St Ann's Bay.

The present yearly Cocoanut crop is from 60,000, to 70,000, and there are many young walks which will soon come in to bearing. There is also a fine young Orange Walk just coming into bearing producing last crop 125 barrels, also well established banana fields.

The pimento crop is from 150 to 200 bags yearly. Besides abounding in Cedar, Braziletto, Fustic and other valuable woods, this property is well known for its good bearing lime trees.

The water supply is abundant having two rivers and many springs running through the property with the advantage of a gutter within a few yards of the house.
For further particulars and permission to view please apply to Arthur Colthirst, Esq on the property or to B. STINES, Auct. Com. Agt. 143 Harbour St, Kingston.

July 5, 1897
High Class Day School for Girls

Vauxhall Brown's Town Kingston
Conducted by Miss Hollar and a Competent Assistant
The above School will be opened on July 26 1897

The course of instruction will comprise English Language, Composition, Arithmetic,
Geography, History and Literature, Religious Knowledge, French, Algebra, Euclid,
Botany, Calisthenics and Needlework,
Terms payable quarterly.
Pupils under 12 years £6 per annum
Do   over do do   £8 per annum
EXTRAS 1. Music 2. Drawing £4 each per annum
Books that are required will be supplied and charged.
Further information if required may be had on application to
MISS HOLLAR
20 Bray Street
Brown's Town, Kingston

REFEREES:- Rev. W. C. Murray, D.D., Rev W. Pratt, M.A. G.P. Myers, Esq., Rev J. Massiah, B.A. J.L Ramson, Esq.M.A. W.D. Smedmore Esq., W. H. Mitchell Esq., M.A.

3 mths 3t 3c wkly   June 12

August 7, 1897
DeLEON At No 26 Hanover St. Spanish Town, CHARLES A DELEON late inspector of poor for Saint Catherine, leaving a widow and a large circle to mourn their loss.
Not gone from Memory,
Not gone from Love
But gone to his Fathers' house above.

August 21, 1897
MUSGRAVE HOUSE
Brown's Town
For the Sporting Season
Muzzle and Breach Loading Guns
Cartridge Shells, Diamond Grain Powder
Revolvers and Cartridges, etc etc
J.H. Levy & Co
Musgrave House
246

1897

GENTS HATS
A Large Assortment Hard and Soft
Felt Hats which we will sell for 1s
To 4s each

Ladies Hats
We have just opened case of Ladies
Sunbean Hats from 6d to 2s 6d ea,
Also White Fancies 3s to 5s each.

TWEED, TWEED, TWEED
1 Bale Cord. French Serge, 5s to 10s a
yd

CORSETS,CORSETS,CORSETS,
A general assortment from 1s6d to 10s a pr

BRACES,BRACES,BRACES
1 Case men's all webb 6d to 4s a pair

PIPES,PIPES,PIPES
1 Case assorted Briar wood 3d to 4 s each

FLANNEL,FLANNEL, FLANNEL
Welsh and Saxony 6d to 3s per yard
Fancy Flannelettes 3d to 6d per yard

RUGS AND QUILTS
Coloured comfortables and Eider Down
Quilt, 5s to 16s each
White Honey Comb and Marsaille Quilts
3s6d to 16s each
Coloured Altambra 1s6d to 8s each
Carriage Rugs and Shawls
Carpets and Carpeting 9d to 3s yd, to 10s each
China Mats 72x36 3s each
Table Covers in Damask and Cloth, floss
Ends

STATIONERY;
Account Books, Letter Books, Exercise
Books 1 ½ to 1s 3d each
Note Paper and Envelopes of superior
Quality
Pens, Penholders, Blotting Paper, Slipper
patterns
Felt patterns 2s 6d, Canvas patterns 1s 3d

Bags and Baskets
Telescope Travelling Bags 2s 6d to 8s ea
Ladies Hand Bags 1s to 8 s ea
Carpet and Leather Travelling Bags
Fancy Baskets,
Market Baskets
Work Baskets Nests Trunks,
1 Case Toilet Waters,
Cologne, Toilet Soaps, etc, etc

CARRIAGE DEPARTMENT
Light 2 and 4 Wheelers, with and with
Out hoops will be sold cheap,
Carriage material in all its branches

Selected Vital Records from the Jamaican Daily Gleaner
Ready made wheels.
BICYCLES
Ladies and Gents Bicycles
Boys Tricycles
Girls Velvet Cushion Tricycles
J.H. Levy & Co

August 26, 1897
PARNTHER-GEDDES-At Coke Chapel Aug. 24th by the father of the bride, assisted by the father of the bridegroom and the Rev. G.H.B. Hay, the Rev. DAVID D. PARNTHER, B.A. Wesleyan Minister to Miss ELIZABETH M. GEDDES.

September 16, 1897
The Elections
St Ann

St Ann-Nominations for Parochial Board St Ann, No 2, division took place at the Court House today before Mr. W.G. Nunes, Returning Officer. The following candidates were nominated; Arthur Townend, Rev. W.H. Atkin, A.J. Hart, A.J. Webb, R. Heming, J.D. Ormsby, J.A. Miller, Rev. Geo House, A.N. Dixon. The contest is going to be a lively one, only 4 members are wanted for here.

Moneague-No 2 Division nominated as follows: Hemming Charles, N. Brown Hamilton Allen Henry, Samuel Henry, Henry Charles, Wesley Royes, George H. Atkinson, Revd George Sutherland, Alfred N. Wesley. Election contested Poll next Wednesday.

Brown's Town- There has been no contest here. The following gentlemen were nominated : Joseph Henry Levy, Henry William Miller, James Emanuel Myers, John Robert Scholes, and James Philip Hall, declared elected.

Ocho Rios- Edmonds Frederick, Harrison Edmund, Hubert Ewen, Frank William duly nominated. Election contested. Poll will be taken next Wednesday.

September 20, 1897
Lazarus-At Falmouth on Saturday 22the inst. Captain H. Louis Lazarus, 25th New York Cavalry, Veteran of the Civil War in the 57th year of his age and MIRIAM his devoted and beloved wife in her 47th year. They leave 3 sorrowing sons, 2 sisters and other relatives to mourn their sad loss.. "May their dear Souls rest in peace"
[A companion piece in the same issue from Falmouth tells more about their unexpected deaths. It says Mrs. Lazarus being a Jewess was buried in the Jewish burial ground and Mr. Lazarus was interred in the public cemetery]

September 25, 1897
Mr. Robert Merrick Watson, of this city against whom a provisional order in bankruptcy in the Supreme Court was made on the petition of Mr. W.H. Bird on the 22nd inst. Yesterday filed notice of his intention to deny or dispute the allegations contained in the petition, and to apply for the revocation of the provisional order. The matters will be argued in Chambers on Friday 1st October next.

October 13, 1897
CHAMBERS
Before Mr. Justice C.R. Lumb, L.L.D.
Mr. WATSON'S PROVISIONAL ORDER
An application of Mr. W.H. Bird to revoke a provisional order against R.M. Watson (his late partner) was made in Chambers yesterday. Mr. P. Stern appeared on behalf of the

debtor, and Mr. Cargill represented the petitioning creditor. After hearing the argument, His Honour revoked the provisional order with costs.

Brown's Town
October 1st, 1897
NOTICE
The Subscriber having sold out his business at St. Ann's Bay carried on by him under the style of Levy, Isaacs & Co, The Retail portion to Mr. Solomon Isaacs, and the Wholesale to Messrs. Wm. Cover, Jr. and A.C. Dunkley, takes this opportunity of thanking his patrons at St Ann's Bay for the liberal support accorded him during the time he carried on business there, and bespeaks for his Successors the same support and confidence.
The Liabilities of Levy, Isaacs & Co will be settled by the Subscriber while all parties indebted to both establishments will please settle with the respective purchasers, but accounts due on acceptances must be settled with the subscriber.
J H. Levy

t & c 2 wks   Oct 6

St Ann's Bay
October 1st, 1897

NOTICE
Referring to the advertisement of Mr. J.H. Levy announcing the Sale of his Retail and Hardware business to me, I beg to inform the public that same will be carried on under the firm and style of "Isaacs & Co" on the same lines as the old firm, keeping a full assortment of every description of Fancy and Staple Goods, haberdashery, Hardware &c &c which will be kept up by regular shipments from England, the United States and the Continent. Mr. MacContel's continuance as manager coupled with the Subscribers' personal supervision is a guarantee that the best attention will be paid to all customers.
Sol Isaacs
t&c 2 wks   Oct 6

St Ann's Bay
October 1st, 1897
Referring to the above, the Subscribers having entered into partnership will carry on business as general merchants, Saint Ann's Bay under the style of "Cover, Dunkley & Co" they solicit from the public the same generous support awarded to their predecessors, and will receive regular consignment of Fish, Cargos Beer, Whiskies &c &c also get fresh supplies of Dry Goods and breadstuffs by every steamer, and also purchase every description of island Produce at highest prices. It is also their pleasure to announce that they will add to the present business a retail Dry Goods and Fancy Department under the management of polite and efficient salesmen and every satisfaction guaranteed.
Wm COVER JR.
A.C.DUNKLEY
t & c 2 wks   Oct 6

October 15, 1897
VERLEY- On the 14th instant, in Kingston, the wife of Leo. C. Verley of a son.

October 20, 1897
CLEMETSON At the Sanitorium Montego Bay on the 11th inst ABRAHAM BRANKER CLEMETSON of Union Hill St Mary. Aged 55 years.

October 20, 1897
THE YELLOW FEVER
When we wrote the article on the 9th instant announcing the existence of yellow fever in Jamaica we stated that the fact was known abroad. A correspondent kindly supplied us with an example of the information that was being published. It seems that the New York Sun had printed something on the subject and this was copied into other journals. Here are the headlines in the Boston Herald of the 7th inst.:-"Almost a Panic-Yellow Fever in Jamaica Rapidly Spreading -Creole and Foreigners Alike Attacked-Fear that Little Can Be done to Check the Scourge-Virulent Cases Among the European Soldiers-The Disease Invade the Army Station in the Hills. [More] – This of course proves how necessary it is for exact intelligence on the subject to be supplied in our local press.

October 26, 1897
St Ann's Bay
NEW BUSINESS
Our well known townsman, Mr. W.A. Gaynor, (late manager of Messrs. Kerr & Coy's tavern shop) has now started his own business in this town. He has opened a nice little dry goods store, and being so well known and respected, we feel sure he will go up the ladder and make his mark. We also hail with pleasure the new firm of Messrs. Cover, Dunkley & Coy; they are making elaborate fixings for their retail department and will be opened to the public in a week or two. We wish these gentlemen success.

October 29, 1897
FOURNIER At 6.55 p.m. on the 28th inst. in his 33rd year, at Mizpah Cottage, Rosedale Avenue (West Race Course)- the residence of his aunt, Mrs. R. McCormack, ERNEST FOURNIER late of Port au Prince and Jacmel (Haiti). Funeral moves at 4.30 this afternoon. Friends will please accept this intimation.

November 9, 1897
BROWN'S TOWN, ST ANN
        A grand concert with tableaux is expected to come off in the St Mark's Church Schoolroom on the 11th inst (Thursday Evening) a new instrument (piano) will be used on the occasion. Several ladies and gentlemen will be taking part. We are sure the inhabitants of Brown's Town have a treat to look forward to.
        The harvest festival that came off on the 24th ult. was a success although it may fall short by a few pounds of last year's collection etc., taking the general depression into consideration there is no reason to complain and we are sure the energetic Rector is satisfied. We hear the St Mark's Church choir intends early next year to give another Hymnal Oratorio. This something that everybody will look forward to with very great pleasure. Business dull. Health of the community good as usual.
        The piano has just arrived.

December 4, 1897
The Yellow Fever
YELLOW FEVER CASES TO THURSDAY DECEMBER 2

Parish	No of Cases	No of Deaths
Kingston & St Andrew	25	31
Port Royal	4	2
Manchester	32	10

Portland	3	3
Westmoreland	1	1
St Thomas	1	1
St Catherine	4	—
St James	1	1
Total	131	49

December 6, 1897
ISAACS-AT Hadds Penn, Westmoreland, on Sunday the 21st November, 1897, FREDERICK ISAACS of the above Penn, aged 59 years. "May his Soul rest in peace".

December 17, 1897
THE CUSTOS OF ST ANN
The Editor of the Gleaner.

Sir, St Ann is surprised at the appointment of Mr. Cox as Custos as everyone fully expected Sir Henry's game was to wait until the eve of his departure and appoint another gentleman whose name had been mentioned, but he was evidently afraid of public opinion.

If Jamaicans were ever deluded with the idea, that the Governor ever cared for them this last action of his will certainly open their eyes.

Mr. Cox though he maybe rich and intelligent man has no more claim to the Custosship (nor I am sure did he aspire to it,) than the veriest pauper in the Parish, then why should Sir Henry go out of his way to appoint a man but a resident of 4 years in the island, (and that confined to the four corners of Claremont) a magistrate and custos in one day, over the heads of the old and experienced magistrates of this parish. The answer is plain. Those who were entitled to it from long service happened, poor men to be Jamaicans, such men as Mr. T.B. Scott and Mr. J.H. Levy. The latter gentleman was fitted and in every respect entitled to the position. The parish and the Magistracy have every confidence in him. Mr. Scott may be objected to because of his failing eyesight, but he is a gentleman and a native and senior Magistrate of this parish and has always acted as Chief Magistrate with ability and satisfaction. The keynote of Sir Henry's administration has been the benefitting of all but the natives, no reward given for long and faithful service. No wonder then that Jamaica was rich when he came. He leaves us all beggars and yet there will be many fools who in the face of such wrongs are ready to sign elaborate addresses and give him a grand send off. There is one thing certain and that, is he will never so use signature of
A Native
St Ann, Cave Valley, P.O.

December 22, 1897
FACEY-JOHN SAMUEL FACEY, Funeral will move from 105 North Street at 4.30 this evening. Friends and acquaintance are requested to accept this intimation.

December 28, 1897
Maxwell, after five days' illness at Retirement Manse on the 20th of December 1897 JEANNIE M TARBET the beloved wife of the Rev. John Maxwell, Church of Scotland, St Elizabeth. Deeply lamented by her many sorrowing friends.

December 29, 1897
VALENCIA-At Pumpkin Ground Pen, Gregory Park a 1 a.m. on 28th inst JOSE M. VALENCIA. Deeply regretted.

December 31, 1897

MILLER-HIRE- On the 22nd December 1897 at Dunkeld Mile Gully, Manchester (MAY) AGNES STEWART HIRE eldest daughter of H.F. Hire and Agnes Hire to R.J. Miller, by Revd. D. A. McKellop assisted by Rev. J.M. Cass. No Cards.

1898

January 4, 1898
Lefranc-At her late residence, 36 East Race Course, at 6.30 yesterday morning CATHERINE MATILDA DALLAS, relict of the late John LeFranc. Funeral at 4 p.m. Friends please accept this the only intimation.

January 5. 1898
VICKERS-On the 15th December, at Melrose, Half-way Tree, ISABEL, wife of Edward Vickers Resident Magistrate, in her fifty-fourth year.

January 7, 1898
Yesterday's Gazette announced that Mr. Edward Vickers, Supernummery Resident Magistrate has been provisionally appointed to act as R.M. for Kingston in the room of Mr. A Can. W. Lucie-Smith who has been transferred to the Colony of British Guiana; also the appointment of Mr. H. S. Fisher, to act as R.M. for Manchester in the room of Mr. William Wissilhouse Fisher who has left of England on leave and Mr. Leonard Grey to act as Clerk of the Courts of Kingston for Mr. H. S. Fisher.

January 10, 1898
RAMSON-ORMSBY-On Wednesday the 19th Dec, 1897 at St Saviour's Church, St Anne, by the Ven Archdeacon Ramson, father of the bridegroom, assisted by the Rev. J.J.C. Ormsby, brother of the bride, and the Rev F. L Grange. B.A., JOHN LUCE RAMSON, M.A. to AMABEL HELEN KATHERINA, third daughter of J.D. Ormsby Esq., of Lime Hall St Anne. At home 57 Beeston St Kingston, 26th & 27the January, 1898

January 15, 1898
ESTATE SOLD
Worthy Park Estate in St Catherine was transferred on the 31st December to a new owner. The negotiations were concluded in England. Messrs Talbot and Carpenter, the old proprietors have sold it to Mr. John Calder of Stanimore, St Elizabeth. Mr. J. R. Scarlett, the attorney is well known; he has acted in that capacity for a period of 23 years. He has now gone to his own property Wineford(Winefield?) in St Ann.

January 17, 1898
DUFF-on 4th inst in Brooklyn, U.S.A. ISABELLA MILBOUROUGH, Relict of the late William Duff of Kingston, Jamaica

Selected Vital Records from the Jamaican Daily Gleaner

January 18, 1898
ESCOFFERY-At her residence, 40 Rose Lane at 8/30 GRISILDA ESCOFFERY the beloved sister of Mortimer Escoffery. Funeral at 4.30 this afternoon. Friends and acquaintances please accept this intimation.

January 24, 1898
DACOSTA- On Saturday 22nd inst. at her mother's residence, 91 King Street, RACHAEL LOUISE, widow of the late Jacob R. DaCosta. Deeply mourned by all who knew her. "God's will be done".

January 25, 1898
JANSEN-At her residence No 20 King St., Spanish Town on the 21st January, 1898, JESSIE JANSEN, born Gordon, the much beloved wife of Otto Arthur Jansen of Magdeburg, Germany.

January 28, 1898
CALDER-DOUGLAS-On the 19th January 1898 at Holy Trinity Church, Duke St Kingston, Jamaica by His Lordship Bishop Gordon, assisted by the Rev. Fr. Collins, Mulry, and Lynch, JULIA MARY second daughter of Geo. A. Douglas, Supt Gen Penitentiary to Wm. Jameson Calder Inspector Jamaica Constabulary second son of Wm. Calder North Berwick, Scotland.

February 5. 1898
MAGNUS-At Eton Villa, South Camp Road, the wife of Eugene M. Magnus of a daughter on the 31st Ultimo.

February 7, 1898
CUNDALL- Yesterday at 'Surbiton" Half-way Tree, GERTRUDE the wife of Frank Cundall. Funeral at 4o'clock this afternoon.

February 9, 1898
BYLES-At the "Lawn", Spanish Town on Sunday 6th inst, GEO DUNCAN BYLES eldest son the late R. L. Byles. R.I.P.

February 17, 1898
THE WESLEYAN CONFERENCE-First Day.

The Western West Indian Conference of the Wesleyan Methodist Church met within Edmondson Hall yesterday morning at 10 o'clock. After devotional exercises by the retiring Vice-President, the Rev. William Clarke Murray, D.D. and Rev. Thos P. Russell, the Rev Thomas M. Geddes, President Elect of the West Indian Conference was inducted into office. The Rev Dr. Murray in a short but exceedingly happy speech introduced the President who was received by the brethren with acclamation.

The President then addressed the brethren. He referred to matters of interest to the Church and concluded by expressing the hope that the clouds which now hang over us will soon be dispersed.

The roll being called the following Representatives were found to be present
KINSTON District
Rev. Thos. M. Geddes, Ex-Officio
Rev. F.O. Miller
Rev. Caleb Reynolds
Rev. G.H. Baron Hay
MONTEGO BAY District

1898

Rev. John Duff, Ex-Officio
Rev. John Grant
Rev. W.A. Griffin
Rev. J. A. MacIntosh
Rev. C.C. Wallace
ST ANN DISTRICT
Rev. W. Clarke Murray, D.D. Ex-Officio
Rev. R.M. Parnther
Rev. W. H. Atkin
Rev. W. J. Williams
Rev. J. Kissock Braham, B.D.
MORANT BAY DISTRICT
Rev. Thos P Russell, Ex-Officio
Rev. S. L. Lindo
Rev. W J. Maund

Neither the ex-officio nor elected Representatives from the Hayti district was present. It was intimated to the Conference that Mr. Pocott (Picot?)the Chairman of the District had had recent severe family bereavement which no doubt, accounts for his absence.

The Rev. Wm. Clarke Murray D.D., was reelected Vice President. The Rev. John Duff was re-elected Secretary.
More.

February 18, 1898
Ashenheim-DeCordova- On Wednesday evening the 9th Febry, 1898 at Glenhurst Kingston by the Rev. S. Jacobs, LEWIS, son of J. L Ashenheim, Esq. to ESTELLE LILLIAN, only daughter of the late F. J. deCordova, both of this city. At home St. Quintins; Viaa, Lisant Road from 7 p.m. on Wednesday the 22nd inst. No Cards.

DeCordova-Ashenheim-On Wednesday evening the 9th February, 1898 at Glenhurst, Kingston by the Rev. S. Jacobs, MICHAEL, second on of the late F. J. DeCordova, Esq. To JUDITH, youngest daughter of J. L Ashenheim, Esq, both of this city. At home at May Ville on Wednesday afternoon the 23rd inst from 5 to 7 o'clock. No Cards.

HUIE At her residence, Barriff Castle, Falmouth, Sunday 13th February 1898, SUSAN WILLIAMS HUIE, aged 84 years, leaving a sister and several nephews and nieces to mourn their loss. R.I.P. Scotch papers please copy.

February 22, 1898
The Methodist Conference then took the Final Draft of stations and resulted as follows-
FINAL DRAFT OF STATIONS, 1898
I-THE KINGSTON DISTRICT.
Chairman Thomas M. Geddes, Financial Secretary, Caleb Reynolds.
Kingston (Coke) Thomas M. Geddes, Caleb Reynolds, Charles C. Wallace Port Royal, Geo S. Lamb, Supernumerary.
Kingston (Wesley) Geo. H. B. Hay
Red Hills and Providence, George Lockett, T.M. Sherlock, Red Hills
Clarendon, Samuel T. Brown
Manchester, Fred O. Miller
Mount Fletcher, Alex. M. Smith
Grateful Hill, Arthur F. Lightbourn
Turks Island, Charles G. Hardwick.

Selected Vital Records from the Jamaican Daily Gleaner

II. THE MONTEGO BAY DISTRICT

Chairman John Duff; Financial Secretary, John A. McIntosh

9.Montego Bay, John Duff, William H. Sloley who shall give 6 months to the Bath Circuit.

10.Lucea, David D. Parnther, B.A.

11.Falmouth, Jonathan Grant

12.Duncans, John A. McIntosh, N. Surgeon, Ulster Spring

13.Mount Ward, William R. Griffin

14. Sav-la-Mar William Baillie, one to be sent.

15. Black River Achilles Lambert

15. Mountain Side, James C.A. Smith.

III. THE ST ANN DISTRICT

Chairman Wm Clarke Murray, D.D.; Financial Secretary R.M. Parnther

17. Spanish Town, Albert H. Aguilar, E.G. Cook, Linstead.

18. St Ann's Bay, William H. Atkin

19. Watsonville J. Kissock Braham, B.D.

20. Ocho Rios H. Gilles Clerk.

21. Beechanville, Robert M. Parnther.

22. Bensonton, William J. Williams, one to be sent.

23. Brown's Town, W. Clarke Murray D.D.

24. Edmondson, Manasseh Barkerr

25. Mount Hunie, Nathan A. Bacquie

26. Guy's Hill and Hampstead Theo A. Glasspole

IV. THE MORANT BAY DISTRICT

Chairman Samuel L. Lindo, Financial Secretary William J. Maund

Morant Bay Clifford M. Clarke

Port Morant Henry T. Page

Bath, William J. Maund

Manchioneal, Hilton C. Quinlan

Port Antonio Samuel L. Lindo

Buff Bay, Reginald W. McLarty

Yallahs, Albert L Johnson.

THE HAYTI AND SANTO DOMINGO DISTRICT

Chairman, Thos R. Picot, Financial Secretary, W. S. Smith.

Port au-Prince, Westmore S. Smith

Petit Goave, An Evangelist

Gonaives, Vacant

Jeremie, Henri Bellonce

Les Cayes, August Albert

Cape Hayti and Monte Christy, Thomas R. Picot

Puerto Plata Adolphus Cresser

Samana and Sanches. Elijah Mair Wil. Emerson Mears, Jacob James Supernumerary

San Domingo, An Evangelist

CENTRAL AMERICA

Panama, Alexander W. Geddes, W. J. Jacobs, one requested.

N.B. 1. James O Mann, has the permission of the Missionary Committee in London to return to England

2. Thomas P, Russell's state of health demands for him immediate rest and change.

THOMAS M. GEDDES,   President,

JOHN DUFF, Secretary.

1898

March 1, 1898
JUDAH-On Saturday morning the 26th February 1898 in Saint Jago de la Vega, POPHAM BASDEN JUDAH, Solicitor

March 12, 1898
Codner-At No 7 West Avenue, Kingston Gardens, on 24th Feb, 1898, the wife of J. W. Codner of a daughter

FFRENCH-In her 71st year, ELIZA FFRENCH relict of the late Mr. George Ffrench. The funeral moves from No 44 Johns Lane at 4.30 this afternoon.

March 17, 1898
ROBERTS-BRISCOE-At St Matthew's Church, Claremont on Thursday 10th March, 1898 by the Revd. J.T. H. Chandler, FREDERICK WILLIAM TALENT of St Ann's Bay to SARAH ELIZA, youngest daughter of William Drew Briscoe of Claremont. No Cards.

March 22, 1898
LITTLEJOHN-In Garden City, Long Island Wednesday 9 [March] 1898 at 4.30 p.m. JEANNIE M. Littlejohn, daughter of the late Samuel T. Armstrong and wife of the Rev. A.N. Littlejohn, Bishop of Long Island.

March 24, 1898
DEPASS-JACOB HENRY DEPASS, aged 58 years. Funeral will move from his late residence, Kendal, St Andrew at 4.30 this afternoon.

DELVANTE-DELGADO-On the 16th March, 1898 by the Rev. S Jacobs, MICHAEL DELEVANTE of Colon, Isthmus of Panama to ALETHIA, third daughter of the late Albert Delgado of Kingston, Jamaica. No Cards.

April 1, 1898
HENRIQUES-Sarah- At 10o'clock yesterday morning at her late residence, 28 East St., Sarah Henriques the beloved mother of Benjamin Harris, Proprietor Harris Express. Friends and acquaintances are requested to attend the funeral at 4.30 this evening. Carriages.

April 19, 1898
Among the Schools
TEACHERS WANTED
On Thursday last the under mentioned School Managers were in want of teachers. Rev. F. Edmonds, Ocho Rios P.O. for Parry Town School, Rev. J. K. Braham, B.D. Moneague P.O for Moneague school and Rev. J.P. Hall, Brown's Town P.O. as additional women teacher for Brown's Town Church of England school.

April 21, 1898
REBEIRO-Last night at 9 o'clock at his residence No 54 Duke St Kingston. T. NUNES REBEIRO late of Stony Hill, St Andrew. Friends and acquaintances will please accept this the only intimation. Funeral at 4 .30 this evening.

Selected Vital Records from the Jamaican Daily Gleaner

April 23,1898

SCOTT-CRUM-EWING-At Belhaven.U.P. Church, Glasgow on 31st ult., by the Rev R.S. Drommond M.A. D.D. assisted by the Revd. Charles Watson, M.A. D.D. Largs, CHARLES CUNNINGHAM SCOTT, eldest son of John Scott C.B. of Halskill, to JANE COVENTRY CRUM, 4th daughter of the late Humphrey Ewing, Crum Ewing and Mrs. Crum Ewing, 28 Belhaven Terrace, Kelvrade, Glasgow, and grand daughter of the late Humphrey Ewing Crum Ewing, of Strathleven.

April 26, 1898

LINDO-At 2.30 yesterday morning ARCHIBALD LINDO, fourth son of Henry Lindo Esq. of Orange Grove, St Catherine from Joselyn Cottage, Musgrave Avenue. Funeral at 8.30 this morning.

48½ Hanover St

MRS REBEIRO begs through this medium to think her many friends and acquaintances for their very kind expressions of condolence during her sad bereavement.

April 28, 1898

It is with pleasure we announce that of the nine junior candidates, entered from Hampton High School for girls, for the Cambridge Local Examinations held last December, all were successful. M. Rattigan took II Class Honours, with distinction in French. P. Pearce, A. Logan, I. DePass, A. Hewitt, each took III Class Honours; M. Sailman, L. Shaw, E. Webster, and B. Hendricks satisfied the examiners.

May 4, 1898

PERSONAL

Mr. J. W. Gruber begs through the medium of this paper the acceptance of his expression of sincere appreciation of, and thanks to, his numerous friends and acquaintances both in and out of the parish of Saint James who have either called addressed cards to, or written him letters of sympathy and condolence in his recent painful bereavement through the sudden death in London of his son, a medical student of St Bartholomew's Hospital at the close of a five year course in that institution, after a University training in St John's College Cambridge. Montego Bay 2nd May, 1898

May 3, 1898

The Gazette of Thursday last had the results of the Cambridge Local Examination which was held at several centres in the Island in December last. The results show further advance on the part of the schools

May 11, 1898

PORTER-At Marble Hall, Rae Town at 12.45 p.m. on the 10th inst. WM COLORIDGE PORTER. Friends and acquaintances please accept this invitation. Funeral moves at 4p.m.

May 18, 1898

DUMETZ-LONGMAN-At St Michael's Church, Kingston on Wednesday the 11th inst, by the Rev R.G. Ambrose,Dumet, grandson of Matthew Whitmore Esq. of Norfolk England to ELMA ADA daughter of the late Thomas W. Longman of Southampton, England. English papers please copy.

1898

DUQUESNAY PHILIP HAROLD, infant son of Phillip and Emma L. Duquesnay at their residence 39 North Street. Funeral at 4.30 this evening. Friends and acquaintances will please accept this the only intimation.

June 10, 1898
HENDERSON-On Tuesday, June 7th at Barriffe Hall, Oracabessa, G.E. Henderson, Baptist Minister in the 81st year of his age. He landed in Jamaica in 1842 and was the senior minister in connection with his denomination in the Island.

June 15, 1898
STONE-AT Hammersmith, England on 21st May FRANCES ELIZA widow of the late Rev. John Campbell Stone, formerly Rector of Portland and of St Elizabeth, in he 82nd year.

June 22, 1898
ROBERTSON-At Alma Brown's Town St Ann, Jamaica on Saturday 4th June, 1898 the wife of G.D. Robertson of a son.

Among the passengers who sailed in the mail steamer yesterday afternoon for England was Mr. Scotcher, the gentleman who was introduced to the Jamaica Agricultural Society as one wishful of organizing a line of steamships between this island and England. According to what Mr. Scotcher told the Agricultural Society, he is now on his way home armed with information as to the potentialities of the fruit trade that Jamaica might prosecute with the mother country. He intends to call a meeting in London and will raise the capital for the organization of a line of fruit steamers forthwith. So he asserts.

LAMB-BRANDON-On 18th inst at Parish Church, Kingston by the Rev M.C. Clare, BEATRICE BERTHA RUTH, eldest daughter of Mortimer Brandon, Esq., to Rae Town, to WILLIAM LAMB, Esq., second son of James Donald Lamb, Esq. Of St Thomas D.W.I.

June 22, 1898
These scholarships have been awarded on the results of last December's examinations as follows-
SENIORS
Jamaica Scholarship of £200 per annum tenable for three years (as already announced)
Husband G.S. Jamaica High School
Scholarships of £60 per annum tenable for three years
Allwood S.G., York Castle High School
Sulman M.R.H. Potsdam School
Scholarships of £15 per annum for one year
Boys
Pearman, J. O'H Potsdam School
Powell F.C. Potsdam School
Bayley H.H.R. Jamaica High School
Lewis C.C. Potsdam School
Girl
Hollar L.C. Barbican High School
JUNIORS
Scholarships of £10 per annum for one year
Boys

Sharp L.C. Jamaica High School
DoddI.A. Potsdam School
Murray R.M. York Castle High School
MacDermot J.H. Jamaica High School
Foster F.A. Jamaica High School
Dodd R.W. Potsdam School
Smith J. A. York Castle High School
Burrowes B. Wolmer's Upper School

Girls
Pearman, C.C. Private Tuition (declined)
Rattigan M. A. Hampton High School
L Miller Barbican High School

July 4, 1898 (Most of July Missing)

SIMS-COVER-On Wednesday June 29th, 1898 at he Parish Church, Kingston by the Rev. M.C. Clare, THOMAS JAMES, son of the late Thos J. Sims of Wettersham, Kent, England, to ELLA ELIZABETH, youngest daughter of the late Charles S. Cover, of "Enfield," Brown's Town St Ann. No Cards.

AUGUST MISSING

September 10, 1898
THE HARBOUR
PASSENGERS-In the R.M. steamer Atrato yesterday morning. From Southampton – Miss E. Lewis, Miss Small, Mrs. W. P. Livingstone and child, Mr. S. H. Davies and manservant. Rev. and Mrs. C. D. Hindle, and infant Mr. And Mrs. Cowper and two children, Miss Armstrong (2) Mr. B. Edwards. Mr. Edward Bourke. Mr. W. C. Humphrey. C.C.A. Reid, Miss A Smith Miss Sinclair Mr. A Dews. From Barbados-Hon S.C. Burke, Mr. and Mrs. I.R. Reece, two children and nurse. Miss E. B. Johnson. One assisted emigrant 15 recruits W.I.R. and four deckers. From Jacmel 10 deckers and 35 in transit.

September 12, 1898
MYERS-At Portsea, St. Elizabeth, on the 9th inst, AMITHY, widow of the late Michael Myers of Portsmouth, England Aged 84 years. Deeply lamented by her numerous relatives and friends. "Not lost, but gone before"

September 22, 1898
The following is the list of guests at Myrtle Bank Hotel. Hon. D. S. Gibson, Hon J.H. Levy, Mr. C.J. Levy, Rev J.P. Hall wife and son. Mrs. Pratt, Capt Cunningham, Mrs. J.N Garguilo Mr. A.E. Silvera, Mr. F. R. Kennedy, Mr. Jm D. Mather, Mr. H. A. Davis, Cap and Mrs. J. D. Hart. Mr. J. W. Smith Snr C Marconel Snr Jose B. DeDelman Mr. O Mehoney Mr. R. Funtion, Mr. John Hoyt. More, unreadable on my copy.

September 23, 1898
The Rev Caleb Reynolds is to be congratulated on the success of the co[] held in the Wesley Mission Allman Town on Wednesday. More.

1898

The Singapore Free Press says-Mrs. J.M. Vermont is, we are glad to say reported to be recovering from the effects of the serious accident which occurred to her on board ship on the voyage out from Europe" Mrs. Vermont is well known in Jamaica where she formerly resided.

October 7, 1898
GENTLE-At Hampstead, Trelawny, on Sunday 2nd instant, ALEXANDER BOLTON GENTLES only son of William and Catherine Gentles and Nephew of Thos. Gentles of Falkirk Scotland. Aged 40¾ years.

October 11, 1898
News from the Parishes
Brown's Town

A Concert was held in Brown's Town, St Ann in aid of the sufferers to the recent hurricane in St Vincent on the 4th October under the patronage of his Honour the Custos, the Hon Dr. Johnston M.L.C. Mr. J.H Levy, Chairman of the Parochial Board. His Honour E. Leslie Thornton, Acting Resident Magistrate for the parish the Justices of the Peace and Ministers of the several denominations. The programme was as follows:

Pianoforte Duet, The Priests March Ithdu Mrs. Johnstone & Miss Isaacs
Song xxx's Lullaby Lane Miss Levy
Pianoforte Solo (1) Parkainus Shuffle
(20 Kemolin Two Step
Miss Johnston
Song Good Company Inspector Clark
Pianoforte solo-The Corsair F. Cowen Mrs. Delgado
Song Winds in the Trees—Mrs. Isaacs
Recitation Human Nature Mast Delgado
Pianoforte Twilight Fancies
Bonser Mrs. Phillpots
Song (comic) All Cooks look alike Mr. W.L. Levy
Pianoforte solo Vals Arabesque Lack Mrs. Hutchies
Song Leaving Home Miss DaCosta
Pianoforte duet Garde de Coer
Mrs. W. Costa & Miss M Cover
Song My Lost Dream Levey Miss Levy
Solo and Chorus Never Alone
Mrs. and Misses Johnston
Legerdemain   Professor Shield

Mr. Thornton presided over the entertainment. He was met by Mr. J.H. Levy J.P. Mr. Chas Costa, J.P. Mr. C.F. Delgado J.P. and the reverend Dr. Murray. After Mr. Thornton had been introduced to the audience by Mr. Levy, he spoke of his own personal knowledge of St Vincent, the destruction and devastation which had taken place there.

The room was well filled with an appreciative audience. The ladies and gentlemen taking part in the programme acquitted themselves excellently well and thanks are due to them for their kindness in taking part. It would be invidious where all have done their best and so well to make further comment. Special mention must however be made of Professor Shield whose tricks were very cleverly done. The money taken at the door amounted to £17 7s 6d.

Selected Vital Records from the Jamaican Daily Gleaner

Hurricane Relief Fund
Collected by J.H. Levy Esq.

J.H. Levy & Co	£2 0 0
George E Henderson &	
Mrs Henderson	£2 0 0
J.B.Thomson & Co	£1 1 0
Delgado Bros	£1 1 0
J.E. Kerr & Co	£1 1 0
Brown's Town Dorcas Society	£1 0 0
Rupert E. Fonseca	£ 2 0
J.P.M. Rose	2 0
Psyche	2 0
C.R.T.	2 0
G.H. Cooper	2 0
	£8 13 0

October 15, 1898
WESTMORELAND-At Esher on the 12th October HENRY STEWART WESTMORELAND eldest son of the late the Hon Henry Westmoreland of Gibraltar. Aged 68? Years.

October 18, 1898
GENTLES-At Hampstead, Trelawny on Sunday October 2nd ALEXANDER BOLTON, beloved husband of J.E. Gentles only son of William and Catherine Gentles and nephew of Thos Gentles of Falkirk, Scotland. He leaves one child who with them mourns his loss.

October 21, 1898
RAMSON-At 57 Beeston Street, Kingston on the 18th instant the wife of John L Ramson of a daughter.

October 27, 1898
ELLIS WOLFE- Last night at his residence Racencroft, South Camp Road ELLIS WOLFE in his 81st year. Funeral at 8.30 Friday morning. Friends will please accept this intimation.

October 31, 1898
BROWN-KOCH-On the 20th Oct, 1898 at Church of the Ascension, West Brighton, New York, J. Sutton-Brown now of this city, to Gertrude Marie Koch.

November 5, 1898
BROWN-KOCH Gertrude M. Koch to J. Sutton Brown at Church of the Ascension, Staten Island, New York 20th October 1898

November 11, 1898
ISAACS-MORTLOCK-on the 27th Oct at the Parish Church, Montego Bay, by the Rev. J.W. Austin, assisted by Rev. C.B. Davis of Sav-la–Mar, Dr. S.A. Isaacs of Sav-la-Mar to Maude Cecil Aileen only daughter of the late F.W.Mortlock, late Collector of H.M. Revenue, and Grand daughter of the late F. Cheetham Mortlock, Esqr of Abington Hall Cambridge, England (English papers please copy).

262

1898

November 15, 1898
DUFF-MARY ELIZABETH- the beloved wife of Charles Percival Duff at 43 Oxford Street, Kingston. Friends and acquaintances please accept this intimation and let your carriages attend. Funeral moves at 5 o'clock this evening. "Not my will but Thine be done"

November 19, 1898
We regret to announce the death of Mr. William Cover late of Hopewell Penn, St Ann. Mr. Cover died on Wednesday night last at 9 o'clock. The funeral took place at the Episcopal Church last Evening. Mr. Cover was a penkeeper, and a Justice of the Peace of long standing.

November 21, 1898
COVER-At Richmond Villa, Brown's Town on the 16th Nov. 1898 WILLIAM COVER, JNR of Hopewell, Dry Harbour and principal of the firm of Cover & Co of St Ann's Bay in the 47th year of his age.

November 1898
J.H. Levy among others was staying at Myrtle Bank Hotel.

November 28, 1898
EWEN On the 15th day of November, instant, at Falmouth, Trelawny the wife of Guy Seymour Ewen of a son.

MRS ELLIS WOLFE and Daughter and the other Members of the family of the late Ellis Wolfe, avail themselves of this medium to express their heart felt gratitude for the numerous kind expressions of sympathy tendered them since their sad bereavement.

November 30, 1898
MALABRE-On the 25th inst at No. 133 East Street, Kingston, the wife of Arthur A. Malabre of a son.

SILVERA-At his residence 105 North Street, at 8 o'clock on the 29th inst. RICHARD A. SILVERA the beloved husband of the late Helen Silvera. Funeral moves at 4 o'clock this evening. Friends and acquaintances please let your carriage attend. "All thy conflict ends in everlasting bliss"

HAUGHTON At the Bungalow, Ocho Rios, on the 15th inst., ROSA ALICE HAUGHTON, second daughter of the late John Haughton James of Roaring River, St Ann's Deeply regretted. English papers please copy.

Neish-At Escombe, Old Harbour, yesterday, 8th Dec. 1898 at 9 a.m. in the 55th year of her age. MARY beloved wife of James Neish. M.D. Canadian papers please copy.

December 13, 1898
GARSIA-At 14 Studley Park Road Kingston on the 10th inst., at 2 p.m. BERONA CAMILLA, aged 33 years, the fond and beloved wife of Eustace G. A. Garsia leaving 3 children and a number of relatives to mourn their irreparable loss.
"Her languishing head is at rest,
"It's aching and sighing are o'er

Selected Vital Records from the Jamaican Daily Gleaner

"That quiet immovable breast
"Is moved by affliction no more"
"She Sleeps in Jesus"
Foreign Papers please copy.

December 14, 1898
Mrs. William Cover Jr., of Hopewell St Ann, adopts this method of returning thanks to the numerous kind friends who in her bereavement have proffered their condolence.

December 28, 1898
SCARLETT-BOETTCHER-At the Cathedral, Spanish Town by the Rev. E.J. Wortley, Rector, JOHN HENRY SCARLETT, second son of John R. Scarlett of Winefield, St Ann's to Annie Vhangiera? eldest daughter of Gustav A. Boettcher, Esq. of Spanish Town, Jamaica.

December 31, 1898
Mr. Rudyard Kipling has been paid for his Navy articles in the Morning Post at the rate of £20 per thousand words. This makes about £40 for the ordinary newspaper column.

1898
Popular Men
On the subject of popular men and in reply to the query "Does this meet with popular approval? "Humboldt" writes Decidedly no, I send you the following twenty-five names which I think are much more popular than those mentioned by "K"
HON P. Stern
Archbishop Nuttall
Rev G.H. Baron Hay
Dr Love
Hon S.C. Burke
Hon C. B. Berry
Mr. W.C. Murray
Hon Rev. H. Clarke
Hon D. A. Corinaldi
Mr. C.M. Farquharson
Hon J. T. Palache
Mr. Arthur Levy
Col. Pinnock
Mr. J. Smicle
Rev. W. Clarke Murray D.D.
Rev W. Gillies, D.D.
Mr. W. Morrison M.A.
Dr. C Whitney
Mr. G.A. Douet
Mr. W. Cradwick
Mr.E. Astley Smith
Rev. W. Graham
Mr. G. Lustac Burke
Mr. Charles Higgins
Mr. E.J. Sadler
Montorvillo writes: In your issue of today's date, under the heading of "popular Men appears a list sent in by K". May I submit the following names as being still more popular

1898

J.T. Palache
Philip Stern.
Wm Morrison A.A.
T.B. Lyons
S.C. Burke
Dr Lumb
Archbishop Nuttall
C.J. Ward,
L. F. McKinnon
Judge Northcote
T.B. Oughton
Mr. Justice Vickers
Oscar Marescaux.
D.S. Gideon
Dr Mogge.

1899

January 3, 1899
MacNish New Year's day 1st January, 1899 At Eden Lawn, Norman Road, Kingston. The wife of James Hunter MacNish of a son and daughter.

January 6, 1899
BARHAM-LYONS-On Wednesday 28th Decr 1898 at Port Maria, AMY IDALIA , eldest daughter of L.I. Lyons, to SIGNISMUND CYRIL second son of the late A.S. Barham. At Home, Sunday 8th and Monday 9th inst. No Cards

A fourth mistress is wanted for the Wolmer's Girls' School. The salary is £70 a year. Candidates for the position should state qualifications, including special subjects.

MacNish-At Eden Lawn, Norman Road on the 4th inst, the infant son of James Hunter and Rilla May MacNish.

January 16, 1899
Gariques-On Friday the 6th instant at Bethany, St Ann, in the 73rd year of his age, FRED NEWTON GARRIQUES, son of Harry Lord Garriques, late of Yarmouth Estate, Vere.

January 19, 1899
SMITH-At 'Dungarvan' St Andrew, on Wednesday morning, 18th inst, the wife of R.P. Smith of a daughter.

January 30, 1899
DELEVANTE-At 27 Charles Street on the morning of 28th inst. The wife of M. Delevante of Colon of a son.

WRIGHT- At Spanish Town on Saturday 28th inst, ALEXANDER WRIGHT

DeMERCADO-At 70 Lawes Street, WALTER DEMERCADO, eldest son of the late Joseph DeMercado. Funeral at 4 p.m.

February 7, 1899
ORRETT-At "Annandale," Elletson Road, on 4th February, the wife of George Orrett, of a daughter.

Selected Vital Records from the Jamaican Daily Gleaner

February 8, 1899

The Rev. Caleb Reynolds who had been recently confined to his residence owing to indispositions has recovered, and was able to conduct services at Ebenezer Chapel on Sunday morning last and at Coke Chapel in the evening.

February 11, 1899

ELLIS-LEVY-On the 10th January at All Saint's Church, Hyeres, France, by the Rev. R. Tahourdm, and previously at the British Vice-Consulate, AUGUSTA son of Major C.D.C. Ellis, La Lucuette Hyeres, to MARY, daughter of the late Henry Westmoreland of Jamaica, and widow of the late E.G. Levy of Jamaica.

CRIDLAND-On Monday 6th inst at Providence, Anchovy, St James, THOMAS CRIDLAND, late of Roaring River Estate, Westmoreland. Aged 78 years.

MELHADO-AT his late residence No 6 Johns Lane at 11a.m. on the 27the January, 1899 SAMUEL MELHADO in the 60th year of his age. Panama and American papers please copy.

February 18, 1899

SARGENT-On the 17th inst at 11.45 o'clock after a short illness, EDWARD L. SARGENT, a native of Georgetown Demerara, B.G. Funeral at 4:30 this afternoon. Friends and acquaintances will please accept this intimation and attend. Requiescat in Pace. Demerara "Chronicle" and "Argosy" please copy.

February 27, 1899

EVA CORINALDI, relict of the late Horatio Corinaldi of Montego Bay, in her 90th year. Funeral at 5 o'clock this evening from the residence of her son-in-law A.H. Morales, Phebe Ville, Victoria Avenue.

February 28, 1899

BRANDON-Last night at 94 Orange Street, AMANDA BRANDON, sister of Jacob Brandon and Daniel I Motta. Funeral at 4.30 this afternoon.

March 2, 1899

SMITH-SHERLOCK- On 28th Feb, at Wesley Church, by Rev G.H. Baron Hay, J Ramby (sic) Smith to Sydney Matilda only daughter of C.M. Sherlock Esq., of Trevennion Lodge St Andrews

MURRAY of Pneumonia on 30th Febry (sic) at Trenton, New Jersey, U.S.A. CONNIE second daughter of John Murray, Kingston.

March 6, 1899

POOLE-At his residence, Camperdown, Half-way Tree, on the 3rd inst CHARLES FREDERICK POOLE.

Obituary
MR C.F.POOLE

It is with much regret that we announce this morning the death of Mr. C.F. Poole, the well-known cricketer. The deceased had been in ill health for some time past, and on Friday last he succumbed to the malady from which he had been suffering.

Mr. Poole was an Englishman and came to Jamaica nearly four years ago. He kept a school at Camperdown in the parish of St Andrew, and was much liked by his pupils. He was very popular in sporting circles, especially in cricket. He was a member of the Kingston C.C. where he was held in high estimation by the members. He was also a member of the Jamaica team of cricketers which visited Barbados and Demerara in September 1896 and he played for Jamaica in the following year against Mr. Priestley's teams of English Cricketers. The deceased was married and has a brother Mr. E.A. Poole.

The funeral took place on Saturday. We tender our sympathy to his bereaved relations.

March 11, 1899
ORMSBY-On Thursday, 9th March, at Sav La Mar, the wife of Rev S. O Ormsby of a daughter.

ALBERGA Laetitia Ann-The beloved wife of William Benjamin Alberga, on the 7th March, 1899 in her 80th year after a short illness.
On the Resurrection morning
Soul and body meet again
All the graves their dear restore
Father Sister Child and Mother, meet once more.

March 14, 1899
STOCKHAUSEN-At Solomon's Villa, Brantford Road on the 12th inst the wife of J.H. Stockhausen of a daughter

REID-CHARD- At Mandeville on the 19th inst. By the Rev Henry Clarke, Jnr. CECIL ALEXANDER, M.R.C.V.S (Edin) Veterinary surgeon, second son of George Reid, Esq., J.P. Campbelton Pen, Hanover, to ELIZA JANE only daughter of the late Henry Chard recently of Edinburgh, and formerly of Wolverhampton, England and Mrs. Chard.

March 15, 1899
LOWCOCK-On the 17th February, 1899, at Cambridge Villa East Twickenham, SOPHIA LOWCOCK beloved mother of Mrs. Mortimer Brandon, aged 92. By Cablegram.

March 16, 1899
The LATE ARCHDEACON RAMSON,
Our Black River correspondent writes. " Quite a gloom was cast over this town on Thursday morning last when a telegram was received, announcing the death of the Rev. Archdeacon Ramson at his residence, Kew Cottage, Bethel Town. Immediately on receipt of the telegram, the bell of the Parish Church was tolled for the space of half an hour as a token of respect to the deceased and at 5 o'clock in the evening it was tolled again. On Sunday 12th, a memorial service was held in the Church (and a very solemn service indeed it was). Special hymns were sung for the occasion, among them the well known one: -
"Now the labourer's task is o'er
Now the battle day is past
Now upon the farther shore
Lands the voyager at last
Father in Thy gracious keeping
Leave me now thy servant sleeping"
More

Selected Vital Records from the Jamaican Daily Gleaner

March 22, 1899

CHANDLER-On the 21st inst. At Rosedale Kingston, the wife of W.C.R. CHANDLER of a daughter.

March 24, 1899

MANLEY-At his residence Roxburgh Manchester, T.A.S. Manley at 7 p.m. on Wednesday evening the 22nd inst. American papers please copy.

March 29, 1899

STEWART-In Brown's Town, Saint Ann, at the residence of her son-in-law, Mr. George H. Cooper, after a long and painful illness, JULIA E STEWART, widow of the late Thomas Stewart, Esquire, of Retirement Pen, Westmoreland aged 85 years.

April 21, 1899 (only one in April)

Perkins-On the 19th inst at St Paul's Rectory, Balaclava, the wife of the Rev. F.H. Perkins of a daughter.

Lewis On Thursday morning the 13th inst. At Greenwich Park, St Ann's in the sixty seventh year of his age, JOHN COLSTON LEWIS, leaving a sorrowing wife, sons and daughters to mourn their loss.

May 25, 1899

DELAPENHA-SAMPSON-At Sunshine Villa, Mandeville, on the 10th inst. SYBEL BLANCH, fourth daughter of Uriah and Ella Louise Delapenha, to LYNDON EVELYN SAMPSON of same place. No Cards.

May 26, 1899

BROWN'S TOWN LITERARY UNION

The opening of the above Association will take place at the Court House, Brown's Town on June 1 at 7.30 p.m.

The chief feature will be a debate. Mr. J. Stewart of the Church school will move "That the Press has been a bigger factor that the Pulpit in the elevating of Mankind. Mr. W. Miller present clerk of the Courts will oppose.

The chair will be taken by Mr. J. H. Levy who has given a suitable building for the reading room.

The public are cordially invited and it is to be hoped that the ladies and gentlemen of the town will show their appreciation by their presence of the movement which will supply a long felt want among the young men.

July 3, 1899

GARSIA-Yesterday at 12.45 p.m. at his residence no 5 Eat Street, GEORGE GARSIA, aged 78 years, the beloved husband of Elizabeth E.A. Garsia, leaving a sorrowful family and many friends to mourn his irreparable loss. Funeral will move at 5 p.m. Friends and acquaintances of the family will please accept this intimation.
"Not gone from memory not gone from love
But gone to his Father's home above"   RIP

July 6, 1899

FARQUHARSON-SMALL-At Dunrobin House, Mandeville, on the 28th June by the Right Rev C.F. Douet, assistant Bishop of Jamaica, CLARENCE CARGILL the youngest son the C.S. Farquharson of Savanna-la-Mar to MABEL IDA BLAIR, eldest daughter of J.A. Small of Newland Park, St Andrew, and of Caenwood, Portland

1899

TAYLOR-PAYNE-GALLWEY- At the Cathedral, Spanish Town, on the 29th June by the Revd. Canon E.J. Wortley, assisted by the Revd. C.M. Buckley, FREDERICK EGBERT TAYLOR, Engineer of the Rio Cobre Irrigation Works, Spanish Town, son the Hon E.B.G. Taylor, C.M.G. late of Nassau, N.P. Bahamas, to CAROLINE LUCILLE, widow of the late Lionel P. Pagne-Gallwey and daughter of Edward B. Lynch, Esq. of Durham House, Spanish Town.

July 13, 1899
ISAACS-LAND- At "St Andrews" Halfway Tree, on the 5th ulto., by the Rgt Revd C.F. Douet, D. D. Assistant Bishop of Jamaica, and the Revd. H.H. Isaacs, M.A. Rector of St Andrews FRANK NEL ISAACS to AMY MARY BLANCHE, daughter of the late Dr. J.C. Land of Spanish Town, and adopted daughter of her Uncle and Aunt, the late Dr. and Mrs. Hamilton of Clifton Mount, Jamaica.

FOR RENT
The following desirable residence in Brown's Town
 The Big Yard Premises consisting of Entrance room sitting room dining room, drawing room and 6 bed rooms, with all necessary outbuildings.
 Old Market premises consisting of Front hall center hall, drawing room and 4 bed rooms with all necessary outbuildings.
 The Upper part of Lannaman's Premises consisting of Entrance hall, drawing room, front piazza, and 4 bed rooms, with all necessary outbuilding.
 Also the residence of Wakering Pen about 6 miles from Brown's Town, consisting of entrance hall, dining room, drawing room 4 bed rooms, with stables and all necessary outbuilding, and grass for reasonable number of horses.
 The above will be rented at reasonable rates to suit the times. J.H. Levy & Co

July 17, 1899
CHANDLER-At Ivy Bank, Brentford Road, Kingston, at 4 o'clock p.m. on Saturday the 15th July, the Revd. C.R. CHANDLER, aged 74 years. R.I.P.

July 27, 1899
GOLDSMITH-At her residence, 142 Orange Street, yesterday (Wednesday) morning, Mrs. FRANCES RIPLEY GOLDMITH; relict of the late John William Goldsmith. Aged 80 years. Funeral at half past four o'clock this afternoon.

Mr. W.A.Vickers of Fontabelle Estate Sav-la-Mar is shortly going on a visit to the other West Indian Islands. He will be away for about 6 or 8 wks.

A man named O'Conner died last week at York, in Westmoreland. He is said to have been 112 years of age. He was formerly a slave at Chester Castle Estate.

July 28, 1899
ISAACS At Balcarres, Shooter's Hill, the wife of Cecil R. Isaacs, of a son. July 25th.

August 7, 1899
SCARLETT-MATTHEWS At Winefield Penn, Saint Ann, on the 2nd inst. By the Revd. J.C. Chandler, FANNY MARY ELIZABETH, daughter of John R. and Elizabeth Mary Scarlett, to CHARLES D. MATTHEWS of Devon, England.

Selected Vital Records from the Jamaican Daily Gleaner

August 9, 1899
BURKE-ROPER-On August 7th a the Parish Church, Kingston, by the Ven Archdeacon Downer, SAMUEL CONSTANTINE BURKE B.A. Barrister of Law, eldest son of the Hon. S. Constantine Burke, Custos of St Andrew, to CHRISTINE MARY youngest daughter of the late Hon. Findlater Roper, L.L.B. Barrister at Law, Custos of St Ann.

August 14, 1899
HENRIQUES-CHARLES COHEN, - at his residence Blenheim Villa, corner Victoria Avenue and Elletson Road. Funeral at 5.30 this evening.

August 16, 1899
We understand from our correspondent at Port Antonio that the report that Mr. Levy of Brown's Town had taken premises at Port Antonio is not confirmed, and is therefore incorrect.

August 22, 1899
SMEETON-HENDERSON-On the 21st inst., at the Cathedral, Spanish Town by the Rev. Canon E.J. Wortley, assisted by the Rev. C. McK. Buckley, M.A. SAMUEL PAGE SMEETON to JEAN, younger daughter of the late John Henderson, of Kingston, Ontario, Canada.

August 23, 1899
TODD-In Rhodesia, South Africa, FREDERICK LAMONT, second son of the late Utten Thomas Todd, Jr. Orange Valley Estate, St Ann, and of Mrs. J.P. Hall, The Rectory, Brown's Town, Age 25 years.

August 24, 1899
MOTTA-DACOSTA-At Tryall, Port Maria, the residence of the bride's father, on Wednesday the 16th inst., by Mr. S.S. Lawton, acting minister of the United Congregation of Israelites, EDGAR CECIL, eldest son of Daniel I. Motta, of this city, to ETHEL LILIAN, eldest daughter of Abraham R. Da Costa. At Home at Leighton, 4 Blake Road, on Saturday and Sunday 2nd and 3rd prox from 4 p.m.

August 25, 1899
MILHOLLAND-Last night at his residence, 54 East Queen Street, John MILHOLLAND age 71 years. Funeral at 4p.m.

September 2, 1899
ROBBINS-VERMONT-At the Cathedral, Spanish town on the 30th inst, by the Revd. Canon E.J. Wortley, assisted by the Revd. C.M. Buckley, M.A. HENRY ROBINS M.D. C.M. Trinity University, Toronto Canada to MARIETTE LOUISE eldest daughter of the late Henry Scott Vermont J.P., St Mary, Land Surveyor.

September 5, 1899
CALDER-At Kingston on the 3rd inst the wife of W. Jameson Calder Inspector of Constabulary of a daughter.

Inspector Calder who is in charge of the police in the parishes of St James and Hanover is now in Kingston on leave of absence.

1899

September 13, 1899
ESCOFFERY-At No 32 Laws Street on Monday 11th instant the wife of Charles Jos. Escoffery, of a daughter.

September 14, 1899
BROWN-At the Farm, Pedro, St Ann's on 2nd inst., after a lingering illness HARRIET AUGUSTA, youngest daughter of the late Hamilton Brown, Snr., of St Ann. "May her soul rest in peace."

September 22, 1899
CAMPBELL-At Beryl Villa, McWhinney St. Kingston on the 11th inst., the wife of Colin Campbell of a son.

September 27, 1899
BRODBER-MOORE-A quiet wedding took place in the Parish Church, Black River on 20the Sept., 10 a.m. when Mr. HENRY BRODBER of Trelawny led to the Altar Miss MARGARET ELIZABETH MOORE, only daughter of Archibald Moore of (Shrewsbury) The bride received several presents.

September 28, 1899
FACEY-This morning at 3.40 a.m. at his residence 44 Duke street, GEORGE SAMUEL FACEY. Funeral will move at 4.30 this evening. Friends and acquaintances please accept this intimation.

October 5, 1899
The Rev W.C. Murray D.D. of Brown's Town is in Kingston for a few days.

October 19, 1899
SILVERA-On 13th inst at Oracabesa St Mary the wife of V.E. Silvera of a daughter.

Not many issues between October and the end of year.
December 27, 1899
BRAHAM-At Gray's Inn Estate, Annotto Bay on the evening of the 19th December 1899 in his 65th year, Henry Braham Esq., J.P. leaving a large circle to mourn their loss. "Not dead but gone to sleep. English papers please copy.

1900

January 2 - March 31, 1900

January 2, 1900
RUTTY-ISAACS -On Tuesday 26th Dec. 1899, at the Wesleyan Church, Brown's Town St Ann, by the Revd W. Clarke Murray, D. D.   FRANK SWIRE RUTTY TO MARY IDA LOUISE   eldest daughter of Abraham and Hannah E. Isaacs of Brown's Town, St Ann's.

February 23, 1900
FOURNIER-- At 42 Orange Street in this city, on the 21st inst. the wife of A Fournier of a daughter.

March 2, 1900
TRENCH--At Hazelymph, St James on the 26th February, the wife of Dutton Trench of a son.

Sale of Properties listed under J.H. Levy Name

Includes land at Tabernacle
58. Tavern Premises at St Ann's Bay belonging to Mrs R. Watson.

March 29, 1900
A Valedictory Concert at York Castle (At Which Grandfather Mitchell sang and made speeches). Uncle Clarence and R Murray are also mentioned as participating

NP418 April 1, 1900 - June 30, 1900

April 17, 1900
A subscriber offers congratulations to Miss M.C. Johnson of Hopeton, Alexandria P.O. on the success of her pupil Miss M. W. Cover of Hopewell Dry Harbour P.O. whom she prepared for the Cambridge examination in December last and also to Miss Williams of Brown's Town on having put Miss Cover through with the musical part

April 26, 1900
PLANT-CATHCART -At St Michael's Kingston on Tuesday 24th April, 1900 by Right Revd, Bishop Douet, D.D. assisted by Revd R.G. Ambrose, WILLIAM HENRY PLANT, Head Master Titchfield School, Port Antonio to ETHEL GRACE CATHCART, second daughter of W.L. Cathcart, J.P. Abbey, St Thomas, and sister of Mrs Vancutlenburg, Kingston. No Cards.

Selected Vital Records from the Jamaican Daily Gleaner

April 27th, 1900
ISSACS- On the 26th inst at Villa Field, St Mary HENRY ISSACS formerly of Kingston. The funeral will leave the Kingston Railway Station at 8.30 this morning.

April 28, 1900
ISAACS- At Griff. St Andrew on the 25th instant, the wife of F.N. Isaacs Esq of a daughter.

May 10, 1900
BRANDAY-DESNOES - At Holy Trinity Church on 2nd May 1900 by Rev Wm Gregory S.J. assisted by Rev John Collins S.J. WILLIAM CHARLES third son of Louis Peter Branday to LEONTINE EMILY eldest daughter of Peter Blaize Desnoes.
No cards. At Home Glencournie Cottage Kingston Gardens. Wednesday and Thursday, 16th and 17th inst.

MUIRHEAD- At Denbeigh Estate on the 5th instant, J.W. MUIRHEAD aged 65 leaving four children to mourn his loss.

May 15, 1900
MUIR - On the 12th instant at the residence of her daughter 125 East St ELIZA CAMPBELL relict of the late John Edward Muir of Falmouth, Trelawney and eldest daughter of Charles McKenzie of Tain Rossshire, Scotland.
Is Coelo Quies
Scotch and Canadian Papers please copy

May 16, 1900
WATSON-At Windsor House, Brown's Town on Saturday 12th inst Mary J Watson relict of the late Richard Watson of St Ann's Bay and mother of Mrs J.H. Levy of Windsor House, Brown's Town in the 70th year of her age.

May 19, 1900
ADVERTISEMENT

YORK CASTLE HIGH SCHOOL----Governor and Chaplain--Rev W.J. William, Head Master W.H. Mitchell Esq M.A. assisted by 5 resident Masters---A First Class Education, Music, Drawing, Painting. The most healthy locality, extensive play grounds. Prospective and Honours List on application to Governor.

also

HIGH CLASS DAY SCHOOL FOR GIRLS. VAUXHALL, Brown's Town, Kingston conducted by Miss Hollar and Two competent Assistants.
The above School will be reopened after the Midsummer Holidays on Monday 24th July
The course of instruction will comprise English Language, Composition, Arithmetic, Geography, History and Literature, Religious Knowledge, French, Algebra Euclid
Calisthenic and Needlework
Terms payable quarterly
Pupils under 12 years £6 per annum
do over 12 years £8 per annum
Extras - Music Drawing £4 each per annum.

1900

Books that are required will be supplied and charged. Further information if required may be had on application to MISS HOLLAR 20 Brae St, Brown's Town REFEREES-Rev W. C. Murray D.D. Rev W. Pratt, M.A. G. P Myers, Esqr, Rev J. - Sfassiah, B.A. J. L Ramson, Esq M.A.. W. D. Smedmore, Esq W. H Mitchell Esq, M.A.

Brown's Town
30th January, 1900

NOTICE

All persons indebted to my old firm of J.H. LEVY & Co and LEVY ISAACS & CO are requested to TAKE NOTE that all accounts due and overdue to the Head Business and the several Branches must now be settled as it is necessary to close the Books at an early date

Those not complying with this request will find their accounts placed in the hand of my solicitor, and NOTICE is also given that as it is necessary to realize all mortgagees and other securities held by the Old Firms, those so indebted are requested to make immediate arrangements for the settlement and so prevent forced realization. J.H. LEVY

June 9, 1900
ROBINSON-COCKING On Wednesday the 6th inst, at the Parish Church, Port Maria, St Mary, by the Ven Archdeacon Downer assisted by the Rev J. H. Graham, Rector of Port Maria, HERBERT CHARLES,Solicitor, youngest son of the late Charles Arthur Robinson, Esq, of this city, to FLORENCE MACDONALD, eldest daughter of Ralph M. Cocking, Esq of Bishop Mount, St Mary.

July 2 - September 29, 1900

July 12, 1900
WOLFE- At his residence in New York City, U.S. A. on Wednesday 11th July 1900, DAVID eldest son of the late Ellis Wolfe of this City - By Cable
July 19, 1900
FISHER on the 7th inst at "Bel Air" Norman Road, the wife of F.Chas Fisher of a daughter.

July 25, 1900
CROOKS - At Black River on Thursday night the 19th inst, Mrs SARAH CROOKS aged 54 years, relict of the late Archibald Crooks of Trelawny , deeply regretted by relatives and friends R.I.P.

July 30 1900
NARROW ESCAPE FROM AKEE POISONING-- We learn that a party of six persons in Kingston who partook of a dish of akee and codfish on Friday last were nearly fatally poisoned as it was they suffered intensely and medical aid had to be requisitioned. It is supposed that the akee must have been in a state of semi decomposition to have produced this result.

August 13, 1900
JOHNSTON - At Toronto, Canada, on July 25th 1900 after a painful and lingering illness, MARGARET JOHNSTON, aged 43, eldest sister of Dr James Johnston of Brown's Town.

Selected Vital Records from the Jamaican Daily Gleaner

August 14, 1900
DELISSER-DELISSER- Miss BLANCHE. DELISSER of Kingston, to HENRY GEORGE DELISSER of Richmond, on Wednesday 8th August, 1900

August 25, 1900
LEVY- Last night at his residence, 42 East Queen Street, JACOB LEVY aged 51 years. Funeral will take place at 5 o'clock this evening. Friends will please accept this intimation aand let you carriage attend. Father in Thy gracious keeping Leave me now thy servant sleeping.

{A later piece describes this Mr Levy as coming to Kingston from Lucia and was associated with St Andrew's Kirk}

August 31, 1900
FISHER At Bel-Air Norman Road, VETA FAITH,. the Infant daughter of Rebecca and F. Chas Fisher Funeral at 7.30 a.m. The Lord giveth and the Lord taketh away. Blessed be his Holy Name.

September 8, 1900
LEVY -On Thursday, the 6th inst at Sunningdale, No 12 North Avenue, Kingston, Gardens, the wife of H. E. Levy of a son.

September 18, 1900
TRENCH-PASCOE - At the Parish Church Kingston, on Tuesday the 11th instant by the Revd M.C. Clare. B. A. assisted by the Revd S. O Ormsby, CHARLES LEPAER, Solicitor of Kingston and eldest son of J.S. Trench Esq Collector of Taxes for Clarendon to FRANCES ELLA, second daughter of W. C. Pascoe, Esq of Kingston.

September 21, 1900
ROBERTS-NETHERSOLE On the 18th instant September at St Michael's Church, Kingston, by the Rector Rev. R. G. Ambrose, Leila third daughter of John C. Nethersole, Mandeville, formerly of Kingston to Michael Joseph Mcdonnell Roberts, of Liverpool, England. No Cards

September 22, 1900
WEDDING AT MONTEGO BAY-- The Wesleyan Church was the scene of a [pretty wedding pm Thursday Whilst Mr Sammuel Hart champions were fighting in the parochial contest, his son Mr Edmund Hart was married to Miss Ella Duff, daughter of the Rev John Duff. No couple enter upon their new life with more "well wishes" from a whole community. The ceremony will be remembered for the good sense shown by the absence of all 'grandiosely and fortes quietness. The church was full but the rowdy element which has been so objectionable at recent weddings was kept out by the police under Corporal Anthony. At ten o'clock the bride leaning on her father's arm walked to the alter followed by the bridesmaids:- Misses Effie and Evelyn Duff, the sisters of the bride and Misses Ruby Hart, Florrie Hart, Julia Hart, Beatrice Hart and Violet Hart, sisters of the Bridegroom. Mr Duff performed the ceremony, Mr Ansell Hart acting as bestman. The bride was dressed in a beautiful white silk dress trimmed with white lace, her hat being a white toque with ostrich feathers. After the ceremony a large party of relations gathered to breakfast at Upton. The newly married pair left about three o'clock for Homewood amidst a shower of good wishes rice and old boots. Nearly a hundred

presents have been received by the happy couple as tokens of the wishes of all who know them.

September 26, 1900
HART-DUFF ON the 20th inst, at the Wesleyan Church, Montego Bay the Rev. John Duff, Edmund son of Mr Samuel Hart to Ella daughter of the Rev John Duff, both of Montego Bay.

October 1, 1900- December 31, 1900

October 1, 1900
WHITELOCKE - HART At the Parish Church, Montego Bay on Thursday the 27th ultimo, by the Rev. C. Walton Austin, CHARLES OLIVER TATE, youngest son of the late Hon Hugh Anthony Whitelocke of Bulstrode, Westmoreland, to ESTHER BEATRICE, eldest daughter of Philip A. Hart of Kingston. No Cards.

October 2, 1900
ROBINSON-MORAIS On Thursday 20th September, 1900 at St Michaels Church, Kingston, by the Rector, Rev.R.G. Ambrose, ERNEST ALFRED, second son of the late Charles Robinson of St Ann, to Myra, youngest daughter of the late Amos Morais of this city.

October 25, 1900
HART- At Woodmere, New York U.S.A, on the 21st September, of Apoplexy ANDREW BERTRAM (BERTIE) AGE 36 youngest son of the late John J. Hart.

November 1, 1900
NETHERSOLE - At Mandeville on 31st October at 8 p.m. JOHN CROSBIE NETHERSOLE , aged sixty-three. Funeral will leave the Railway terminus at 2 p.m. November 1st for St Michael's Church Kingston.

November 21, 1900
NUTTALL- On Monday 19th November, at Half-Way-Tree St Andrew, the wife of E. Nuttall of a daughter.

December 12, 1900
NASH- pm the 1st December at Osborne, Dry Harbour, the wife of W. J. Nash of a daughter

December 20, 1900
SUTTON - On the 2nd Instant at Mandeville the wife of LEONARD SUTTON of a son

1901

January 4, 1901
Wedding

The Parish Church St Ann's Bay was the scene of a very pretty little wedding on the 26th ins. when Mr Hugh Pullar was married to Miss Clara DeLisser, second daughter of Mr Henry DeLisser. The Revd Mr Ripley officiated, assisted by the Revd. Fraser. The service was fully choral and the church was beautifully decorated for the occasion. The bride was given away by her father. She wore a handsome gown of white corded silk trimmed with chiffon, with semicourt train and veil of tulle surmounted by a spray of orange flowers; she also carried a beautiful shower bouquet composed of Eucharist lilies and maiden hair fern. The bridesmaids who were charmingly dressed in pink mousseline-de-soie were Miss deLisser (sister of the bride), Miss Nellie Pullar sister of the bridegroom) Misses Lena and Minnie Brown, Misses Nettie and Marion Arscott (cousins of the bride) and little Misses Iris and Nina Lyon (nieces of the bride). There was a large gathering of friends and relatives at the ceremony and a reception was afterwards held by the bride's sister (Mrs Lyons) at her residence. Amongst the guests we noticed Dr and Mrs Cox, Revd and Mrs Ripley, Revd and Mrs House, son and daughter, Mr Fred Clerk and sister, Mr and Mrs Hopwood, the Misses Lyon, Inspector Harrel and several others. The presents were numerous and costly.

January 7, 1901
DESNOES - At his late residence. No 5 North Street, on Sunday 6th January 1901 PETER BLAIZE DESNOES. Funeral this afternoon at 4 o'clock.

February 13, 1901
COVER-GAYNER - On 7th Feby 1901 at 6 p.m. at St Mark's Church Rio Bueno, by the Revd. Wm Noble, WILLIAM ARSCOTT, eldest son of the late Wm Cover Sr of Annadale,[sic] St Ann's to JULIA BERTHA, daughter of the late J.W. Gayner of Bridewater, St Ann's

March 15, 1901

ROBINSON- At Bedford, England on the 14th inst, GERALDINE wife of Inspector Church and eldest daughter of the late Chas. A. Robinson of this city.

April 27, 1901
MOTTA- At Leighton, 4 Blake Road on 24th instant the wife of E.C. Motta of a son

Selected Vital Records from the Jamaican Daily Gleaner

May 20, 1901
GALLANT - At residences, Siloah, on Friday, the 17th instant, at 2.30 p.m. COLIN son of Wm Gallant of Scotland, aged 64 Beloved husband of Matilda Gallant, leaving 7 children and grandchildren to mourn their loss. "Safely, safely gathered in God Himself the soul will keep"

August 20, 1901
HAIRS - On the 16th instant at 4 a.m. at Church Street, Montego Bay ANN WOOSTER aged 82 years formerly of Exeter, Devon, England leaving several children to mourn her loss "Asleep in Jesus" English papers please copy

August 22 ,1901
MENNELL At Chilton, Westmoreland on Thursday 15th August 1901 of acute pneumonia, GEORGE POLACK MENNEL aged 25 years, fifth son of John W. Mennell.

October 28, 1901
THOMAS - On the 27th instant at Pembrook Cottage, Half-Way-Tree the wife of the Rev C. R. G. Thomas of a son.

November 25, 1901
RAMSON At 57 Beeston Street, Kingston, on Sunday morning 24th instant the wife of the Rev J. L Ramson of a son

December 11, 1901
ISAACS- At the residence of H.G. Jervis on Saturday the 7th instant ESTHER, relict of the late Joseph Isaacs Esq of Falmouth at the age of 90 after a long illness.

December 12, 1901
COLES-MACDERMOT - On 12th December at St Matthew's Church, Allman Town, Kingston, by His Grace the Archbishop of the West Indies assisted by the Rev Canon MacDermot Uncle of the bride and the Rev H. Scotland, Chaplain, Up Park Camp CHARLES HERBERT COLES M.A. Oxon Warden of the Theological College and Rector of St Matthew's (son of the late Lewis Coles of London) to ISABEL , daughter of Mrs Macdermot, The Lodge, Arnold Road, St Andrew and the late Rev Hugh C.P. MacDermot Rector of Arthur's Seat, Clarendon. No Cards. At home Thursday January 2nd, 1902

1902

January 3, 1902
Beverland   At Dry Harbour, St Ann   On Friday morning December 27th 1901 Mrs. Susannah Beverland the beloved mother of William James Nash and Mrs. E. B. Stephenson, in the 77th year of her age leaving several relatives and many friends to mourn her loss.

Cover-Williams- On the 31st Decr. 1901 at the Parish Church Kingston by the Ven. Archdeacon Downer, assisted by Rev J. L. Ramson. M.A.   Charles Arscott second son of the late Wm Cover Esqr. Snr. of Armadale St Ann's to Alice Augustus Swinhoe second daughter of Wm Rowe Williams, Esqr. of Calcutta, India

January 6, 1902
DeLisser At Colon on 2nd January, 1902 Solomon B. DeLisser second son of Henry deLisser, St Ann's Bay

January 11, 1902
The Mr. DeLisser whose death appeared in our issue of the 6th instant is a brother of Mrs. J. J. Lyon of St Ann's Bay.

Mrs. E. B, Stephenson begs through this medium to thank her many friends for their kind sympathy during her sad bereavement.

January 25, 1902
A Fournier and Co were advertising Boxes for fruit shippers at 42 Orange Street.

February 4, 1902
Lopez At 5 East Parade, on the 2nd inst, the wife of C. Aug Lopez Dentist, of a daughter. English and American papers please copy.

February 7, 1902
CAMPBELL at Brampton Villa, St Ann's Bay, on Monday the 3rd instant, after 25 days illness, EDITH MAUD, the dearly beloved wife of Colin Campbell, Storekeeper, leaving a husband 4 young children, relatives and numerous friends to mourn her irreparable loss. "She fell asleep into the bosom of her Saviour and now she rests in peace".
February 14, 1902

HARVEY-DAVIS At Mears Clarendon, on Monday the 10th inst. after a few days illness, Louisa Emily, the beloved wife of Alfred Harvey-Davis and fourth daughter of the Revd C. A. Winn, of Ballintoy, St Ann's

Selected Vital Records from the Jamaican Daily Gleaner

February 26, 1902
HENDERSON-At the Baptist Mission House, Brown's Town on Tuesday, Feb 5th Caroline Box Henderson, aged 79 years. She was connected with the Jamaica Baptist Mission for more than sixty years.

March 3, 1902
McCrea- At Hazeldene, Port Antonio, on 28th February, the wife of J. Elliot McCrea of a daughter.

March 8, 1902
Isaacs -At Torrington, Sav-la-Mar, Jamaica on the 4th inst., the wife (nee Mortlock) of Dr S. Isaacs of a son. English and Mexican papers please copy.

March 15, 1902
CAMBRIDGE LOCAL EXAMINATION
The Results
Boys
Class I Under 19 years who have obtained honours R.M.Murray Jamaica High School r,e,l,g,m. Religious Knowledge, English, Latin,Greek, mathematics

Boys Class Class III C. St L. Hogarth Wolmers' School,

Students not under 16 years of age who have passed the examination as juniors C. O. Cover Jamaica High School W. H. Costa Potsdam School, W. W,. Maxwell, Potsdam School

Girls Senior N. E. E. Hollar Wolmer's High School

March 17, 1902
LEVY - On 15th inst. at 59 Surdan Road, London, Louisa, relict of the late Chas. Levy (By Cable)

March 19, 1902
Camac- At New Park, Brown's Town St Ann, on the morning of the 13th inst. Charlotte Niven, the eldest and dearly beloved daughter of the late David Camac, native of Belfast, Ireland, leaving a sorrowing mother and other dear relatives to mourn their irreparable loss.

She is not dead, the child of our affection,
But gone unto that school:
Where she no longer needs our poor protection,
And Christ himself doth rule.
(English papers please copy).

March 19, 1902

Advertisement

To PINE & ORANGE GROWERS
_____

1902
READ THIS:

Messers J. W. Meddleton & Co
Kingston,

Huntly, Brown's Town P. O.

Dear Sirs, Please send me round to Dry Harbour per first coastal boat 2 gallons more of your "Demon" Insecticide. I have found it splendid for killing ants, in fact I think it really does more than is claimed for it. I could scarcely get a pine-apple to come to perfection on account of ants before I used that " Demon"

I remain, Yours truly,
(Sgd) H. Q. Levy

Seven shillings per Gallon

One Gallon makes 40

J.W. Middleton & Co

Hardware Merchants, 130 Harbour St

April 2, 1902
Lindo At Laurisdale May Pen after one day's illness, Herbert Lindo, son of Alexander Joseph Lindo late Custos of St Mary, age 64 years verse

April 10, 1902
Cooke on Friday, the 21st ultimo, at Eltham Pen, Saint Ann, the residence of her father, T. B. Scott, J.P St Ann the wife of Wilbert M. Gerrard Cooke of a son.

April 11, 1902
Myers At Top Hill, the residence of her brother, A. J. Hendriks on Sunday the 5th instant, Mrs. Julia F. Myers eldest daughter of the late Frederick and Euphemia Hendriks in her 76th year.

April 14, 1902
Townend Michelin. On the 9th day of April, at the parish Church, St Ann's Bay, by the Rev J. Chandler, Mary Alice Stewart eldest daughter of Arthur Townend Esq. to Victor Alfred, youngest son of the late William Michelin, Esq.

April 25, 1902
Wedding
    We briefly noticed yesterday the wedding of Mr. C. S. Kelly of Kingston to Miss N. Ormsby, daughter of Mr. J. D. Ormsby of Lime Hall. From further particulars to hand we learn that the marriage took place at St Saviors, the ceremony been performed by the Revs J. T. H. Chandler, S. O. Ormsby and J. L. Ramson. M.A.. The church was beautifully decorated for the occasion.

The bride was attired in white silk and carried a bouquet of orange blossoms. There were four bridesmaids, who were dressed in white muslin trimmed with yoke and open worked sleeves, and they carried white wands trimmed with bunches of flowers and silver ribbons, which they held up at the entrance to the church in order to allow the bride to pass beneath. She was preceded by ten little maidens beautifully dressed in blue muslin and wearing sprigs of lily of the valley.

The whole arrangement was very pretty and well carried out. The bride was given away by her eldest brother the Rev J. J. C. Ormsby. There was large number of friends present and after the ceremony the party went to the late residence of the bride where the usual refaction was enjoyed and the usual toasts given. An Opportunity was given the guests to view the presents which were both beautiful and numerous. Dancing began at eight o'clock and lasted until two in the morning; the newly married couple leaving, however, at half past eleven for Endeavour where the honeymoon is to be spent.

May 1, 1902
OGILVIE-VICKERS ON the 29th April 1902, at St Andrew's Parish Church, Halfway Tree, by the Ven. Archdeacon, C. W. Downer, assisted by the Rev Canon E. J. Wortley and the Rev. J.B. Ellis, M.A, CHARLES MCDONALD OGILVIE, Solicitor, eldest son of Dr James Ogilvie, J.P. F.R.C.S. E Health Officer, Kingston, to ALICE EMILY, fifth daughter of Edward Vickers, Esq., B.A. Cantab, Barrister-at-Law, Resident Magistrate for Kingston.

May 3, 1902
Roxburgh-- At Annandale, St Ann, on the 2nd inst, Thomas Francis Roxburgh, Esq. in his seventy seventh year.

May 5, 1902
About the funeral of Mr. Roxburgh, and

Two slight corrections are necessary in our sketch of the late Mr. T. F. Roxburgh. Dr Roxburgh was pastor of Free St Georges Glasgow and not Edinburgh. Mr. Roxburgh went to St Ann before 1870 residing at Woodfield. But he became owner of Annandale in 1870.

May 10, 1902
Allwood - At his residence, Woodhall Chapelton, on Wednesday the 7th inst, James Allwood late Resident Magistrate for Clarendon,

May 24, 1902
McDonald, At 106 King Street on 22nd May 1902, the wife of Ronald McDonald of a son.

June 198, 1902
Clerk--At Lanequenet, on the 11th June, Eliza Frances, relict of the late James Otway Clerk, in her 84th year

July 13, Fort de France
Last night and today Montpelee was in eruption.

1902

Arscott, Charles Dussard on Sunday the 13th inst, at his residence Berry Mill (sic) St Ann (Berry Hill)

August 13, 1902
Motta.--At Holywood on the 7th inst. the wife of Edgar C. Motta of a daughter.

August 15, 1902
Littlejohn-Hart on Wednesday 13th instant at St Gabriels Church May Pen, by the Revd. J. D. Junt Herbert Melville youngest son of the late Revd. D. R. Littlejohn, Rector of Trelawny, to Marie Gertrude youngest daughter of Philip A. Hart, Esq. J. P. St James. No Cards.

September 2, 1902
Morris-On the 28th August 1902 at Ballitoy, St Ann, the residence of his father-in-law Louis Alexander Morris of New Court, Trelawny, Superintendent of Parochial Roads and Works.

September 4, 1902
Terrible Disaster in Martinique---Mont Pelee Spreads More Havoc, Over 1,000 Lives Lost

September 5, 1902
Levy-DeSouza At St Mark's Church, Brown's Town St Ann, on Tuesday August 26th William Lionel son of J.H. Levy Esq. of Brown's Town to Harriette Viva Erminie daughter of the late D. C. De Souza of Falmouth, Trelawny. English and American papers please copy

September 24, 1902
Byles-At Milford, Brown's Town, St Ann on 19th September 1902, the wife of A. S. Byles of a daughter

October 8, 1902
At Tobolski on the 29th September, the wife of Robert L. Young, of a daughter

November 4, 1902
Dallas At Budgate House, Norman Crescent on the 3rd inst Frank P. McD. Dallas. Funeral at 4 p.m. this afternoon.

November 15, 1902
Wedding

Todd-Comrie

Malvern Nov 13 one of the prettiest and most successful weddings that has ever taken place in Santa Cruz Mtns was celebrated at St Mary's Church on Wednesday the 12th instant at 3.30p.m. The contracting parties were Mr. Utten Thomas Todd of Sportsman's Hall, Trelawny and Miss Ida Arabella Comrie of Fernhurst, Malvern, only daughter the late Walter Comrie of Bog Estate Vere

Column mentions her mother and her brother Mr. Sterling Comrie and best man Dr Costa. The marriage ceremony was performed by the Rev Mr. Hall of Brown's Town the step-father of the bridegroom. Lots of Maxwells mentioned as guests

December 17, 1902

Lynch- On Sunday 14th December, 1902 at St Ann's Bay Jamaica, W. I. the wife of John M. Lynch of a daughter. English papers please copy.

1903

January 5, 1903
McConnell-At "the Mission" Duncans on 27th December the wife of D. G. McConnell of a daughter

January 6, 1903
Stephenson-At Rose Garden, Priestman's River, P.O. Portland on the 31st December, 1902, the wife of T.J. Stephenson of a son

February 23, 1903
Orrett-At the Grove, Halfway Tree, on the 21st inst. the wife of E. G. Orrett of a daughter

March 9, 1903
Crum-Ewing- At Brampton Mandeville on the 5th instant, the wife of Humphrey E. Crum Ewing of a son

March 13, 1903
Ormsby At St Michael's Rectory, on Thursday, March 11th wife of Rev S. O. Ormsby of a daughter

Only first 3 months in detail from microfilm
Only a few items were available on line for the period April to December
Most issues were the Kingston Freeman of New York

April 6, 1903
Opening Service will be held at Pedro River, St Ann in connection with the New Wesleyan Chapel on the 15th inst. The dedicatory Sermon will be preached by the Rev. W. Clarke Murray, D.D., President of the Conference. An after meeting will be held at 2 p.m. when addresses will be delivered. Special collection will be taken in aid of the building.

June 25, 1903
McKella—Depass On June 24th at Innesleigh, Elletson Road, by the Rev. S. O. Ormsby, of St Michael's Church, CHARLES McKELLA, to ETHEL MARIA, eldest daughter of T.E. dePass, ex-Inspector of Jamaica Constabulary.

June 27, 1903
STEPHENSON-SMALL—On the 18th inst. at St Peter's, Hope Bay by the Rev. Wm. Lund, MARY LAURA HARRIS fourth daughter of the late J.A.E. Small, Esq., of

Caenwood, Portland, to EDMUND CHARLES, eldest son of Mr. and Mrs. Stephenson of 'Bridgewater," St Ann.

1904

January 6, 1904
MICHELIN At Oxford, St Thomas-ye-East on the 31st ultimo, the wife of V.A. Michelin of a son.

January 9, 1904
CLARK- At Grantham, Highgate, on 7th inst, Herbert Harvey, son of Mr and Mrs Harvey Clark, aged one year and eight months.

January 14, 1904
GUNTER-BRAHAM-On Wednesday, 6th January 1904 by the Rev Canon Wortley (cousin of the bride) at St Augustine's Church, Porus, Manchester, Godfrey George, son the late C. E. Gunter J.P formerly cashier of the Colonial Bank, Kingston, Ja, to Lillian Amy, second daughter of H. Spence Braham. J. P. of TuBrook, Porus, Manchester.

January 19, 1904
ST ANN'S BOARD. A Meeting of the Parochial Board of St Ann was held on Thursday the 7th Jany, 1904. Present: J.H. Levy Esq, chairman, A. J. Webb, Esq, vice-chairman, A. W. Douet, A. N. Sutherland, W. S. Groves, Colin Campbell, His Honour the Custos and H. S. Allen, Esq.

January 27, 1904
WOLFE-AT her residence, Ravenscroft, South Camp road, at 6:30 o'clock last evening, Emily Wolfe, relict of the late Ellis Wolfe. Funeral at 4:30 o'clock this afternoon.

AGRICULTURAL--- Instructive Report by Mr. R. L. Young--Cotton Experiments-- Lecturing alone does no substantial good. Mr Robert L. Young Local Instructor for St Ann, has forwarded his monthly report to the Secretary of the Jamaica Agricultural Society.

January 29, 1904
Mr Sydney Sutherland has been appointed a Justice of the Peace for St Ann.

February 3, 1904
A.A. Bullock of Brown's Town and L. S. Bullock, of Montego Bay take this medium of thanking their friends for sympathy during the illness and death of their brother W. DeLeon Bullock.

Selected Vital Records from the Jamaican Daily Gleaner

February 4, 1904

SHARPE-AT Windsor, St Mary on Sunday 31st January, 1904, Caroline Isabella, the beloved wife of Revd. F. H. Sharpe leaving an aged mother, a sorrowing husband, a large family circle to mourn their irreparable loss. Age 59 years. "Father in They gracious keeping, Leave we now our loved one sleeping."

February 6, 1904

WESLEYAN BODY--Surrender of the Old constitution.--A Resolution Passed-- High Appreciation of Dr. W. Clark Murray's Work.

February 19, 1904

Crosswell--At 52 King Street. N.E.. corner of Barry Street on the 19th February, Eleanora Crosswell, relict of the late Noel Croswell, age 86 years. Funeral at May Pen Cemetery this afternoon at 4 o'clock.

February 25, 1904

LOPEZ-WILKIE--At St George's Church on Wednesday 17th February by the Revd A. C. Sutcliffe, Leopold Fitzherbert, eldest son of Edmund Lopez, Esq to Louise Matilda, eldest daughter of Robert Wilkie, Esq., of London, England. At Home at 14 Blake Road on Monday evening, 29th instant--No cards

Isaacs- At St Ann's Bay, on Sunday, 21st, while bathing in the sea, Ivan Dudley Isaacs in his 21st year. "Peace; let him rest; God Knoweth best."

February 27, 1904

PRIESTNAL-SPRATT-- On Tuesday, Feb 23rd, in the Wesleyan Church, Brown's Town, St Ann, by the Rev W. Clarke Murray, D.D. assisted by the Rev J.P. Hall (Rector) and Rev G. H. Lea (First Hill) Rev. William, Preistnal of the North St Congregational Church, Kingston. to Sarah Mary (Minnie) youngest daughter of the late Mr William Costa of Brown's Town.

March 10, 1904

Honniball- On the 6th instant at 10 South Camp Road, Kingston, the wife of R. Dunscombe-Honiball of a daughter.

THE RUSSIAN-JAPANESE WAR- Struggle in the Far East.

March 19, 1904

RAMSON-In New York, on the 9th inst, Aubrey De Cresse Ramson (Jim) second son to the late Archdeacon Ramson, age 39 years.

March 21, 1904

Cambridge examination--Results for last December.

April 12, 1904

PERSONAL - Mrs C. P. Delgado of Brown's Town and Mr A.L. Delgado of Falmouth, express their sincere thanks to all their friends who sent letters of condolence and cards to them during their late sad bereavement.

May 2, 1904

ROXBURGH-ROXBURGH- On Thursday the 28th April 1904 at Mount Plenty, St Ann, the residence of the father of the bride by the Revd. Henry Scott assisted by the Revd. H.

1904

Hope Hamilton, Katherine Julia, eldest daughter of Adam Roxburgh, Esq to Kenneth Laurence, eldest surviving son of T. Laurence Roxburgh, Esq, assistant Colonial Secretary, Jamaica

May 12, 1904
Isaacs-At Torrington, Sav-la-Mar, Westmoreland on the 9th day of May 1904, Solomon Isaacs, Esq J.P. of St Ann's Bay in his 67th year. "At Rest".

May 14, 1904
DaCosta-At Devon Lodge, St Andrew, on Thursday, the 12th inst, the wife of Alfred H. DaCosta of a daughter.

May 17, 1904
James-At Windsor, St Mary on Friday 13th May, 1904, Mrs Mary Ann James relict of the late Haughton James of Old Harbour and Mother of the late Mrs F. J. Sharpe, leaving one son and a large circle of relatives to mourn their loss. Age 83 years.

June 17, 1904
Walder-At Tan-y-Bryn, Walderston, on the 12th instant, the wife of Alfred Walder of a daughter

June 25, 1904
CLERK-HENDRIKS At St George's Church, Kingston, on Wednesday, June 22nd, 1904 by Rev C. H. Coles, M.A. Robert Thomas Clerk to Evelyn Beatrice Hendriks. No Cards.

June 28, 1904
FEARFUL CATASTROPHE AT BOG WALK

July 13, 1904
FARQUHARSON At his residence "Beckford Lodge" Sav-La-Mar, suddenly on Saturday night 9th instant, William Neilson Farquharson, in his 80th year.

July 14, 1904
DELEON- At her residence Ebenezer Villa, Sandy Gully, St Andrew, Mrs Elvina DeLeon. Funeral at 4 p.m. today.

July 16, 1904
Issacs- At "Torrington" Savanna-la-Mar on the 6th inst, the wife of Dr S. A. Isaacs, of a son.

July 21, 1904
COLES - On the 20th inst, at Glencairn, Up-Park camp P.I., the wife of Rev C. H. Coles, M. A., Oxon, of a daughter.

August 5, 1904
Isaacs on the 3rd instant, at Griff, St Andrew, the wife of Frank N. Isaacs of a daughter.

Isaacs - The wife of Cecil R. Isaacs of a son August 1st.

August 15, 1904
Clarke At Richmond, St Ann on the 11th August, the wife of Fred L Clarke of a son.

Selected Vital Records from the Jamaican Daily Gleaner

August 14, 1904

WINS RHODES SCHOLARSHIP--Mr R. M. Murray Selected for Jamaica--His Splendid Career--Comes First Out of Five Candidates Presented--Meeting of Committee.

A meeting of the Jamaica Selection Committee in connection with the Rhodes Scholarship was held at Headquarters House yesterday to select the candidate for the scholarship for the year 1904.

The members of the committee present were His Excellency the Acting Governor, His Honour the Acting Chief Justice, the Hon Thomas Capper, Superintending Inspector of Schools, His Grace the Archbishop, Dr. G. C. Henderson, and Mr W. Scott Evans, Acting Secretary.

Five candidates went up before the committee, and it was decided to award the scholarship to Mr Reginald Myrie Murray, of Jamaica College, age 22, a son of the Rev W. Clarke Murray, D.D. Wesleyan Minister, and a brother of Dr E.E. Murray of Kingston who won the Jamaica Scholarship some years ago and Mr Arthur E. Murray, Solicitor of Kingston, who took a very high place in the competition for the same scholarship in another year.

Mr Reginald Myrie Murray, was born at York Castle, St Ann, and was educated at the York Castle School until it was given up in December 1900. He then went to the Jamaica College in January 1901. He remained in the school there for one year, and during that time he won one of the Jamaica £60 scholarships and he has been a student in the collegiate department of the College since then up to the present time.

While at York Castle Mr Murray was successful in the Junior Cambridge examinations on three occasions, and on the last occasion he passed with six distinctions and also won the book prize for Jamaica. He entered for the Senior Cambridge examination twice at York castle and passed with five or six distinctions. While at the school at the Jamaica College, Mr Murray was again successful in the Senior Cambridge Examination. He passed with first-class honours in several subjects, and he has never failed in these examinations.

Mr Murray has passed the London Matriculation Examination, and also the first division of the Intermediate B.A. examination of London. Since September 1903, Mr Murray has been assisting in the teaching work at the College.

This young gentleman is also an enthusiastic athlete. He was Captain of the cricket and football club in connection with the Jamaica College for a part of 1901. He also belonged to the Kingston Rovers football club which competed for the Challenge Shield, and he ran second in the half mile flat race at the Half Holiday Association sports last November.

We understand that it was Mr Murray's intention to take the final B. A. examination in London next year and then to read for the science degree at Oxford.

We congratulate the young gentleman on his brilliant successes and on being selected as the Jamaica candidate for the Rhodes Scholarship, and wish him further success in his future studies.

1904

August 30, 1904

A SHOW OF HORSEKIND TO BE HELD IN ST ANN- The Plans Fully Discussed at a Meeting in Brown's Town Last Week. WAY OPENED TO PURCHASERS FROM KINGSTON--Mr Barclay and others Advise Local Promoters of the Course to be Followed.

A public meeting was held at the Town Hall, Brown's Town, St Ann, on Saturday last to consider the question of holding an Agricultural Show in the district.

There were present Messers, J. H. Levy, H. Q. Levy, L. A. Hopwood, Charles Costa, Purchas, Cover, Davis, Daly, Hirst, Cradwick, Barclay, Young, Revs. Dr W. Clarke Murray, J. P. Hall, E. Arnett and others.

Mr J. H. Levy was voted to the chair.

Mr Levy said while he thought Brown's Town was a most convenient and suitable district for holding an agricultural show, they must remember that such an undertaking involved a great deal of work, and one of the first questions they must ask themselves was whether they were prepared to carry through the work once they put it in hand. The proposed show would not be in competition with the St Ann's Show because it would be tapping quite a different district and would be held at a different time of the year to the St Ann's show. Brown's Town was a large settler's district and was also the centre of the large settler's district of the Dry Harbour Mountains and the pens and plantations in the lowlands. He would like to hear expressions of opinion from those present on the subject.

Mr Young said this show had been arranged to be held last November and they had gone so far as to put the prize list in hand, and to get posters printed, but the hurricane of last August had blown the prospects of that show away. He thought that the time was ripe and that the people were now ripe for a show to be held in Brown's Town. He had been working among the settler's population in the Dry Harbour mountains and he could tell them that he had spoken so much about the proposed show that already the settlers were beginning to brush up their stock, although it was not proposed to hold the show until about February. He had arranged with the Secretaries of local Societies to have district Committees and they were also arranging to have small local shows first. These shows would not be any great extent, but simply a kind of inspection of stock as they went along. He had invited Mr Barclay, the Secretary of the parent Society, to attend the meeting as he had had experience of nearly all the shows that were held in the island, and had their figures at his finger's end. He would ask him to speak on the matter.

Mr Barclay said he had brought with him the balance sheets of two representative shows and he had spoken to a good many people in Brown's Town before coming to that meeting, so that he had been able to prepare two different estimates of the proposed show for them, showing minimum and maximum figures. It had been his experience that it had always been most difficult to have a surplus from any show. It had not been easy, indeed, to make ends meet at most of them and it had too often happened that the credit side of the balance sheet had been woefully disappointing. Therefore all their estimates and calculations should be carefully made, and they ought not to be too sanguine over the matter. The most important point in connection with proposals to hold show was the consideration of the matter of finance. He had had, unfortunately for his peace of mind, a great deal to do with this particular aspect of shows. He would read his minimum and maximum estimates and would be glad to hear criticisms of them, and so they would be able to get what might be nearest the actual.

The meeting critiqued the figures and finally adopted the estimates of probable receipts and expenditure which showed a small surplus.

Mr Hopwood said that in his opinion there was always something wanting in shows, and he proposed that a Stock Fair be held in connection with this proposed show. The Show stock would be at one part of the ground and Fair stock at another, and all people who had anything to sell, could, on payment of a small fee, bring their stock. He hoped if this feature of the show was well advertised that buyers from Kingston and elsewhere would come, see the show, and at the same time be able to make purchases at the fair. He would not have stock sold at auction, but simply that people could attend the show and make their own bargains.

On the motion of the Rev. Dr Murray, seconded by the Rev Mr Hall, this idea was adopted.

The Chairman said that one of the first things to be done was to get a Secretary. A great deal of work devolved upon him so that a person who was willing and enthusiastic over the matter must be secured.

Rev Mr Hall proposed that Mr R. L. Young be appointed secretary and Mr Charles Costa, treasurer.

Mr H. Q. Levy seconded, and this was agreed to.

The next point discussed was where to hold the show.

Various places mentioned, but on Mr. Young stating that he had asked the Hon. George McGrath for the use of his property, "Minard" for the show, and that that gentleman had kindly agreed, Mr H. Q. Levy proposed, seconded by the Rev Mr Hall and it was agreed, that the show be held at "Minard" and that the thanks of the meeting be accorded to Mr McGrath for his kindness.

As regards the time for holding the show on the motion of the Rev. Dr Murray, seconded by Mr. Charles Costa, it was resolved to hold it on the second Thursday in February.

The names of a large number of gentleman were submitted, to be asked to act as a General Committee, from which an Executive Committee, of those gentlemen readily available to meet in Brown's Town could be elected.

It was decided to ask the Hon. H.E. Cox, Custos of St Ann, and the Hon George McGrath, Custos of St Catherine, to act as patrons of the show.

It was also agreed that the name of the show be the western St Ann Agricultural Show.

August 31, 1904
STEPHENSON At Bridgewater on the 28th August and interred at Rio Bueno on the 29th, Edmund Brown. Peace perfect peace.

1904

September 3, 1904
MUSCHETT-EDBURY At the Parish Church, Lindstead, on the 31st instant, by the Rev
C. R. G. Thomas, Gilbert Chas. Muschett to Eda Venetia Estelle Edbury

September 10, 1904
NETHERSOLE - At Belfast, Cleveland Road, on the 9th September, the wife of Ernest
B. Nethersole of a son.

September 12, 1904
HART-TRENCH-At St Gabriel's Church May Pen, on Wednesday, September 7th 1904,
by the Revd J.K. Hunt, Ansell, second son of Samuel Hart Esq, J.P. of Montego Bay to
Lizzie Louise, third daughter of the late J.S. Trench Esq, Collector of Taxes.

September 12, 1904
LOPEZ-On Sunday at 1.25 p.m. at his residence 28 Rosemary Lane, Asher Lopez aged
74 years. Friends and acquaintances of A. Leo Lopez please accept this only intimation.
Please let your carriage attend. Funeral moves 4.30 sharp this evening.

September 20, 1904
Mary Ann DaCosta--At Good Air, St Andrew, on Saturday morning the 17th inst, Mrs
Mary Ann DaCosta, relict of the late Henry Willoughby DaCosta, merchant of Kingston,
deeply regretted by her family and a large circle of friends and acquaintances. "The
commencement of a better life".

September 26, 1904
Casserly At Ocho Rios, on e 20th September, the wife of Owen B. Casserly of a son.
English and American papers please copy.

October 3, 1904
WHITTINGHAM-HELWIG-At Eccleston's Chapel, St Ann's on 28th September, by Rev
A. Cresser, assisted by Rev. M Barker, Elmos Japhat, son the J.W. Whittingham, Esq, of
Falmouth to Alice Caroline, Daughter of Mrs Frederica Helwig of Clarksonville, St
Ann's.

October 8, 1904
ROXBURGH At Annandale, St Ann, on the 6th instant, Catherine Gibson, relict of the
late Francis Thomas Roxburgh. Age 83 years

October 8, 1904
Mount Pelee in eruption--The Martinique Volcano Belches Lava--Phenomenon observed-
-Dust Clouds Observed in Windward Islands--Fears in St Vincent.

October 12, 1904
DEATH OF MR F.W. HOLLAR. Late Vice-Chairman of the City Council. --Died Early
yesterday--The End came Rather unexpectedly. Was A self-made man. It is with great
regret that we announce the death of Mr F. W. Hollar who, up to Monday afternoon,
filled the position of Vice-Chairman of the Mayor and council of Kingston.
        The sad event took place at 3 a.m. yesterday, and the end was so unexpected
that the news came like a shock to all his friends when it became known ....Mr Hollar
was a native of Port Royal, and although he resided in the city, Port Royal was still his
headquarters where he engaged in carrying out work for the naval and military

departments........Mr Hollar was 59 years of age and leaves two sons, and a daughter, Miss Hollar who is one of the mistresses at Wolmer's School and who left Jamaica on the Port Kingston on that vessel's return voyage home.

The funeral took place yesterday and was largely attended. The Mayor and all the City Councillors attended, as well as a number of members of the Masonic craft, of which Mrs Hollar was a prominent member.

To his widow and sorrowing relatives we tender our sincere condolence.

October 18, 1904
HOLLAR-At his residence, Vauxhall, Kingston, Francis White Hollar. "Thy will be done" English and American papers please copy.

October 24, 1904
RAMSON-At St Luke's Parsonage, Up-Park Camp, on Saturday morning, 22nd inst, the wife of the Rev J.L. Ramson of a daughter.

BROWN'S TOWN. --- Concert of Miss Maud Cover L.R.A.M.
Brown's Town, October 21. As intimated in the daily papers and by placards, the concert got up by Miss Maud Cover L.R.A.M. came off Thursday evening 20th inst. The day opened gloomily, and there were several showers of rain, off and on. Towards evening the rain ceased, and although many from a distance were disappointed a goodly number assembled.

The room was tastily decorated with flags and flowers, and the following programme was successfully carried through:-

Part I

1. Violin Solo...Allegro brilliant..Ten Have ...Miss Cover
2. Song Tell Her I Love Her so ....De Faue... Mr H.Q. Levy
(I never knew Granddad could sing)
3. Pianoforte Solo...Fantaisie Impromptu...Chopin.. Miss Cover
4. Quartette...True Love... Misses Cover, Dr Levy, Mr C. Levy
5. Song ....Love's Coronation ...F. Alyward...Misses Cover
6. Song...."Let her Drowned"... Mr A Sewell
7. Pianoforte Solo...2nd Movement Sonate Op 87..E .Grieg...Miss May Cover
8. Violin Solo.....Miss Cover

Part II

1. Pianoforte Duet...Hungarian Rhapsodie...Liszt Misses Cover
2. Recitation
3. Song (a) The Birds go North....Willeby
(b) The Sweetest flow that Blows...Willeby   Miss Cover
4. Pianoforte Solo.. The Moonlight Sonata...Beethoven Miss Cover
5. Song..The Whistling Coon...Mr Sewell
6. Quartette In this Hour of Softened Splendour... C.
        Pinsuti..Misses Cover, Dr Levy, Mr C. Levy
7. Violin Solo..Sonata Op 45, 2nd Movement. ..E. Grieg Miss Cover
8. Song ...Mr W.L. Levy

1904

The items were well chosen and effectively rendered. Special mention might be made of the violin solos and song by Miss Cover, the duet by the Misses Cover and the quartette by the Misses Cover, Dr and Mr C.E. Levy. The lighter or humorous songs contributed by Messers Sewell and W. Levy added to the general pleasure of the evening.

October 25, 1904
Farquharson--At Dunrobin, Mandeville on Sunday Morning, October 23rd Isabelle Gordon, the dearly loved wife of Mr C. S. Farquharson.

October 26, 1904
INGRAM--At Brown's Town on the 17th instant, Eliza, relict of the late Thomas Ingram of Orange Hill, St Ann. "Thy will be done"(English and American papers please copy)

November 11, 1904
Gunter--On Monday the 7th November 1904 at Tragaunter Camperdown, Kingston the wife of Godfrey George Gunter (Solicitor) of a daughter

November 19, 1904
HALL At Holme Lea, Taptonville, Shefield, England aged 69 years, Mr William Greaves Hall, J.P.

An advertisement for the Moneague Hotel lists T.J. Sims, Moneague as the person to" Write or wire for accommodation and for buggy to meet you at Ewarton".

December 2, 1904
Mrs Hollar and daughters beg through this medium to return thanks to their numerous friends and acquaintances for their kind letters of sympathy received during their recent sad bereavement.

December 6, 1904
VALVERDI-DELISSER At St John's Presbyterian Manse, on Saturday, December 3rd, by the Rev S. R. Braithwaite, Oscar Byron Valverdi, to Evelyn Murray Delisser.

December 20, 1904
In a report on the telephone company and the effect of the hurricane of 1903 it is stated that "There were 358 instruments in operation yielding a monthly revenue of £236 10s 9d" Presumably all in Kingston.

1905

January 23, 1905
Clark--At Nonsuch St Mary, on Thursday, 19th January, 1905, the wife of Harvey Clark of a son

January 24, 1905
Barrett-On the night of the 21st January 05, Cas J Moulton Barrett of Clifton, Falmouth Age 91. R.I.P English papers please copy.

January 28, 1905
Hire-At Knowsley Park Manchester, on the 22nd inst, H. F. Hire aged 62.

February 4, 1905
OLD FAMILY OF JAMAICA--Tributes to the Late C. Moulton
Barrett. The Funeral Ceremony--Love Letters of Robert and Elizabeth Browning. (C. Moulton Barrett was Elizabeth Brownings brother)February 14, 1905

CALL FOR JAMAICA LABOUR FOR THE PANAMA CANAL. -Important Message Prepared by the Governor For Presentation to Legislative Council.--Report of the Conference with Mr Taft. Despatch From British Consul at Panama, Telling of the Coming of Jamaicans

February 15, 1905
THE AGRICULTURAL SHOW IN ST ANN---A Detailed Description of an
exhibition that was highly successful---SPLENDID EXHIBITS IN SEVERAL CLASSES. -- Some Features that Helped Largely Towards the Success of the The Brown's Town Show--Report by Two qualified Agricultural Experts.

The much-talked-of and long expected Agricultural Show of the Western St Ann Agricultural Society, which was held at Brown's Town on Thursday 9th inst., exceeded by a hundredfold in most directions the most sanguine prognostications. Wedged in between days of doubtful weather, the Show day was an ideal one. A fresh breeze blew, light clouds drifted over the blue of the sky, and so the heat of the day was nicely tempered and the people could move about with pleasure. The show grounds, Minard Penn, belonging to the Hon. Geo. McGrath, kindly loaned for the occasion, are beautifully situated and were in perfect order. The common looked green and fresh and was adorned in all directions with thousands of banners and flags floating in the breeze. There was a regular street of booths, selling all sorts of refreshments, most of them gaily decorated, while the show buildings had more flags that was ever seen at any show. A large Union Jack proudly waved in the centre of the show grounds, another waved over the office, and another over the agricultural products shed. There was a great crowd of some five thousand people present, while the hundreds of buggies packed around the ring were filled with a galaxy of beauty and fashion, not only from St Ann alone, but from our sister parishes Manchester contributing quite a number, including the genial Secretary of Kendal Show, Mr. G.A. Bonnitto, anxious to see the great rival of the Show held at Kendal.

There were also many tourists present, nearly the whole of those at Moneague Hotel having come over. Some distinguished personages present were Lord Walsingham, Col. Blagrove, Col Matthias and Professor Cossur Eward of Edinburgh, who, by the by, is now spending part of his honeymoon in Jamaica. Remarks and exclamations were heard on all sides commenting on the beauty and picturesqueness of the scene, while some the strangers gave it as their opinion that they could not have imagined such a gathering possible in Jamaica. So the show was a good advertisement of the good behaviour of the people, their enthusiasm, and the quality of our stock and agricultural products. Too great praise cannot be bestowed on the behaviour of the crowd; a better conducted concourse it would be impossible to imagine. There was not one single case of drunkenness, disorderly conduct or riotous behaviour reported for the day, nor even after the Show. The police were merely there as an assurance of the safety of private property rather than for the idea of keeping order. Can it be wondered at then that people of St Ann are so proud of their parish not only as the garden of Jamaica, but as a well behaved parish, containing a peasantry who are a model of sobriety and good conduct ? Where else could we find all classes working together in such harmony, with only one object in view-- the success of our "show". Besides the large proprietor contributing his pound, the poor artisan, even the sugar pedlar, etc, contributed voluntarily to the fund of the show to keep up the honour and prestige of the parish they all love so well.

AGRICULTURAL PRODUCTS

For the Agricultural products two sheds had been built, 60 feet long, and the exhibits were simply prodigious. They commenced to flow in from the previous evening, and by 9 a.m. when they should have been all arranged and the judging commenced, the whole scene was still one of jumble and chaos apparently. The numerous volunteers who were put down to act as clerks did not materialize in the morning until they were looked for and got together, and then only half could be got but with the able management of such veterans as Messrs, Barclay and Cradwick, together with the experienced assistance of the Messrs Heining who have done so much for the ---------Arnett, the exhibits were put in shape for judging by noon, when really the judging should have been all over. The judging was in full swing till after 4 o'clock, when it was time to begin to hand back the exhibits. It was the old story of little assistance and heavy burden on a few. The bluff secretary of the show, Mr Young, was all over the place looking anxious, worried-- and yet happy. In such classes as ground provisions, meals and starches the exhibits assumed mammouth proportions, and there never has been such an extraordinary show of yams anywhere. In spite of the bench being 60 feet, set for their accommodation, many were but seen having to go under the bench. In this class alone thirty prizes were awarded and 22 extra prizes were given, all equivalent in second prizes. The display of citrus fruits was a very fine one, better oranges could hardly be obtained in any part of the island. There was a large competition in boxes packed for export. The common Jamaica oranges took the palm, and those produced by Mr Corlett, Knuttford, who took several prizes, were a revelation to the fancy grow orange man. The grapefruits in fineness of texture and smooth appearance if displayed in a shop in London or New York would surely have tempted the money out of anybody's pocket. The unfortunate thing here is with all the agricultural products was the lack of room and the short time left for arranging so that none of the exhibits were displayed in full advantage, else it would have been an impressive show. At last we have seen something like an exhibition of coffee worthy of Jamaica outside of the Port Royal Mountains show which is always marvellous. The exhibits were also of a high order, but some of the best failed to get prizes, through not being dried enough, which is a common fault both with coffee and cocoa. The cocoa, on the other hand, though well represented, was not of a very high order. There were some splendid exhibits of kola powder and there was a good demand for it for sale. The manufactured articles were all out in strong force, such as home-made saddles, baskets, etc.

In the ladies' classes there was a great turn out of exhibits, and there were some really splendid displays of plain and fancy work. There was a very fine show of lace bark articles from Cave Valley district. The preserves were very attractive and were in fair quantity. There was a pretty good show of dairy articles, the eggs showing up better than at any shows since the old Kingston shows were held. The butter was nothing extra in the way of quality, but the competition was good. So large was the number of exhibits of agricultural products and fancy work that a great many sent from a distance were unopened and consequently not judged.

HORSEKIND ENTRIES.

The entries for horsekind numbered over 160, a large proportion belonging to small settlers classes which were well filled. The settlers brood-mare class was a specially good one with 16 entries.

The riding and driving classes were also filled and there was splendid competition. In the class for over 14.2 driving, the first prize was taken by a small settler who, before the show, had to be strongly persuaded to take his chance against his bigger neighbour. One of hardest classes to judge was that for the ladies. It is seldom that there is such good competition and such good riders perhaps only at Kendal Show. After deep consideration the judges awarded first prize to Mrs Turner, a visitor staying at New Hope, St Ann, and second to Miss Fisher. Another very interesting class that deserved some comment was that of the native stallions in which the judging commenced. We were anxious to know how the judges who were both breeders of thorough-breds would treat Mr. Webb's half-bred hackney which, to our minds, was one of the finest of the class bred in Jamaica-but we had our doubts as to his being preferred to Mr Sewell's through-bred Silver Bead, which is by Black Beed out of Tilda, a Timbale mare. However, Ivanhoe, the Hackney, got first and Silver Bead second. On the other hand a half-bred colt of Silver Bead, Lilly Bead, took first prize in the 1903 class for fillies and the championship prize of the Show. It was bred by Mr. Arnett, one of the local instructors, and was afterwards sold for £20 to one of the judges.

CATTLE CLASSES

In the cattle classes there was keen competition, there being over 100 entries, and here again the small settler showed up to great advantage, more so than in horsekind, and we feel certain that if the two classes had competed against each other the majority of prizes would have been in favour of the small man. It made us proud of the St Ann peasantry to turn out such splendid stock, and we doubt if any other parish could have provided such a sight. Mr C. Lopez, one of the Judges, was so pleased and impressed with the display of settlers'cattle that with praise-worthy philanthropy he awarded 40s in -

--the most---an act which was very much appreciated by the recipients when they heard of it.

The remaining entries were as follow:-Sheep 10, goats 26, pigs 16, dogs 17, poultry 28, rabbits 5.

Among the sections the goats showed up very well indeed and the pigs magnificently, Mr. F. L. Clark having his huge Poland China sow there weighing nearly 600 lbs. The dog classes are seldom up to much in Jamaica and there was nothing striking at this show. The poultry classes showed up better than most shows--mostly through Mr. F. L Clark's exhibits of brown leghorns, light brahamas, plymouth rocks and Indian games. The rabbit section were mostly filled up by good Belgian hares or half-bred.

The Society for the Protection of Animals awarded 20s in prizes for the best kept domestic animals, one being awarded for a mule, two for donkeys and one for a dog, to small settlers animals which were all presented in surprisingly good trim.

The horticultural section was a great success, the only drawback being that the buildings were too small for the exhibits. Mr. Hopwood made a very fine exhibit of growing strawberries in bamboo pots, all stages up to ripe strawberries. He also showed a cluster of apples grown at his place, Lillyfield in St Ann, where he has made quite a success in growing apples of large size, good appearance and good flavour.

GENERAL

The show was opened by the Custos of the parish, Mr. Cox, who arrived soon after 11 o'clock, and was received by the chairman, Mr. J. H. Levy, Dr. Johnston, the clergy of the town and some other gentlemen of the show committee. After an exchange of complimentary speeches the show was declared open, the Brown's Town Band playing for all it was worth as if to make a reputation.

One of the side shows was a display of seedling canes sent up by the Island Chemist in charge of Mr. Percival Murray, superintendent of the sugar experiments, who attended to give all the necessary information concerning them, and to explain all the improvements made in the implements for testing sugar.

Messars Delgado & Co of Falmouth, presented a very nice exhibit of aerated waters, which was well spoken of. The Custos, Mr. Cox, made a very interesting exhibition of the tea grown at Ramble, and gave away free samples. We may say here that those people who did not like this tea from first samples sent out before the special machinery for treating it was installed, and experience gained in the curing will find that the tea that is now presented as good if not better than any of the imported teas. It is quite a different article from that first sent out.

The school exhibits were very satisfactory. Miss Townsend who acted in conjunction with the Rev. Mr. Geddes, was high in praise of the Baptist School exhibit, which took first prize. She assured us about the darning and patching exhibits that she had seldom seen better, even in England. She particularly commented on the cleanliness of the copy books. In summing up Miss Townsend said that if all the day school masters took such pains over the children as this particular one had evidently done then indeed there would be good hopes for the success of day schools in the near future.

The finances of the show will be all right and should certainly leave a substantial balance to the good as the money for admission will probably amount to above £120, while the entry fees are far more than estimated and the subscriptions substantial. We think Western St Ann should be particularly proud of its show.

THE PRIZE LIST

The following is a list of the prizes awarded at the show:-

HORSEKIND.
Judges:-Messrs. A. C. L. Martin and E. W. Muirhead.

Class 2. Native stallion: A. J. Webb's Ivanhoe 1st; Hon. Henry Sewell's Silverbeed 2nd.

Class 3, A jenny stallion: John Williams 1st

Class 5. Native brood mare, over 14.2 Hone. Henry Sewell's Bay mare Victoria 1st; H. Q. Levy's Zettie 2nd.

Class 6, Native Brood Mare, 14.2 and under: W. A. Cover's bay mare Topsy 1st; H. Q. Levy's Phyllis 2nd.

Class 7. Settlers Brood Mare, any height: Alex Green 1st Thomas Campbell 2nd Chas Craig highly commended.

Class 8 Mare and mule cub at foot: Col Blagrove's Madge 1st H.Q. Levy's Jess 2nd.

Class 9. Native Foal of 1903 R. L. Young's Lillyhead 1st; Guy Purchas's Straker, 2nd.

Class 13, Young Mule of 1903:Colonel Blagrove, Orange Valley, 1st Colonel Blagrove, Cardiff Hall 2nd.

Class 15, Young Mules of 1904 H. Q. Levy 1st; Colonel Blagrove 2nd.

Class 18, Native proof ass: W.A. Cover's Dandy 1st Alex. Hopwood's Colombia 2nd.

Class 21 Pair carriage horses over 14.2 Hon Geo. McGrath's certificate, D. W. Daley 1st; A. Corlett 2nd.

Class 23, Single buggy horses over 14.2: J.L. Rattray's Blue Jackett 1st; Leslie W Levy's Lance 2nd

Class 25 Lady's riding horse: Mrs Power 1st, Miss Fisher 2nd

Class 26 Saddle horse over 14.2 Sterling Fisher's Nora 1st Leslie Levy's Lance 2nd.

Class 27 Saddle Horse, 14.2 and under: S. M. Browne's Cyclone, 1st Dr. Chas. Levy's Joker 2nd Guy Purchse' Molly high commended.

Class 29 Native Carriage Mule (single) Leslie Levy's Lassie 1st, Moses Stewart 2nd

Class 30 Native saddle Mule C. M. Cahusac 1st; Leslie Levy's Lassie 2nd

Class 31 Three Dray Mules: Hon Geo. McGrath 1st Col Blagrove Cardiff Hall 2nd.

Class 33 Lady's driving class (single) J.A. G. Smith's Nimble 1st D. W. Daly's Juliette 2nd

CATTLE

Judge, Messrs A.W. Douuet, Clarence Lopez and Adm Roxburgh.

Class 1, imported bull: Rev J. P. Hall's Aberdeen Poll Angus: the British Empire" 1st

Class 3 Native bull four years and upwards ; Hon Geo McGrath 1st A. Lovell Simons 2nd.

Class 4 Indian bull 4 years and upwards; Hon Henry Sewell 1st: Cardiff Hall Pen 2nd; Hon Geo McGrath high recommended

Class 5 Settlers bull: Thomas Campbell 1st Jas. Scarlett 2nd Robert Linton (special prize by Mr Lopez)

Class 6 Native bull dropped 1902 Tobolski Pen 1st

Class 8 Native bull (dropped 1903) A.B. Rerrie 1st; Alex Hopwood 2nd

Class 9 Indian bull (dropped 1903) Tobolski Pen Maharajh Cardiff Hall Pen 1st, 2nd, 3rd.

Class 10, breeding cow: Harry Stephenson 1st, Tobolski Pen "Dove" 2nd Cardiff Hall Pen highly commended Hon Henry Sewell Highly commended.

Class 12, heifer of 1902 Cardiff Hall Pen 1st Hon G. McGrath 2nd H.J.(sic) Levy commended

Class 13, heifer of 1903 Hon G. Mc Grath 1st H.Q. Levy 2nd.

(continued) I did not continue it but H.Q. Levy finally got a first in Bull calf of 1904. J.S. Cover won several produce prizes

February 22, 1905
Jackson - At his residence, Waltham, Mandeville, Henry Jackson, on the 19th February, 1905 at 8.30 a.m. Aged 66.
Jesu, Lover of my soul.
Let me to Thy bosom fly,
Safe into the Heaven guide
O, receive my soul at last.

March 10, 1905
At Spitzkop, St Andrew, on the 9th March, the wife of C. W. Doorley, of a daughter.

1905

McDowell-Saturday, March 4th, at the residence of his brother, the Rev. Samuel McDowell, Carronhall, James the second son of the late Andrew McDowell, Partedown, Ireland

March 13, 1905
Cover--At Moneague, St Ann, on 8th March, Elizabeth Cover, relict of the late Charles S. Cover of "Enfield", Brown's Town, St Ann.

March 16, 1905
DaCosta--On Tuesday the 14th instant, at his late residence, 3208 Columbia Avenue, Philadelphia, U.S.A. Henry Rodriques DaCosta, late of Kingston, Jamaica in his 78th year by Cable

March 25, 1905
Scarlett At 145 Kings Street, on the 24th instant at 9.p.m. Eliza Steel, widow of the late John Gallimore Scarlett of Rose Hill, St Ann, and beloved mother of Mrs L.G. Garcia. Funeral will move from the above residence at 4.30 p.m. to day. Friends and acquaintances please accept this the only intimation.

Not gone from memory,
Not gone from life,
But gone to her Father's home above

March 25, 1905
Mrs Rattigan, mother of Mr L.A. Rattigan is very ill in Kingston.

April 5, 1905
Fournier--At 23 Charles Street at 6 p.m. on 4th April, 1905, Alphonse Pierre (Peter) eldest son of Alphonse and Essie Fournier, aged 11 years and 9 months. Funeral will leave the house at 4.30 p.m. to day for the Catholic cemetery. Please accept this intimation.

April 6, 1905
At Bel Air on the 2nd inst, the wife of F. Chas. Fisher, of a son.

Coles--On February 17th, 1905 at Johannesburg, South Africa, from heart failure, following on wounds received in the South African War, Ernest Harcourt Coles, formerly of the 8th Troop of the Imperial Yeomanry, son of Lewis Harcourt Coles, of London, captain of 1st Middlesex.V.B. Royal engineers (Long Service Order) and nephew of the Rev. C. H. Coles M.A. Up-Park Camp, Jamaica "Dulce et decorum est pro patria mon" "Out of weakness made strong, waxed valiant in fight, turned to fight the armies of the aliens"

April 7, 1905
Column on the funeral of Peter Fournier who was a pupil of St George's College, Winchester Park.April 17, 1905

Rattigan--At quarter past 2 o'clock yesterday, at 12« Kings Street, Mrs Ann Rattigan (aged 92) the mother of Mr. L. A. Rattigan, Collector of Taxes for St Catherine.
Tis Sweet !
Oh! So very Sweet !!
To be at Home !!!

Selected Vital Records from the Jamaican Daily Gleaner

In Heaven!!!!

April 18, 1905
Mossman - At Hampstead House, St Mary, on the 14th inst. Jessie M. Mossman, relict of the late Archibald Mossman of Linstead. Aged 82 years. "Rest comes at Last"

April 25, 1905
Allwood- At Knutsford, St Andrew, on the 20th April, Henrietta Allwood, widow of the late James Allwood, in her 89th year.

April 27, 1905
Honiball-At 10 South Camp Road, Kingston, on the 22nd inst., the wife of R. Honiball, of a son.

May 2, 1905
Duff-Davis--At the Parish Church, Lucea on Wednesday, 26th April by the Venerable Archdeacon C. Henderson Davis, assisted by the Rev. A. Parker Kennedy, Rector of the Church, Percy Granville, son of the Rev. John Duff, to Jane Anita Winifred, daughter of A. E. Davis, Esq, Lucea. American and English papers please copy.

May 27, 1905
LIVING JAMAICA WORTHIES

III. WILLIAM CLARKE MURRAY. D.D.

There are some men in whom moderation is so strong a quality that it becomes the marked characteristic of their lives. They are usually, the Whigs of politics, combining as they do a desire for progress with a conservative instinct which keeps them from going too far. They move slowly and carefully, but they always do move; they are never stationary; and although not apt to regard new theories with a rapturous enthusiasm are never impervious to ideas or hopelessly prejudiced. The best class of such men are generally acknowledged to be a valuable element in any community: they do not only represent the ballast of the State but are also a propelling power of moderate force. One such individual is undoubtedly the Rev. William Clarke Murray, D.D. whose name is a household word in Jamaica, and who is universally respected for his sober common-sense and the integrity of his character. A little over seventy now, he has lived a full and busy life, and is a witness to the truth that character, industry and intelligence are amongst the most valuable possessions of any man, and are the most potent factors in a useful and successful career.

To achieve success in this world is the ambition of the majority. But there are different kinds of success, and what appeals to one man does not appeal to the other

This low man seeks a little thing to do,
Sees it and does it.
That high man with a great end to pursue
Dies ere he knows it.

It all depends upon your standards and your ideals; and many a one whom the world calls a failure has really lived his life nobly and would not exchange his humble lot for the wealth and honour which others acquire by restless seeking and striving. And one's ideals are largely the result of one's temperament and attitude of mind. Some live a life of thought, some a life of action. Some would devote themselves to laying the foundations of great industries, others to directing and controlling great masses of men, others, again, to labouring amongst the poor, the down-trodden and the oppressed of society. But what ever career a man chooses, we may be sure that the secret of his success (unless he be a genius and so stands in a category apart) will be found in the possession by him of the qualities of intelligence, integrity and industry. He may possess more of one and less of the other; but he must possess some of all three. However intellectually brilliant he is, if he has not character he must eventually fail. However honest and hard-working he is, he must always remain in the lower ranks of life if he has but little intelligence. The fact is that, granting ordinarily favourable circumstances, we shall succeed or fail in life according to our possession or lack of these three essential qualities. The more we have of them and the finer proportion they bear to each other, the better for us; the less we have of them the greater their disproportion, the more are we handicapped in the arena of the world. The individual himself may not see this: if he be clever he may rejoice in his cleverness and never give a thought to what he lacks in other respects. But sooner or later he will suffer for his defects, for this in the law of more existence.

Now in the Rev, William Clarke Murray we find patient industry, sober intelligence and sterling integrity admirably combined. In his youth he had not many of those advantages which come to the more fortunate. Perhaps the best tuition he ever got was what he received for a year or two from Mr Charles Allen, an ex-Jesuit priest, who gave him some instruction in mathematics and the classics. At seventeen he left school, and from that time to this-- from seventeen to seventy--he has been working, quietly, steadily, perseveringly, gaining recognition without directly seeking for it and earning the esteem of all who can appreciate the qualities of his personality. And all his life he has been a learner. Some persons imagine that a man's education is finished at school or college, whereas it is only begun. Every professional man knows how much he learns of his profession by experience and the exercise of his own faculties; every one knows something of the treasure that is to be found in books and in life. Now, William Clarke Murray had a receptive and inquiring mind, and so at an early age he gave considerable time in reading, his attention being chiefly devoted to theological, philosophical and historical subjects. From the age of seventeen to twenty two he was connected with the Department of the Clark of Works in the Naval Dock Yard in Port Royal; but all this time he did not neglect his studies. And he had found his true vocation. While a clerk he had done some lay-preaching, and when he finally left Port Royal it was with the determination to obtain a systematic training for the ministry. He did not, however, enter any college, but found employment at one as an Employed Lay Teacher in the Wesleyan body, and in 1858, after passing his examination, was appointed a minister of that Communion. How he gradually rose until he occupied the highest positions in the Wesleyan Church, and came to be appointed to all kinds of honorary posts by the Government, and succeeded in winning the respect and esteem of the whole island--all this is matter of common Knowledge. And throughout his whole career his great characteristic, moderation, has been conspicuous. He has taken part in many public discussions and has advanced views that were at the time considered "dangerous". But he was urbane and moderate even in the midst of disputes and his efforts seem always to have been directed towards producing an atmosphere of intellectual calm. He loves to steer a middle course. To the more enterprising voyager who would run his bark into strange seas with never a thought as to what might befall him there, this carefulness and caution must often be tantalising. But it must also be a consolation to him to find so steady a mariner sometimes commending some bold adventure of his and rather sympathising with than reproving his enthusiasm. He instantly sees that the carefulness of this man is not the result of narrowness of mind but the inevitable expression of an even balance of temperamental traits and impulses.

William Clarke Murray selected the ministry as his vocation. He might have chosen some other field for the exercise of his energies, but he preferred to follow the true bent of his mind. By so doing he has become an influence in the island; what he says is listened to with respect, and there are few of his confreres who do not speak of him in terms of high regard. Surely this is something for a man to be proud of. The Greeks with wise philosophy have warned us to count no man happy till he is dead, for no one can tell what sudden reverse of fortune he may not experience. But in this instance it will not be unwise to count the subject of this character-study as happy, though happily not yet dead. For no reverse of fortune could take from him the esteem of the people and the respect of those who know him.

May 30, 1905
Brown-On Sunday May 28th, Steerfield, St Ann, Mrs Dorothy Brown, at the age of 64 years, leaving ten orphans to mourn her irreparable loss. "Thy will be done"

May 31, 1905
Labor exodus from Jamaica--Kingston Athenaeum and Panama Canal--It will be of benefit-- Lessons which the emigration will teach. (Debate "Will the employment of Jamaica labour in the construction of the Panama Canal be of benefit to this country)

June 3, 1905
Burbidge--Amy Maud, beloved wife of George Arnold Burbidge, and eldest daughter of Mrs Ella Cover, at 147 King street on the 31st ult. Aged 26 years "Thy will be done"

June 5, 1905
Harty -At Bushy Park, near May Pen, on Monday, 29th May, Sarah Shevan, eldest daughter of William Harty and his wife Jessy, formerly of Chapelton.

June 7, 1905
LOPEZ-ABRAHAMS On the 17th ult., at Christ Church, Egbaston, Birmingham, England, by the Revd. Canon Owen, Marie Louise, eldest daughter of Thomas Abrahams, Esq., Tavanue, Chapelton, Clarendon, to Manly Thomas Lopez, also of Tavanue, Chapelton.

June 15, 1905
Lopez On the 10th instant, at Weggis, Switzerland, the wife of Leo.

June 16, 1905
Lopez Suddenly on Sunday, June 4, 1905 Isaac, beloved husband of Sophia Lopez. Funeral from late residence, 69 West 97th Street, New York

Lopez- on Wednesday, June 7, ten a.m.. F. Lopez of a daughter.

June 20, 1905
Hart At Brentford Lodge, Brentford Road, St Andrew, on the 17th inst., the wife of Ansell Hart of a son.

1905

June 21, 1905
Muschett At Catadupa on June the 16th, the wife of G.C. Muschett of a daughter

MacDonnel At Winsfield St Ann on the 3rd June 1905, Mrs Jane MacDonnel, beloved and regretted by numerous relatives and friends "Rest in Peace"

June 24, 1905
Sickness on the Isthmus--More Yellow Fever Cases are Reported--Must be eradicated--Governor Promises Proper Sanitary System--Vitrified bricks wanted.

July 1, 1905
Crum-Ewing At Grey Abbey, Mandeville, on 23rd inst., the wife of H.E. Crum-Ewing of a son.

July 8, 1905
DaCosta On Thursday morning, 6th July, at her residence, "Elton Grove" Mandeville, Sophia, relict of the late Alexander DaCosta and the beloved mother of G.A., A.E. and A.G. DaCosta. Aged 83 years.
Father in Thy gracious keeping
Leave me now thy servant sleeping

July 11, 1905
Walcott At Richmond, Saint Mary, on Monday, July 10th Mary Jane Walcott in her 91st year

July 15, 1905
NELSON - On Friday evening, 14th July instant, at her residence, No 1 Beckford Street, Spanish Town, Ellen Emily Nelson, relict of the late Edward Colin Nelson, and second daughter of James Samuel Facey, Esq. Funeral will take place on Sunday morning the 16th instant, at 8.30 a.m. Friends and acquaintances will please accept this only intimation.

July 17, 1905
LOPEZ At Clifton Villa, Spanish Town, on Sunday, 9th July, the wife of Dr A.C. Lopez of a son.

July 19, 1905
DEATH of MR ISAACS (By Telegraph) Brown's Town, Tuesday July 18 Mr Abram Isaacs, otherwise know as "Mass Bram" one of our esteemed and prominent townsmen, died here suddenly at two o'clock this morning.

July 22, 1905
ISAACS - On the 18th at Brown's Town, St Ann, Abraham Isaacs, in his 60th year

August 4, 1905
Nash- At 2 p.m. on Wednesday, 2nd August at "Abbotstown," Hope Road, the wife of E. J. M. Nash of a son.

McHardy Alexander Campbell, on Wednesday, 2nd August, 1905. He was called to the ministry of the Gospel in 1891 and spent several years in earnest, faithful service till failing health compelled his resignation. "Man in Christ"

Selected Vital Records from the Jamaican Daily Gleaner

August 8, 1905
WEDDING BELLS
Orrett-Harrison

A very pretty wedding was celebrated at St Michael's Church on Wednesday the 2nd inst when Mr. Henry Macaulay Orrett, Principal Clerk at Mr Haggart's office, and youngest son of the late Mr. George Denniston Orrett was united to Miss Lily Muriel Harrison, youngest daughter of the late Thomas Harrison, Esq, Surveyor General. The wedding ceremony was performed by the Rev S. O, Ormsby (more)

August 15, 1905
REV. STEWART"S DEATH..-Funeral in Falmouth. Falmouth August 13 --The body of the late Rev E.A. Stewart, who died in Kingston, was brought here for interment last night.

The coffin was placed in front of the altar at the Parish Church, where it remained for the night, a number of persons sitting up all night with it in the Church. The funeral took place at 9 a.m. today. A large concourse of people turned out this morning to attend. All the gentlemen of the town and surroundings were present. The Revd. E.A. Stewart became rector of Falmouth Church about the end of October 1878, succeeding Mr Garrett, and during the past thirty-five years performed his duties faithfully and well, endearing himself to his congregation and becoming generally respected by the community at large. About two years ago he had to retire from active work on account of illness and was succeeded by the Revd J. B. Hall. He resided at "Armagh" latterly, about five miles from the town, drawing a pension as island curate of the Rio Bueno, which place he left to take charge of Good Hope Church, when he came to Falmouth where he reared a large family consisting of four sons and five daughters all of whom and a widow the sister of Richard and William Todd Esqs with the exception of one daughter, are left to mourn their loss. The bereaved family have the heartfelt sympathy of the whole community.

August 29, 1905
SMITH - On 27th instant at Chancery Hall, St Andrews, Mrs Frances Euphemia Smith, relict of the late Rev John Smith, Rector of St Ann's Aged 89 years

September 9, 1905
Lynch At Port Antonio on the 4th day of September, 1905, the wife of E.L. Lynch, Esq of a son.

September 21, 1905
Doorly In New York on Wednesday 20th instant, Mary E. Doorly, relict of the late James G. Doorly, District Engineer, Jamaica--By Cable.

September 30, 1905
Cleghorn At Gatun Republic of Panama Sept 18th, 1905, Mrs Martha Cleghorn, wife of Dr. A. Cleghorn, artist, at the age of 28 years. R.I.P.

October 16, 1905 (Monday)
Earth Tremor Shakes Island--Two Other Violent Shocks of Earthquake--Worse than last one. Another severe shock of earthquake occurred on Saturday morning. It was felt in Kingston at 9.27 o'clock and lasted fully a minute. The oscillations at first were from north to south and then from east to west. The shock was more prolonged and violent than that which shook all Jamaica on Thursday evening.

1905

October 24, 1905
Whitelocke On the 16th October, 1905 at Bulstrode Park, Westmoreland, the wife of Charles O. Whitelocke, of a son.

November 8, 1905
Royes At 5.30 p.m. yesterday at "Devereux Ville" (NW corner Waterloo and Windward Roads) Charles John Royes, late of Knapdale, St Ann, in his 74th year. Funeral will move for May Pen Cemetery this evening at 4.30 punctually.

SEND GREETINGS TO YOUR FRIENDS ABROAD.

PICTORIAL POST CARDS

The Views set forth on these Cards are clean and bright, and are tastefully finished. They are well fitted to convey to friends abroad or in the island excellent impressions of scenery and life characteristic of much of the Island. The following is a list of some of them:

A Distant View of Kingston Harbour
A View Near Newport
Cane River Falls
Near View of Constant Spring Hotel
Distant View of Constant Spring Hotel
Gordon Town
Near View of Port Antonio
View of Port Antonio Harbour
A Family View, Kent Village, Bog Walk
A Halt in the Fern Valley
A study in Black and White
A Washing Scene, Near Old Harbour
Richmond Railway Station
River Scene
Waterfall, Road to Newcastle
Lych Gate, Half-Way-Tree
River Falls
"Home Sweet Home"
Bamboo Glade, Worthy Park
Native Wedding Party
Brown's Town Market
"A Corner in Pines"
Going to Ground
Mandeville Market
Pimento, Coffee, etc
Sugar and Rum, "en route" Newcastle, looking towards Kingston
Mending Our Ways
Barbecues for Drying
Royal Palms, Spanish Town

Price 1d each, post free 1«d, or 9d per doz, post free 10d

313

Selected Vital Records from the Jamaican Daily Gleaner
Coloured Views 2d each, post free 2«d

The EDUCATIONAL SUPPLY COY
16 King Street, Kingston
W.R.Gillies, Manager.

November 10, 1905
Daniel On Tuesday, November, 7th, the wife of H. Hood-Daniel of a daughter

November 11, 1905
The charge for advertisements of Births, Marriages and Death 3/- per insertion or three insertions for 7/6

MacLachlan-- At Valley Minor Penn, St Ann, on the evening of October 21st, 1905 Robert Steel Maclachlan, of Edinburgh, Scotland, in the 81st year of his age.
" For we which have believed do enter into rest,'
There remaineth therefor a rest to the people of god." Scotch papers please copy.

November 16, 1905
A BRILLIANT WEDDING--Marriage of Miss Verley to Mr Bradley. - LATEST SOCIETY EVENT--List of The Guests and Array of Presents--Some of Dress worn (The marriage of Mr Richard Walter Bradley to Miss Flossie Ivy House Verley, youngest daughter of the late Mr Louis Verley at St Andrew Parish Church yesterday afternoon..........(More)

November 21, 1905
Scarlett At Water Valley, on the 16th instant, the wife of J.H. Scarlett, of a daughter.

November 29, 1905
Death of Mr Maxwell, J.P.--Shoots himself on His property by Accident. Suddenly Went Off. Details of the Sad Occurrence Last Saturday

News has been received in Kingston announcing the death, under very sad circumstances, of Mr George R. M. Maxwell, a Justice of the Peace for the parish of Westmoreland, which occurred at his residence at Darliston on Saturday last. From information which we have been able to gather Mr Maxwell accidentally shot himself, death following almost immediately

It appears that on Saturday the 25th inst, while Mr Maxwell was in his house at Darliston, he saw a mongoose run into the wall of his cow pen, a few chains from the house. He called one of his sons and two servants and along with them he proceeded to the cow pen taking his breech leading double barrel gun with him. After arriving at the cow pen, it is said the mongoose had gone and he sent his son and the servants to the other side of the wall and told them to put fire to it in order to chase out the mongoose. The gun which Mr Maxwell had taken out with him was loaded and according to the statements of the persons who were with him, the gun at this time was between his knees. The trigger of the left barrel was on full cock and the muzzle resting on Mr Maxwell's right shoulder. After the servants and the son of Mr Maxwell had gone to the other side of the wall and were engaged in putting the fire there, they heard the gun fired and when they looked round they saw Mr Maxwell struggling on the ground and bleeding from the throat. The gun had evidently gone off by accident. He died almost immediately after the gun went off. The face of the deceased was much disfigured.

A post mortem examination was performed on the body by Dr Harvey, The D.M.O. at Sav-la-Mar. Much sympathy is felt for the relatives of the deceased gentleman who has met such an untimely death.

December 5, 1905
Priestnal--On Sunday, 3rd December, at the Congregational Parsonage 28 North Street, Kingston, the wife of the Rev Wm Priestnal of a son.

December 6, 1905
Sims On the 3rd inst. at Moneague, the wife of R.J. Sims of a son

December 12, 1905
MAY-NETHERSOLE On the 5th inst. at St Michael's Church, Kingston, by the Rev J. Massiah, B.A. Rector of the Parish Church Montego Bay, assisted by the Rev S. O. Ormsby, Rector of St Michael's Donald Raynes McFarlane, son the the late Donald McFarlane May of Kingston, to Blanche Allen, daughter of the late John Crosbie Nethersole of Kingston.

Deeember 16, 1905
RHODES SCHOLARSHIP-- Life at Oxford as Seen By the First Scholar From Jamaica. WORKING OF THE PLAN --(By R.M. Murray, of Jamaica)

In writing this article I do not presume to evolve any ideas of my own on such a magnificent educational scheme. (I use the word educational in its true sense), but it is my purpose mainly to set forth some facts on the subject which I have gathered from speeches delivered at various time by Dr. Parkin, from reading and from conversations held with different scholars.

I need hardly dwell upon the details of the scheme; they are too well known to call for repetition here. The late Cecil John Rhodes directed that scholarships to the value of £300 per annum should be awarded to young men from certain parts of the British Empire, from the United States of America and from Germany. He provided that annually there should be eight from South Africa, seven from Australia, eight from Canada, three from the Atlantic Islands and the West Indies, about forty from the States, and five of £250 from Germany. This means that after Sep 1906, there will be over two hundred Rhodes Scholars continually in residence at Oxford, and the annual expense will amount to over £60,000.

The liberality of such a bequest, coupled with the unique nature of its conditions, leads one to enquire the purpose and idea which the founder had in view. Cecil Rhodes was a profound imperialist; he believed that the English-speaking race was the greatest factor in bringing about the progress, and up-building of mankind; this set conviction broadened into the dream of the unity of these peoples for the spreading of the British Empire throughout the world. He desired, accordingly to impress upon the young Colonial the advantages that would accrue to the Colonies as well as to the Mother Country from retaining the Empire intact as it is today, and so he conceived the idea of providing for sending men to Oxford at a time when their minds would be ready to receive impressions, that their views of life and manners might be broadened and that they might gain such experience as would serve them in good stead when they returned to their countries to occupy positions of greater or less influence.

The question my reasonably be asked "why was Germany included in the bequest?" The explanation was given by Mr Rhodes himself in the following word, "a good understanding between England, Germany, and the United States of America, will secure the peace of the world, and educational relations form the strongest tie.

The Scholars are distributed among twenty one colleges and are not confined to any particular one. The idea that was furthest from the mind of Rhodes was that of Clubbing together; he wanted the men to assimilate English ideas and to rub shoulder to shoulder with every sort and condition of person. There is, however, one function at which all gather annually and that is a dinner, provided for, in the will. All who are able are requested to attend, and the Trustees invite "such guests as have shown sympathy with the views expressed by the Founder" On Friday the 24th November Lord Miller took the chair, and Mr Rudyard Kipling was the chief guest. After the dinner the Chairman proposed the toast of the King, of the President of the United States, and on the Kaiser. These were replied to by various representatives and also of "The memory of Cecil John Rhodes" Dr Parkin, among either things, said that a record was being kept of the past of every Rhodes Scholar, of his career at Oxford, and that the Trustees intended keeping it as far as possible of his future life. Each year a pamphlet would be sent to every scholar containing a general account of the progress of his fellows in different parts of The world. This would be an additional tie binding together those who had known each other during their college days at Oxford.

It is difficult to conceive of the magnitude of the scheme, and of the enormous difficulties which the trustees had and still have to face. In connection with this, it was my good fortune to be present at a paper read by Dr Parkin at the Royal Colonial Institute Northumberland Avenue, London; he said "when the will of Mr Rhodes was first published, the admiration everywhere expressed for the greatness and nobility of its conceptions was qualified by much criticism. Many of its suggestions were considered impracticable and grave doubts were expressed as to the possibility of framing from them a working scheme. He wished qualities to be measured which were not measurable; he desired to draw into a single educational atmosphere men reared in widely different communities, with divergent educational ideals; he planned to select his scholars by new agencies and according to new standards; he had evidently outlined his views without detailed knowledge of the conditions under which they would have to be worked out. From all these difficulties, which were patent upon the very face of the testament, the sanity of the testator provided a way of escape--first, by the selection as his trustees of a group of men accustomed to deal with large affairs on general principles; and secondly, by leaving them, after giving an outline of his views, the widest possible directions in giving these effect" I need hardly remind the reader "of the amount of blood that was drawn" over the question of eligibility in the case of our colony.

The benefits that a colonial may be expected to derive from an Oxford Education naturally depend very largely upon the traits of character in the individual, but, broadly speaking they may be summed up under the following heads, the first place he will, we will take it, obtain a degree in course of time, a degree which is universally acknowledged as one carrying prestige and weight, in as much as it indicates a standard of intellectual ability and literary attainment which, if coupled with the necessary quota of common-sense, will fit him for occupying a position of responsibility in some sphere

316

of usefulness. Secondly, it will give him power and a broader view of the world, enabling him to realize situations and grapple with them more successfully.

Again the social life of Oxford must certainly rub the rough edges of even the roughest diamond. There are features in it which are perhaps unique throughout the world, features which scarcely lend themselves to description in words, but contribute so largely to stamp the bearer as an Oxford man.

One of the main traits of Oxford life is its devotion to manly exercise; the very atmosphere breathes a desire to become physically fit; this has -------so many of its men to ---strenuous and useful lives after they have gone down and out into the world.

Again, one gets the opportunity of hearing the finest speakers and preachers in Great Britain, and of consulting libraries such as the Radcliffe and The Bodleian.

During the vacations one travels on the Continent and has the opportunity of learning French and German and the customs and manners of life obtaining in these countries, and of visiting the chief towns and places of interest in Europe.

And now we come to the question, "Does the Colonial in return do anything for Oxford, over and above that which the average undergraduate who spends three summers at the Varsity does?"

It may resonabley be expected that "the invasion of Oxford by Colonials" will prove advantageous to the colonies and England, and hence to the Empire, in diffusing, not only among the Colonials who meet one another here from all parts, but more especially among the Englishmen at Home, a better knowledge of Greater Britain.

One cannot help being amazed, not to say annoyed, at the lamentable ignorance displayed in England as to the elements of the geography of the Empire, ignorance which often fringes upon indifference. I was reading a leading article published a few weeks ago in a contemporary of the Gleaner in which reference was made to the unwillingness evinced by merchants and men of means in England to invest their capital in ventures in Jamaica. I think, and I am sure I am one among many who hold this view, that their retinence may justly be adduced as an instance of this poor and inaccurate knowledge shared by so many in the mother country. If then the greater numbers of colonials who are entering Oxford are instrumental in awakening an interest in the lands that be over the seas, the scheme of Cecil Rhodes will have accomplished much towards the upbuilding and preservation of the British Empire.

December 21, 1905
Lindo Keith infant son of A.B. Lindo and Jennie Lindo, at their residence 2B Slipe Pen Road at 4.30 p.m. yesterday, aged 11 months. funeral at 4 o'clock this afternoon (Thursday) They will be done.

1906

January 3, 1906
The death is announced of the Attorney General of Panama, Gabriel Guisado Costa.

January 4, 1906
At 1 p.m. on Wednesday, January 3rd, 1906, Sarah A. Walker, relict of the late John Walker, late bailiff of Kingston district court. Friends and brethren of Mr. E. Wilkins are requested to attend the remains of his mother-in-law from her residence No 38 Johns Lane to the place of interment at 4 p.m. this afternoon. (Thursday)

January 5, 1906
Muschett. In Panama on the 14th December, 1905 after a short illness, Gladstone Muschett, aged 17 years and 2 months. "Sleep on Beloved, We will meet again".

January 18, 1906
On the 27th December, the Right Rev C.F. Douet D.D. late assistant Bishop of Jamaica.

January 31, 1906
Wortley. At the Rectory, Half-Way-Tree on the 30th inst., Selwyn Wortley aged 20. Funeral at Half-Way-Tree Church at 8 am today.

February 5, 1906
Lefranc. On the 3rd inst., Marie Helene wife of Izett E. Lefranc and 3rd daughter of John S. Codner.

February 6, 1906
Feurtado. Yesterday at 26« East Queen Street, wife of W.A. Fuertado, Jnr, of a son.

February 17, 1906
Dayes-Magnus. At St Georges Church on Monday 5th February, 1906 by Revd Canon Kilbourn, assisted by the Ven Archdeacon Downes, Harold W. W. Dayes (Solicitor) youngest son of the late James Dayes, to Lena Maud Louise, eldest daughter of Fred A. Magnus. At home "Camerson Villa" (Villa Pen Road) on Monday the 19th inst from 5 p.m.. No cards

February 24, 1906
Whitelocke. At "Balstrade Park" [sic] Westmoreland on the 19th instant, the wife of Fred M. Whitelocke of a son.

Selected Vital Records from the Jamaican Daily Gleaner

March 9, 1906
Costa. On the 5th March 1906, Anastasia, relict of the late William Costa of Brown's Town, St Ann. In her 85th year. Philadelphia papers please copy.

March 10, 1906
Motta. At Glenwyn, South Camp Road on Saturday, 3rd instant, the wife of Edgar C. Motta of a son.

March 12, 1906
Sewell. At Arcadia Penn, Trelawny, Jamaica on 9th instant, Hon. Henry Sewell.

March 30, 1906
Farquharson. At the Bungalow, Black River on 22nd instant, the wife of W.N.C. Farquharson of a son.

April 9, 1906
Millar. On Saturday the 7th April 1906 at Clifton House, Mandeville, Jamaica, Robert Millar in the seventy-second year of his age. "Forever with the Lord, Amen so let it be". (Scotch papers please copy)

April 10, 1906
Lynch. On Sunday April 8th 1906 at Durham House, Spanish Town, Jamaica W.I. Mary Blizard Wilhelmina, the wife of Edward B. Lynch, Esquire. Aged 65 years.

April 12, 1906
Sherlock- At his residence, Cheshunt Lodge, Norman Road, on Wednesday, morning, Charles McClelland Sherlock, J.P. Aged 53 years. Funeral at 8 o'clock this morning.

April 16, 1906
Dennison- At May Hill, Manchester on Tuesday 10th instant, Sarah Dennison. Aged 84.

May, 1906
Rutty- On Saturday, 28th April 1906. at Sea Villa, St Mary, the wife of F. S. Rutty of a son.

May, 1906
Trench - On Monday 30th April, 1906, at Lake Ville, Brentford Road, the wife of C. Lepoer Trench of a son.

May, 1906
Galbraith- At Sevenoaks, St Anns, Jamaica, on Tuesday 8th May, 1906, aged 25 years, Ragna, nee Eversen, beloved wife of William Anderton (sic)Galbraith. R.I.P. Norwegian and Mexican papers please copy.

May 18, 1906
Hart-Bonitto-- At Locksley Hall, 2 Clovelly Road, City; the residence of the bride's father, on Sunday the 13th instant Karl Wilford, son of the late Edmund Nathan Hart, Esq. of St Ann's Bay, to Esther, youngest daughter of John Bonitto, Esq. "At Home" at Locksley Hall, on Sunday the 20th inst. from 5.30 p.m. No cards

1906

May, 1906
Milne--On the 23rd May, Douglas James, infant son of Mr & Mrs W. A. Milne.

May 28, 1906
Mrs Robert Miller and family of Clifton House, Mandeville; beg through this medium to express their kind thanks for and appreciation of the many cards the letters of sympathy received during their irreparable loss.

May 31, 1906
Verley- At Brighton, England, on the 30th May 1906, Dr Reginald Louis Verley. Aged 56 years. By Cable.

June 7, 1906
Clark-- On the 23rd May, 1906, at Detroit, Michigan, U.S.A. Francis Jane, relict of the late Wm. Carey Clark, M.D. of Brown's Town, St Ann. Aged 64

July 2,1906
DISSOLUTION OF MARRIAGE.--Divorce case Tried at St Ann's Court--KILBURN VS KILBURN-- Petitioner's Story of unhappy Married Life. (Arthur Levy was the Advocate for the petitioner).

BROWN'S TOWN--Literary Association.

Members of the Brown's Town Literary Association are reminded that the "Social Evening" in connection with the association will take place at the Court House, Brown's Town, on Wednesday 11th instant, commencing at 8 p.m. The chair will be taken by Mr J. H. Levy, one of the Co-presidents of the Association. A paper entitled "The Art of Poetry, with special reference to the rise and development of English Poetry" will be read by Mr C.A. Bicknell, and will be followed by a musical programme, to be rendered by some of the members of the Association, arranged under the direction of Mr Clarence L. Levy. Non-members of the Association may obtain tickets of admission upon application to the Hon. Secretary, Mr. E. S. Lindo, or to members of the Managing Committee. The latter are particularly requested to attend the meeting of the Committee at the Court House on Wednesday 4th inst. at 5 p.m. as there are a number of new members to be proposed for election, and other business to be dealt with.

July 4, 1906
Sutherland --At Charles Town, Buff Bay, on Friday 29th June, Robert A. Sutherland, the beloved husband of Frances Sutherland. Aged 60 years. Rest in Peace.

July 10, 1906
Judah-- At St Jago de la Vega; on the morning of the 9th July, Charles Theophilus Judah in his 59th year.

July 11, 1906
BROWN'S TOWN SCHOOL BOARD.--Taking over New Government Building. -- Praise for Contractor--Thanks Returned to the Honorary Supervisor (J.P. Hall)

July 13, 1906
At Upton, Montego Bay, on Thursday morning 12th inst. the wife of Rev. T.W. Halliday of a son.

Selected Vital Records from the Jamaican Daily Gleaner

July 23, 1906

BOURKE-- On Saturday 21st July at 5 a.m. at his residence 155 King St. Wellesley Bourke, Solicitor. (Also a 3 column obituary, in which it says he was born 61 years ago)

ORRETT-- At 16a Lower Charlotte Street, Kingston, on Sunday 22nd inst. at 5.30 a.m. George, eldest son of the late George Denniston Orrett. Funeral at 5 p.m. Monday 25 July.

GIFFORD--At Brown's Town on the 17th instant, George L. Gifford. Aged 50.

July 24, 1906

RUTTY--At Barnstaple, Trelawny, on the 19th July, Willard Dorian aged 3 years 8 months, elder son of Ernest W. Rutty and Winifred Rutty. "Asleep in Jesus"

July 28, 1906

CLARKE-MCDONALD- On the 26th inst., at the Baptist Chapel, Brown's Town, St Ann, JNO ISAAC CLARKE of Buff Bay, to SARAH URINA, youngest daughter of Mrs Isabella McDonald. Central American papers please copy.

August 9, 1906

AGRICULTURAL DEVELOPMENT--Last Week's Show at Brown's Town. MORE PRIZE WINNERS-- Awards Made in the Minor Products Classes.

Among the winners:

Tomatoes: 1st H.Q. Levy
1 doz sweet potatoes: Highly commended H. Stephenson
1 doz oranges: 1st Col Blagrove, Orange Valley
1 doz Tangerines: 1st H.Q. Levy
Pimento 10 lbs Plantation: 1st H.Q. Levy, 2nd Col
Blagrove O.Valley
Nutmegs: 1st Mrs Cotter
Lime Juice:, 1 bottle 1st Col Blagrove O. Valley
Pimento Dram: 1 bottle: 1st H.Q. Levy

August 10, 1906

WATSON- On Monday morning the 6th instant (August) at Pell-River in the parish of Hanover, Robert Watson, Esquire, aged sixty years. Scotch and Australian papers please copy.

August 16, 1906

DU Quesnay -- At his residence No 19 North Street, PHILIP LEMERCIER DU QUESNAY, third son of Theodore L. DU QUESNAY at 12 p.m. 15 inst. Funeral at 5 p.m. today. Friends and acquaintances will please accept this intimation. R.I.P.

August 31, 1906

MICHELIN-- At Bellevue, St Ann, on Sunday 26th inst. Letitia, relict of the late William Michelin.

September 8, 1906

ORMSBY- At his residence, Lime Hall, St Ann, on the 5th September, Joseph Dussard Ormsby, in his 69th year.

1906

September 13, 1906
MUIRHEAD- At Springfield, Trelawny, on the 8th inst, Mary Adelaide Muirhead, relic of the late Andrew Muirhead. Aged 72 years

THE COLONIAL MINERAL & AERATED WATER CO
(Late A. Fournier & Co)
Really High-Class Table Waters

Note Well Our Trade Mark (Royal Palm)

There are lots of others and for that reason we wish you to know our Trade Mark so that when you order you will be sure to order the "ROYAL PALM BRAND" of the COLONIAL MINERAL & AERATED WATER CO. SODA WATER WITH THE BITE, Kola Champagne, Dry Kola, Ginger Ale, Cream Soda, Ginger Beer, Lemonade &c, &c. All of the very Best -because we use the VERY BEST Materials in our Manufactures.

Manager and Manufacturer- Mr A. Fournier
Proprietors- Fred L. Myers & Son
Office and Factory: 23 Port Royal Street, Kingston.

September 21, 1906
LOCKE - At her residence, Logwood Pen, DIANA LOCKE, on the 9th September, Aged 95 years of age.
Asleep in Jesus blessed sleep
From whence none ever wake to weep
Sweet truth to me ! I shall arise
And with these eyes my Saviour see.

September 22, 1906
PASCOE - At No 99 King Street, on the night of Monday the 17th instant, Frances Ann, relict of the late William Pascoe of St Ann. Aged 96.

September 23, 1906
Gayner-- On the 11th September 1906, at the Dairy, Miss Charlotte E. H. Gaynor. Aged 77

September 27, 1906
LOPEZ- On the 25th instant at No 2 Lissant Road, to Dr and Mrs C. A. Lopez (nee Parcells) a son. (English & American papers please copy

October 1, 1906
Honiball- On the 26th instant at No 28 South Camp Road, the wife of R. Honiball of a son.

October 11, 1906
LEVY - At his residence Black River, on the Tuesday morning 9th October 1906, at 5 o'clock , after five days painful illness, GEO ELIA LEVY, aged 75, leaving a widow, seven children and a large circle of relatives and friends to mourn his demise.

Selected Vital Records from the Jamaican Daily Gleaner

October 13, 1906

FISHER- At "Mahogany Hall," Trelawny on the 8th September, J. Wauchope FISHER in his 85th year

October 16, 1906

FARQUHARSON--On 13th October, at Malvern, St Elizabeth, HON J.M. FARQUHARSON C.M.G. Custos of the parish. Age 80 years and 11 months.

October 17, 1906

REUBEN-DELISSER--At South Camp Road, by Mr S. Corinaldi, on the 14th October S. R. Reuben to Rose A. DeLisser, daughter of Alfred V. Delisser.

October 20 1906

KILBURN-HISLOP-- At St George's Church, Kingston, Jamaica; on the 17th inst., John Bertram, second son of the Rev. Canon Kilburn, Rector St George's Kingston, to Hazel Carrie, only daughter of S.H. Hislop, Agent United Fruit Company, Kingston.

October 29, 1906

LINDO--At Sunnyside, Linstead; on the 22nd October, Oscar Eric, eldest son of Robert and Constance Lindo. Aged 6 years and 8 months. "Is it well with the child.....Its is well".

LITTLEJOHN--At Seabank Water Lane, SUSAN JOCELYN, daughter of the late Rev. D.R. Littlejohn, Rector of Trelawny. Funeral at Half-Way-Tree Church, to move from 14 Water Lane at 2 p.m. today. (English and Scotch paper please copy)

November 10, 1906

BROWN'S TOWN SCHOOL BOARD.--Interesting Reply to the Serious Charges Contained in Governor's Letter to Board of Education.
-- SOME COUNTER-CHARGES OF MISSTATEMENTS.-- Amount Required for New School Building.--PROMISES OF THE PAST.

November 13, 1906

DIXON-- at his residence, Cocoanut Grove, Ocho Rios, St Ann, on Tuesday, 6th inst., CORNELIUS A. DIXON. Aged 70 years. Deeply regretted by his relatives and friends. "Peace, perfect peace"

THE ST ANN PRODUCTS COMPANY
Purchase all the year round.
Coffee, Pimento, Wax, Honey, Skin, Dyewoods, Sarsaparilla, and every description of Island produce.
HEAD OFFICE-BROWN'S TOWN, ST ANN
Corn Meal Manufactured from Native Corn a Specialty. Supplied in Barrels and half barrels and forwarded to any part of the Island.
Certificates of Merit have been awarded for our Meal at the following Agricultural Shows:-- Kendal, December 1904; Minard, February 1905; Clarke Town, April 1905.
Thicket, August 1905; St Mary, July 1906.
Silver Medal, Mount Pelier, March 1905

November 20, 1906

ALLWOOD-- At his residence "The Den" Lucea, on Friday 16th inst., JOHN ALLWOOD (late clerk of Parochial Board, Hanover) at the age of 70 years.

1906

December 15, 1906
SEES A NEW JAMAICA-- Dr. W. Clarke Murray on the Coign of Vantage already Gained. WHAT IS NOW NEEDED. (By the Rev W. Clarke Murray, D.D.) including picture.

I gladly embrace the opportunity offered me by the GLEANER to express kind gteetings to my fellow-country-men of all classes and conditions at this glad season. The year has been full of goodness and mercy. Divine Providence has graciously saved us from disasters and distructions which have been the sad lot of many communities, and some of them not far from our shores; and instead a spring has taken place in our material condition and interest. Let us be grateful for these blessings; and let us hail the higher benefits which our Saviour's advent brought; welcome them into our hearts and lives; and henceforth seek help from the same strong son of God to act as men and women placed by the grace of infinite live on the ground of redemption from all wickedness and wrong, and to all righteousness and holiness.

Recalling the features of our country's life when first we essayed to do some public service, we are filled with thankful surprise at the marvellous changes which our Educational, Religious and other formative forces have effected. We are indeed living in a new Jamaica; and a better one. Some of our earnest and good workers (to whom the country owes a large and lasting debt of gratitude), under the pressure of their ideals, are impatient of delays, and are tempted to think, and sometimes to speak, as though they had laboured in vain. We do ourselves regretfully confess to this in moments of solicitude and depression. But our two generation of educational and generally progressive efforts have been emphatically marked by great progress in every department of our manifold life. The proofs are many and patent; and therein we do rejoice, year, and will re-rejoice.

We have attained a coign of vantage, and must move on with more intelligent purpose, and firmer determination. We must strengthen the things that are good and useful, and resolve and apply ourselves with all diligence to remedy those that are harmful and hindering.

May reference be made to two points in our general character in which there is room for much improvement?
1. A recognition of the principle of Mutuality; by which we mean, acting in a reciprocally right spirit and manner one to another. This principle touches all the relations of life, whether natural or formed by choice. Relationship means duty of a mutual character; involves obligations that bind both sides, and which should be intelligently recognized and faithfully discharged. The husband and the wife, the parents and children, the brother and the sister, the lover and his betrothed, the employer and the employed, the tradesman and his patrons, the seller and his customers, the minister of religion and his members and congregation, the medical man and his patients; the newspaper editor and his readers, the lawyer and his clients, the teacher and his pupils, the government and the citizen--between these, and every other conceivable relationship, there are duties sacred and binding and every earnest, honest and conscientious effort should be made to fulfill them. Can we say that as a people our sense of responsibility on this matter has so possessed us that we have striven at our best to do our duty one towards another, and have only failed when to do, and to do well, has been absolutely beyond our power? It would be no difficult, though a painful matter, to furnish illustrations of failure drawn from many quarters of our many sided social life; but we leave our readers to supply these from personal knowledge, as the writer does from his own experience.

MORE EXCELLENT WAY

In view of our failures to keep up a high practical standard of mutual justice, let us resolve to strive after a more excellent way. Let us do better in the future. Our self-respect, convenience, comfort and good character would thereby be secured the peace, prosperity, and happiness of others would be promoted and the country's general well-being enhanced. We are all, whatever our rank or station, wearing the garment with which our country is to be decently and honourably clad, and he who is false to duty breaks a thread in the loom, and the flaw will appear somewhere as a sad disfigurement. Let our patriotism then prompt us to and endeavour, strong and sustained, to array our country in the best role without blemish or defect.

My other point is:--
2. The avoidance of a spirit of Litigation. Law is a product, and also a producer of, civilization.

Law has its important uses, and we are thankful for our judicial provisions, and for the general wisdom and justice of our legal administration. But is not the legal machinery too frequently put in motion to settle disputes that never should have arisen, and which mutual good-will, patience, a little commonsense and concession would have settled? It is quite amazing and painful to see the number of men and women who attend our courts; to note the very frivolous and trivial matters that are made occasions for litigation; and to consider the money expended in fees and fines that might have served important personal and family uses; and the "bad blood" and social and family ruptures that follow are sadly depressing and very deplorable. Is there any reason why this foolish and hurtful practice should continue? Ought we not to summon up a better spirit--a spirit of forbearance, forgiveness, peace and good-will on the one hand, and of justice, kindness, and righteousness on the other? Many have so lived, and are so living: Why not all? This is the blessed Christmastide. The angels of old sang "Peace among men in whom Good is well pleased".

Let us throw open our beings to the loving message from the skies; and we shall then assuredly live in peace among ourselves. Let this Christmas season be seized to heal all hurts; to right all wrongs; to unite all divisions that should not be; to settle definitely the question of our rights, peaceful relations to God and man; and let us go into the New Year, should we be spared to do so, resolved to live in the truce of God, and to sound it far and wide until we reach the glowing sun's departed beam.

1907

Jan. 2 1907
Isaacs at Hopeton on the 29th December the wife of Frank Isaacs Esquire of a Daughter.

Jan. 4 1907
Isaacs at York cottage 176 Orange Street at 1130 p.m. on the 31st December 1906 Rebecca widow of the late Henry I. Isaacs formerly of Chester Castle, Hanover.

January 14 1907 was the day of the big Earthquake that devastated Kingston. The Gleaner was not published for several weeks.

Feb. 11 1907
Barker-Duff At Mt Ward Hanover on the fifth instant by the fathers of the bride and the bridegroom William Henry youngest son of the Rev. M. Barker to Evelyn Marion youngest daughter of the Rev. John Duff.

Fraser- Judah. In St. Jago de la Vega on Wednesday 23rd January 1907 Walter Mortimer Fraser chief clerk Surveyer general's department to Alice Victoria Phillpotts younger Daughter of G. F. Judah searcher of Records and Registries and Genealogical searcher.

Pringle-At Cape Clear on Wednesday 23rd Jan. at 10.30 p.m. Amy Zillah the beloved wife of John Pringle A most of devoted wife and mother.

Feb. 12th 1907
Tait At the public hospital Kingston on the 10th instant as a result of the injuries sustained during the earthquake of the 14th ultimo Charles Walter Mayor of Kingston retired chief clerk of the public Works departments and grandson of the late William Tate's of Tate fields Aberdeenshire Scotland Lieut RA A devoted husband and father English, Scottish American and Canadian papers please copy .

Feb. 16 1907
Verley At 38 Gold Street Louise Adelaide aged 37 years Funeral at 4 30 p.m. today please accept this the only intimation. Gone but not from memory. Colombian papers please copy.

The New Gleaner---From Rev. W. Clarke Murray, D.D.

Selected Vital Records from the Jamaican Daily Gleaner

The first issue of the "New" GLEANER came to hand this morning and I was make glad by its arrival. Deeply did I sympathize with you all; and greatly did I miss the paper. Let me thank you for the fine spirit of your article, "Towards the Future" and for your appreciative remarks on the Archbishop. It is sudden calamity, like the earthquake, that brings out the real character of men. And we thank God for such glimpses of what our holy Christianity can effect. It is the difficulty of life that draws out and develops the qualities that make men, and we are thankful to recognise them in the staff of the GLEANER and its directors, as in so many other of our stricken citizens. We fell stiffened for life's duties by the manifested fortitude, firmness and resolves. May gracious Heaven propitiously smile benedictions, helpful and tender, on all!
W Clarke Murray, Brown's Town, Feby 12th 1907

February 18, 1907
Miller-Killed by falling walls, on Monday 14th january, William Arthur, fifth son of the late Rev J. E. Miller. R.I.P. Mrs Miller and family take this medium of thanking their friends for the many kind expressions of sympathy received in their late sad bereavement.

February, 26, 1907
LYNCH- On Sunday the 24th February 1907 at St Jago Park, Spanish Town, Edward Bancroft Lynch, late Deputy Keeper of Records in his eightieth year.

March 2nd, 1907
Victims of the Earthquake—An Alphabetical list of the Dead--- Admissions to Hospitals—Names of patents who Died after being Admitted. Compiled for the Gleaner

March 9, 1907
Clarke At Richmond Estate, St Ann the 5th inst, the wife of Fred L Clark of a son.

March 11, 1907
Results of Cambridge Local Examinations.

Revised List of the Earthquake Victims (The admitted to Hospital were now in alphabetical order). [See World Gen Web Jamaica page for list.]

March 14, 1907
Maynier On January 14th Mrs Julia Maynier relict of the late Adolph Maynier, killed by falling walls in the vicinity of Holy Trinity Church.

April 9, 1907
CATHCART On the 8th instant, at the residence of Mr Van Cuylenburg, Lunatic Asylum, WILLIAM JAMES CATHCART, J.P. for St Thomas.
Funeral will leave the Asylum at 6 p.m. today and friends of the family are kindly requested to accept this the only intimation.

April 12, 1907
COTTER, On the morning of the 9th of April, 1907, at 'Torrington' ELLA M COTTER beloved mother of Duncan, Arundel and Harry Cotter. English papers please copy.

April 20, 1907
DELGADO- At Panama, on Wednesday, 10th April the wife of R.L. Delgado of a son. Cuban and Spanish papers please copy.

1907

April 24, 1907
DOUGALL-At Pemberton Valley, Oracabessa, on the 15th instant, the wife of William Dougall of a son.

Brown's Town Hotel is advertized.

April 25, 1907
RIPLEY-On the 3rd April at the Nursing Homes, Beech Bungalow, Haslemere, Surry, ELLA MAUD the beloved wife of the Rev R.J. Ripley, formerly Rector and Canon of the Cathedral, Spanish Town, aged 32, and EVELYN their infant daughter who died on the 2nd April.
Lord, all Pitying Jesu blest
Grant them Thine eternal rest.

THOMAS Henry Charles Binney, at Beckenham, Kent, England on Good Friday, at 3 p.m. HENRY CHARLES BINNEY THOMAS, father of Rev. C. M.G. Thomas, St James's Rectory, St Elizabeth.

May 4, 1907
MYERS-BARROW-AT "Collar Japise" Kingston, on Wednesday, 20th March, 1907, ALFRED DECORDOVA, youngest son of Fred L. Myers to Sybil May, second daughter of the late Charles E. Barrow. No Cards.

May 14, 1907
MALABRE At 146 East Street on the evening of the 11th EMLIE DUVERGER relict of the late Arnold Louis Malabre in her 79th year

Dr E.E. Murray, has removed his dispensary to No 73 Duke Street opposite the Franciscan Convent, where his patients can see him.

May 17, 1907
BICKNELL In her 67th year, at Brown's Town , St Anne on the morning of the 13th inst. Catherine Ann, relict of the late H. J. Bicknell, Resident Magistrate. Rest in Peace

May 22, 1907
ST ANN SLANDER CASE IN THE CIRCUIT COURT---Lawrence Case against Inspector Purchas—Verdict for the defendant-Jury decides without Hearing the Defence—Appeal consider Likely.

The special jury case of Mrs Lillian Lawrence wife of ex-Sergt Mayor Lawrence, against Inspector F.A.G. Purchas of St Ann to recover £50 damages for slander, for second hearing in the Kingston Circuit Court yesterday before his Honour Mr Justice Vickers, acting Senior Puisne Judge.

May 25, 1907
Scott-At Brown's Town St Ann, on the 14th of May James Wilson Scott after 5 ½ days illness, aged 76 ½ years. 'Lo he giveth His beloved sleep'
English, Scotch and American papers please copy.

Selected Vital Records from the Jamaican Daily Gleaner

May 27, 1907

SUTHERLAND-PRAWL-At Holy Trinity Church, Linstead, on the 22nd May, ROBERT ARNOLD, schoolmaster, Port Royal, to Zipporah Beatrice Maud, daughter of William B. Prawl of Port Royal. Cuban papers please copy.

June 19, 1907

CLARKE-At Richmond Estate, St Ann on the 17th instant, the infant son of Fred L and Nora Clarke, age 3 months.

Friday June 21, 1907
WEDDING BELLS
COVER-REECE

AT Mandeville Parish Church on Tuesday evening (June 18), Mr E.R.D. Cover of Santiago Cuba was joined in wedlock to Miss Anne Reece, eldest daughter of His Hon Mr L R. Reece, Resident Magistrate for Manchester and Mrs Reece. At a few minutes to 3 o'clock the bridegroom accompanied by his brother Mr J G Cover entered the Church and at 3 o'clock the bride leaning on the arm of her father, walked up the isle the choir singing, "The Voice that Breathed o'er Eden' She was attired in a beautiful dress of while China silk, prettily trimmed with silk motifs and true lovers' knots. The bridal bouquet was exceptionally pretty. Miss Vanda Reece, her sister, who was Bride's maid was dressed in white Crep de Chine with silk ribbon made up into butterflies and wearing a pink sash.

The ceremony was performed by Rev H. Clarke Jnr. Afterwards Mr and Mrs Cover left the church amidst a rain of flowers and rice for the "King Edward Hotel" where the reception was held.

The steps of the hotel were beautifully carpeted with rose petals. The table was beautifully decorated by Mrs Archambeau, the owner of this lovely hotel, who spared no effort in making everything attractive. In front of the bride and bridegroom's chairs, a silver trail of flowers artistically draped with white bells, asparagus and Eucharist lilies hung prettily over the table. Each spray was fastened with a true Lover's knot of white satin ribbon. The cake also was beautifully decorated with roses and wreaths formed in the icing with real orange blossoms.

Besides Mr and Mrs Cover, the following were the guests present: Mr and Mrs I R. Reece , father and mother of the bride, Mr Charles Reece, uncle of the bride, Mr RH. Reece brother of the bride, Miss Vanda Reece, sister of the bride, Master Reece brother of the bride, Mr. J.G. Cover brother of the bridegroom, Hon. Arthur Levy was absent having been away at Legislative Council, Inspector T. Alexander and Mrs Alexander, Miss V Levy, Miss M Levy, Dr Geo Cooke, Miss Kathleen Cooke, Rev. Henry Clarke and Mrs Clarke and Miss May Clarke.

Mr and Mrs Cover will remain at the King Edward Hotel for some days and afterwards will proceed to Santiago.

June 28, 1907

ARCHER-GARCIA At Stratheden House 145 King St Kingston, on Monday 24th instant by the Rev. Canon Kilburn, JOSEPH LEOPOLD ARCHER third son of David Archer Esq, J.P. of Trelawny and St Ann, to FLORENCE LOUISE ISABELLA, eldest daughter of the late George Garcia, of H. M. Customs, and Granddaughter of the late John Gallimore Scarlett of St Ann.

1907

June 29, 1907
FOGARTY-At Schawfield, in the parish of Trelawny on the 21st June, 1907, DANIEL MICHAEL, youngest son of Daniel Fogarty of Lottery and grandson of Patrick Waugh, of Abuthnot, St Ann.July 4, 1907

MAXWELL-At Philadelphia, United States of America from injuries received from the earthquake at Kingston, Jamaica on the 14th Jan 1907, E.L. MAXWELL relict of the late John Maxwell of Baltimore and mother of Major J.W. Maxwell now stationed at Edinburgh, Scotland. English and Scotch papers please copy.

July 10, 1907
COOPER-ERIC VIVIAN PATRICK, the fourth and dearly beloved son of Alberax & George H. Cooper late of Brown's Town St Ann Ja Age 15 years and 3 months. Verse.

July 12, 1907
HOGG- At Mount Brighton, Gordon Town on Wednesday July 10th, 1907 at 6 p.m. FANNY the beloved wife of Robert Hogg aged 70 years. Verse.

July 13, 1907
COOPER-At Riverdale Hospital, New York on June 26th, 1907, ERIC aged 15, the youngest son of George and Alberta Cooper, late of Brown's Town, St Ann. (Next day) 272 East 22nd St New York, format as first notice

July 16, 1907
CASSERLY-At Weetfield, St Mary on Saturday the 6th July 1907, the wife of Owen B. Casserly of a son. Still born, (English papers please copy)

August 2, 1907
NASH-In Toronto, Canada on the 29th July, after a brief illness in her 25th year, VIOLET SARAH wife of H.O.Nash, and beloved daughter of L.L. and Wilhelmina Fraser of St Ann's Bay. Only resting in peace, perfect peace.

September 3, 1907
ARCHER-SCOTT At Falmouth, on Thursday, 9th August by the Rev C.G. MacGregor, Rector of the Parish Church. BEATRICE RUTH "Trixie" DAUGHTER OF David Archer, J.P. of Trelawny and St Ann, to MATT SCOTT, J.P. of Falmouth, Trelawny youngest son of the late Matthew Scott of Coatbridge, Lanarkshire, Scotland. Scotch and American papers please copy.

October 11, 1907
VERLEY-AYRE-June 19 at St Nicholas Church, Withernsea, Yorkshire by the Rev C. Ray, Vicar assisted by Rev W. W. Bragg, JAMES CECIL LIONEL eldest son of the late James Louis Verley J.P. of Abbey Court St Andrew Jamaica to VIOLET JOSPHINE, youngest daughter of the late H.H. Ayre J.P. of Withernsea.

November 1 1907
GROOM In Montego Bay on the 27th inst after a long illness, Francis Groom of Snape Abbey Suffolk, England in his 72nd year. Verse.

SMITH At his residence , Brown's Town, St Ann on Wednesday at 5 p.m. RICHARD SMITH an old and respected citizen of this town, leaving a wife, two sons and three daughters to mourn their irreparable loss.

Selected Vital Records from the Jamaican Daily Gleaner

November 19, 1907
DUFFUS-HOLWELL-At the parish church, Half-way-Tree, on the 12tth November, 1907, by the Rev E.J. Wortley and S.O. Ormsby, WILLIAM ALEXANDER only son of George Duffus of Aberdeenshire, Scotland, to EMILY HENRIETTA MARY (HETTER) only daughter of the late Frederick B.C. Holwell.

November 20, 1907
DUNKLEY-PASCO-On Tuesday, the 12th November, 1907 at St Luke's Church, St Andrew by the Rev C.R.G. Thomas assisted by the Rev J.L. Ramson and S.O. Ormsby, LESLIE HILL eldest son of A.C. Dunkley Esq. of Brown's Town, St Ann, to Florence Clara Louise eldest daughter of W. G. Pascoe, Esq of St Andrew, (late of St Ann).

November 22, 1907
VERLEY-NORFOLK-On Saturday 16th November, 1907 at the Parish Church, Half-way-Tree, Jamaica, by His Grace the Archbishop of the West Indies, assisted by the Revd. Canon E.J. Wortley, REGINALD CHARLES M.B., ChB., MRCS, LRCP, B Sc (Edin) son of the late James Louis Verley, Esquire J.P. of "Abbey Court", St Andrew, to HELEN eighth daughter of the late Robert Norfolk, Esquire. J.P of Grimsby, Lincolnshire.

November 23, 1907
HART-At Norms Lodge, St Ann Bay on the morning of the 16th November ISABELLA (Bell) the beloved wife of Albert J. Hart leaving a large circle of relatives and friend to mourn their loss. For many months she was a great sufferer, but bore her illness with Christian resignation, relying on a Glorious hereafter and at peace Perfect peace. Verse. English, American and Colon papers please copy.

November 28, 1907
HALL-At the Rectory Brown's Town, St Ann, on Saturday 23rd November in his 17th year, REGGIE the dearly beloved son of the Rev J.P. and L. Hall. Died from Typhoid fever. God's will be done.

December 5, 1907
MCCrea –On the 29th November, 1907 at Titchfield Hill Port Antonio the wife of J. Elliott McCrea of a son

December 19, 1907
OSMOND-ISAACS December 16, 1907-Married at St Mark's Church, Brown's Town, St Ann HENRY A.W. OSMOND, son of the late Capt. Osmond, R. N. to W. E.E. ISSIE ISAACS, daughter of the late A. Isaacs and Grand-daughter of the Rev. T. B. Cahusac. English papers please copy.

December 24, 1907
Mr Albert Jos Hart & Mrs Clara Arscott, husband and sister and other members of family return thanks for letters telegrams cards and other messages of sympathy received during their recent sad bereavement.

1908

January 2 1908
LEVY- At Black River on Wednesday 25th December, 1907 at 5 p.m. after a short and painful illness, Edwin, the third son of the late George E. Levy, Esq, Aged 27 years. He leaves a sorrowing mother and a large number of relatives to mourn his demise.

January 14, 1908
Thwaites-In Loving and Affectionate Memory of W. A. Thwaites, Killed 14th January, 1907

January 17, 1908
MURRAY-ABRAMS. On December 29th, 1907 at New York City by the Rev Miner Lee Bates, J. HERBERT MURRAY second son of John Murray Esq of Kingston Jamaica to Harriett third daughter of Carl Abrams Esq of Kingston NY. New York and Denver papers please copy.

January 30, 1908
MORRIS on the 24th inst at Toronto Penn, St Ann's Bay, IRINE LOUISE and baby after "Giving Birth" The beloved wife of F.A. Morris Leaving 2 small boys a husband sister, relatives and friends to mourn their irrparable lost. She rests in the Lord.

February 12, 1908
MALABRE-DUQUESNAY-On the 29th January at Holy Trinity Church by the Rev Father Dinand assisted by the Rev Father Redock, MARIE EMILY eldest daughter of Mr and Mrs C. Arnold Malabre to CHARLES LEMERCIER. At 'Home" on Saturday 15th February afternoon and evening at No 5A Race Course.

February 18, 1908
SCOTT At Edinburgh Scotland on the 27th January 1908, REGINALD WILLIAM HALDANE SCOTT, J.P. Montego Bay St James, eldest son of the late Dr. William Scott of Falmouth, Trelawny.

February 19, 1908
DaCOSTA-At 11.15 a.m. yesterday at her late residence "Newchatel" No 17 South Camp Road, ROSA, relict of the late David Hoffman Da Costa, and mother of Altamont E. DaCosta. Funeral will leave from the above address this afternoon at 5 o'clock. Friends will please accept this intimation.

Selected Vital Records from the Jamaican Daily Gleaner

February 25, 1908
WALKER-At Osborne Estate, Annotto Bay, St Mary on 19th February 1908, the wife of Clarence Alvin D. Walker of a son.

February 27, 1908
LINDO-LINDO-ARTHUR son of the late Alfred Alexander Lindo to IRENE D'Aguilar eldest daughter of Alexander Joseph and Marian Lindo, at the Amalgated Congregation of Isrealites on the 29th January, 1908. At Home at No 5 Blake Road this Saturday and Sunday evenings from 6 o'clock. No Cards.

March 3, 1908
RITCHIE-On Sunday, 1st March, 1908 at Inverary Four Paths, MARY ANN RITCHIE aged 72 years. Scotch papers please copy.

March 6, 1908
DELGADO-SELLAR-On Sunday 1st March, at the Parish Church, Falmouth by the Rev C. G. McGregor, ALICE MAUD second daughter of Mr and Mrs Peter Seller of the Roch to DONAT ALFRED DELGADO of Falmouth.

March 9, 1908
FOGERTY At Clarks Town, Trelawney on the 29th February 1908 MARY GORDON FOGARTY of Schawfield, widow of Daniel Fogarty of Lottery and last surviving daughter of Patrick Waugh.

March 10, 1908
DOORLY on the 8th March, 1908, the wife of C.W. Doorly of a son.

March 14, 1908
LEVY At Kingston on the 13th March 1908 at 5 p.m. ISAAC LEVY Son of the late HON ISAAC LEVY of St Catherine.

March 21, 1908
The recent Cambridge Local Examinations. Full List of the Passes for Jamaica

March 25, 1908
ANDRADE On the 21st inst, at No 22 White Church Street, Spanish Town, MIRIAM LOUISE the beloved wife of Jacob A.P. M. Andrade and daughter of the late S. S. Lawton, Of Kingston.

March 28, 1908
PARNTHER- At Beecham Ville, St Ann on Tureday 24th March SARAH ELIZABETH the beloved wife of Rev. R. M. Parnther

April 1, 1908
RITCHIE-COSTA At St Mark's Church, Brown's Town, St Ann, on 26th March, WINIFRED eldest daughter of Charles Costa of Orange Valley St Ann to F. A. Ritchie DMO Annotto Bay. English papers please copy.

VERLEY On the 28th inst, the wife of STUART L.VERLEY of a son.

1908

April 6, 1908
SQUIRE At Aionslie House, Manchester Square on the 4th inst. SAMUEL MONTAGYE the dearly beloved son of Harold and Aimee Squire. Aged 14 years and 4 months.

April 8, 1908
ANDERSON-On the 26th March 1908 at Guantanamo Cuba in her 97th year REBECCA ANDERSON, widow of the late Richard Anderson of St Ann, and sister of the late John Codner. English and Foreign papers please copy.

April 23, 1908
ESCOFFERY At Laughlands House, St Ann, on the 15th inst. the wife of C. J. Escoffery of a daughter.

May 4, 1908
CARGILL-MORRIS At St Peter's Church, Westmoreland on April 28th 1908, JOHN HENRY youngest son of the late Dr Cargill of 'Monaltrie' St Andrew to Gwendolen Isabel Halton youngest daughter of S. H. Morris, Esq of 'Blue Castle', Westmoreland.

May 5, 1908
NETHERSOLE- ON THE 15TH April 1908 at the Vicarage, Horsley, Derby England, Emily, relict of the late John Crosbie Nethersole.

May 8, 1908
FINE FUNCTION-Deaconess High School at Brown's Town—DISTRIBUTION OF Prizes-An Operetta Creditably staged by the Children.. [Mostly Delgado and Brown children mentioned in prizes given].

May 9, 1908
LITHERLAND-HELWIG. At Boston Mass, 29th April by Rev William L. Clarke, Vicar of Accension Church, ROBERT A. LITHERLAND to JOSEPHINE eldest daughter of Mr and Mrs Geo Helwig, Ocho Rios, St Ann's.

May 11, 1908
ABRAHAM-LEACH On the 7th May by the Revd Father Bridges at Rose Lawn, Spanish Town the residence of the bride's parents, MR FRANK L.O. ABRAHAM of 70 Cambridge Gardens, North Kensington, London to MARY ISABEL LEACH eldest daughter of Mr and Mrs J. V. Leach.

May 13, 1908
Advertisement by Dr F. N. SCOTLAND for spectacles. His consulting Rooms at 55 East Queen St (Corner Duke St) and Opposite the Bank of Nova Scotia.

May 18, 1908
MOTTA At No 11 Marine Gardens on 12th inst, the wife of Edgar C. Motta of a daughter.

June 3, 1908
STEPHENSON- On Tuesday the 2nd inst, the wife of W. A. STEPHENSON of a son.

Selected Vital Records from the Jamaican Daily Gleaner

June 4, 1908
WORTLEY–At Compton Halfway Tree, on June 1st the wife of E. Jocelyn Wortley of a son.

June 10, 1908
MURRAY-LEVY At the Methodist Chapel Brown's Town, St Ann on the 3rd June, 1908, PERCIVAL WATERHOUSE MURRAY, third son of Revd W. C. Murray DD. to ETHEL MAUDE, second daughter of J. H. Levy Esq, J.P. of Windsor House Brown's Town.

Marley-Walker – At Half-way Tree Parish Church, on Thursday the 4th inst by the Rev E. J. Wortley, Robert Marley to Helena Maud Walker both of St Andrew.

June 17, 1908
LINDO- on Friday morning 12th instant at Falmouth, ESTHER LINDO age 81 years

June 19, 1908
DAYES Lena SYBIL infant daughter of Harold W. W. and Lena Maud Dayes on Thursday 18th inst Aged 6 months. Funeral moves from 11 Arnold Road this afternoon at 5 p.m. She is not dead but sleepeth.

June 20, 1908
WALCOTT- At his residence 8 Norman Road, Kingston on the 19th instant, RICHARD AUGUSTUS WALCOTT age 29 years. Funeral will leave the residence for Railway Station at 9.45 am.m. this morning.

June 25, 1908
Chinese Influx in Jamaica-The matter considered by the Council of the Merchants Exchange yesterday Afternoon—Opinions expressed by the Members on the subject. Merchants Exchange Decide that they are Unable to Endorse view of Montego Bay Citizens Association. Member Testify as to Honesty of the Chinaman.(Front page article)

June 26, 1908
GOFFE at Grantham, Highgate on the 19th inst the wife of C.F. F. McTavish Goffe of a son.

July 7, 1908
Pictures of the various phases of the Eclipse of the sun which took place on Sunday June 28

July 9, 1908
WEDDING BELLS—Fashionable Marriage at Half-Way Tree. A pretty and fashionable wedding took place at the Half-Way Tree Parish Church yesterday afternoon when Lieut. James Claude Buchanan of the West India Regiment was married to Miss Zillah Irene McDonald Cocking daughter of Mr Ralph M Cocking, Chief Clerk at the Administrators General's Office (p10).

July 14, 1908
Olympic Games: Great Gathering of the World's Athletes. Fund for Entertainment. Amazing Magnitude of Stadium Arrangements (London, 1300 athletes).

1908

July 21, 1908
DALY At "Success" in the parish of Saint Elizabeth on the 16th inst, RICHARD WALSH DALY of Cork, Ireland. English papers please copy.

VAUGHN At Bocas del Toro, on Thursday 25th June, JOHN GRAVES VAUGHAN, in his 67th year. What most I prize it near was mine, I only yield thee what is Thine. Thy will be done.

July 24, 1908
GRANT-HELWIG-On the 16th inst, at Eccleston Chapel, Cave Valley, by the Rev D.D. Parnther. M.A. assisted by Revs M. Parker and W. Head, WALDENAR ECCLESTON second son of the late R. S. Grant, Esq. J.P. of Vere to FLORICE LOUISE third daughter of the late Henry Helwig Esq of Clarkson Ville, St Ann.

July 15, 1908
GALBRAITH – At Green Castle, St Ann on the 21st July 1908 MRS ANNA MARY GALBRAITH. Aged sixty four.

July 29, 1908
CROSWELL-SOUTAR. At Richamond, Half-way Tree on the 23rd July 1908, by the Rev Father Rodock, S. J. ALFRED NOEL, 2nd son of the late Abram Noel Croswell and USA HORTENSE, eldest daughter of Simon Soutar, Esquire, J.P. St Andrew. No Cards.

August 6, 1908
BROWN'S TOWN NOTES—(From our Correspondent) Brown's Town August 4. Miss Rose Cato the organist of St Marks Church has relinquished her post after serving faithfully and well for the past 15 years. Miss Sibil Ingram is at present the organist.
The Rev J. N Cosby of Philadelphia the curate appointed to assist the Rev Hall gives a favourable impression as one interested in his work.

August 10, 1908
STEWART–FFRENCH MULLEN- At St Georges' Church Kingston on the 6th August, 1908 by the Reverend J.L. Ramson, MURIEL SOPHIA VON REITZENSTEIN, youngest daughter of Dr & Mrs Ffrench Mullen and grand daughter of the late Massy Onge Esq., Newberry Hill and Haystown House Country Dublin Ireland to FREDERIC WILLIAM LAMONT STEWART fourth son of the Reverend E. A. M. Stewart, of Rosecrea, Tipperary Ireland and the late Rector of Falmouth, Jamaica.

August 13, 1908
At Sea Villa, Port Maria on the night of Monday 3rd, wife of Frank Rutty of a son.
August 18, 1908
DODD in Spanish Town on the 14th inst., after a few hours illness MARJORIE CONSTANCE the only and dearly beloved child of John and Mollie Dodd. Aged 5 years and 11 months Jesus called a little child unto Him

August 19, 1908
GAYNER At Dairy, St Ann on the 13th August 1908, Mary Olivia. Aged ninety-one.

August 22, 1908
SCOTT At Clifton , Falmouth on the 19th inst, the wife of Matthew Scott of a daughter

Selected Vital Records from the Jamaican Daily Gleaner

August 26, 1908

NEWMAN At Scrogie Hall St Ann on Sunday the 23rd the wife of Chas H. Newman of a son.

September 2, 1908

SUTHERLAND At Moneague, St Ann on Thursday 27th August, ALFRED NATHAN SUTHERLAND in his 64th year.

September 3, 1908

DOORLY On the 2nd September 1908, CHARLES MARTIN infant son of C. W. and M. C. Doorly, Aged 6 months.

September 5, 1908

DUFFUS At St Ann's Bay on Sunday the 30th August 1908 the wife of W.A. Duffus of a son.

September 11, 1908

WEDDING BELLS

The marriage took place on the 1st inst at Ballintoy, St Ann of Hugh Gauntlet, deputy clerk of the Courts for St Ann, to Charlotte August widow of the late Louis A. Morris of New Court Trelawny and daughtrer of the Rev Chas Augustus Winn of Ballintoy, St Ann

September 16, 1908

LITTLEJOHN-At Tantallan, Manhattan Road, St Andrew, on the night of Sunday 13th inst, the wife of H. M. Littlejohn of a daughter.

LITTLEJOHN At Tantallan, Manhattan Road St Andrew on the morning of the 15th instant in the 74th year of her age, LUCY, widow of the late Revd. D. R. Littlejohn, Rector of Trelawny and dearly loved mother of H.C. & H.M. Littlejohn of this City. English Scotch and Canadian papers please copy.

September 24, 1908 p 9,

City Wedding—The Marriage of Mr Wellesley Bourke—Ceremony at the Church—Bishop Collins on the Dignity of Matrimony. (Wellesely Bourke, solicitor and Miss Annie Isabel Robinson, daughter of the late Mr Rose Bigham Robinson of the parish of St Mary. A lot of Cockings at wedding)

October 3, 1908

WALCOTT-On Tuesday 29th September 1908 STANLEY Emanuel, eldest son of Gerad Stanley Rawlins and Florence Walcott at Berekfod Cottage, Savanna-la Mar Aged 7 years and 9 months. Jesus called a little child unto Him.

October 13, 1908

BOURKE-ROBINSON At Holy Trinity Church Kingston on the 23rd day of September 1908, by His Lordship Bishop Collins, assisted by Rev Fathers Harpes, Gregory, O'Hara, Redock and Macdermott, WELLESLEY BOURKE of Kingston, Solicitor, eldest son of the late Wellesley Bourke, Solicitor to ANNIE ISABEL third daughter of the late Rose Bigham Robinson J.P. of Greer Park, Saint Ann.

CHANDLER Yesterday at his residence 116 ½ Duke St , Nathaniel Chandler the beloved husband of Isabell Chandler at 5 o'clock p.m. Funeral at 4.30 this evening. Verse.

338

1908

October 14, 1908
MAXWELL At Nazareth on the 4th October AMBERZENE GERALDINE dearly beloved wife of Jos. A. Maxwell. Thy Will be done.

October 15, 1908
HOUSE On the 5th inst at Wilkinsburg, PA U.S.A. the wife of Lawford House of a son.

October 19, 1908
MUSCHETT-GORDON – At Saint Peter's Church Alley, Vere, on the 15th October 1908 HERBERT R. MUSCHETT second son of the late William R. Muschett of Claremeont, Old Harbour, to KATE E. Gordon. eldest daughter of the late James R. Gordon of Earliston, Vere

October 20, 1908
Sanftleben At "Lucea View" Lucea Jamaica on Saturday 17th instant, the wife of Henry C. L. Sanftleben Esqr., J. P. Hanover (Newphew of Hon Geo A. L. Sanftleben Custos of Hanover) of a daughter. English & American papers please copy.

October 24, 1908
ONE OF THE MOST NOTABLE SONS OF Jamaica
picture of J.H. Levy. Mr J. H. Levy, Chariman of the Parochial Board, St Ann. Mr J. H. Levy of Brown's Town whose portrait we present to our readers this morning is one of our best known public men. He needs no introduction to our readers. Mr Levy is a Jamaican and a Jamaican of who we can all feel proud. In St Ann his native parish, he is looked up to and respected by and high and low alike and the Cognomen of the People's Joe with which he has been dubbed is a title that he can be proud of. (More)

October 29, 1908
JEFFREY-SMITH At Ravenworth, Spanish Town, on the 28th inst Laura wife of Charles Jeffrey-Smith Jr. Toronto, Canada.
Thy will be done. Canadian Papers please copy

November 5, 1908
TAFT IS ELECTED—RESULTS OF THE United States Election. A Republican Sweep. Some Amazing results of the Great Contest Whirlwind Campaigning Over. By Direct WI Cable Co from New York November 3.

November 5, 1908
The Hon Arthur Levy Manchester's Member in the Legislature

November 6, 1908
St Elizabeth's Member of Council. The Hon Charles E. Isaac.

November 11, 1908
TOWNSEND-At Westwood High School, Stewart Town, E. Townsend, relict of W. Townsend Esq of Abingdon, England, November 6th 1908 "Fallen Asleep". English papers please copy.

December 14, 1908
The Building of the Fine New Catholic Cathedral for Kingston.

Selected Vital Records from the Jamaican Daily Gleaner

December 19, 1908
SOUTHBY At Arlington , Mandeville on December 15th the wife of T.G. Southby of a son.

December 24, 1908
RUTTY- At 'Sea View' Oracabessa, St Mary, at 1 p.m. Sunday 20th December 1908, Joseph W. Rutty late of Barnstaple Trelawny Age 71.

December 30, 1908
SUFFRAGETTE MALADY FOUND. Have Tarantism, Says a London Doctor. Cold Baths a good Cure.

December 31, 1908
p 13 A FATAL FALL-Sad death of young Mr Sanftleben. Gloom cast over Lucea. Evidently Took Ill and Fell Into the Sea. (John Sanftleben son of Custos)

1909

January 6, 1909
CASSERLY - At Nutfield, St Mary on the 27th ulto the wife of O.B. Casserly of a son,

January 15, 1909
INSTRUCTOR'S WORK

Mr H.Q. Levy who is at present one of the instructors at the agricultural course at the Mico, will take up work in Portland and St Mary on the 24 th inst. He will carry on the duties of agricultural instructor in those parishes until the end of February at which time Mr Cardwick is expected to return to Jamaica.

February 23, 1909
GOVERNOR PRAISES WORK OF RETIRING OFFICER-- The strenuous Career of Mr L. A. Rattigan--Our system of Taxation--General RECOGNITION of Valuable Services Rendered. [Picture]
Mr Luke Augustus Rattigan was born in 1848 at Amity Hall in the parish of St Ann His parents Luke and Ann Rattigan of the same place were descendants of two Irish Families Luke Rattigan of Killarney and Dennis Wetford both of whom settled in Jamaica and were large slave owners of the long ago.. Mr Rattigan was educated at Walton, St Ann, and after leaving school in 1865 he "struck out" as a private classical tutor in a clergyman's family the Rev Horatio Reece Webb

March 15, 1909
MORRICE - At Richmond, St Mary on Sunday 14th inst FREDERICK G. MORRICE. Funeral will move from "Trevorton"Half-Way-Tree Road at 8.30 a.m. this morning

Mr Morrice's Death.
Mr Fred Morrice who was up to a short time ago in the office of Mr E. A. H. Haggart died at Richmond, St Mary yesterday morning. His body was brought over to Kingston for interment.

Mr Morrice was recently in Panama and he returned here in poor health.

March 16, 1909
DUQUESNAY- On Saturday the 6th March at Charlottenburgh, Saint Mary, the wife of C. L. Duquesnay of a son.

Mr. and Mrs Frank L. Fraser beg to thank their numerous relatives, friends and acquaintances for their kind letters of sympathy during their recent sad bereavement.

March 19, 1909
RITCHIE -_ At Gibraltar, Annotto Bay on the 16th instant, the wife of Fred A. Ritchie DMO, of a son

April 24 1909
HORN -WALCOTT- On the 20th inst at Christ Church, Morant Bay, JOHN HORN JR younger son of John Horn Esq E.L. J.P.. of Thominsen Kinrosshire N. B. and Oakburn, Windermere, to MINNA ISABELLE MENNELL,   Younger daughter of Mr and Mrs Walcott of Serge Island.

May 13, 1909
LEVY- At Brown's Town, St Ann, on Sunday May 9th the wife of W. L. Levy of a son [Jack?]

HELWIG- At "Cosy Cottage", Borobridge, St Ann's on Sunday 9th May at 5.10 p.m. CLARA LOUISE beloved wife of C.J. Helwig

May 20, 1909
DUQUESNAY - At 9.30 o'clock last night at 147 King Street, Kingston, Theodore Lemercier Duquesnay. Funeral at 5p.m. today. Friends and acquaintances are asked to accept this, the only intimation.

July 1, 1909
[Front page] DEATH OF REV DR WILLIAM CLARKE MURRAY-- A Venerable Preacher Has Passed Away--HIS GREAT LIFE'S WORK-Efforts for the Real Advancement of the People FACTS ABOUT HIS CAREER.

July 5, 1909
THE LAST SCENE---Passing away of the Rev Dr Clarke Murray--FUNERAL ON THURSDAY LAST---Touching and appropriate remarks by Rev W.J. Williams.

July 8, 1909
MURRAY - William Clarke, Wesleyan Methodist Minister at Brown's Town, Saint Ann, on Wednesday the 30th of June. Age 78th years (sic).

July 16, 1909
LIFE OF THE LATE DR. W. C. MURRAY-- In Memoriam Service at Brown's Town -- REV R. PARNTHER'S SERMON--The Great work Accomplished by the Departed Preacher.

September 4, 1909
DUNKLEY- At Kendal, St Andrew on the 2nd instant the wife of L.H. Dunkley of a son

September 25, 1909
[Picture] Mr Fred A. Judah Mr Frederick A. Judah one of the candidates for election to the Mayor and Council on the platform of the Party of Progress.

1909

November 5, 1909
AGRICULTURAL

The Work of Mr Levy in Trelawny's Parish---

Mr H.Q. Levy the agricultural Instructor for Trelawny states in his report for the month of October, that he visited Mr Gillespie's property, Claremont, on the 6th to have a look at his cotton. Mr Gillespie was away from home but Mr Levy was informed that on account of the continued rainy season, the cottonbols would not open, and that the crop was likely to be a failure. The statement he (Mr Levy) verified for himself by having a look at the fields. He had visited the Rio Bueno plot twice during the month and it was looking well.

Mr Levy proceeds to mention the several plots he visited during October. These were at Goodwill, Manchester, White Hall, Duncans and Granville. "I have had some trouble with the Goodwill Plot" continues Mr Levy "as there seems to be some friction between the owner of the land and the schoolmaster, who is in charge of the cultivation. Anyhow so far I have managed to calm down things a bit.

During the month I visited the Lowe River and Troy districts, but as on the previous occasions of my visit I met very unfavorable weather and could not get through much work. Still I managed to visit a fair amount of Holdings and give instruction in the pruning of coffee, cocoa and bananas, which is sadly needed throughout Trelawny. The seasons have been splendid in Trelawny for the last few months. In fact, they have not had such regular seasons for a great number of years. The canes are looking fine. I have never seen them looking better. The crop promises to be the heaviest in recent times if sufficient labour can be marshalled to do the necessary work. This is the problem that faces the Trelawny planter

"During the month of November I want to pay special visits to Banana cultivations of both small settlers and large land owners, as I find the art of suckering to produce spring fruit is almost an unknown one in this parish.

November 12, 1909
HART - At 143 East St. Kinsgston at 7 p.m. on 8th November, Elizabeth widow of late T. P. Hart Inspector of Constabulary, St Ann's Bay

November 17, 1909
In loving memory of my wife Isabel Hart who departed this life November 16th 1907

"When the weary ones we love
Enter on this rest above
Seens the earth so poor and vast
All our live's joy overcast
Hush! Be every murmer dumb Til I come

A.J. HART, St Ann's Bay 16 Novemmber 1909

November 20, 1909
At Roslyn, St Mary on the 9th inst the wife of C. H. Clemetson Goffe of a daughter

Selected Vital Records from the Jamaican Daily Gleaner

November 27, 1909

DELISSER-REDPATH - A. Geo Delisser son of Mr A. G. Delisser of Falmouth to Miss Josephine Redpath the second daughter of Mr C. W. Redpath of Running Gut, St James, on the 24th November, 1909 ceremony performed by the Rev. Halliday of Montego Bay.

November 29, 1909

DeLISSER - At 12 p.m. on Saturday 27th November 1909, ANDREW DeLISSER age 65 years son of the late George DeLisser of Falmouth Jamaica and father of Stanley DeLisser, Kingston Ja. English and American papers please copy.

November 30, 1909

At "Torrington" Winchester Raod, Half-Way-Tree on the 27th inst, the wife of Wellesley Bourke, Solicitor of a son

December 8, 1909

COVER At 12.10 last night Miss MAUD COVER. Funeral move(s) at 4 p.m. this afternoon from the nursing home at East Street

Decmeber 10, 1909

COVER - December 7th 1909 after a short illness at Kingston, Jamaica MAUD ANDERSON, eldest daughter of the late William Cover Jr of Hopewell, St Anns and of Mrs E. J. Cover of Bon Accord, Kingston. English and Colon papers please copy.

Decmeber 20, 1909

ADAMS-COVER On the 17th by the Rev J. L. Ramson M.A. W. N. A. Adams Inspector of Police to LOUISE (SUE) second daughter of S.M. Cover of St Ann.

1910

January 3, 1910
Picture Staff and Scholars of Westwood High School for Girls and two column piece on The High School at Westwood.

January 6, 1910
Robinson- On the 3rd inst. at Truro, St Andrew, the wife of Kenneth A Robinson of a son.

Notice

Miss Mabel Cover having decided to take up and carry on the work of her late sister, Miss Maud Cover will be pleased to receive pupils for the Pianoforte at Bon Accord Cross Roads P.O.

January 17, 1910
At 36 South Camp Road on Saturday 15th inst., wife of P.W. Murray of a son (Percival)

January 28, 1910
Murray- At New York U.S.A. on the 16th January, Herbert John Murray, youngest son of John Murray of Kingston, Jamaica.

February 1, 1910
Snaith, William George at his residence at Morant Bay on Saturday morning January 29, 1910. Asleep in Jesus.

February 2, 1910
ROPER at Grier Field St Ann on Wednesday the 26th January, Lena Maude Forbes, the beloved wife of Frank Roper.

February 8, 1910
Scenes of the disastrous floods in the capital of France
Pictures.

February 14, 1910
First Mention of Halley's Comet
February 26, 1910

Selected Vital Records from the Jamaican Daily Gleaner

WALCOTT-At Cooksville, Ontario, Canada on the 16th February the wife of W. Mennell Walcott of a daughter

March 5, 1910
At Weymouth Dorestshire, England on February the 11th to Mr. and Mrs. F.G. Southby of Jamaica a son.

March 21, 1910
THOMAS EDWARD ESCOFFREY Druggist of Port Antonio, Died 20th Feb 1910 Aged 61 years. Verse. Foreign Papers please copy.

March 26, 1910
ISAACS On the 23rd instant at Fairholme, Santa Cruz Mountains, CHARLES EARLE ISAACS M.L.C. in his 74th year

April 11, 1910
DRIVER-SUTHERLAND-At the Church of the Holy Trinity, Philadelphia. U.S.A by the Rev Floyd W. Tomkins, D.D, FREDERICK BETTS, eldest son of Alfred Driver Esq. of Ridley Park, Pa to MABEL WILLMOTTE, fifth daughter of the late A. N. Sutherland of Moneague, St Ann.

April 12, 1910
KIRKLAND-At No 86 Hanover St. Kingston on Sunday morning 10th April instant. LETTIA JANE KIRKLAND, widow of the late Robert Kirkland of the parish of St Thomas in the 88th year of her age. "Blessed are the dead who die in the Lord"

April 18, 1910
Power-On the 26th March 1910 at 21 Sinclair Mansion's N. Kensington, London the wife of Ambrose Power Esquire, of a daughter.

COTTRELL-At Ancon Hospital Panama on the 7th inst. RICHARD JOHN COTTRELL Suddenly of heart failure aged 32.

April 22, 1910
Picture of Mount Etna crater in recent eruption p 7.

April 23, 1910
PICOT-GRUBER-At the parish Church St Ann's Bay on the 20th April by the Ven Archdeacon Sharpe assisted by the Rev John Chandler rector and the Rev Herbert Sharpe, Charles Henry son of the Rev Picot of Port-au-Prince, Hayti, to Sarah Louise, fourth daughter of E. C and Mrs. Gruber, St Ann's Bay.

April 25th 1910
Front page Story: Many Nations Lament the Death of Mark Twain.
Picture

April 26, 1910
ISAACS-At Montego Bay on Sunday, April 10th, 1910 after a long and painful illness PHOEBE eldest daughter of the late Isaac Isaacs.

ORRETT-AT the Grove, Half-way-Tree, FRANCES VERGO widow of the late John Orrett. Funeral at 5 p.m. today

1911

April 30, 1910
MACFARLANE BYLES-On Tuesday the 26th inst. by the Rev Canon Ripley, Parish Church Kingston, Granville G. MacFarlane to Marion Constantia Byles, both of Spanish Town.

MOSSMAN-WARD-At 3 p.m. at the Kingston Parish Church on Wednesday, 20th April, 1910, Charles Percival to Clara Eugenie second daughter of J.W. Ward of St Andrews by His Grace the Archbishop of the West Indies assisted by the Rev R.J.Ripley.

May 6, 1910
SCOTT-At Jarrett's wharf-house on the 30th April, the wife of Mathew Scott, of a son.

May 7, 1910
LE ROI EST MORT! VIVE LE ROI!

THE CODRINGTON BICENTENARY---History of the College and Some Facts about the Founder And the family From Which He Came

May 12, 1910
HOW Halley's Comet now appears here.

May 19, 1810
ALBERGA-At "Cricklewood" 29 South Camp Road on Monday 9th May the wife of Lucien Alberga of a son.

May 26, 1910
On the 22nd instant at Sportsman's Hall a son to Mr. and Mrs. Utten Todd.

May 27, 1910
ANTHONY-SUTHERLAND-At Easton, Pennsylvania, U.S.A. on May the 14th 1910 BURT LUTHER younger son of the late Captain Merritt Anthony of Fort Scott Kansas to CHARLOTTE AGNES (Lottie) sixth daughter of the late A N Sutherland of Moneague, St Ann, Jamaica B. W. I.

May 31, 1910
RITCHIE-At Gibraltar, Annotto Bay, on Sunday 29th May inst. the wife of Fred A. Ritchie, D.M.O. of a daughter.

June 3, 1910
GRANT-COCKING-At the Parish Church, St Andrew on Wednesday 1st June, by the Rev E. J. Wortley, CECIL A.W.GRANT to MABEL MARCELLA MACDONALD, daughter of Mr. and Mrs. R. S. Cocking of Widcomb, Saint Andrew.

HOPWOOD-At Peterfield, Westmoreland on Sunday morning 29th May, HERBERT HOPWOOD, third son of the late S. M. Hopwood.

June 14, 1910
ABRAHAMS-MOXSY-On June 2nd 1910, at St Paul's church Chapelton, by the Rev C.P. Muirhead, DOROTHY daughter of Sidney Moxsy Esq., Suttens Chapelton to THOMAS (Junior) son of Thomas Abrahams, Esq. of Tavanore, Chapelton. No Cards.

Selected Vital Records from the Jamaican Daily Gleaner

June 17, 1910
GOFFE-ISAACS-At Half-way-Tree church on Wednesday 15th June by the Rev E. J. Wortley, Lesline Gertrude youngest daughter of the late A. A. Isaacs, Esq. of St Ann's to Alexander Davidson Goffe, J.P. of Oxford, St Mary.

STEDMAN-At her residence 40 Hanover Street, EMILY (Minnie) beloved daughter of James Stedman and sister of Mr. W. C. D'Aguilar. Funeral at 4.30 this evening. Friends please accept this the only intimation.

June 21, 1910
WALCOTT-At Winefield on the 16th June, 1910 MRS SARAH ELIZA WALCOTT aged 80 years.

June 25, 1910
COVER-FINDLAY-On the 22nd June 1910 by the Rev H. Sharpe at St Matthew's Church, Claremeont (Saint Ann) Mary Christine Copeland, second daughter of William Grant and Elsie Findlay of Darliston, Westmoreland to John George Corlett Cover, youngest son of the late William and Sarah Cover, (Snr) of Saint Ann. No cards. Foreign papers please copy.

June 30, 1910
LITTLEJOHN-At Tantallon, 3 Manhatten Road, St Andrew, on 28th inst. the wife of H.M. Littlejohn of a daughter. English and Scotch papers please copy.

July 1, 1910
HORN-At Woodstock, Buff Bay on Monday 27th June, Minna Isabel wife of John Horn, a daughter. English and Scotch papers please copy.

July 4, 1910
CUNHA-BERTIE youngest son of Mr. and Mrs. Herbert A. Cunha aged 22 years and 3 months. Funeral at 5 p.m. this afternoon from Chatsworth, South Camp Road. Friends are requested to attend. Sometimes Darkness, Now Light (Canadian papers please copy).

July 11, 1910
COSTA-On 5th instant at Glasgow, St James, Isaac Costa, M.B. London. English papers please copy.

Picture Mr. J. H. Levy

July 14, 1910
LINDO At Aboukir, Cave Valley 12th inst. Rev Samuel Leonard Lindo, Wesleyan minister. Third son of the late Rev S.L. Lindo Ages 26. Verse.

July 19, 1910
Picture The Hon Arthur Levy. Tributes to the Member for Manchester.

July 27, 1910
WALCOTT-At her residence, Bloomsbury, Saint Elizabeth on 23rd instant at 7 am. Georgina widow of the late William Vaughan Walcott and second daughter of the late Charles Mais of Savanna-la-Mar in her 85th year. (English papers please copy)

1911

August 15, 1910
BRIDAL BELLS.--- A Fashionable Wedding at Mandeville.---ITS REGIMETNAL ASPEPCT---Bride and Bridegroom Pass under Swords of Officers.

At Mandeville Parish Church on August 11th a pretty military wedding took place between Captain W. H. Nightengale 1st Battalion West India Regiment and Mary Louisa Poole, daughter of Mrs. Poole and the late Charles Baker Poole. and niece of the Hon Arthur Levy. The bride was attended by Miss Hastings and two train-Bearers Miss Fay Westmoreland and Master Bar Griffiths........Over 70 people attended the reception. Later in the day captain and Mrs. Nightengale left for Chippenham kindly lent by the uncle of the bride.

August 191, 1910
MUNROE-At Mackfield, Westmoreland on Sunday Evening, 14th August 1910, ANTHONY JOHN MUNROE aged 64 years. English and Canadian papers please copy.

August 20, 1910
RAMSON-At 97 Church St. Kingston on Friday 19th inst. at 5.45. p.m. LILLA JANE the beloved wife of H.E. Ramson, late of the Civil Service, Jamaica. Funeral at 5 o'clock this afternoon. Friends and acquaintances please accept this the only intimation.

August 27, 1910
CRUM-Ewing-At Knockpatrick Mandeville on the 22nd inst., the wife of Humphrey E. Crum Ewing of a daughter.

September 8, 1910
LINDO-On the 5th instant at Crig Millar, Hope, the wife of Mr. Percy Lindo of a son.

September 27, 1910
DaCOSTA-At 7 o'clock last night at 57 East Queen Street, Ivan Rodriques daCosta, proprietor of the Commercial Bar in the 64th year of his life. Funeral leaves the above address at 4.30 o'clock this afternoon for Holy Trinity Church and afterward to the Catholic Cemetery. Friends and acquaintances will please accept this the only intimation.

October 6, 1910
Panton Jnr. On Tuesday 4th Oct. the wife of Geo.B. Panton. Jnr of a son. American papers please copy.

October 7, 1910
BROWN-On Tuesday 4th October, at "Argathney" Brown's Town St Ann, the wife of William Brown, Jnr. of a son

October 15, 1910
EVERSLEIGH-SMICLE-On Monday 3rd Oct. 1910 by the Rev. Floarde Howard assistant Rector of St Cyprian's Church, New York, KATHERINE the 3rd daughter of the late Hon. Josiah Smicle to MR. CHAS W.B. EVERSLEIGH of New York, U.S.A.

October 24, 1910
At London, England on Wednesday the 12th instant, the wife of Alfred H. DaCosta a son.

Selected Vital Records from the Jamaican Daily Gleaner

November 2, 1910
HUMPHRIES-On Sunday 22nd ult at 6A Melbourne Road, the wife of R.C. Humphries of a daughter.

November 12, 1910
TOWNEND-ON November 6th the wife of Vincent William Townend Esq., Jnr of Cedar Valley, St Ann and St Mary's Teignmouth, Devon, England of a son. English and Irish papers please copy.

November 14, 1910
ARCHER-At Falmouth, DAVID ARCHER, J.P. on Thursday 10th inst., aged 67 years.
Father in Thy Gracious keeping
Leave we now Thy servant sleeping.

November 24, 1910
FEURTADO-At his residence Cottage Grove, 32 Upper Elletson Road, WALTER AUGUSTUS leaving a beloved wife and 6 children. Funeral at 4 p.m. sharp this evening. Friends please accept this the only intimation.

November 28, 1910
ROBINSON-In St Andrew on the 26th November, 1910, FLORENCE MACDONALD, the beloved wife of Herbert Charles Robinson.

December 1, 1910
TODD-At the Ridge, St Ann, on Sunday 20th November, Mary Annette, 4th daughter of the late U.T. Todd, Esq.

December 3, 1910
CALDER-SARAH-At her late residence 16 Wildman Street, Sarah relict of the late James Calder, Aged 74 years. Friends and acquaintances please accept this the only intimation. Funeral at 4.30 p.m. today. R.I.P.

December 7, 1910
STEPHENSON-Alice Powell, Oscar Ville, Glengoffe, the beloved wife of A. J. Stephenson on 2nd December. Verse.

December 14, 1910
HOLLE-At the Rock, Trelawny, Reginald Christopher Holle, the beloved son of John George and Harriett Julia Holle of Brown's Town St Ann in his 26th year.

December 16, 1910
TRENCH-On the 9th December the wife of Maxwell D. Trench Esq of a son. English and Scotch papers please copy.

December 29, 1910
FINDLAY-At Costa Rica on the 19th inst. after a short illness, EDWIN LEWIS FINDLAY youngest son of William G. and Elsie Findlay of Darliston, Wetsmoreland. By cable. Scotch, Canadian and American papers please copy.

1911

January 3, 1911
TRENCH December 13th 1910 at Glasgow, Scotland. Frances Charlotte, widow of the late Honourable Daniel Power Trench, and mother of Dutton Trench aged 86.

January 12, 1911
Columns about the Verley trial.

Visit of Mr. Bernard Shaw

January 13, 1911
MUSCHETT- At his residence "Byebrook" near Santa Cruz, St Elizabeth on the 26th December, 1910, Peter Armand Muschett, father of A.E. Muschett of Georgia, Duncans aged 74 years. Thy will be done.

STEPHENSON-JENSEN-At Christ Church, Port Antonio at 5 p.m. on Thursday 12th inst. by the Rev Alf. Whitehouse, M.A. assisted by the Rev. E. E. Brice, Aubrey Douglas, youngest son of the late Edmund Stephenson, Esq. of St Ann, Jamaica to Kierstine Eline Albertha, elder daughter of Captain Chresten Marinus Jenson, of Frederikshavn Denmark.

January 17, 1911
The Life and Work of an esteemed citizen—An interesting chat with Mr. H.A. Cunha [Picture]

January 26, 1911
HELWIG-At Culloden Pen, St Ann, the wife of Caleb J. Helwig on the 12th inst. of a son. American papers please copy.

January 25, 1911
BOVELL-HAUGHTON-At the Parish Church Kingston, on the 18th inst., by His Grace the Archbishop of the West Indies, assisted by the Ven. Archdeacon Downer, the Rev R. J. Ripley, Rector of the Parish Church, Kingston and the Rev J. Messiah B.A. of Montego Bay, Conrad William Kerr Bovell, of the Uganda Police, son of C.P. Bovell, Esq of Hatfield, Westmoreland, to Edith Margaret Haughton, second daughter of R. S. Haughton, Esq. of Cavaliers, St Andrew.

Selected Vital Records from the Jamaican Daily Gleaner

January 27, 1911

At Montego Bay, St James, on Monday 15th inst. the wife of C. W. Redpath, Esq. of Running Gut Estate, St James of a daughter (American papers please copy).

January 31, 1911

At 'Farm Hill' Ocho Rios, the wife of Anton Hamilton Doorly of a son (Scotch and American papers please copy).

February 8, 1911

VOMITING SICKNESS—Capt. Potter of the R.A.M.C arrived in Kingston a couple of days ago from Duncan's in Trelawny, where he had been investigating cases of vomiting sickness and went to Stony Hill to make similar investigations. He returns to Duncan's to-day.

February 27, 1911

MANLEY MRS MARGARET ANN MANLEY of Belmont, Guanaboa Vale, on Saturday 25th February 1911, at 5 a.m. at Mary Villa, Church St. Kingston.

February 28, 1911

JACKSON-McLAUGHLIN-On the 23rd February 1911, at St Andrew's Kirk, Kingston, by the Rev. KJ Martin, DUDLEY SAMUEL JACKSON of George Town, Grand Cayman to LILLIAN CATHERINE MAUD McLAUGHLIN of Kingston, Jamaica youngest daughter of E. N. McLaughlin, and Mrs. McLaughlin. (Canadian and American papers please copy).

March 9, 1911

HAIRS-At Roseville, Montego Bay on March 3rd 1911, after a month of suffering borne with Christian fortitude and resignation, ELIZABETH HAIRS eldest daughter of the Lawrence and Ann Hairs. verse.

March 10, 1911

MOTTA – At 71 Church Street the residence of his mother-in-law (Mrs. M Magill) Samuel Simonds (of Riverdale) Funeral moves at 4.30 this evening. Friends and acquaintances please accept this the only intimation. Father in thy gracious keeping, Leave we now thy servant sleeping.

March 13, 1911

STERLING William, who died 11th March 1911, aged 54 years. We cannot Lord Thy purpose see, But all is well that's done by Thee.

Cambridge Exam Results p 13

March 14, 1911

At Romanoff, St Andrew, 12th March the wife of J. Sutton-Brown of a son.

March 25, 1911

HOSACK- On the 22nd inst. at London. JANE LAWTON HOSACK, widow of William Hosack, in her 92nd year.

1911

March 29, 1911
At Nutfield, St Mary on the 21st inst. after a brief period of suffering, Amy the dearly beloved and only little daughter of Mr. and Mrs. O.B. Casserly, aged 5 years and 3 months. Thy will be done.

March 30, 1911
GARSIA, Died on the 16th March at the residence of her son, 740 Nashville Avenue, New Orleans. Adelaide Eliza relict of Alexander Garsia of Kingston, Jamaica.

April 10, 1911
BATLEY-DELISSER-ON 6th April, 1911 at St Marks Church, Brown's Town, Saint Ann, by the Rev J.P.Hall, Richard Clarkson Batley of Yorkshire England to Ethel Louise DeLisser of Brown's Town, Jamaica.

In the piece on p 10. It says that the groom was from Philadelphia, PA. The bride was Miss Ethel Delisser of Enfield. Uncle Clarence was the best man, flower girl Miss N. Levy.

April 11, 1911
SOUTHBY-on April 7th at Braemar, Malvern P.O. the wife of T.G. Southby of a son.

REBECCA RITCHIE At No 13 South Camp Road, on Monday 10th inst. at 5.30p.m.Funeral will leave from the above address at 4 o'clock precisely. Friends and acquaintances please accept this the only intimation. Verse.

April 13, 1911
TINGLE-On the 12th instant at Widcombe, St Andrew, the residence of her nephew, Amanda Daughter of the late James Randolph Tingle of Aboukir, St Ann.

April 21, 1911
PHILLIPS-At the Eye and Ear Hospital, New York, on the 13th inst. of Meningitis, August Leach DeLeon youngest and best beloved son of Joseph and Catherine Phillips aged 22 years and 5 months. God rest him.

April 22, 1911
GARCIA-JENSEN-At Christ Church, Port Antonio at 7.30 a.m. on Thursday 20th inst. by the Rev A. Whitehouse, M.A. assisted by the Rev. E.E.Brice, ROBERT DONALD MELBOURNE, eldest son of the late G.D.Garcia, Esq of H.M.Customs, Kingston, and grandson of J.G. Scarlett, Esq. of "Rose Hill" St Ann to AMY LOUISE JOSEPHINE younger daughter of Captain Chresten Marinus Jensen of Frederickahavn, Denmark. American, English and Danish papers please copy.

p6 a long description of the above wedding including a list of some of the presents and by whom given.

April 26, 1911
DOORLEY – At Chiswick London, on the 22nd April, 1911, Dorothy the eldest daughter of C.W. and M.C. Doorly aged 7 years.

Selected Vital Records from the Jamaican Daily Gleaner

May 3, 1911

On the 20th April at St Josephs, The Grove, St Andrew by the Ven Archdeacon Downer, assisted by the Rev Canon MacDermott, John Ridell son of the late W. Ridell Walker to Annie widow of the late Charles Cottman Snape of Devonshire, England.

May 8, 1911

COOLIES ARRIVE-Over eight Hundred Came on Friday Last. WILL BE LANDED THIS WEEK-The various Estates Where the immigrants will go.

May 10, 1911

MACDONALD-At Brenford, 1 Ivy Road, St Andrew, on Wednesday 3rd May 1911, the wife of Ronald Macdonald of a son.

May 16, 1911

AIKEN-At Banbury, Sav-La-Mar, Jamaica, B.W.I. on the 11th inst. ROBERT AIKEN in his 69th year. Canadian and Scotch and English papers please copy.

May 22, 1911

MCLEAN-O'MEALLY-At Kingston on the 16th inst. by the Rev J.L. Ramson, M.A. JOHN W McLean, J.P: of Lloyds, St Davids to Martha Leonara, third daughter of the late Rev Patrick O'Meally of Ulster Spring, Trelawny and grand daughter of the late Louis Valois Sicard, of York Castle, St Ann.

May 23, 1911

BAQUIE-At No 151 King Street on the 22nd May, 1911 at 1.40 p.m. Minervina Matilda, (Minnie) eldest daughter of the late R.C.J. Baquie. Funeral leaves residence at 4.30 p.m. "Them also which sleep in Jesus will God bring with Him

p 13 [Picture] Mr.C.A.Cover B.A. NEW INSPECTOR –the appointment of Mr Charles A. Cover. A sketch of his career. We publish above the picture of Mr. Charles Arscott Cover B.A. the headmaster of Rusea School, Lucea who has been appointed to the position of Inspector of Schools. Mr Cover was born at Armadale, Dry Harbour Mountains about 40 years ago. He received his education at York Castle High School from 1881-1889. While there he passed the Junior Cambridge Local Examination with Honours and the London Matriculation in the 1st Division. He passed the London Intermediate Art in 1892 and took the final B.A. in 1895 with Honours in English. He became a teacher on the staff of York Castle in January, 1889 as a junior master taking English and Mathematics in the higher forms till July 1896 when he succeeded Arnold Larson, Esq, M.A. as Classical Master and became Greek Tutor to the Theological students of the college. This post he held till September 1897 when he succeeded the late A.E. Tomlinson Esq,B.A. as Headmaster of Rusea School, Lucea. Secondary Education in Lucea received a great impetus under Mr Cover. The school improved in attendance and efficiency. It was removed to more commodious buildings, girls were admitted and the commercial side was more fully developed. Many of his pupils have passed from the school into good positions in this island and abroad. Five pupils have won Drax Scholarships three of which were opened to the whole island. Mr Leslie Levy, a recent Jamaica scholar and now a Barrister at Law in Kingston, passed from the Rusea's School as a Drax scholar. Attention has been paid to the physical as well as the mental and moral development of the children. Athletic sports and School library and literary and debating society are features of the school.

1911

May 27, 1911
Addison John at Huntly, Brown's Town on the 20th inst.

May 26, 1911
VERLEY-At Norwalk Con. U.S.A. on Monday 22nd May 1911, Frank Louis son of the late Louis Francis and Eliza Jane Verley aged 46.

May 29, 1911
HELWIG-on 22nd May at Alma Brown's Town P.O. St Ann, the wife of William C. Helwig of a son.

McCubbin –At Clarendon Park, the residence of her daughter Mrs. Teresa Fray on the 24th inst. MRS ANDREW McCUBBIN aged 93 years relict of the late Andrew McCubbin Esq. of Stenrear Wightonshire, Scotland and J. P. of St Elizabeth and Hanover.

Red Eve by H. Rider Haggard is still serialized.

June 1, 1911
COSTA-AT his residence, Orange, St. James on Friday May 26th JOHN ALEXANDER COSTA One more to welcome us in the Great Beyond. American papers please copy.

June 8, 1911
COOPER-At Twickenham Park, Ocho Rios Wednesday 7th June 1911 at 2.30 p.m. in the 81st year of her age, REBECCA AMELIA relict of the late Wm. Cooper, of Twickenham Park and formerly of Falmouth, sister of Thomas B. Scott of Etham St Ann. J.P leaving two sons (R.P. Cooper of Annotto Bay and John B. Cooper (sic) of Kingston also five daughters and a large circle of relatives and friends to mourn their loss. Her remains will be laid to rest at St John's Church Yard, Ocho Rios. Verse. English and American papers please copy.

June 17, 1911
SHERLOCK At 17 Arbour Street, Sourthport England HANNAH widow of the late J.T. Sherlock of Clondulane and Britway Co. Cork, Ireland and mother of Capt J.E. Sherlock, R.M.U.C.

A CORONATION FETE Myrtle Bank Hotel Tuesday, June 20th 1911 at 4 p.m.— Arranged by the Friends of Wesley Church. The full Band of the W.I.Regiment will be in attendance. Coronation Tree. Motor Boat, Motor Car and other attractions Concert at 8 p.m. Refreshment Tables. Tickets 1s, Children 6d.

p 13, Examination in Music Here—The Publication of the Pass List-Successful Candidates-Examination that were Held in April and May

June 20, 1911
BROWNE At No 12 Norman Road, at 5 p.m. on the 19th inst. FLORENCE IDA BROWNE, daughter of the late William Browne, Custos of Hanover. Funeral this evening at 4 o'clock.

June 24, 1911
KING GEORGE THE FIFTH IS NOW REALLY AND TRULY CROWNED.
Front Page headline with pictures of the King and Queen Mary.

WINN –At his residence Ballintoy, St Ann on Monday 19th instant Rev. CHARLES AUGUSTUS WINN. Aged 86

Saturday June 24, 1911 CORONATION Number, price one penny.

Monday June 26, 1911
HOW THE CORONATION OF THE KING WAS CELEBRATED IN VARIOUS PARISHES OF THE ISLAND LAST THURSDAY. Brown's Town J.H. Levy gave the speech. "The procession from the Court House to St Mark's Church next followed and there were present in order of Procession a squad of police under command of Sergeant Murphy. Hon J.H. Alwood, Messrs J.H. Levy, Chas. Costa and Alex Hopwood, Dr Johnson and Dr Miller (in hood and gown) H.Q. Levy and J.J. Millner, H P Rubie and W. J. Nash, A.S. Byles and H.Isaacs, Dr Wilson and Dr C P Smith (in hood and gown)D.I. Morris, D.W. Daly A.M.Brown, J.J. Harris, T.A.D. Shaw, G Campbell, R Moss and A. Barret…"..Fireworks were displayed at night in the Norman Market and the town was well illuminated with lanterns.

WESTIN-Marie wife of Henry Westin, Minneapolis, Minn. and daughter of Charles J. Brandon of this City on the 13th of June of a son.

LINDO-At her residence, 55 Lake Lane on the 26th inst. SARAH LINDO (beloved mother of Mortimer Lindo and Chas Lindo in her 97th year Funeral moves a 8 a.m. sharp. Please let your carriages attend .Thy will be done. Panama papers please copy.

Picture of Rev R.J. Ripley, Rector of Parish Church Photo by A.Duperly and Son.

July 4, 1911
GARSIA EUGENIE ELIZABETH, beloved wife of Francis George Garsia, at her residence, Hurstwood on the Constant Spring Rd, St Andrew at 7.25 p.m. on the 3rd inst. Funeral moves at 4.30 this afternoon. Friends and acquaintances please accept this intimation. Let your carriages attend.

July 8, 1911
At Pimento Valley, Lacovia on 28th June, 1911 the wife of W. A.L. Cawley of a son.

July 10, 1911
First photographs received from London showing scenes connected with crowning of King and Queen.

July 22, 1911
Picture of Rev C. H. Coles. A.M. column RECTOR"S WORK—Brilliant Career of the Rev. C.H. Coles. His Labours in Jamaican (born in London).

July 26, 1911
PARSONS-BODDEN-On the 12th inst., at the Presbyterian Church Georgetown, Grand Cayman, by Rev R.C. Young, M.A. Edmund Samuel second son of Edmund Parsons, Esq. J.P. ex-Custos Cayman Islands to Mary Annie, second daughter of Arthur Bodden, Esq. Collector of Customs, Georgetown. Mobile Ala papers please copy.

1911

HELWIG On 23rd July Rose, beloved wife of Chas. L. Helwig of Rosebank, Alexandria. We cannot Lord Thy purposes see, but all is well that's done by Thee. American papers please copy.

BOETTCHER-On the 23rd inst. at the Nursing Hostel, Kingston, Thomasine Elizabeth Margaret widow of the late Gustav Boettcher of Spanish Town. Verse.

July 27, 1911
A POPULAR LADY PRINCIPAL-Miss H Ormsby A.C.P. Principal of the Colonial High School for Training Girls.

July 28, 1911
JENSEN AT Port Antonio on 26th July, Frances Louisa, the beloved wife of Captain C. M. Jensen and mother of C.A. P. Jensen, Mrs. A.D. Stephenson and Mrs. R.D.Garsia aged 54 years Verse R.I.P English, Danish and American papers please copy.

August 7, 1911
GALBRAITH-On the 8th July, the wife of Chas A. Galbraith, of a daughter.

DEATH GALBRAITH-On the 8th of July, the infant daughter of Marie Louise and Chas. A. Galbraith.

GALBRAITH-On Wednesday August 2nd at West Toronto, Canada the beloved wife, Marie Louise Coplin of Chas. A Galbraith and the youngest daughter of Capt. and Mrs. Bastian.

August 8th, 1911
It adds to the Galbraith passage in deaths by saying "Youngest daughter of Capt. Frank Bastian and Marian, his wife of Savanna-la-Mar Jamaica leaving three little girls in their 8th, 7th and 5th years of age (English, American and Australian papers please copy.)"

August 10, 1911
BODDEN-TAYLOR-At St Michael's Church Kingston, Reginald Eden Bodden, eldest son of Arthur Bodden, Collector of Customs, George Town, Grand Cayman, Grandson of Wm. Eden and Great Grandson of the late Hon. Wm. Eden Custos, to Ruth Isabel Taylor youngest daughter of the late Geo.Wm Taylor of the Audit Office.

August 12, 1911
LANNAMANN-At Brown's Town, St Ann, Thursday the 10th August 1911, ELIZA the beloved wife of George Lannamann aged 73, leaving a large family to mourn their loss. Verse.

August 14, 1911
TOWNSHEND-August 8 at DevonSide, St Ann, BEATRICE 3RD daughter of Arthur Townshend, J.P.

An old man who has passed his century. Burton who is 112 years old. p5

August 16, 1911
Correction Townend August 8th At DevonSide, St Ann Beatrice 3rd daughter of Arthur Townend J.P.

357

Selected Vital Records from the Jamaican Daily Gleaner

August 18, 1911

Sherlock-At Oracabessa on the 13th inst. at the residence of Mr. and Mrs. S. M. Roche, Mary the beloved mother of Mrs. E.S. Lindo, Mrs. J Kissock Braham of Brown's Town, J.E. and H. T. Sherlock. Asleep in Jesus.

August 24, 1911

COVER-On the 19th August, 1911 at Cranston, Woodford Park St Andrew, the wife of J.G. Cover of a daughter.

Phillips-Died at Melrose House, 117 Duke Street, in her 77th year on the 22nd inst. Elizabeth Catherine widow of the late George Phillips, J.P. formerly of Montego Bay, but later of New York, leaving four sons and four daughters.

August 25, 1911

picture Mr. H.A. CUNHA, Vice president of the Council of the Association (Sunday School Association). One column of the Jamaica Sunday School Association. Mr Herbert A Cunha presided.

September 1, 1911

RECENT DEATH-Sad End of Well-Known William Keating. Coroner's enquiry held-Verdict of Accidental Drowning Returned by Jury.

September 2, 1911

MOTTA-Constantia at 2.50 a.m. widow of the late Daniel I. Motta. Funeral will leave from Spicer's Beach, No 6 Harbour St on Sunday morning at 8.30.

September 11, 1911

MURRAY-WILLIS-On the 9th August 1911 at the Church of the Ascension, New York City by Rev Percy Stickney Grant, D.D. William Forbes eldest son of John Murray Esq.; of Kingston, Jamaica to Mary Cathleen, third daughter of the late Robert Willis Esq. of Dublin Ireland.

September 15, 1911

HOGG-At Waltham Cottage, Mandeville on 11th September 1911 at 5.30p.m. Maise Lillian infant daughter of F.A. and M.A. Hogg aged 4 months and 11 days. Verse.

September 19, 1911

MCDONALD-MOSSMAN-At Saint Michael's Church Kingston by the Rev S.O. Ormsby, William Osborne to Imogene Lucinda of Linstead.

October 6, 1911

SCENES DEPICTING THE BROWN'S TOWN WATER FAMINE

October 10, 1911

CHAIRMAN OF THE ST Ann's board.

The annual election of Chairman and Vice-Chairman of the Parochial Boards of the Island take place during the month of October most they have already taken effect, those left will all take place by next week.

Among the most popular of those already elected is Mr. J.H. Levy of St Ann whose picture is shown above.

Mr Levy has been elected sixteen years in succession – a factor that testifies fully to the appreciation he is held in by his fellow parishioners.

1911

October 16, 1911
HOLLAR JOHN-Aged 37 years on Sunday 15 October at the Public Hospital after a short illness. Funeral moves from the Hospital at 1 p.m. today for interment at Port Royal at 4 p.m. The deceased is brother of Frank and Horatio Hollar.

October 17, 1911
PELOUX-BOURKE-On 7th October 1911 at the cathedral Port au-Prince Haiti, by the Archbishop of Haiti, Louis Peloux of Port au Prince to Kathleen (Lena) Bourke third daughter of the late Wellesley Bourke, Solicitor

October 24, 1911
GREAT GENEROSITY OF COL WARD-Gives Gift of 3,000 pounds to Equip New Theatre. His Munificent Act. Front page.

October 30m 1911
LEVY-DUNKLEY-ON 24TH INST BY Rev J.P. Hall, Clarence Edgar youngest son of J.H. Levy Esq. to Eva Maud, daughter of A.C. Dunkley, Esq.

p 13 WEDDING BELLS Marriage Ceremony Performed at Brown's Town. Mr Levy Miss Dunkley. Brilliant Scene at St Mark's Church a Few Days ago............his groomsman (his brother L.W. Levy) Her father give her away....preceded by the choir in surplices and Master George Dunkley and M. Bullock pages carrying the pink satin cushions upon which the Bride knelt at the altar. The Bridesmaids were Miss Kitty Dunkley nicely attired in an apron dress with spotted voile and a girdle around her waist, Misses Marie Dunkley, Elma Nash, Violet Levy, Sally Young, Nina Dunkley, Amy Bullock, Majorie Levy and Eileen Tucker all of whom were dressed in pink and white and carrying trays of flowers. They were recipients of a gold heart each the gift of the Bridegroom to them.
     Large Number of guests. Among those present were Mr. and Mrs. J.H. Levy, Mr. and Mrs. H.Q. Levy, Mr. and Mrs. W.L. Levy, Mrs. M.A. Allwood, Mrs. J.P. Hall, Mrs. and Miss Thomson, Mrs. H. M. Scott, Mrs. Edith Shirland, Miss Gertrude Shirland, Mrs. Chalmers, Mr. C.P. Carlton, Miss Una Jeffrey-Smith, Mrs. and Mrs. George Henderson, Miss Henderson, Mr. and Mrs. J.K. Barham and daughters, Mr. and Mrs. H.G. Gauntlett, Mr. and Mrs. Nash and Misses Nash, Mrs. Ella Stephenson, Mrs. and Miss Murray, Mrs. Young and Mr. R. Young. Mr. and Mrs. H Delisser, Mr. and Mrs. Frank Fraser, Mr. L. H. Dunkley, Mr. and Mrs. Hopwood and Mrs. Clara Arscott, Mrs. D Arscott, Mr. Arscott, Mr. and Mrs. E.S. Lindo, Master Sol and Arthur Lindo, Miss Ethel King, Rev R. Mettam, Mrs. G Tucker, Mr. and Mrs. Percy Murray, Miss Nellie Dunkley, Mr and Mrs. Dunkley and Mr. W. A. Dunkley.......... The guests were entertained at Richmond Hotel which was handsomely decorated and the newly wedding pair left by motor car for Runaway Bay to spend their honeymoon and within the next week will leave for Mandeville their permanent Home.

November 1, 1911
HOPWOOD-At her late residence, 24 Rum Lane, Miss Ellen Hopwood age 96 years aunt of the Hon. Arthur Levy M.L.C. of Manchester. Funeral will move at 4 o'clock this afternoon, Friends please accept this only intimation.

Selected Vital Records from the Jamaican Daily Gleaner

November 4, 1911

BROOMFIELD ROSEY CHRISTIANA –At Newport Manchester, Jamaica, the beloved sister of Albert Roland McDaniel gentleman, City and Parish Kingston, 29th October 1911, Aged 48 years Verse (Columbian papers please copy).

November 6, 1911

SMITH-At Yonkers, New York, on Friday 3rd inst. Rev. J.C.A. Smith late of Claremont (By cable)

November 7, 1911

McDONALD-At Indermann, Grange Hill on the 3rd inst. MALCOLM McDONALD aged 90 years.

November 14, 1911

At Lucky Valley, the wife of Mr. Peter Herbert Dupee of a son.

November 16, 1911

DENNOES-On the 14rh inst. at Croiston Cross Roads to Mr. and Mrs. L.P. Dennoes, a daughter.

November 17, 1911

SCOTLAND-At 5 South Camp Road at 5.30 p.m. on 16th November, Rev.Horace Scotland. Funeral moves for May Pen at 4.30 o'clock this afternoon.

MURRAY-On Tuesday 14th November,1911 at Fairy Hill, Portland, John Murray aged 86. "Victorious through Christ"

November 23, 1911

FINDLAY – At his residence No 35 ½ Highholborn St, Robert the beloved husband of Mrs. Evalina Findlay aged 88 years. Funeral at 4.30 p.m. today. Friends and acquaintances please accept this only intimation. Father in Thy Gracious keeping, Leave we now Thy servant sleeping.

November 28, 1911

THE HISTORY OF THE ROMAN CATHOLIC CHURCH p 10

November 29, 1911

THE DEATH CALL-Passing Away of Mr. J.W. Gruber—DIED AT Montego Bay The body taken to St Ann's Bay for Interment.

December 1, 1911

On the 29th Nov, 1911 at Goshen, Moneague, the wife of Leicester L Roper of a daughter.

December 2, 1911

GRUBER-At his residence, North St. Montego Bay on Sunday 26th November at 2.30 p.m. JASPER WILLIAM GRUBER aged 69 years and 6 months.

December 9,1911

THOMPSON-CAMMAC-At St George's Church Kingston on the 7th December , 1911 by the Rev.J.L.Ramson, M.A. Stanley Leonard, eldest son of Mr. and Mrs. E.T.

1911

Thompson of Stony Hill to Barbara Rubinia (Ruby) daughter of the late Robt.M.Cammac, Halfway Tree, St Andrew.

LECESNE-At Gayle, St Mary on the 5th inst., the wife of Dr G.I. Lecesne of a daughter. English and West Indian papers please copy.

December 16, 1911
BODDEN-McFARLANE-On the 10th inst. at the Methodist Church, Colon, by the Rev Elliott MrA.W. Bodden of Duncans to Miss Laurel McFarlane of Falmouth, Jamaica.

December 21, 1911
AIR FLIGHTS IN Jamaica [Picture} Mr. Seligman and his monoplane in Flight.
Advertizement (next page) Aviation Meet Jesse Seligman-Aviator of the Moisant International Aviators, Inc. New York West India Regt. Band in Attendance. Today Only ! Gates Open at 3 p.m. Flying at 4 p.m.
at Knutsford Park. Popular Prices, Admission to Grand Stand 4 s To Wooden Stand 2s And to the Enclosure 1 s.

1912

January 23, 1912
ISAACS-Charlotte Emily at her residence, No 4 St Andrew's Lane on the 22nd January 1912. Funeral will move at 8.30 this morning. Asleep in the arms of Jesus.

January 24, 1912
ISAACS- Under very sad circumstances on Tuesday 23rd inst., at 11 a.m. Samuel A.Isaacs. Funeral will leave his late residence, "Tukay Ville" on the Dallas Pen Road (off the Constant Spring Road) at 4.30 o'clock this (Wednesday) afternoon. Friends and acquaintances will please accept this the only intimation. American papers please copy.

January 25, 1912
EDUCATIONAL--Opening of the St Ann High School for Boys--A PLEASANT FUNCTION-Secondary School Established By Rev. J.W. Graham.

(From a Correspondent).
On Monday 22nd inst., an event of great moment as regards the Parish of St Ann in particular and the whole island in general, took place in the progressive town of Brown's Town, when the St Ann High School for Boys was formally opened.

The Rev. J. W. Graham, M.A., on his return from Costa Rica about a year ago, tried to establish a school at Claremont; but the inducements offered were not sufficient, and a request from Grand Cayman was being seriously considered-to start such a school in the Dependency-when an invitation was extended to him by the Rev. J. Kissock Braham, B.D., to remove to Brown's Town. Mr. Graham agreed to do so, and the school is now located in this town.

The Principal was fortunate enough to secure the premises known as Rockville, the property of Mrs. Delgado. The house is a large one being 55 feet in length and 50 in width. It has eleven apartments and there is accommodation for at least twenty boarders. On the lower floor which is 13 feet below the upper, the schoolroom is 50 x 20 with a second apartment about half that size which will be used as a common room for the boys. A grassy plot in front provides a playground for the short recess, while a large field at Egypt has been kindly placed at the disposal of the school by the Rev. J. Kissock Braham for cricket and football.

At 4 p.m. on Monday an interesting function took place in the schoolroom at which there were present Mr. and Mrs. J. H. Levy, Mr. and Mrs. E.S.Lindo, Mrs. H.F. Isaacs, Mrs. J.A. Thomson, Miss Braham, Revs J.P Hall, J.P. J. Kissock Braham, B.D, Hon J. H. Allwood, M. L.C, Dr W. H. Miller, M. P.B. Messers. H.Q. Levy and Chas. Thompson.

Mr. Graham in a few words asked that Mr. Levy should take the chair.

Mr. Levy in acceding to the request said it gave him great pleasure in doing so, as his sympathies were entirely with the movement to establish a secondary school in the town. He felt sure that there was

A BRILLIANT FUTURE

in store for the school, and he would do all in his power to help to make it a success.

Mr. Braham then offered prayer, after which the Principal outlined the scheme which he had conceived with regard to the work of the school.

The Rev J.P. Hall, Rector of Brown's Town was the next speaker, and he urged that a high ideal should be maintained in the work.

The Hon. J.H. Allwood followed. He welcomed the school and the Principal to the town, and looked forward to the day when the glories of Walton and York Castle would reappear in Brown's Town, and that Government recognition would be given to the school. He announced that he would offer a prize of books to the value of one pound to the boy who made the best progress during the school year.

Mr. Braham spoke on the necessity for developing character in school, and he also offered a prize of a similar amount for good conduct.

Mr. Lindo joined with the others in wishing the school success, and said that Mr. Braham deserved the thanks of the community for his untiring efforts in getting the school established.

Dr. Miller and Messrs Harry Levy and Charles Thomas followed in a similar strain.

The Principal thanked them all for the kind and encouraging words they had spoken and promised to do all he could to meet their expectation.

Letters of regret were read from Messrs C.A. Cover, B.A., J. Dickenson, H.F. Isaacs, and Dr. Wilson, who were unable to attend but who sent their best wishes for the success of the venture.

The school opened with 20 boys and it is expected that within a few weeks the number will increase to 30 as some of the boys promised were unable to put in their appearance on Monday.

January 30, 1912
PHILLIPPS-At No 30 Ladd lane, Kingston on the evening of the 29th inst. Rudolph Phillipps eldest son of Mr. William H. Phillipps of this city. Funeral moves at 4.30 p.m. to-day. Friends of the deceased and of the family are kindly requested to attend.

NEWMAN-Florence Dalay, beloved wife of E. L Newman at her late residence, Ridgewood, No 5 Kensington Road, after a short illness. Funeral at 7.30 o'clock this morning (Tuesday). "He giveth His beloved sleep".

January 31, 1912
STEELE-On Monday January 29th at Mount Charles, Elisa, widow of Charles James Steele, London, mother of Mrs. John Maxwell, Giddy Hall, St Elizabeth.

February 5, 1912
AGRICULTURAL
Recent Meeting of the Stewart Town Branch---Work of Instructor--Fine Appreciation of the Service of Mr. H.Q. Levy.

1912

The monthly meeting of the Stewart Town Branch of the Jamaica Agricultural Society was held on the 25th ult.

Mr. John Stockhausen presided and among those present were: Messrs. H. Q. Levy. A. N. Bernard, J. Johnson, Thos. Morland, E. Eagan, W. Cunningham, Chas. McFarlane, W. Richards and Angelo Bemett.

This being the first meeting of the year, the chairman took the opportunity of welcoming the instructor and referring to his invaluable services to the branch, his regularity in attending and his success as an instructor.

Mr. Levy replied thanking the chairman for what he termed his "very flattering remarks. They had had a very trying time during the past year, but he hoped that success and prosperity would crown their efforts in the future. Notwithstanding the fact they had just passed through a severe drought, he was glad to see the banana fields around looking up so well. He wished to see the branch wielding a powerful influence in the parish not only agriculturally, but socially making or helping towards good citizenship.

He then went on to tell of his attendancy of the half yearly meeting of the Parent Society. The most important matter to the branch that was then discussed was: "a standard measure for oranges" which was brought forward by the Claremont branch.

The speaker then touched on tomato cultivation which he said, was much neglected. He went on to give some valuable hints as to its cultivation.

Mr. Levy informed the meeting that the pedigree boar promised from the Farm School was ready to be taken away.

The secretary was instructed to see to this.

The corn competition was considered and several members entered their names.

Final arrangements were made for the local show to he held on Thursday 8th Feb.

February 6, 1912
WALKER-At his late residence "Tiverton" Devon (Manchester), on the 2nd February David Walker in his 80th year. Deeply regretted.

February 8, 1912
DUFF-Katherine Lucy-AT Kingston on Sunday the 4th inst. Aged 70 years.

February 13, 1912
THE BUSINESS OF TRELAWNY--Matters Discussed by the Parochial Board--Lighting Falmouth--Mysterious Vomiting Sickness Again Makes its Appearance.

February 15, 1912
THE CHINESE BURIAL GROUND---Dedication Ceremony on Sunday Afternoon Last. Gathering of Chinese. The address Delivered by His Grace the Archbishop.

On Sunday afternoon last the Archbishop of the West Indies dedicated the Southern section of the Chinese Burial Ground situated at Leader's Lane near Kingston. There was a very large attendance of Chinese and others. Among those present were Mr. and Mrs. Thoms Leahong, and Miss Leahong, Mr. E. Wongeam and family, Mr. and Mrs. Tie Ten Quee, Mr. and Mrs. Chin Peow Fook, Mr. Lae Kin Kee, Mr. James Solomon, Mr. Wong San Kook, Mr. Shin San, Mr. Leakong, Snr., Mr. Saltau, Mr. and Mrs. James, Mr. and Mrs. Man Yenn, Mr. and Mrs. David Mar, the Misses Chin Fook, Mrs. and the Misses Emanuel, Mr. Earnest Charles and Mr. Wun. Many other members of the Chinese community in Kingston and the neigbourhood numbering in all almost 300, attended the function. Mr. Charles Emanuel was unavoidably absent through sickness.

Selected Vital Records from the Jamaican Daily Gleaner

The visitors included the Sisters of the Deaconess Home, Mrs. Ripley, Mrs. Ramson, Mrs. Richardson, Miss Evans, Mr. and Mrs. S.R. Cargill, Mr. and Mrs. H.H.Cargill, Mr. H H E. MaClaverty and many members of the Kingston Parish Church and of the Pinfold Mission. The clergy present were Rev Canon Wortley, Rev. Canon Harty, Revs R. J. Ripley (who arranged for the service) J.L. Ramson, P. B. Richardson and G. H. Thompson. More.

February 20, 1912
HOBSON-GRUCHY-At St. George's Church Kingston on Feb 17 '12, by his Grace the Archbishop of the West Indies assisted by the Rev. J. L Ramson, George Frederick Harman Hobson eldest son of the late F.S. Hobson Esq., manager of the Colonial Bank, Dominica to Gladys May eldest daughter of Lt. Col L.G. Gruchy.

CLERK-DOUGALL-On the 14th February at Banes Oriente, Cuba by the America Episcopal Bishop of Cuba and the Archdeacon of the Province of Santiago, Amy eldest daughter of Mr. and Mrs. John H. Clerk of Wales, Trelawny to James A. Dougall, Banes, Cuba.

COVER-Howard Cathcart at "Brooklyn" Half-Way Tree on Sunday 18th Feb. 1912. Eldest son of Mrs. E. J. and of the late Wm. Cover of St Ann's aged 29 years.

February 22, 1912
Advertizement

February 23, 1912
GOOD SOCIETY--A Branch of the Y.M.C.A. for Brown's Town--MR. J.H. LEVY'S SPEECH.

(From our Correspondent)
Brown's Town February 19--A meeting in connection with the formation of a branch of the Y.M.C.A. was held in the Court House of this town on Sunday last.

A large gathering of men of all creeds and denominations were present among whom were Messrs. J.H. Levy (Chairman) Revs. J.P. Hall. J. K Braham, J. W. Graham,

1912

Messrs. E. S. Lindo, H.Q. Levy J. A. Thomson, W.H. Brown jr A.C. Dunkley, T.A Bramwell.

The meeting was opened and closed with hymn and prayer.

The Chairman in introducing Mr. Nuttle, the Assistant Secretary of the Association expressed his satisfaction and appreciation of such a large gathering. He explained that he the Chairman was not very conversant with the rules and regulations of the Association but was cognizant of its world-wide importance and influence. He regretted it had not found a home in Jamaica before but now that it had come he sincerely hoped it would be encouraged and maintained. He felt sanguine that such an institution was greatly needed at this time, as never within his 50 years residence in Brown's Town each decade of which has been marked by some improvement and social advancement) did he observe such lack of earnestness among the young men in things that edify. The age was characteristic of callousness, thriftlessness and indifference and if the Y.M.C.A. through their influence could impart some moral fibre to the young men that will help to

FORM AND DEVELOP

character it would be a blessing of inestimable benefit. He concluded by expressing his willingness to assist in the movement.

Mr. Nuttle said he appreciated the welcome given him by such a large gathering. He spoke of the origin aims and influence of the Y.M.C.A as already narrated by correspondents of other places where meetings are held.

He illustrated the Y.M.C. A. as triangular in its objects, by many vivid and interesting incidents memorable among which is one of the young men leaving home with advice and expressed desire of the old folks that "he should always be a man". [Not readable-ink smeared]

A committee was formed to work in the establishment of a branch and a vote of thanks was given Mr. Nuttle for his helpful address.

February 28, 1912
At New York on the 23rd inst. of pneumonia, SIDNEY CHARLES WOOD, eldest son of Charles R. Cahusac of Orange Grove, Westmoreland, aged 19 years. (By Cable)

February 29, 1912
WRIGHT-On 25th instant at Richmond Hotel, Brown's Town of pleurisy and subsequent heart failure, SARAH E. WRIGHT of New York city.

March 4, 1912
IN MEMORIAM
VASSALL-At Southfield, on the Santa Cruz Mountains, St Elizabeth, there passed away in quiet sleep on the first of March 1910, DIANA ELIZABETH, beloved wife of Richard Vassall, and mother dear of Annie, Addon, Francis Charles, Samuel and Joseph.
So loved so mourned,
Death's best, a path that must be trod,
If we would ever pass to God.

March 9, 1912
THE CAMBRIDGE EXAMINATIONS--Results Achieved by the Jamaica Students-- FULL LIST OF PASSES--Noteworthy Position Secured by Two Senior Wolmer's Girls.

Appended is a list of Jamaica Passes in the recent Cambridge examinations. It is noteworthy that the two senior girls of Wolmer's School who have obtained first-class honours are the only two girls to obtain such honours in the Colonies. etc
[Not a full list]

Selected Vital Records from the Jamaican Daily Gleaner

Senior Boys
Students under 19 years of age, who have obtained Honours
Class II
Escoffery G.S. l,m, Jamaica College

Class III
Manley N.W. m, Jamaica College
Young, L.B. m, Jamaica College
Calder, C.A. m, Potsdam School

Students under 19 years of age who have satisfied the examiners
Cawley, L.E. Jamaica College
Gruchy S.G. Wolmer's School
Nethersole S.C. Potsdam School
Parris, I.E.R. Brown's Town High School

Junior Boys
Students under 16 years of age who have obtained Honours

Class I
McDonald G.S. r,h,l Wolmer's School
Watson C.E. m, Potsdam School
Class II
Snaith K.O. bk, Jamaica College

Class III
Ashenheim, L.E. bk Jamaica College
Calder, J. N. Potsdam School
Halliday T.M. Potsdam School

Students under 16 years of age who have satisfied the examiners

Veira L.C. Jamaica College
Aikman. C.W. Jamaica College
Hopwood K.A. a Manchester Sch

Students not under 16 years of age who have passed the Examination as Juniors
Evans []C. Wolmer's School
Oppenheim P.G. Montego Bay Government Secondary School
Orrett J.P. Montego Bay Government Secondary School

SENIOR GIRLS
Students under 19 years of age who have obtained Honours
Class I
Leake, V.M. r,h, Wolmer's High School
Parkinson A.E. e, bk, Wolmer's High School

Class II
James I.F.A. r,e,h Wolmer's High School
Johnson, I. J. Wolmer's High School
Lopez A.K. e, Wolmer's High School

1912

Class III
Reid H. L. Wolmer's High School
Students under 19 years of age who have satisfied the Examiners:
Goubault. E. M. Hampton School
Roxburgh E. M. e, Hampton School
Butler W. I. R. St Andrew's School Halfway Tree

Students not under 19 year of age who have satisfied the examiners
Jeffrey-Smith M.R. Westwood High School

JUNIOR GIRLS
Students under 16 years of age who have obtained Honours
CLASS I
Cowper, M.R. r,e,h,ge, f, sc, Wolmer's High School
Class II
Foster P.R. Hampton School

Students under 16 years of age who have satisfied the Examiners
Costa A.M. Hampton School
Davis N.U. W. Deaconess High School, Brown's Town

THE PRELIMINARY EXAM. BOYS
Students under 14 years of age who have obtained Honours.
CLASS I
Mais E.N. r,e,g,m. Potsdam School
CLASS II
Riddell, C.E. e,g,m. Wolmer's School
Browne, F. A. fm, al, Potsdam school
Nethersole E.E. fm, Potsdam School
CLASS III
Walcott A. L. Wolmer's School
Student under 14 years of age who have satisfied the examiners
Ashenheim, N.N. St Andrew's School Halfway Tree,
Duff, C.S. St Andrew's School Halfway Tree
Gruchy C. L. C. Wolmer's School
Nunes, F. V. Wolmer's School
Segre, L.E. Manning's School, Savanna-la-Mar

Student between 14 and 16 years of age who have satisfied the examiners
Clerk C.A. Jamaica College
DaCosta F. N. Jamaica College

GIRLS
Students under 14 years of age who have obtained Honours
Class III
Oppenheim G.V. r, Westwood High School
Students under 14 years of age who have satisfied the examiners
Andrade, D.V. Cathedral High School
Cohen H.M. The Home School, Brentford Road, St Andrew
O'Sullivan, E.L. Church High School, St Ann's Bay
Parker, V.E. Brown's Town High School
Stockhausen, L.L. H, Westwood High School

Allwood, V.M. Home tuition
Students between 14 and 16 years of age who have satisfied the examiners;
Andrade F. L Cathedral High School,
Hopwood I. ST M. Titchfield Secondary School
Nash M.E. Holmwood Girls School
Nash A.M.E. Deaconess High School, Brown's Town.

March 12, 1912
GALBRAITH-CAMPBELL--On the 6th March 1912 at the old Parish Church of Saint Thomas in the Vale by His Grace The Archbishop of the West Indies, assisted by the Rev. E.P. Williams, Rector, EDWARD SCARLETT GALBRAITH, son the late Edward Harman Galbraith and grandson of the late Rev. Edward Galbraith, Rector of Lucea, to MARJORIE EDGILL, daughter of Mr. and Mrs. Dugall Campbell of Rosehall, St Catherine.

PROPOSED EARLY CLOSING BILL--The Opposition of Mr. J. H. Levy to the Measure--No Necessity for it--The Baltimore Merchants Want the Saturday Nights.

The Editor,
Sir, I noticed that the Hon. member for Kingston has given notice to bring forward during the present session of the Legislative Council his Famous "Shop Assistants' Bill" having made some amendments since he withdrew it at the last session.

I have not seen the details of the new bill, therefore am unable to say if he has eliminated the clauses that appeared objectionable in the first one, but this I know, that no law restricting the hours of labour, and giving the shop-keepers and merchants the weapon, whereby they can reduce the pay of employees, will be of any use to the country, and a bill of this nature will defeat its own object.

I see no necessity for legislation to regulate the hours of service for shop or any other class of wage earners in this country. The merchants and shop-keepers in Jamaica are not tyrants and if their clerks desire relaxation from work at a reasonable time, I am sure they need only ask for it, and are there not numerous public holidays?

I should have thought that a legislator like Mr. Simpson would have advocated more work and more pay for the people, instead of legislating to deprive them of what they are in the receipt of, for this will be the outcome of the bill if it becomes law.

A bill of the kind, no doubt, is popular among certain classes, but these will be the greatest sufferers when it is put into operation. Then something may be said for the merchants. If they are compelled by law to open their stores at 8 o'clock in the morning and close at 4 in the afternoon, besides giving half-holidays a good bit of the business will be driven into the hands of those whom the law does not reach, which would hardly be fair.

I see no necessity for the bill, and think it is an ill-conceived measure, and will work a great deal of hardship. If Mr. Simpson does not withdraw it, it should be thrown out, then he will at least get the credit of having tried to do something for the clerks, though in a mistaken direction, and my opinion is that in the end they will bless him more for his good intentions that if he had succeeded in getting it passed into law, as the clerks would be left with reduced wages, and much enforced spare time on their hands.
I am etc,
J.H. Levy
Brown's Town
March 9, 1912

1912

P.S. Since writing the above, I noticed the Merchants' Exchange has made some pronouncement on the bill. Needless to say I entirely concur in their condemnation of the measure.

March 18, 1912
KERR-JARRETT--To Mr. and Mrs. F. M. Kerr-Jarrett on 14th inst. a daughter

Lauder, Rebecca.--At Linstead on Monday 11th March, 1912 after a very short illness, leaving an only daughter to mourn her irreparable loss. R.I.P. English and American papers please copy.

Isaacs-At her residence Farnleigh, South Camp Road on Saturday 16th March, 1912 ELIZA, relict of the late Andrew Henry Isaacs of Kingston, Jamaica

April 4, 1912
MANY DEATHS--Children Dying form the Vomiting Sickness--Brown's Town Report--Suggestion that Free Literature Should be Circulated.

From our correspondent
Brown's Town, April 2, Within the past three or four days half a dozen or more children have died in this district from vomiting sickness. In one home, it is reported there were four children, three of whom succumbed to the attack of this dreadful scourge. In another where there were two, the mother observed froth in one of the children's mouth, and that it could not speak. She hurried off to the doctor with it, only to find, on reaching the dispensary, that the child was dead. On returning home, she discovered that the other child had also taken ill and died.
If this disease is so virulent in its attacks, would it not be wise for the authorities to circulate free literature among the people on the treatment of the disease (if it really exists) to enable them to adequately cope with the attacks, until medical assistance could be obtained?

April 9, 1912
INGEWERSON-REID--At Woodlawn, 49 South Camp Rd., Herman August Ingewerson, of New York, to Ivy Ethlin Reid, fifth daughter of J. Bolton Reid, Esq., of this city and sister in law of F.A. Steele, Esq., of the Hamburg American Office, on Wednesday, 3rd April by Rev. R. J. Ripley. English and American papers please copy.

FRENCH-MULLEN-At "The Cedars" Claremont, St Ann on Sunday 7th April, suddenly, VINCENT, fifth son of the late Laurene and Jane French Mullen of Ardmulchan Tuam, County Galway, Ireland. R.I.P. America, English and Irish papers please copy.

April 12, 1912
POSTS-Mr. Richard Reece Going on Leave of Absence--May Retire Later On. Probable that Mr. A.V. Kingdon Will Succeed Him.--Other Changes to be Made.

We understand that His Honour Mr. I. Richard Reece, Resident Magistrate of the combined parishes of Manchester and St Elizabeth will go on leave of absence in the early part of May. It is also stated that the learned Resident Magistrate will go on his pension at the expiration of his leave..............
The retirement of Mr. Reece will certainly be a loss to the lower branch of Judicial service. Educated at St. John's College, Cambridge, in 1870, he graduated as a Bachelor of Arts and was called to the Bar of the Inner Temple a year later. He was

made a Justice of the Peace at Barbados in 1871 and Coroner for the parishes of Christ Church and St George in that colony in 1873. Then he acted as Provost Marshall and Sergeant at Arms in 1874: acting Police Magistrate of St. Michael's parish in 1875; acting Judge of the Assistant Court of Appeal in 1875-1877 and 1879. He was afterwards Commissioner of Probates and acting Solicitor-General in 1880. The he became Registrar of Friendly and Building Societies in 1880; acting Attorney General and ex-officio member of the Executive and Legislative Council of Barbados, Chief Justice (on two occasions for special purposes) and Chancellor of the Diocese. He was the

SOLE COMMISSIONER

appointed to report on a complaint of the Vestry of St Michael's (Barbados) against the Bridgetown Water Works; afterwards appointed Commissioner to report on the working of the Courts of Inferior Jurisdiction; Commissioner to investigate charges against rioters in Barbados and subsequently was selected as Judge of the Assistant Court of Appeal in Grenada.

In 1884 to 1885 Mr. Reece acted as Chief Justice of St. Vincent and after holding several important appointments in that colony, he was selected as Commissioner by the Secretary of State for the Colonies to perform special duty in Grenada. It was in 1888 that he was appointed a Resident Magistrate of Jamaica and how painstaking and impartially he discharges his important duties, are well known to those who practice in his Courts

ABSENCE WILL BE REGRETTED

Our Malvern correspondent writes;

"His Honour the Resident Magistrate for St Elizabeth will be away for the next three months on leave of absence. His absence will be very much regretted generally, his sympathetic nature having won for him high esteem among the inhabitants of these parts.

[From Alumni Cantabrigensis-online from Ancestry.com

Reece, Isaac Richard.
College: ST JOHN'S
Entered: Michs. 1866
Born:
Died: Aug. 11, 1929

Adm. pens. at ST JOHN'S, Oct. 5, 1866. [Eldest] s. of Isaac, planter [of Pilgrim House,Barbados] (and Elizabeth Mary). B. [Jan. 1, 1847], at Newton, Barbados. Bapt. Feb.6, 1847. Matric. Michs. 1866; B.A. 1870. Adm. at the Inner Temple, Jan. 22, 1868.Called to the Bar, Jan. 26, 1871. Acting Provost Marshal and Sergeant-at-Arms,Barbados, 1874. Acting Solicitor-General, Barbados, 1880. Acting Judge of Assistant Court of Appeal, 1880-2. Resident Magistrate in Jamaica, 1888-1913. Married and had issue. Died Aug. 11, 1929; buried at Half Way Tree, St Andrew's, Jamaica.
Brother of William (1871) and Abraham (1874). (Inns of Court; Foster, Men at the Bar; W. Cowper.)

April 16, 1912
DUFF-SANFTLEBEN-At the Parish Church, Lucea on the 11th inst. by the Ven. Archdeacon Henderson Davis assisted by the Rev. J. I. Kirschmann, John Hartley Duff M.A. eldest son of the Rev. John and Mrs. Duff to LILIAN only daughter of the Hon. and Mrs. Sanftleben. American English and foreign papers please copy.

1912

April 17, 1912
[Frontpage]
TERRIBLE DISASTER OCCURS TO THE WHITE STAR LINE TITANIC-Vessel Struck Iceberg and Has Foundered--The Great Loss of Life--Over Fifteen Hundred Persons Believed to be Drowned--The Insurance at Lloyds [Picture of Titanic]

April 22, 1912 (Monday)
ORRETT-BRANDAY-On the 10th inst. E.G. son of the late John Orrett to Mabel Florence, youngest daughter of the late L.P. Branday.

FRASER-On April 16th, WILHELMINA, beloved wife of L.L. Fraser of St Ann's Bay, Ja. (Toronto papers please copy)

ADVANCEMENT OF EDUCATION--Deaconess High School at Brown's Town--THE PRIZE DISTRIBUTION--Enjoyable Function Held on Thursday Night Last.

(From Our Correspondent)
Brown's Town Friday--The annual breaking-up and prize distribution of the Deaconess High School of this town took place in the school room on Thursday night.
The room was tastefully and beautifully decorated with flags and flowers. The attendance was larger than on any previous occasion.
Among those present were: Rev J.P. Hall and Mrs. Hall, Mrs. L. Johnston, Miss Edith Johnston, Mrs. Allwood, Miss V. Allwood, Miss Hicks, Mrs. Addison and Miss Addison, Miss Townsend, Miss May Jeffreysmith, Mr. and Mrs. E.S. Lindo, Miss King, Messrs, J. H. Levy, H.Q. Levy, W.A. Cover, L.W. Levy, W.L.Levy, C.A. Cover, P.A. Calton, Mrs. Young, Mr. and Mrs. S.M. Brown, Mr. and Mrs. C.E. Levy, Mrs. A.S. Byles, Miss Byles, Mr. and Mrs. Gauntlett, Mr. and Mrs. H.P. Stephenson, Mr. and Mrs. W. Helwig, Mr.and Mrs. Nash, Mr. W.A.Dunkley, Miss Dunkley, Mrs. Hopwood, Mrs. Dickenson, the Misses Dickenson, Mrs. Stewart, Mr. and Mrs. Davis, Mr. and Mrs. C.L. Phillips, Mr. H B. Brown, Mrs. Barrett, Miss Brown, Misses Kennedy, Murray, Costa, Mr. C.F. Lynch, Miss G. Miller, Mr. H.F. Isaacs and daughter and others too numerous to mention.
The operetta staged by the pupils was called "The Congress of Nations." with Miss Braham as pianist, the following were the representative characters: Misses Geraldine Turner, (England;) Nina Levy (Ireland;) Rose Harty (Wales;) Elma Nash (Scotland;) Edna Moss, (Russia;) Elsie Cover (German;) Edna Atkinson (Chinese;) Beryl Byles, (Spanish;) Sally Young, (Hollander;) Ada Stewart (Turk;) Nesta Nash, Swiss;) Nouchette Davis, (Negro;) Constance Coates, (Italian;) Elsie Geddes (Hindoo) Madge Stewart (American) Mary Masters (Australian.)
Trolls--Emily Davis and Violet Levy; Nymphs--Sybil Hopwood and Cora Hopwood; Dryads--Kitty Chalmers and Dorothy Graham; Fairies: Marjorie Levy and Elsie Stephenson.
Misses Turner, Nash, Stewart, Atkinson, Davis and Dunkley (as professor) did their part well but the star of the evening was beyond doubt--Miss Nina Levy; she was so natural bold and expressive in her delivery at that she entirely captivated the audience. The singing was on the whole good but again the juniors (Fairies, trolls, nymphs and dryads,) excelled in both their singing and dancing.
The Hoop Drill was the next item. It consisted of 34 children crossing and re-crossing each other in various evolution of an intricate march. The accuracy and precision with which it was executed redounds highly creditable to the skill an intelligence of the pupils especially considering the small space in the platform on which it was performed and the tender ages of the performers.

Selected Vital Records from the Jamaican Daily Gleaner
REPORT OF THE HEADMISTRESS

Rev. J.P. Hall read the headmistress report of the school for year 1911-12, which was as follows:

"The work has gone on without any serious interruption during the past year. In the 2nd term of the year there was an outbreak of measles in the school just before the examination commenced, and this has made a considerable difference in the prize giving this year, Notable instances are Sylvia and Nina Levy who by losing a term's marks lost also their chance of obtaining prizes although they had done excellent work the other two terms; prizes being awarded for three terms work.

"The number of pupils in the school has varied during the year but little, our minimum being 25, and the maximum 34 our present number.

"There have been three examination held during the year, and the results have been on the whole satisfactory. This term our manager, the Rector, set the papers for history, Scripture and Prayer Book knowledge.

"Nine pupils sat for the various musical examination last year, of these seven passed. Primary Minnie Brown and Nouchette Davis, Elementary: Elma Nash, Beryl Byles, Constance Coates and Louise Miller. Lower division : Gertrude Sutherland. Nearly all these girls have been entered for a higher grade than they took last year, and we trust that the results will be as satisfactory or more so.

"Three pupils sat for the Cambridge Examination at the end of last term, two passed. These were Nouchette Davis (Junior) and Elma Nash (Preliminary).

During the school year Mrs. Foster visited the school and gave the girls an interesting address on F.F.S. ideals and the work done by the Society. Her husband , Major Foster, accompanied her to Brown's town.

"I am glad of this opportunity of expressing my gratitude to the many kind friends who have in one way or another given me their ready cooperation when I needed their help. We are indebted to Mr. Hall for her kindness in lending a waggon and mules thus enabling the children to have a fine picnic at the sea side.

Mrs. Levy was "a tower" of strength at the tennis tournament, and throughout the year the pupils have enjoyed the privilege of playing tennis on her lawn.

Mr. Leslie Levy was the originator of the 1st tournament and offered the prize of a racquet. The Headmistress gave the 2nd racquet, and on both occasions, Mr. H. Levy undertook and carried through to the entire satisfaction of all, the arduous duties of umpire. Our thanks are due to these gentlemen and to Mr. Nash and several others who as already stated assist cheerfully when there is help needed.

Mrs. Addison has kindly given the language prizes this year, and the Archbishop, Bishop Joscelyne and Mrs. J. Whitehouse have also continued their yearly prizes, as will be seen from the prize list.
UNA JEFFREYSMITH, Headmistress

THE PRIZE WINNERS
The prizes were distributed by Mrs. Hall and following are the prize winners.
Form IV Nouchette Davis; Form III Constance Coates: Form II Nesta Nash. Form I. Emily Davis.
Prayer Book Knowledge--Edna Moss, French Nouchette Davis; Latin Edna Moss, Drill Elma Nash; Scripture, Geraldine Turner, Jamaica Geography, Edna Moss.
Cambridge Junior--Nouchette Davis, Preliminary, Elma Nash; Music Nesta Nash; Drawing, Constance Coates, Conduct, Elma Nash.

Rector Hall who is manager of the school, in expressing his sincere satisfaction of the report said Miss Jeffreysmith was indefatigable in her work, and most successful in her teaching. He felt fully repaid for his efforts in establishing the school which was now well known throughout the island and doing good work. He also expressed his appreciation of the services rendered by Miss Johnson (in music) and Miss Ida Braham (assistant teacher).

A hearty vote of thanks was accorded Mrs. Hall for distributing the prizes, and Miss Jeffreysmith for providing such an interesting and appreciative entertainment.

Indeed may the old maxim be applied 'Labor omnia vincit".

April 23, 1912

FIRST LIST OF THE SURVIVORS

(Transmitted from the Carpathia by ways of the Olympic)

The following list of passengers from the Titanic and placed on board the steamship Carpathia contains all the name sent from the Carpathia. [Follows an alphabetical list, also a list of First Cabin Passengers Missing]

April 24, 1912

HART-ROTHENBERG-At "The Sevigny," New York on the 11th April, Dr. S.C. HART, son of Samuel Hart of Montego Bay to HILDA, daughter of Mrs. Rachel Rothenberg of Cincinnati, U.S.A.

April 26, 1912

BOURKE-on 24th inst. at "Torrington" Winchester Road, Half-way Tree, the wife of Wellesley Bourke, Solicitor, of a son

April 30, 1912

TRENCH-Josephine Elizabeth, relict of the late J. Trench at Gonville, St Andrew, on 29th inst. Funeral moves from Gonville, Oxford Road for Half-way Tree on Tuesday 30th inst., at 5 p.m.

April 30, 1912

WEDDING BELLS

Marriage At Holy Trinity Cathedral Yesterday

About 100 invited guests, and four or five hundred other spectators principally of the gentler sex, attended at Holy Trinity Cathedral yesterday afternoon to witness the marriage of Miss Muriel Isabel Desnoes a daughter of the late Peter B. Desnoes, of this city, to Mr. John Patrick Walsh, who resided in Kingston some years ago, and is now Attorney-at-Law practising in New York.

The bride entered the sacred edifice at 2.5 leaning on the arm of her uncle, Dr. H.F. Malabre. She wore a dress of white Messaline satin trimmed with real point Duchesse lace. The court train of the same material was carried by Master Reginald Branday. Miss Desnoes carried a lovely shower bouquet of lillies.

Her bridesmaids were Miss Hilda Desnoes (a sister of the bride) and Miss Ivy Jones, and they were attired in blue Messaline satin, trimmed with Ninon point lace.

Mr. Herbert Malabre was bestman.

The marriage ceremony was performed by His Lordship Bishop Collins, S. J., assisted by Fathers Mulry Gregory, Krels, and Howle.

His Lordship, before he united the young couple in the bonds of matrimony, give an earnest address on the sanctity of marriage.

The reception was held at No ? North Street, the home of the bride's parents, and was largely attended.

Mr. and Mrs. Walsh, who have been the recipients of many costly, pretty and useful presents, will sail on Friday for New York.

Selected Vital Records from the Jamaican Daily Gleaner

May 3, 1912

DUFF-COOPER-On Tuesday 30th April at the Parish Church, Kingston, ALAN DALLAS second son of Mr. and Mrs. C.F. Duff to MARY HELEN, only daughter of Mr. and Mrs. John Cooper of Bellevue, Pennsylvania, U.S.A.

May 13, 1912

MOTTA-At Clieveden, Hope Road on Friday 10th May, the wife of Edgar C. Motta of a daughter. (Fay)

May 14, 1912

FOWLER-Henry Edward on the 10th May 1912 at Strawberry Pen, St Ann aged 71 years. English and American Papers please copy.

May 16, 1912

BAQUIE- At Bryan's Pen, May Pen on Wednesday 8th May, the wife of Rev. N.A. Baquie of a daughter.

May 30, 1912

JUNOR-At Montego Bay on the 26th inst., the wife of T.A. Junor of a son.

June 4, 1912

WATER SCHEME--Permanent Supply for Dry Harbour Mountains---A PUBLIC MEETING HELD--Resolution of Thanks to Mr. J. H. Levy & Hon J.H. Allwood.

(By Telegraph From our Correspondent)

Alexandria, June 1. A very enthusiastic and representative public meeting was held at Charlton yesterday. Every section of the community was represented, and resolutions were passed urging on the Government the necessity of at once supplying Dry Harbour Mountains with a permanent water supply.

Mr. J.H .Levy, the chairman of the Parochial Board, of St Ann presided, and in a very eloquent speech traced the history of the Cascade scheme, in connection with the Parochial Board.

The Hon. J.H. Allwood, in a brilliant speech, which lasted over one hour, related a history of circumstances, showing that the Government was in a position to supply the dry areas of the island with water.

The speech was punctuated with cheers.

A resolution of thanks, moved by the Rev. Kissock Braham, was presented to the hon. gentleman for his service in the Legislative Council and also to Mr. Levy for his years of faithful services in the parochial Board, and having been chairman half the time.

Messrs. Helwig, Wint and Rev. Braham were appointed as the committee to prepare a petition to the Governor, regarding the water supply scheme.

The meeting was most successful.

June 12, 1912

HENRIQUES-HERON-By Registrar on the 5th June, SIMON CECIL, youngest son of I.C. Henriques of Kingston, to HAZEL LOUISE, eldest daughter of the late A. Geo, Heron of Cocoa Walk, Manchester. (English and American papers please copy).

June 13, 1912

MUSICAL EXAMINATION HERE-Publication of the Results Which have Just Arrived--THE SUCCESSFUL PUPILS--The Pass List in Various Divisions of the Examinations--[Not a complete list]

376

1912

The following are the results of the examinations of the Associated Board of the Royal Academy of Music and the Royal College of Music held in Jamaica in 1912.

LICENTIATE ASSOCIATED BOARD
Sole Performer Examination
Miss Muriel Sant, St Andrew's School, pianoforte
LOCAL CENTRE EXAMINATIONS
Advanced Grade
Miss G.E.C. Smith, Hampton School, pianoforte
Intermediate
Miss D. Constantine, Hampton School, pianoforte
Miss B. Jeffrey-Smith, Spanish Town, pianoforte
Miss G.E. Williams, Miss Mabel Cover, pianoforte
Rudiments of Music
Miss M.I. Morand, Miss Mabel Cover.
Miss D. Constantine, Hampton School
Miss B. Jeffrey-Smith, Spanish Town
Miss M.K.M.Lynch, Hampton School
Higher Division-Distinction
Campbell, Ellen J., Miss L.A. Trench, L.A.B. Piano
Higher Division-Pass
Avis Costa, Hampton School, Piano
Duff, Hilda, Miss M. Morrison, Mandeville piano
Marchalleck T.E.L. K. Miss H. Ormsby, Kingston Piano
Lower Division-Pass
Cathcart Gladys, Hampton School,
Davis Sybil, Miss Hilda Cover
Cowper Florence, Miss Mabel Cover, Piano
Lord, Madeline, Miss Morrison, Mandeville Piano
Elementary Division Distinction
Constantine Stella, Hampton School, piano
Delgado, Violet, Hampton School,
McCrea Olive, Hampton School
Muschett, Carmen, Hampton School
Lindo, Francis W., Miss E.D.Llewellyn, Kingston, piano
Elementary Division-Pass
Purchas, Gwendoline, Miss Ashby, Mandeville, piano
Lynch Doris W. Miss Ashby Mandeville
Sanftleben Elise, Hampton School piano
Harty Rose, Miss Una Jeffrey-Smith
Davis Nouchette, Miss Una Jeffrey-Smith, piano
Hopwood Sybil, Miss Una Jeffrey-Smith,piano
Ormsby Barbara S., Miss H. Ormsby, piano
Oppenheim, Gladys, Miss A.M. Townsend, Westwood, piano
Goffe Ruby, Miss A.M. Townsend, Westwood piano
Primary Division Distinction
Lannaman, Nina M. Miss H. Ormsby Piano
Lannaman, Zillah, Miss H. Ormsby
Primary Division-Pass
Facey Muriel, Miss Foster, Cross Roads, Piano
Hollar, Vida,L. Miss Lucia Hollar, Brentford Road, Piano
Braham, John, Miss Una Jeffrey-Smith Brown's Town, Piano
Nash Nesta, Miss Una Jeffrey-Smith, Brown's Town, Piano

Lindo, Solomon, Miss Una Jeffrey-Smith Brown's Town, Piano
Lindo, Arthur, Miss Una Jeffrey-Smith Brown's Town, Piano
Stewart, Madge, Miss Una Jeffrey-Smith Brown's Town, Piano
Young, Sally, Miss Una Jeffrey-Smith Brown's Town, Piano
Gayner, Sydney, Mrs. MacFayden-Smith, Kingston, Piano
Rattigan, Winifred, Miss M.A. Rattigan, Kingston, Piano
Murray Edna, Miss A.M. Townsend, Westwood, Piano
Stockhausen, Enid, Miss A.M. Townsend, Westwood, Piano
Primary Theory
Lord, Madeline, Miss M. Morrison, Mandeville
Rudiments of Music
Hudson M.L. Miss H. Ormsby, Kingston.

June 14, 1912
TODD- On the 4th inst. at the Ridge, St Ann, RICHARD UTTEN TODD, eldest son of the late Utten T. Todd.

June 18, 1912
GEDDES-At her residence No. 1 Law Street, on the 16th June, "MAY" eldest daughter of the late Rev. R.M. Geddes and sister of the Rev. A.W. Geddes and T.H. Geddes Esq., "Light after darkness, Peace after pain"

June 21, 1912
RUTTY-At Mason Hall, St Mary on the 18th inst., wife of F.S. Rutty of a son.

June 22, 1912
WENCK-COCKING-At New York, U.S.A. on the 20th inst. HANS WENCK of Leipzig, Germany, to LAURA MACDONALD, daughter of Mr. and Mrs. Ralph Cocking of Widcombe, St Andrew.

June 25, 1912
BOURKE-In Paris, France on 31st May 1912 ELIZABETH MARY (LIZZIE) BOURKE, sister of the late Wellesley Bourke, Solicitor.

July 5, 1912
HART-At Montego Bay on Tuesday 2nd July DUDLEY EDMUND, aged 10 years, eldest son of Edmund and Ella Hart.

Advertizement

1912

July 10, 1912

RATTIGAN-On July 9th at 145 King Street, JESSIE ANN, beloved aunt of Mrs. H. Duquesnay and Miss A. DaSilva. Funeral moves at 4.30 o'clock this afternoon. Friends and acquaintances please accept this, the only intimation. "Asleep in Jesus"

July 11, 1912

THE PRIZE DISTRIBUTION AT WOLMER'S SCHOOLS.--Excellent Work Being Done By the Institution--HEADMASTER'S REPORT--Interesting Speeches Delivered at Function Yesterday.

At the annual prize distribution in connection with the Wolmer's School took place yesterday afternoon on the school grounds commencing at 5 o'clock. His Worship the Mayor, who is also chairman of the Trustees of the school, presided, and His Excellency the Acting Governor distributed the prizes.

Others in the large gathering present were: His Lordship Bishop Collins, Hon J.R. Williams, Major Wyndham (A.D.C. to the Acting Governor) Revs. W. Pratt, and J. Randall, His Honour Mr. A.V. Kingdon, Dr. Angus Macdonald, Dr. McCrindle, Colonel Gruchy, Messrs. F. Cundall, W. R. Durle, C.T. Burton, J. Tillman, Henderson-Davis and F.D. Robertson.

The Mayor opened the proceedings by extending a hearty welcome to His Excellency the Acting Governor and His Lordship Bishop Collins. There was not much, he said to chronicle this year, except the usual round of success. The girls had done exceedingly well, and the boys had done well also. One girl especially in the Cambridge Junior division had passed higher than any girl had passed in this examination in any part of the British Empire, and this was something that Wolmer's School, and the whole island could be proud of. They thanked the Governor and the Government for the grant of £500 to the school this year and in doing so he would say that the Trustees treated this grant as an earnest of further favours to come (Applause) More.

THE PRIZE LIST

Girls

Forms I and II. Form Prize: Jane Webb. General Progress: Marguerite Randall, Rachel Osborne. Neatness: Kathleen McDonald. Good Conduct Edith Sandford, Gwendolyn Samuel

Form III (b) Form Prize: Daisy Connolly. Latin Prize: Betty McDonald

Form IV (b) Form Prize: Olive Connolly, Gertrude Morris, General Improvement: Beryl Hart. Botany Doris Livingston.

Form IV (a) Form Prize: Marjorie McCrindle, Ivy Grannum: English Essay (Prize presented by Mr. L.C. Levy): Dorrit Thompson. Botany: Constance Gleadle.

Form V (b) Form Prize: Ivy Lopez. Mathematics Cora Bell. English Literature: Ivy Lopez

Form V (a) General Progress (Prizes presented by Mr. W. Gillies): Beryl Stewart, Lilian Macpherson; English Literature: Doris Sowley. History: Mary Cowper.

Form VI French: Alma Parkinson.

Cambridge Local (Honours)

Junior (Class III) Bessie McCrindle; (Class I) Mary Cowper.

Senior (Class III) Helen Reid, Audrey Bell Jessie Leake. (Class II) Iris Johnson, Lelia James, Amy Lopez. (Class I) Alma Parkinson, Vera Leake.

Higher Local

(Class II)-Mabel Rouse

Old Girl's Prize

Mary Cowper.

Prizes presented by Cambridge Local Committee

1st Junior Mary Cowper

1st Senior Vera Leake

Picture Prizes

Form III (b) Improvement in French Pronunciation Form VI Roman History (Average 72%) prize presented by Mr. F.C. Cundall.

BOYS

Form VI L.M. Moody, V.L. Ferguson, W. W. Buckley

Form V G.P. F. Allen, S.M. DeSouza

Form IV G.S. MacDonald, A.E. B. Shirley

Form III B.D. Webster, R J. Curphey

Form II (a) C.E. Riddell, E. L Jack

Form II (b) A.B. Adams, R. O. Bell. special N.W. Hall

Form I (a) Seniors E.S. Kemble, L.G. Robertson

Form I (a) Juniors W. H. M. Cowper, C. A. Adams Special: A.K. Astwood, L.A. Murad, S.C. Helwig.

Form I (b) K.E. Roberts, A. Stephens

Special prizes-Mathematics: F.R. Soltau, Merit: R.H.S. Livingston.

Cambridge Certificates

Seniors (Honours) G.P.F. Allen, V.L. Ferguson, W.W. Buckley. Pass S. G. Gruchy, G.W. T. Knight

Juniors (Honours) G.S. MacDonald, A.E.B. Shirley, G.R. Soltau. Pass L.S. Hendrick, H.A. Munroe, H.H. Darby, L.C. Evans, C.A. Fairweather, B.H.D. Webster.

Preliminaries (Honours)C.E.Riddell, E. L. Jack. A. L Walcott. Pass -S.A. Brown, H. A. Campbell, F. A L. Dick, C.L.C. Gruchy, N. W. Hall, F.V. Nunes, C.C. Sandford, R.G.Williams, F.G. Marsh, and G.C. Roberts.

A Vote of Thanks etc.

July 17, 1912

WORK OF EDUCATION IN DRY HARBOUR MOUNTAINS--Annual Meeting of the Teachers' Association--ADDRESS BY MR. COVER.

(From our correspondent)

Dry Harbour Mountains, July 12--The annual meeting of the Dry Harbour Mountains Teachers' Association was held in the Brown's Town Government Schoolroom on Friday, 28th ultimo. The minutes of last meeting being confirmed, the Secretary read the annual report which showed much improvement on the preceding year. The retiring President then delivered his address reviewing the year's work, telling of successes and failures and encouraging the members to take up the work of the new year with renewed enthusiasm. The Association, he pointed out had evidently come to stay for whereas in the past an Association formed in these parts could only exist for a year some even dying the very day of their birth, this Association since its formation by the present secretary, Mr. Wint had been steadily growing and though it experienced a certain amount of failure during the year had certainly had a very active and useful twelve months indeed for a 2 year old Association. It could boast of more active work than many older ones.

The election of officers for the year was then taken. Messrs I.J. Elliot, G.R. Brown and I.H. Edwards were nominated for the office of President, and Mr. Edwards was elected. For Vice president Messrs. Brown, T.E. Coote and S.J. Palmer were nominated and Mr. Brown Elected. Mr. D. Theo . Wint was unanimously re-elected

1912

Secretary. For treasurer, Mr. A. J. Clarke, Miss Veitch and Webster were nominated and Miss Veitch elected.

The Rev J.W. Graham. M.A. who was prevented on account of illness from addressing the last meeting being now present was then introduced. Mr. Graham was warmly received and the members cheered heartily as he rose to address s them...
Mr. C.A. Cover, Inspector of Schools followed Mr. Graham.
[speech].

July 23, 1912
MUIR-At 3 p.m. on the 22ns July 1912 (MAGGIE) dearly beloved wife of Ivan Muir, Government Railway and daughter of Mr. and Mrs. P. A. Moodie, City. Funeral at 5 p.m. to-day, 139 East St. Friends and acquaintances please accept this the only intimation. "Asleep in Jesus"

IN MEMORIAM
BOETTCHER-In sorrowing and loving memory of our beloved, devoted and unselfish mother, Thomasine E.M. Boettcher, who fell asleep in Jesus July 23rd 1911. "Peace prefect peace with loved one far away, In Jesus keeping we are safe, an they. M.G. B.

July 27, 1912
IN MEMORIAM
JENSEN-In loving memory of FRANCES LOUISA, dearly beloved wife of CHRESTEN MARINUS JENSEN, and mother of Mr. C.A.P. Jensen, Mrs. A.D. Stephenson and Mrs. R. D. Garcia, who fell asleep on the morning of the 26th July, 1911 (Verse).

July 29, 1912
SUTHERLAND-DUNBAR-At Christ Church, Port Antonio on Wednesday 24th inst., by the Rev. Verity, PERCIVAL SUTHERLAND to KEITHA. DUNBAR, eldest daughter of A.E.Dunbar of Williamsfield.

CURRENT ITEMS
Mr. J. H. Levy of Brown's Town returned from his visit to the Isthmus on Saturday last by the United Fruit Company's steamer S.S. Marta

August 2, 1912
BURROWES-On the 1st day of August, EDNA BURROWES, beloved infant of Mr. and Mrs. A. L Burrowes, after a short and acute illness, Aged 3 years.
Not gone from Memory, Not gone from love, But gone to her Father's home above.

August 3, 1912
SCOTLAND-At 1 o'clock on the morning of the 3rd August, Lavinia Scotland, mother of Dr. S. M.G.W. and T.A. Scotland, and Mrs. Pomier. Funeral will leave from her late residence Arnold Villa, Arnold Road, at 8 o'clock on Sunday morning the 4th.

August 6, 1912
FOR ATHLETICS--Fine Sports Held at Brown's Town Last Week---A SUCCESSFUL AFFAIR--The List of Officers and the Successful Competitors

(From Our Correspondent)
Brown's Town, August 2--An athletic meeting and gala day, under the auspices of the Brown's Town Cricket Club, was held yesterday, at Coronation Park. The heat and

drought being still in power, not a drop of rain attempted to challenge their rights or dispute their supremacy.

The officers in charge of the management of affairs were at work from early morning and at 10 o'clock, when all fixtures and decorations were complete, the neglected recreation and pleasure ground presented an inviting and almost park-like appearance.

The appreciation of the efforts put forth to provide healthy, recreation and amusement, so distinctly manifested by the presence of such a large crowd, together with the keen and lively interest evinced in all that went by, fully justifies your correspondent, asserting that it is one of the most, if not the most, successful athletic demonstration held here for many a long summer day.

It is impossible to here enumerate the many persons present, as from all appearances it would seem that there was not more than two or three families un-represented, within a radius of seven or eight miles of this town.

From a pecuniary standpoint also, the undertaking was an unqualified success; a larger amount was collected at the gates, than on any previous occasion of similar events. The side-lines were well patronized, and special mention would be made of the roaring success of "throwing at the ring" under the management of Mr. H.F. Isaacs, also of the bull beard and fishing well, under management of Messrs. R.B. Miller and A. Solomon, respectively. The bar in the charge of Messrs. F.W. Hamilton and M. L. Crawford who had an exceptionally busy time, was ably managed. Mesdames Cato, sisters assisted by Mr. J. A. Dickenson, conducted the department of ice cream and cakes, the demand for which far exceeded the supply.

The following were the officers of the athletic sports:
Judges: Messrs. W. J. Nash, H. Q. Levy, P. Blagrove, A. S. Byles and J. Stockhausen.
Starters: Messrs. R.M. Murray, W. L. Levy and E. A. Stockhausen.
Handicappers--Messrs R.M. Murray and C.O. Cover.
Competitors Stewards -Messrs. A.E. Murray, C.O. Cover and S.M. Brown
Secretaries-Messrs C. L Phillips and T. A. Bramwell.

RESULT OF THE EVENTS

The events and results are as follows:-
100 yds Handicap (boys under 12 years) 1st Edward Byles; 2nd Egbert Irons.
120 yards Handicap (boys under 16 years) --1st A.E. Byles, 2nd C.A. Byles.
100 yards (Men)(scratch) 1st E. D. Gayle 2nd T. Marston
220 yards open to members of the B.T.C.C. 1st T.A. Bramwell; 2nd C.E. Lurch
High Jump 1st C.E. Byles 2ns T. Marston and D.Reynolds, tied.
440 yards open 1st C.E. Byles, 2nd E. D. Gayle
Sack Race 1st E.D. Gale; 2nd T. Marston.
880 Yards Handicap 1st C.E. Byles; 2nd R. Bramwell
Potato Race (ladies) 1st Miss M. Bramwell and Miss F.A. Hall tied; 2nd Miss Iris Brown
Long Jump-1st T. Marston; 2nd C.L. Phillips
Obstacle Race 1st W.G. Coore; 2nd E.D.Gales
1 Mile Walk 1st R. Bramwell; 2nd H. Embden.
Donkey Race 1st McGhie (Buller) 2nd Cunningham (Nicholas)
2 miles Marathon Handicap 1st C.E. Byles (scratch) 2nd W. Brown (5 yds)
Tug of War (Civilian vs Police) 1st Civilian (Messrs E.A.Anderson (cap) Jas. Campbell, Hy Brown, Wm Jarret,, Geo Brown, T. Richards and Jas. Whilbey).

In the costume football match, a prize for the most original costume was kindly offered by Miss Lena Murray. Mrs. J. H. Allwood and Mrs. J H. Levy were asked to judge, and they conferred the prize on Jas. F. Coates (working girl costume).

After the costume football match, Mrs. J. H. Allwood, who was asked and kindly consented, distributed the prizes, which were both valuable and useful.

1912

August 10, 1912
MUSCHETT-ANNA MARIA, beloved mother of R.C. Muschett of Retreat, St Mary, and A.E. Muschett of Georgia, Trelawny, at her residence Byebrook near Santa Cruz on the 4th inst. aged 72.

August 12, 1912
CARMAN-DUFF-on Wednesday, Aug 7, by the Rev. R.J. Ripley, RALPH, eldest son of Mr. and Mrs. Henry Carman, London, England, to MAUDE STUART, eldest daughter of Mr. and Mrs. C.F. Duff, Trevenion Park, St Andrew.

August 23, 1912
VERLEY-ELIZA JANE, widow of the late Louis Francis Verley at 4.40 a.m. Thursday 22nd August, 1912 a her late residence Ivy Green, St Andrew.

August 24, 1912
COOPER-Died of heart failure in New York at 223 West 16th St., August 14th at 4 p.m. ALBERTHA, the beloved wife of George H. Cooper (late of Brown's Town) after a long and Painful illness, leaving a husband, two sons and other relatives and friends to mourn their loss. Thy will be done.

August 30, 1912
CLERGYMAN WHO IS LEAVING JAMAICA [Picture] The Rev. C.H.Coles. M.A. Columns Work Here of Rev. C.H. Coles--A Fine Appreciation of the Reverend Gentleman.

September 2, 1912
MAY-At 27 Eridge Road, Tunbridge Wells, Kent, on the 10th August, 1912, the wife of D. Raynes May of a son.

September 2, 1912
EDWARDS-CHARLES JAMES, at his residence at Standfast, Brown's Town, St Ann, on the afternoon of Monday, August 26th. Age 81. Verse. Costa Rican and Panamanian papers please copy.

September 4, 1912
THE TITANIC WRECK--Story of a Jamaican
    New Orleans, August 23--Today's "Picayune" says: Eskbert Blake, Jamaican, after escaping from the White Star Liner Titanic when she struck an iceberg and went down, has worked his way to New Orleans and was yesterday employed as helper in the kitchen at the Hotel Monteleone. Blake said that he was mess boy on the great trans-Atlantic greyhound when she was making her first race across the ocean, and was one of the two Jamaicans in the crew who escaped. The story of Blake's escape in one of the lifeboats is thrilling.
    "When the boats were being lowered and we knew that there was no chance of the great steamship remaining afloat until day light, I with others made a rush for the boats" he said. "The captain saw me as I raced across the deck, and when I did not obey his command to halt, he fired his pistol at me twice. There were no others trying to get into that particular lifeboat, and I managed to crawl over the side of the ship and find a place among those who were being rescued".

"Blake said that until they were picked up they suffered extreme torture from cold, and the stories which he tells bear out the details of the sinking of the Titanic as were published at the time.

"Blake said that he shipped from New York for England on the Pickford and Black liner Sinjeamine, and joined the crew of the Titanic when she steamed on her first voyage.

September 5, 1912
SILVERA-BRADSHAW-At the Seventh Day Adventist Church on Tuesday evening the 3rd inst. EVADNE, daughter of the late Wm. Bradshaw of this City (coach builder) to DONALD SILVERA of St Mary. The party were the recipients of numerous presents.

CURRENT ITEMS
The Rev. C.H. Coles M.A. sailed for Boston on Tuesday on the S.S. Admiral Schley accompanied by Mrs. and Miss Coles.

Dr R.S. Turton D.M.O. for Stony Hill leaves for England to-day on the Elders and Fyffes steamer Tortuguero accompanied by Mrs. Turton.

September 9, 1912 (Monday)
THE PASSING AWAY OF A COUNCIL MEMBER. [Picture] Late Hon. Arthur Levy.

THE DEATH OF HON. ARTHUR LEVY. His Sudden Demise on Saturday Night Last.--Brilliant Life ended.

It is with deep regret that the "Gleaner" this morning announces the death of the Hon. Arthur Levy, member of the Legislative Council for Manchester, which sad event took place at his home in Mandeville, on Saturday night. The honourable gentleman had been in failing health for some years past, but no tidings that his condition was in any way serious had reached the city up to Saturday, and the news of his demise will come as a distinct shock to his large circle of friends and admirers throughout the length and breadth of Jamaica.

Mr. Levy had a very winning personality which gained for him the genuine liking and respect of all who knew him; and in his own parish, Manchester, he enjoyed a popularity such as few other public men do. All classes of the community looked up to him, not only as their political leader, but as a man whose life entitled him to their respect and esteem. He will be keenly missed in Mandeville and in Manchester, where his name was, of a truth, a household word.

SKETCH OF HIS LIFE

The Hon. Arthur Levy was a son of the late Mr. Joseph Levy of Mandeville, and was born about 72 years ago. Deciding to enter the legal progression he came on to Kingston, and served articles with the late Mr. Marsh, a well known solicitor of the day. Mr. Levy was admitted to practise in the Courts of this island as far back as 17th February, 1862, and at the time of his death was the second oldest solicitor on the roll. Mr. James Daly Lewis being about four months his senior. He went into partnership with Mr. J.T. Palache, and practised his profession in Manchester. Soon after the late Mr. R.A. Walcott was articled to the firm, and on his passing as a solicitor, was admitted to partnership, the firm being known as Levy, Palache and Walcott. After being in existence a few years, the partnership was dissolved, and Mr. Levy practised alone. On the 11th June 1874, he was made an Advocate of the Jamaica bar, and for years past was the only holder of that title in Jamaica--he was the last of the Advocates. For a short time Mr. Levy acted a s

Judge of one of the (then) District Courts of Jamaica. He recently took into partnership Mr. Solicitor W. H. Coke of Mandeville

Mr. Levy was one of the shining lights of the profession of law in this island, possessing as he did, all the qualifications of a successful counsel. He was an erudite lawyer, and an able advocate, his special forte being his cross-examination of witnesses, a faculty he had achieved by a close study of the people of Jamaica, their way and mannerisms. He appeared in many of the biggest cases fought out in the Jamaica Courts, and was one of the counsel for the policyholders in the historic insurance trials at Mandeville and Montego Bay.

POLITICAL CAREER

As a politician, Mr. Levy also made his mark. In the Legislative Council he brought his legal training and great abilities to bear on all debates in which he took part--he verily, as he himself was wont to say, "microscopically" examined the subject matter of debate, before passing his judgement on it. His colleagues on the elected side of the House held him in the greatest esteem a feeling which was shared to the fullest by the official and nominated members. In the early days of his political life, he was a stubborn and skilful yet none-the-less graceful fighter, and brilliant speaker, but in recent years ill-health prevented his being in regular attendance at the Council meeting. He, however, always tried to be present when important matters were down for consideration, and was in the House a portion of the time during the last session.

He launched out on his political career when well past middle life, standing for St. Elizabeth, for the representation of which parish he was defeated by the late Hon J.M. Farquharson. On the retirement of Mr. J.T. Palache, Mr. Levy was elected for Manchester, which seat he kept up to the time of his death. He was also a member of the Parochial Board of the Parish for many years and both in the Legislative Council and at the Board rendered his parish useful and meritorious service. He was very good raconteur, and chairs would be drawn in closer when his time came round to tell a story.

He was a prominent member of the Mandeville Parish Church--was, in fact, a leader of Church and social life of Mandeville. He returned from a health trip abroad last year, and was arranging to go back to England this month.

The interment took place at the Mandeville Parish Church yesterday afternoon, the funeral being very largely attended. Mr. V.E. Manton the Kingston representative of Mr. Levy went over to Mandeville yesterday to pay his last respects to the deceased gentleman. Mr. Levy is survived by three sisters, two of whom reside in this island, and to the sorrowing relatives and his hosts of friends the "Gleaner" tenders its sincere condolences.

September 10, 1912

THE DEATH CALL--Passing Away of the Hon. Arthur Levy.--HIS SUDDEN DEMISE.--Large Funeral on Sunday Afternoon: The Governor Present.

(From Our Correspondent)

Mandeville, Sept 9--Your correspondent reports the death of the Hon Arthur Levy with great and heartfelt sorrow. The sad event took place at his residence her on Saturday night after a very brief illness.

The deceased gentleman had only come in that morning from one of his properties (Chippenham) where he and his sister, Miss V. Levy had been spending a few days. He returned home apparently quite well and in the best of health, and was so up to about 4.30 p.m. when he had a stroke from which he never recovered. He was sitting on his verandah after tea when he was attacked by the stroke. Dr. Cooke and Beard were called in but to no avail, as the honourable gentleman breathed his last at five minutes to eleven.

His remains were interred at the Mandeville Parish Church yesterday at 5 p.m. The Revs. Mr. Pike and A. Brown performed the funeral ceremony. At five minutes to five the funeral cortege moved from the gate of his home, headed by Police Guards of Honour on horseback and the bearers, Messrs W.H. Coke, J.M. MacGregor, W.E. Lewis, G.G. Gunter, R.C. Bacquie, Clarence E. Levy, E.W. Muirhead and T.P. Leyden. In the procession there were no less than 50 carriages. On reaching the town a squad of police under command of Inspector Alexander, joined and headed the procession, and so the remains of a popular and much respected man were taken to its last resting place.

THE GOVERNOR PRESENT

At the Church gate, among many others, were to be seen His Excellency the Governor, and Major Wyndham as also the Custos of the parish, the Hon J.P. Clark. Here and there amongst the crowd were to seen eyes dimmed with tears, chief among the mourners being Mr. J. Daly Lewis.

The funeral was attended by people who lived miles from this town, and had it been a week day when the news could have been better circulated the attendance would have been twice as large.

The deceased gentleman had been ailing for some time past; but not seriously and had been to America and England for treatment. He had however, never taken to his bed with any long illness, and apart from experiencing pains at certain times, he was apparently quite strong.

He was one of the oldest practising solicitors, having started as far back as 1862. The oldest of his brother practitioners and friend is Mr. J. Daly Lewis. As a lawyer, Mr. Levy was most successful, which need hardly be said as his fame was widespread.

He left three sisters, the Misses V. Levy and M. J. Levy and Mrs. Toole (sic)[Poole] as also two nieces and one nephew, Mrs. K. Doorly, Mrs. O.H. Nightengale and Mr. C. A. Poole to mourn their loss, and to them great condolence is to be conveyed. Mr. Levy was a Mason, and he died in his seventieth year.

September 11, 1912
PORTER-At 10.40 p.m. on the 10th inst., at her residence No 32 Barry St., Kingston, MARGARET ANN daughter of the late James T. Porter of Falmouth, Trelawny. Age 53. Funeral moves at 4.30 p.m. Friends and acquaintances please accept this the only intimation "He giveth His beloved sleep".

September 18, 1912
At Brown's Town
(Special by Wire)

Brown's Town Sept 17--Interest in the parochial election held here today reached fever heat between the hours of eleven and noon. The total number of votes polled in the Brown's Town District was 70, the Bethany station 56, and Cave Valley 21. The result of polling was as follows:

J.H. Levy........................ 123
W. Levy...........................122
H.J. Wilmot   99
T. Bramwell   98
J Allen   94
The above were elected.

There was a large crowd at the Court House and a lively scene followed what with speeches Etc. Mr. J.H. Levy expressed himself satisfied that he still had the confidence of the voters. Other speakers were Messrs W. Levy, Bramwell, Wilmot, Allen and Wint.

1912

September 20, 1912
Advertizement

SAINT ANN HIGH SCHOOL
Brown's Town
Principal: Rev. J.W. Graham. M.A.
Boys prepared for Cambridge Local and other exams.
VIVA VOCE SPANISH TAUGHT
A limited number of Boarders can be taken
For Prospectus and fuller information, please address
THE PRINCIPAL

September 20, 1912
LITTLEJOHN-At "Cootesworth" Retirement Crescent on the 19th inst. the wife of H.M. Littlejohn of a son.

September 23, 1912
MOWATT-GRUBER-in Brooklyn, N.Y. U.S.A. the Rev. A.J. W. Mowatt of Dublin, Ireland, to NELLIS ELISE, third daughter of Edmund Chas. Gruber, J.P. of St Ann.

West Indian papers are requested to announce the marriage on August 31st, at St. Marylebone Parish Church, W, by the Rev. A.H. Lash, cousin of the bride, assisted by the Rev. Cavendish Moxon, of Walter John May of 24 Upper Wimpole street, and Gerrard's Cross, to Violet Madge, third daughter of Dr. and Mrs. S.G. Littlejohn of Gerrard's Cross.

September 25, 1912
HOOD-DANIEL At Ballyhooly Mandeville, on the 24th the wife of H. Hood Daniel of a son.

LINDO-On September 4th at 102 Elspeth Road, London, W.S. England, IRENE BEATRICE, second daughter of the late Henry Lindo of Holmwood, Rae Town, Kingston.

September 27, 1912
REPORT OF JAMAICA SCHOOLS COMMISSION--The Progress of Secondary Education in Jamaica. AN INTERESTING REVIEW--The Changes Made as a Result of Mr. Piggott's Visit.
[The following schools were reported as Endowed Schools and were treated in detail]
Munro and Dickenson's Schools, St Elizabeth;
Wolmer's School, Kingston;
Manning's School, Sav-la-Mar;
Rusea's School, Lucea;
Tichfield Schools, Port Antonio;
Beckford and Smith's School, Spanish Town;
Manchester School, Manchester
Vere Schools Vere;
Montego Bay Secondary School, Montego Bay.

October 5, 1912
POPHAM-OLIVIER-October 3rd 1912, ARTHUR EWART HUGH POPHAM, of the British Museum, London to BRYNHILD, second daughter of Sir Sydney Olivier, K.C.M.G. and Lady Olivier.

ROBINSON ISABEL ANN, at Trafalgar, Claremont, St Ann, daughter of the late Robert Robinson of Lancashire, England and of "Trafalgar" Claremont, after a short illness in her 80th year.

October 21, 1912
KIRKLAND-At his residence 310 Adelphi St. Brooklyn on the 25th Sept., 1912 ROBERT MACDONALD KIRKLAND, the beloved uncle of Mr. Chas. MacKensie-Muir, St Ann's Bay. Well done thou good and faithful servant.

October 26, 1912
FIGHT DISEASE--The Investigations Made Into Vomiting Sickness--The Official Report--Cost of the Visit of Major Potter R.A.M.C. to Jamaica--Questions in the Council.

October 28, 1912
INTERESTING DESCRIPTION OF PANAMA CANAL--The Vivid Impressions of Mr. J. H. Levy--EXCELLENT SANITATION--Not a Fly or Mosquito to be Found on the Canal Zone.
(From our Correspondent)
Dry Harbour Mountain, Oct. 24
Friday last J.H. Levy Esq., chairman of the parochial Board of St Ann who recently went on a visit to the Isthmus, by request delivered an address on the Panama Canal at the meeting held in the Government schoolroom, Brown's Town. The address was a most interesting one throughout and was listened to with marked attention.
Mr. Levy was received with applause and said:
Gentlemen: This paper was prepared after my visit to the Isthmus of Panama with the object of sending to the Y.M.C.A. of this town the members having requested that I should do so, but for some reason other it did not materialize, and I have now consented at the invitation of Mr. D. Theo. Wint to read it at this meeting. I express the hope that you will be tolerant of defects, and if you find anything to be appreciated you will credit it to the efforts to please a community in which I have lived so long, and love so much, rather that to any claim to literary style or rhetorical effect.
SEEING THE CANAL
I have selected this short but xxx title as the head lines of my little talk to you about the Canal, as I think it better illustrates my short visit to that great hive of industry and mammoth undertaking, than any other that I could select. I may, however, say that the title is not original, as it is the name of a little Pamphlet issued by the Canal Commissioners for the benefit of those who visit the Isthmus for the purpose of seeing the Canal by the observation trains with expert guides, but as I did not avail my self of this means (except for a short distance) my experience and my talk to you will be more in the nature of personal observation by routes selected on the recommendation of those on the spot and by the amiable Captain of the boat on which I travelled from Jamaica. It is right, however, to say that a good deal of the history anterior and subsequent to the building of the Canal by the American is derived from literature published by the Canal Commissioners or others interested in the great work, as I do not wish to pose in borrowed plumes, so frankly make admission of the fact.
Before proceeding, I wish it to be understood that this is no lecture, my object is less ambitious, and you must accept what I am going to tell you, as more in the light of talking to my fellow townsmen who like myself, are interested in the great undertaking to building the Canal, and its possible bearing on the destinies of this Island.
It may be thought by those who have only given cursory consideration to the subject of the building of the Canal, that the idea first originated with the French, which after

failure, was taken up by the American, and who are now doing the work; but this is not the case. For the benefit of those who have not studied the subject, I propose to give an abridged account of its history.

The transit across the Isthmus of Panama, connecting the Pacific with the Atlantic Ocean by an interoceanic canal had been a matter of thought since the year 1580. Several ideas were formulated from this time on, and not until the sixteenth century did it assume tangible form; nothing was done until 1828 when surveys and explorations were made with the view of determining whether the undertaking was feasible or not. Different routes were considered, but in process of time, all were abandoned save two, that by Nicaragua and that by Panama. After the discovery of gold in California in 1849, an American Company established a provisional transit by means of stage and boat across Nicaragua, and formulated some plans for completing the system by the construction of a Canal. These plans were not carried out, owing to various complications, some of them of an international character. In 1872-1875 complete surveys were made of both routes by the United States Government and the Panama route declared to be the best and most feasible. At this period, however, a Frenchman named Wyse secured from the Columbian Government a concession for building the Canal: it is said that his surveys and explorations were incomplete, but armed with the concession from the Columbian Government, he returned to France and secured the cooperation of deLesseps. An International Scientific Congress met in Paris in 1879 and a Panama Canal company was formed with deLesseps as head, and the Wyse Concession was purchased. It was estimated at the time that it would cost $169,000,000 to build the Canal. Shares were taken and the Canal commenced in 1881. The Canal was to have followed much the same route as that of the Railway from Colon to Panama, and was to be a sea-level Canal, with a depth of nearly 30 ft, and a bottom width of 79 ft., the distance was to be about 47 miles. It was, however, soon discovered that a sea level canal could not be built for the money estimated, and that a lock canal was necessary. It is said that the French made many mistakes and in 1889 they abandoned the work. To this time it is said it had cost $260,000,000. In 1894, however, a new French Company was formed to carry on and complete the work: and after operating for some time, also abandoned the undertaking. At this time it is said that about 12 miles of the entire length of the Canal had been finished by the French; this, however, did not include the more difficult portion of the work. It is said that never in the history of any great undertaking was there ever such lavish expenditure of money,

EXTRAVAGANCE AND GRAFT,

as was experienced by the building of the Canal by the French: a great deal of the machinery proved to be entirely unsuitable and useless, indeed there is to be seen to-day along the banks of the present canal, tons upon tons of large pieces of machinery lying among jungles and debris, of no use whatever.

It was soon after the Spanish American War that the United States Government announced its intention of building the Canal, and in 1904 the French Company offered to sell their rights to the United States Government, and price fixed was $40,000,000. Previous to this, say in 1903, the Treaty between the U.S. and the Columbian Governments was signed, whereby the U.S. was to secure a lease of the necessary slip of land for the building of the Canal for a hundred years, renewable at the pleasure of the U.S. This Treaty, however, was rejected by the Columbian Government; then followed the establishment of the Panama Republic, and a treaty was then signed by the U.S. and the Panama Republic, which gave the land to the U.S. for ever, say five miles of either side of the Canal (now called the Canal Zone) on payment of $10, 000,000 and an annual payment of $250,000 after 9 years, at which time it was calculated the Canal would be finished. This bargain with the Panama Republic following the rejection in the first instance of the treaty by the Colombian Government will recall to many the severe strictures that were heard on many sides against the U.S. Government over this bargain and the ceding of Panama and Colon from the possession of the Columbian Government. However, with these matters we have nothing to do, for out of evil (if there were any) good will assuredly come. The building of the Canal will mark a new era in the history of nations, and make for the progress and prosperity of the entire world, and it is doubtful if any other nation could or would have undertaken so stupendous a work as building the Canal with the same amount of certainty, and success as the American Nation as on my visit I was not only struck with the stupendous nature of the work, of its mammoth organization carried out without a hitch, but with the well-studied nature of the sanitation of the entire Zone, its perfect system in every detail, and of the lavish and unstinted expenditure of money everywhere, without, as far as I could see, extravagance or waste. I will not, however dwell here on this phase of the undertaking, as I hope as I proceed, to give a few condensed details of what is being done, but I thought by bringing in these facts at this stage it would help to demonstrate the idea of which I have given expression, that is how well equipped the Americans were to undertake the work, and that there were no obstacles in the way of their carrying it to completion, as against other nations who were less equipped, and less enterprising.

Having brought my talk down to the period of the completion by the United States of America of the bargain with the Panama Republic to build the canal, and their taking the same over, I will now tell as best I can what

THE AMERICANS HAVE DONE

during the seven or eight years of their occupation of the territory known as "The Canal Zone" containing about 448 square miles of land. The entire length of the Canal, from deep water in the Atlantic to deep water in the Pacific is about 50 miles, its length from shore line to shore line about 40 miles; the bottom width of the channel, maximum about 1,000 feet; the canal is to be provided with a system of dams and locks. The vessels passing through the locks will be propelled by electricity, no vessel being allowed to use its own power. The estimated time for a vessel to pass through the Canal is 10 hours, being 3 hours through the locks and 7 hours through the open water-way; that is no vessel will be allowed to proceed at a greater speed than 5 miles an hour. The Americans have estimated that it will cost to build the Canal the large sum of $375,000,000 or £75,000,000 of our money, but I may here say that in my opinion it will cost nearer $500,000,000 or £100,000,000 sterling.

Up to some period of last year it was estimated that 182,537,000 cubic yards of excavation had been done by the Americans, besides appropriations for Railway Tracks, work on the dams and locks, and various other constructional and electrical work etc., costing over $218,000,000. The total number of people engaged at work at this time was nearly 36,000 daily. The pay to the labourers, including West Indians is from ten to twenty cents per hour, or the average of about 6/[shillings] sterling per day, while skilled labourers could earn from 8/ to 10/ per day and more. It would be tedious for you to listen to further details in long and wearisome figures giving the details of the cost of respective departments, how manned, and so on, suffice it to say in this connection, that it is estimated that more than three fourths of the work has been completed, and that the year 1915 will see the final finish, and that soon after, the ships of all nations will be passing through the Canal. It is estimated that the distance saved by vessels going to Panama from the United States instead of going via Cape Horn, as they now have to do will save 10,000 miles by going via the Panama Canal.

I will now tell you as briefly as I can my personal observations of the work, and I will ask you to make allowance both for brevity and lack of consecutive detail.

PERSONAL OBSERVATIONS

I left Kingston on the s.s. Prinz August Wilhelm on Saturday the 20th July, the vessel sailing at 10 a.m. and on Monday at 7 a.m., we were going up the harbour at

Colon, thus making the voyage across in about 45 hours. At about 8.30 we were all ashore investigating and inspecting conditions in Colon, and I may here say that I was struck with its complete sanitation and cleanliness. I had of course heard of the greatly improved conditions to eight or ten years previous, but it was certainly a great revelation to me to find a complete system of sewerage, concrete side-walks, streets clean as a new pin, and everywhere, cleanliness and sanitary completeness rivalling our larger and older city Kingston. On enquiry, I found that the new state of things were coincident with the American Treaty and purchase of the Canal Zone that the Panama Republic was required to keep the city in a perfect state of cleanliness and sanitation, and to which the Canal Company made a substantial contribution, and had the power at any time, not only to enforce, but to do the sanitation themselves in case of failure by the Panama authorities. I found too, that several new docks were being built at Colon with the evident intention of overtaking the increased trade that would come to it after the completion of the Canal; it is admitted on the Isthmus, that Colon, much more that Panama, will benefit by the Canal, for while at the Pacific end vessels are likely to enter and pass through the Canal without stopping, at Colon on entering the Atlantic they will stop for coaling after taking in stores, before proceeding on their journey, and certainly, this view of the matter appealed to even my lay mind as being a reasonable conclusion to this end. The P.R.R.Co., which is an adjunct of the Canal Company, are now building a very large hotel in Colon to contain 1,000 rooms with all modern and up-to-date conveniences in order to meet the contingency spoken of. The Hotel is to be of reinforced concrete, the first of its kind in Colon. I may say that ninety percent of the houses in Colon are of wood, and all are provided with mosquito netting, even the smaller houses (and those I took to be houses of the working people) are similarly protected. In this connection, I may here state, that from the time I landed in Colon, and all through my roamings on the Zone and in Panama, I never saw a mosquito or a fly, the reasons for which I will give later on.

The Cold Storage of the Isthmus is in Colon, situated at Cristobal, the greatest and most perfect institution in the world, the place from which all meat, vegetables, and fruit are supplied for the feeding of the thousands working on the Canal. I visited this place which is considered one of the show places of the Isthmus, and I found it well worthy of a visit and quite up to, if not exceeding, all I had expected to find. I was treated with great courtesy by the management, and to my surprise and delight the manager of this department was an Englishman who had lived in Jamaica for some years, and was apparently glad to see one coming from Jamaica. The Cold Storage proper consists of a number of stores, but under the same roof, in which are stored hundreds of carcasses of oxen, sheep and pigs, and eggs, butter, fish and vegetables and fruit, each having a separate room colder than ice, if I may say so, one room in particular was 15 degrees below zero.

Before entering these cold rooms, a heavily lined coat is given you, as one would actually freeze if one went in without this precaution. I was shown over the entire place from one room to the other, and I was amazed to find the

EXTREME ORDER AND CLEANLINESS.

that everywhere abounded, and the great system of perfect organization that existed. I was told by the manager that ten train loads of beef and other stuffs leave Colon every morning for all sections of the Canal, Panama and other places and that 120,000 people were fed from the supplies from the Colon Storage every day. A steamer from Chicago brings a supply of beef, mutton and other necessaries every week.

I then visited the power house, the bakery, and the laundry, all in connection with the cold storage and belonging to the Canal Company. I saw in the Laundry a great many Jamaican girls that I knew, all at work and apparently satisfied; the Manager told me that of the hundreds employed in the storage rooms-none received less than $10 gold per week. I considered the Cold Storage of Colon, one of the greatest things I saw, and anyone going there, should not miss seeing it.

At 10.25 I took the train for seeing the Canal enroute for Panama, we stopped off at Culebra Cut and having first gone over the Culebra Cut, where I saw the sliding hill recently reported, and I having luncheon at the Y.M.C.A. restaurant, took the sight-seeing train for Pedro Miguel, where we were shown over the Locks, Dams, and other constructional works. From there we went to the Miraflores Dam down the east side to the locks, and thence by the track on the west side of the Canal to Corozal, then to Balboa to view the Pacific entrance to the Canal, and then on to Panama where we stayed that evening at the Tivoli, a fine hotel built by the Canal Company. Neither at this hotel nor at and of the other hotels controlled by the Canal Company is liquor or spirits of any kind sold. Needless to say no spirits or even beer is sold at any of the hotels or restaurants controlled by the Y.M.C.A. and at almost every station along the line there is an hotel or restaurant run by this great and worldwide association. The charge for a good luncheon with iced tea at these places is only 50 cents or 2/.

The next day (Tuesday) we spent in seeing Panama. Like Colon, most of the houses are of wood, but there are more stone buildings than in Colon, and all protected by the inevitable mosquito netting. The streets were clean, and everywhere there was evidence of careful and persistent sanitation. I visited several of the Historic buildings and Public Institutions, and was everywhere met with extreme courtesy. There are a great many shops and bazaars in Panama, many of them owned by the obsequious Chinamen who appear to be in flourishing condition. The same evening we returned to Colon, arriving there at night.

The best part of the trip for the seeing the Canal was reserved for Wednesday, the Captain of the ship with whom I had gone over having arranged for a motor boat to take us to the Gatun Locks, the part of the Canal most advanced, it took us about an hour to get there, the distance by water being about six miles. We passed through a part of the canal which had been constructed by the French, and which will be used by the Canal Company. I may here say that although the French Company had to abandon the building of the Canal owing to monetary troubles and other disabilities, a good bit of work that they performed, has been found to be of great use to the present Canal Company, and though the routes in some places have been abandoned for others found more practicable, yet, as pioneers in preparing the waterway, the present company has found the work more easy; besides this, though a good lot of the machinery brought out by the French was found useless, there are others of which the Americans have been able to make use, so that when they paid $40,000,000 to the French, they had good value for their money, as it is estimated that they got fully $42,000,000 worth of work and materials for the $40,000,000 they paid.

THE GREAT LOCKS.

Arriving at Gatun, we left the boat for the scene of observation, and for two and a half hours we walked the entire length of the locks and made careful inspection of the locks and large iron gates that were being prepared for holding in the water, and filling and emptying the canal during the progress of ships passing through; some of the gates were already finished, and others in course of construction. It is estimated that these gates will weigh from 300 to 600 tons each, and measure 62 feet high. It is said that it will require 92 leaves for the entire canal, estimated to weigh 57,000 tons. The lock gates will be operated by electricity; the locks will be filled and emptied through a system of Culverts; several are already finished and are a marvel of ingenuity and engineering skill. It is said the average time taken to fill and empty a lock will not be more than about 15 minutes. The dimensions of all locks at Gatun, Pedro Miguel and Miraflores will be the same say 1,000 feet long with a width of 110 feet. Each lock will be a chamber with walls and floor of concrete; the walls are 15 to 50 feet wide. I stood on the top of one of these walls and looked down, and never saw more perfect work in my life.

Passing from the locks, we went to the tower or look-out, and here had the most welcomed thing we had had on the whole excursion-a glass of cold iced water. From this tower we viewed the canal from the east side, where the dams have already been erected to control the water of the Chagres River-it was while going over the road to reach this tower, that I picked up the piece of rock here shown. I may here frankly state that nothing that has been written, nor anything one can see with the eyes, lacking those of an expert, can adequately or accurately describe the magnitude of the work at this point. As far as the eye can encompass are seen hundreds of workmen employed in all kinds of work; trains coming and going laden with rock and debris taken from the bed of the Canal, depositing it either on the banks, or carrying it long distance to fill up swamps and depressions in the land; machinery and stack of girders or iron plates strewn over the entire ground! It is certainly a most wonderful sight, and one thing that struck me as being most remarkable, was the ease and comparative comfort with which all the workmen did their work; there was no hustling nor confusion; no headmen or supervisors bawling; everything seemed to be carried on with the precision of clock-work!

Another remarkable thing that I observed, was that along almost the entire length of the cut itself, and along the banks, railway lines are laid, and one sees hundreds of trains being operated; some taking the dirt and stones that are being thrown up by the steam shovels at work; others carrying stones and other materials for the workmen. It is said that there are one hundred of these steam shovels constantly at work; no fewer that 315 locomotives and 360 drills, while there are over 1,000 cars, 30 dredgers, besides 57 cranes, 12 tugs, pile drivers, 70 barges and lighters and 14 launches and other appliances. This I think, will give some idea of the magnitude of the work, and of the perfect organization.

I had almost omitted to say that many of the trains are operated to take labourers from one point of the Canal to another, and for carrying them to central points for meals. The labourers, and indeed the whole staff working on the Canal, are fed from the Commissaries established along the line by the Canal Company, they are charged so much per meal, which amount is deducted from their pay at the end of the week. From these commissaries the labourers and others get their clothing, and indeed anything that they require. I was told in Colon, that this system has

DESTROYED THE TRADE

of the shop-keepers, as it is no longer necessary for the labourers to buy their supplies at the shops, as they can get them from the various Commissaries, and cheaper than the shops can sell, as the Canal Company pays no duty on the goods they import from the United States of America, whereas the shop-keepers are taxed heavily. Large townships are established the whole length of the line, and every house or hamlet, lighted with electricity supplied from the electric plant established at Gatun. It was a pretty sight to see the lights on every hill or slope, as you travel by train from Panama. It is interesting also to note that at all these sections there are regularly equipped hospitals, sanitary inspectors, and every appliance that may be needed in case of accidents or illness. To illustrate:-One of the Captain's party that went with us to Gatun, got a nail through his boot, and he immediately went to one of these hospitals on the way, and had his foot cauterized. I saw it done myself, and we were put on one of the trolleys, and sent to meet our party; there was no charge by the doctor, indeed, he invited us to stay for dinner.

NO FLIES OR MOSQUITOES.

In earlier stages of this paper or I may say "talk," I promised to tell you how it is that in Colon, and indeed the entire length of the Canal Zone into Panama, no mosquitoes or flies could be found; the secret is this: On all the elevations or on the hills overlooking the canal, there are large oil tanks containing crude petroleum, and along the banks of the Canal on both sides, are large iron pipes (I should say about 4 inches in diameter) and the oil is sent through these pipes and deposited in every swamp, every trench throughout the improvised towns, on the banks of the river and lakes, and indeed, in every place where there is the least settlement of water. In this way, with the additional work that is being carried on of filling up every swamp, can easily be seen how this death to the mosquito and fly is brought about. Of course, the whole Zone reeks with the smell of the oil, but it has the desired effect, and one gets used to it after a time.

While on the subject of sanitation, and having assured you of the perfect system that obtains on the Isthmus, you will excuse my digressing a little, and talking about what I consider a kindred subject that I noticed on my recent trip. I refer to the precautions taken by the Health Officers in Colon, in inspecting every passenger on the ship in which I travelled, before allowing them to land. Unlike the English Officers of Health, who consider that it is official etiquette to take the word of the Medical Officer of the ship, that there has been no illness on board, or no infectious disease at the last port of call, the Colon Health Officers order all the passengers, whether they be first, second, or steerage, to be mustered, and they are called each by name and pass in review before him, the Purser of the ship having one list and he another, and each name is ticked off as the passenger is called. He scrutinizes everyone as he or she passes him, and if he sees an unsteady gait, or the slightest cause for suspicion, that passenger is turned back, and kept for the last, and then he or she is specially examined before being allowed on shore. In fact, the morning we landed, three or four of the passengers were treated in this way. You will thus see that in addition to the strict Sanitary Laws existing on the Isthmus, and the precautions taken to ensure healthy conditions among the people, rigid precautions are also taken to prevent the introduction of any infectious disease that may be brought from other places.

The last halt in my travels was at Gatun, but as you will see, I have travelled over a considerable extent of territory outside this particular place in order to get in matter bearing on the subject, as may be of interest to you.

We returned to Colon Wednesday afternoon, and the balance of the time, until I embarked on the Santa Marta for Jamaica on Thursday, was taken up with further sightseeing in Colon. Leaving Colon Thursday, I got back to Kingston Saturday, having been away exactly one week. I found this quite long enough to see the Canal, and no one who desires to go to the Isthmus for this purpose, need remain away any longer. I found the trip instructive and educative, and am fully repaid from all I saw and learnt.

I would advise all who can spare a week, to do the same, as it will be money and time well spent. It costs really very little, and the amount spent will not be regretted. (Cheers)

I thank you gentlemen for the courtesy in asking me to address you and for the patient and indulgent hearing that you have exercised in listening to me, and I can assure you that it has been a great pleasure to me in acceding to your request (Applause).

A VOTE OF THANKS

Rev. W. Graham, M.A., amid cheering, rose to move a vote of thanks to Mr. Levy. The lecture had been a most interesting one, the most complete thing of the kind ever given in Jamaica (he believed) or published in a Jamaica newspaper. He asked that the Press be requested to publish the address in extenso so that the whole island could enjoy it. He had been over the Canal Zone and was therefore particularly fascinated by the address which so completely took him over grounds he had some knowledge of. He would mention by the way that the idea of cutting the Panama Canal was first conceived by an Englishman some seventy years ago (cheers)

Mr. George R. Brown seconded the vote of thanks, which was warmly supported by Messrs. Wint and Walters, and carried unanimously.

1912

November 1, 1912

BENEDICT-DALY- At St. Stephens Church, Boston, on the 15th October, by the Rev. Frederick C. Lauderburn, assisted by the Rev. Thomas S. Cline, MARY MAUD, second daughter of Mr. and Mrs. John Daly of Paisley, Jamaica to GEORGE LAWRENCE BENEDICT of Boston, Mass, U.S.A.

November 12, 1912

HOPWOOD-At his home "Devon" Manchester, on Saturday night at 10.15 o'clock, JOSEPH HOPWOOD aged 70 years. American and Canadian paper please copy.

November 12, 1912

QUINLAN Nov 6th at 26 Rum Lane, Kingston, ALICE MAUD SARAH QUINLAN, the dearly beloved sister of Rev. Hilton Cheesborough Quinlan, Wesleyan Minister, Laban C. Quinlan and Sydney Stead Quinlan, passed peacefully to rest at 12.30 a.m. after much suffering, in her 63rd year, Loved and Missed She was strong in faith. Antigua and St Lucia papers please copy.

November 15, 1912

KEELING At St Jago Park, Spanish Town, on the 14th inst., the wife of A.L. Keeling, of a son.

ROPER-On Sunday 11th November at 5 p.m. JOSEPH ROPER, of St. Margaret's Bay, Portland at port Maria. Verse.

November 23, 1912

EXTENDED ACCOUNTS OF DAMAGE WROUGHT BY HURICANE--Heavy Loss is estimated--Full list of the Identified Dead in Monday's Great Catastrophe in Town of Montego Bay--Building in Gully Course to be Prohibited--Governor Discusses with Magistrates and Board Members the Best Means of Dealing with the Situation--Steps Taken to Cope with the Conditions.

STORMY WEATHER AT BROWN'S TOWN
(from our correspondent)
Brown's Town, Nov 18--We have been experiencing stormy weather since Saturday night. The climax of the situation was reached this morning, when from about 5 o'clock, the blowing raged strong and fierce.

The well known water -settlements Egypt Pastures, Tabernacle, Mission Yard and Gun Pond- have had a much larger intake than usual, forming miniature lakes. The rain fall for the past two days is about nine inches.

With the wind blowing heavily in a north-easterly direction, the only saviour from devastating destruction is apparently the intermittent showers, which seem to keep in check the force of the wind.

Trees have been uprooted in all directions, blocking all means of communication. Ground crops, are it is reported practically, or wholly, submerged. The damage to bananas is extensive; no loss of life or other property has been heard of; nor can the value of the damage done be ascertained.

The mails due to arrive here this morning have not been heard of between here and Moneague.

November 27, 1912

ESTWICK-BROMFIELD-On Sunday 24th inst., at Up Park Camp, by the Rev. C.E. Jarvis, EDWARD ESTWICK (of Barbados) Segt W.I.R. to MARY BROMFIELD, daughter of Mr. and Mrs. David Bromfield of Potsdam, St Elizabeth. (Barbados papers please copy).

November 29, 1912
LITTLE BERTY HOLLAR-At his father's residence, Halmah, on the Lady Musgrave Road. Funeral moves at 4 p.m. to-day Friday. He will gather in His own.

MORE RAIN AT BROWN'S TOWN
(From our Correspondent)
     Brown's Town, Tuesday--The weather broke out again yesterday and torrential showers of rain fell. The streets were flooded and the district of Stand Fast situated at the lower portion of the town was nearly washed away. The roads have been severely cut up. Indeed were it not for their beautiful formation and solid substrata a far greater amount of damage might have been done. The exterior walls of one or two houses have fallen in, but no serious loss has been reported: there is apparently more rain to follow.
     Your correspondent is now able through the courtesy of the hon. member for the parish and the chairman of the Parochial Board, who have been motoring through the Dry Harbour mountains with a view to ascertaining the amount of damage done to property, etc. by the recent storm and weather, to give an extended account.
     The gentlemen, proceeding from this town, made their first call at St.D'Acre where they visited and inspected the Cottage Hospital under the care of Dr. Hargreaves, the popular D.M.O. of the district and found the verandah of the building blown away and the guttering destroyed. They also learnt that the hospital was nearly flooded during the heavy rain and wind, trees on the premises were uprooted and all cultivations in the locality, especially bananas, had been totally destroyed. Their next stop was made at Aboukir, the property of the chairman, and there they found that the verandah of the old hospital was blown off and the entire building and door of the coffee factory demolished. Banana cultivation and fruit trees destroyed. From thence to Cave Valley similar destruction met the eye. They found on leaving this last place complete devastation and ruin on all sides, all cultivation were wholly wiped out and the coffee crop partially destroyed. Mr. Bernard, proprietor of Cave Valley Estate, suffered to an alarming extent both in loss of cultivation and stock. The gentlemen were much struck at the extent of the damage and entertain the gravest fears for suffering and hunger in the ensuing year. They report that all yam cultivation at Bog Hole, upon which the inhabitants of this and adjacent districts depend for food supplies are completely ruined--one cultivator losing some 6.000 hills of yams, another 20 heads of stock, whilst the loss to others in goats, pigs and donkeys is alarming. Fully 300 acres of small cultivations have been wiped out. They got as far as "Wasp Cave" on the Clarendon road and could go no further--the road as well as adjoining cultivation being covered for a considerable distance with water. A passage (except by boat which was improvised and used to go across) was impracticable.
     The gentlemen have been deeply impressed with the situation and destruction to the once thriving and prosperous township of Boro Bridge and intend representing the conditions observed to the Government with a view to obtaining government aid for the planters of the district.
     In regard to Watt Town and districts in that neighbourhood, damages have been done to cultivation, the coffee crop has been partly whipped off. Bananas, corn and other crops destroyed, and several houses blown down whilst the roads are in need of repairs.
     The promptness with which these gentlemen have enquired into the loss and distress among the people in the stricken districts is not only commendable but amply serves to testify to their genuine interest in the welfare of the constituency they represent.

1912

November 30, 1912

The Gleaner regrets to learn that Mr. C.T. Pascoe of the "Temple of Fashion" is lying seriously ill at the Nursing Hostel. An operation had to be performed on Thursday.

December 12, 1912

JONES-CUNHA-December 10th, at Coke Church by Rev. Arthur Kirby, assisted by Revs. W.J. William and J.W. Wright, Rev. Edward Armon Jones, eldest son of Edward Jones Esq., of Liverpool, to Daphne Helena, third daughter of Mr. and Mrs. Herbert A. Cunha of Chatsworth, South Camp Road, Kingston Jamaica.

DUFF-At his residence, West Lincoln Road, St Andrew, on 9th December, 1912 William Duff, late of the Government Audit Office staff age 68 ½ years.

December 13, 1912

SHARP-On the 6th inst., at Biddeford, James Henry Sharp (Engineer) in his 67th year.

December 18, 1912

KIRKLAND-on the 16th inst. in Kingston, WILLIAM DICKSON KIRKLAND OF Ayr, Scotland.

ORRETT-At No 2 Lower South Camp Road on the 17th inst., MISS ADELAIDE ORRETT. Funeral leaves late residence at 4 p.m. today. R.I.P.

December 23, 1912

WEDDING BELLS--Marriage Celebrated Mandeville Recently--The R.M.'s Daughter--Pretty Wedding at Coke Church on Wednesday Last.

(From Our Correspondent)

Mandeville, Dec 17--A very pretty wedding took place here today in the parish Church when Mr. Arthur William Lemonious Clerk was married to Miss Vanda Moore Reece, daughter of His Honour Mr. I. Richard Reece. The church was beautifully decorated by the friends of the bride. Miss Clerk, sister of the bridegroom, acted as bridesmaid with two pages following whilst Mr. Clerk a brother of the bridegroom, acted as groom's man.

The ceremony was performed by his Lordship Bishop Joscelyne, assisted by the Rev. E.B. Pike. After the ceremony they went to the Newleigh Hotel where the usual repast was partaken of and thereafter the happy couple left for Chippenham by motor car where they will spend their honeymoon.

December 28, 1912

CLERK-REECE-At the Mandeville Parish Church on the 17th inst. by His Lordship Bishop Joscelyne, assisted by the Rev. E.V. Pike, ARTHUR WILLIAM LEMONIOUS, eldest son of J.H. Clerk Esq. of Wales, Falmouth, to VANDA MOORE, youngest daughter of Mr. and Mrs. I.R. Reece.

MANY DEATHS--Vomiting Sickness in the Porus District-VISIT PAID BY DOCTORS--The Parochial Board Asked to Give Aid to the Needy.

December 31, 1912

ISAACS-At Torrington, Sav-La-Mar on the 26th December, the wife of Dr.S.A. Isaacs of a daughter. (English and American Papers please copy.

Selected Vital Records from the Jamaican Daily Gleaner

CRUM-EWING-At Kingston, on December 30th 1912, ALEXANDER CRUM-EWING, of Dunbartonshire, Scotland, and of Caymanas, St Catherine. Aged 86. Funeral will move from 5 South Race Course at 4 p.m. today (December 31st) for Half-way Tree.

1913

January 15, 1913
[Picture] The old Kingston Court House on Election Day: about 70 years ago.

January 16, 1913
MANY DEATHS--More People Dying From Vomiting Sickness--LATE NEWS FROM PORUS--The Need of a Resident Doctor in the Town.

January 18, 1913
STEWART-DACOSTA-At All Saints Kingston, 12th inst., CYRIL CHARLES, son of A.T.Stewart Esq. of Stewarton, St Elizabeth to Mabel Eulalie, daughter of J. DaCosta Esq., of St Mary. (American and Panamanian paper please copy).

January 20, 1913
SCARLETT--In Canada on the 2nd January 1913, ANNA GRACE SCARLETT in her 80th year.

CROSSWELL-At Half-Way Tree on the 6th January, the wife of A. Noel Crosswell of a daughter.

January 23, 1913
FATAL DISEASE--deaths Reported from the Vomiting Sickness--POOR PEOPLE STIRCKEN--Dr Seidelin is Still Engaged In His Investigations.

January 25, 1913
TOWNEND-At Barnes, Oriente, Cuba on the 16th inst., to Mr. and Mrs. Arthur E. Townend, a daughter (nee Rerrie).

January 29, 1913
[Picture] Mr. P. Anderson Cover, Composer of "Dearest" Waltz

A FINE MUSICIAN--The Work of Mr. P.A. Cover as a Composer--His Brilliant Talent.

Mr. P. Anderson Cover, the composer of "Dearest" Waltz, whose picture is produced above, was born at Huntly, St Ann on the 22nd February 1873, and is one of a very musical family.

He received his first lessons in music from Mrs. Minnie Hedmann, the wife of the Rev Arthur Hedmann, being enabled by her kind, careful and interested tuition to take a high place at York Castle College advancing his musical studies under Messrs. C.E. Sterry and E.P. Sibthorpe; and eventually succeeded Mr. Sibthorpe as music master and organist which position he resigned after nearly six years' service. While at York Castle, Mr. Cover published a pretty little song, " A Serenade" to Longfellow's words, "Stars of the Summer Sky".

Being urged by his friends, Mr. Cover hopes in time to be in a position to give more of his compositions, which include marches, hymns songs, etc., to the public.

Another waltz, "Venus" s in the publishers' hands, and another in the manuscript stage.

Mr. Cover is the principal of the High School, Balaclava, the climate of which town, he says, is inspiring to a composer.

As a composer, he shows decided originality, not one bar of "Dearest' which by the way, can be obtained from Astley Clerk, Cowen Music Room, 14 King Street can be pointed to as "like so and so". It is a pretty waltz, with the true waltz swing, and what is best is the genuine product of Mr. Cover's own brains.

"Gleaner" readers who have not yet got a copy should write at one to Mr. Astley Clerk; the price is 2.1 post free.

February 7, 1913
ROPER-On the 4th inst. the wife of L.L. Roper of a son.

ADDISON-At her residence in Gt. George Street, Savanna-la-Mar on 1st February 1913 ALICE widow of the late John Addison son of John Addison of Scotland at the age of 92 years, leaving one son and several grand and great grand children to mourn their loss (English papers please copy)"Through the Cross, To the Crown".

February 12, 1913
LEVY-At Kalonah, Mandeville, wife of Clarence E. Levy, of a son. Feb. 11th, 1913 [Arthur]

March 1, 1913
DREAD DISEASE--The Vomiting Sickness Has Claimed Many Victims.--CASES IN ST. ANDREW.-Dr. Seidelin Has now Seen Scores of the Victims--THE MALADY DISAPPEARING.

March 4, 1913
NASH-MOORE-On the 22nd February at the Colon Parish Church, MISS MAY NASH of Manchester, Jamaica to Mr. SIDNEY MOORE of Louisiana, U.S.A.

ISAACS-At Ivy Cottage" Brown's Town, St Ann, on the 25th Feb., 1913, ELIZA eldest daughter of the late Abraham and Sarah Isaacs. Aged 86. Much beloved and mourned by a large circle of relatives and friends.

March 8, 1912
THE CAMBRIDGE EXAMINATION--Results Achieved by the Jamaica Student-A FULL LIST OF PASSES.--Miss M.E. Cowper Has Topped Colonial List of Girls

March 14, 1913
RUSSELL-MURRAY-At East London, Cape Colony South Africa, THOMAS FRASER (eldest surviving son of the late Rev. Thos. Porter Russell to OLIVE CAROLINE.

1913

March 27, 1913
MAXWELL-At Bloomsbury, Saint Elizabeth, on the 23rd March 1913, GERTRUDE JOHNSON, the youngest daughter of the late George Robert and Elizabeth Christiana Maxwell. Aged 17 years. Verse.

March 31, 1913
[Front page Picture] The Ceremony at Half-Way Tree on Friday When the Memorial Tower was Dedicated. Caption: The Scene at he dedication of the King Edward Memorial Clock Tower.

March 31, 1913
HOLLAR-On Sunday, 30th, JANET CONSTANCE (Nettie) aged 13 years, beloved daughter of Mr. and Mrs. F.L. Hollar. Funeral moves at 4.30 p.m. 31st inst. from Ravensworth, 56 Brentford Road. Friends and acquaintances please accept this intimation. Safe in the arms of Jesus.

POLACK-At Newport, Manchester on the 28th March 1913, MARY POLACK, widow of the late Myre Polack and sister of the late Mrs. Joseph DeLeon in her 77th year. "He giveth his Beloved rest".

April 4, 1913
NASH, GEORGE. In his 72nd year on the 22nd March at Mandeville, eldest son of the late Geo. William Nash, Emporium Jamaica and Dover, England. (English, Australian and American papers please copy).

April 16, 1913
MURRAY-HITCHINS-On the 12th April at St. George's Church, Kingston by His Grace the Archbishop of the West Indies assisted by the Rev. J.L. Ramson, M.A. FRANK E.MURRAY of the Colonial Bank fifth son of the late Mr. A. Pilgrim Murray and Mrs. Murray of Saint Philip, Barbados, to HILDA VICTORIA, second daughter of Mr. and Mrs. A.W. Hitchins of Hadley, St Andrew, Ja.

MAXWELL, CHARLES H.C. At his late residence No 9 Spanish Town Road yesterday. Aged 81 years. Funeral moves at 4 p.m. this evening. R.I.P.

April 21, 1913
DELISSER-ALFRED GEORGE--Wednesday evening at 6.30 at his residence Water Square, Falmouth the beloved husband of Josephine in his 53rd year. Verse.

May 1, 1913
PHILLIPPS-LUCIA MARIA FREDERICA, the wife of Joselin L. Phillipps, at Langston Road, Rollington Pen, at 6 o'clock last evening, after a long illness. Funeral will move from her late residence at 5 o'clock last evening. Friends and acquaintances please accept this intimation and attend.

May 2, 1913
CHAIRMAN OF THE ST ANN BOARD RESIGNS [Picture] caption: Mr. J. H. Levy.

WATER SUPPLY--The Resignation of the Hon. J.H.Levy Yesterday.--A MOTION OF CENSURE?
(Special by Wire)

401

(From our Correspondent) St Ann's Bay May 1. At the meeting of the Parochial Board of St Ann, held here to-day, the Hon. J. H. Allwood moved in effect, that the Board appoint a committee to consist of Messrs. Allen and Bramwell and himself to take steps to secure the water supply for the dry districts of the parish, which the Board had delayed to do till now as the money voted by the Government was likely to be used otherwise.

On division, the motion was carried. Messrs. Cameron, Roxburgh, Tennant and Deleon, voting against, and Messrs Allwood, Bramwell, Allen, Baines and Brown for. The chairman, Mr. J. H. Levy, declined to vote.

The chairman regarded the motion as tantamount to a vote of censure, and handed in his resignation after the adjournment.

Mr. Levy had held the position of chairman of the Parochial Board of St Ann for more that 20 years having been re-elected from year to year.

Friday May 2, 1913 Editorial
Mr. J.H. Levy's Resignation of the Chairmanship of St Ann's Board.

Only a few days ago we referred in these columns to the successful working of representative institutions in St Ann's parish, and described the Parochial Board as a sort of "happy family" in which an excellent Chairman, Mr. J.H. Levy was loyally supported by the Custos, the Hon. H.E. Cox, and the member for the parish in the Legislative Council, the Hon J.H. Allwood. Indeed, we attributed the satisfactory financial position of the Board and the smooth running of the local administrative machinery, in large measure to the co-operation of these three influential gentlemen. But "the unexpected always happens," as the late Lord Beaconsfield once said. Readers of the "Gleaner" will be surprised-and most of them will be sorry as well as surprised to learn that Mr. Levy is no longer Chairman, and that this resignation of a position which he has filled with honour and distinction for something like thirty years, was brought about through a vote of "no confidence" which Mr. Allwood moved and to carried at yesterdays meeting of the Board. A rupture between old friends is always regrettable; but it is doubly so when the severance of the tie is likely to affect detrimentally the welfare of a large community. The question of providing the dry districts of the parish with water a question concerning which the member for St Ann has displayed a vast amount of zeal and enthusiasm is responsible for the unhappy turn that events have taken. Perhaps the true inwardness of the movement that culminated in Mr. Levy's resignation of the position of Chairman yesterday, will never be revealed; for it generally happens that, in all such cases, forces are at work which do not appear on the surface. What is known, however, is that for a few months past the staunchest political supporters of Mr. Allwood have not been satisfied with the attitude taken up by Mr. Levy on the water supply question -have been disposed to accuse Mr. Levy of indifference to the real needs of his fellow parishioners, and of standing in the way (consciously or unconsciously) of the realization of the policy so ably and earnestly advocated by Mr. Allwood. The first sign of the gathering storm which came under our notice was the passing of a strongly worded resolution on the subject at a Branch Agricultural Society's meeting in the Dry Harbour Mountains district some weeks ago. That resolution expressed regret that the Parochial Board had not taken advantage of the grant from the Government to build tanks in the locality. The next sign of the growing discontent was the publication in this journal of a characteristically outspoken letter from Mr. D. Theo. Wint, in which the Board was severely censured for its negligence and in which also reference was made to a somewhat unfriendly encounter between Mr. Levy and Mr. Allwood on the vexed question of supplying the dry area with water.

The Last Magnanimous Stand.

1913

The third act of the drama was played yesterday at St Ann's Bay. According to our correspondent's telegram, Mr. Allwood moved a resolution to the effect that a small Committee (consisting of himself and two other members of the Board) should be appointed to take steps to secure for the dry districts to the parish the water supplies which the Board had too long delayed to obtain; more especially as there was every chance that the Government would use the money which had been ear-marked for such a purpose, to carry out other schemes in other parts of the colony. Our correspondent did not wire us the "ipsissima verba" of Mr. Allwood's motion; so we do not profess to have given the exact wording of it in what we have just written; but we daresay we have given the substance of the resolution with tolerable accuracy. If so, the "slap in the face" to the Board (and particularly to its honoured Chairman) was unmistakable; and we cannot help thinking that Mr. Levy was right in regarding the motion brought forward by the hon. legislator as "tantamount to a vote of censure" on his attitude and conduct. In these circumstances, what did Mr. Levy do? We ask our readers to observe the dignity, the self-respect, the independence with which he acted. He could easily have defeated the resolution. In spite of the fact that the attendance was small, and that two or three of the Chairman's ardent supporters were absent, four members voted against the motion, and only five (including Mr. Allwood himself) in favour of it. Although so much was at stake, Mr. Levy declined to vote. He could have voted, and thereby created a tie; in which case, he would have been in a position to defeat the resolution by means of his casting vote. But pride, we presume, forbade him to rally to the rescue of his own reputation as an efficient and patriotic parochial administrator-to do anything to prevent the vote of "no confidence" in him from being passed, if the majority of his colleagues on the Board were willing to pass it. We have often admired Mr. Levy, we have often appreciated his manliness and magnanimity, during the course of that portion of his public career (extending over a quarter of a century) of which we have personal knowledge. But never have we so profoundly admired him as at the present moment. He could have saved himself and his position -he could have triumphed over Mr. Allwood quite easily---but he refused to do so. And a man who can do that, has in him the stuff of which heroes are made. We feel sure that in every part of St Ann to-day, the feeling will prevail that the parish has lost the services of one of the most capable and disinterested men who have ever looked after the management of its affairs. And if strong pressure is not brought to bear immediately on Mr. Levy to withdraw his resignation, we are confident that a few months hence (when Mr. Allwood's Committee has failed to do anything more than the Parochial Board has done) a request will be addressed to him by all sections of the electors to resume his old position. In our opinion, Mr. Levy has been treated most ungratefully by Mr. Allwood and his friends. The ex-chairman has served the parish and its people with a fidelity and self-sacrifice worthy of the highest praise; and even in the matter of obtaining water supplies for the dry area, he has done all that he possibly could have done. In a letter from his pen which we had the pleasure of publishing the other day, he had no difficulty in defending his conduct and explaining why the Dry Harbour Mountains district was still without the tanks that had been promised it. The "grant," which he was blamed for not having taken advantage of, never existed except in the imagination of his critics; and whatever chance there was of getting that grant from the Government at an early date, disappeared when the hurricane struck the western parishes in November last and necessitated the spending not only of the Government's cash balances but also of the colony's Reserve or Insurance Fund of £100,000. Although misrepresented and humiliated by some of his fellow-parishioners, however, Mr. Levy may rest assured that the overwhelming majority of his fellow countrymen recognise the value of the services he has rendered to Jamaica in general and St Ann's parish in particular, and that they hold him even higher esteem to-day than ever before.

Selected Vital Records from the Jamaican Daily Gleaner

May 3, 1913
ISAACS-At Torrington on the 30th April at 2 a.m. BARBARA NOELLE, the infant daughter of Dr. an Mrs. Isaacs, aged 4 months and 4 days. English and American papers please copy.

May 5, 1913
THE DEATH CALL--Sudden Demise of Deputy Inspector General-- A SHOCK TO KINGSTON--His Great Impartiality and Strict Devotion to Duty.

It is with deep regret that we announce this morning the death of Deputy Inspector-general McCrea at his residence, 88 Hanover Street, in this city at 10 o'clock on Saturday night last.

The news will come as a great surprise to his many friends in Kingston who saw him out about as usual up to Saturday evening. Indeed, it was a great shock to the officers and men at Sutton street goal, when the news reached that station on Saturday night, as Mr. McCrae was there all Saturday performing his duties and showed no signs of illness.

On Saturday afternoon he took a drive up to the Liguanea Club, where he spent a few hours returning to his residence at Hanover street, and subsequently took ill.

Dr. Frank Saunders was quickly summoned to the house, but in spite of all that was possible to be done, the Deputy Inspector-General passed away at about 10 o'clock.

Mr. McCrae went on a fortnight's leave to Chapelton recently, and since his return to the city on Monday last, he had been performing his duties as usual. His intimate friends, however, observed that he was not looking as well as he always did, but still he went about his work without complaining. His death will create a vacancy among the officers of the force, which cannot easily be filled, for despite the fact the Mr. McCrea was not as popular an officer as his predecessor was with the public, he was nevertheless a most efficient man

A STRICT DISCIPLINARIAN,
an honest upright gentleman. Even the men under him, who when they erred in some way or another, had to be disciplined, would always speak of his impartial manner and of the kind sympathy underlying the firm hand. He watched over the interest of his men with a keen zealous eye and to the man who showed ability, who displayed intelligence in the discharge of his duty, Mr. McCrea showed every consideration and never allowed an opportunity to pass without recognizing or rewarding by promotion, such men

SON OF AN ADMIRAL
Mr. John Harry McCrea came from distinguished English family. He was a son of Admiral McCrea of the British Navy, and was born in England. He came out to Jamaica when quite a young man. and started out in the planting line at "Whitfield Hall" in the parish of St Thomas, where he was engaged in the cultivation of Cinchona. He was made a Justice of the Peace for St Thomas, and at one time served as a member of the Parochial Board of that parish.

Mr. McCrea entered the Police Force as a sub-Inspector on the 25th April, 1887. He served first in Kingston as a sub-Inspector, and afterwards in St. Elizabeth, going from that parish to St. Mary, where he commanded the division for some time. He was next transferred to the Clarendon division, where he served from 1891 until January 1909 when he was appointed Deputy Inspector-General and Officer Commanding the Kingston Division in succession to Mr. A.H. Webster Wedderburn, who had retired on pension.

On several occasions in the absence of the Inspector-General, Mr. McCrea acted as Inspector General. He married a Miss Macdonald daughter of the late Hon. Wm

Macdonald of "Water Valley" and then Custos of St Mary. He has two daughters and a son. The latter has just left school in England and gone to Canada.

Mr. McCrea's record in the Force has been a most creditable one all through. His career was particularly marked by his strict devotion to duty and in the fearless, impartial manner in which he discharged the duties attached to the responsible office he held. He did duty after the Riot at Montego Bay and was also in command of the Kingston division a the time of the Car Company's Riot. He figured prominently in the latter on account of the arrest of two citizens which he ordered at he beginning of the trouble.

Mr. McCrea was the author and compiler of "the Sub-Officer's Guide" a book which is most useful, not only to the members of the force but to the public as well. The deceased was 50 years of age. More.

May 5, 1913
McCREA--At his residence, 88 Hanover Street, Kingston, suddenly at 10 p.m. on Saturday May 3rd, 1913, HARRY McCREA, Deputy Inspector General, Jamaica Constabulary. Aged 50 years.

May 9, 1913
ST ANN BOARD--Special Meeting Called by The Vice Chairman--MR. LEVY'S RESIGNATION--Motion to be Proposed Asking Him to Continue Services.

(Special by Wire) From a Correspondent. St Ann's Bay, May 3--By order of the Vice-Chairman, a meeting of the St Ann Parochial Board was convened in the Board's office this morning, when there were present: Messrs. Roxburgh, Cameron, Tennant, Dillon, Hart and Baines, the object of the meeting was to decide what steps would be taken in connection with the recent resignation of Mr. J.H. Levy, Chairman of the Board, for so many years past.

It was agreed to call a special meeting on Thursday, the 8th inst., for the passing of a resolution of unbounded confidence in Mr. Levy, and for presenting a letter to him, praying the withdrawal of his resignation.

This meeting will be called at 2 p.m.

At 7 o'clock on the same evening a public meeting of the parishioners will be called in the Town Hall, for a like purpose.

The division on the Hon. J.H. Allwood's motion, which resulted in the chairman's resignation, was as follows: For the motion: Messrs. Allwood, Bramwell, Allen, Fowler, Brains and Brown (6) Against: Roxburgh, Cameron, Tennant, Dillon and Hart (5).

May 6, 1913
COVER-On Friday the 2nd inst., at 3 Geffrard Place, the wife of C.A. Cover, of a son.

VIEWS EXPRESSED BY READERS----Resignation of Mr. J.H. Levy From the St Ann Board.

THE RESIGNATION OF MR. J.H.LEVY

Sir-- I thank you for your leader in the Gleaner which reached me today, so far as it expresses an appreciation of the efficient services of Mr. J.H. Levy, as Chairman of the St Ann's Parochial Board for the past twenty years. I have lived in the parish for thirty-eight years, and have been conversant with the work of the Board and its Chairman, since the day of the Hon. Michael Solomon, and I think I speak the general opinion of the older inhabitants, when I say that no one has earned the confidence and respect and gratitude of his fellow-parishioners more fully or generally than Mr. Levy. I say earned it; because his chairmanship was no sinecure. He has at great personal sacrifice been for so long the leader in all our parochial affairs, and I am sure that the majority will feel that the parish has sustained a great loss by the retirement of one whose ability, and energy and experience in all public matters, made him the safeguard to parochial life at a time when so many younger, and perhaps more zealous, men are coming forward as our guides and counsellors, who will need the older heads to steady them. I know nothing of the personal conflict between the Hon J.H. Allwood and Mr. Levy, in their official positions, to which you refer. I regard both as personal friends, and refuse to enter into that side. The only source of any dissatisfaction which has recently arisen toward Mr. Levy, as Chairman, has been (so far as I have heard) that he did not secure, at the time when it is said he might have done it money that was available for a water supply for the Dry Harbour Mountains, and which is not now available, as it has been necessary to use it to feed the hungry and relieve the distressed that have been brought to destitution by the recent hurricane. I we grant this (though I do not admit it as proved) then the

MATTER RESOLVES ITSELF

into a claim that the need of the Dry Harbour Mountains for a better water supply is paramount, and more pressing than the relief of the multitudes in the western parishes, who were so suddenly plunged into destitution. This I don't think, any one would dare to assert, though the contention simmers down to that.

Mr. Levy and all of us, hoped that the money, which was wisely secured for a general water supply mainly through Mr. Allwood's efforts would have removed one of the great hardships, which oppresses this part of the island in times of drought; and this would have been the case, if a greater calamity had not befallen our neighbours. The storm, however, made their present distress far greater than ours, and I believe that the majority of our people, who have suffered so often through drought, would yet be quite ready to wait a little longer in their present condition, if the money expected to build them tanks, has had to be diverted to save life, or to provide shelter for those destitute through the calamity that has befallen them

I do not know whether Mr. Levy can be induced to resume his position on the Board. I fear not. But I would like publicly to express my regret that anything should have been said or done by residents in this parish, and especially in this part of St. Ann, where Mr. Levy's public services are so well known to wound him in any way, or to make it appear that we, as a people, are ungrateful or unappreciative, of the self-denying services he has rendered to us all. No man have given more freely of his time and energy for the public good, and no one has filled the position of chairman more efficiently, and he well deserves the grateful public recognition which many of us are glad to give him.
I am , etc
GEO. E. HENDERSON
The Chapel,
Brown's Town,
May 3rd, 1913

May 7, 1913
MAY ROBERTS--On the 16th April at St Mark's Islington, London, N. by the Rev. F.W. Ainley, M.A. Vicar of St. Andrews, London. N., GEORGE CYRIL McFARLANE MAY of the Colonial Civil Service, Southern Nigeria, to MINNA CONSTANCE, daughter of the Rev. James and Mrs. Roberts, Late of Gordon Town, Jamaica.

1913

May 9, 1913

THE ST ANN PAROCHIAL BOARD EULOGISES THE STERLING WORTH AND WORK OF MR. J.H. LEVY--resolution Passed at Special Meeting Yesterday--MOTION IS EXPUNGED--Late Chairman Cordially Invited to Resume Old Position.

(By Telegraph from our Correspondent)

St Ann's Bay. May 8--The special meeting of the St. Ann Parochial Board, convened to deal with the resignation of Mr. J.H. Levy as its chairman, came off at the Board's office at 2 o'clock this afternoon. There were present: Messrs Adam Roxburgh, Vice-Chairman: A.J. Hart, H.J. Wilmot, A.B. Geddes, E. C. Baines, H.G. Tennant, Joseph Cameron W. L. Levy and Rev. J .T. Dillon.

The Vice-Chairman opened the proceedings by stating the object of the meeting. He said the meeting was called to give effect to the resolution he had given notice to move, and to endeavour to remove from Mr. Levy's mind the impression that the Board had no confidence in him, and desired to censure him, which actuated him in handing in his resignation on the carrying of the resolution which stood in Mr. Allwood's name. The speaker eulogized Mr. Levy very highly and expressed deep regret at the incident which had occurred. He referred to Mr. Levy as being the man who knew more about the administration of the Parochial Board than any other individual, and spoke in very feeling terms of his zeal and devotion to the work of the Board. He said that while he was certain that every one who voted for the resolution did so with the purest motives, he was sorry the Chairman took it as a vote of want of confidence, as he was sure that no one who was present intended to convey to Mr. Levy the pain which must have resulted in his tendering his resignation. He stated that Mr. Allwood had written to him expressing his great confidence in Mr. Levy, and his regret at the turn affairs had taken.

The speaker read a part of Mr. Allwood's letter in that connection, and said he wished the resolution would be passed unanimously:

Telegrams from Messrs. J.C. Allen and T.A. Bramwell were then read heartily agreeing with the spirit of the resolution, as also letters from Messrs. H.A. Fowler and Hamilton Brown.

A RESOLUTION

The Vice-Chairman then moved the following resolution: "That the Parochial Board of St Ann hereby expresses and places on record the high appreciation it entertains of the unwearied and efficient services rendered to the Board, and to the parish it represents, by its highly esteemed Chairman, Mr. J.H.Levy. The Board expresses its unabated confidence in Mr. Levy, and his ability to preside over its meetings, and to guide its effort for the betterment of the parish and its inhabitants.

"It conveys to Mr. Levy a declaration of its sincere loyalty and the earnest hope that he may long be spared and be blessed with the health and strength needed for the high position he occupies as Chairman, which position the Board feels he adorns in an exceptional degree."

The Rev. Dillon endorsed the Vice Chairman's sentiments and seconded the resolution, which was carried unanimously.

The Rev. Dillon addressed the Board on a resolution he proposed to move. He said in effect that mistakes were made in the very best Legislative assemblies, and the Board was no exception to the rule. Very often mistaken resolutions were passed by small majorities, which bound the whole body, and brought it to public censure, which was the present position of the Board. A

MISTAKE HAD BEEN MADE

The Vice Chairman had taken a first step to rectify it, and Mr. Allwood a second in the letter read. He, (the speaker) desired to take the third step, and did so in moving the resolution standing in his name. He would do so without criticising anyone, or offering any comment on anything that had gone before.

Selected Vital Records from the Jamaican Daily Gleaner

The Vice Chairman called Mr. Dillon's attention to section 2 of bye-law 3 which required that notice of his motion should be given to the Clerk fourteen days before the meeting and sent by the Clerk to the members seven days before.

Mr. Dillon replied by quoting section one of bye-law fourteen which provided that it shall be competent for the Board to rescind, or expunge any resolution with or without notice of motion on the ground of irregularity, provided it be so expunged at any general or special meeting of the Board within one month from the passing thereof. He contended hat Mr. Allwood's motion was irregular in so far as it was not put in the hands of the clerk fourteen days before the meeting, at which it was moved, and challenged the clerk to deny that he had not received it within fourteen days.

The Clerk explained that in handing in his resolution, Mr. Allwood had called his attention to the fact that as it was not a motion involving expenditure of money, under section one of bye-law eight, the motion could come on.

The Vice Chairman said that it had been the custom of the Board for years, not to stick to the letter of bye law fourteen, but to discuss motions as Mr. Allwood's was done.

Mr. Dillon insisted that the bylaw should operate, and the Vice Chairman finally allowed the resolution, which was seconded by Mr. A. J. Hart, to be put. It is as follows:

"That the resolution moved by the Hon J.H. Allwood at the meeting of the Board on the 1st inst. appointing a special committee consisting of the Hon J.H. Allwood and Messrs. T.A. Bramwell, H.J. Wilmot and H.A.Fowler to secure water for the dry districts of the parish, be rescinded and expunged from the minutes of that meeting.

The motion was carried.

Mr. Baines declined to vote.

It is learnt that Mr. Levy has expressed himself as being unable to withdraw his resignation as long as Mr. Allwood's resolution remains on the minutes.

In the circumstances it is now quite open to Mr. Levy to return to the Board.

MR. ALLWOOD'S LETTER

Following is the full text of the letter of the Hon J.H. Allwood, sent to the Vice Chairman, of the Board, reference to which is made above:-

Dear Sir,

"Referring to the resignation of the Chairman and to the resolution to be moved to-morrow, expressing confidence in him, and the desire of the Board that he should resume the position, I have the honour to ask you to be so good as to convey to the Board my own expression of confidence in Mr. Levy, and commendation of his efficient and self-sacrificing services to the parish during a long term of years and my earnest wish that he should accede to the wishes of his fellow members and to the parishioners generally, and withdraw his resignation. Personally, I felt much regret that my motion appointing a special committee to deal with the water question should have caused Mr. Levy pain and occasioned his resignation, and I need hardly assure the Board that such was very far from the object of my motion, its only purpose being to secure some immediate action on behalf of the suffering people in the dry districts of the parish.

"With respect to M. Dillon's motion to rescind this resolution, I am of opinion that it is not in order, and is contrary to the rules of the Board; but I take the liberty of suggesting to the mover and the members of the Board, that the same effect which I assume is aimed at by he motion, will be secured if the name of Mr. Levy is added to the Committee, and that he be substitute and as Chairman thereof in place of myself.

"The personnel of this Committee was selected from among members representing the districts affected by drought, in the hope that thereby greater impetus would be given to the progress of the work entrusted to them.

"I am emboldened to make the above suggestion to the Board in the earnest hope that it may settle the controversy which has been aroused and enable the Board to continue peacefully and without acrimony to discharge the important duties entrusted to it.

"I have further to say that I opened up communication with the Government on Friday last, and on Tuesday the hydraulic engineer of the Public Works Department visited Brown's Town, and also with some members of the Committee and Mr. Levy, the plans and estimates for the Brown's Town supply were gone into and the site visited, and we understand that the engineer will report to the Governor during this week. The relation between Mr. Levy and the Committee during this conference were of a cordial and amicable character.

I find it impossible to be present at the Board's meeting to-morrow, hence I take the liberty of conveying my views to the Board through you, in the hope that my suggestion will be received in the same spirit of friendliness with which they are put forward.

I am etc.,

(Sgd) J.H. Allwood
St Ann's Bay,
7th May, 1913

May 10, 1913

POPULARITY OF MR. J.H. LEVY-Parishioners Ask Him to Resume Chairmanship--PUBLIC MEETING HELD--Unfortunate Incident was Result of a Misunderstanding.

(By Telegraph From Our Correspondent)

St Ann's Bay, Friday--A public meeting called to deal with the question of Mr. J.H. Levy's resignation as chairman of the Parochial Board for this parish, was held here last evening. The gathering, which was a very large and representative one, was presided over by Mr. Adam Roxburgh, vice-chairman of the Board.

The chairman, in very eloquent speech, spoke in the highest possible terms of Mr. Levy as a man, as a merchant and as chairman of the Parochial Board. He declared that the recent unfortunate trend of affairs was the result of a misunderstanding as it was absolutely impossible for Mr. Levy to have been neglectful over what had been his life's aim i.e. a water supply for the dry districts.

Letters were read from Messrs. Arthur Townend and A.N. Dixon expressing their hearty accord with the aim and object of the meeting, as was also a letter, signed by nearly 100 residents in and around Ocho Rios, expressing unbounded confidence in Mr. Levy, and begging that gentleman to withdraw his resignation and resume his old place as chairman of the Board.

VOTE OF CONFIDENCE

Mr. A.J. Webb moved a vote of confidence in Mr. Levy, and at the same time asking that gentleman to resume the chairmanship of the Board.

The resolution followed the general terms of the one passed at the Parochial Board's meeting earlier in the day, and published in yesterday's Gleaner.

Mr. H.G. Tennant seconded in a lengthy speech, in which he spoke of Mr. Levy as a chairman par excellence, and dealt very ably with Mr. Levy's methods at the Board, and his successful administration.

The motion was carried without a dissenting voice and amidst uproarious applause.

A deputation, consisting of Messrs. A.J. Webb, J.J. Lyon, A.W. Rerrie, H.G. Tennant and the Rev. E.A. Jones was appointed to wait upon Mr. Levy next Tuesday, and convey to him the resolution as passed.

Rev. E.A. Jones proposed a vote of thanks to M. Roxburgh, for presiding. Mr. A.J. Hart seconded the motion, which was carried unanimously. Mr. Roxburgh suitably replied, and the meeting terminated.

May 10, 1913 Editorial

HAS HARMONY AND AMITY BEEN RESTORED AT THE ST. ANN'S PAROCHIAL BOARD?

The parochial situation in St. Ann is still somewhat unsatisfactory, and, if anything, it is more complicated than ever. At the special meeting of the Board which was held on Thursday afternoon, a vote of wholehearted confidence in Mr. J.H. Levy as the Chairman was unanimously adopted; and handsome tributes were paid by those who spoke on the motion to the valuable services which that gentleman has rendered to the parish for fully a quarter of a century. In connection with the vote referred to, a letter from the pen of the Hon. J.H. Allwood to the Vice-chairman of the Board, was read; and no letter could possibly have been couched in more appreciative language, or conceived in a more friendly spirit. The surmise which was expressed in these columns several days ago, viz. that Mr. Allwood, in bringing forward his motion to appoint a Committee to expedite the work of supplying the dry districts with water had no desire to disparage the services of Mr. Levy, or diminish his influence and authority, or would his susceptibilities, was corroborated in every detail by the hon. member for the parish. Indeed, it would be difficult to find in the political and administrative literature of this colony--or for that part of it, any other British colony-- a more generous and manly document than the one addressed by Mr. Allwood to Mr. Roxburgh; and we cannot help thinking that, after such a display of confidence in, and appreciation of the work of Mr. Levy-after Mr. Allwood had publicly express his desire to be associated with the other members of the Board in their expression of loyalty to the Chairman --it was a mistake for the Rev. J. T. Dillon to bring forward his resolution with regard to the rescinding and expunging from the minutes, the motion passed at the previous meeting on the initiative of the representative of the parish in the Legislative Council. In his letter Mr. Allwood pointed out "a more excellent way" -a way by which all difficulties would be smoothed away, and all friction or misunderstanding overcome in a manner satisfactory to all the parties concerned. He pointed out that justice would be done to the Chairman if his (Mr. Levy's) name were added to the Committee; and he further stated that he would glad to see Mr. Levy accepting the chairmanship of the Committee instead of himself. Why was not that friendly and generous suggestion acted on-more especially after the Vice-Chairman's resolution expressing complete confidence in the unalterable loyalty to Mr. Levy, had been passed unanimously and with Mr. Allwood's cordial approval?

Magnanimity in Public Men

Our Correspondent says that it was rumoured in St. Ann's Bay, before the special meeting was held, that Mr. Levy was not prepared to re-consider his resignation as long as Mr. Allwood's resolution remained on the minutes. But we have some hesitation in accepting such a report as accurate. We have known Mr. Levy for a great many years; and, whilst he is in some ways, a proud spirited man-the pride he possesses is of the right sort-still we have never seen any evidence of small-mindness in him, nor have we ever had reason to believe him capable of acting from personal pique rather that from a sense of public duty, in a matter affecting the vital interests of his fellow-parishioners. Moreover, the attitude taken up by the Vice-chairman, when Mr. Dillon rose to move his resolution, was in our opinion, in, inconsistent with the idea that he story which had gained currency was true. We do not suppose that any man in St Ann's parish knew better than Mr. Roxburgh the feelings that animated Mr. Levy and the line of action he was prepared to take. And yet Mr. Roxburgh tried in a gentle way to dissuade Mr. Dillon from proceeding with his motion--though when the matter was pushed to a decision he did not hesitate to support or vote for that motion. It was scarcely conceivable to us that so close a friend of Mr. Levy as Mr. Roxburgh is, and has long been, would have suggested the postponement of Mr. Dillon's resolution had he known that rescinding and deletion of Mr. Allwood's motion at the previous meeting was a "conditio sine qua non" to the return of Mr. Levy as Chairman of the Parochial Board. What we now fear is that the member for the parish will be tempted to regard himself has having been insulted, and treated in an utterly harsh and contemptuous manner by the rejection of his peace proposals. And very few intelligent outsiders will venture to deny that, if Mr. Allwood should decide to regard the latest action of the Board as a distinct "slap in the face" to himself, he would have ample justification for so doing. Yet we hope, for the sake of the parish, which both he and Mr. Levy have served so long and so well, that he will trample any such temptation under foot--that he will show the same magnanimous spirit in his conduct now has he displayed in the letter which was read at Thursday's meeting of the Board. It would be infinitely regrettable if, as a result of any personal disappointment and irritation, Mr. Allwood's interest in securing water supplies for the dry districts of St. Ann, were to be diminished to the slightest possible extent. Public necessities should leave no room for the exhibition of personal antagonisms. We venture to express the earnest hope that matters will be allowed to rest just where they are that further recriminations will be carefully avoided and that Mr. Levy and Mr. Allwood will now, not only find it possible, but deem it urgently necessary, to work harmoniously together in order to secure for the dry districts of the parish adequate storage tanks, such as the prolonged drought of recent years have proved to be absolutely essential for the maintenance of public health and individual comfort. There can be, there need be, no rivalry between Mr. Levy and Mr. Allwood' and we are sure that no intelligent resident of St Ann has any desire to play off the one against the other. Both gentlemen have a work to do for the parish which no other man can do quite so well. And if the electors want to see Mr. Levy resuming the Chairmanship of the Parochial Board, they have equal confidence in Mr. Allwood as their representative in the Legislative Council.

May 16, 1913

HOPWOOD-At his father's residence Hope-Ville, Mandeville on the 10th instant, WILFRED STANLEY, in his 44th year. "In his lifetime, greatly loved at his death, deeply lamented".

WEDDERBURN-At Petersfield on Wednesday, 14th inst., WALTER WEDDERBURN, leaving 3 sons and 3 daughter to mourn their loss. Aged 84 years.

May 16, 1913

GOOD WORK OF MR. J.H. LEVY--His Recent Resignation From Parochial Board.--A VOTE OF CONFIDENCE.
(From a Correspondent).

A representative public meeting took place at the St. Ann's Bay Court House on Thursday, the 8th inst., over which the vice-chairman of the Parochial Board, Mr. A. Roxburgh, presided.

Among those present were: Messrs A.J. Webb, a former vice-chairman of the Board; A.B. Rerrie, J. J. Lyon, A.J. Hart, H. Tennant, G. Hunt, W. Levy, L. Reece, S. Thompson, Revds. A. Jones and J. Dillon, Dr. Myers, Messrs J. Cameron, G. Casserly, C. Hay, J. Ogle, R. Hobson, J. Miller, and Inspector Knowles.

Letters were read from Mr. Arthur Townsend and Mr. A. N. Dixon, supporting the vote of appreciation passed as hereunder:-

Selected Vital Records from the Jamaican Daily Gleaner

The Vice-Chairman, in opening the meeting, said that there was no necessity to enter into the history of the matter; there had been a misunderstanding which had led up to the Chairman of the Board (Mr. J.H.Levy) resigning his position, and they had convened this meeting to pass a vote of confidence in him as Chairman of the Board, and to shew their appreciation of his many years of able and useful work to the parish, and to endeavour to get him to retain his seat as Chairman of the Board; and before going any further, he read a letter from the Hon J.H. Allwood, regretting that his motion had had this effect as he only meant by the appointment to the committee to renew action in obtaining water supplies for the dry districts; and expressing his own vote of confidence in Mr. Levy, and commendation of his efficient and self-sacrificing services for the parish during the long term of years, and it was his earnest wish that Mr. Levy should withdraw his resignation. (Received with cheers).

The Chairman of the meeting then read Mr. A.N. Dixon's letter who voiced the feelings of every thoughtful and intelligent parishioner, "that from the history of Mr. Levy's lengthened service in the public interest, he would never consciously leave a stone unturned to secure the end, which he has made the very object of his daily life, namely to provide a proper water supply where it is urgently needed; and that the people of St Ann will not countenance or indeed tolerate this form of treatment to any citizen who faithfully and loyally performs his share of public service:. (Loud Cheers)

The Chairman, commenting on this letter, said that these were the views of one of the most far-seeing men in the parish, whose experience and judgement commanded attention and respect in every section of the parish.

A petition from Ocho Rios was presented, which was largely signed, asking the Chairman of the Board to withdraw his resignation and continue his activity as Chairman as his absence from the Board would be a public loss, and expressing their unabated confidence in him as Chairman of the Board, and their appreciation of his services to the parish.

The Chairman said that it was therefore, the universal belief of every inhabitant that Mr. Levy had accomplished a great deal for the parish, and no Chairman of the Board had ever devoted so much time and labour in the public interests over such a long period of years as Mr. Levy; so that it was their duty that he should rest under no aspersion, and that they should express the fullest confidence and appreciation of his service as Chairman of the Parochial Board of St Ann, and ask him to withdraw his resignation (Loud Cheers).

RESOLUTION PROPOSED

Mr. A.J. Webb then moved:--

"That this meeting of residents in and around St Ann's Bay having learnt that Mr. J.H. Levy of Brown's Town has resigned his position as Chairman of the Parochial Board of St Ann, hereby expresses the feeling of profound regret with which the intelligence has been received by all classes of the community, records its high appreciation of Mr. Levy's services to the parish during many years of public life, both as a member of the Legislative Council and of the Parochial Board. It recognizes gratefully the unselfish and self-sacrificing nature of those services, and declares its conviction that much of the prosperity enjoyed by the parishioners by reason of the comparative low rate of taxation for local purposes, is due to the ceaseless care and wise foresight of the Chairman of the Parochial Board; whilst, on the other hand, the progressive and enlightened policy of the Board is clearly to be seen in the improved sanitary condition of the towns and the excellence and ever increasing mileage of the roads under its care. All of which bear witness, that under Mr. Levy's Chairmanship, the Board has been kept alive to the interests of the inhabitants, and to the necessity of moving with the times.

"This meeting therefore hopes, and hereby tenders to Mr. Levy its earnest request, that he will reconsider his determination to resign his position at he Parochial

Board, and trusts that he will continue to perform the duties so efficiently discharge in the past".

Mr. Webb in speaking to the motion, said that he had been in the past for a long time associated with Mr. Levy and could bear testimony to the excellent work he had done at the Board and for the great amount of time and energy he expended on the public interests. As vice-chairman, he had on one occasion to act for Mr. Levy for a few months, and the volume of work that had to be dealt with made him doubly welcome the Chairman's resumption of the office. (Laughter). He was, therefore, in a position to say that Mr. Levy was pre-eminent among the chairmen of the Parochial Boards of the island in length of service and devotion to the public welfare. (Loud Cheers).

Mr. Tennant, in seconding the motion, shewed the interest the St. Ann Board had always taken in the water supply question. Long before there was any talk of a Government grant, the Board had formulated a scheme, whereby a tank would be put in every district of the parish out of Parochial Funds, and already several tanks had been built, the last one having been erected at Alderton, and the provision in the Parochial Estimates for this years was to erect a tank at Stepney in the Dry Harbour Mountains District, whether there was a Government grant or not, the very district which was now accusing the Board of inaction. The settled policy of the Board had been, that cost what it may, the Board would secure for every district an adequate water supply, and where it was most urgently needed would first be supplied, and the correspondence that had taken place shewed that this Board had lost no time in trying to get a Government grant and which was now pledged to them. From the time he had been at the Board, he could testify to and admire the administration of the Chairman, and the Dry Harbour Mountains had the greatest interest of the Chairman, who had used his utmost endeavours to get as much benefit as he could for this portion of the parish, especially in regard to water supplies. First came the Cascade Scheme, which was to benefit every district from Cave Valley to Dry Harbour; and for years that was tried to be got, but the spring was inadequate, and they knew how keen the Chairman was to get this to give every house in the Dry Harbour Mountains water; then there was the Dornock water supply, and an extensive catchment scheme to give Brown's Town water. As Mr. Dixon had said, not a stone had been left unturned to get water, both by the Chairman and the Board.(Loud Cheers).

The motion was put to the House and unanimously carried, and a deputation, consisting of Messrs. A.J. Webb, J.J. Lyon, A. Rerrie, H. Tennant and the Rev A. Jones was appointed to convey this resolution to the Chairman, and to use their influence to get him to continue his services to the parish.

Mr. W. Levy, who was present, thanked the meeting for their very kind mention of his father's work, and was proud at the way the people of St Ann's Bay had taken up his cause (Cheers)

The Rev. A. Jones moved a vote of thanks to Mr. Roxburgh for presiding over their meeting. Seconded by Mr. A.J. Hart and carried.

Mr. Roxburgh thanked the meeting.

The meeting then adjourned.

May 17, 1913
THE WINNER OF THE JAMAICA SCHOLARHSIP [Picture]
Mr. G.S.Escoffery.

PROGRESS MADE BY HIGH SCHOOL--Prize Giving Day at St Ann Training Institution.--THE ANNUAL REPORT-- Rev. J.W. Graham Congratulated on Success of His Work.
(From Our Correspondent)

Selected Vital Records from the Jamaican Daily Gleaner

Brown's Town May 16, Despite the rain which fell yesterday afternoon, a fairly large number of the residents in and around this town assembled at the St Ann High School in response to the invitation of the Principal to witness the first annual prize-giving in connection with the institution.

The proceedings began at 5 o'clock when the Principal called the meeting to order and requested Rev. J.P. Hall, Rector of Brown's Town, to take the Chair.

Mr. Hall expressed his pleasure in being present and deferred his remarks to a later stage in the proceedings. He then called on the Principal the Rev. J. W. Graham to read the report on the school for 1912 which he did as follows:

THE REPORT

"The St Ann High School was started in February 1911 at Claremont, immediately on my return to the island from Costa Rica. That locality did not however, lend itself to the development of such an institution: and in October of that year I accepted the invitation of the Rev. J. Kissock Braham, B.D. to transfer the school to Brown's Town.

The School began the Epiphany Term last year in the building with 21 boys, of whom four were my own and four were boarders who came with the school from Claremont. Two of the remaining thirteen were also admitted as boarders.

"The work of the school for 1912 was, on the whole, satisfactory. We had the usual drawbacks associated with beginnings: but I am glad to say they were not such as could not be overcome by an expenditure of energy, aided by the kindness of those friends who are interested in the work. The growth of the school has been slow, but I hope, sure. The year closed with 27 boys in attendance, being an increase of six for the year under review.

The school course was arranged to follow, as far as it maybe possible, the line of the Cambridge Local Examination. At the 1st examination, four candidates succeeded in satisfying the examiners, and their certificates will be presented to them today. As they were all over 14 years of age they were not eligible for marks of distinction.

"During the year under review, arrangements were made for a course in manual training in connection with the Government School in this town. Twelve boys began the course in May but the instructor left in September and the work was suspended. It was resumed in January, and the exhibits to the work before you is partly the result of the 1913 classes. This school is as far as I know the only secondary school in the island with the exception of Titchfield which has a manual training department attached to it.

"With regard to sports, I regret to say that there has not been sufficient interest displayed by the boys. Through the kindness of Mr. Braham a part of the common at Egypt was prepared at considerable expense as a football ground. For the first few months a certain amount of enthusiasm was evinced, and good sport was the result. Unfortunately, the enthusiasm waned, and I am afraid has now died out altogether. I am now making arrangements to start the Boys Scout movement in connection with the school which I hope will meet with a better fate.

" I cannot close this report without expressing my deep gratitude to all those who, in one way or another, have helped to make the work a success so afar. I must specially convey my thanks to those whose names will appear later on as donors of prizes, for the very ready and generous response to my appeal. With out their substantial aid, the function in which we are how taking part would have been impossible.

"I must also tender my thanks to all the friends who have taken the trouble to come here this afternoon, which I take it is an outward and visible sign of their interest in the school. Specially the Rev. Frank R. Cocks, M.A. of Woking, England, who has kindly consented to distribute the prizes:

"The Chairman introduced the Rev Frank R. Cocks, M.A. who had been specially asked to distribute the prizes.

1913

Mr. Cocks spoke a few words expressing his pleasure at being present, and his appreciation of the work which he understood was being done in the school. He thought it a great advantage to have a school of its kind here. He then distributed the prizes as under.

PRIZE LIST 1913

Upper Division

Good conduct, Silver medal (Presented by Rev. J. Kissock Braham, B.D.): Percival H. Gale.

General Improvement, Silver medal (Presented by Hon.J.H. Allwood, M.L.C.): Harold A. Graham

Religious knowledge (Prize presented by His Grace the Archbishop):John K. Braham.

English, Prize (presented by C.R. Thomson, Esq.): J Noel Thomson

History (Prize presented by L.A. Rattigan, Esq.): H.A. Graham

Geography, (Prize presented by Mrs. Philpotts): J. K. Braham

Mathematics, (Prize presented by His Honour the Custos): P.H. Gale

Drawing, (Prize presented by Rev J.P. Hall J.P.) P.H.Gale

Manual training (Prize presented by J.H. Levy, Esq.): P.H. Gale

Dux, Cambridge Examination prize presented by C.L. Philips, Esq.): Noel Thomson.

LOWER DIVISION

Good conduct, (Prize presented by Alex. Hopwood, Esq.): Edward Braham

General Improvement (presented by A. Hopwood, Esq.): Rupert Lyon.

Elementary Science, Silver medal, (presented by Hon P.C. Cork, when Acting Governor): Frank E. Graham.

Religious knowledge, (presented by His Grace the Archbishop): Frank Graham

English (presented by C.R. Thomson, Esq.), Frank Graham.

History (presented by L.A. Rattigan, Esq.):Frank Graham

Geography: Fred A. Paterson

Mathematics (presented by His Honour the Custos): W.E.L. Trewick.

Drawing, (presented by Rev. J.P. Hall), Frank Graham

Diligence, (presented by John A. Thomson, Esq.): Robert Byles

Home work, presented by J.F Isaacs, Esq.): Edward Braham

Manual training (presented by J. H. Levy Esq.): W.E.L Trewick.

FORM PRIZES

Form IV.--Harold Graham

Form III- Leonard Thomas

Form II Rupert Lyon

Cambridge Certificates: John Noel Thomson, Harold A. Graham, Richmond Braham and Percival Gale.

The rector spoke of the school as supplying a long felt need in the community, and congratulated Mr. Graham on the success which had so far attended his efforts. He congratulated the boys who had won prizes, and urged the others to strive for a similar distinction next year.

Mr. Braham said that he felt it particularly fitting that he should say something on the occasion as he had been dubbed (and he was far from resenting it) the Godfather of the school. He felt it had far exceeded his most sanguine expectation. Knowing however, Mr. Graham's ability, scholastic attainment and power to impart what he knew, he would be very much surprised if it were otherwise.

The chairman asked Messrs. H.F. Isaacs, C.R. Thomson, J.A. Thomson and Miss Turner (Local headmistress of the Deaconess High School) and Mr. H.G. Gauntlett to say a few words.

In all instances they spoke appreciatively of the work of the school and hoped for its further success.

The chairman then closed that part of the proceeding by one more urging the boys to apply themselves to their studies with a view to taking their places in the world in future years.

He thanked the audience on behalf of the Principal for their presence, and Mr. Cocks for finding time during his short holiday in Jamaica to show his sympathy with the educational side of life in the island.

Refreshments were then served to the boys and visitors and all left feeling that the function was a successful one.

June 5, 1913

RAFFINGTON-On 31st May at Green Castle, St Ann, ELLEN RAFFINGTON, aged 83, eldest daughter, of the late Dr. Thomas Raffington. R.I.P.

June 7, 1913

[Frontpage]TO SIT IN LEGISLATIVE COUNCIL ON TUESDAY--[Picture]
Mr. J.H. Levy , the able Chairman of the St Ann Parochial Board, who will take his seat in the Legislative Council next week as a nominated member.

DETAILED REPORT

Pursuant to adjournment the Honourable Legislative Council met at Headquarters House at 2 p.m. yesterday afternoon.
Present:
His Excellency Brigadier-General Sir William Henry Manning, K.C.M.G., C.B., Governor, President
Ex-Officio Members.
Hon. Philip Clarke Cork, C.M.G. Colonial Secretary,
Hon. Ernest St John Branch, K.C. Attorney-General,
Hon John D'Aeth, I.S.O., Acting Director of Public Works,
Hon Alfred Henry Miles, I.S.O., Collector General,
Nominated Members
Hon. Sir John Pringle, K.C.M.G. Custos, St Mary.
Hon. Louis John Bertram, C.M.G. Auditor-General,
Hon. Dr. John Errington Ker, S.M.O.
Hon. Herbert Henry Cousins, Director of Agriculture.
Hon. James Rowland William, Director of Education.
Hon. Dugald Campbell.
Hon. John Barkly Lucie-Smith, Postmaster for Jamaica.
Elected Members
Hon. J.H. Allwood, St Ann.
Hon. David Aurelius Corinaldi, St James,
Hon. J.M. Farquharson, St Elizabeth.
Hon. F.R. Evans, Westmoreland,
Hon. H; Cork, St Thomas,
Hon. A.A.Fleming, St Catherine.
Hon. Edmund Archibald Henderson Haggart, St Andrew,
Hon. C. W. Hewitt, Hanover.
Hon. Hubert Ashton Laselve Simpson, Kingston.
Hon. Stephen Samuel Stedman, Portland
Hon. Rev. Walter Booth Esson, Manchester.

1913

THE MINUTES

The minutes of the last meeting were read and confirmed.

NEW MEMBERS

Mr. J. H. Levy, nominated member, and Col. A.E. Barchard, acting G.O.C. were sworn in as members of the Council.

More.

RECENT EXAMINATIONS IN MUSIC HELD HERE--Publication of the highly Interesting results--THE DIFFERENT SCHOOLS--Long List of the Successful Candidates in Jamaica.

The following are the results of the examination of the Associated Board of the Royal Academy of Music and the Royal College of Music held in Jamaica a short time ago: [Not a complete list]

LICENTIATE ASSOCIATED BOARD(Solo Performer's Examination)
Miss G. DePass, Pianoforte
Local Centre Examination
Advanced Grade
B. Jeffrey-Smith, Pianoforte, Spanish Town.
Intermediate Grade
Florence Scudamore, Pianoforte, Hampton
Hilda Duff, Pianoforte, Brampton
Madeline Isaacs, Pianoforte, Brampton
Miriam Rattigan, Pianoforte, Kingston
Beryl Scudamore, Pianoforte, Brampton
Rudiments of Music
Hilda Duff, Brampton School
Madeline Isaacs, Brampton School
Miriam Rattigan.
Florence Scudamore, Brampton School
Beryl Scudamore, Brampton School
Avis Costa, Hampton School
Louise deSouza, Hampton School,
Ruby E. Mills, Hampton School
SCHOOL EXAMINATION
Higher Division
Gladys Reid, Piano, Hampton School
Lilian Gruber, Piano, Hampton
Edith Livingston, violin, Mr. H.E. Rombey, Kingston
Lower Division
Elise Sanftleben, Piano, Hampton School
Carmen Muschett, Piano, Hampton School
Dorothy Nuttall, Piano, Miss A. Bickwith, Cross Roads
Inez Martinez, Piano, Miss I. Facey , Cross Roads
Rose Harty, Piano, Deaconess High School, Brown's Town
Lilian Calder, Piano, Miss Edith Marson, Malvern
Sibyl Hart, Piano, Brampton School
Hilda Cohen, Piano Duke Street Convent
Barbara Ormsby, Piano, Colonial High School
Elementary Division
Violet Levy, Piano, Deaconess High School, Brown's Town

Nesta Nash, Piano, Deaconess High School, Brown's Town
Sally Young, Piano Deaconess High School Brown's Town.
Sydney Gayner, Piano (Distinction)Miss McFadyen Smith, Kingston
Moira Escoffery, Piano, Brampton School
Barbara Isaacs, Piano, Brampton School
Pearl Snaith, Piano, Mrs. Parkinson, Cross Roads
Winifred Rattigan, Piano, Miss M. Rattigan, Kingston
Stepanie Isaacs, (Dis.). Piano Convent of Mercy, Alpha
Vera Magnus, piano, Mr. E.P. Sibthorpe, Kingston
Daniel Marchelleck, Piano, Ven. Archdeacon Simms, Jamaica College
Vera Dixon, Piano, Mr. A.M. Soutar, Kingston
Ena Muschett, Piano, Miss Mildred Thomas, Malvern
Edna Murray, Piano, Westwood High School
Sylvia Silvera Piano, Westwood High School
Nina Lannamann, Piano, (Dis.) Colonial High School, Kingston
Zillah Lannamann, Piano, (Dis.) Colonial High School, Kingston
PRIMARY DIVISION
Doris Motta, Piano, Miss A. A. Carter, Kingston
E. Rutty, Piano, Miss H. Davis, Port Maria
Vivian Morris, piano, Deaconess High School, Brown's Town
Edna Atkinson, piano, Deaconess High School, Brown's Town
Elsie Stephenson, piano, Deaconess High School, Brown's Town
Elsie Geddes, piano, Deaconess High School, Brown's Town
Sylvia McConnell, piano, Deaconess High School, Brown's Town
Alice Roper, piano, Brampton School, Mandeville
Mary Scudamore, piano, Brampton School, Mandeville
Donald Motta, piano, Brampton School, Mandeville
Anthony Isaacs, piano, Brampton School, Mandeville

June 19, 1913
WAR OF WOMEN--Sentences Passed on many Militant Suffragettes.--MUST DO
HARD LABOUR.--Defendants Also Ordered to pay costs of Prosecution--BOUND
OVER TO KEEP PEACE.
(Special Service Cable)
[By Direct W.I.Co., via Bermuda]
London June 17--Mr. Justice Phillmore passed sentences on the Militant
Suffragettes today as follows:--Miss Annie Kenney, eighteen months; Mrs. Beatrice
Saunders, fifteen months; Miss Harriet Kerr, twelve months; Miss Rachael Barrett, nine
months; Miss Agnes Lake and Miss Laura Lennox, six months each and E. Clayton, the
chemist, twenty-one months.
All prisoners were committed to the third division which entails hard labour.
Each defendant was ordered to pay one seventh of the cost of the prosecution, and they
were bound over to keep the peace for a year after the period of imprisonment.

MORE DAMAGE DONE.
London, June 17--The Library of St. John's College, Cambridge, has been closed to the
public following the discovery that the backs of some 3,000 books had been slashed. A
"Votes for Women" card was found nearby.

June 21 1913
WELLER-MAY-At Rosedale, Trinity Church, B.N. Bottom by the Honble. and Revd
W.B.Esson, assisted by the Rev. Nathan Bacquie, JAMES WILLIAM, third son of the

1913

late Mr. and Mrs. William Weller, Black River to DOROTHY AMANDA, third daughter of Mr. and Mrs. George May of Cliff Villa, Rosedale.

SMITH-At Hill View, Church Lane, St Andrew on Wednesday 18th instant at 2 a.m. ESTHER MARGARET BROWNEL (Nellie) the second daughter of the late Joseph Gordon Smith of Eastwood Park, St Andrew.

July 5, 1913
MURRAY-At "The Lodge", Arnold Road, Kingston, on Thursday July 3rd the wife of Dr. E.E. Murray, of a daughter (Kathleen)

TIE QUEE FAT-At Nan Tow, China on the 9th May 1913, the father of Tie Ten Quee and Willie Tie Ten Quee of this city age 69 years. Deeply regretted.

July 14, 1913
COVER-ELLA JANE, Wife of the late Geo. Cover of St Ann, on the 12th inst. at her residence 133 East Street at 8 p.m. leaving a daughter and son and several friend to mourn their irreparable loss. Peace perfect Peace.

July 25, 1913
NEW "MOVIES"--Opening of Cross Roads Theatre Last Night.--FINE ENTERTAINMENT--Instructive and Amusing Pictures Thrown on the Screen.

July 26, 1913
JENSEN-In loving memory of Frances Louisa, dearly beloved wife of Chresten Marinus Jensen, and mother of Albet Kierstine and Amy, who left us on the morning of the 26th July, 1911

July 28, 1913
MOTTA-BRANDON-At Emma Ville, South Camp Road on Wednesday the 23rd inst., ALFRED EVELYN, son of the late Daniel I. Motta to IRIS SELNA, daughter of the late Isaac S. Brandon. At Home at Emma Ville, South Camp Road on Wednesday and Thursday evenings the 30th and 31st inst. from 7.30.

August 12, 1913
OUT ONCE MORE-Mrs. Pankhurst Set Free From Holloway Jail--AND UNUSUAL RECORD--Members of Deputation Arrested at House of Commons.

London July 25--Mrs. Pankhurst was released from prison again last evening. She was taken from Holloway to her flat in Westminster in a motor ambulance. According to a suffragette statement she was "broken down and practically at death's door". Dr. Flora Murray, who is medically attending her at her flat, last night called in three consultant doctors. When she was arrested on Monday last at the Pavillion, Mrs. Pankhurst threatened to "Hunger, thirst, and walk" strike. She was sentenced on April3 to three years penal servitude, and the diary of her subsequent movements is as follows:
April 12 Released
May 26 Rearrested.
May 30 Released
June 14 Rearrested.
June 16 Released
July 21 Rearrested
July 24 Released.

August 16, 1913
MUIRHEAD-Katherine Fitzhenry Muirhead, beloved wife of Easton W. Muirhead of Mandeville, on 12th inst. in her 46th year, after many years of patient suffering.

HOPWOOD At his residence Hope Ville, Mandeville, on the 11th inst., JAMES HOPWOOD, leaving a wife, four children and grand children and a large circle of friends to mourn their irreparable loss. Aged 76. Thy will be done. (English and American papers please copy)

WEDDING BELLS-Fashionable Wedding at Spanish Town.--CATHEDRAL CROWDED--Dr Wilson of Brown's Town and Miss Una Jeffrey-Smith
An extremely pretty wedding took place in the Cathedral at Spanish Town on Thursday afternoon, when Miss Una Jeffrey-Smith, second daughter of Mr. and Mrs. C.A. Jeffrey-Smith, was married to Dr. W.E. Wilson of Brown's Town, St Ann.
The Cathedral was tastefully decorated with flowers, the service was choral; and the whole building was so crowded that there was no standing room left unoccupied.
Precisely at three o'clock the bridal party arrived. The bride who was given away by her father, was gowned in ivory white charmuese satin, draped with pearl ornaments and wore a magnificent court train. Her veil was held with orange blossoms.
The train bearers were the nephew and niece of the bride (Daisy and Charlie Jeffrey-Smith, attired in page costume caskate greenaway.
The bride's mother wore grey duchesse satin draped in figured rose ninon and carried a bouquet of scarlet roses. The bridesmaids wore blue ninon draped with pink satin and carried bouquets of pink roses also gold swastika charms, gifts of the bridegroom.
The bestman was Mr. L.C. Jeffrey-Smith.
The Rev. Canon Hendrick, assisted by Revs. C.M. Buckley and G.C. Hedmann, performed the ceremony, which occupied just half an hour. When it was over the party drove to Durham House, the residence of the bride's parents, where the newly wedded couple received the guests.
The usual toasts were drunk and Mr. and Mrs. Wilson left for Eton Hall, St Ann, at about 5.30 o'clock, the guests remaining until nearly seven.
The presents were numerous. The bridegroom presented the bride with a beautiful sapphire and diamond ring. The bride gave the bridegroom an engraved ring. The guests present were:
Canon and Mrs. Hendrick, Rev. and Mrs. Buckley, Rev. and Mrs. Hedmann, Dr. and Mrs. W.D. Neish, Dr., Mrs. and Miss Huntly Peck, Major Drummond, Mr. and Mrs. Knetcht, Mr. and Mrs. Ryley, Mr. and Mrs. Bateman, Mr. and Mrs. Frank Billingslea, Mr. T. Sharp, Mr. and Mrs. H. Smith, Mr. R. L. Rivett, Mr. and Mrs. Gilpin Hudson, Mr. and Mrs.Herbert G. deLisser, Mr. R. Bloxham, Mr. and Mrs. W. Jones, Miss Townend, Miss Thomson, Mr. McKella, Mr. Aitken, Mr. and Mrs. Hay, Mr. and Mrs. Brooks Douet, Miss Daisy Wortley, Mrs. and Miss Stephenson, Mrs. Janzen, Sister Madeline, Mr. A.Simms.

LIST OF PRESENTS
Following is the list of presents:
Bishop and Mrs. Joscelyne, set of cut glass finger bowls; Canon and Mrs. Hendrick, pair silver candlesticks; Rev. Mr. and Mrs. Buckley, pair silver photo frames; Rev. Mr. and Mrs. Hall, silver vases; Rev. Mr. and Mrs. F.C. Hedmann, pair silver pepper and salt castors; Dr. and Mrs. Hargraves, set silver tea spoons, tong and sifter; Rev. Dr and Mrs. Turner (London), Bread board and silver tray; Dr. W. E. Smith, silver

tongs; Dr and Mrs. Lopez(Panama) crumb tray and scoop; Dr. and Mrs. Peck, picture with mirror; Dr. and Mrs. Neish, set of fruit knives; Maj. Drummond, silver vase; Mr. and Mrs. Jeffrey-Smith cheque; Mr. L.C. Jeffrey-Smith wedgewood china tea set; the Misses Jeffrey-Smith, set of silver and case; Mrs. Miller (Edinburgh), silver and spiral vases; Mrs. and Miss Scott, embroidered tea clothe; Miss Barron (New York), sofa cushion; Mr. Webb, tea set; Mrs. Rebeiro, crochet cloths; Mr. and Mrs. Knetcht, cheque; Mr. and Mrs. Ryley, pair silver candlesticks; Mr. and Mrs. T. Sharp, silver ink pot; Mr. and Mrs. Billingslea, silver sugar castor; Mr. and Mrs. Howard Smith, tete-a-tete breakfast tea set; Mr. and Mrs. Bateman, silver bon-bon dish; Mr. and Mrs. Jones, fruit forks; Miss G. Millon, set silver serviette rings; Mrs. and Miss Scott, embroidered tea cloth, Miss W. Isaacs, knitting; the Misses Thompson, sugar tongs: Mr. and Mrs. Thompson, silver bell; Mr. and Mrs. Lindo, sugar bowls and scoop; Mr. and Mrs. Dunckley, fruit knives; Mr. R.A. Bloxam, individual butter, sugar and Jam spoon in case; Mr. and Mrs. Stockhausen, egg stand and spoons; Mr. and Mrs. Hay, silver clock; Mr. and Mrs. A. Hall, half dozen silver tea spoons, Mr. C. Aitken, silver sandwich tongs; Mr. and Mrs. Yanzen, silver cut glass knife rests; Miss D. Peck, ivory fan; Mr. and Mrs. Hudson, silver butter dish and knife; the Misses Hudson, silver bell; Master C. N. and Miss D. Jeffrey-Smith, oak and silver gong; Mr. Brennan, silver butter dish; Mr.and Mrs. deLisser, silver fish slice and fork; Mr.and Mrs. McKella, 1 dozen brass finger bowls; Miss Haydee Fiddes silver ink well; Miss D. Wortley, drawn thread cloth; Miss Murray, embroidered cushion; Nurse Green, 3 vases; Mr. and Mrs. Books Douet, set of lace bark doyles; Mr. and Mrs. C. Levy, set of fruit knives; Mrs. Millener, 2 silver serviette rings; Mr. and Mrs. J. Dodd, cut glass silver scent bottle.

August 18, 1913
HOGG-Colin Alexander Chisholm, at his late residence No 4 Sutton Street, at 7.30 o'clock last evening, in his 74th year. Funeral will move from the above address at 4.30 p.m. today. Friends please accept this only intimation. Had he asked us we should say Lord we love him, let him stay.

August 20, 1913
GAETJENS-BOURKE-On the 31st July 1913 at the Cathedral, Port-au-Prince Haiti, RAOUL GAETJENS to MARIE LORINSKA BOURKE, fourth daughter of the late Wellesley Bourke, solicitor.

August 23, 1913
WILSON-JEFFREY-SMITH-On 14th August, at the Cathedral, Spanish Town, WILBERT EDWARD WILSON, M.D. Brown's Town to UNA JEFFREY-SMITH, second daughter of C.A. Jeffrey Smith.

August 27, 1913
BROWN-On the 23rd inst. at Hermon Hill, Dry Harbour, ESTELLE EVANGELINE, eldest daughter of Rev. and Mrs. S.T Brown. verse.

August 30, 1913
The following guests registered at South Camp Road Hotel during the fortnight ended Thursday, 21st inst.,:
Mr. and Mrs. C.A. Michelin and two sons, Plantain Garden River, Mr.A.C. Bancroft, Stokes Hall P.G.River; Mr. J. H. Watson, Costa Rica; Mr. E. Bouppacher, Spanish Town, Mr. and Mrs. J. B. Smith, Washington, D.C. Mr. L.G. Silvera, Port Maria; Mr. W.H. Rerrie, Montego Bay; Mr. W. Morris, Westmoreland; Mr. E. Roden, England; Mr. H. Vandenburg, Port Antonio; Mr. W.S. Pickwick, Port Maria; Mr.J. H.Snelson,

Bristol Pa; Mr. S.G. Snelson Palmyra, N.J.; Mr. James Gilliland New York City; Miss Louise C. Ball, New York City; Mr. and Mrs. G.E. Scudamore, Port Antonio; Mr. J. R Howe, Kingston; Mr. W. Hugh Walker, Claremont; Mr. S. Scudamore, Montpelier; the Misses Scudamore, Port Antonio, Master R. Scudamore, Port Antonio. Mr. Lionel J. Hawthorn. Guilsbro, Montego Bay; Mr. David Horn, Kellets; Mr. A. Livingston Hirst, London; Rev Jno A. McIntosh, Ramble; Mr. W. E. Percy, New Orleans; Mr. F.S. Thomson, Kingston; Mr. B.H. Segre, Sav-la-Mar; Mr. Leslie W. Levy, Brown's Town; Mr. R.A. Tavares, Sav-la Mar; Mr. W.G. Eggins, Kingston; Mr. E.H.Delvaille, Sav-la-Mar Mr. D. Geo McConnell, Alexandria; Miss Sylvia McConnell, Alexandria, Major. W.O Little, Windermere, England Mr. Percy Fox, St Ann.

September 5, 1913
NIGHTENGALE-At the Villa, Mandeville, on 2nd September, the wife of Capt. W.H. Nightengale, 1st W.I. Regiment of a daughter.

CURRENT ITEMS
The Hon. J.H. Levy of Brown's Town and Mrs. J.H. Levy, returned from New York yesterday on the U.F. Coy's steamer Tivives.

September 9, 1913
FOWLER-BRAHAM-At Retirement, St Ann, on Wednesday 3rd Sept., HORACE ALEXANDER, second son of the late H.E. Fowler of Shawbury, St. Ann, to AGNES MAUD MARIA youngest daughter of John R. V. Braham of Retirement Pen, St Ann.

September 10, 1913
BOVELL-At St Leonard's on Sea, Sussex, England, on the 9th inst., the wife of Capt. C.W. K. Bovell, Uganda Police, of a son.

September 12, 1913
TORONTO SHOW--Mr. J.H. Levy Replies to Mr. J. Barclay's Letter.--PACKING OF EXHIBITS--More Time Should be Allowed in Getting Up he Articles.

THE EDITOR,
Sir,--I am sorry that Mr. Barclay has forced me to return to one of the subjects of your interview with me on my return to the Island, i.e., the Toronto Exhibition, as I would have preferred to have left the matter where it was. What I said was not intended to cast any discredit on the Jamaica exhibits at the exhibition, or on the Agricultural Department, which was responsible for sending on the exhibits. Indeed, I tried to do full justice to the Jamaica Court, which was very attractive, and creditable to the Island, taking into account the short time allowed for getting up the exhibits.

What I wanted to emphasize more particularly, was that more time should be allowed for getting up and preparing the exhibits; and all that Mr. Barclay says in this respect in his letter is quite correct, and was fully known to me. I thought my letter would help to strengthen his hands and the Agricultural Society in future.

As regards the packages in which the exhibits were packed, I feel sure that Mr. Barclay could not have seen all of them, as he would have noticed several, with Chinamen's names and all kinds of marks; in many instance not stenciled, but marked with a brush, and badly marked too. They may have come from the independent exhibitors mentioned by Mr. Barclay, but there is no doubt that the packages presented an unfavourable contrast to those from the other islands and from the different sections of the Dominion, that were pouring in at the time. A cooper or any ordinary storeman could have scraped off all old marks from these packages. Mr. Barclay is wrong in saying that on the day in question, I entered the Exhibition as a privileged guest. It was one of the days of unpacking before the Exhibition was actually opened, and there were thousands of people besides myself. And as it is generally conceded that this time is among the best for advertizing (unpacking days) there is little wonder that so many people were there. Certainly, after the packages were opened, the exhibits displayed, and the packages packed away, the court looked very nice; and as said before, great credit is due to Mr. Cradwick for its appearance. At the same time, with my interest in the Island, I could not help remarking and commenting on what I thought was not creditable to the Colony, in the shape of these old and ugly packages.

I intend no censure on the Agricultural Society, or its able secretary, and I shall be surprised if my observations do not bear good fruit in the future.
I am etc.,
J.H. Levy,
Brown's Town
Sept 10, 1913

September 19, 1913
KIDSTON-TRENCH-At Parish Church, Kingston, on 17th inst. by Rev. Ripley, MALCOLM GLEN, 3rd son of William H. Kidston, Esq. of Helensburg, Scotland, to GLADYS, only daughter of Dutton Trench Esq. of Hazelymph, Cambridge, Jamaica.

September 20, 1913
REV. J.P. HALL
The Rev.J.P. Hall, rector of the Anglican Church at Brown's Town, was a passenger on the s.s. Prinz August Wilhelm yesterday from New York.

September 24, 1913
TODD-At Sportsman's Hall, Jackson Town on the morning of the 19th September, 1913, the wife of Utten T. Todd of a daughter.

September 25, 1913
MacGregor-At St Luke's Hospital, New York city, on the 20th inst., at 9 p.m. in his 66th year, the Rev. CHARLES GEORGE MacGREGOR, rector of the Parish Church, Falmouth. Funeral New York 24th inst. By Cable.

PANTON--At Manchioneal, ANNIE on 19th September, Aged 19 years. Not gone from memory, Not gone from love, But gone to her Fathers' home above.
Panama and Costa Rica papers please copy.

October 15, 1913
DUFF-On Monday night at Annotto CHARLES PERCIVAL, late of the Kingston General Commissioners in his 56th year leaving four children to mourn their loss. R.I.P.

October 16, 1913
DAVIS-At Ingleside, Brown's Town, St Ann, on Friday 10th October, 1913, ALISON HARVEY WINN, aged 13 years, third and beloved daughter of Alfred Harvey and the late Louisa Emily Davis.

October 18, 1913
FORREST-At Vineyard, St Elizabeth, on the 12th October, 1913, ANN, in her 96th year, relict of the late Sanford Forrest of South Kensington, England. The old chair is vacant, Oh we miss her.

October 20, 1913

FISHER-HARTY-In the Wesleyan Chapel, Stewart Town by the Rev. J. Kissock Braham B.D. on Sunday afternoon, JOSEPH FISHER of Mt. Pleasant Pen, St Ann, to LAURA ALICE, daughter of the late Albert J. Harty, and Mrs. Georgiana Harty, and the grand daughter of the late Rev. W. C. Harty, Congregational Minister, First Hill Trelawny.

FINE WELCOME FOR GOVERNOR--Receives Many addresses at St Ann's Bay-- NEEDS OF THE PARISH--Water Supply Must come Before the Public Parks.
(By Telegraph From Our Correspondent)

St Ann's Bay, Monday--His Excellency the Governor, accompanied by Capt. Dennistoun, acting A.D.C. and Mrs. Dennistoun, arrived her to-day at 12 o'clock from Shaw Park.

The Governor who was attired in uniform, was met by a guard of honour of sixteen constables under Inspector Knollys and Sergt. Major Magee. His Excellency inspected the guard and then drove along the main street, which was prettily decorated, and went to the Court House where the school children, who had assembled on both side of the entrance, sang Rule Britannia.

On entering the Court House, the Governor was met by Hons. J.H. Allwood and J.H. Levy, Senior Magistrate. Here an address was presented by the Hon. J.H. Allwood, on behalf of the people of St Ann. In this address a cordial welcome was accorded His Excellency, and he was asked for increased transport facilities, water supply for dry districts, and harbour improvements.

His Excellency thanked Mr. Allwood for his hearty welcome, and expressed the pleasure it gave him to meet with members of the Legislative Council, the Magistracy, as well as the Parochial Boards and all those who help to direct the welfare of the island. He would consider the points submitted when funds permitted. He paid a tribute to the ability of Mr. Allwood.

MAGISTRATE'S ADDRESS

Another address was then presented to His Excellency by Hon J.H. Levy, on behalf of the Magistrates of this parish, in which a most cordial welcome was accorded him. The Justices of the Peace praised His Excellency for the keen interest that he has taken in the affairs of the island since his coming into this colony. They also commended him for touring the island so as to have an opportunity of seeing the general condition of the colony and obtaining information at first hand.

The Governor replied, showing his appreciation of the remarks made. He was greatly interest in the loyalty of the inhabitants of this island, and it was a pleasure to him to see how His Majesty the King was venerated here.

THIRD ADDRESS

Yet another address was presented by the Hon J.H. Levy, as Chairman of the Parochial Board on behalf of the Board. The Board clearly showed its appreciation of the Governor's visit, and at the same time urged upon His Excellency the claims of his parish upon the Government. The following were among the claims: Enlarging the town of St. Ann's Bay, granting the townsfolk a recreation ground; giving this parish a branch railway.

In replying, His Excellency pointed out that his visit this time was purely official, but he hoped to return to their beautiful parish. The Board's demands were not exactly modest, but would think over the various matters submitted to him. At any rate he thought it better to see after water supply before thinking of public parks.

1913

His Excellency then went upstairs where Justices of the Peace, Members of the Parochial Board and several other gentlemen were introduced to him.

After visiting the public hospital etc., the Governor was entertained at luncheon by the Magistracy at Osborne Hotel.

His Excellency left at 4.20 along with the Hon J.H.Levy to visit the alms house at Priory.

DAUGHTER IN JAIL

London, Oct. 14.--Sylvia Pankhurst, daughter of Mrs. Emmeline Pankhurst, who was arrested by the police last night but afterwards managed to make her escape, is again in Holloway Street jail to-night. After her success last night she announced that she would speak at Poplar today. The police were wide-awake and caught the young women just as she was entering the meeting in disguise.

Miss Pankhurst screeched and fought desperately. She was aided by a mob of East End roughs who are the hereditary enemies of the police and who tried to rescue her. The police were too numerous, however, and Miss Pankhurst is back again on a hunger strike at the old spot.

Suffragettes gathered in the hall for some time previous to the meeting and were prepared to fight the police. A number of them carried short lengths of knotted rope and other weapons, and in the hope of preventing the police from identifying Miss Pankhurst several women who resemble her in physique wore bandages on their heads and had painted their eyes black as if they were suffering from yesterday's scrimmage with the police, when Syliva escaped.

The ruse failed as the police know Miss Pankhurst too well, and when she walked into the entrance of the hall with her head bandaged and the blackest of black eyes she was immediately pounced upon by the constables and rushed into a taxicab.

October 22, 1913
NIGHTENGALE-On the 18th inst. at Sierra Leone, West Africa, CAPTAIN W.H.NIGHTENGALE of the West India Regiment.

October 23, 1913
HOLLAR-At 36 King Street, Spanish Town on Monday the 20th inst., SYDNEY, the infant son of Simeon and Ethel Hollar, aged 5 months and 2 weeks. The remains were interred a Ebenezer cemetery, the Rev. Mr. Thomas of the Wesleyan Circuit officiating. "Asleep in Jesus".

October 29, 1913
SNAITH-At Morant, Morant Bay on the 25th October, Marjorie Anne, beloved wife of W.H. Snaith. Deeply regretted.

November 5, 1913

PROPERTY MARKET

FOR SALE OR RENT

"BELGRAVIA" A charming upstairs residence in Brown's Town in the parish of St. Ann, the most bracing climate in the Island, with an acre of land abounding in fruit trees and pimento.

Don't miss this opportunity

For further particulars please apply to

M.P. DaCosta

Auctioneer, Real Estate Commission Agent and Valuator, 149 Harbour St. Kingston.

Selected Vital Records from the Jamaican Daily Gleaner

November 11, 1913
JUDAH--At No. 1A Wild Street, Passmore Town, on Saturday, November 8th, after three hours illness, LOUSIA JUDAH, the beloved mother of Mrs. Julia Chevannes, and mother in law of M.A. Chevannes.

November 15, 1913
HOYT-At Melvin Hall, Montego Bay on the 3rd to Mr. and Mrs. F. M. Hoyt, a son

HOLLAR- At Panama on the 8th inst., JAMES WILBERFORCE HOLLAR, son of the late William J. Hollar and brother to George, Simeon, and William Hollar. Aged 37.
Father in thy gracious keeping,
Leave we now Thy servant sleeping.

November 18, 1913
MacMAHON-LEVY-On November 6th, 1913, in New York City, U.S.A. THOMAS J. MacMAHON of Cambridge, Mass, to ELLEN CATHCART, widow of Isaac Levy of Jamaica.

SHERLOCK- At the residence of her son-in-law W.A. Hewett, on Saturday 15th inst., at 8.30 p.m. FRANCES SHERLOCK, relict of the late Thos Sherlock, of Kingston. The eternal God is thy refuge, and underneath are the everlasting arms. Deut. 33.27

PASCOE-On board S.S. Santa Marta on Saturday 15th instant, ALMA, in her 51st year R.I.P.

November 28, 1913
ORRETT-On Thursday 27th inst., at 3.30 p.m. at 20 Harbour Street, Kingston Mrs. ELIZA ORRETT, IN HER 87TH YEAR. Funeral at 4.30 p.m. today.

November 29, 1913
THE "VOMITING SICKNESS" IN THIS ISLAND
Report Prepared by Dr. Harold Seidelin. HIS VISIT TO JAMAICA--Observations of the Expert as a Result of His Tour.

1913

Thursday: (Pickwick Papers, 2 acts) and other good
attractions
Sunday's Performance begins at 8.30 p.m.
Genuine Vaudeville Acts for 1 week beginning Friday
Night "The Three Appolos" straight from the Hippodrome,
New York. Acts changed Friday, Monday, Wednesday.
PRICES: 9d and 1/6, box seats 2s. Children 6d, 9d & 1/.

WARD THEATRE
Fisher Amusement Company
THE BIGGEST PROGRAMME IN TOWN
Wednesday December 3rd:
1--Parcel Post Johnny....................Comedy
2-- For his Brothers Crime.........Dramatic
3--Where the Mountains Meet..........Scenic
4--The Three Queens..... A Gripping Drama
5-- Look not upon the Wine...........Drama
6--The Early Bird...................Comedy
7--The Under Study........... A Story of the Stage
8--From Pen to Pick...... Comedy

DRESS Circle 1/6 Par. 1/ Gallery 6d

December 8, 1913
LT-COLONEL CHARLES JAMES WARD, C.M.G.- At "Arran" Seashore Gardens,
Harbour Street, Kingston on Sunday 7th inst., at 2 p.m. LT COLONEL CHARLES
JAMES WARD. The funeral will leave Seashore Gardens at 4 o'clock today (Monday).

December 12, 1913
CLERK-At Banes, Cuba on the 9th inst., to Mr. and Mrs. A.W.L. Clerk, a daughter.

December 16, 1913
DIXON-On Friday 12th inst. at Prospect, St. Mary, the wife of F.E. Dixon of a son.

NETHERSOLE-AGNES CAROLINE wife of John Mapletoft Nethersole, at 6.30 on the
15th instant. The funeral leaves 47James St., at 1 p.m. today for St. George's Church.

December 18, 1913
NEWS FROM THE RURAL PARISHES
Ideal Seasons Being Experience at St. Elizabeth--the Cambridge Exam. Wesleyans at
Brown's Town Holding Series of Festivities.

BROWN'S TOWN NOTES:
(From our Correspondent)
        Brown's Town, Dec. 15--The Cambridge Local Examinations began here at
11.30 am. to-day. Thanks to the Rev. J.W. Graham, Principal of the St Ann High School,
this important town has been made a centre, a distinction which has not fallen to the
parish since the closing of York Castle. There are 31 candidates sitting in the St Mark's
Church schoolroom, kindly lent for the purpose by the Rev. J.P. Hall. Of these 15 are
from the St Ann High School, 11 from the Brown's Town High School, and 5 from the
Deaconess High School.

Selected Vital Records from the Jamaican Daily Gleaner

Mr. R.M. Murray, B.A. is the examiner, assisted by a local committee, composed of some of the ladies and gentlemen of the town. The Wesleyan Chapel of this town is having a series of Festivities. But two weeks ago the new pipe organ was installed and an organ recital, in which several ladies and gentlemen, including Mr. B. DeC. Reid of Mandeville Y.M.C.A. Band, Mr. and Mrs. C.E. Levy and others took part was given the night following.

Yesterday the harvest festival services were conducted by the Rev. A.W. Geddes, when inspiring discourses were given and the services well attended.

Miss Ida Braham, through whose untiring zeal and perseverance the attaining of the pipe organ is an accomplished fact, presided at the instrument. Mrs. P.W. Murray rendered a solo at the night service and both the Church and Sunday school choirs, under the choirmastership of Mr. C.L. Phillips, acquitted themselves creditably

Within the next two weeks, on Sunday 28th inst., Rev. C.W. Andrews, B.A., B.D who is now travelling in this island in connection with the missionary work of the Methodist Church, is expected to preach here.

The only event of any magnitude now being looked forward to for the Xmas season is the grand athletic sports and gala day to be held at the Coronation Park on Friday, 26th inst. Extensive preparations are being made for this event and all signs of success is in evidence. It is proposed to give fireworks at night and a bon fire will be made.

The following are the event of the day:--100 yard flat race, (Handicap) for men; 100 yard flat race (handicap for boys under 12 years); 100 yard flat race (handicap for boys under 16 years) 220 yards flat race for members (Brown's Town CC) 440 years flat open; 880 years handicap; 1 Mile walking race; 2 miles marathon race; long jump; high jump; three legged race; sack race obstacle race; bun race; wheel barrow race; egg and spoon race; ladies thread the needle race; ladies donkey race; 1 mile cycle race.

1914

January 7,1914

SOME CASES IN CHAMBERS—Interpreting Will of Late Mr.Hyman Levy—THE POINT INVOLVED—Injunction Against the Registration of Title to Land.........
Another Matter

The next case called on was that of Levy vs. Phillips. It was to have the decision of the Court on certain points that have arisen under the will of the late Hyman Levy. Mr. Hector Josephs, K.C. instructed by Messrs. Millholland, Ashenheim and Stone appeared for the plaintiff, whilst Mr. H.M. Radcliffe represented parties interested under the will.

Mr. Josephs said the court was asked to decide a narrow point on the question of construction under the will of the late HYMAN Levy. The testator provided that his estate should go to his widow and on her death to his two daughters Rachael and Georgianna during the time they remain unmarried. But in case of either being married he devised and bequeathed his property to his children, eight in number, including either of his two children, Georgianna and Rachel. Both daughters died unmarried and the question has arisen as to whether there is an intestacy, as to the real estate or whether the remainders to the several children took effect.

Mr. Josephs argued that there had been an intestacy or in the alternative that each of the unmarried sisters took an eighth of the estate absolutely on the death of their father and that on their death intestate and unmarried their share devolved to their brother. The further hearing of the summons was adjourned.

January 9, 1914

FORMATION OF SCHOOL BOARDS—Members Appointed for The Various Parishes—DUTIES OF THE BOARDS—The Functions to be Carried Out in Regard to Education.

Under the provision of Section 3 of Law No 3 of 1910 as substituted by Section 3 of Law No 35 of 1912, and of Section 4 of Law No 3 of 1910, the Governor has appointed the following persons to be Members of the Parish School Boards of the several Parishes of the Island:-

PARISH OF KINGSTON

Revs. M.J. O'Shea,S.J., W. Pratt, M.A., J. W. Wright, J. F. Gartshore, M.A., P. B. Richardson, P.F.X. Muiry, S.J. and R.J. Ripley. W.T. Connolly, Esquire J. L. King, Esquire, B.A. L.L.B., M.D. Farrier, Esquire, Mrs. Arthur Kirby, T.H. MacDermot, Esquire, E.V. Lockett, Esquire, B.A., Inspector of Schools.

PARISH OF ST ANDREW

Selected Vital Records from the Jamaican Daily Gleaner

The Reverend E.J. Wortley, R. Mair, Esquire, The Reverend G.D. Purdy, The Reverend R.M. Sherlock, The Lady Principal of Shortwood Training College, The Reverend G.I. Young, The Reverend J. W. Wright, W.H. Landale, Esquire Mrs. K.H. Bourne, The Reverend E.A. Edwards, F.H. Deerr, Esquire, M.A. Inspector of Schools.

PARISH OF ST THOMAS
Revs. A.N. Thomson, E. Mowl, W. H. Evers, J.A. Bowen, J. Grant, W. P. Sibley, A.E. Hollis, Esquire, J H. Williams, Esquire, C.U. Bogle, Esquire, W.T. Lannaman, Esquire, A.C. Bancroft, Esquire, W.F. B. Phillips Esquire, H.G.C. Murray, Esquire, E.V. Lockett, Esquire, B.A. Inspector of Schools

PARISH OF PORTLAND
Revs. P.A. Conahan, F.S. Grange, B.A., D.D. Parnther, A.V. Petgrave, W.J. Thompson, E. Mair, W.P. Sibley, P.H. Thompson, Esquire, A. E. Ffrench, Esquire, R.C. Geddes, Esquire. J. W. Hill, Esquire. F.B. Brown. Esquire. Mrs. Alma Swift, P. Urquhart, Esquire, M. A., Inspector of Schools.

PARISH OF ST MARY
Revs. R.H. McLaughlin, W.T. Graham, B.A. J MacNee, W.D. Henderson, H.H. Hamilton, C. Reynolds, J.C. Sharpe, Esquire, The Reverend A.A Barclay. The Honourable Sir John Pringle, M.B. K.C.M. G. The Reverend J. G. Hay, P. Urquhart, Esquire, M.A., Inspector of Schools, The Reverend R.H. MacLaughlin, Acting Inspector of Schools.

PARISH OF ST ANN
Revs. E.A. Jones, G.E. Henderson, C.H. Swaby, J.K. Braham, B.D., J.P. Hall, W.S. Lea, J.T. Dillon H. Fowler, Esquire, R. Bramwell, Esquire, The Honourable Colonel E.A. Moulton-Barrett, C.M.G., J.H. Levy, Esquire, Mrs. Louise Johnston. A. Young Esquire, B.A. Inspector of Schools, The Reverend R.H. McLaughlin, Acting Inspector of Schools.

PARISH OF TRELAWNY
Revs. W. S. Lea, J. Kingdon, H.G. Clerk, A.F. Lightbourne, R. B. Prentice, A. G. Eccleston, E.P. Messado, Esquire, The Honourable F.S. Ewen, W. Fitz-Ritson, Esquire, J.N. Helwig, Esquire, The Reverend R.H. McLauglin, Acting Inspector of Schools.

PARISH OF ST JAMES
Revs S. McDowell, B.A. MaCalla, T. W. Halliday, M. B. Burgess, G.S. Grey, J.A. Jones, A.H. Browne, Esquire, A. B. Lowe, Esquire, The Reverend H. L, Webster, The Honourable W. Coke Kerr, J. Shore, Esquire, Edmund Hart, Esquire, J. H. Duff, Esquire, M.A. Inspector of Schools, The Reverend R. B. McLaughlin, Acting Inspector of Schools.

PARISH OF HANOVER
Revs J.M. MacDonald, W. W. Finlason, W.M. Christie, T. W. Halliday, D. A. Rothnie, A. Cresser, The Honourable C. W. Hewitt, The Reverend J. I. Kirschmann, The Reverend B. C. Lumsden, P. E. Corinaldi, Esquire, E. Melville, Esquire, the Reverend J. A. McIntosh, J.H. Duff, Esquire, M. A. Inspector of Schools.

PARISH OF WESTMORELAND
The Venerable Archdeacon C. Henderson Davis, F.K.C., Revs C.C. Wallace, A.G. Kirkham, I.A. Dell, J. Carnegie, H. Clarke, T.J.R. Phillips, A. Sooley, Esquire, Hugh

Clarke, Esquire, The Honourable W.A.S.Vickers, J. W. Mennell Esquire, J.H. Duff, Esquire, M. A. Inspector of Schools, W. Mornan, Esquire Inspector of Schools.

PARISH OF ST ELIZABETH
Revs Canon C. Melville, S.C. Ashton, S.I. Marson, H. W. Cope, W.J. Driver, Stafford Maxwell, Esquire, A. N. Williams, Esquire, The Reverend J. R. Gale, The Honourable J. M. Farquharson, F.B. Bowen, Esquire, W. Mornan, Esquire, Inspector of Schools.

PARISH OF MANCHESTER
The Reverend J. Watson, The Rt. Reverend Bishop Westphal, B.D. Revs R. Johnston M.A. B.D, M.F. Johns, W. Baillie, F.P. Wilde, B.D., W.C. Morrison, A. C. L Martin, Esquire, S. H. Glanville, Esquire. S. A Hendrick, Esquire, The Honourable The Reverend W. B. Esson, D.D. Phillips, Esquire, G. Hicks, Esquire, Inspector of Schools.

PARISH OF CLARENDON
Revs. J. K. Phillips, R.J. McPherson, C.H. Baker, G. Lacey, N.A. Baquie, J. D. Hunt, S. Negus, R.B. Thompson, Esquire, U. T. McKay, Esquire, S.M. DeRoux, Esquire, The Reverend J. A. S. Linton, E.R. C. Earle, Esquire, M. B. Lon, M.R.C.S. L. H. C. P., G. Hicks, Esquire, Inspector of Schools, C.D. Neilson, Esquire, Inspector of Schools.

PARISH OF ST. CATHERINE
Revs. W.H. Stole, T. G. Somers, J.R.M. Cass, Canon S.P. Hendrick, S.A. W.A. Tucker, T.M. Sherlock, H.H. McLaughlin, The Honourable A.A. Fleming, A.E. Wigan, Esquire, W.D. Neish, Esquire, L.R.C.S. L.R.C.P. Edin., G.H. Deerr, Esquire, M. A. Inspector of Schools, C.D. Neilson, Esquire, Inspector of Schools.

January 10, 1914
Guide to Tourists
Brown's Town
Richmond Hotel

LITTLEJOHN-At his residence, "Cathlaw" Gerrard's Cross, Bucks, England on the 16th December, 1913, DR. SALTERN GEORGE LITTLEJOHN, third son of the late Rev. D.R. Littlejohn, Rector of Trelawny, Jamaica. Aged 68 years.

Advertisement
ST ANN'S PRODUCT CO.,
Brown's Town
Dealers in every description of Island Produce for which Highest Prices are paid.
WHOLESALE MERCHANTS
Manufacturers of Meal from Native Corn also Stock Feed
We have the most up-to-date steam plant for curing and grading Coffee in the island and now offer to the public Superior Quality High Mountain Coffee Sherry brand roasted and ground in 1 lb and ¼ tins.
CERTIFICATES OF MERIT
Have been awarded for our meal at the following Agricultural Shows:
Kendal, Dec. 1904; Minard, Feb Thicket, Aug. 1904, St Mary, Jul 1905; Clark's Town, April 1908.
(J.H.Levy)

Selected Vital Records from the Jamaican Daily Gleaner

January 12, 1914

SHERLOCK, MARY ANN—wife of the late C.M. Sherlock at her residence, 9 Norman Road on Saturday January 10th at 10.30 p.m.

STEEL-HART—On Wednesday the 7th January 1914 at the Parish Church Saint Ann's Bay, Beryl Violet daughter of Mr. and Mrs. Dan Hart of Hartlands, Saint Ann's Bay to HERBERT TOWNLY son of (the late) William Sydney and Madeleine Warwick Steel of Bexley England. (English papers please copy).

January 13, 1914

RECENT DEATHS—Case of Vomiting Sickness in Clarendon—Demise of School Boy—Doctor Says that George Peart Died from Heart Failure.

January 15, 1914

LATE MRS. SHERLOCK

A memorial service for the late Mrs. C.M. Sherlock will be conducted by the Rev. W.J. Williams in Wesley Church on Sunday morning 18th inst., at 11 o'clock. Will the friends of the family and the members of Wesley please make this known?

Because of special services to be held on the three following Sundays it is impossible to arrange otherwise.

January 20, 1914

Advertisement

RICHMOND HOTEL
Brown's Town
(Situated in the Garden Parish
of the Island)
Every attention and comfort
Provided for guests
For further particulars apply
RICHMOND HOTEL or
Tourists' Information Bureau
Kingston

January 21, 1914

Current Items

Mr. L.A. Rattigan writes from "Belgravia", Brown's Town on the 17th inst., as follows: "Weather here this morning delightful, crisp and cold. Temp 53 deg at 6 a.m. 6.30 now 10 a.m. bright sunshine.

LAND DISPUTE IN ST THOMAS—Wesleyan Body and the Bath Corporation—Issue Before Umpire—A Land Surveyor will First Decide the Boundaries.

January 23, 1914

NICHOLSON-At 2.30 a.m. on January 22nd at the residence of her nephew Dr G.C. Henderson, Miss SOPHIE NICHOLSON in the 97th year of her age.

SHAKESPEAREAN COMPANY WHICH HAS BEEN ATTRACTING BIG HOUSES AT WARD THEATRE [Picture] Caption: Members of the Glossop-Harris Shakespearean Company, which has had a very successful season in Jamaica. (22 people)

January 24, 1914

LATEST PICTURE OF THE PRINCESS WHO IS ON A VISIT TO JAMAICA

1914

[Picture] Her Highness Princess Marie Louise of Schleswig-Holstein

January 27, 1914
COVER-At Musgrave Avenue, Kingston, on the 24th January, 1914 SAMUEL MORRIS, eldest son of the late C.S.Cover of Enfield, St Ann.

January 30, 1914
Front Page. PRINCESS ON TOUR—Drove Through Parish of St Ann Yesterday—Met Hearty Welcome—Presented with an Address on Reaching Brown's Town—The Splendid Decorations.

(By Telegraph From Our Correspondent)
      Moneague. Thursday. Princess Marie Louise of Schleswig-Holstein passed here at ten o'clock today by motor car, accompanied by his Excellency the Governor. They did not call at the hotel but journeyed on the Ocho Rios road.

AT ST ANN'S BAY
(By telegraph from Our Correspondent) St Ann's Bay, Thursday. Princess Marie Louise and party arrived here at 11.30 a.m. and lunched at the Osborne Hotel. The police guarded the entrance. The town people did not know in time that the Princess would have passed through here hence there were no decorations. The Princess left for Falmouth at 1 p.m.

PRESENTED WITH ADDRESS
(By Telegraph from Our Correspondent) Brown's Town Thursday—Today at ten minutes past two p.m. Her Highness Princess Marie Louise accompanied by His Excellency Sir William Manning, Governor and Mrs. Dennistoun, arrived at the Square of the lower section of this town. Immediately on the arrival of the Princess the band in attendance under Mr. R.M. Edwards, struck up the National Anthem and played two bars of it.

      The Governor then alighted and was met by the Hon. J.H. Allwood, M.L.C., and Mr. J.H. Levy, Chairman of the Parochial Board of St Ann.

      His excellency presented the Hon J.H. Allwood, Mr. J.H. Levy and Dr. Miller to the Princess and thereafter Mr. Allwood asked and obtained permission of Her Highness to present the address of welcome which had been prepared.

      The hon. Gentleman then read the address which runs thus:

      "To Her Highness the Princess Marie Louise of Schleswig-Holstein

"May it please your Highness on behalf of the inhabitants of western Saint Ann and as we feel assured, voicing the sentiments of the whole parish, we beg to offer to your Highness a loyal and hearty welcome to the parish of St Ann. To the people of this parish, as in all parts of the Island the visit of a relative of our Sovereign Lord the King is ever a cause of gratification and joy, and this feeling is enforced in the case of your Highness who has evinced

SUCH A DEEP INTEREST
In the population and affairs of the West Indies. We trust that your Highness will enjoy good health during your stay amongst us that that the natural beauties and historical associations of the country parts of the Island and especially of St Ann, will prove a source of interest and pleasure to you. Assuring you of our deep loyalty to and affection for the throne and person of His Most Gracious Majesty the King. Signed on behalf of the Inhabitants of Western St Ann, by J.H Allwood, M.L.C. and J.H. Levy, Chairman, Parochial Board St Ann.

      Her Highness in replying said:

      I thank you for your kind address of welcome. Please convey to all my appreciation.

Selected Vital Records from the Jamaican Daily Gleaner

Her Highness was presented by Miss Enid Levy, the tiny granddaughter of Mr. J.H. Levy with a casket tied with purple ribbon containing a beautiful array of violets very nicely and neatly arranged.

Mr. Levy also presented Mrs. Dennistoun with a nice bouquet of white asters.

After the address and reply, Hon J.H. Allwood called for three cheers for the Princess which were heartily responded to, and before the party drove off Mr. A.S. Byles called for three cheers for His Excellency which were also well responded to.

His Excellency then shook hands with Hon J.H. Allwood, Mr. J.H. Levy Dr Miller and Mr. A.S. Byles and the party drove off amidst cheers, the Princess bowing graciously in acknowledgment thereof.

Through the energy of Mr. C. L. Phillips, who may well be termed the handy man, assisted by Mr. R. B. Miller and Mr. Jacobs and others, the decoration of the section between the Court Street and Musgrave Square was both picturesque and attractive. Banners of welcome to Her Highness, and flags and bunting were to be seen on either side and across the street, waving playfully with the breeze.

An arch constructed of cocoanuts and bamboo palms and other natural productions of the vegetable world of this island majestically span the wide street from Musgrave to Norman House. This was decked with flowers, crotons, and other shrubs interwoven here and there with flags and decorations and orange fruits. The arch displayed as far as possible the vegetation of the tropics.

In front of this hung the banner

GOD SAVE THE KING

And before this, the address and short ceremony which cannot fail to leave indelible impressions on the minds of those who witnessed it.

In spite of the short notice of the coming of the Princess, a fairly large crowd of people was present, and the school children of the Deaconess High School and the Government School marshaled his host and rendered a few patriotic songs. By the arrangement of the police, under command of Inspector Knollys, there was no crowding of the thoroughfare and unnecessary jumbling of the crowd.

The sun shone brightly, but the atmosphere was cool and enjoyable.

The party, as already announced in the Gleaner, is expected to pass through to-morrow (Friday) on their way from Falmouth, and to breakfast at Enfield with the hon. Member for the parish.

February 5, 1914
COVER-LAWRENCE WILLIAM, aged 19, beloved son of the late William Cover Jr. of St Ann, Jamaica and Mrs. E.J. Cover at Panama, January 25th 1914, leaving bereaved relatives to mourn their irreparable loss.

February 7, 1914
Personal
Mr. and Mrs. J. R. Smith, Dr Sherlock, Mr. A.M. Sherlock and W.M. Sherlock desire through this medium to thank their numerous friends and sympathizers for their kind letters of condolence during their recent sad bereavement.

LATE DR. W. CLARKE MURRAY
(From our correspondent)

Brown's Town. There was break in the service of the Wesleyan Chapel on Sunday last just before the collection and Mr. Levy conveyed the pleasing news to the congregation that the initial steps had been taken and the tablets and tombstone in memory of the late beloved and esteemed Dr. W. C. Murray were procured and lying in the chapel yard ready for erection. The monument is estimated to cost £100; of this amount £45 has been subscribed voluntarily by friends and admirers throughout the island, among whom are Sir Sydney Olivier and His Grace the Archbishop; £40 has been contributed by Dr. Murray's family and for the remaining £15 he asked permission of the family to extend the privilege of contribution to the members of the Brown's Town, Edmondson and Stewart Town Circuits.

He desired to say that he (Mr. Levy) was making no begging appeal for the £15 as the family was quite willing to pay same, but he thought if an opportunity of contributing were not offered the members and friends in the circuit in which Dr. Murray last ministered, they would feel aggrieved and slighted: consequently he had made the remarks above mentioned and he trusted they would be appreciated and acted upon. Stone and mortar he continued, was an insignificant memorial of a man of Dr. Murray's worth and usefulness; but it was some token of the esteem in which he was held.

Mr. Levy emphasized that no collections were to be made and the amount was only to be contributed by members of the congregation. Of course if any outsiders desired to contribute they could do so and he would be willing to receive sum of from 1/- to 2/6 or more.

Work had actually begun in connection with the erection and soon the chapel will be adorned with the tokens of memory of a departed worthy friend.

February 10, 1914
WORK OF SYNOD—Wesleyan Ministers Discuss Church Matters—Draft of Stations—Efforts to Make the Year One of Spiritual Advance.

FINAL DRAFT OF STATIONS, 1914
Kingston, Coke—Arthur Kirby, A. Reginald Thomas, William J. Turnbull, Geo. Lockett, Supernumerary Theological Institution, Jas. T. Hudson, B.A. B.D.
Kingston, Wesley.-William J. Williams, Joseph W. Wright, John Duff, Supernumerary
Clarendon- Nathan A. Baquie
Manchester.—William Baillie
Mount Fletcher.—Elijah Mair
Grateful Hill- Terence M. Sherlock
Montego Bay- Thos. W. Halliday
Lucea.-R. Mettam.
Falmouth.- H. Gillies Clerk
Duncans.-Arthur F. Lightbourne, One to be sent, S.T. Brown, Supernumerary.
Mount Ward.-John A. McIntosh
Sav-la-Mar.- Chas. C. Wallace
Black River.- H. T. Page
Mountain Side.- One wanted. A.M. Smith, Supernumerary
Spanish Town.- Wm. H. Sloley
St Ann's Bay.- E. Armon Jones
Watson Ville.- M. Britton King
Ocho Rios.- Caleb Reynolds
Beecham Ville and Bensonton.-Alex Geddes, Thos. Whitfield (Bensonton). Robt.M. Parnther, Supernumerary
Brown's Town and Edmondson.- J Kissock Braham, B.D. Man. Barker, One to be sent
Guy's Hill and Hampstead.- Walter J.Jacob
Morant Bay.- Jonathan Grant
Bath and Port Morant.- Wm J. Evers
Manchioneal.- Adolphus Cresser
Port Antonio and Buff Bay.- David D. Parnther B.A., Adolphus N. Walker B.A. Buff Bay
Yallahs.- One to be sent, H.C. Quinlan, Supernumerary

Selected Vital Records from the Jamaican Daily Gleaner

Turks Island.- Christopher H. Tice

Panama and Colon.-Chas G. Hardwick, Fred. Parker (Colon)

Costa Rica.- Edward A. Pitt

Bocas Del Toro.- Mortimer C. Surgeon

W.J. WILLIAMS, Chairman,

J. KISSOCK BRAHAM, Secretary

The afternoon session was devoted to the "Conversation of the work of God" The membership statistics reveal

20, 667 Full and accredited members

1,286 on Trial

9,284 Junior Members

A net decrease of 276 members, but an increase of 139 on trial and 568 junior members. There are 393 local preachers, 1,305 class leaders, 464 students, 157 Sunday Schools, 1,276 Sunday School Teachers and 15, 470 Sunday School scholars, 31 Christian Endeavour Societies, 1,830 members, Wesley Guild 13, with 938 members.

February 13, 1914

FRASER-At Brooklyn, New York on the 12th LILY beloved daughter of Mary and the late Walter H. Lewis. Verse.

WINN-At 5.30 a.m. on Friday, 6th inst., at her residence "Woodbine Cottage" Mandeville, ZIPPORAH FRYER WINN, widow of the late Rev. C.A. Winn of the parish of St Ann, aged 81 years. English papers please copy.

February 17, 1914

LYNCH- on 15th February, 1914 at Falmouth, Jamaica, B.W.I. the wife of John M. Lynch of a daughter. English and American papers please copy.

ONE OF THE COMPLETED LOCKS OF THE GREAT PANAMA CANAL [Picture]. Completed Lock Looking East Towards Colon. The above picture is the latest to arrive here showing how the work on the great Panama Canal is nearing its completion. The view shows a lock just completed, giving a splendid idea of this wonderful engineering feat.

February 19, 1914

NOVELIST WEDS AGAIN AT AGE OF SEVENTY-FOUR—[Picture] Mr. Thomas Hardy British Novelist, author of "Far from the Madding Crowd" and "Tess of the d'Urberfiles" and many other works known throughout the world, married recently Miss Florence Dudgale, his Secretary and typist. Mr. Hardy's first wife died in 1912. He is in his seventy-fourth year. The bride Miss Dugdale, is the author of many tales for children.

February 19, 1914

CATHCART- At Port Antonio on the 18th inst. MAY L. the wife of W. H. Cathcart, the Clerk of the Courts, Portland.

February 24, 1914

GARCIA-IVAN CECIL-The beloved brother of Eustace Stanley and Vera Louise and affectionate nephew of Mrs. E. Nash, aged 21 years. Funeral moves from his late residence 143 Princess Street at 4 p.m. today. Friends and acquaintances please accept this the only intimation. "We duly yield thee what was thine, Thy will be done".

1914

February 24, 1914

A SOCIAL EVENT—Mandeville Ball was a Brilliant Function—A COMPLETE SUCCESS-Reflected Credit Upon Mrs. Leyden and Friends.

(From our Correspondent) Mandeville Feb. 23—What may be termed, and was, a brilliant function came off at the Court House here on Thursday night last, in the form of a fancy dress ball. The Court room was suitably decorated for the night's enjoyment. The function was a success from every point of view and certainly did credit to Mrs. Leyden, who got it up, and to those who helped her in making it the success it was. The function was chiefly got up for the children, and the little ones undoubtedly showed their appreciation by the way they enjoyed themselves. The various costumes were all neat and well got up. The Y.M.C.A. band was in attendance, under Mr. B. Dec. Reid, A.V.C.M. and rendered the necessary music, to the delight of the happy parties present: and the many encores that the band had to respond to went to show that the musicians have greatly added to their reputation. Dancing started at 7.30 p.m. for the benefit of the little ones, whilst the older heads remained until 3 a.m. when the last waltz was played and the function broke up to the regret of all.

Miss Ruby Gideon, as "Fashions for All" and Miss Doris Hart, as "Gipsy Fortune-teller" got the prize for over 14, whilst Master Allan Anderson, as "Knave of Hearts" and Miss Joyce Motta, as "Fairy" got the children's prize.

The following ladies and gentleman were present:-Mr. and Mrs. A.E. Sampson, Master Aubrey Sampson, "Trick bicycle rider"; Miss Adele Vaz, Mr. W. L Thornton Sharp, Miss A. DaCosta, Miss Conlin, Miss Manson, Miss Randell, Mr. H. B. Sturridge,"Italian Peasant"; Mr.J.A.V.Thomson, "Devil"; Mr. D. Jacobs, Miss A. Harding, Mr. and Mrs. H.E.Crum-Ewing, Master Crum Ewing, "Clown"; Mr. and Mrs., Ernest Wilson, Miss Edna Wilson, "Cherry Ripe"; Miss Olive Wilson, "Colleen Bawn"; Mr. H.H. Heron, Miss E. Maxwell, "Fortune Teller"; Miss Eva Maxwell, "Dutch Girl"; Miss Cecily Maxwell,"Celia"; Miss Stewart, "Lady of the 20th Century"; Mr. and Mrs. Macgregor, Miss E.M. Dixon, "Pierrette"; Miss Barbara M. Isaacs, "My Great-great-grandmother"; Master L.A.C. Isaacs, "Little Jack Horner"; Mr. and Mrs. C.R. Isaacs, Master E. Fulford,"Pierrot" Miss C. Fulford, "Priscilla"; Miss E. Fulford, "Japanese"; Miss M. Burke, "Titania"; Miss F. Sharp, "Fairy"; Mr. and Mrs. A.S. Phillips, Mr. V. Henriques, Mrs. Smith, Mr. Hall, Miss A. Anderson, "Boo-Peep"; Miss D. Nash, "Dutch Girl"; Master G.Anderson, "Bubbles"; Mr. S. Glanville, "Grecian Sailor"; Mrs. E. Anderson, Master Allan Anderson, "Knave of Hearts"; Miss Glanville, "Kashmere Girl"; Miss S Glanville, "Kashmere Girl"; Miss Glanville, :Gipsy"; Miss S. Hart, "Pierrette (Modern)"; Miss M. Morrison, Miss O. Lewis, "Sun Flower"; Miss M. Hall, "Puritan Maid"; Miss R. Lehenan, "Indian"; Miss Hilda Harty, "Butterfly"; Miss A. Bartlett, "Tucker Girl"; Miss W. Bartlett, "Red Riding Hood"; Miss M. Motta, "Ancient Greek"; Master Donald Motta, "Knave of Clubs" Miss T. Labostillh, "Dutch Girl"; Miss E. Labostillh, "Chinese Lady"; Miss D. Henriquez, "Gipsy"; Miss K. Essling, Alsatian Peasant"; Miss Gwen Lord, "Cinderella"; Miss K. Charley, "French Waiting-Maid"; Master L. Cox, "Pierrott"; Mr. H. Lewis, "Master"; Miss Lewis, "Lady of the Georgian Period"; Miss M. Elliott, "Spanish Dancing Girl"; Mr. C. Farquharson, Mr. Duncan, Misses Joynt, Master A. Heron, "Little Lord Fauntleroy"; Master R. Heron, "Greek Brigand"; Master H Heron, "Highlander"; Mr. and Mrs. Griffith, Master G. Griffith, "Sioux Indian Chief"; Master J. Griffith, "Knave of Hearts"; Mrs. Lynch, Mr. Saunders, Miss I. Morrison, Miss H. Mossman, "Early Victorian"; Miss O. Davidson, Mr. C. Jackson, "The Moon"; Miss P. Griffith, "Folly"; Miss Paton, Miss E. Lewis, "Italian girl"; Mr. G. Lewis, "20th Century Gentleman"; Mr. S.J.A. Stewart, "Gentleman of 20th Century"; Miss Paton, Mr. Brandt, Mrs. Williams, Mr. Williams, Miss Benson, Mr. Hume, Miss Clough, "French Fisher Wife"; Miss Farquharson, "Pierrette"; Miss M. Farquharson, "Pyjama Girl"; Dr. and Mrs. . W.G. Farquharson, Mr. St John Laing,

"Spanish Knight Templar"; Mrs. Pengelley, Miss Pengelley, Mr. E. Pengelley, Miss C. Pengelley, "Cherries"; Mrs. Harty, "Lady of 20th Century"; Master R. Harty, "Chauffeur"; Mr. T. Harty, "Gentleman of the 20th Century, Miss Pawsey, "Turkish Lady"; Mr. R.B. Daly, Miss N. Alford, "Bride"; Miss Lena Daly, "Moonlight"; Miss E. DeL. Forde, "American Fisher Girl""; Mr. Hutchinson, Miss O. Leyden, "Folly"; Mr. and Mrs. Leyden, "Turkish Gentleman and Madame Angot"; Master N. Leyden, "Boy Scout"; Mr. I. Leyden, "Ancient Greek"; Mr. Cox, "Souador"; Master K. Motta, "Page"; Miss Joyce Motta, "Fairy"; Mr. G. H. Linden, Mrs. L.A. Isaacs, Mrs. J. Lord, Miss M. Sampson, "Five O'Clock Tea"; Miss Doris Hart, "Gipsy Fortune Teller," Miss Ruby Gideon, "Fashions for All" and Mrs. Simpson.

March 2, 1914
WINNERS OF SCHOLARSHIPS-Success of Miss Cowper and Miss Johnson.—A Definite Statement-Great Success Achieved by Pupils of Wolmers School.

The Gleaner is now in a position to announce the names of the winners of the Girl's Scholarships, which was causing anxiety in certain quarters as the announcement was not made at the same time as the Boy's Scholarship.

We are reliably informed that the winner of the Girl's Scholarship for 1914 is Miss M.E. Cowper, while the additional scholarship for this year goes to Miss I.J.Johnson.

Both young ladies are students at Wolmer's Girls School, and are to be congratulated on their success. Miss Cowper is a daughter of Mr. William Cowper M.A., Headmaster of Wolmer's Boys' School, and in the junior Cambridge Exam she came out at the top of the list.

One of the causes of delay in making the announcement is, we understand, due to the fact that it was only a few days ago that the Legislative Council passed the vote for the additional scholarship.

The winning of these two Scholarships by Wolmerians reflects the highest credit on the teaching staff at that institution, which, it will be remembered also carried off the Jamaica scholarship for Boys this year.

March 5, 1914
COVER-On Tuesday 3rd inst., DOROTHY FLORENCE LORD, the beloved child of Charles Arscott and Alice Augusta Swinhoe Cover, aged six years and four months.

March 10, 1914
KIPLING TALKS TO BIG AUDIENCE—How the World of Travel Is Changing— Geography by Smell—The Great Prospects which the Future now Holds out.

March 11, 1914
Glanville-On Sunday 8th inst., at her residence Fern Hill, Manchester, ELIZABETH GLANVILLE widow of the late John Glanville, Manchester.

March 13, 1914
THE CAMBRIDGE EXAMINATIONS—Results Achieved by the Scholars in Jamaica—Full list of Passes—the splendid Work Done by Many of the Students.

Appended are the name of the successful scholars who sat for the Cambridge Local Examinations held in Jamaica in December last: -

The side letters denote that the candidate to whose name they are prefixed was distinguished in the following subjects respectively: -

1914

a. Arithmetic (Junior only); ag. Agricultural Science; am, Applied Mathematics; b, Botany; bk, Book keeping; ch, Chemistry; cn, Chinese; d Drawing; dh, Dutch; ds, Domestic Science; e, English Language and Literature; f, French; g, Geography; gk, Greek; gn, German; h, History; j, Logic; l, Latin; m, Mathematics; ms, Mensuration and Surveying; mu Music; n, Natural History; p, Political Economy; pg, Physical Geography; ph, Physics; phl, Physiology and Hygiene; r, Religious Knowledge; s, Shorthand; sc Experimental Science; sp, Spanish.

Senior Students are not eligible for marks of distinction unless they are under 19 years of age; and Juniors are not eligible unless they are under 16 years of age.

SENIOR BOYS
Students under 19 year of age who have obtained honours, Class III.
Don, E.G.A., Jamaica College; phl Curphey, T.J., Patterson L.V. l,gk Ferguson, V.L. Wolmer's School; l, gk Lee W.R. Potsdam School; h,l McDonald G.S. Wolmer's School.
Students under 19 years of age who have satisfied the examiners, but are not included in the foregoing class: -
Bell, E. A., bk DaCosta F.N., Doran E.D.A., Morales, E.McL., Patterson, E.S., Stockhausen, A.C., Buie-Tomlinson, G.P., Veira, L.C., Hollar, F.G., Jamaica College; Ashman C.E., Bancroft, O.R., Connery, J.E., Gadishaw, E.A., Wolmer's School; Gregoire, F.L., St George's College; Hendriks, L. St.C. Wolmer's School; Hopwood K.A., Manchester Middle Grade School; Lewis, L.L., St George's College; Lyon O.A. Beckford and Smith's School, Spanish Town; Marsh, B.C. Wolmer's School, Martin, S.A., St George's College; Rennie, A.B., Wolmer's School; Rubie, M.P. Vere Trust Secondary School; fVendryes, B.L., St George's College; McCulloch, W.E., Morales, C.McL., Jamaica College; Arnold, L.E., Alberga, C.L., Bliss, L.R., Montego Bay Government Secondary School; Corinaldi, W.R., Trinity, Montego Bay; Ellis, H.H.A., Murray D.A., Packer, A.H.C., Tomlinson, A.E.O. Montego Bay Government Secondary School; Burke, P.G. Manning's School.
Students not under 19 years of age who have satisfied the examiners:-
Gayle, S.S. Jamaica College; Parkins, G.V., Private tuition; Knight, G.W.T. Calaber College; Manley N.W., Jamaica College.
JUNIOR BOYS
Students under 16 years of age who have obtained honours, Class I:
l,f,m,bk,s Ashenheim, L.E. r,m, Dickenson, W.N., Jamaica College; r,e,h,l,gk,m Riddie, C.E., Walcott A.L. Wolmer's School.
Class II
Edmonds, F.S., Jamaica College, r Hall N.W. r Jack, E. L., Wolmer's School
Class III
Ashenheim, N.N., Edmonds, E.A. r Phillips, R.O., r,e Thomson, G.A.P., Jamaica College; Brown, S.A., Gruchy C.L.C., Wolmer's School.
Students under 16 years of age who have satisfied the examiners but are not included in the foregoing Classes:-
Braham, R.R., Braham J.K., St Ann High School; Coore, C.R., Brown's Town High School; Vermont-Graham, H.A. St Ann High School; Isaacs, L.C. St Ann High School; Morrison J.L., Brown's Town High School; Malabre, L.M.A., r bk Sanford C.C., Tucker, Jamaica College; r Alberga L.P., Bronstorph, F.L. Campbell, J. A., Wolmer's School; Craig, S.H. Titchfield Secondary School; Dick, F.A. L., Wolmer's School; Francis, P.F., Manchester Middle Grade School; Kemble C.S. Nunes, F.V., Wolmer's School; Swainson, W. L., Vere Trust Secondary School; Watson, W.E., Wolmer's School. Carnegie, H.A., Duff, C.S. Calabar High School; Miller, P.R., Montego Bay Government Secondary School; Segre, M.A., Manning's School.
Students not under 16 years of age who have passed the examination as Juniors:-

Bramwell, E.L., Dixon, E.D. Gordon, A.J. Brown's Town High School; Moss C.V., Brown's Town High School; Palmer, E.E. St Ann High School; Clerk, C.A., Goubalt, A.L., Scott, S.L., Sinclair, A.V., Thomson, A.O. Jamaica College; Byles A.L.S. Wolmer's School; Hendriks, A.R. New College; Lewis, H. V., Manchester Middle Grade School; Macpherson, F.R., Wolmer's School; Williams, V.G., New College; McDonald, F.B., Orrett, F.C., Calabar High School; Box, A.A., Rusea's School, Lucea; Davis, A.A., Rusea's School, Lucea; Gallimore S.B., Montego Bay Collegiate School; Aitken, J. H. Montego Bay Government Secondary School; Mair, L.A., Manning's School.

SENIOR GIRLS

Students under 19 years of age who have obtained honours, Class II.

Foster, P.E. Hampton School;

Class III

Marson, E.H. Hampton School; e McCrindle, B.W.R., MacPherson, L.E., Wolmer's High School

Students under 19 years of age who have satisfied the examiners, but are not included in the foregoing classes:-

Donald-Hill, J., Fraser, F.A., Levy D.L., McCaulay. S.I. Millar, H.E., Mudie, M.M.P., Powell, I.L., Smith, E.V., Hampton School; Andrade F.A. L., Colonial High School; Barham M. Home School, 15 Brentford Road; Gale, J.R. L., Wolmer's High School for Girls; r,e Hudson, M. L., Ormsby, N.E. Colonial High School; Thompson, D.M. Wolmer's High School for girls; Thomas, M. H. R., C. of E. High School for Girls; Wallace, A.C.L., Manning's School; Roche, H.E., Westwood High School

Students not under 19 years of age who have satisfied the examiners:-

Jeffrey-Smith I.A., Private Study

JUNIOR GIRLS

Students under 16 years of age who have obtained honours Class III.

r Lamb L.E. Westwood High School.

Students under 16 years of age who have satisfied the examiners, but are not included in the foregoing class:-

Smith I.M., Brown's Town High School; Constantine S., Donald-Hill B., d Ramson, E.M., Reid, F.L. Spence, L.G. Hampton School; Andrade, D.V. Colonial High School; Balfour, E.D., Wolmer's High School for girls: Bonitto, L.M., Colonial High School; Connolley, E.D., e Edwards, G.O., Wolmer's High School for girls; Grosett, A.J., Titchfield Secondary School; Leahong,U.A., Colonial High School, Mein, I.R. Titchfield Secondary School; Ormsby, B.S., Colonial High School for girls; Purdy, R.C. Private School, Williams, R.C., Wolmer's High School for girls; Bingham, L.M. Wallace, E.M.L., Miller, E.E.L., Church of England High School for girls; Goodin, L.M. Mannings School, r Chisholm, B.M.H., Westwood High School; r Stockhausen, L. L. Westwood High School.

Students not under 16 years of age who have passed the examination as Juniors:-

Dunkley, M.A., Moss F.E. L., The Deaconess High School, Brown's Town; Hylton, B.S., Nash, E.A.M., Smith, G.M., Hampton School; Brathwaite, W.E. Wolmer's High School for girls; Dunn, M.A., Colonial High School; Harrison, L.E., Hodelin, E.F., Wolmer's High School for girls; Lazarus, G.L. Deaconess Home High School; Ormsby H.V., Walcott, I.E. B., Colonial High School; Watson E.S. Wolmer's High School for girls; Moodie E.M. Titchfield Secondary School; Barron, R.I., Logan. A.A.L., Murray E. I., Riche, R.L., Westwood High School.

PRELIMINARIES

Boys

Students under 14 years of age who have obtained honours: Class I

r Prendergast C.E., Jamaica College; g Stockhausen H.W., Jamaica College; e,al, Adams, C.A., Wolmer's School; Murad, W.H., Wolmer's School

1914

Class II

Lindo E.A., Jamaica College; Levy V.L. Wolmer's School

Class III

Fraser, N.J. Wolmer's School

Students under 14 years of age, who have satisfied the examiners, but are not included in the foregoing classes.

Graham F.E.C. St Ann High Sch; Parker, P.T., Brown's Town High Sch.; Arscott, P.L., Jamaica College; Cathcart, L.H.H. Jamaica College; Don, C.S.D. Jamaica College; Harty I.L.M. Jamaica College; Lawrence, H.S. Jamaica College; Marshalleck, D., Jamaica College. Nethersole, H.G. Jamaica College; d Plant, H.A., Jamaica College, Thomas, A.C.V., Jamaica College, Bloomfield, C.A., Wolmer's Sch.; Bradbury, B.T. O'L, Colonial High Sch.; Constantine, R.G., Titchfield Secondary Sch.; l Cruchley F.H., St George's College, Dunkerley, L.L., Beckford and Smith's Sch., Spanish Town; Ffrench, L.S.C., Titchfield Secondary Sch.; Ilgner H.O.L., Vere Trust Secondary Sch.; Somers, F.G. Beckford and Smith's Sch., Spanish Town; Bellamy, A.A. Titchfield Secondary School; Carnegie, E.S.T., Calabar High Sch.; Matheson, H.I.C., Calabar High Sch.; Mornan, A.K. Calabar High School; Turner, G.W. Calabar High Sch.; Levy R.C., Govt Sec. Sch., Montego Bay; Clare N.A. St. L., Rusea's Sch., Lucea; Chambers, H.C. W. Manning's Sch.

Students between 14 and 16 years of age who have satisfied the examiners:

Bramwell, H.A. Brown's Town High Sch.; Burke, R.A. Jamaica College; Isaacs, F.K., Jamaica College; Mills, A.A. Ja. Col; Muir R.C. L. M., Ja. Col; Stockhausen, J.M. Ja. Col.; Strudwick, B.G. Ja Col; Williams, L.G. Ja. Col.; Brown, A.V., New Col.; Byles J.H., Wolmer's Sch.; Chance A.E. Kingston Grammar Sch.; DeLisser, O.L. New Col.; McCulloch, I.D., Wolmer's Sch.; Mossman, O.V., Vere Trust Secondary Sch.; Samuda, H. A., Manchester Middle Grade Sch.; Shelton F.O., Titchfield Secondary Sch.; Stimpson, R.K.A., Wolmer's Sch.; Streadwick, R.D. St.G., Wolmer's Sch.; Sullivan, A.M., Titchfield Secondary Sch.; Sewright, E. McK., Wolmer's Sch.; Clark, L.D.M., Dixon, E.D., Excell, S.G., Levy L.A., Shaw J.A., Montego Bay Government Secondary Sch.

Girls

Students under 14 years of age who have satisfied the examiners:-

Levy V.C. The Deaconess High Sch., Brown's Town; Levy L.M., The Anglesea Sch.; Myers, E., The Anglesea Sch.; Williams, C.L.G., Deaconess Home High School; Muir, M.C.McK. Colonial High Sch.; Chisholm, D.A.L., Vernon, K.A., Bloomsbury Sch.; Aguilar, G.W., Manning's Sch.; Brown, A.L., Westwood High Sch.

Students between 14 and 16 years of age who have satisfied the examiners:-

Jones, S.H., The Deaconess High Sch., Brown's Town; Lynch D.H.W., The Deaconess High School, Brown's Town; Parris G.V. Brown's Town High Sch.; King, R.D. Titchfield Secondary Sch.; Marshalleck, B.S.L., Colonial High Sch.; Sale, A.M.B., Colonial High Sch.; Thelwell I.L., Titchfield Secondary Sch.; Sutherland N.S., Titchfield Secondary Sch.; Watson, I.L., Rusea's Sch., Lucea; Kennedy, P.E., Rusea's School, Lucea; Anderson, Z; Manning's School; Hall H.L. Hendricks, I.J. L. Lewis, G.E. Ottey, B.L., Ottey, L.L Vaz. T.M.A.E. Williams, M.E. Whitelocke, M.C., Manning's School, Eccleston, L.E., Goffe R.E., Heron, D.H. Ritson, E.M. Westwood High School.

March 14, 1914

ROBINSON-At Truro, St Andrew, Mrs. Ken Robinson of a son.

March 26, 1914

MUIR-At Lauriston, Hope Road, on Wednesday, March 25th EMMA LOUISA. Funeral leaves Lauriston at 4.30 this afternoon.

Selected Vital Records from the Jamaican Daily Gleaner

March 28, 1914
BROWN'S TOWN NEWS
(From our Correspondent)

Brown's Town Tuesday—The erection of the tombstone and tablet in memory of the late beloved Dr. W. Clarke Murray is well nigh completed and the unveiling thereof will be arranged for at no distant date.

The St Mark's Church is arranging to hold a service on Thursday night, 29th April, at which the Assistant Bishop is expected to administer the rite of confirmation. The candidates are now being prepared by the rector. It is rumoured that this church is now raising the wherewithal to provide a pipe organ to cost between £500 and £600.

One of the best-attended and well-arranged funerals of recent days passed, through the upper and lower portions of this town today. The deceased was Mr. Edward Campbell of Standfast and was a member of Dr. Johnston's Tabernacle for many years. He held the position of Superintendent of the Sunday School in connection with the chapel to the time of his death. He was a worthy example of hard work, and industry, just the type of man the country needs to-day. The cortege led by the choir of the chapel, Sunday school teachers and members, proceeded from the residence of the deceased at Standfast right through the town to Tabernacle, where the burial service was conducted by Dr. Johnston and from thence back to Standfast, where the remains were interred. Among those in attendance at the funeral were the Hon. J.H. Allwood, Mr. J. H. Levy, Mr. L.W. Levy, Mr. D. L. Morris, Mr. J. Dickenson, Mr. A. Fullerton.

March 30, 1914
JUNOR-At Esperanza, Westmoreland, on the 27th inst., the wife of T.A. Junor of a daughter.

March 31, 1914
ELLIOTT –At Franleigh, May Pen, on Sunday, 29th March. Sarah Sophia, relict of the late E.C. Elliott, J.P. of Vere, Clarendon. "What our Father does is well". English and Canadian papers please copy.

IN MEMORIAM
HOLLAR-In loving and affectionate memory of Janet Constance (Nettie) daughter of Mr. and Mrs. Francis L. Hollar, who died on the 31st March, 1913. Verse.

PANAMA CANAL—Great Armada will Assemble at Opening of Waterway—BIG VESSELS TO MEET—Entertainment for Crews will Surpass Anything Yet Done.

April 2, 1914

Advertisement

1914

Shares bought and sold
Auditor--Victoria Mutual Building Society
Jamaica Co-Operative Fire Ins. Co
The Standard Life Ass. Co., etc etc.
Cable Address: WINCHESTER
Jamaica
P.O. Box No. 76

April 9, 1914
[Front page Pictures] OUR COMING MEN: SUCCESS ACHIEVED AT CAMBRIDGE
EXAMINATION

April 16, 1914
OUR COMING MEN: SUCCESS GAINED AT CAMBRIDGE
EXAMINATION.[Pictures]
We publish above the second batch of photographs of successful scholars who have
passed with honours Cambridge Local Examination. Another lot will appear later.

April 18, 1914
MOTTA-At "Maryfield" St Andrew on Friday 17th April, 1914, the wife of Alfred E.
Motta of a son.

April 22, 1914
Duquesnay-At 5 Norman Crescent, on the 18th inst., the wife Theo. LeMercier
Duquesnay of a son.

LATE DEATHS IN PARISHES—East Indian who Died Suddenly from Convulsions—
VOMITING SICKNESS—Cases that have Occurred in Trelawny and Manchester—NO
INQUESTS ARE NECESSARY.

April 25, 1914
A NEW doctor—Success of Mr. G.E. Valentine—It is gratifying to announce
that Mr. Gilbert E. Valentine, who was educated at Wolmer's School and carried off the
Jamaica Scholarship some six or seven years ago, has completed his medical studies in
Aberdeen University, Scotland and passed the final examinations for the degrees of M.B.
and M.Ch. The distinguished student has also taken the degrees of M.A. and B.Sc., and
has therefore, fully maintained the scholarly traditions of his native land.
Word has just been received that young Dr. Valentine has secured an
appointment on the staff of the Royal Asylum in Montrose, and has settled down to the
discharge of his duties in that Institution.
All his old friends in the colony will be glad to receive this news of his success.

April 28, 1914
MAY-At his residence at Douce, Crooked River at 11 a.m. on Wednesday the 22nd
April, 1914, SAMUEL MAY leaving a widow and son to mourn their irreparable loss.
"He is not dead, but sleepeth".

Selected Vital Records from the Jamaican Daily Gleaner

April 29, 1914

MURRAY-At her residence, "The Lodge", Arnold Road lower St Andrew, yesterday Tuesday 28th at 6 a.m. SARA BRIDGET, the beloved wife of E.E. Murray. Funeral moves from the house at 8 a.m. today.

KEELING-On the 27th inst., the wife of A.L. Keeling of St Jago Park, Spanish Town of a son.

April 30, 1914

WEDDING BELLS-Mr. H. Roper and Miss D. Douet Joined In Wedlock—Ceremony Yesterday—Honeymoon is being Spent at Shaw Park St Ann.

A quiet and fashionable wedding was celebrated at the Half-Way Tree Parish Church yesterday morning, the contracting parties being Mr. Harold Roper, the manager of the Atlantic Fruit Company's estates in St James and Miss Dorrit Douet, a daughter of the late Mr. George Douet.

The bridesmaids were Miss Winnie Douet, Miss Marjorie Burke and Miss Alice Roper, whilst Mr. Wolverston filled the role of groomsman.

Canon Wortley officiated, and the service was fully choral.

The bride was given away by Mr. A.W. Douet, her uncle, and a large number of friends and relatives witnessed the ceremony.

After the knot had been tied, the party repaired to the rectory, where a reception was held. Mr. and Mrs. Roper then left for Shaw Park, a property belonging to Sir John Pringle, K.C.M.G., where the honeymoon will be spent.

Mr. and Mrs. Roper have been the recipients of many valuable and useful presents.

May 2, 1914

CURRENT ITEMS

Colonel C.B. Blagrove, C.B., was among the passengers who sailed on the Oruba yesterday for Southampton.

COLTHIRST-SCOTT—At Highbury St Ann on 29th ult. By the Rev. C.H. Swaby, DONALD FORBES, second son of A.C.C. Colthirst, Esq. to Laura Minnie Helena, 2nd daughter of the late T.B. Scott, Esq.

May 2, 1914

OBITUARY

DEATH OF MRS. E.E. MURRAY OF THIS CITY.

The death occurred on Tuesday this week, of the wife of Dr. E.E. Murray. Born at Elma, Arthur's Seat, Clarendon, she was the third daughter of the late Rev. H.C.P. MacDermot, niece of the Rev. Canon H.M.F. MacDermot, and sister of "Tom Redcam".

The affection and esteem which her life inspired in all circles where she was known, was shown by the gathering round her grave, not alone by the numbers that thus did honour to her memory, and by the representative character of the assembly, but by the deep spontaneous love and sympathy shown.

Her life was a pure flame of self-sacrifice and loving desire to serve others. She shrank from praise and never entered in the smallest degree on public life, but with her crystal-like simplicity of character and noble self-abnegation there was combined an intrepid bravery. When Kingston was on fire after the terrible earthquake of 1907 she came down into the city and, with one or two others, was instrumental in rescuing her

1914

brother who was buried in the ruins in Harbour Street, at what was then the Jamaica Times office.

A great lover of birds, animals and flowers, her tender heart also responded unceasingly to the calls of suffering human beings, no matter what their rank or degree, and no matter what their trouble. Her marriage was an ideally happy one, but in her happiness the beautiful unselfishness of her nature shone out, and hardly anyone who knew her but will remember her for some act of kindness or thoughtfulness. Her death falls as an overwhelming sorrow on her husband and immediate relatives, but its shadow falls on every circle where she was known.

The funeral service was performed by the Rev. Canon Wortley, assisted by the Rev. E. B. Brice, and the grave in the Half-Way Tree Church yard was covered and banked in by the beautiful flowers in the form of wreaths and crosses that were laid on it.

OFF TO THE SHOW
(From Our Correspondent)
Brown's Town, April 30. Today the town is as if deserted, a large number of the people from this end having gone to attend the agricultural show at Stewart Town, Woodlands Common. Several motor cars are plying for hire between here and the grounds and quite a stir and confusion is seen in the going to and fro of the many vehicles. Nearly all business houses have been closed so as to allow of the employees attending the show.

A CONCERT
A successful concert came off in the Elliot school room, Richmond, on the 30th April, notwithstanding the inclement weather the people turned out after the showers and there was a good house. Mr. J.A. Banks, a resident in the district was asked to preside over the meeting. The minister of the Church being unavoidably absent.

May 5, 1914
WALKER—At No 1, Bow Street, Rae Town, Kingston, on the evening of Monday the 4th May, EMMIE, the beloved wife of William J. Walker. Funeral will leave the house at 4.30 this afternoon for St Andrew's Kirk.

May 9, 1914
GOOD WORK OF JAMAICA COLLEGE-The Prize Distribution Function yesterday Afternoon—CREDITABLE REPORTS-Sound Advice Given to Pupils by Assistant Bishop,
The annual prize distribution in connection with the Jamaica College came off yesterday afternoon at the College. There was a fair attendance of parents and friends and the function, proved a most enjoyable one.

The chair was taken by His Lordship Bishop de Carteret, and among those present were: His Lordship Bishop Collins, Mr. Hector Josephs, K.C., Dr. C.A.H. Thomason, Lieut. Colonel Gruchy, Ven. Archdeacon Simms, M.A. (Headmaster), Rev. J. L Ramson, M.A., the Hon. Robert Johnstone, Acting Col. Secretary, Mr. F.E. Reed, Rev. W.F. O'Hare, S.J., Mr. Wm. Cowper, M.A. Mr. J.M. Nethersole, Dr. Maunsell, Rev. A. N. Thomson, Mr. A. deC. Myers, Mr. R.H. Smith, M.A., Mr. R.M.Murray, B.A., Mr. C.A. Warner, Mr. J. A. Bulman.

....

THE PRIZES
The prizes were then distributed by His Lordship as follows:
FORM VI
C.McL. Morales (Languages and Mathematics)
FORM V

Selected Vital Records from the Jamaican Daily Gleaner

E.D.A. Doran (Mathematics) W. E. McCutloch (Science and Drawing)
FORM IV
(Seniors)
E.G.A Don (Languages, etc.) F.N. DaCosta (Mathematics) L.C.Veira (Science and Drawing)
(Juniors)
W.N. Dickenson (Languages) L.E. Ashenheim (Mathematics)
FORM III
G.A.P. Thomason (Languages) E.A. Edmonds (Mathematics) E.A. Edmonds (Drawing)
FORM II
H.W. Stockhausen (Languages and English) H.A. Plant (Science and Drawing)
FORM I
H.W. Bolton (Languages etc.) W.A.D. Cover and S.E.L Ferreira (Mathematics) W.A.D. Cover (Science)

His Lordship in handing the prize for mathematics in Form IV juniors to Master L.E. Ashenheim congratulated him on the many distinctions gained at the Cambridge exams.

The headmaster said that although beaten by a phenomenal Wolmers boy, who got distinctions in six subjects, Master Ashenheim was the first boy in Jamaica in four subjects (Loud applause)..........

May 14, 1914
YOUNG-Claire, wife of R.L. Young of Brown's Town, St Ann's Bay, in Kingston at 9 a.m. on the 13th. Funeral at St Ann's Bay this afternoon.

May 15, 1914
DeLEON-On the morning of 14th inst. at 14 Rae Street, Rae Town, ALICE MAUD, the beloved wife of W. L. DeLeon in her 38th year, leaving two children and a large circle of relatives and friends to mourn their loss. R.I.P.

May 16, 1914
TOWNEND-At Los Angeles, Banes, Oriente Cuba on the 3rd inst., the wife of Arthur E. Townend of a daughter

May 18, 1914
MURRAY-On the 17th day of May, 1914 at 20 Bray Street, Kingston, SARAH ELIZABETH, eldest daughter of the late Elias Murray of Port Royal. Aged 78 years. Funeral moves at 8 o'clock this morning.

May 19, 1914
Personal
Mrs. Urcella May of Crooked River adopts this medium of returning thanks to her numerous friends and well wishers for their kind letters of sympathy and messages of condolence during her recent sad bereavement.

Dr. E.E. Murray begs through this medium to very sincerely thank all those who have by telegrams, cards, letters, and in other ways, shewn sympathy for him in his recent sad bereavement.

May 19, 1914

PROMINENT RESIDENT OF ST ANN—History of the Life and Work of Mr. Albert Joseph Hart—Long Lived Family—Has served Parish on Parochial Board fro Fully 17 years.

(Written specially for the "Gleaner" by our Saint Ann's Bay Correspondent)

Mr. Albert Joseph Hart, whose photograph we have the pleasure of reproducing above, comes of a well-known, respected and long-lived family. His parents were Mr. and Mrs. Aaron Hart of Montego Bay—his mother being a niece of the late Sir Jacob Adolphus. He first saw the light of day on 10th March 1841At Reden Wharf-now known as the Bogue Island in "noble" St James.

His mother and father both died at the advanced age of 84 years. One of his uncles, Jacob Jacobs, died at the age of 79 and an aunt, Mrs. Daniel Levy, reached the age of 88. There are also Mr. Ellis Hart (aged 82) and Mr. George Josephs (aged 88) still living. Mr. Samuel Hart of Montego Bay is a brother, and Mrs. Georgiana Nunes of Kingston Gardens, a sister of the subject of our sketch. Reference was made in the columns of the "Gleaner" to Mrs. Nunes who has seen her fifth generation.

Mr. Hart's early education was received from Rev. J.K. Hepburn, of Montego Bay. He afterwards went to the Montego Bay Academy where he completed his education under Rev. Geo. Miller. That he was a clever youth can be easily seen from the business ability that he possesses in his mature years. His power of concentration, his quickness of figures, the ease and intelligence with which he converses on almost any topic, his knowledge of Biblical facts and Hebrew, and the general unimparing of his intellectual powers at this age speak volumes for him.

He is popularly known as "Mass Albert" and is a favourite with all classes of the community. There is no gentleman who is more approachable or who will exhibit a keener interest in anything that concerns the welfare of any of his fellowmen.

As a Jew, he is a firm believer in the Hope of Israel, but although he will take a firm stand for his religious tenets, he will not despise a man on account of that man's religious belief differing materially from his. He is always ready to co-operate in any thing that tends to the betterment of his fellowmen.

The respect with which he is held was undoubtedly evinced during his recent illness when, during all hours of the day, rich and poor were to be seen wending their way up the stairs to see "Mass Albert".

A LOVER OF ANIMALS

His hobby seems to be the keeping of pet animals-especially birds – and the rearing of flowering plants; and we think that it can be said with safety that a keener admirer of these is hard to find.

"Mass Albert" made his advent to St Ann's Bay in 1869. He was employed by the old and reliable firm of Messrs. Chas. Levy and Co. as mercantile clerk, second in charge of the establishment. He served in this capacity for seven years. On account of the ability that he displayed, Mr. Levy wanted him to have opened a branch at Port Maria, but just about the same time the firm shut down business in Kingston, and so the opening of this new branch was out of the question.

In 1871 he was married to a daughter of the late Mr. David Morris, of Ipswich, England a cousin of the late Mr. Charles Alexander of Kingston. He subsequently decided on opening business here pour soi compte, and with the aid of Messrs Bravo Bros., Mr. Solomon and others he did so in 1873, with the full consent of his then employers – Messrs Levy and Co. In 1875 Messrs. Levy and Co., closed business here, but Mr. Hart's own business has been going on ever since, with the exception of about 3 years (1889-92) when accompanied by his wife, he took a trip to New York.

Along with Messrs. M. Solomon, Alexander Lake, D. Carvalho, H. DeLisser and a few others he was instrumental in founding the Seville Lodge (530 S.C) in 1871 and he had the honour of being its first Secretary and Treasurer. The above named Lodge is one of the most historic in the island - having at one time over 90 members enrolled. They also established Mar Lodge which had a membership of over 30.

There is a long list of noble men in connection with the Seville Lodge who have gone to their rest, and A.J. Hart alone remains as the oldest resident founder of it. It may not be out of place to mention that his mother Lodge was the Athole Union of Falmouth.

SERVED ON THE BOARD

He has also creditably served his parish in the capacity of member of the Parochial Board for fully 17 years. Some idea of his usefulness on the Board can be had from the fact that at the time he was chairman of every committee. He became a member in 1894 and remained as such until 1898, when he resigned. He again served from 1900 to 1909 and from 1911 to 1912. All this time he was returned for the Saint Ann's Bay division. Then in 1913 [Picture] he was returned for the Claremont and Moneague divisions and is still serving them.

It may be well here to state that when Ocho Rios was unrepresented, Mr. Hart acted on a committee for them (in conjunction with Rev. Atkins) for over 6 months, and went up weekly to see after the work.

After the hurricane of 1903, he again rendered yeoman service, serving in the capacity of Chairman of the Local committee to distribute doles, for rebuilding houses that were destroyed, as well as distributing articles of clothing, etc. This involved an expenditure of over £597 and letters (which he still has in possession) were sent him from the Central Board congratulating him on the splendid success that he had achieved.

Mr. Hart does not work for thanks or commendation. He aims only at having the satisfaction that he is doing what he can.

The greatest blow of his life came in 1907 when he lost his beloved wife. He has never quite recovered from that blow, and as soon as the anniversary of the death comes round readers of the "Gleaner" can always see from his "In Memoriam" that the event is still fresh in his memory, but to make use of his own words that he used when spoken to on this subjects some time ago, "God has been with me and I bow to His will". May "Mass Albert's" smiling face long continue among us.

May 20, 1914
KERR-JARRETT-At Catherine Hall on the 16th inst., to Mr. and Mrs. Kerr-Jarrett, a daughter.

YOUNG-In Kingston on 13th May, 1914, CLAIRE, beloved wife of Robt. L. Young of Hawkhurst, St Ann in her 48th year.
"We miss her voice, her touch and the true helping of her willing hand,
Till through the storm and tempest safely anchored just on the other side,
We'll find her dear face looking through deaths shadow, not unchanged, but glorified".

May 21, 1914
BROMFIELD-Mary Ann, at the residence of her son C.D. Rowe, 27 East Queen St. last night at 8 o'clock. Funeral moves at 4.30 o'clock this evening. Friends and acquaintances of Mr. C.D. Rowe are requested to accept this the only intimation.

May 22, 1914
PASCOE-WILLIAM GEORGE, at his late residence, Clevedon, St Andrew, in his 65th year.

1914

JAMAICA COLLEGE
ANNUAL ATHLETIC MEETING
The annual athletic meeting in connection with the Jamaica College came off successfully at the college grounds yesterday afternoon, in the presence of a large number of spectators.
Following are the results:
Throwing the Cricket Ball
G.L. William (94.0.8)...1
E.A. Edmond...2
100 Yards Under 12
D. Chambers...1
G.L.Reid..2
Time 13.3
One hundred Yards Under 16
B.G. Strudwick..1
R.A. Burke..2
L.A. Malabre..3
Time 10.9-10
One Hundred Yards Over 16
A.O. Thomson..1
S.L. Scott..2
Time 10.4-5
100 yds Under 13
H. Lawrence...1
W. DeLisser...2
Time 13 secs
220 yards Under 16
R.A.Burke...1
B.G.Strudwick...2
Time 25 secs
Long Jump Open
A.O. Thomson (18.2 ½)...1
R.A.Burke (18.1½)...2
High Jump Under 15
R.A.Burke, 4 ft 10..1
V.E. Prendergast 4 ft 8.......................................2
440 Yards Over 16
S.L. Scott..1
W.N.Dickenson...2
220 Yards Under 14
N. Ashenheim..1
H. Chambers...2
220 Yards Under 13
W. Crosswell..1
C.Don...2
Time 30 3-10
440 Yards Under 16
L.A. Malabre..1
R.A. Burke..2
B.G. Strudwick..3
Time 58 1-5

449

Pole Vault

R.A.Burke...1

E.G.A. Don..2

220 Yards Under 12

A.Sangster...1

H. Macglashan...2

D. Chambers..3

High Jump Over 15

D.P. Thomson (5 ft 1)...1

A.O. Thomson...2

440 Yards Under 13

C.Don...1

W. Crosswell...2

Time 70.2-5

220 Yards Over 16

H.O. Thomson...1

P. Stines..2

Time 25 secs

880 Yards Open

J.M. Burke..1

S. Stockhausen..2

W.N. Dickenson...3

220 Yds Consolation Race

S. Ferriera...1

May 23, 1914

GREAT ABILITY-Mr. H.A. Cunha is one of City's Astute Financiers--RECENT APPOINTMENT--The Decision given in Late Insurance Arbitration Proceedings--

We published yesterday the full text of the award which Mr. H.A. Cunha, the well known accountant and auditor, give in the arbitration proceedings between Mr. Ferreszade and the Yorkshire and Jamaica Cooperative Fire Insurance Companies.

As will be seen from the award, the assured, Mr. Ferreszade has only been allowed a little less than half the amount he claimed, viz., £2,013 12s 9d.

Mr. Cunha, the umpire, has gone very carefully into the matter and his decision is regarded as being sound.

[Picture, Mr. H.A. Cunha]

It is understood that Mr. Ferreszade has decided to bring an action against the two companies to recover the full amounts under the policies which he carried with them. The suit will be launched by Messrs. Morrison and Morrison.

The solicitors who are acting for the Insurance Companies are Messrs. Milholland, Ashenheim and Stone.

Mr. Cunha, whose picture is published herewith, is one of the most capable business men in the city and an appreciation of his ability as a financier was shown a couple of weeks ago, when the directors of the Myrtle Bank Hotel Company, offered him the appointment of secretary of that concern.

Mr. Cunha has accepted the appointment, and hopes to do for the company what he did for the late Sir Alfred Jones (in connection with the old Myrtle Bank and Constant Spring hotels), viz., to make it a success.

1914

May 26, 1914

SERIES OF OUTRAGES-Militant Suffragettes destroy some more valuable pictures—
WILD SCENES IN COURT—Magistrate on bench is bombarded with bags of flour—
The Harangue of a Militant.
(Special Service Cable) (By Direct W.I. Co., via Bermuda)

London, May 22-A militant suffragette today slashed and damaged five
pictures in the National Gallery. Among them were four valuable paintings by Giovanni
Bellini. As Friday is Student's Day at the National Gallery, all rooms were thronged with
young artists engaged in copying masterpieces.....................Pictures damaged in the
National Gallery were a Madonna and child with infant saints, a portrait of Girolamo
Malatini, Saints John, and Christopher and the doge, a landscape with the death of Saint
Peter, and Christ's Agony in the garden. Apparently they were not irreparably injured.

CHAINED TO CHAIR

London, May 22—The King and Queen listened to the harangue of a militant suffragette
this afternoon, while they were attending a matinee at His Majesty's theatre. A woman
rose in the stalls and began to address the King. "You Russian Czar," she shrieked; and
then the attendants found that she was chained to the seat and they had to cut through a
link before she could be removed. While this was in progress a half dozen women in
different parts of the theatre started shouting at His Majesty. One of them jumped up and
began to speak, and when she had been thrown out others began. Eventually all the
disturbers were ejected and the police on duty outside had a hard struggle to rescue them
from the hostile crowd.

June 4, 1914

PERSONAL

R.L. Young of Hawkhurst Farm, and Mrs. H.Q. Levy of Brown's Town, and their family,
desire to express grateful thanks and appreciation to their many friends throughout the
island for kind sympathy in their recent sad bereavement.

LATE ROBBERY-The Big Theft of Jewellery from Mr. Abraham's Store—ANOTHER
"FIND" MADE—Discovery of the Tools That were Used on the Job.

City detectives, working along with the man Nelson (who found Mr. Roland
Abrahams' stolen jewellery in a burial ground on the Spanish Town Road on Saturday
last made another find yesterday in connection with the matter.

Some little distance from where the jewellery was dug up searchers came
across the "tools" used in breaking into the store, and then to cut through the door of the
steel safe. These consisted of, as far as can be learnt, four drills, a powerful bit, and a
long screw attachment for the drills. The towel, which was also taken from Mr. Roland
Abrahams' store, and in which it is believed the jewellery was wrapped up has also been
found.

The detective department is trying to locate Paul Dennis of Cuba, with a view
to bringing him back to Jamaica in connection with the robbery.

June 6, 1914

WHITELOCKE-At "Bulstrode Park" Westmoreland, Jamaica on 1st June 1914,
CHARLES OLIVER TATE WHITELOCKE, youngest son of the late Hon. Hugh.
Anthony Whitelocke, aged forty-seven years. English and American papers please copy.

June 13, 1914

DALLAS-At No 10 Foster Lane, ELLEN, beloved wife of T. Douglas Dallas. Funeral moves from the residence at 4.30 this afternoon for St. Andrew's Kirk, thence to the place of interment. Friends and acquaintances will please accept this intimation.

June 15, 1914

WILSON-At "The Quarters", Brown's Town, St Ann, on Wednesday June 10th the wife of Dr. W.E. Wilson of a daughter.

June 15, 1914

GOVERNOR VISITS BROWN'S TOWN--Presides at Prize Distribution of Deaconess High School--KEEN ON EDUCATION.--Excellent Work being Done in the Schools Of the Island.

(From Our Correspondent)

Brown's Town, June 11.- The annual prize distribution of the Deaconess High School of this town came off at the school room on Wednesday at 4 p.m.

The room was tastefully decorated with evergreens and shrubs and the seating of the room was neatly arranged. In spite of threatenings of a thunderstorm, a goodly number of parents and friends attended. Among those presents were: His Excellency Sir William Manning, Capt. and Mrs. Dennistoun, Hon J.H. and Mrs. Allwood, Miss Turner (headmistress), Mr. J.H. Levy, Revs. Henderson and Hall, Manager and Rector (on the platform); Mr. and Mrs. A.C. Dunkley, Mr. and Mrs. C. E. Levy, Dr. Miller, Mr. G.A. Cocks, Miss Cocks, Mrs. James Johnson, Mrs. Hall, Miss deLisser, Rev. and Mrs. Graham, Mrs. Tucker, Miss Fraser, Miss Sutherland, Mrs. Harty, Mr. and Mrs. Jno. Lynch, Dr. C.F. Smith, Mr. H.Q. Levy, Mr. and Mrs. J. A. Dickenson, the Misses Ethlene and Hilda Dickenson, Mrs. H.F. Isaacs, Mrs. Jeffrey-Smith, Dr. Wilson, Mr. and Mrs. E. Helwig, Mr. Bailey, Mrs. Ella Stephenson, Mr. L.W. Levy, Mr. C.F. Jacobs, Mr. R. Moss, Mr. and Mrs. J.A. Thomson, Miss Monica Thomson, Miss Miles, Miss Ruby Lindo, Mrs. H. Stephenson, Mr. C.R. Thomson, Mrs. Hopwood and children, Mr. and Mrs. A.S. Byles, Mr. A.E. Murray, Miss Lena Murray, Mrs. J.H. Levy, Mrs. Henderson, the Misses Alice and Elsie Henderson, Miss Ingram, Miss Coates, Mrs. Simpson, Miss Frazer (assistant teacher) Miss McGregor, and the pupils of the school and others.

Some minutes after 4 o'clock, His Excellency accompanied by the Hon. J.H. Allwood, Capt. and Mrs. Dennistoun and Mrs. Allwood, arrived and was escorted to the platform, while a verse of the national Anthem was sung.

Rev. Mr. Hall thereafter extended a welcome of Irish founding, he said to His Excellency: he appreciated very much his presence and the honour conferred on the school by His Excellency's consent to distribute the prizes. It was another evidence of His Excellency's interest in education. Brown's Town, he continued was becoming well known as an educational center. It now possessed two high schools for boys, one high school for girls and a private school, and from the latest published records of the Government, it had the largest Government Elementary School in the island. This school now had over 500 children with 73 marks.

The aim of the Deaconess High School, he proceeded, was not only to impart sound knowledge, but build character and make good citizens. The school was fortunate in securing the services of Miss Turner, who was an efficient headmistress and splendid teacher and worker, and assisted by a competent staff, the school gave promise of making its influence felt in the community.

Miss Turner, the headmistress, was then asked to read the report for the year, which is as follows:-

THE REPORT

1914

The year has been fairly uneventful. We seem to have been gathering ourselves together and putting ourselves in order. It has been a year in which we have been strengthening our stakes and lengthening our cords, and now we are ready to go forward. We have been gradually increasing in numbers, and have now reached a total of 35 scholars, 18 of whom are borders.

The staff has been changed by the appointment of Miss Fraser as senior mistress, and of Miss MacGregor. There are now six forms in the school, and we have been able to establish the fourth, fifth, and sixth forms in class rooms adjoining the school, which is a great improvement. We are, however, outgrowing our class rooms-the fifth form is almost out of the door.

As regards examination work our record is fairly successful. Out of eleven candidates who entered for the practical examinations of the Associated Board of the Royal Academy and Royal College of Music, in April of last year, ten passed. We entered fifteen for the same examinations this year and are still awaiting results. Five scholars entered for the Cambridge Local Examinations in December last, all of whom passed. But of course, we consider the preparation for examinations as one of the lesser departments of our school work. The purpose of education, as everyone knows, is to prepare the young, not for examinations, but for life. We want each of our girls, as she leaves us, to be in some measure prepared to take her place as a citizen in the world. And in order to do this, she must be developed- not only intellectually, but also morally and physically. Success and usefulness in the world depend upon character, and therefore we put before everything the building up of the characters of those committed to our care. Jamaica needs trained and disciplined women, as well as men, if she is to prosper. And so we would before all things train up our girls to be good citizens- to take their stand- to be strong enough to fight against evil – and to be themselves a power for good in the world. And therefore although we may not possess scholars of brilliant mental capacity, (though we know not what latent talent may be lying dormant in some of them), I think we have a right to be encouraged when we look at our school. For there are signs which show promise of something far more valuable than ability to pass examinations-signs of grit-signs of ability to tackle hard work-signs of love of knowledge for its own sake and of joy in work for work's sake all of which are signs that we are alive. And so long as we can feel that we are alive, then, I think, there is promise of great hope for the future.

PRIZE WINNERS

The reading of the report was followed by the long-looked for and eagerly awaited distribution of prizes by His Excellency and the presentation of their certificates to those who had been successful in the Cambridge Local Examinations.

The following is he list of prize winners:

Form Prizes

Form I: -Dorothy Purchas
Form II: - Enid Isaacs
Form III.- Nina Dunkley
Form IV. - Nina Levy
Form V. - Sylvia Levy

II Cambridge Certificates
Cambridge Junior.-- Edna L. Moss
Cambridge Junior.-- Marian M. Dunkley
Cambridge Preliminary.--Violet C. Levy
Cambridge Preliminary.-- Sybil H. Jones
Cambridge Preliminary.-- Doris Lynch

III Special Subjects

Scripture, First prize presented by the Archbishop.- Sybil H. Jones

Scripture, Second prize-Violet C. Levy.

English presented by Miss Elizabeth Schoept--Sylvia Levy

History, presented by Miss H.L. Powell--Nina Dunkley

French--Eileen Tucker

Geography--Cora Hopwood

Mathematics--Sybil H. Jones

Prayer Book, presented by Bishop de Carteret--Valentine Lynch

Cambridge Junior presented by Miss Elizabeth Schoept--Edna L. Moss

Cambridge preliminary--Violet C. Levy

Good conduct, presented by Sister Madeline--Enid Geddes

IV. Essay Prizes

English essay, presented by Mrs. Bourne, Sybil H. Jones, History essay presented by His Excellency Sir W.H. Manning-- Nina Levy.

The last prize- and the prize par excellence-was the one presented by His Excellency himself for English History. This prize had been competed for by the writing of essays, various subjects having been given for the competitors to choose from. Before the presentation of this prize, therefore Nina Levy, to whom the prize had been awarded read her essay.

The essay, which showed considerable grasp of the subject "Marlborough-the man-the General" was very much applauded, and His Excellency, in presenting the prize to the youthful composer, congratulated her on winning his prize and on the excellence of her essay. The prize was a two-volume edition of Carlyle's "French Revolution" bound in leather.

THE GOVERNORS REMARKS

Having completed the distribution of the prizes, His Excellency gave a delightful address to the school.

He said he was very glad to be present at the prize distribution of the school. It was not the first time he had had the privilege to address school girls, as short time ago he addressed a branch of this school in Kingston on a similar occasion. The report read by the Headmistress only emphasized what he had heard of the excellent work being done by High Schools in the island. He endorsed what had been said, that the object of education was not only the inculcating of book-learning, but the building up of character. The air and atmosphere in which the teaching was given had an important effect upon after life. The building up of character in a school was of vast importance. The character of the rising generation should be the care of the present. If neglected, then there must and could only be one result, that those who followed would not have the example before them, which he trusted, they themselves had always had. It behooved them to remember what they learnt. They would have to go out into the world and it would be useful in various ways. Most of what was learnt they would remember, but some they would probably forget. What they remembered would prove useful to them, but of greater importance was the moral training, the teaching of which, if followed in life would prove more useful to them and make them good and honourable women and worthy citizens of the island and the Empire to which they belong. As had been pointed out, they were here not only to imbibe book-knowledge, the importance of which he would not undervalue, but he trusted what they learnt would be for their betterment, and would remain with them, building up character. He desired to say a few words to the staff of the school. He desired on behalf of the island, to thank them for their work and to encourage them in further endeavours. He knew, he said how carefully the mistresses were chosen, and from the teaching he knew the work carried out was excellent. He desired, as Governor of the Island to encourage them. He appreciated very much the importance laid upon the moral training and because of that he was here to express his appreciation of the teaching imparted, and to encourage and wish for this school and other schools of the island success. (Cheers).

HON.J.H. ALLWOOD

The Hon. J.H. Allwood, with his usual eloquence and graceful delivery, said he was projected into the programme for the purpose of moving a vote of thanks to His Excellency. In an interesting speech he paid tribute to His Excellency's willingness to always take part in what is good and uplifting. He assured him that not only as his coming appreciated by those immediately connected with the school, but by the whole community. He said His Excellency's visit happily synchronized with the coming of the rain, as a heavy shower had fallen at Enfield on the arrival of His Excellency, and where he is now staying. His Excellency, he said, had braved the long and dusty journey and the boredom of country life to distribute the prizes.

He then congratulated the winners of prizes on their achievement, and encouraged those who had not won prizes to strive and work harder with the hope of securing prizes at the next distribution. He hoped the school would advance and grow, and in the near future one of the girls of the school would win the blue ribbon of secondary education in Jamaica-the Girl's Scholarship.

He had much pleasure in moving a vote of thanks to His Excellency for being present to distribute the prizes.

Rev. Mr. Graham said he too was projected into the programme for the purpose of seconding the vote of thanks to His Excellency. He took it for granted that His Excellency's presence that afternoon was an indication of his interest in secondary education. He was always at a loss to understand how so much money was spent year by year in elementary education and little or no provision was made for those men from whose pockets a large portion of the moneys were obtained. He hoped the time was not far distant when the matter would be taken up and considered by the Governor and the hon. Member of the parish, and he would see on the next estimates of the colony ample provisions made, not only for elementary education, but secondary education.

SCHOOL CONCERT

The ceremony was brought to a close by the school concert. The programme consisted of songs rendered by the school, pianoforte solos, Latin, French and English recitation. Proceedings were finally concluded by the singing of the Doxology.

The school possessing no suitable grounds, a reception was held at the Richmond Hotel, to which all the guests were invited.

Prize days are always glowing days in school annals, but all those connected with the school will look back to June 10th, 1914 as a day which stands out very specially among red-letter days, owing to the kindness of His Excellency the Governor in coming down and cheering both the school and the staff by his presence among them.

The programme for the concert was as follows:-
Song A hunting we will go 18th century ………The School
Recitation……… Ode XIII Horace ………..Nina Dunkley
Piano Solo…. Liede Ohne wore Gullitt……..E. Helwig
Recitation…………The Lost leader…..Browning…. Nina Levy
Piano Duet………Spanish Dance……Kirchner…..V. Levy and E. Stephenson
Recitation………..Adieu de Marie Stuart……..Beranger….S. Levy
Piano Solo ………Scarf Dance……….Chaminade…………R. Harty
Song………Dulce Domum………17th Century…………The School

THE DOXOLOGY

The Governor and party left for Enfield, being the guests of the hon. member for the parish.

June 16, 1914
Advertisement

CLIFTON HOUSE SCHOOL
(Gordon Town)
Headmaster: W. Hugh Walker Esq. (Int. B.A. London, etc)
Assisted by a competent Staff
HOME SCHOOL. SOCIAL LIFE A FEATURE
Preparation for Public Schools, Army, Navy, Public Service
And University Exams
Boys return on Thursday April 23
The Headmaster will be at Clifton on and after Sunday,
April 19, from 2-6 p.m. Otherwise by appointment
The school will probably move to more spacious premises either in St Andrew or St Ann.
No immediate vacancies.

COLONIAL HIGH SCHOOL, Kingston, Jamaica
Reopens 5th May, 1914, Girls and Boys in separate departments
Staff-Mrs. W.G. Twiney (nee Miss H. Ormsby) H.C.P. Higher Cert. N.F.U. University
training with distinction. Ablett's Drawing Hons.
Mr.W.G. Twiney B.Sc., Hons. Lond. F.C.S.
Miss L. Trench L.A.B. and a large number of certificated assistants.
Borders from home or abroad taken—Girls any age, but only small boys as boarders.
Reduction for brothers and sisters. All drinking water boiled. Healthy locality, large
building. Tennis court. Only respectable and well behaved children taken. Healthy
moral tone and good training. Preparation for Cambridge locals, Matric. Col of
Preceptors, Musical, Pitman's and other exams. Physical drill and all school subjects
taught. Preparatory class for young children. Special attention to English and
Arithmetic, Spanish, book-keeping and shorthand in upper forms. Typewriting extra.
Individual attention to backward children. Astonishing progress for quick pupils. School
equipped with science apparatus. Scientific agricultural principles with practical
demonstrations, needlework for girls and carpentry for boys-small scholarships offered to
bright and industrious pupils. Students of either sex may be prepared by correspondence
for Senior, Matric. Or Post Office Exams. Apply to the Principal 9 North St.

June 20, 1914
THE RESULTS OF THE EXAMINATIONS IN MUSIC—The Complete List of The
Successful Candidates—DIFFERENT DIVISIONS—Success Achieved by Pupils from
the Various Schools.

The following is the list of successful candidates at the examinations held this
year in connection with the Associated Board of the Royal Academy of Music and the
Royal College of Music:-[Not a complete list-extractor]
LICENTIATE OF THE ASSOCIATED BOARD.
Solo Performers examination.
Miss Grace M. Fisher, Miss Hannah L.R. Mordecai, Hampton School, Violin
LOCAL CENTRE
Advanced Grade
Miss Ellen Campbell, Miss L. Trench, Oxford Road, Piano; Miss Katie Craig, Mrs. Helen
Shirley, Singing; Miss Florence A. Fraser, Hampton School, Piano; Miss Constance
Gunter, Miss Gray, Piano (honours); Miss N.B. Muirhead, Miss E.V.Smith, Hampton
School, Piano.
Intermediate Grade

1914

Miss K.I. Abendana, Hampton, Piano; Miss G.E.M. Akin; Miss Trench, Oxford Road, Miss Carmen Cover Piano; Miss Constance Gunter, Miss Gray, Harmony; Miss Dulcie Humber, Hampton, Piano Miss Amy Lyon, Westwood High School, Piano; Miss Eulalie Manherty, Cathedral Deaconess High School, Spanish Town, Piano; Miss T.E. K. L. Marshalleck, Colonial High School, East St., Piano; Miss Mabel Watson, Miss L. Trench, Oxford Road, Piano.

Rudiments of Music

Miss K.I Abendana, Hampton School; Miss Carmen Cover; Miss Dulcie Humber, Hampton School; Miss Una Leahong, Colonial High School, East St.; Miss Claire Magnan, Miss L. Trench, Oxford Road; Miss Eulalie Mannhertz, Cathedral Deaconess High School, Spanish Town; Miss T.E.K.L. Marshalleck, Colonial High School, Kingston; Miss Ethel Marson, Hampton School; Miss Lucy Miller, Mrs. Helen Shirley, Cross Roads; Miss Gladys Reid, Miss Gladys Smith, Hampton School; Miss Mary Smith, Convent of Mercy, "Alpha"; Miss Mabel Watson, Miss L. Trench, Oxford Road; Miss Olney Watson, Kingston; Miss Lena Wilson, Hampton School.

SCHOOL EXAMINATION

Higher Division

Violet Delgado, Carmen Muschett, Rebecca Fisher, Lena Wilson, Elise Sanftleben, Enid Farquharson, Constance Mais, Hampton School, Piano; Ethel Smith, Hampton School, Violin; Norah Muirhead, Avis Costa, Hampton School, Singing; Inez Martinez Miss Beckwith, Piano; C. Phyllis Chandler, Miss Bovell, Piano; Dorothy Scarlett, Miss Braithwaite, Islington, Piano; Lilian Calder, Miss M.P. Miller, Malvern, Piano; Dora Morales, Miss Agnes Morales, Montego Bay, Piano; Doris Hart, Sybil Hart, Ruby Gideon, Miss Morrison, Mandeville, Piano; Hilda Cohen, Convent Immaculate Conception, Piano.

Lower Division

Olive McCrea, Zillah Lannamann, Annie Don, Hampton School, Piano; Enid Farquharson, Doris Levy, Hampton School, Violin; Phyllis Milholland, Miss Beckwith, Camperdown, Piano; Nesta Nash, Miss C.S. Hicks, Dry Harbour, Piano; Sydney Gayner, Lena Marsh, Mrs. McFadyen-Smith, Piano; Dorothy Thomson, E. Silveira, N. Escoffrey, Gladys Casseres, Barbara Isaacs, Neale Hargreaves, Miss Morrison, Mandeville, Piano; Daniel Marchelleck, Ven. Archdeacon Simms, Jamaica College, Piano; Ena Muschett, Helen Whitelock, Miss Thomas, Montpelier, Piano; Sarah Young, Miss Turner, Deaconess School, Brown's Town, Piano; Edna Murray, F. Cecelia Thomason, Miss Townsend, Westwood, Piano.

Elementary

Elly Bolton, Miss K. Bolton, Gordon Town, Piano; Mary Leon, Eva Messado, K.M. Clarke, Irene Dickson, Miss W. Clerk, Falmouth, Piano; Kathleen Dougall, Ellie Rutty, Miss Hilda Davis, Port Maria, Piano; Beryl Facey, Miss Facey, Brentford Road, Piano; Marian Calder, Miss Miller, Malvern, Piano; Joyce Sampson, Eugenie Labastille, Aileen Joyce, Donald Motta, Aileen Bartlett, Miss Morrison, Mandeville, Piano; Vida Hollar, Ivy Lamb, Enid Braham, Mrs. Parkinson, Brentford Road, Piano; David Marchalleck, Ven Archdeacon Simms, Piano; Linnette Squire, Edeline Soutar, Miss A.M. Soutar, Kingston, Piano; Sybil Cunningham, Miss Sylvia Sowley, Ivy Road, Piano (Dist) Violet Broderick, Miss Sylvia Sowley, Ivy Road, Piano; Ethel Sanftleben, Thomas Briscoe, Angele Reynado, Ruth Finlay, Marguerite Todd, Miss Thomas, Montpelier School, Piano; Elsie Geddes, Elsie Stephenson, Deaconess High School, Brown's Town, Piano; Cora Meikle, Eunice Roberts, A. Louise Brown, Elsie Cover, Gladys Eccleston, Ruth Hall, Miss Townsend, Westwood, Piano; Donald Hart Miss L. Trench, Oxford Road, Piano; Sybil Hart, Olive Roberts, Colonial High School, Kingston, Piano.

Primary Division

Gertrude Archer, Doris Ikin, Olive Isaacs, Miss Gladys Akin, Kingston, Piano; Elsa Lannamann, Miss Bovell, Half-way Tree, Piano; Helen Farquharson, May Farquharson, Miss L.L. Clark, May Pen, Piano; Olive Messado, Irene Dickson, Miss Winnifred Clerk, Falmouth, Piano; Eric Levy, Miss Collymore, Montego Bay, Piano; Mary Milliner, Helen Milliner, Miss Ida Milliner, Stewart Town, Piano; May Coke, Daphne Cooke, Beryl Escoffery, Elma Joyce, Winnifred Bartlett, Kathleen Charley, Gwen Lord, Cherry Pengelly, Rosita Lehman, Maisie Motta, Miss Morrison, Mandeville, Piano; Eugenie Labestille, Miss Morrison, Mandeville, Violin; Myrtle Muschett, Ruby Renado, Beryl McDermot, Miriam Levy, Miss Thomas, Montpelier, Piano; Linda Helwig, Enid Helwig, Cora Hopwood, Ruby Lindo, Leila Lynch, Enid Isaacs, Viola Thomason, Annis White, Deaconess Home School; Brown's Town, Piano.

Grammar of Music I

Sydney Gaynor, Linda Bonito, Augustine Hudson, Lena Marsh, Miss McFadyen-Smith, Kingston Gardens; Hilda Dickenson, Miss Townsend, Westwood.

Grammar of Music II

Barbara Ormsby, Olive Owen, Beryl Marchalleck, Edna Roberts, Colonial High School, Kingston

June 22, 1914

THE MUSIC EXAM

The Editor

Sir Will you please publish the following corrections to the list of successful candidates at the recent Music Examinations which appeared in your columns today:

Miss H.I.R. Mordecai (Hampton School) passes the L.A.E, Solo Performers Examination, taking Pianoforte as her subject and not violin.

Miss Carmen Cover, who passed the Local Centre Intermediate Division, Piano, was taught by Miss Winifred Saunders. Etc.etc.

E.H. HAUSE

Actg. Hon. Representative of the L.A.B.

Kingston

June 20, 1914

June 25, 1914

THE FIRST LARGE STEAMSHIP TO PASS THROUGH PANAMA CANAL [Picture]

The steamship Allianca, belonging to Panama Railroad Company, is the first large vessel to pass through the Gatun locks of the Panama Canal. That steamer was recently sent through the locks for the purpose of testing the electric locomotives that will be used to tow vessels through the locks. The test was a success, the locomotives handling the four thousand ton steamship easily and speedily. It took the Allianca one and one-half hours to pass through the locks.

June 26, 1914

ACTION TO RECOVER COST OF FRUIT SUPPLIES—Special Sitting of the R.M. Court at May Pen—W. March vs. H.Q. Levy—His Honour Decides The Action in Favour of Plaintiff.

(From our Correspondent). May Pen, Wednesday—At a special session of the Resident Magistrate's Court held here today, before His Honour Mr. C.H. Yorke-Slader, the case of W.F. March versus H.Q. Levy was heard.

The plaintiff was represented by Mr. G.G.Gunter, while the defendant conducted his own defence. The defendant's agent had contracted to take all the fruit that the plaintiff could supply on a certain day. On the day in question defendant informed the plaintiff that he did not require all the fruit; they were left at the station, and the plaintiff sued for damage of £10 9/ the value of fruit refused.

Mr. W.F. March commissioned land surveyor said Petgrave, the agent of Mr. Levy came to me and contracted with me to take all the English bananas I could supply on Monday the 11th May. The fruit was sent to the station, but only a portion was taken. After waiting a considerable time I sent two of my men to Petgrave and told him that the people were complaining; he then took another load of the fruit. I saw Mr. Levy after the night train left about 3 o'clock. I asked him what about the bananas, the draymen want to go away. He said he would take no more bananas from me. I told him "Petgrave ordered the fruit and so I brought them and now he tells me you say not to take any more". Mr. Levy said Petgrave told him he ordered 200 stems from me and he could not take any more. I told him I could not force him to take them but I would put them under the tree on which his license was fixed. I told him Petgrave had ordered all the English bananas. He said Petgrave told him he only ordered 200 stems. I told him Petgrave was mistaken. Witness continuing said I had the bananas put under the tree and counted and covered them. Next day I counted and graded them before Webbe and Robinson. I then consulted my solicitor at Chapelton. There was no change of selling English bananas that week or I would try and sell them.

Cross examined by Mr. Levy witness said: Lots of marketable fruit were left back at Chapelton Station.

Mr. Levy: Has it ever been your practice to take these orders in writing?

Witness: It is quite a common thing to take orders verbally as I did from Petgrave.

How many acres have you in banana cultivation? Witness: About 150 acres.

Mr. Levy: It is very desirable to get three quarter cutting isn't it?

Witness: When it is possible.

Mr. Levy: You get your fruit off earlier don't you?

Witness: Yes and it benefits the succeeding crop.

His Honour: Is it cheaper than the American Fruit?

Witness: No

Mr. Levy: If you cut fruit on the 11th of May when do you get full fruit in June?

Witness: By the end of May

Mr. Levy If you cut your three quarter fruit you may have a certain amount of risk?

Witness: Certainly

Mr. Levy How many stems of three quarter fruit would you get from 150 acres of land at that time the 11th May? I may be able to get 1,500 stems.

His Honour: If Petgrave had made this contract it is binding on him.

Mr. Levy: Has Petgrave ever been over your cultivation either at Ivy Lawn or Trout Hall
Witness: No

Did he know you had 150 acres in cultivation? Yes I told him so.

Have you ever got an open order for English fruit before? Yes.

I put it to you Mr. March, whenever you cut fruit for the Atlantic Fruit Company you are asked how many fruit you can cut first? The agent would say send all the bananas and say how many you can cut.

It is only sometimes they would ask how many can you cut? But more often they say cut all you can. That is sometimes they limited and sometimes unlimited orders.

Suppose on Saturday afternoon the agent wrote and said

SEND ALL THE ENGLISH FRUIT

you had but let me know how many you are sending. You sent to tell him you can supply 1,000 stems. Isn't he at liberty to reduce the amount before you cut on Monday? - Not if my orders have been given to cut already. If the reduction came before I sent my cutters he would be at liberty to reduce the order.

Mr. Gunter: Mr. Levy is airing what he knows about fruit contract, but he is wasting time.

Mr. Levy: Have you never heard of a case where after a man began to cut he is stopped?

Witness: Only in the case of contract fruit and then the company pays for what ever remains on the fields and ripen and even those that remain on the trees and ripen. In this case I never got an order to stop cutting.

Mr. Levy: Your Honour I am going to prove he did get an order to stop cutting.

His Honour: It is up to you, Mr. Levy

Mr. Levy: he got notice at a sufficiently early time in the day to stop cutting.

Mr. Gunter: You have changed your front.

Mr. Levy: You saw me at the railway station during the day?

Witness: Yes

I asked you if you were supplying fruit?-Yes

At that time you had how many cart loads in the station? I had five cart loads.

What did I say to you? You asked me how many loads have you?

What time was it? It was about 5 o'clock in the evening.

What is the customary load for a cart of bananas? Between 40 and 60 stems according to size.

THE NEXT WITNESS

The next witness, Harold Tapper, said I am employed to Mr. March as chauffeur. I saw Petgrave at the store of Mr. Thomas Abrahams. He told me to tell Mr. March to send whatever English fruit he could on Monday. I gave the message to Mr. March the same evening. On Monday morning I got Mr. March's car ready and I saw old Green and Mr. Petgrave come up in Ivy Lawn at seven o'clock. Petgrave waited for Mr. March on the verandah. Somebody called Mr. March and he came down to him. Petgrave told Mr. March he would take all the bananas he could supply him today. Mr. March asked what per 100 do you give? Petgrave said £10. Mr. March did not accept, so Petgrave said £10 10s 6d and they decided accordingly. Mr. March sent for the cutter who came to the verandah. Mr. March told him to cut the English fruit. Petgrave also told him to cut whatever English bananas he could get. Old Green was at the verandah at he time and heard the agreement. I then took Mr. March to Trout Hall and returned to Chapelton. I saw the bananas arrive at the station and saw Petgrave receiving them. I saw Mr. Levy come there at 5 o'clock. He said to Mr. March: I hear Mr. Petgrave is taking fruit from you. Mr. March replied "yes". After the drays were left outside, Mr. March sent me to Petgrave about 7 o'clock to ask him why he won't unload the drays, so that the draymen might go back. He said I don't think I can take anymore of the bananas. Mr. March sent me back later at about one o'clock in the night. I told him Mr. March asked what about the fruit? He said: "I don't know. I am not boss, wait till Mr. Levy comes".

Robert Green the next witness said: I live at Red Hills in Clarendon. On the 11th May I went to Mr. March yard before he woke about eight o'clock (laughter). While there I saw Mr. Petgrave: he was waiting on the verandah with me. Mr. March came out and Petgrave asked him for English bananas. He didn't tell Mr. March how many. He told him he must cut all his English bananas. They agreed at £10 10s 6d per 100 stems. Adolphus Blake, the next witness, who cuts Mr. March's bananas, corroborated the former witnesses as to the contract having been made.

EVIDENCE OF THE CHECKER

Mr. A.T. Webb said, I am a member of the Church of God and do not take the oath. He therefore repeated the affirmation after His Honour. He was a checker of fruit and checked these on the 10th May.

Cross-examined by Mr. Levy: You have checked English ¾ fruit before for the United Fruit Company? Yes

Have you ever noticed the quality of ¾ fruit the United Fruit Company take? Yes. Sometimes I check ¾ fruit for them

His Honour: Does the United Fruit Company require a higher grade?

460

Mr. Webb: There are occasions when the United Fruit Company ship to England.

Mr. Gunter: Is this a new defence?

Mr. Levy: How long would bananas take to ripen under the conditions which existed in that yard?

Witness: According to the quantity of covering, fruit generally ripen according to the heat developed among them.

Don't you know the amount of damage done to fruit in packed up cars? Yes

How long would these fruit take to ripen? In cool chambers they would ripen from 11 to 17 days.

How long would it take three quarter bunches to ripen? Under those conditions they would have ripened in 10 days.

Suppose they didn't ripen within three weeks would you consider them good fruit? I would say something was wrong, they should have ripened within 18 days.

You drew down a load of fruit for Mr. March, did you? Yes

Was there a certain amount of American fruit amongst them? Yes the heap I checked contained both English and American fruit.

As a matter of fact, each cart load contained a certain amount of English and American Fruit? Yes

Do you remember me going to you at a certain part of the day on Monday giving you instructions as to whose fruit you should take? – Yes

Mr. Gunter: I object to that.

R. Newman stated that he drew two loads of fruit for Mr. March: the first was taken the second was refused. The fruit he drew first were mixed. The English fruit from Mr. Levy the others for the Atlantic Fruit Company but the second load were all English fruit for Mr. Levy.

The case for the plaintiff having closed, His Honour asked Mr. Levy if he would go up first to give evidence for the defence.

Mr. Levy: Your Honour, I don't see that you have any case against me at all. The man who checked the fruit, who is the chief witness against me, said they were-

His Honour: They would be entitled to judgment against you as the case stands.

Mr. Gunter: It is necessary that Mr. Levy give evidence in the case first and especially so as he is his own advocate.

DEFENDANT'S EVIDENCE

Mr. Levy said: I am agent in the parish of Clarendon for United Fruit Company and purchase fruit at Chapelton station and other places. On the 9th May I got information from my company through a telegram as to the purchase.

Mr. Gunter: I object

Mr. Levy continuing; I instructed Petgrave to procure a certain quality of fruit.

Mr. Gunter: I object

His Honour: Just wait Mr. Gunter

Mr. Levy: I got this telegram (produced).

Mr. Gunter: I object.

His Honour: You are dealing with the United Fruit Company. We are dealing with your contract with Mr. March.

Mr. Levy: I gave instructions to Petgrave. On Monday 11th May I was in the Chapelton station yard when Mr. March, the plaintiff, came in his motor car. It was sometime near one o'clock. At that time there were about 5 loads of fruit in the yard belonging to the plaintiff. I went round to all the carts and found out that they belonged to Mr. March. At that time I was not aware that Mr. March was supplying any fruit that day to the Atlantic Fruit Company. On information given to me by Petgrave previous to that I went to the plaintiff and said to him "how many fruit are you cutting?" He said: "Between 400 and 500 stems" I said: "I don't know what you are going to do with them because Petgrave tells me he only ordered 4 loads of fruit from you". The plaintiff made absolutely no reply, but walked away towards his motor car and I went to my business. I then went round and collected the checks and counted the amount of fruit then delivered. As a matter of fact, I wanted to see if I could take any more fruit from the plaintiff. I gave certain instructions to my selectors. At three o'clock I left the station yard for my residence, stopping on the way to speak to suppliers all the time. When I got to Mears I was there some time. I got in my motor car and went up towards Frankfield. When I was going, I saw men cutting fruits on Mr. March property. I remained at Frankfield half an hour. It was 5 o'clock when I left Frankfield to go back on my way back I saw men still cutting fruits on Mr. March's property. I stopped opposite to where they were cutting and noticed the fruit being brought out, some were English and some American fruit. I went home changed car and went back to the station. After being there a considerable time, some time during the night the plaintiff came to me and said: "What about my fruit if you are not going to take them". I replied: "I had already told you only four loads were ordered from you. As a matter of fact I have taken more". Petgrave had told me he only ordered four and I

REFUSE TO TAKE ANY MORE

The day after receiving Mr. March's letter I was down at the station and I went towards the pile of fruit left down there, lifted some of the trash and examined the fruit so far as I could see. I found a good deal of exceedingly small fruit and a good proportion of it was round full America fruit.

His Honour: What do you call poor fruit?

Witness: What we call poor fruit in the trade, are those that have suffered from poor soil or something of the sort.

Witness continuing said: I didn't count them or disturb them: in any way. Sometime after that I noticed the heap of banana started ripening. Only a few days after they were placed there.

Mr. Gunter: You are an independent kind of an agent are you not?

Witness: It all depends.

You insist on taking out license in your own name? And you can buy as much as you like on your own risk?-Yes

And when you buy on your own risk and lose, you don't like it? Now why didn't you take these fruit, did you get vexed with Mr. March? No.

You were over loaded were you not? Had you exceeded your limit?- I had got my limit.

You had been receiving fruit from contractors during that day?- Yes

You had turned down lots of contract fruit? I refused to purchase a lot of open fruit.

You know what you mean by open fruit as distinguished from contract? – Yes

I put it to you Mr. Levy, that when contract fruit is ready to be cut it is up to you to pay for it or lose it altogether.

Witness: What do you mean by lose it altogether?- We pay for it whether we take it or not.

Mr. Gunter: On this occasion you had got all you wanted when you refused Mr. March's fruit? I had not.

But you just told us you made some effort to take some of the fruit. Would you have been vexed with Mr. Petgrave if he had given an order for an unlimited supply from Mr. March? I certainly would.

Don't you think speaking as a man of the world that Petgrave would have been a fool if he had readily admitted his fault? Are you not the Banana King of Chapelton"?

Witness: That is just what I am saying.

Mr. Gunter: But I want to tell you, you are not Lord of all you survey.

Many witnesses for the defence were examined, including Mr. Petgrave, who most emphatically denied ever giving an unlimited order to Mr. March.

1914

JUDGMENT FOR PLAINTIFF

At this stage His Honour summed up the case. "In a case like this" he said, "where I have a very sharp conflict it is very difficult to arrive at a proper verdict. There is one thing Mr. Petgrave said in his evidence that is rather strong in favour of the plaintiff's case. He said if the English fruit had remained till the following week Mr. March would have got £11 5/ instead of the price he actually got. Then I have to take the evidence of the people who were at Ivy Lawn. All these all bear out that Mr. Petgrave gave an open contract.

I do believe that Mr. Levy had nothing to do with the getting up of the people for the evidence. I do believe there was an open contract given to Mr. March, and when Mr. Levy spoke to him he only went on carrying it out. I cannot help being forced to the conclusion that the open contract was given to Mr. March and improperly given.

I don't believe that all the fruit left there, was marketable fruit and therefore the plaintiff is not entitled to full amount of damage.

What I do is to divide the thing in half.

Mr. Gunter: Although the good fruit predominated, your honour?

His Honour: What I will do is to make it 2-3, I cannot in a matter like this, get at the thing minutely and accurately and I make it 2-3, that is I award judgment for the plaintiff for £6 19/4 with cost and solicitor's cost.

June 30, 1914
[Front page] ARCHDUKE FRANCIS FERDINAND AND HIS WIFE ARE SHOT DEAD IN THE MAIN STREET OF THE BOSNIAN CAPITAL

July 3, 1914
SMEDMORE- WILLIAM DEY at his residence, 49 Beeston St., on Thursday, 2nd July.

July 3, 1914
INTERPRETATION OF WILL OF THE LATE COLONEL C.J. WARD—Hearing of Appeal by the Supreme Court Yesterday.—Beneficiaries' Move—The Grounds of Appeal From the Decision of Chief Justice—Arguments Being heard.

Wanted
To sell Ranch, Kootenay Lake, B.C. Canada, 20 acres, good house, 500 apple trees planted 5 years. Daily steamers to town in summer, train in winter. Near two hotels. English settlers, Church, etc $8,000. For full details apply Rev. C. Reynolds, 15 South Camp Road.

To Sell Rockville, a palatial residence, containing twelve apartments in the upper storey with all accommodations, including a fine range of out-rooms and three large water butts. Situated in Brown's Town, St Ann. Late residence of the Delgadoes. Original cost £1,200. Will be sold cheap. Very seldom such an offer is made to the public. Apply at one to J. A. Thomson & Co., Auctioneers and Commission Agents, Brown's Town P.O.

July 4, 1914
HART-At Hartmont, Montego Bay, July 2nd to the wife of Edmund Hart, a daughter

July 7, 1914
UNSETTLED CONDITIONS CAUSED BY THE ASSASSINATION IN AUSTRIA
[Picture] Rulers who control the Peace of Europe: Emperor Francis Joseph, Emperor William, Crown Prince of Servia, The Tsar, King Peter of Servia. The riots in Austria which followed the assassination of the heir to the throne, have been threatening the

peace of more that one European country. The terrible event which has thrilled Europe is another illustration of how well stifled is the anxiety always present in the minds of European politicians and diplomats about the unstable conditions prevailing in the Balkans and even in the dual monarchy itself. The various rulers, whose portraits are shown above, are lending every effort to preserve peace in the terror ridden monarchy.

July 8, 1914
DEANS-WRIGHT-On Wednesday 1st July 1914 by Rev. S.I. Moodie assisted by Revs. Grange and Binger, CLAUDE, son of the late H.P. Deans of Kemnay Grove to HILDA, daughter of A.Q. Wright Esq., of St Ann. (American papers please copy).

July 9, 1914
PRIZE DISTRIBUTION AT WOLMER'S—A Pleasing Function took Place yesterday Afternoon—Reports Presented—Institution Which is Doing Splendid Work in The Community.

Girls Prize List
Forms I and II. Gwen Sinclair, First place in form; Cecile Burton second place in form; Lena da Costa, improvement; Sybil de Souza Nature Study.
Form IIIb Helen Thwaites, first place in form; Eunice Edwards, second place in form
Form IIIa Edith Williams, first place in form; Ismay Wilson, second place in form.
Form IVm Edna Russel, first place in form; Amy Constantine, second place in form.
Form IVb Florence Cowper, first place in form; Dahlia Whitbourne, second place in form.
Form IVa Betty Macdonald, first place in form; Gladys Edwards, distinction in Junior Cambridge.
Form V. Beryl Hart, first place in form; Elsie Lindo, second place in form; Elsie Lindo, Botany; Mavis Alberga, Shorthand; Winnie Braitewaite, Improvement; Ruby Mornan, Improvement; Gertrude Morris, English. Form V. improvement in French pronunciation
Form VI- Bessie McCrindle, Honours in Senior Cambridge; Lilian Macpherson, honours in Senior Cambridge; Lilian Macpherson, Old Girls prize.
Form VIa – Vera Leake, Mathematics; Iris Johnson, Scholarship work: Mary Cowper, French; Mary Cowper, Scholarship work.
The prizes and Cambridge certificates were then distributed to the girls.

Boys Prize List
Form VI V.L. Ferguson, G.S. McDonald
Form V- T.J. Curphey
Form IV- C.E. Riddell, A.L. Walcott, L.S.C. Hendriks (seniors)
Form IIIa R.O. Bell, A.B. Adams, N.W. Hall (Juniors)
Form IIIb C.A. Adams, L.R. Wynter, C.S. Kemble, W.H. Murad, and W.H.M. Cowper, Special
Form IIa V.L. Levy, L.N. Goldring
Form IIb A. B. Cunningham, C. C. Calame
Form Ia A.C. Marsh, O.R. Parkinson
Form Ib C.A.Cover (special) H.S.Hall, A.R. Murad.

July 16, 1914
KINGSLEY-JOHNSTON—At Brown's Town, St Ann, on Tuesday, July 14, by the Revd. J.P. Hall, GERTRUDE, younger daughter of Dr. and Mrs. James Johnston, to Dr. ROLFE KINGSLEY of New York City U.S.A.

1914

July 18, 1914

PRIZE GIVING-Pleasing Function in Connection With St Ann High School-PRINCIPAL'S REMARK—The Full List of the Winners in the Different Divisions.
Brown's Town, July 15

The St Ann High School, of this town, closed its midsummer session this afternoon, when the certificates gained at the last Cambridge Local Examination and the prizes for 1913 were distributed by the Rev. J. Kissock Braham, B.D.

The Principal, Rev. J. W. Graham, give a verbal report of the work of the school during 1913 and explained that the prizes which would be distributed were awarded on the results of the last Cambridge local Examination, the detailed report being taken as the examiner's report. He had decided on this course, owing to the fact that he had boys of his own in the school. He was gratified however, to find that the prize list of 1913 was, with one exception, identical with that of the previous year. Boys could not expect to win prizes unless they applied themselves with diligence to their work.

Mr. Braham then presented the prizes and certificates as follows:-
PRIZE LIST 1914

Upper Division

Old Testament, John Braham, Presented by C.G. Longley, Esq.

New Testament, Richmond Braham, Presented by Rev. J.P. Hall

English, Harold Graham, Silver watch presented by H.E. the Governor.

History (English) John Braham, presented by Mrs. Phillpotts

Mathematics, Harold Graham, Presented by Hon. Geo. McGrath

Physiology and Hygiene. A.E. Palmer, Presented by P. Blagrove, Esq., J.P.

Drawing, Noel Thompson, Presented by J.H. Levy, Esq., J.P.

General Improvement, John Braham, Silver medal, Presented by Hon. J. H. Allwood, M.L.C.

Dux, Cambridge Local Junior, Harold Graham, Presented by C.R. Thomson, Esq.

Middle Division

Religious Knowledge, Frank Graham, Present by Rev. J.P. Hall

English, Frank Graham, Presented by C.R. Thomson, Esq.

English History, Frank Graham, Presented by Alex. Hopwood, Esq.

Geography Frank Graham

Mathematics W. E. L . Trewick, Presented by Hon. Geo. McGrath

Drawing, Frank Graham, Presented by J.H. Levy Esq.

Dux, Cambridge Prelim. Frank Graham Presented by C. L. Phillips, Esq.,

Lower Division

Religious Knowledge, E. Braham, Presented by Rev. J.P. Hall

English Edward Braham, Presented by C.R. Thomson, Esq.

English History, Eric Hopwood

Geography Edward Braham, Presented by A. Hopwood, Esq.

Mathematics Eric Hopwood, Presented by Hon. Geo. McGrath

Diligence, Robert Byles, Presented by J. A. Thomason, Esq.

Good Conduct Edward Braham, Silver Medal, Presented by Rev. J. Kissock Braham

Cambridge Certificates

Juniors: Braham, J.K., Braham R.R., Graham, H.A. Two certificates in this grade, Isaacs L.C. and Palmer, A.E. had been forwarded to the boys, who have left the school.

Preliminary: Graham F.E.

Mr. Graham explained that there was one prize not yet awarded. Sir John Pringle had kindly given a prize for Jamaica Geography, and the papers were in the hands of the examiner, who had not yet sent in his award.

Selected Vital Records from the Jamaican Daily Gleaner

July 20, 1914

Mrs. Smedmore and family beg through this medium to thank their friends for the many kind letters and cards of condolence received during their recent sad bereavement.

EDGAR-HALLIDAY-At Coke Church, Kingston, by the Rev. Thomas W. Halliday, brother of the bride, assisted by the Rev. W.J. Turnbull on Saturday, July 18th, Herbert Wedderlie, son of the late Sir James David Edgar, K.C.M.G. of Toronto, Canada, to Fannie Henrietta, daughter of William Halliday, Esq., of Mandeville, Jamaica.

July 27, 1914

EUROPE IS NOW FACED WITH WAR OF NATIONS-Austria Hungary Has Made Demands on Servia to which it is thought the Last Named Country Will be Unable to Accede-A VIRTUAL ULTIMATUM IS SENT TO BELGRADE—Feared that Struggle if it Takes Place will Lead to Conflagration that will Draw In Several of the Big European Nations—REPORTED STANDS OF RUSSIA AND GERMANY.

July 27, 1914

HOLLINGSWORTH, JOHN—At "Westra" Lincoln Road, (off Brentford Road) on 26th inst., JOHN HOLLINGSWORTH, aged 67 years. Funeral will move for Half-Way Tree Church to-day at 4 p.m. Friends please let your carriage attend.

July 27, 1914

HENDRIKS-Yesterday at 10 a.m. T.B. Hendriks, late of Government Savings Bank. Funeral moves this afternoon at 4.30 from 15 Brentford Road for May Pen Cemetery.

July 28, 1914

SUCCESSFUL SCHOOL FUNCTION-Annual Prize Giving Day at Institution at Brown's Town-Mr. ALLWOOD PRESIDES—Report Showing that the High School is Steadily Progressing.

Brown's Town July 25.—The breaking up and annual distribution of prizes and Cambridge certificates in connection with Brown's Town High School, took place in the Baptist School room on Friday last.

A larger and more truly representative gathering has never been seen in this locality at any similar function. Beginning with the first citizen of the parish-the honourable member of the Legislative assembly-there was a happy admixture of all classes colour and creeds, prominent among whom was our worthy patriot and esteemed Chairman of the Parochial Board..........................

THE PRIZE LIST

C.R. Coore awarded by Hon.J.H. Allwood, M.L.C. 1st Cambridge Junior
A.J. Gordon awarded by J.H. Levy, Esq., for passing Cambridge Exam
C.V. Moss awarded by A. Bramwell Esq., for passing Cambridge Exam
I.M Smith awarded by C.L Phillips Esq., for passing Cambridge Exam
E.J. Bramwell awarded by C.C. Solomon (New York) for passing Cambridge Exam
H.L Morrison awarded by Headmaster for passing Cambridge Exam
A.J. Gordon awarded by Col. E. Moulton-Barrett for English
Miss I.M. Smith awarded by Col. E. Moulton-Barrett for English
S.Jarrett awarded by A. Barrett, Esq. for Good Conduct
P.T. Parker, prize awarded by Educational Supply Co. for 1st Cambridge Prelim
H.A. Bramwell, prize awarded by E.E. Roger, Esq. for Cambridge Prelim. Exam
G.V. Parris, prize awarded by Rev. J.P. Hall for Cambridge prelim Exam.

1914

A.J. Gordon, prize awarded by L.R. Edwards, Esq., for 1st on mid-summer Exam (Form IV)

V.F. Murphy for passing 1st on Mid-summer Examination (Form III) Prize awarded by L. L. Ingram, Esq.

N.Parris for passing 1st Midsummer Exam.(Form II) Prize awarded by Mrs. E.S. Lindo

J. Hylton for 1st in Form Ia on Mid-summer Exam. Prize awarded by E.E Rogers Esq.

CAMBRIDGE CERTIFICATES

Junior Passes: C.R. Coore, A.J. Gordon, C.V. Moss, H. L . Morrison, I.M. Smith, E.L. Bramwell, D. Dixon.

Preliminary Passes: P.T. Parker, H. A. Bramwell, G.V. Parris.

July 29, 1914

AUSTRIA YESTERDAY DECLARED WAR ON SERVIA: EUROPE IS FACED WITH GENERAL CONFLAGRATION—Fight Between Slav & Teuton-Tsar Nicholas of Russia in a Burst of Impatience Declares that His Country has Stood Austria's Provocation Long Enough—Hostilities Began Before War was Declared—The Russian Minister of War Declares that it is His Belief that War is Inevitable Between Muscovite and the Austrian—SERVIANS FIRE ON FRANCIS JOSEPHS' SOLDIERS.

EUROPE IS ONCE AGAIN IN STORM—Formal Notice of the Declaration of War was Sent by Austria to Foreign Diplomats at Vienna in the First Instance—SERVIAN TROOPS BLOW UP BRIDGE OVER DANUBE—Efforts Made by Foreign Secretary Sir Edward Grey to Bring About Peace and the Delimitation of the Theatre of War— BRITISH FLEET RECALLED TO PORTLAND, ENGLAND

July 31, 1914

NATIONS OF EUROPE, GREAT AND SMALL, WAIT ON THE WORD OF THE CZAR TO DETERMINE WHETHER THEY SHALL BEGIN "BATTLE OF ARMAGEDDON"

The Peace of Europe, and its Dependence is Upon Whether the Ruler of Russia will Declare War on Austria or Not—GERMAN ORGAN COUNSELS PEACE WITH CZAR—London "Times" Says that if France is Menaced or the Safety of the Belgian Frontier, Britain shall Act with Promptitude-EMPEROR FRANCIS JOSEPH WRITES A MANIFESTO

August 1, 1914

EUROPE A VAST ARMED CAMP, STANDS ON THE ABYSS OF UNIVERSAL WAR. AUSTRIANS ARE SHELLING BELGRADE: WORLD STOCK MARKETS ARE IN PANIC.

The Worlds Navies

Country	Built	Building
United Kingdom	592	84
France	370	26
Russia	177	83
Germany	316	38
Austria-Hungary	114	20
Italy	145	52
U.S.A.	167	40
Japan	178	7

The Worlds Armies

Great Britain	275,000
France	1,250,000
Russia (European Russia Only)	1,200,000
Caucasus	250,000
W. Siberia	180,000
E. Siberia	275,000
Germany	2,250,000
Austria Hungary	810,000
Italy	750,000
U.S.A. (Regular Army)	65,000
Japan	750,000

August 1, 1914
MURRAY-At the Bungalow, Hope Gardens, on the 26th July to Mr. and Mrs. P.W. Murray, a daughter.

August 5, 1914
[Front Page] GERMANY DECLARES WAR AGAINST GREAT BRITAIN. 2.15 a.m. – His Excellency the Governor informs us that Germany has declared war against Great Britain—A special Gazette will be published early to-day and another later on- M.Delcasse, Foreign Minister for France. Mr. John Redmond Announces that Irish men of All Creeds will Unite for the Defence of the British Empire.

MONDAY'S EARTHQUAKE SHOOK A LARGE SECTION OF ISLAND—Some Buildings in Port Antonio have been Damaged.—WALLS ARE CRACKED—Earth Movement was Very Heavy at All the Points—NO LOSS OF LIFE REPORTED

August 8, 1914
PERSONAL
Mrs. Facey and other members of the late T.B. Hendriks' family beg through this medium to return sincere thanks to their many friends and acquaintances for the expressions of sympathy in their sad bereavement.

Church News and Services
Our Ocho Rios correspondent, writing under date 3rd int. states:- "A silver tree entertainment was held yesterday in the Geddes Memorial Church in aid of the seating of the church, and was a success. The tree was stripped of its bags of 'silver' fruit by the Misses Reynolds and others, the collection totalling £30 12s 6d. The musical portion of the service was well rendered".

August 13, 1914
MANLEY-At his residence, Black River, on Monday morning, 10th August, at 1 o'clock, SAMMUEL SMITH MANLEY, aged 64 leaving a widow and other relatives to mourn their loss.

ORRETT- At Gayle, St Mary, on the 9th August, 1914, after a very short illness, ROSA EUGENINE ALICE, the beloved wife of Charles Orrett, J.P.

August 17, 1914
EDUCATIONAL-Results of the Royal Drawing Society's Examination.—THE HAMPTON SCHOOL—The results of the examinations of the Royal Drawing Society

which were held in June, have come to hand. Two of the pupils of Hampton School, Winifred M. Farquharson and Enid M. Ramson, have during 1913 and 1914 gained honours in all the six divisions of the examination, and are therefore entitled to the Full Honours Certificate awarded by the Society. More.

August 19, 1914
CANAL NOW OPEN
[By Direct W.I. Co., via Bermuda] Washington, August 18. With the passage through the Panama Canal today of the War Department Liner Ancon, the great waterway becomes free and open to the vessels of commerce, and of war of all nations on terms of entire equality, in accordance with the provisions of the HayPauncefote treaty.

Vessels drawing not more that thirty feet of water may now make the passage. Any of the foreign Warships now in the Atlantic and Pacific waters can make the trip. Twenty-four hours is the limit of time a belligerent vessel can remain within the Canal except in cases of distress, and a vessel of war of one belligerent cannot depart within twenty-four hours from the departure of a vessel of war of another belligerent.

THE POPE IS ILL
[Rome, Aug. 17]-The Pope was yesterday ordered to bed for a complete rest. He is suffering from gouty catarrh and the intense heat which prevails is contribution to weaken him. His Holiness has not been well for several days and the war in Europe has much depressed him. Yesterday his condition was worse. His doctors have ordered that all audiences by suspended. HAS HIGH FEVER

London, August 18-A dispatch to the "Daily Chronicle" from Milan says that the Pope is in a state of high fever, and that his condition occasions serious alarm.

August 21, 1914
Dr. Charles I. Levy who has been on vacation in the country, will return to Kingston to-day and resume his practice on Saturday (tomorrow).

August 22, 1914
WHITING-At Richmond, 17th August, 1914, CLINTON DUDLEY, eldest son of Mr. and Mrs. W.T. Whiting of Falmouth.

DEATH OF THE HOLY FATHER—The Body of the Late Pope Laid Out in State—SISTER FOLLOWS HIM—Death of Father Wernz The General of the Jesuit Order.

August 24, 1914
SIMPSON-At Cheshunt Lodge, Norman Road at 2 p.m. Saturday, August 22nd, ELLEN SIMPSON, aged 96 years, aunt of the late C.M. Sherlock.

NOTICE TO CUSTOMERS
Following is a copy of the price of foodstuffs etc., on sale at retail provision and grocery establishments conducted by Chinese in Kingston. The increase is due to the rise in the price of all articles, on a basis of fully 30 per cent. The ruling prices are subject to a change according to market fluctuation:

Rice (white and brown)... . 6d qrt
Baking-flour (best quality Three Stars)...................................... 3d qrt
Medium Flour...2½d qrt
Cornmeal.. .....2½d qrt

Selected Vital Records from the Jamaican Daily Gleaner

Corn	3d qrt
Beef	10d lb
Pork	10d lb
Codfish (First quality)	7d lb
CottonseedOil	1s 3d qrt
1 lb NestlesMilk	7½d
½ lb NestlesMilk	3½d
Margarine per lb	1s 1½d
Oleo per lb	1s
Compounds, per lb	1s
Sardines per Tin	3½d
1 lb Tin Butter	2s 3d
Fresh Herrings	6d
Shepherd Brand Milk	5d

August 27, 1914
GREAVES-At Rosebank, Stewart Town, Trelawny, On Monday 24th Aug., after years of great suffering, Mrs. ELIZABETH GREAVES, aged 92. May she rest in peace.

September 2, 1914
HONIBALL-On 31st August at "Bostonville" Annotto Bay, to Mr. and Mrs. O.D. Honiball, a son.

September 5, 1914
WHITE-WALKER- At the Free Methodist Church, Beecher Town, St Ann, On Thursday 27th August, 1914 by the Rev. G.A. Miller assisted by the Rev. Caleb Reynolds, SAMUEL, son of Mr. John White, Circuit Steward of Ocho Rios Circuit, to BEATRICE, eldest daughter of James Walker of Beecher Town. American Costa Rican, Panamanian papers please copy.

September 7, 1914
PLANT DISEASE—Messrs P.C. Cork and H.Q. Levy Visit Field At Balcarres—OBJECT OF JOURNEY—How the Places where Disease Had Occurred, were Treated.

We understand that Mr. P.C. Cork, C.M.G., formerly Colonial Secretary, and Mr.H.Q. Levy a member of the Board of Management of the Jamaica Agricultural Society, visited Balcarres on Wednesday last.

As newspaper readers are aware, it was at Balcarres that the Panama Disease was first discovered, which subsequently led to the destruction of a field of bananas belong to a Mr. McFarlane. The outbreak of the Panama Disease and the measures which were adopted by the Agricultural Department in dealing with the disease, loomed largely in the enquiry which was recently conducted by the Commission appointed by His Excellency the Governor to enquire into the working and general development of the Department in question. The report of the Commission is now before His Excellency the Governor.

From what can be ascertained, fresh representations have been made to the agricultural authorities and we learn that the object of the visit of both Messrs. Cork and Levy to Balcarres last week was for the purpose of making investigations on behalf of the Jamaica Agricultural Society as to how the places where Panama disease had occurred had been treated, and what precautionary measure had been taken to prevent the progress of the disease.

The report of the two gentlemen will be presented at the next meeting of the Board of Management of the Jamaica Agricultural Society.

1914

September 9, 1914
Parents and other to kindly note that the Deaconess High School for Girls, Brown's Town will reopen on Monday September 14th, instead of Monday 7th as first arraigned. For particulars and terms apply to Rev. J.P. Hall, Brown's Town, P.O.

FOR ALL WE HAVE AND ARE
By Rudyard Kipling
(Copyright, 1914, all rights reserved) London, September 2, 1914
(This Poem was unfortunately crowded out of yesterday's Gleaner)

I
For all we have and are,
For all our children's fate,
Stand up and meet the war!
The Hun is at the gate.
Our world has passed away,
In wantonness o'erthrown.
There's nothing left to-day
But steel and fire and stone.
Though all we knew depart,
The old commandments stand
"In courage keep your heart!
In strength lift up you hand!"

II
Once more we hear the word
That sickened earth of old:
"No law except the sword,
Unsheathed and uncontrolled!"
Once more it knits mankind;
Once more the nations go
To meet and break and bind
A crazed and driven foe.

III.
Comfort, content, delight-
The ages' slow-bought gain-
They shriveled in a night.
Only ourselves remain
To face, the naked days
In silent fortitude,
Through perils and dismays
Renewed and re-renewed.
Through all we made depart,
The old commandments stand
"In patience keep your heart!
In strength lift up you hand!"

IV
No easy hopes or lies
Shall bring us to our goal
But iron sacrifice
Of body, will and soul

471

There's but one task for all-
For each one life to give.
Who stands if Freedom fall?
Who dies if England live?

September 14, 1914

METROPOLITAN THEATRE
3d & 6d High Grade Moving Pictures & Music 3d &6d
Tomorrow Night Our Prize Night
Programme
THE COLONEL'S WARD, Part 1....................................Drama
THE COLONEL'S WARD, Part 2.................................Drama
THEIR FIRST UNDRSTANDING......................................Comedy
LOVE'S VICTORY..Drama
THOSE TERRIBLE CHILDREN...Comedy
HOLLAND..Scenic
THE ENGRAVER...Drama
ILLUSTRATED SONG
Two performances each night 7.15 and 9.15
Doors open at 6.30.

MOVIES LIMITED—Cross Roads
This Theatre is under the distinguished patronage of His Excellency the Governor.
Latest and most reliable War news Nightly.
-TONIGHTS PROGRAMME-
THE OUTLAW...Drama
CONCENTRATION...Comedy
THE ETERNAL DUEL..Drama
THE CHARMED ARROW....................................Drama
BRINGING UP HUBBY....................................Comedy
Two performances each night 7.15 and 9.15. Gates open at 6.30. Prices of admission 6d
and 1s
-:COMING:-
Tuesday.—Our "Silver" Prize Drawing-10 Prizes
Wednesday.- The Necklace of Rameses 3 Acts
Thursday.- Our "Electro" Prize Drawing- 10 Prizes.
Saturday.- Our Cash Prize Drawing of two Prizes. Four Pounds and One Pound
Remember keep your coupons, they are good from Sunday to Saturday.

THE PALACE
Kingston's Best and Most Up-to-Date Moving
Picture Theatre.
LATEST WAR NEWS SHOWN NIGHTLY
Tonight our Coupon Night
Programme
HUNTING THE GAME IN A LARGE CITY
Or the Capture of the Underground Crooks,
Exciting Drama in 3 Parts,
THE WHITE CAP................................Comedy
MARIE BRICCA...Drama
ILLUSTRATED SONG BY Mr. WRIGHT
Our Next Coupon Night, Wednesday 16th.

1914

Coming

Thursday.—by Special Request—BALOO IN 2 REELS
LA CIGALE and RORY O'MORE
FRIDAY.-PATRON'S NIGHT—Special Feature-The
Original QUO VADIS, in seven reels
The World's Master piece-by Cines.
Two Performances each night at 7.15 and 9.15
Prices of Admission........................6d and 1s
Gates open 6.30. Prices of admission 6d & 1s. Boxes 1s 6d

There is Money in Moving Pictures
IN EVERY TOWN IN JAMAICA. Let us equip you a
Place complete for cash or credit. Only a small
Capital required. No former experience necessary,
Which is free to you. The LARGEST STOCK OF
FILMS FOR HIRE IN THE WEST INDIES, consisting
Of all the AMERICAN and EUROPEAN
Makes.
COLONIAL FILM EXCHANGE,
40 Church Street, Kingston.

September 15, 1914
ROBINSON—At his residence No 19 Barry St. on Saturday night CHARLES EDWARD, leaving a widow, family and friends to mourn their loss, aged 51. Thy will be done.

September 16, 1914
WEDDING BELLS-Mr. O.K. Henriques and Miss R. Melhado

A pretty little wedding was solemnized last evening when Mr. O.K. Henriques, the genial and popular member of the firm of Henriques Bros. (Industrial Works and Garage) of this city, was joined in holy wedlock to Miss Rebecca Melhado, daughter of the late Mr. Chas. Melhado of Old Harbour.

The ceremony was performed at the residence of the bride's uncle Mr. S.C. Henriques on the South Camp Road, by the Rev. M.H. Solomon of the United Congregation of Israelites. The bride who was given away by her brother, Mr. Cyril Melhado, looked charming in a dress of embossed voile, with a train of white satin and orange blossoms with a veil and cap of orange blossoms and lace. She was attended by two bridesmaids, Miss U. Henriques and Miss Phyllis Melhado.

After the ceremony, the guests adjourned to the banqueting room where the health of the bride and bridegroom was proposed and drunk, with becoming felicity.

Mr. S.C. Henriques father of the bridegroom, also took the opportunity of announcing the engagement of another son, Mr. Rudolph Henriques, Jamaica's scenic artist to Miss Henriques of New York.

We join their many friends in wishing Mr. and Mrs. O.K. Henriques a long and prosperous married life.

September 28, 1914
WARD- Killed in Action in France, CAPT. A.C. WARD, D.S.O., the Lancashire Fusiliers, third son of the late Charles James Ward, C.M.G. aged 36. R.I.P.

473

Selected Vital Records from the Jamaican Daily Gleaner

September 30, 1914
LORD-At Rodon's Pen, Old Harbour, on the 27th inst., ELIZA FANNY, relict of the late Charles Payne Lord of Clifton, Gloucestershire, England

HORN-On the 9th September at his residence, Oakburn, Windermere, England, JOHN HORN, D.L. J.P. of Homanean Kinross, Scotland, in his 79th year.

October 5, 1914
GIVEN FINE WELCOME TO ST ANN—Mr. York Slader Takes His First court at Brown's Town.

(From our Correspondent) Brown's Town, Friday- His Honour Mr. C.H. Yorke-Slader took his seat on the bench here to-day for the first time. A number of gentlemen were present in the Court House, among them, being: Mr. J.H. Levy, Hon. J.H. Allwood, Dr Miller, Messrs. A.E. Murray, L.W. Levy, J. Lee, C.J. Helwig, C. Jacobs, E.L. Phillips, H.F. Isaacs, D.T. Wint, R.A. Bramwell and H.O. Gauntlett, Deputy Clerk of the Courts.

Addresses of welcome were given by Mr. J.H. Levy, Senior J.P. and Chairman of the Parochial Board for the parish, Hon.J.H. Allwood, and Mr. H.G. Gauntlett, Deputy Clerk of the Courts.

His Honour in replying, said he was pleased to come to the parish and to be met in such a friendly manner. There was in the parish of Clarendon, from which he had come plenty of work, both criminal and civil. He was glad to observe that there is very little crime in this parish.

He hoped he would be borne with if at any time during his administration, he appeared tedious and lengthy, he would endeavour to do justice to all parties coming before him with out favour or affection.

The business of the court was then proceeded with, and several civil cases disposed of.

October 6, 1914
McCONNELL-At Berry Hill, St. Ann, on the 29th September, the wife of D.G.McConnell of a son.

October 8, 1914
MAY BE DUE TO A POISON—Dr Scott's Deductions On Mysterious Vomiting Sickness-WEIGHT OF EVIDENCE—Result of Investigations Is Against the Bacteriaemia Theory-SHOULD WASH OUT STOMACH.

October 14, 1914
MENNELL-At Chilton, Darliston on Sunday 11th October, 1914, ZEBULON E.L. (Bill) youngest son of John W. Mennell in his 27th year, an invalid from his birth.

October 20, 1914
DUFF-To Mr. and Mrs. J.Hartley Duff on the 14th instant, a daughter.

October 31, 1914
RAMSON-At Mary Villa, 155 Church St., Kingston, at 11.50 a.m. on 30th inst., HELEN GERTRUDE, aged 20 years, youngest daughter of H.E.Ramson. Funeral at 8.30 this morning. Friends and acquaintances please accept this only intimation.

1914

November 2, 1914
CASSERLY-At Fort George, Annotto Bay to O.B. F.K. Casserly, a daughter on the 10th October. [November 4- O.B. and K Casserly]

November 3, 1914
CUNHA-At "Industry" on the 2nd November, MARIE LOUISE, the beloved wife of C.L. Cunha. Funeral leaves for Half-way Tree cemetery at 4 o'clock this evening.

November 5, 1914
ROBINSON-COOKE-At Grace Church in the city of New York on the 11th September, 1914, PERCIVAL LESLIE ROBINSON of Cuba son of Mr. A.L. Robinson of Grier Park, St Ann to ALICE, third daughter of Mrs. Cooke, of 115 Rue Borghese, Paris.

November 5, 1914
THE CANADAIAN TROOPS LEAVING TO TAKE PART IN THE GREAT WAR [Pictures] The picture on the left shows Colonel Samuel Hughes, Canadian Minister of Militia leaving the flagship of the cruiser convoy. The scene on the right, the troops waving their last farewell.

Colonel Hughes, in a farewell message to the troops on their way to fight for Great Britain in Continental Europe, showed that upward of thirty-three thousand Canadians of English, Irish, French, Welsh, Scotch, American and German ancestry embarked within six weeks from the day they heard the call to arms, having passed that time perfecting themselves in rifle shooting and camp life.

November 6, 1914
THE SYRIANS HERE

A good deal of apprehension has arisen amongst the Syrians in Jamaica as to whether they will be put under arrest and treated as prisoners of war.

The feeling of unrest is due to the fact that war has been declared by Great Britain on Turkey, and most of the Syrians here come from Assyria, which is dominated by Turkish rule. It is true that some of the Syrians are British subjects, inasmuch as they have been granted letters of naturalization. Those who are not Britishers are, however, fearing that they will be treated as enemies.

A representative of the Gleaner called at Headquarter House yesterday afternoon and enquired as to what action the Government proposed to take in the matter. He was informed that the Governor had caused a proclamation to be issued with regard to the outbreak of war between Great Britain and Turkey and the position of the Syrians here. Beyond that proclamation, no further action had yet been taken.

November 7, 1914
SYRIANS HERE-Letter from Mr. Antonio Issa Denouncing Action of the Porte
THE EDITOR
Sir,-The Syrian community throughout the island, I am sure, greatly deplore the outbreak of hostilities between Turkey and Great Britain.

One would hardly have imagined that Turkey would have been so rash as to wage a war against a Power that has been for more that century its staunchest friend and protector. It is however, abundantly clear that German intrigues lie at the very root of the trouble between the two Empires. I need hardly assure the Government as well as the general public, that the Syrian residents here have absolutely no sympathy whatever with the Turks, in this, their latest aggressive and wanton war. Our fervent hope and prayer is that England, and her Allies will emerge victorious from this struggle, despite the ill-advised intervention of Turkey, at this juncture.

Furthermore the hope is earnestly expressed, that at the end of this war, we may see our country freed once and for all, from the Turkish misrule and tyranny, for we are thoroughly convinced that our unfortunate country can never hope to obtain any appreciable degree of progress, either materially or socially, under the present Mohammedan Turkish rule. The very religion of Turkey is a stumbling block in the path of unity, progress, and civilization.

We Syrians in Jamaica, in common with the inhabitants of this island are law-abiding citizens, devoted and intensely loyal to the British Crown and Government, as we have already assured His Excellency the Governor in a memorial addressed to him, at the outbreak of the war in August.

It is quite obvious, and there is no gain-saying the fact that England stands in this war for honour, freedom, and justice and by God's help she and her Allies will eventually triumph.

Thanking you, Mr. Editor for publishing this letter,

I am etc.,

ANTONIO ISSA

142 Harbour St.,

Kingston,

6/11/14

November 10, 1914

McGRATH-Died in Hospital at Boulogne on the 5th November from wounds, received on the battlefield on the 31st October, LIEUTENANT NOEL GEORGE SCOTT McGRATH of the Second Dragoon Guards (Queens Bays) and eldest son of the Hon. George McGrath of Charlemont, Ewarton. Aged 28

November 12, 1914

GEDDES-On the morning of the 11th instant, REBECCA GRACE GEDDES, aged 74, widow of the late Rev. T.M. Geddes, and mother of the Rev. A.W. Geddes, and T.H. Geddes.

November 14, 191

WOOLER-GENGE-At the Parish Church, Kingston, on Nov. 4, by the Rev. R.J. Ripley, Dorothy Gladys, daughter of T.Taylor Genge, of Clifton, Bristol, to Edmund Upton Wooler, of Hyde Hall, Trelawny.

LEVY-On 12th inst, to Mr. and Mrs. L.C. Levy, at Spanish Town, a daughter

November 17, 1914

RAMSON-To Rev. J.L. Ramson and Mrs. Ramson, St George's Rectory, Kingston, at 10 15 p.m. Saturday, 14th November, a son.

November 23, 1914

IN MEMORIAM-Work and Worth of the Late Mrs. T.M. Geddes-THE SERVICE AT COKE—Eulogy Passed on the Deceased Lady by the Rev. Arthur Kirby.

November 27, 1914

SERVING KING AND COUNTRY—List of Jamaican who are now Fighting for The Motherland—SOME ON FIRING LINE—Col. E. Moulton-Barrett is at the British War Office—MANY NAMES KNOWN HERE.

1914

We have received from a correspondent, the following provisional list of the sons of Jamaica on active service. We shall be grateful if those who can do so will send in any additions or corrections with will enable us to make the list correct and complete.

KILLED

Capt. A. Ward D.S.O. Lancashire Fusiliers, son of the late Hon C.J. Ward, Kingston.

Lieut N. McGrath, Queen's Bay, son of the Hon. Geo. McGrath, Ewarton.

Lieut. W.B. Gosset, Royal Field Artillery, son the Hon B.S. Gosset, Bull Bay.

NOW SERVING

Capt. D.D. Alexander, Gordon Highlanders, son of the late Hon A.H. Alexander, Inspector of Immigrants

Capt A.C. Alexander, Seaforth Highlanders, son of the late Hon. A.H. Alexander, Inspector of Immigrants.

Midn. A. Ashton, R.N., son of the Rev. S.C. Ashton, Malvern.

K.W. Calder, Hon. Artillery Co., son of the Hon J. V. Calder, Ewarton.

Lieut. E.F. Coke, Fort Garry Regiment, 1st Canadian Contingent, son of E.F. Coke, Mile Gully.

N. Coke, 2nd Canadian contingent, son of E.F. Coke, Mile Gully.

Capt. Conran, R.E., Indian Army son of Mr. W. Conran, St Ann.

Lieut. P Conran, Lancashire Fusiliers, son of Mr. W. Conran, St Ann.

H. Cox, son of the late H. Cox, Kingston.

Lieut. DeCordova, York and Lancashire Regiment, son of Mr. J. DeCordova.

G.J. Dodd, end Canadian Contingent, son of Mr. J.H. Dodd, Kingston.

Major E. French, R.A.M.C. Kingston

G. Gould, 2nd Regiment King Edward's Horse, son of Mr. Geo. Gould, Kingston.

C. Gray, 2nd Canadian Contingent, son of Mr. W.B. Gray, Kingston

Lieut. R.G.C. Harvey, Suffolk's, son of Dr.C.E. Harvey, Sav-la-Mar

Lieut. Haughton, R.E. son of Mr. R.S. Haughton, Kingston

Dr.H. Harty, R.A.M.C., son of Mr. T.H. Harty, Alley

Comr. A. Harrison, R.N., son of the late Hon. Jas. Harrison, Morant Bay

L.S. Isaacs, 5th Bat. 2nd Brigade, C.F.A.(1st Canadian Contingent), son of Mr. L.A. Isaacs, Mandeville.

A.F. Kemble, son of Mr. F.A. Kemble, Kingston.

Lieut. T.N.C. Kemp, 9th Ghurkas, son of Mr. T. Kemp, Constant Spring.

Kirkham, son of the Rev. A.G. Kirkham, Sav-la-Mar

Lieut. H. Kerr, Royal Scots, son of the late W.L. Kerr, Trelawny

R. Kerr, son of Mr.H.F. Kerr, Montego Bay

Capt. S. Lewis, R.A.M.C. Royal Irish, son of Mr. J.D. Lewis, Mandeville

A. Lopez 3rd East Surreys, son of Mr. C. Lopez, Chapelton

M.McFarlane, son of Mr. A.B. McFarlane, Kingston

Lieut. D. McGrath, R.N., H.M.S. Lancaster son of the Hon. Geo. McGrath, Ewarton

Lieut. W.H. Miles, Dorsets, son of the Hon A.H. Miles, Kingston.

R.D. Miles, 2nd Canadian Contingent, son of the Hon A.H. Miles, Kingston.

A.Moxey, Irish Regiment, son of Mr. S. Moxey, Kingston

McCrindle, son of Dr. McCrindle, Kingston

H. Mais, son of Mr. C.L. Mais, Kingston

D. McPhail, 2nd Canadian Contingent, son of Mr.J.H. McPhail, Bog Walk.

Hon Col. E. Moulton-Barrett, West Kents, Albion St Ann

Lieut. E. Moulton-Barrett, West Kents, Albion, St Ann

Major O.H.G. Marescaux, D. Staff A. War Office, son of the late O. Marescaux, Kingston.

Mid D. Neish, R.N. H.M.S. Iron Duke, son of Dr. W. Neish, Spanish Town.

L Nugent, 2nd Canadian Contingent, son of Mr. H.P. Nugent

Lieut. E.P. Nosworthy, R.E., 1st Indian Contingent, son of Mr. R. Nosworthy, Kingston.

C.W. Nosworthy, son of Mr. R. Nosworthy, Kingston.

Midn. A. H. Nosworthy, R.N. H.M.S. Vixen, son of Mr. R. Nosworthy.

Fleet Payr., Geo. Osmond, R.N. son of the late Capt. G. Osmond R.N., Malvern.

Major .M. Ogilvie, Kingston

Lieut. J. Phillippo, son of Mr. E. Phillippo

Dr Neil Sinclair, R.A.M.C., son of Dr. E.A Sinclair, Negril

Lieut. D.P. Stephenson, North Staffordshire, son of the late D. Stephenson, Kingston.

Lieut. C. Sharp, R.A.M.C. son of Mr. T.H.Sharp, Spanish Town.

Capt. H. Saunders, Ghurka Rifles, son of Dr A. Saunders, Kingston

Capt. H Sewell, son of the late Hon H. Sewell, Arcadia

Commr.J.D. Stewart, R.N.,H.M.S. Magnificent, son of the late W. Stewart, Shaw Park

Lieut. E.A. Sturridge, King's Liverpool, son of Dr. E. Sturridge.

E. Taylor, son of the late Hon. Capt. Taylor, Moy Hall.

E.V.S. Thomas, 1st Regiment King Edward's Horse, son of the Rev. E.J. Thomas.

Lieut. H. Thomas, Royal Marine Light Infantry, son of Inspector H. Thomas, Black River

Lieut. E. Thomas, Royal Field Artillery, Inspector H. Thomas, Black River

Lieut. B. Thomas R.N., son of inspector H. Thomas, Black River

Thomas, son of Inspector H. Thomas Black River.

B.W. Williams, 2nd Regiment, King Edward's Horse, son of the Hon J.R. Williams, Kingston.

Lieut. W. Wynne, R.N. H.M.S. Blenheim, son of the late W. Wynne, Mandeville

Lieut. H.N. Walker, Welsh Regiment, son of Mr. L. Walker, St Ann

M. Wortley, son of the Rev. Canon Wortley, Half-way Tree

Wortley, son of the Rev. Canon Wortley, Half-Way Tree.

Midn. Wright, son of the late Inspector General, E.F.Wright.

November 28, 1914

FIGHTING ON BATTLE LINE.-Further List of Jamaicans Taking Active Part in the War. –HOLD COMMISSIONS-Many Sons of colony Are Officers in the Regiments—IN CANADIAN CONTINGENT

In yesterday's Gleaner we published a provisional list of the sons of Jamaica on active service. In compliance with our request for additions or corrections which will enable us to make the list accurate and complete, we have received the following additional names of those who are serving their king and country at the front:-

Dr Reginald Charles Verley, a Lieutenant of the R.A.M.C.

Midshipman Roger B. Gibb R.N. H.M.S. Zealand, son of the late Dr.J.M. Gibb, veterinary surgeon

Eustace M. Clough, Queen's Own Rifles, Canadian Contingent, son of the late David G. Clough, Kingston.

Maynard McFarlane, second Lieut. In the 5th Battalion Middlesex Regt., son of Mr. A.B. McFarlane, of the Mico College.

Adolph Orrett, Canadian Rifles (2nd Contingent) son of Charles A. Orrett, J.P. Gayle St Mary

Claude Orrett, London Scottish Regiment, son of Mr. William H. Orrett, Solicitor

Captain Musson, Indian Army, son of the late Hon. S.P. Musson, Island Treasurer, and grandson of the late Hon John Orrett.

M.H.B. Cox, Canadian contingent, son of the late Mr. T.P. Cox.

1914

December 1, 1914

AT FIRING LINE—Some More Jamaicans Who have Answered Country's Call-AFLOAT AND ON LAND—Islanders Hurry to Motherland from all Parts of the World.

Following is a further list of Jamaicans who are now serving the Empire in its mighty trial of strength with German militarism:-

Major Robert Pierce, Royal Irish Inskilling Fusiliers. Major Pierce's father, was the late Rev. Edward Pierce, of St. Michael's Church, who with his wife and four of their children were drowned in the Essequibo River, Demerara, many years ago.

The present major, who was then a small boy, swam to a rock in the stream and was saved. His elder brother (who was then at school in England at the time) was killed in the South African War, while serving with the Cape Mounted Rifles.

C.E. Osmond, Sec. Lieut., Hon Artillery Co., London; son of the late Mr. G.W. Osmond, Capt. R.N. of Malvern Chase, St Elizabeth.

A.K. Tate, First Canadian Contingent, son of the late Mr. Lawrence Tate, of Shaftston, Westmoreland

A.G. Westmoreland, First Canadian Contingent, son of the late Mr. Harry Westmoreland, of Esher, St Mary

A.H.Graham, Second Canadian Contingent son of Mr.A.A.H. Graham of Port Antonio, Portland

Herbert Jarrett-Kerr, Lieut. Third Lahore Expeditionary Force, son of Mr.H. Jarrett-Kerr, of Phoenix, Trelawny.

Thomas Kerr, Lieut. R.N. Submarine "A5", son of the late Mr. W. L. Kerr of Trelawny

W. Pengelly, and C. Pengelly, First Canadian contingent, sons of J.C.T. Pengelly, Balaclava

Lennox-Sloane Lt., R.N., son of Mrs. G.T. Dewar, Trelawny

Norman Moore, Lt., R.N.H.M.S. "Edgar", Grandson of the late Mr. John Cameron, Windsor, St Ann.

Leslie Rerrie, son of Mr. C.A. Rerrie

F.W.D. Pratt, son of Mr. E. Pratt, St. Ann's Bay

C.H.S. Buckley, 28th Bat., The London Regiment (which is now in France) son of the Rev. C.M. Buckley of Pratville.

Major J. Gwynne Griffith, 23rd Lancers T.A.D.A. Adjt-General, 2nd Cavalry Division, 1st Expeditionary Force, son of Mr. F.A. Griffith, and brother of Mr.H.W. Griffith of Hodges, Black River.

Lieut. Errol S.E. Rerrie of the 3rd East Yorkshire Regiment, a son of Mr. R.P. Rerrie, solicitor of Montego Bay and grandson of the late Hon, Alex. Rerrie and Wm J. Ewen. Having just left college when war broke out, and formerly belonging to the Territorials, he got his commission right away.

Letters received here by the relatives and friends of Jamaicans at the front, might also be of interest to the public. We shall be glad to receive these letters and publish extracts from them.

December 7, 1914

COOPER-HALE-In Calvary Church, New York on Sunday, 22nd November at 4 p.m. by the Rev. Alexander Brown, HAROLD NORMAN, second son of George H. Cooper, late of Brown's Town, St Ann to ADELAIDE AGNES, eldest daughter of E. Harvey Hale, Esq., of Mansfield.

December 8, 1914

A GRAND BALL—New South Camp Road Hotel Opens with Brilliant Function-LARGE ATTENDANCE-Mr. Evelyn Gives His Guests a Most Delightful Time.

.........Over two hundred guests responded to the invitations for dinner and dance, and quite an enjoyable time was spent by all.............................There was quite a select crowd, notable among those present being, Mr. J. Tapley, Mr. J.B. Stiven, Mr. and Mrs. Hector Josephs, Mr. R.E. Nunes, Dr. Grossett, Mr. A. Grossett, Dr. A.E. Norton, Mr. Altamont DaCosta, Mr. H. E. DaCosta, Dr. Lewis Crooks, Dr. Levy, Mr. and Mrs. H.W. Dayes, Mr. H.E DaCosta, Mr. Cecil deCordova and a good many others, including officers of H.M. Army and Navy.

December 9, 1914
REYNOLDS-STEPHENSON-At the Parish Church, Kingston, on December 2nd, 1914 by the Rev. R.J. Ripley, CHARLES R.S. third son of Caleb Reynolds, Wesleyan Minister to FLORENCE MILDRED youngest daughter of the late Edmund Stephenson of Dry Harbour, St Ann.

December 10, 1914
MAIR-At St Ann's Bay, Saturday 5th December, CATHERINE JONE, the beloved wife of J.W. Mair, Inspector of Nuisances (late Serjeant-Major Jamaica Constabulary) St Ann's Bay. She sleeps in Jesus. American and Costa Rican papers please copy.

December 14, 1914
COX-On 10th inst. at "Ramble Tea Estate" St Ann, HERBERT EDWARD COX, for over 16 years Custos of that Parish.

December 22, 1914
LEVY-STEWART-On the 17th inst at the Mandeville Parish Church, by the Rev. E.B. Pike, ARTHUR EMANUEL, son of the late Hon. Arthur Levy to FLORRIE youngest daughter of the late Louis Stewart, Esq. of Old England, Manchester. NO CARDS. English and American papers please copy.

December 30, 1914
WEDDING BELLS
(From our Correspondent)
        Saint Ann's Bay, Saturday, Dec. 26—One of the prettiest weddings that have ever graced this town for a long time came off at the Parish Church here on Wednesday last. The contracting parties were Dr. A.E.C. Myers, district medical officer, (son of G.P. Myers, Esq., member of the city Council and ex-Mayor of Kingston) and Miss Edna W. Fraser, (daughter of L.L. Fraser, Esq., one of our most popular businessmen).
        The wedding came off at 4 p.m. and Rev. C.H. Swaby, performed the ceremony. The groomsman was Mr. G.D. Myers, (brother of the bridegroom) while the bridesmaid was Miss Florence Fraser (sister of the bride).
        The Church was tastefully decorated for the occasion, and the large number of persons that thronged the sacred edifice spoke in unmistakable terms of the esteem that they have for the happy pair.
        The bride looked charming in her dress of white satin. She was given away by her father.
        The presents, which need not be her detailed, were valuable and numerous.
        After the ceremony the happy couple repaired to the residence of the bride's father where their health was drunk. They subsequently motored to the Moneague Hotel where a part of the honeymoon will be spent.
        To Doctor and Mrs. Myers Saint Ann's Bay wishers long years of happiness.

1914

December 31, 1914

MYERS-FRASER- On 23rd inst. at Parish Church, St Ann's Bay by Rev. C.H. Swaby, ALGERNON EDGAR CYRIL (D.M.O.) son of G.P. Myers, Kingston, to EDNA WILHELMINA, daughter of L.L. Fraser, St Ann's Bay.

1915

January 4, 1915

JUDAH-At Spanish Town at noon on 31st December 1914, GEORGE FORTUNATUS JUDAH, aged 83 years. R.I.P.

January 6, 1915
HEDMANN At Bloomsbury, Montego Bay, on Sunday 3rd January 1915, the wife of the Rev. G. Clinton Hedmann, of a son

McCarthy-Louisa relict of the late Justin McCarthy, at her late residence, Clan Carthy, on the 3rd inst at 3.30 p.m. Funeral moves at 4 o'clock this afternoon.

January 8, 1915
KEELING ERIC DAVID, at St Jago Park, Spanish Town on Thursday 7th January at 11 o'clock the beloved younger son of Mr. And Mrs. A.L. Keeling, aged 8 months. Funeral at Half-way Tree Church at 10.30 o'clock a.m.

January 9, 1915

St Ann's Product Coy
Brown's Town
Dealers in every description of Island
Produce for which Highest
Prices are paid
WHOLESALE MERCHANTS
Manufactures of Meal from Native
Corn also Stock Feed.
We have the most up-to-date steam
Plant for curing and grading Coffee
In the island and now offer to the
Public Superior Quality High Moun-
tain Coffee, Cherry Brand, roasted
And ground in 1 lb and ¼ lb tins
CERTIFICATES OF MERIT
Have been awarded for our meal at the
Following Agricultural shows:
Kendal, Dec 1904; Minard Feb
Thicket, Aug 1904; St Mary, July
1905; Clark's Town April 1902

FOR SALE

The following Freehold Properties in
St Ann

Situated at BROWN'S TOWN
The extensive premises known as
The BIG YARD PREMISES with
Engine and Boiler; Coffee sizing,
Drying and Roasting Machinery and
Cornmeal Plant, all in good order.
Premises known as COCK SHOP
Premises with three ranges of
Buildings all having frontage on main
Street.
Commodious business premises
Known as Musgrave House with
Fixtures consisting of Modern Show
Cases, Mahogany Counters etc.,etc
Premises known as OLD MARKET
PREMISES with dwelling and shop.
Premises known as LYON'S SHOP
PREMISES
Premises known as LONDON HOUSE
Two storey building
Situated at Burrobridge;
STORE PREMISES and RANGE OF SHOPS,
Also 3 acres of land in cultivation
Situated at Dry Harbour
WHARVES consisting of spacious
Wharf Stores and Offices
Two detached Shops and House
Known as WHITE HOUSE
Acres of land recently planted
In Cocoanuts.
Also FIVE BOATS in good order
Situated at RUNAWAY BAY
WHARF with new pier and fruit
Shed. Also Cottage and Offices
Standing on three acres of land
Situated at Moneague
Premises consisting of Livery
Stables, Coach House and Out rooms.

Applications to inspect may be made up to 31st January 1915 to Mr. J.H.LEVY at Brown's Town and full particulars together with terms and conditions of sale ma y be obtained either from Mr. J.H. Levy or from Mr. H. Davonport, Chartered Accountant or Mr. H.H. D'Costa, both of 14 Port Royal St Kingston.

January 16, 1915
MICHELIN-At her residence, Retreat, St Mary, on the 15th inst., Olivia, the beloved wife of Henry Michelin, mother of Mrs. J. L. Dixon, Kingston; Edgar and Ennaline Michelin, Retreat; Mrs. A.C. Morris; Gayle; Mrs. R Bariffe, Oracabessa, and several others to mourn their irreparable loss.

IN MEMORY OF LATE DR.MURRAY—Tablet and Monument Unveiled in Brown's Town, St Ann—THE SPEECHES MADE—Ceremony Performed by Rev. W.H. Williams, Chairman of District [Picture]
(From Our Correspondent)Brown's Town Jan 14. The unveiling of the tablet and monument erected to the memory of the late reverend Dr. W. Clarke Murray took place at the Wesleyan Chapel yesterday. Unfortunately in consequence of continuous showers of rain from early morn the attendance was not as was expected. Among those present were the immediate relatives of the deceased gentleman, the family of Mr. J.H. Levy and the Stewart Town branch of the circuit was presented by Mr. Jno. Stockhausen. There sat on the platform Revs. Braham (chairman) Rev W.J. Williams and Mr. J.H.Levy.
More.

January 20, 1915
REYNOLDS-At Harmony Hall, St Mary on the morning of Monday 18th inst., MARY ANNIE, the beloved wife of Rev. Caleb Reynolds Wesleyan Minister, aged 61 years leaving a sorrowing husband and 7 children to mourn their loss.
"I long of household voices gone
"For vanished smiles I long;
"But God hath led my loved one on,
"And He can do no wrong.

January 21, 1915
DOUET, Mrs. ELLEN, died at 22 Dalmore Road, Dulwich, on Dec 31st wife of the late Right Rev. C.F. Douet, D.D. , Assistant Bishop of Jamaica. R.I.P.

February 2, 1915
WESTMORELAND Mrs. MARGARET, relict of the late Alexander Westmoreland on the 31st January 1915, at her residence 67 Wildman Street. Funeral moves at 4.30 this afternoon. Friends and acquaintances accept this the only intimation.
"Asleep in Jesus"

February 3, 1915
Availing themselves of this medium, the Rev. Caleb Reynolds and family tender their grateful appreciation, to the many kind friends who sent telegrams, cards and letters of sympathy in connection with their recent sore bereavement.

February 4, 1915
LOPEZ-HOFFMANN-On Sunday January 31 at Holy Trinity Cathedral, by His Lordship Bishop Collins, S.J.D.D. Assisted by very Rev. Father Harpes, S.J. and Rev. Father Keller, S.J. FABIAN PATRICK LOPEZ, nephew of James Dunn, Esq. to INEZ LELIA, third daughter of E. B. Hoffmann, Esq.

February 9, 1915
ROPER-At the Nursing Hostel on the 5th inst. The wife of Harold L. Roper of a son.

February 13, 1915
WESTMORELAND-At Wakefield Pen on the 11th inst the wife of Percy Westmoreland of a son.

Selected Vital Records from the Jamaican Daily Gleaner

February 20, 1915
IN MEMORIAM
DUFF-In loving memory of my dearly beloved sister Theodosia Roberts, who departed this life on the 24th February 1914, after a short and painful illness, deeply mourned by her friends and relatives. Verse. JOHN DUFF & FRIENDS

February 27, 1915
DALLEY-MUSCHETT-On the 22nd February, 1915 at St Georges' Church, Savanna-la-Mar, by the Rev. C.V. Fraser, Rector of St Paul's Church, Harry Alexander, engineer of Amity Hall Clarendon, eldest son of Mr. And Mrs. J.B. Dalley of Montego Bay to Lynette May, eldest daughter of Geo. M. Muschett of Sav-la-Mar and his late wife Clara. Montreal and Philadelphia papers please copy.

March 1, 1915
VERLEY-At Spring Garden, St Catherine, on Saturday February 27th LEOPOLD CHARLES LOUIS VERLEY. J.P. in his 40th year. Buried at Tamarind Tree Church, Old Harbour on Sunday February 28th.

March 2, 1915
DAWSON-GRANT-On Feb 25 by the Rev. Brooks at The Methodist Episcopal Church, West 23rdSt, New York. JONATHAN ALEXANDER DAWSON, of Brown's Town, Jamaica to JOSEPHINE GRANT of Kingston, Jamaica

March 4, 1915
FULLERTON-Mary Rose, at Brown's Town, St Ann on the 23rd February 1915 Aged 86. The dearly beloved mother of A.D. Fullerton and four other children.
Sleep on Beloved;.......
We loved thee well, but Jesus love thee best
New York, Nicaraguan and Cuban papers please copy.

March 13, 1915
The final match in connection with the Billiard Tournament of St Andrew's Club was played on Wednesday night last between Dr. Levy (owing 100) and R.B. Harris who received 40. The game was 500 up and was witnessed by a large number of spectators. It resulted in a victory for Dr. Levy the scores being Dr Levy 500 and Mr. Harris 71.
[Uncle Charles Levy]

March 18, 1915
BYNDLOSS –At his residence Athol, St Andrew at 4 a.m. yesterday THEODORE HENRY. R.I.P.
Foreign papers please copy.

March 22, 1915
HEDMANN-At his residence, Mt. Felix on the night of Wednesday 17t March, Jacob Elias, 4th son of the late Gothard and Sophia Hedmann, and brother of Rev. A.A. Hedmann. English and American papers please copy.

March 23, 1915
THE CAMBRIDGE EXAMINATIONS-Publication of the Results which were Received Yesterday—Full List of Passes—The Splendid Work Done by a Number of The Pupils
    The results of the Cambridge Local Examinations for 1914 arrived in Jamaica yesterday from England and are as follows: [extractor: not complete]

The small letters denote that the candidate to whose name they are prefixed was distinguished in the following subjects respectively:

a Arithmetic (junior only)

ag Agricultural science

am Applied Mathematics

b Botany

bk Book-keeping

ch Chemistry

d Drawing

dh Dutch

da Domestic Science

e English Language and Literature

f French

g Geography

gk Greek

gn German

h History

j Logic

k Sanskrit

l Latin

m Mathematics

ms Mensuration and Surveying

mu Music

n Natural History

p Political Economy

pg Physical Geography.

ph Physics

phi Physiology and Hygiene

r Religious Knowledge

s Shorthand

sc Experimental Science

sp Spanish

Senior students are not eligible for marks of distinction unless they are under 19 years of age and juniors are not eligible unless they are under 16 years of age.

SENIOR BOYS

Student under 19 years of age who have obtained honours.

Class I

Ashenheim L.E. Jamaica college

r, gk Riddell C.E. Wolmer's school

f, m Halliday, T.M. Potsdam School

Class II

Dickenson W. N. Jamaica College

Edmonds, R.S. Jamaica College

Curphey T.J. Wolmer's School

Gadishaw, E.A. Wolmer's School,

Patterson L.V. Wolmer's School

m MacLeod, N. J. Potsdam School

m Mais, E.N. Potsdam School,

Swaby, C.L. Potsdam School

m Wallace, H.A.Potsdam School

Class III

Janzen, G.A. Jamaica College

r Jack E. L Wolmer's School

h l gk McDonald G.S. Jamaica College

m Nation B.C. O'B Potsdam School

Nethersole E. L. Potsdam School

Student under 19 years of age who have satisfied the examiners but are not included in the foregoing classes.

Coote C.R. Brown's Town High School

Gordon A.J. Brown's Town High School

Isaacs L.C. Brown's Town High School

Moss C.V. Brown's Town High School

Morrison, H. L. Brown' s Town High School

Bell F.A. Jamaica College

Alberga L.P. Wolmer's School

Byles A.L. St C., Wolmer's School

Students not under 19 years of age who have satisfied the examiners

Turner A. G. St George's College

Comber L.T. Calabar High School

Morales C. McL. Jamaica College

Wilson R.E. Private Tuition

JUNIOR BOYS

Students under 16 year so age who have obtained honours

Class I

n,r,e,l,gk,m Adams, A.B. Wolmer's School

e,m Bell R.O Wolmer's School

r,h,l,f Lyon L.C. Potsdam School

r,h,m MacLeod, D.R. Potsdam School

r.m. Scudamore W.S. K Potsdam School

r,e,h,g,l,f, m Swaby E.E. Potsdam School

Class II

Ashenheim N.N. Jamaica College

Cowper W.H.M., Wolmer's School

r,h, Lockett M.B Wolmer's School.

Class III

Muir R.C. L. M. Jamaica College

a,r Wynter, .L.R. Wolmer's School

Henriquez C.S. Potsdam School

Students under 16 years of age who have satisfied the examiners but are not included in the foregoing classes

Bramwell H.A. Brown's Town High School

Parker P.T. Brown's town High School

Lindo E.A. Jamaica College

Stockhausen H.W. Jamaica College

Levy V.L. Wolmer's School

Murray F.H. Titchfield Secondary School

Watson E.E. Potsdam School.

Students not under 16 year of age who have passed the examination as juniors

Murphy V.H. Brown's Town High School

Thomas L.T Brown's Town High School

Akin JC. L. Jamaica College

Harty W.A. Jamaica College

Penso N.B. Wolmer's School

1915

Lord C.W. L. Potsdam School
Hutchinson R.A. Manning School, Savanna-la-Mar
SENIOR GIRLS
Students Under 19 Years of Age who Have Obtained Honours
Class II
Hart B.E. Wolmer's High School
b k Lindo E.C. Wolmer's High School
McCrindle M.R. Wolmer's High School
Class III
Cover B.B., Wolmer's High School
a Mornan R.W. Wolmer's High School
Morris G.E. Wolmer's High School
Students under 19 Years of Age who Have Satisfied the Examiners, but Are not included in the Foregoing Classes
Levy S. G. The Deaconess High School Brown's Town
Parker V.E. Brown's Town High School
Ramson E. M. Hampton School
Alberga M.V. Wolmer's High School
Ormsby H.V. Colonial High School
r Chisholm B.M. H. Westwood High School
Stockhausen L.L Westwood High School
JUNIOR GIRLS
Students under 16 years of Age who have Satisfied the Examiners but are Not Included in the Foregoing Classes
Levy N.L. Deaconess High School Brown's Town
Levy M.L. Hampton School
Hendriks G.R. Wolmer's High School
Martinez L. Wolmer's High School
Sutherland, U.S Titchfield Secondary School
Heron D.H. Westwood High School
Marchalleck T.I. K. L. Colonial High School

CAMBRIDGE PRELIMINARY LOCAL EXAMINATION
Only Students under 14 years of age are eligible for marks of distinction
BOYS Class I
al Lawrence H.S. Jamaica College
Cathcart L.H.H. Jamaica College
Chambers, H.C. W. Jamaica College
Nethersole, H.G. Jamaica College
Class III
r Don C.S.D. Jamaica College
d Plant H.A. Jamaica College
McHardy A.E. Wolmer's School Kingston
Students under 14 years of Age who have Satisfied the Examiners But are not included in the Foregoing Classes
Walker L.S. Brown's Town High School
Arscott P.L. Jamaica College
Bolton H. W. Jamaica College
Cover W.A.D. Jamaica College
Dunkerly L.L. Jamaica College
Ferreira S.E.L. Jamaica College
Kelly C.O. Jamaica College

Marchalleck D. Jamaica College
Reid F.L Jamaica college
De Souza D.A. Jamaica College
Seivright W. McK Wolmer's School
Sherlock P.M. Calabar High School
Walcott A.H.C. Wolmer's School
Keeling G.I. Government Secondary School Montego Bay
Halliday H.F. Government Secondary School Montego Bay
Bingham L.E. Manning's School
Students between 14 and 16 years of Age Who Have Satisfied the Examiners
Collins F.S. Brown' s Town High School
Isaacs P.D. O. Brown's Town High School
Harty T.L.M Jamaica College
Stockhausen J.M. Jamaica College
Cahusac F.M. Manning's School Jamaica
GIRLS
Students Under 14 years of Age who has Obtain Honours
Class III
Roberts E. T. Colonial High School Kingston
Students Under 14 year of age who Have Satisfied the Examiners But are not included in the foregoing Classes
Dunkley N.D. Deaconess High School, Brown's Town
Levy C.I.L. Deaconess High School
r Facey B.M. D'E The Home School Brentford Road
Fraser M.C. Cathedral High School
Cover E.S. Westwood High School
Arscott C.M., Westwood High School
Students Between 14 and 16 years of Age who have satisfied the Examiners
Ramsay D.B., Cathedral High School
Edwards, B.K., Bloomsbury School
Eccleston G.L. West wood High School

March 25, 1915
GRUBER-In ever constant memory of Harold, who died in New York on the 25th March 1914. Verse. C.H.

March 29, 1915
Chandler, Reginald- Youngest son of Mrs. I. Chandler and late Nathaniel Chandler of 116½ Duke Street, Kingston at Boston, Mass. U.S.A. on the 15th March, 1915 Verse

March 30, 1915
LEVY- Wife of Clarence E. Levy, a daughter on 27/3/15 [Alison]

April 1, 1915
RAFFINGTON-At Green Castle, St Ann on the 27th March, 1915, MATTHEW GALLIMORE RAFFINGTON, age 79 son of the late Dr. Thomas Raffington. R.I.P.

April 7, 1915
DESNOES-At Crolston, Repon [sic] Road on the 3rd inst. To Mr.and Mrs. L.P. Desnoes a son.

April 8, 1915
GOSDEN-DUFFUS-At Holy Trinity Cathedral on Tuesday the 6th inst., by Rev. Fathers Harpes and Rowle, Oscar Joseph of Nicaragua to Hilda Claire, daughter of the late Edward Duffus and Mrs. Ambrosine Duffus of 56 East Queen Street. No cards. Foreign papers please copy.

The Brown's Town section of the Reserve Regiment will have their first Church Parade on Sunday, the 11th inst. They will assemble in the station yard and march to the St Mark's Church where they will attend the 11 o'clock service.

April 9, 1915
Mrs. Byndloss her son, and daughter beg through this medium to thank all those who so kindly sent cards, telegrams, and letters of condolence to them in their sad bereavement.

April 10, 1915
OGILVIE-At Belleisle, Grange Hill by accident on April 3rd, Charles Philip Ogilvie. Aged 49 years. West Indian and English papers please copy.

April 24, 1915
ISAACS-ANDRADE-On 21st April 1915 by Rev. S.O. Ormsby, at the residence of the bride's father Frederick Leopold Isaacs to Gladys Alithea Lucille Andrade, of Spanish Town.

Mr. F.L. Isaacs, chief warder at the St Catherine District Prison, was married at Spanish Town on the 21st inst to Miss Gladys Alithea Lucille Andrade. Rev. S.O. Ormsby performed the wedding ceremony, which took place at the home of the bride's father.

Master J. Richard Reece of Mandeville, has been awarded an open scholarship tenable at Potsdam School. He was prepared at the Marley Rectory School, Adelphi.

The McGill Entrance Examination comes off on June 15th. All who intend sitting should apply to Rev. W. Graham, Cross Roads, for a form, which must be sent in before May 15th. None will be received after that date.

April 26, 1915
In fond memory of CECIL CONSTANTINE LEVY the beloved son and brother who was suddenly called away on the morning of the 26th April 1915. Verse. MOTHER BROTHER & SISTERS.

April 28, 1915
IN MEMORIAM
Of SARA BRIDGET (MacDERMOT) MURRAY beloved daughter, sister wife and mother who passed into the Unseen, April 28th 1914."Absent only in the body"

May 4, 1915
MAY-At Richmond Lodge, Eridge Road, Tunbridge Wells, Kent, on the 10th April 1915 JOHN, the beloved and youngest son of Blanche and Raynes Donald MacFarlane May.

May 6, 1915

SCUDAMORE-OWEN-At the Church of the Holy communion Paterson, New Jersey on the 21st ult., by the Rev. Vernon Ruggles, William Edward to Helena Louise, second daughter of Mr. And Mrs. L.E. Owen.

May 10, 1915

DeLEON At Kelvin, Mico College on May 8th 1915, the wife of F.A. deLeon of a daughter.

May 11, 1915

Mrs. Ffrench-Mullen has arrived from Costa Rica by the S.S. Chagres.

Mr. Stanley deLisser returned from New York yesterday on the United Fruit Company's steamer Carrillo.

May 17, 1915

Notice of Dissolution

NOTICE is hereby given that the partnership hitherto subsisting between us the undersigned carrying on business at Annotto Bay in the parish of Saint Mary as General Dealers and Dry Goods Merchants under the style or firm of Hylton, Arscott & Co has been dissolved by mutual consent as from the Twenty third day of March one thousand nine hundred and fifteen as far as concerns the said ETHELRED DUSSARD ARSCOTT who retires from the said firm.

NOTICE is also given that all debts due to and owing by the said late firm will be received and paid respectively by JOHN ROWLAND HYLTON who will continue to carry on the said business under the style of firm of J.R. Hylton" Dated the 7th day of May 1915

J.R. Hylton,

The continuing partner

E.D.Arscott

The retired partner.

May 18, 1915

RITCHIE-At Liscard, Richmond, on Saturday 15th inst., the wife of Fred. A. Ritchie, D.M.O., of a son. [Herbert]

May 19, 1915

HOUSE-At New Jersey U.S.A. on the 4th inst., ANNA beloved wife of Rev. George House and loving mother of Mrs. Fred Clarke

May 20, 1915

FOWLER-At Phoenix Park Penn, Moneague, on Wednesday the 12th May 1915 the wife of H.Alex. Fowler, of a son.

May 21, 1915

DIXON-On Wednesday the 19th inst., at Prospect, St Mary, the wife of F.E. Dixon of a daughter.

May 29, 1915

NASH-At Williamsfield Dry Harbour St Ann, Jamaica on the 25th May 1915, WILLIAM JAMES NASH aged 67 years. English, Scotch and American papers please copy.

June 5, 1915

SCHLEIFER-on Tuesday 1st June, at Highgate, the wife of H.S. Schleifer, of a son. Both doing well.

DR L.T. Henriques and his brothers Vis, Leo, Massena, and Sydenham beg through this medium to return thanks for the many letters, cards and telegrams of condolence received during their recent sad bereavement.

LAMONT-WILLIAM- At his Daughter's residence 81½ Church Street on Monday the 7th inst. Aged 74. Funeral leaves at 4.30 p.m. today.
Friends and acquaintances please accept this the only intimation. He sleeps in hope of coming up in the first resurrection.

June 10, 1915
DOYLE-On 8th June at Dainty Villa, Hope Road, to Mr. And Mrs. J.J. Doyle a daughter. Both Well.

June 12, 1915
HOGG-JAMES- at his residence Cambridge, St James on the 1st inst., after a long and painful illness. Aged 67. Rest in Peace.

June 15, 1915
MURRAY-On the 11th instant, at "Sutton's Pastures" Vere, the residence of her son, George Dorset Murray, Johanna Elizabeth Murray, relict of the late William Ritchie Murray, in her 96th year. Scotch and English papers please copy.

June 17, 1915
LATE MUSICAL EXAMINATIONS-Tests Conducted Here By Associated Boards Of England-COMPLETE PASS LIST-The Candidates sat at Various Local Centres and at Schools.
The following are the results of the examinations of the Associated Board of the Royal Academy of Music and the Royal College of Music held in this island in the current year.
Pass List [extractor: not extracted completely]
L.A.B. Solo Performer's Examination Miss Ethelyne Soutar.
Local Centre Examinations
Lilian J. Calder, rudiments of music
Sybil D. Cawley Hampton School rudiments of music
Stella Constantine Hampton School, rudiments of music
Carmen Cover, advanced piano
Florence Cowper, intermediate piano and rudiments of music
Sybil Hart, Brampton School, Mandeville, intermediate piano and rudiments of music
Constance M. Isaacs Hampton School, advanced piano
Edna Garland-Murray, Westwood High School, rudiments of music
Carmen Muschett, Hampton School, intermediate piano and rudiments of music
Barbara Ormsby Colonial High School, rudiments of music
Ada Stewart, Retreat School Anchovy rudiments of music
SCHOOL EXAMINATIONS
Stella Constantine Hampton School, higher piano
Zillah Lannaman, Hampton School, higher piano
Constance Isaacs Hampton School, higher singing
Ena Muschett Hampton School higher piano

Beryl Escoffery Miss Monica Nixon, elementary piano
....

Edith Harty, Deaconess High School, Brown's Town, higher piano
Violet Levy, Deaconess High School, Brown's Town , higher piano
Elsie Geddes, Deaconess High School, Brown's Town, lower piano
Enid Geddes, Deaconess High School, Brown's Town, Elementary piano;
Sylvia McConnell, Deaconess High School, Brown's Town, elementary piano
Leila Lynch, Deaconess High School, Brown's Town, elementary piano
Viola Thomson, Deaconess High School, Brown's Town, elementary piano
Enid Isaacs, Deaconess High School, Brown's Town, elementary piano
Enid Helwig, Deaconess High School, Brown's Town, elementary piano
Lena Heming, Deaconess High School, Brown's Town, primary piano
Vera Veira, Deaconess High School, Brown's Town, primary piano

June 28, 1915
LEACH-On May 7th 1915, one of the victims of the torpedoing of the Lusitania NEAL JOHN LEACH, aged 25, eldest son of J.C. and K.T. Leach of Spanish Town, St Catherine. R.I.P.

The Rev. J.F. Gartshore M.A. and Mrs. Gartshore are expected to arrive here tomorrow on the Elders & Fyffes' steamer Cavina from England where they have been on furlough for the past few months.

June 29, 1915
JEFFREY-SMITH-At his residence, Durham House, Spanish Town, St Catherine, on the 28th inst., Charles Augustus, late Superintendent of Public Works. Funeral at 4 p.m. today.

July 2, 1915
VINCENT-TOWNEND-1st July 1915 to Mr. And Mrs. W. Vincent-Townend of Cedar Valley, St Ann and St Mary and Teignmouth, Devon, England, a daughter.

July 15, 1915
The Roll of Honour of Young Jamaica. The following are the names and addresses of those who passed the medical examination at Up-Park Camp on Tuesday last and who will form a part of Jamaica's War Contingent. List of Names and Addresses follows.

July 17, 1915

FOR SALE
Valuable Properties in St Ann
AT BROWN'S TOWN
That spacious and centrally situated store known as MUSGRAVE HOUSE, substantially built of stone, two storeys with fixtures comprising mahogany counter and shelves, glass cases, combination safe, large plate glass Windows, iron verandah in perfect order. The most desirable stand for business in Brown's Town
AT RUNAWAY BAY
WHARF PREMISES, new pier, office and plenty of land. Suitable for the fruit or other trade.
Immediate possession can be given. Offers will be received by A.H. D'Costa & H. Davenport 14 Port Royal Street, Kingston and J.H. Levy, Brown's Town. Permission to inspect may be obtained and other particulars given if needed by J.H. Levy.

July 21, 1915

HARRIS-LINDO-July 14th, at Coke Church, Kingston by the Rev. Arthur Kirby, assisted by Revs. J.E. Rundall, and W.J. Williams, Herbert Leslie, youngest son of Mr. And Mrs. A.L. Harris of Kingston to Lena 4th daughter of the late Rev. S.L.Lindo and Mrs. Lindo. At Home at "Wynville" South Camp Road, after September 1st 1915.

July 23, 1915

McCrea-At Putney Lodge, 12 Water Lane, Kingston on Thursday 22nd at 9 a.m. ELLEN McCREA nee Bolton. Funeral at 4.30 this afternoon.

In sorrowing and loving memory of our beloved and devoted mother Thomasine E.M. Boettcher, who fell asleep in Jesus, July 23rd 1911. Verse. M.G.B.

July 26, 1915

JENSEN-In loving memory of Francis Louisa, the dearly beloved wife of Chresten Marinus Jensen and mother of Albert Kierstine and Amy who left us on the morning of July 26th 1911. Verse. C.M. Jensen

July 27, 1915

KERR-Killed in action, 4th Battalion Royal Scot's HENRY KERR, youngest son of the late W. L. Kerr of Orange Valley, Falmouth. Aged 23.

July 28, 1915

Our Brown's Town correspondent writes: -"A concert is being arranged by Mrs. Allwood and others in aid of the Jamaica Contingent Fund. No efforts are being spared to make it a huge success. It will take place in the Court House on Thursday 5th August.

July 29, 1915

TYNDALL-In New York, on 21st July 1915, LOUISA beloved daughter of Mrs. Esther Tyndall of Brown's Town St Ann, Aged 20 years. Deeply regretted. "With Thee is plenteous redemption".

July 30, 1915

ISAACS-HANNAH SOPHIA HAVAGAL (Winnie) on Sunday 25th at Port Maria, third daughter of the late A.A. Isaacs of Brown's Town St Ann.

July 31, 1915

DeLEON-At Red Church Street, Spanish Town, in her 77th year, Victoria Louise DeLeon, widow of the late Charles A. DeLeon, mother of A.H. DeLeon, Deputy Clerk of Courts, St Andrew. R.I.P.

August 3, 1915

UNVEILING OF CLOCK & TABLET—Ceremony Performed at Claremont by Mrs. J.E.L. Cox—MR.. T Dobson's gifts—Mr. J.H. Levy Presides And Many Speeches are Delivered. (From Our Correspondent) Claremont July 30—A rather interesting and long to be remembered event in the history of Claremont took place yesterday. It was the occasion of the unveiling of a memorial tablet and clock the generous gift of Mr. Tom Dobson of Claremont.

Willing hands were busy from early morning on the scene making necessary preparations for the ceremony. A platform erected for the occasion was tastefully decorated. Scarcely had this been done than rain clouds gathered, a heavy downpour of rain fell and delayed the proceedings for nearly an hour.

The gathering (in spite of the rain) was very representative.

Selected Vital Records from the Jamaican Daily Gleaner

Hardly was there a remote corner of the parish unrepresented. Among those present were the Hon J.H. Levy, Acting Custos and Chairman of the Parochial Board of St Ann, Mr. Adam Roxburgh Vice Chairman Parochial Board, Messrs, Sylvester Cotter, J.C. Cameron, A. J. Hart, H.S. Allen, T.S. Bramwell, H. A. Fowler, members of the Parochial Board: H.P. Ruble, Superintendent, P. Arscott, Clerk of the Board. Hon T. L Roxburgh and wife, Messrs. Tom Dobson, J.P. K L Roxburgh, JP.A.H. Davis JP, J.E.L. Cox J.P. Hamilton Brown, J.P., C.N. Heming JP., Rev. R.M. Parnther, H.F. Sharpe, W. Brassington and W. Mumford, Dr. A.G. Curphey and H .Joslen, Messrs J.H. Miller, Allan Young, G. Hunt, J.G. Cover, J.W. Mair, C. L. Reece, F.W.T.Roberts, R.L. Trewick J.Hurst, N.H. Harker E.S. Sharpe and wife J.C. McIntyre and wife G.C. Brown and wife, D.A. Brown and wife, Mrs. H.E. Cox, Mrs J.E.L. Cox Mrs. Hamilton Brown and Miss Brown, Miss Curphey, Mrs. Joslen, Mrs. Fowler and Miss Fowler Mrs. C.M. Heming, Mr. R. Watson, Mrs. A.W. Geddes and Miss Parnther. More.

August 5, 1915
CLERK-In Baltimore, U.S.A. on Monday August 2, EVELYN, beloved wife of R.T. Clerk (of the United Fruit Co., Kingston) The funeral will leave the dock of Half-way Tree soon after the arrival of the S.S.Santa Marta.

August 7, 1915
LINDO-On Friday afternoon, August 6th 1915, ANN LINDO, beloved widow of the late Richard Lindo, aged 107. Funeral will move on Sunday morning at 8 o'clock form No 6 Sutton St. Relatives and friends are asked to accept this the only intimation. R.I.P

August 9, 1915
Special Notice
CLERK-In Baltimore U.S.A. on Monday, August 2, EVELYN, beloved wife of R.T. Clerk (of the United Fruit Co., Kingston). The Santa Marta will arrive so late this evening that the funeral will leave the dock to-morrow (Tuesday) morning at 9 o'clock, calling first at St. Luke's Church, then on to Half-way Tree.

SALMON- At her late residence No 124 Princess Street on August 6th, 1915 MARGARET TAYLOR SALMON ("Grannie Mag") relict of the late Chas. S. Salmon of Kingston and daughter of the late Hon Chas John Royes, Custos of St Ann, beloved mother of Dr. A.J. Salmon of Lucea and Mrs. J.H. Berry of Kingston. Aged 74 years. Requiescat in pace.

August 11, 1915
Mr. William Cowper, M.A. will give readings from the works of Charles Dickens at Wesley this evening at 7.30. The members of the Wesley Guild are requested to be in full attendance. Friends are also cordially invited.

August 18, 1915
HARVEY-McCREA-At St Paul's Church, Chapelton, on Wednesday, 11th August, 1915, by the Rev. R.J. McPherson, assisted by the Rev. J.D. Hunt, Cecil Edward Harvey, third son the late Victor Harvey of Dorset, England to Lena? Marian, eldest daughter of the late Harry McCrea, Deputy Inspector General of Police, Jamaica

August 28, 1915
SMALL-At "The Cottage" Fairfield, Montego Bay on August 24th to Mr. And Mrs. WD.A.B. Small, a daughter.

August 30, 1915
PURCHAS-At the Quarters, Chapelton, on the 26th inst., FRANK DOUGALL, aged 5 years and 9 months, youngest son of C.G. Purchas.

August 31, 1915
WHITING-St Falmouth on the 27th inst (August) Conway eldest son of the late Stephen and Martha Whiting formerly of Cornwall England and late of Garredu, Trelawny. Aged 70. English and Cuban and American papers please copy.

September 2, 1915
TOPPER-SANFTLEBEN-At the Lucea Parish Church by the Rev. W.T. Johnson, 7 a.m. on Tuesday 31st August FREDERICK TIMOTHY SANFTLEBEN TOPPER, J.P. of "Barbican" Estate, Sandy Bay P.O. to RUHAMAH GULIELMA MARTHALENA SANFTLEBEN, only daughter of the late J.W.H. Sanftleben, Esq., J.P., Hanover. English and American papers please copy.

September 3, 1915
WHITELOCKE-At Bulstrode Park, Westmoreland, Jamaica on the 28th August HELEN CAMPBELL Aged 85 years and 11 months, relict of the late Hon. Hug{h} Anthony Whitelocke. English papers please copy.

September 14, 1915
Mr. T. A. Roxburgh, Rhodes Scholar for 1915 left on the Elders and Fyffes' steamer Camito yesterday for England.

Mr. H.W. Dayes the well-known solicitor of this city is we regret to learn, confined to his residence of the past few days, owing to illness.
The finals of the handicap singles of the Liguanea Club Billiard Tournament will take place at the club House on Thursday night the 17th inst at 8.30 p.m. between Dr. Chas. Levy and Mr. P.D. Burnett, 500 up.

September 16, 1915
Messrs. A.D. and A.C. Goffe of St Mary, sailed for New York yesterday forenoon, on the Atlantic Fruit Co's Steamer Frontera.

September 17, 1915
NASH-At her son's residence, Rosebery, Mandeville, on the morning of Monday the 13th September, FRANCILLA relict of James Nash, Mandeville. Aged 93.

Saturday being a Jewish Festival the store of Mr. Edgar C. Motta, The Louvre, 89 King Street, will not be opened.

September 18, 1915
STEPHENSON MAUD, at her residence 144 East Street last night Funeral at 4.30 p.m. today. (American and Panamanian papers please copy).

In the second paragraph in the letter from "Lex" in our yesterday's issue relating to the late Mr. Justice Vickers an error appeared. It was there stated that the father of the late Judge was a Justice for Westmoreland; it should have been "Custos" for such parish.

Selected Vital Records from the Jamaican Daily Gleaner

Mr. Stanley DeLisser will sail for America to-day on the s.s. "Santa Martha," for the benefit of his health. During his absence from the island, Mr. R.S. Mead will represent the interests of the Hamilton Corporation, at 118 Harbour Street, Kingston.

September 20, 1915
HOGARTH-MURRAY-At Seaforth St Thomas, by the Rev. Jonathan Grant, at 2.30 p.m. on Wednesday, 15th September, Cecil St Leger, son of Mr. And Mrs. C.P. Hogarth of Gwendolyne Villa, St Andrew, to Jessie Colville, third daughter of the late Elias A.B. Murray and Mrs. L. E. Murray of Seaforth, St Thomas and niece of the late Rev. Wm Clarke Murray, D.D. English and foreign papers please copy.

A piece in the adjoining column adds " The bride was given away by Mr. E.S. Murray of the Collectorate in Kingston whilst Mr. Oscar Brown was groomsman. A fine reception followed."

BRAMWELL-At Burton Cottage Egypt, on Monday morning 13th Sept., 1915 REBECCA JANE, the beloved wife of Wm Bramwell, of Burton Park, St Ann. "Thy will be done" English papers please copy.

September 28, 1915
Brown's Town News
(From our Correspondent)
Brown's Town, Wednesday-While working on the main road passing Lindale Pen to Stewart Town, Amos Miller, an able bodied labourer suddenly fell down and died. A post mortem examination was performed on the body by Dr. Wilson D.M.O.
Mr. Cramphorn, who arrived from England by one of the late boats, is busy erecting the pipe organ in the St Mark's Church of this town. It is expected that the opening which promises to be a grand affair will take place on Tuesday, 12th October next. It is understood that artistes will-known in musical circles will take part and the evening in looked forward to with enthusiasm.

October 4, 1915
Keeling-On Saturday morning, the 2nd inst at "Norbrook" Constant Spring, the wife of A.L. Keeling of St Jago Park, Spanish Town of a son.

October 5, 1915
WALKER- At Shelton Rectory, England, the REV. W. WALKER, D.D., dearly loved father of W.Hugh Walker of Clifton House School. Friends please accept this intimation. R.I.P.

October 6, 1915
MOTTA-At Hudson Park, St Andrew, on Tuesday the 5th inst., the wife of Alfred Evelyn Motta of a boy.

DUFFUS-Yesterday at 5.30 p.m. at the residence of his mother 56 East Queen street, EDWARD JOSCELYN DUFFUS, Funeral moves at 4.30 p.m. to-day. Friends and acquaintances please accept this the only intimation.

October 8, 1915
VEIRA-At his residence, Mount Salus, St Andrew at 11.05 a.m. on the 6th October JOSEPH VEIRA after two months' illness leaving a widow, son and daughter. R.I.P.

October 11, 1915
PARISH BOARD—The Business of St Ann Transacted by Parochial Fathers.—
ELECTION TAKES PLACE—Mr.J.H. Levy Called to the Chair for the 27th Time.

October 14, 1915
MYERS- At the Hotel Ansonia, New York on Tuesday night 5th inst., Fred L. Myers,
J.P. of this city. Aged 62. Funeral will leave his late residence "Kensington Place" No 1
North St Kingston , on Friday 15th inst., at 4 p.m.

GRANNUM Louise (widow of the late George S. Grannum), yesterday at her residence,
No 20 Studley Park Road, Kingston Funeral to-day at 4.30 p.m. Friends and
acquaintances please accept this the only intimation. Trinidad and Barbados papers
please copy.

WALKER-TOWNEND-At Christ Church, Moneague by the Rev. H. F. Sharpe, on
Wednesday the 6th October, 1915, Gerald Low Napier, second son of C. L. Walker, Esq.,
J.P. of Hopewell, St Ann, to Stephanie Maud, youngest daughter of Arthur Townend,
Esq., J.P. of Devonside, St Ann.

October 16, 1915
SHERLOCK-Frances Reid, relict of Theodore Sherlock, and mother of the Rev. T.M.
Sherlock and Mr. F.H. Sherlock. Aged 93 Rest in Peace.

October 19, 1915
RERRIE-At Montego Bay on Wednesday the 13th instant, at 8.15 p.m. ELIZA, relict of
the late Hon. Alexander Rerrie. Aged 75

October 28, 1915
The members of the family of the late Mrs. Sarah Merrick Watson of Kingston, relict of
Rev. R.E. Watson of Mount Merrick and Point Hill St Catherine desire through this
medium to thank their many friends and acquaintances for their kind expressions of
sympathy and condolence in their recent sad bereavement.

November 3, 1915
TODD-On the 30th October, at The Retreat Pen, Brown's Town, after a long illness,
ARTHUR ROCHFORT TODD, M.R.C.S & L.R.C.P. London and J.P. for St Elizabeth,
late son of U.T. Todd, Jr., Orange Valley, St Ann, and Mrs. J.P. Hall. Aged 42 years.
"His end was perfect peace"

November 5, 1915
THE CALL OF THE MOTHERLAND—Big Recruiting Meeting at Brown's Town on
Tuesday-INSPIRING ADDRESS—Young Men to Come Forward and Enlist For the
War.
(From Our Correspondent)
    Brown's Town Wednesday—The recruiting meeting called by Mr. J.H. Levy,
acting Custos, came off yesterday at the court House. The intermittent showers of rain
pre-doomed the meeting a failure but one was agreeably surprised in entering the Court
Room to find it full to over flowing. The local Reserve Regiment numbering about 35
strong under the command of Captain L.W. Levy previously drawn up in double file in
front of the court House entered the room just before the meeting was called to order and
the National Anthem led by the Band of Mr. Matthew Edwards was struck up by them.

Selected Vital Records from the Jamaican Daily Gleaner

Among those present were Mr. J.H. Levy (Chairman) Dr. J. Johnston, Hon. J.H. Allwood, Major Slader, Messrs J.T Musson, A.E. Murray, S.M. Brown, H.F. Isaacs, J.C. Allen, CF. Crawford, R. Heming, A.W. Kennedy. Chas Campbell. A.J. Banburh, T.A. Bramwell Arthur McGrath, H.Q. Levy, F.L. Miller, A.S. Byles, A. Segree, C.H. Scott, C.R. Thomson, E.A. Mair, P Blagrove, Chas Costa, A.J. Webb, S. Thompson and W. Coore. A number of ladies were also in attendance among whom being Mrs. J.H. Levy, Mrs. Musson, Mrs. and Miss Addison, Mrs. H.Q. Levy, Mrs. and Miss Allwood, Mrs. Slader, Miss R. Lurch and Misses Solomon.

More about the addresses and call for recruits.

November 10, 1915
DELISSER-At Dry Harbour, St Ann, on the 1st November, 1915 ABRAHAM CHARLES W. DELISSER, only son of the late William DeLisser and his widow, Sarah DeLisser, in his 60th year.

November 13, 1915
HONIBALL, EDWARD- At Myersville on the 4th inst., leaving a wife and several children. Panama and American papers please copy.

Dr. Charles Levy, who was indisposed for a few days, will resume his practice to-day.

November 19, 1915
NASH-In Boston, U.S.A. on 7th inst, Elsie Isabel, eldest daughter of the late William Caswell Nash, after a short illness.

November 22,1915
FRANKLIN-KERR-On November 20th at Half-way Tree parish Church, Reginald Franklin, eldest son of Mr. and Mrs. Robert T. Franklin, of Ewelme, Wallingford, Berks, England to Hilda Margaret, only daughter of Mr. and Mrs. L P. Kerr of Saxthorpe, St Andrew.

November 23, 1915
ARSCOTT-The wife of E.D. Arscott, "The Waverly" Falmouth, of a daughter on the 20th November.

November 27, 1915
The Rev. and Mrs. J.P. Hall desire through this medium to express their warmest thanks to the many friends who so kindly sent telegrams, cards and letters of condolence in their recent bereavement.

MEN OF THE FIRST JAMAICA CONTINGENT FOR THE GREAT WAR
List of Men who form the Various Platoons. Our Men in Mother Country.—The Jamaican from every Part of the Island who answered the Call of the Empire and Left for England a short time Ago.

December 1, 1915
MEETING HELD—Convened by Hon J.H. Allwood at St Ann's Bay, Court House. DISTRICTS MARKED OUT—Request is Made that The Literacy Test be Abolished. The meeting convened by the Hon. J. Allwood of the members nominated by the Government to form the official recruiting committee for the parish, took place at he Court House, St Ann's Bay on Tuesday the 23rd November, 1915

Present: The Hon J. Allwood, Messrs J.H. Levy, S.H. Allwood, H. Tennant, C. E. Mellish, Inspector Knollys and Dr A.E. Myers. (J.H. Levy turned down the offer to be chairman).

December 2, 1915
HELWIG-At Ocho Rios, on Wednesday December 1st, GEORGE, in his 63rd year.

December 8, 1915
Among the passengers who left for England on Monday on the Camito were Messrs. A.B. Richardson, C.G. Scudamore, R. Delepenha, who are going to volunteer for service in England.

December 9, 1915
BRAHAM-In Kingston on the morning of December 8th, after a long and painful illness, Herbert Clarence Sherlock, eldest son of Rev. J. Kissock and Mrs. Braham, aged 21 years and 10 days. Thy will be done.

December 11, 1915
HOGG-At New Works, Westmoreland on the 8th December, MARY ADELINE (Min) beloved wife of G.A. Hogg of Courts Office, Black River and much loved sister of Mr. Jackson, Port Antonio. (American and Californian papers please copy.)

December 15, 1915
DOUGALL-At "The Villa" Port Maria, on the 12th inst., Eliza Belle, relict of the late James Dougall, of Sav-la-Mar in her 81st year.

BROWN'S TOWN NEWS
Arrangements for a Christmas Concert
From our Correspondent
        Brown's Town, Monday. His Honour Mr. C.H. Yorke-Slader returned to the parish and resumed his duties as Resident Magistrate. The Deaconess High School broke up on Friday last for the Xmas holidays. The Cambridge Local Examinations are being conducted in the St Mark's school room in this town. Mr. R.M. Murray is presiding examiner.
        The Brown's town Girls club is arranging to give a Christmas concert in the Baptist Schoolroom on Tuesday evening 21st December when songs, recitations and folk games will be given. The brotherhood is also arranging a grand fete on Aberdeen common. The fete will take place on Monday 27th December. The Brown's Town brass band will be in attendance.
        The rose vendors of the Negro Improvement Association were to be seen busily pursuing their avocation throughout the town to-day. The Government elementary school will give holidays during the coming week. There will be a change of staff in the infant department in consequence of the departure of Miss Garsia for another sphere of activity. The Baptists of this town are conducting centenary meetings to-night. Revs. Mr. Halliday and Marston are expected to speak. The Wesleyans had their annual harvest services yesterday.

December 16, 1915
SNAITH- At Oracabessa on Sunday 12th December, IDA De MONTAGUE, infant daughter of Mr. and Mrs. W.Geo. Snaith. Safely gathered in the folds.

Selected Vital Records from the Jamaican Daily Gleaner

December 18, 1915

BROWN'S TOWN—Meeting of the Universal Negro Improvement Association. MR J.H. LEVY PRESIDES-Dr J. Johnston Makes Speech and Asks for More Details of Plan. [Marcus Garvey read a speech]

December 21, 1915

HERCERT [sic] AUGUSTUS CUNHA-At His late residence "Chatsworth" South Camp Road. The funeral will leave for Coke Church at 4.15 from thence to Ebenezer.

December 22, 1915

ARCHER-BROWN-At Christ Church, Port Antonio on the 20th instant, Gerald Alexander, second son of the late Mr. and Mrs. David Archer, of Cave Valley, Saint Ann, to Louie, elder daughter of Mr. and Mrs. A. Augustus Brown of Port Antonio. At Home at Windsor after January 2nd 1916.

December 23, 1915

Title Application

Joseph Henry Levy of Brown's Town in the Parish of Saint Ann Merchant. Application No 6481

14th July 1915

23rd December 1915

All that piece or parcel of land situate in Brown's Town in the Parish of St Ann known as "Big Yard" containing 3 roods 16 perches outlined in red on and of the shape and dimensions and butting and bounded as appears by the place or diagram thereof made by Messrs. Byles and Heming dated the 5th day of July 1915 and being the document numbered 5 among the documents lodged with the application.

December 29, 1915

CALDER-On December 21 of wounds received on December 19 in Gallipoli, KENNETH WILLIAM fourth son of John Vassall Calder of Worthy Park, Ewarton, aged 23.

MAY-on the 7th inst., at Tunbridge Wells, Kent, MINNA CONSTANCE, wife of George C. May of H.M. Civil Service Duala, Cameroon, West Africa.

December 30, 1915

Miss Enid Cunha, Rev. and Mrs. Armon Jones and Mr. and Mrs. T.H. Geddes take this opportunity of thanking their friends and acquaintances for the many telegrams, cards and letters of condolence received during the illness and after the death of their father and mother Mr. and Mrs. H.A. Cunha.

Index

Hon. J.H., 356,
363, 402, 412,
424, 433, 465,
466, 500
Hon. J.H. and Mrs.,
452
J.H., 139, 167, 227,
237, 239, 376,
407, 415, 416,
442, 474
James, 286, 308
John, 190, 324
John Humber, 230
Mr., 218, 229, 402,
405
Mr.J.H., 194
Mrs. and Miss, 500
Mrs. J.H., 373, 382,
495
Mrs. M.A., 359
Philip, 61
R.W., 242
S.G., 217, 259
S.H., 501
V.M., 370
Valda, 373
Alvarez
Miss, 116
Ambrose
Miss, 157
Rev. and Mrs, 157
Rev. R, 242
Rev. R.G., 100,
156, 258, 275,
278, 279
Rev.H., 79
Robert George, 80
Anderson
A.W., 64, 74
Allan, 437
E.A., 382
G., 437
Miss A., 437
Mr., 226
Mrs. E., 437
Rebecca, 335
Richard, 335
Z., 441
Andrade
D.V., 369, 440
F.A.L., 440
F.L., 370

Gladys Alithea
Lucille, 491
Jacob A.P.M., 334
Miriam Louise, 334
Andrews
Archibald J., 135,
216
Hon. W., 161
Mr., 119
Rev. C.W., 428
William, 126
Ansell
Rachel M., 115
Anthony
Burt Luther, 347
Merritt, 347
Arbouin
L.O., 217
Archambeau
Mrs., 330
Archbishop of the
West Indies, 282,
332, 347, 351
Archduke Francis
Ferdinand, 463
Archer
Beatrice Ruth
(Trixie), 331
Cyril, 213
D., 148
David, 34, 83, 145,
330, 331, 350,
502
Gerald Alexander,
502
Gertrude, 458
J.L., 217
Joseph Leopold,
330
Laurie, 213
Mrs., 116
Trixy, 213
Armon Jones
Rev. and Mrs., 502
Rev.Edward, 397
Armsley
Dr., 126
Armstrong
C.H.B., 162
Jeannie M., 257
Miss, 260
Samuel T., 257

Arnett
Mr., 303
Mrs., 227
Rev. E., 295
Arnold
L.E., 439
Miss, 189
Arrowsmith
C.J., 163
Arscott
C.M., 490
Charles D., 206
Charles Dussard,
287
Clara, 332, 359
E.D., 500
Ethelred Dussard,
492
F.H., 218
Marion, 281
Mary Ann, 206
Mary Elizabeth, 24
Mr., 359
Mr. R.W., 27
Mrs. D., 359
Nettie, 281
P., 496
P.L., 441, 489
R.W., 49, 53
W.D., 163
Ashby
A.J., 164
A.J.A., 164
Effie, 187
George M., 135
Kathleen, 186
Miss, 377
Miss A.J., 186
Ashenheim
J.L., 255
Judith, 255
L.E., 368, 439, 446,
487
Lewis, 255
Misses, 157
Mr. and Mrs., 157
N., 449
N.N., 369, 439, 488
Ashman
C.E., 439
Ashton, 477
Midn. A., 477

Index

Rev.D., 99

Bastian
  Capt. and Mrs., 357
  Maire Louise
    Coplin, 357

Bateman
  Mr. and Mrs., 420,
    421

Bates
  Rev. Miner Lee,
    333

Bathurst Hall
  Mrs., 179
  Rev. G., 179, 204,
    205

Batley
  Richard Clarkson,
    353

Batten
  Hon. R., 161

Baugh
  L.D.H., 163

Bawton
  T. Ellis, 201

Bay
  Rev. G.B., 115

Bayley
  Alice, 27
  Charles, 27
  H.H.R., 217, 259
  W.R., 217

Baynes
  Miss Baynes, 227

Beacher
  Eliza Ann Calder,
    59
  John, 59

Beadon
  Rev. F.F., 8

Beard
  Dr., 385

Beckford
  Edward, 184
  Margaret, 184
  Peter, 184
  William, 184

Beckridge
  Frances, 33

Beckwith
  Miss, 457

Bedward, 200

Bell

Audrey, 379
Cora, 379
E.A., 439
Edward A., 50
F.A., 488
Hon. V.G., 161,
  209
R.O., 380, 464, 488

Bellamy
  A.A., 441

Bellini
  Giovanni, 451

Bellonce
  Henri, 256

Belloncle
  Henri, 216

Belmont Pen, 245

Bemett.
  Angelo, 365

Beneckendorf
  Mr. and Mrs. and
    Miss, 157

Benedict
  George Lawrence,
    395

Bengough
  Major General, 224

Benjamin
  Mr. B.Y., 39

Bennett
  Daniel, 83
  George, 193
  Hon George, 193
  Mr., 211, 239
  Sarah, 193

Benson
  Miss, 437
  Mr., 119

Bensyn
  Mr. S., 120

Bernard
  Mr. A.N., 365

Berry
  Alex, 126
  Hon. C.B., 264
  Mrs. J.H., 496
  Rev. C., 102
  Rev. Carey B., 209

Bertram
  Louis John, 416

Beverland
  Susannah, 283

Bicknell
  Catherine Ann, 329
  Charles Arbouin,
    152
  H.J., 329
  Henry John, 152
  Mr. C.A., 321

Bickwith
  Miss A., 417

Bignell
  William, 103

Billingslea
  Mr.and Mrs., 421
  Mr.and Mrs. Frank,
    420

Binger
  Rev,, 464

Bingham
  L.E., 490
  L.M., 440

Binns
  E.E., 217

Bird
  Dr. Reginald
    Wallace, 100
  W.H., 248
  W.W., 100

Bishop de Carteret,
  454

Bishop Douet, 184

Bishop Nuttall, 221

Bishop of Jamaica, 63,
  65, 73, 80, 109,
  152, 184

Blagrove
  Col., 302, 305, 322
  Col. C.B., 444
  P., 382, 500
  Peter, 465

Blake
  Adolphus, 460
  Eskbert, 383
  Lady, 166
  Miss, 4
  Olive, 166
  Sir Henry, 112,
    166, 183, 251
  Sir Henry A., 209
  Sir Henry Arthur,
    138

Bleby
  William H.F., 135

Index

Rev. J.Kissock,
424, 465, 501
Rev.Kissock, 376
Richmond, 415,
465
Róbert B., 10
Rosa Mary
Carroline, 39
Brains
Mr., 405
Braitewaite
Winnie, 464
Braithwaite
Miss, 457
Rev. S.R., 299
Bramwell
A., 466
E.J., 466
E.L., 440
H.A., 441, 466, 488
Miss M., 382
Mr., 402, 405
Mr. T.A., 367
R., 382, 430
R.A., 474
Rebecca Jane, 498
T., 386
T.A., 382, 407, 500
T.S., 496
Wm., 498
Branch
Bertie, 203
Ernest St John, 416
Rev. Canon, 203
Branday
L.P., 373
Louis P., 156
Louise Isabelle,
156
Mabel Florence,
373
Misses, 157
Mr. and Mrs Jno.,
157
Reginald, 375
William Charles,
276
Brandon
Amanda, 268
Beatrice Bertha
Ruth, 259
C.A., 206

Charles J., 356
Constantia, 42
Iris Selna, 419
Isaac S., 419
Jacob, 268
Miriam, 86
Mortimer, 259
Mr., 116
Mrs. Mortimer, 269
Nathaniel, 42, 86
Brandt
Mr., 437
Branker
Alex,, 66
Mary Helen, 66
Brass
Mr., 162
Brassington
W., 496
Brathwaite
W.E., 440
Bravo
Mr., 138
Walter, 139
Bravo Bros
Messrs, 447
Bravo Bros & Coy,
133
Bravo Bros. & Coy,
129, 137
Breakspear
Mary Ann, 127
Thomas, 162
William, 127
Brennan
Mr., 421
Brice
J.R., 7
Rev. E.B., 445
Rev. E.E., 353
Rev.E.E., 351
Bridgewater
Rev., 185, 187
Briggs
Mr., 156
Briscoe
Sarah Eliza, 257
Thomas, 457
William Drew, 257
Brodber
Henry, 273
Bromfield

David, 396
Mary, 396
Mary Ann, 448
Bronstorph
F.L., 439
Brooks
Rev. G.B., 38
Broomfield
Rosey Christiana,
360
Brough
Emma Lamar, 5
Jos., 5
Brown
A., 230, 386
A.L., 441
A.Louise, 457
A.M., 356
A.V., 441
Alexander Alfred
Augustus, 107
Bertha Evangeline,
71
C.A., 145
Charles, 25
D.A., 496
Dorothy, 310
Estelle Evangeline,
421
F.B., 430
G.C., 496
G.R., 380
Geo, 382
George R., 394
H., 190
Hamilton, 24, 115,
273, 407, 496
Hamilton T., 27
Harriet Augusta,
273
Helen, 202
Henry Isaac Close,
165
Hy, 382
Iris, 382
J. Sutton, 352
John Samuel, 60
Lena, 281
Louie, 502
Mary Malvina, 25
Mary Menzies
McGregor, 61

Index

George Henry, 86
J.A.P., 86
Josefa, 86
Buchanan
   James Claude, 336
Buckley
   C.H.S., 479
   Rev. C. McK., 272
   Rev. C.M., 271,
     272, 420, 479
   Rev. Mr. and Mrs.,
     420
   W.W., 380
Buie-Tomlinson
   G.P., 439
Bullock
   A.A., 291
   Amy, 359
   L.S., 291
   L.T., 115
   M, 359
   W.Deleon, 291
Bulman
   J.A., 445
Bunbury
   Rev. Thomas, 28
Burbidge
   Amy Maud, 310
   George Arnold,
     310
Burger
   Beatrice Mary, 204
Burgess
   Rev. M.B., 430
Burial of Paupers, 200
Burke
   Alexander A., 159
   Alexr., 10
   Ella, 192
   Hon. S.C., 260, 264
   Hon.
     S.Constantine,
     272
   J.M., 450
   Katie, 76
   Marjorie, 444
   Miss M., 437
   Mr., 239
   Mr. G. Lustac, 264
   P.G., 439
   R.A., 441, 449
   S. Constantine, 76

S.C., 209
Samuel
   Constantine, 73,
     272
   Sarah Constance,
     73
Burnett
   Mr. P.D., 497
Burrell
   Anne Maria, 65
   Rev. William
     Robert, 65
Burrowes
   B., 260
   Edna, 381
   Jonathan B., 74
   Mr. and Mrs A.L.,
     381
Burton
   Cecile, 464
   Mr., 357
   Mr. C.T., 379
Bussell
   Rev. W., 103
   Rev. W. Kemp, 152
Busultil
   B., 199
   Michael, 199
Butler
   Mr., 157
   W.I.R., 369
Byles
   A.E., 382
   A.L., 488
   A.L.S., 440
   A.S., 139, 145,
     190, 287, 356,
     382, 434, 500
   A.Shamrock, 116
   Beryl, 373
   C.A., 382
   Edward, 382
   Geo Duncan, 254
   J.H., 441
   Marion Constantia,
     347
   Mr., 210, 218, 502
   Mr. A.S., 179, 184
   Mr. and Mrs. A.S.,
     452
   Mrs. A.S. and
     Miss, 373

R.L., 254
Robert, 415, 465
Theophilus Lynch,
   201
Byndloss
   James, 33, 62
   Marie, 96
   Mrs., 491
   Rosamond, 96
   Theodore, 96
   Theodore Henry,
    486

C

C.R.T., 262
Cahusac
   C.M., 306
   F.M., 490
   Hannah Elizabeth,
    24
   Rev. T.B., 332
   Sidney Charles
    Wood, 367
   T. Barry, 24
Calabar High School,
   80
Calame
   C.C., 464
Calder
   C.A., 368
   Hon. J.V., 477
   J.N., 368
   James, 350
   John, 253
   John Vassall, 502
   K.W., 477
   Kenneth William,
    502
   Lilian, 417, 457
   Lilian J., 493
   Marian, 457
   Mr., 149
   Sarah, 350
   W. Jameson, 272
   Wm., 254
   Wm. Jameson, 254
   Wm. Johnson, 101
Calton
   P.A., 373
Camac

Index

Index

Conlin
Miss, 437
Connery
J.E., 439
Connolley
E.D., 440
Connolly
Daisy, 379
Olive, 379
W.T., 429
Connor
Charles, 182
Conran
Capt, 477
Lieut. P., 477
Mr. W., 477
Constantine
Amy, 464
D., 377
R.G., 441
Rev. M. Gregory,
18
S., 440
Stella, 377, 493
Cook
E.G., 256
Cooke
Alice, 475
Daphne, 458
Dr., 385
Dr.Geo, 330
Katheleen, 330
Maximillian Henry
Stoddard, 126
Mrs., 475
Stephen, 126
Wilbert M., 285
Coolies, 113
Cooling
John, 60
Coombs
George, 139
Cooper
Alberax, 331
Alberta, 331
Albertha, 383
Eric Vivian Patrick,
331
G.H., 262
Geo.H., 145
George H., 270,
331, 383, 479

Harold, 213
Harold Norman,
479
Ivan, 213
John B., 355
Mary Helen, 376
Master, 213
Mr., 132, 205, 244
Mr.and Mrs. John,
376
R.P., 355
Rebecca Amelia,
355
Thomas, 70
William, 194, 355
Willie, 213
Coore
C.R., 439, 466
W., 500
W.G., 382
Coote
C.R., 488
T.E., 380
Cope
Rev. H.W., 431
Copper Mining in
Jamaica, 105
Corbett
Arthur, 230
Mr., 167, 184
Mrs., 227
Corinaldi
D.A., 209
David Aurelius,
416
Edith Alice, 67
Edwin Cecil, 67
Eva, 268
Hon D.A., 264
Horatio, 268
Mr. and Mrs., 157
Mr. S., 324
P.E., 430
Sydney.Anna, 67
W.R., 439
Cork
H., 416
Hon. P.C., 415
Josias, 38, 53
Miss, 116
Mr. P.C., 470
Philip Clarke, 416

Rev. Josiah, 27,
153
Rev.J., 57, 123
Revd Josiah, 24
Revd. Josias, 20
Revd. Js., 17
Corlet
John, 9
Corlett
A., 305
Hephsibah, 32
John, 42, 186
Mary Ann, 186
Mr., 179, 302
Rev. John, 32, 45
Cornwall
Rev. P.D.M., 95
Cosby
Rev.J.N., 337
Costa
A.M., 369
Alice, 214
Anastasia, 320
Avis, 377, 417, 457
C., 236
Charles, 295, 334
Chas., 148, 230,
261, 356, 500
Dr., 288
Gabriel Guisado,
319
Isaac, 348
John Alexander,
355
Louisa, 22
Miss, 373
Mrs. W., 261
Sarah Mary
(Minnie), 292
W., 148, 213
W.H., 284
William, 22, 292,
320
Winifred, 334
Winnie, 214
Costume Ball, 109
Cotes
Miss E., 120
Cotter
Amie, 70
Arundel, 70, 328
Dr.Arundel H., 70

Index

Index

Index

Rev. Father, 333

Dixon
A.N., 139, 145,
147, 148, 190,
209, 210, 229,
243, 248, 409,
411
Cornelius, 324
D., 467
E.D., 440, 441
F.E., 427, 492
Hon A.N., 222, 227
Miss E.M., 437
Mr., 181
Mr. A.N., 116
Mrs. J.L., 484
T.C., 139
Vera, 418

Dobson
Mr., 226
Mr. Tom., 495
R., 226
S., 243
Saml., 139
Samuel, 226

Dobyns
Andrew, 10

Dodd
Ann, 53
G.J., 477
I.A., 260
J.H., 477
John, 337
Marjorie
Constance, 337
Mollie, 337
Mr. and Mrs. J.,
421
R.W., 260

Dolphy
Dinah Irene, 89
Isaac, 89

Don
Annie, 457
C., 449
C.S.D., 441, 489
E.G.A., 439, 446,
450

Donald-Hill
B., 440
J., 440

Donaldson

T.H., 217

Doorley
C.W., 306
Dorothy Walrond,
83

Doorly
Anton Hamilton,
352
C.W., 334, 338,
353
Charles Martin,
338
Dorothy, 353
J.H.M., 163
James G., 312
James Graham, 68
M.C., 338
Martin, 83
Mary E., 312
Mr., 157
Mrs. K., 386
Mrs. M.C., 353

Doran
E.D.A., 439, 446

Douet
A.W., 291, 306,
444
Dorrit, 444
Ellen, 485
George, 444
Mr., 222
Mr. and Mrs
Brooks, 420
Mr. and Mrs.
Brooks, 421
Mr. G.A., 264
Mrs., 116
Rev. Bishop, 275
Rev. C.F., 9, 43,
111, 202, 270,
271, 319, 485
Rev. C.J.P., 116
Rev. C.T.P., 76
Rev. Charles F., 65
Roberta Wilmina,
76
Ven Arch., 80
William Maxwell,
116
Winnie, 444

Dougall
Eliza Belle, 501

Geo.A., 145
James, 501
James A., 183, 366
Kathleen, 457
William, 329

Douglas
Geo., 157
Geo.A., 254
Julia Mary, 254
Misses, 228
Willie, 157

Doutlwaite
Mr. T.W., 184

Downer
Rev., 80
Rev. G.W., 43, 58,
60, 66, 76, 84,
103, 108, 122,
127, 161, 184,
203
Ven. Archdeacon,
272, 283, 319,
351, 354
Ven. Archdeacon
G.W., 286

Doyle
Mr. and Mrs. J.J.,
493

Drew
J.J., 79
Mary Emily, 79
Stephen, 79

Driver
Alfred, 346
Frederick Betts,
346
Rev.W.J., 431

Drommond
Rev. R.S., 258

Dron
Mr., 228
Mr. and Mrs., 157

Drummond
Major, 420, 421

D'Souza
David Henriques,
18
Mr. D.H., 18

Duchess of Fife, 133
Duchess of Teck, 133
Dudds

520

Index

Theodore L, 322
Theodore
Lemercier, 45
Ulysses Lemercier,
28
Durle
Mr. W.R., 379
Durrant
John, 145

E

Eagan
Mr. E., 365
Earl
Thomas, 90
Earle
E.R.C., 431
Edward, 128
Edward R..C., 128
Earthquake, 312, 468
1907, 327
Victims, 328
East
Rev. D.J., 123
Eastin
Edward, 164
Eaves
Mr. F., 179
Eccleston
G.L., 490
Gladys, 457
L.E., 441
Rev.A.G., 430
Eclipse of the sun, 336
Edbury
Eda Venetia
Estelle, 297
Edgar
Herbert Wedderlie,
466
Sir James David,
466
Edmond
E.A., 449
Rev. F., 123
Edmonds
E.A., 439, 446
F.S., 439
Frederick, 248
R.S., 487
Rev. F., 257

Educational
Conference, 123
Edwards
B.K., 490
Charles James, 383
Eunice, 464
G.O., 440
G.W., 218
Gladys, 464
H. Launcelot, 83
I.H., 380
L.R., 467
Matthew, 226, 499
Mr. B., 260
Mr. H.B., 157
Mr. R.M., 433
Rev. E.A., 430
Egerton
Mr. and Mrs., 157
Eggins
Mr. W.G., 422
Elliot
Mr. I.J., 380
Elliott
E.C., 442
Miss M., 437
Rev., 361
Sarah Sophia, 442
Ellis
Augusta, 268
Eddley Ernest, 122
Edward K., 122
H.H.A., 439
John, 8, 145, 148
Major C.D.C., 268
Rev.J.B., 80, 81,
108, 121, 126,
170, 184, 286
Rev.J.D., 128
Sir Adam G., 90
Emanuel
Charles, 365
Mrs., 365
Embden
H., 382
Emperor Francis
Joseph, 463
Emperor William,
Crown Prince of
Servia, 463
Ermandez
Miss L., 198

Ernandey
Miss L.J., 214
Erskine
Mr., 116
Escoffery
A., 7
A.C., 111
A.W., 10
A.Walcott, 19
Alexander, 4, 28,
104
Alexander W., 15
Alexander Wolcott,
4
Anne Eliza, 21
Beryl, 458, 494
C.A., 217
C.J., 163, 335
C.S., 111
Charles Jos., 273
G.S., 368, 413
Grisilda, 254
Jesse Eugenie, 15
John, 39
John W., 111
L., 192
Mary Ann, 28
Miss S.L., 198
Moira, 418
Mortimer, 254
Mr. A.W., 21
N., 457
Thomas Edward,
346
Espeut
Hon. W. Bancroft,
155
Essling
Miss K., 437
Esson
Hon. Rev. W.B.,
431
Rev. W.B., 418
Rev. Walter Booth,
416
Estates in Cultivation
in Trelawny. 1877,
48
Estavard
Eugene, 14
Estwick
Edward, 395

Index

Dr. and Mrs., 337
Jane, 371
Laurene, 371
Mrs., 492
Muriel Sophia Von
    Reitzenstein,
    337
Vincent, 371
Fiddes
    Alexander, 8
    Haydee, 421
Field
    Augustus, 33, 82
Fielding
    Mr. S.R., 14
Figueroa
    Colin Grey, 79
    John Hawkins, 83
    Joseph, 83
    William Gray, 79
Findlay
    A.F.C., 217
    Edwin Lewis, 350
    Elsie, 348, 350
    Evalina, 360
    Marie McCulloch,
    75
    Mary Christine
        Copeland, 348
    Rev. Acheson, 75
    Robert, 360
    William, 75
    William Grant,
    348, 350
Finke & Co, 33
Finlason
    Rev. W.W., 430
Finlay
    Ruth, 457
Finlayson
    Ambrose A., 18
Finsi
    Mr. and Mrs
        Lionel, 157
    Mr. G., 157
Fisher
    Chas., 127
    F. Chas., 277, 278,
    307
    Geo., 127
    Grace M., 456
    Hon. J. W., 45

Hon. J. Wanchope,
    216
Hugh Seymour
    Charles Scott,
    108
J. Wanchope, 23,
    63, 108, 324
J.W., 5, 17
John, 10
Joseph, 424
Mary Eliza, 63
Miss, 303, 305
Mr. H.S., 216, 253
Mrs., 216
Rebecca, 278, 457
Sterling, 76, 305
Veta Faith, 278
William
    Wissilhouse,
    253
Fisher Jnr
    Ethel Myra, 127
    Geo., 127
Fitzgerald
    Lord George, 112,
    166
    Mr., 116
Fitz-Ritson
    W., 430
Fleming
    A.A., 416
    Hon A.A., 431
Fletcher
    Charles, 65
    James, 3
    Mary Isabella Jane,
    3
    Osborne G., 144
Floods
    Paris, 345
Fogarty
    D.E., 217
    Daniel, 331, 334
    Daniel Michael,
    331
    Mary Gordon, 334
Fonseca
    R.E., 236
    Rupert E., 262
Forbes
    Rev. Wm., 11
    Thomas, 101

Forrest
    Ann, 423
    E.T., 134
    Sanford, 423
Forrester
    Rev. G., 100
Forster
    Rudolph, 200
Foster
    Edith Constance,
    62
    F.A., 218, 260
    Henry B., 32
    Miss, 377
    Mrs., 374
    P.E., 440
    P.R., 369
    R.L., 62
    Rev. H.B., 32
Fournier
    A., 275
    Achille, 220
    Adrienne, 34
    Alexander, 220,
    238
    Alphonse, 307
    Alphonse Pierre
        (Peter), 307
    Ernest, 250
    Essie, 307
    Hercules, 41
    Honore, 34
    Mr. A., 323
    Peter, 307
Fowler
    H., 430
    H.A., 407, 496
    H.Alex., 492
    H.E., 422
    Henry Edward, 376
    Horace Alexander,
    422
    Miss, 496
    Mr., 405
    Mrs., 496
Fox
    Mr. Percy, 422
Fraenckel
    Mr., 119
    Mr. R., 120
Francis
    Joseph, 38

Index

Garland-Murray
Edna, 493
Garrand
Mr., 120
Garrett
Mr., 312
Mrs., 24
Garriques
Fred Newton, 267
Harry Lord, 267
Henry Lord, 199
Peter Francis, 99
Garsia
Adelaide Eliza, 353
Alexander, 353
Berona Camilla,
263
Elizabeth E.A., 270
Eugenie Elizabeth,
356
Eustace G., 263
Eustace G.A., 110
Francis George,
356
Geo D., 96
George, 270
George Donald, 66
Miss, 501
Mrs. R.D., 357
Gartshore
Rev. J.F., 429
Rev.J.F., 494
Garvey
Marcus, 502
Gaultier
Mr. P., 5
Gauntlet
Hugh, 338
Gauntlett
Edmund
Greenwood, 219
H.G., 415
H.O., 474
Mr. and Mrs, 373
Mr. and Mrs. H.G.,
359
Oscar Greenwood,
219
Walter Charles,
203
Gayle
E.D., 382

S.S., 439
Gayleard
Rev. James, 21
Gayner
Elizabeth Ann, 19
J.W., 281
John W., 15
Julia Bertha, 281
Mary Olivia, 337
Mary Rose, 15
Sydney, 378, 418,
457
Gaynor
Charlotte E.H., 323
Sydney, 458
W.A., 139, 145,
250
Wm., 230
Geddes
A.B., 407
A.W., 136
Adrian Bunting,
136
Alex, 435
Alexander W., 216,
256
Alexander William,
93
Elizabeth M., 248
Elsie, 373, 418,
457, 494
Enid, 454, 494
Isabel, 152
M., 86
May, 378
Mr. and Mrs. T.H.,
502
Mrs. A.W., 496
Mrs. T.M., 476
R.C., 430
Rebecca Grace,
476
Rev., 170
Rev. A.W., 100,
139, 378, 428,
476
Rev. R.M., 378
Rev. T.M., 139,
193, 215, 476
Rev. Thomas M.,
254
Rev. Thos.M., 136

Rev.Mr., 304
Rev.T.M., 79, 155,
185
T.H., 378, 476
Thomas M., 135,
255
Genge
Dorothy Gladys,
476
T.Taylor, 476
Gentles
Alexander Bolton,
261
Catherine, 261
J.E., 262
Thos., 261
William, 261
George
Mr. and Mrs.
Arthur, 157
Gibb
Dr. J.M., 478
Roger B., 478
Gibson
Hon D.S., 260
Gideon
D.S., 209, 265
Ruby, 437, 438,
457
Gifford
George L., 322
Mr., 237
Gilles
Leila, 136
Rev. William, 136
W., 221
Gillespie
Mr., 343
Gillies
Isabelle Sophia, 70
Mr. W., 379
Rev. W., 102, 221,
264
Rev. William, 70,
199
Rev. Wm., 170
Robert, 199
Gilliland
Mr. James, 422
Gillis
Andrew, 119
Rev. Wm., 34

Index

Graves John, 74
Gray
  Annie Louisa, 43
  C., 477
  Miss, 456
  Mr. W.B., 477
  Thomas, 43
Greaves
  Elizabeth, 470
  Mrs., 227
Green
  Alex, 305
  Alfred, 104
  Frederick, 104
  Jane, 104
  Nurse, 421
  Robert, 460
Gregoire
  F.L., 439
Gregory
  Father, 375
  Rev. Father, 338
  Rev. Wm., 276
Grey
  Leonard, 253
  Rev. G.S., 430
Griedhander
  Rev.A., 67
Griffin
  Rev., 116, 154
  Rev. W.A., 255
  Rev. W.R., 123,
    215
  William R., 135,
    215, 256
Griffith
  H.W., 479
  Major J. Gwynne,
    479
  Master G., 437
  Master J., 437
  Miss P., 437
  Mr. and Mrs., 437
  Mr. F.A., 479
Griffiths
  Bar, 349
  Rev. Wm., 71
Groom
  Alfred, 73, 111
  Francis, 331
  Rhoda, 73
  Susannah, 111

Grosett
  A.J., 440
Grossett
  Dr., 480
  Mr. A., 480
Groves
  W.S., 291
Gruber
  E.C., 346
  Edmund Chas., 387
  Harold, 490
  J.W., 28
  Jasper William,
    360
  Joshua James, 28
  Lilian, 417
  Mr. J.W., 258, *360*
  Nellis Elise, 387
  Sarah Louise, 346
Gruchy
  C.L., 369
  C.L.C., 380, 439
  Colonel, 379
  F.G., 80
  Gladys May, 366
  L.G., 94, 115, 151,
    186
  L.S., 218
  Lieut.Col, 445
  Lt Col. L.G., 366
  S.G., 368, 380
Gugan
  Capt., 151
Guilsbro
  Mr. Lionel J.
    Hawthorn, 422
Gunter
  C.E., 291
  Constance, 456,
    457
  G.G., 386
  Godfrey George,
    291, 299
  Mr.G.G., 458
  Thomas, 155

H

H.E. the Governor,
  465
H.R.H. The Prince of
  Wales, 120

H.R.H. The Prince of
  Wales, 120
Haggard
  H. Rider, 355
Haggart
  Edmund Archibald
    Henderson, 416
  Mr., 312
  Mr. E.A.H., 341
Haigle
  A.C., 152
Hairs
  Ann, 352
  Ann Wooster, 282
  Elizabeth, 352
  Lawrence, 352
Hale
  Adelaide Agnes,
    479
  E. Harvey, 479
Hall
  Ann Catherine, 106
  C.S., 127
  C.W.H., 127
  Commander and
    Mrs., 183
  Eustace A., 188
  Geo., 47
  George, 60
  H.L., 441
  H.S., 464
  J.P., 236, 321
  J.Philip, 223
  James Philip, 99,
    248
  Jno. Jas., 21
  John H., 200
  John Herman, 9,
    115
  Louise, 332
  Mary Bevecca, 21
  Miss F.A., 382
  Miss M., 437
  Mr., 437
  Mr. and Mrs. A,
    421
  Mr. C. Vidal, 157
  Mrs., 116, 452
  Mrs. J.P., 272, 359,
    499
  N.W., 380, 439,
    464

Index

Index

Herrmann
John, 49
Hewett
W.A., 426
Hewitt
A., 258
C.W., 416
Hon. C.W., 430
Hicks
Abigail, 86
C.S., 457
Colonel, 86
G., 431
George, 87
Miss, 373
Hidalgo
Florence Leonora,
88
Juan, 88, 100
Juanita, 100
Higgins
Mr. Charles, 264
Hill
A.C., 164
J.W., 430
Hindle
Rev. and Mrs.
C.D., 260
Hire
(May) Agnes
Stewart, 252
Agnes, 252
H.F., 252, 301
Hirst
Mr., 295
Mr. A. Livingston,
422
His Excellency the
Acting Governor,
379
His Excellency the
Governor, 386, 424
His Grace the
Archbishop, 415,
435
His Honour the
Custos, 415
His Lordship Bishop
Collins, 338, 379,
445
His Lordship Bishop
de Carteret, 445

His Lordship Bishop
Gordon, 254
His Lordship Bishop
Joscelyne, 397
His Lordship the
Bishop, 81, 156
Hislop
Hazel Carrie, 324
S.H., 324
History of the Roman
Catholic Church,
360
Hitchins
Hilda Victoria, 401
Hobson
F.S., 366
George Frederick
Harman, 366
R., 411
Hocking
Hon. H.H., 161
Hodelin
E.F., 440
Hodges
Dr., 33
Hodgson
W., 9
Hoffmann
E.B., 485
Inez Lelia, 485
Hogarth
C. St. L., 284
C.P., 498
Cecil St. Leger,
498
Frederick P., 108
Hogg
Adela, 105, 122
Amy Constance,
105
C.C.A, 126
Catherine, 221
Colin, 58
Colin A.C., 221
Colin Alexander
Chisholm, 421
Collin A.C., 71
Elizabeth, 58
F.A., 358
Fanny, 331
Frank Seymour,
122

G.A., 501
Henry J., 27, 51
Henry J.F.H., 51
James, 493
Jane, 71
John Weir, 17
M.A., 358
Maise Lillian, 358
Mary Adeline, 501
Rev. A.G., 28
Robert, 331
Sophia, 27
Thomas, 126
Thomas A., 105,
122
William, 28
Holland
Mrs., 39
Hollar
A.C.J., 164, 172
Anna, 177, 192
Berty, 396
Ethel, 425
F.G., 439
F.L., 401
F.W., 297
Francis L., 442
Francis White, 298
Frank, 359
George, 426
Horatio, 359
James Wilberforce,
426
Janet Constance
(Nettie), 401,
442
John, 359
L.C., 259
Lucia, 377
Miss, 171, 244, 276
Mrs., 299
N.E.E., 284
Simeon, 11, 425,
426
Sydney, 425
Vida, 457
Vida L., 377
William, 426
Holle
Christopher, 350
Harriett Julia, 350
John George, 350

Index

Index

Index

George, 215
Ivy, 457
James Donald, 259
Justice, 170
L.E., 440
Rev.G.S., 203
William, 259
Lambert
Achilles, 215, 256
Lamont
John C., 67
Margaret, 67
William, 493
Lanaman
J.J., 159
Land
Amy Mary
Blanche, 271
Dr.J.C., 271
Landale
W.H., 430
Lane
Edward John, 14
Miss D., 227
Sibylia Elizabeth, 14
William Decimus, 81
Lang
Alexander
Morrison, 86
Lanibb
George S., 135
Lannaman
Geo., 20
J.L., 139
Nina, 377
W.T., 430
Zillah, 377, 493
Lannamann
Eliza, 357
Elsa, 458
George, 357
J.J., 147
Nina, 418
Zillah, 418, 457
Larson
Arnold, 354
Lascelles
Alfred S., 156
Herbert, 156
Lash

Rev. A.H., 387
Latreide
Rev. G. Birket, 94
Laubere
Mrs., 120
Lauder
Rebecca, 371
Lauderburn
Rev. Frederick C., 395
Lawes
Henry Emanuel, 17
Lawrence
H., 449
H.S., 441, 489
Mr. C.J., 120
Mr. S., 184
Mrs. Lillian, 329
Lawton
Miriam Louise, 334
Mr. S.S., 89, 272
S.S., 334
Lay
Armand, 69
Octavio Jose, 69
Layette
Miss, 157
Lazarous
Michael, 20
Lazarus
G.L., 440
Louis, 248
Michael, 21
Miriam, 248
Lea
Rev. G.H., 292
Rev. W.S., 430
Leach
J.C, 494
J.V., 335
K.T., 494
Mary Isabel, 335
Neal John, 494
Leahong
Miss, 365
Mr. and Mrs.
Thoms, 365
U.A., 440
Una, 457
Leake
Jessie, 379
V.M., 368

Vera, 379, 464
Leakong
Mr., 365
Lecesne
Amelia Louisa, 103
Dr. G.I., 361
James C., 178
James Celestic, 123
Lee
J., 474
W.R., 439
Lefranc
Catherine Matilda, 253
George Bolivar, 217
Izett E., 319
John, 217, 253
John Alexander, 79
Marie Helene, 319
Lehenan
Miss R., 437
Lehman
Rosita, 458
Lehong
Henry, 154
Mary Frances, 154
Lennox
Laura, 418
Leon
Mary, 457
Levatt
Edward, 101
Levett
D.L., 220
Viola, 220
Levien
F.S., 197
Sidney Lindo, 206
Levy
A.D.C., 59, 209
A.W., 162, 171
Alexander, 82
Alison, 490
Amos D.C., 70
Arthur, 152, 321, 385
Arthur Emanuel, 480
C.Hope, 166
C.I.L., 490
C.J., 217

Index

Mr. W.L., 237, 261, 298
Mrs., 116, 151, 166
Mrs. Daniel, 447
Mrs. H.Q., 451, 500
Mrs. J.H., 276, 374, 452, 500
N.L., 489
Nina, 373, 453
R.C., 441
Rachael, 429
S.G., 489
Samuel, 114
Sarah Gertrude, 243
Sylvia, 374, 453
V.C., 441
V.L., 441, 464, 488
Victoria, 385, 386
Violet, 359, 373, 417, 494
Violet C., 453, 454
W., 386, 411, 413
W.L., 342, 359, 373, 382, 407
Wilfred, 152
William Lionel, 287
Willie, 210
Willoughby George, 20
Levy & Co
  J.H., 262
Levy & Palache, 49
Levy and Palache, 53
Levy, Isaacs & Co, 132, 188, 249, 277
Lewin
  Raphael DaCosta, 88
Lewis
  A.H., 8
  C.C., 259
  Capt S., 477
  Clarisse, 202
  G.E., 441
  H., 437
  H.V., 440
  Henry Cerf, 200
  J. Daly, 386
  J.C., 230

James Daly, 384
John, 132
John Colston, 270
Julia Victoria, 200
L.L., 439
Lily, 436
Mary, 436
Miss, 437
Miss E., 260, 437
Miss O., 437
Mr., 139, 157
Mr. G., 437
Mr. J.C., 116, 147
Mr. J.D., 477
Mrs., 116, 164
Rev., 90
Rev. D.H., 58
W.E., 386
Walter H., 436
Leyden
  Master N., 438
  Miss O., 438
  Mr. and Mrs., 438
  Mr. I., 438
  Mrs., 437
  R.P., 209
  T.P., 386
Liddel
  Mr. and Mrs., 157
Lightbourne
  Arthur F., 135, 215, 255, 435
  Rev. A.F., 215, 430
Linden
  Mr. G.H., 438
Lindo
  A.B., 317
  A.J., 91
  Ada Mary, 204
  Alexander Joseph, 285, 334
  Alfred, 183
  Alfred A., 82
  Alfred Alexander, 180, 334
  Alfreda Alexandra, 183
  Amos, 151
  Ann, 496
  Archibald, 258
  Arthur, 180, 192, 334, 359, 378

Aug. A., 69
Augustus Rebecca, 151
Chas., 356
Constance, 324
E.A., 441, 488
E.C., 489
E.S., 321
Elsie, 464
Emma, 110
Esther, 336
Francis W., 377
Fred, 126
Frederick, 66, 241
Henry, 20, 110, 151, 180, 183, 258, 387
Henry Alexander, 204
Herbert, 285
Hon. A.J., 86
Irene Beatrice, 204, 387
Irene D'Aguilar, 334
James, 81
Jennie, 317
Keith, 317
Lena, 495
Marian, 334
Maryann, 91
Matilda, 59
Miss, 204
Mortimer, 356
Mr. and Mrs. A.I., 67
Mr. and Mrs. E.S., 359, 363, 373
Mr. E.S., 367
Mr. S.D., 137
Mr.and Mrs., 421
Mrs. E.S., 358, 467
Oscar Eric, 324
Percy, 349
Rebecca, 86
Rebecca Augusta, 82
Rebecca L., 180
Rev., 239
Rev. S.L., 145, 181, 198, 255, 495

Index

Lowcock
  Sophia, 269
Lowe
  A.B., 430
  Arthur, 31
  Ellen Rosalie, 31
Lubbock
  Sir John, 173
Luces
  Anna, 94
Lucie-Smith
  J.B., 76
  John Barkly, 416
  Sir John, 76
  W., 253
Lumb
  Dr., 265
  His Hon. Justice,
    189
  Judge, 172
Lumsden
  Rev. B.C., 430
Lunan
  Mr., 193
Lund
  Rev., 204
  Rev. Wm, 289
Lurch
  C.E., 382
  Miss R., 500
Lusitania, 494
Lyall
  James Charles
    Harold, 204
Lynch
  Caroline Lucille,
    271
  D.H.W., 441
  Dora, 96
  Doris, 453
  Doris W., 377
  E.B., 96
  E.L., 312
  Edward B., 271,
    320
  Edward Bancroft,
    48, 328
  Frances Elizabeth,
    10
  Frank F.M., 80
  John, 436
  John M., 288

Leila, 458, 494
M.K.M., 377
Mary Blizard
  Wilhelmina,
    320
Miss, 96
Mr., 203
Mr. and Mrs. Jno,
  452
Mr. C. F., 373
Mrs., 437
Rev. Fr., 254
Rev. R.B., 19
Revd., 18
Robert B., 10
Valentine, 454
Violet, 96
Lyon
  Amy, 457
  George, 183
  Horatio, 49
  Iris, 281
  J.J., 115, 148, 409,
    411
  L.C., 488
  L.L., 230
  Misses, 281
  Mr.J.J., 116
  Mrs., 116
  Mrs. A., 91
  Mrs. J.J., 283
  Nina, 281
  O.A., 439
  Rupert, 415
Lyons
  Amy Idalia, 267
  F., 92
  J.Jackson, 106
  John E., 90
  L.I., 267
  Misses, 157
  Mr. and Mrs., 157
  Mrs., 281
  T.B., 265

M

M. Solomon & Co,
  132
MaCalla
  Rev. B.A., 430
Macaulay

Sarah, 90
MacContel
  Mr., 249
MacCormick
  Rev. Father, 199
Macdermot
  Hugh C.P., 282
  Isabel, 282
  Mrs., 282
MacDermot
  J.H., 217, 260
  Rev. Canon, 282
  Rev. Canon
    H.M.F., 444
  Rev. H.C.P., 444
  Rev.H.M.F., 71
  Thomas H., 429
Macdermott
  Rev. Father, 338
MacDermott
  Rev. Canon, 354
  Rev. H.M.F., 66
Macdonald
  Betty, 464
  Dr. Angus, 379
  Hon. William, 28
  Hon. Wm., 405
  Miss, 404
  Ronald, 354
  Sibyl Emma, 23
  William, 14, 23
MacDonald
  G.S., 380
  Hon. William, 122
  Mr. and Mrs Jno.,
    157
  Olive, 122
  Rev.J.M., 430
MacDonnel
  Jane, 311
MacFarlane
  Granville G., 347
Macglashan
  H., 450
Macgregor
  Mr. and Mrs, 437
MacGregor
  Charles George,
    423
  J.M., 386
  Rev. C.G., 331
MacIntosh

Index

Manton
V.E., 163, 385
Mar
Mr. and Mrs., 365
March
Mr., 460
W.F., 458
Marchalleck
Beryl, 458
D., 490
David, 457
T.E.L., 377
T.I.K.L., 489
Marchelleck
Daniel, 418, 457
Miss Z., 198
Marconel Snr
C., 260
Marescaux
Major O.H.G., 477
O., 477
Oscar, 265
Marley
Robert, 336
Maroon, 107
Marsh
A.C., 464
B.C., 439
F.G., 380
Lena, 457, 458
Marshall
Joseph Baertra, 51
Marshalleck
B.S.L., 441
D., 441
Maud, 177
Miss T.E. K.L., 457
Zilla, 177
Marson
E.H., 440
Edith, 417
Ethel, 457
Rev. S.I., 431
Marston
Rev., 501
T., 382
Martin
A.C.L., 305, 431
Joseph Francis, 18
Mr. P.W., 157
Rev. James, 63
Rev. K.J., 352

S.A., 439
Martin & Spicer, 104
Martinez
Inez, 417, 457
L., 489
Martys
Gwendoline, 96
Violet, 96
Mason
John, 120
Mr., 119
Massa
Mr., 120
Massiah
Rev.J., 315
Masters
Mary, 373
Mather
Mr. Jm D., 260
Matherson
C.F., 243
O.Leo, 230
Matheson
H.I.C., 441
Matthews
Charles D., 271
Matthias
Col., 302
Maund
Rev. W., 115
Rev. W.J., 255
William J, 215
William J., 135,
256
Maunsell
Dr., 445
Dr. H.E., 139
Inspector, 157
Mrs., 116
Mawbey
J.H., 145
Jno. L., 47
Maxwell, 288
Alice, 13
Amberzene
Geraldine, 339
Cecily, 437
Charles H.C., 401
E.L., 331
Elizabeth, 82
Elizabeth
Christiana, 401

Eva, 437
George R.J., 75
George R.M., 314
George Robert, 401
Gertrude Johnson,
401
James D., 82
Jas., 13
Jeannie M Tarbet,
251
John, 331
Jos.A., 339
Major J.W., 331
Miss, 133
Miss E., 437
Mrs. John, 364
Rev. John, 251
Revd D.S., 13
Revd. James, 23
Stafford, 431
W.W., 284
May
Blanche, 491
D.Raynes, 383
Donald M., 89
Donald McFarlane,
315
Donald Raynes
McFarlane, 315
Dorothy Amanda,
419
George C., 502
George Cyril
McFarlane, 406
John, 491
Minna Constance,
502
Mr. and Mrs.
George, 419
Raynes Donald
MacFarlane,
491
Samuel, 443
Urcella, 446
Walter John, 387
Mayner
Dr., 157
Maynier
Adolph, 328
Mr. and Mrs Jose,
157
Mrs. Julia, 328

Index

McKiennon
  Rev. Campbell, 33
McKinnon
  L.F., 265
McLarty
  Reginald W., 216,
  256
McLaughlin
  E.N., 352
  Lillian Catherine
  Maud, 352
  Rev. H.H., 431
  Rev. R.B., 430
  Rev. R.H., 71, 430
McLean
  John, 43
  John W., 354
McMillan
  John, 75
McNeil Smith
  Julia Alexandria,
  203
  Rev.A., 203
McPhail
  D., 477
  John, 54, 93
  Mr.J.H., 477
McPherson
  Mary, 71
  Rev. R.J., 431, 496
McWhinney
  William W., 75
Mead
  Mr. R.S., 498
Mears
  Wil. Emerson, 256
  Wm. E., 216
Mehoney
  Mr. O., 260
Meikle
  Cora, 457
  Mr., 162
Mein
  I.R., 440
Melhade
  David, 39
  Ernestine, 39
Melhado
  A.D., 163
  Abraham, 89
  Chas., 473
  Cyril, 473

Miss Rebecca., 473
Nathaniel, 161
Phyllis, 473
Reginald, 89
Samuel, 268
Solomon, 161
Mellish
  C.E., 501
Melville
  E., 430
  Rev., 154
  Rev. Canon C., 431
  Rev. W., 67, 113
  Rev. Wm., 93
  William, 135
Mendes
  Henry John, 82
Mennell
  George Polack, 282
  J.W., 431
  John W., 282
  Mr. J.W., 222
  Zebulon E.L.
    (Billy), 474
Mercier
  Rev. Fredk, 107
Merrick-Watson
  Mr. R., 198
Merritt
  Mr. and Mrs., 168
Mesquita
  A.C., 139
  H., 139
Messado
  E.P., 430
  Eva, 457
  Olive, 458
Messiah
  Rev.J., 351
Mettam
  R., 435
  Rev. R., 359
Meyers
  Fred L., 41
  Rev. Joseph, 58
Michelin
  Edgar, 484
  Ennaline, 484
  Henry, 484
  Isabel Maud
    Henriet, 13
  Letitia, 322

Mr.and Mrs. C.A.,
  421
Olivia, 484
V.A., 291
Victor Alfred, 285
William, 13, 285,
  322
Middleton
  J.W., 285
  Mrs., 116
Miles
  Alfred Henry, 416
  Hon. A.H.., 477
  Lieut. W.H., 477
  Miss, 452
  R.D., 477
Milholland
  John, 157, 272
  Miss, 157
  Phyllis, 457
Milholland,
  Ashenheim and
  Stone
  Messrs., 450
Milk River, Bath, 127
Millar
  H.E., 440
  Robert, 320
Millener
  Mrs., 421
Miller
  Aggie, 213
  Amos, 498
  Dr., 181, 184, 220,
    227, 229, 244,
    356, 433, 452,
    474
  Dr. W.H., 140, 148,
    167, 175, 363
  Dr. Wm. Henry,
    230
  E.E.L., 440
  F.L., 500
  Fred O., 255
  Frederick O., 135
  Henry William,
    248
  J., 239, 411
  J. Alexander, 229
  J.A., 139, 148, 190,
    230, 248
  J.H., 496

Index

Index

Index

Orgil
  Jessie, 110
  Jone?, 110
  Lislie Isabel, 110
Orgill
  Harriet, 236
  John J., 116, 134
  Rev. T.T., 236
Ormesby and Son, 132
Ormsby
  Amabel Helen
    Katherina, 253
  B.S., 440
  Barbara, 417, 458,
    493
  Barbara S., 377
  C.M., 198
  Dr., 239, 243
  Dr.C.M., 127
  H., 377
  H.V., 440, 489
  J.C., 230
  J.D., 139, 248, 253,
    285
  Joseph Dussard,
    322
  Miss H., 357, 456
  Mr. J.D., 116
  N.E., 440
  Nellie, 285
  Rev., 109
  Rev. J.J.C., 253,
    286
  Rev. S.O., 269,
    278, 285, 289,
    312, 332, 358,
    491
  Stephen Oliver,
    236
Orrett
  Adelaide, 397
  Adolph, 478
  C., 148, 236
  Charles, 230, 468
  Charles A., 478
  Chas, 184
  Clara Isabel, 152
  Claude, 478
  E.G., 289, 373
  F.C., 440
  Frances Vergo, 346

George, 45, 207,
  267, 322
George Denniston,
  312, 322
Henry Macaulay,
  312
Hon. J.T., 199
Hon. John, 152
J.P., 368
John, 346, 373
Mr., 157
Mr. E.G., 185
Mrs. Eliza, 426
Rosa Eugenine
  Alice, 468
Thomas Hood, 154
William H., 478
Osborne
  Rachel, 379
Osmond
  C.E., 479
  Capt G.., 478
  Capt., 332
  Fleet Payr. Geo.,
    478
  G.W., 479
  Henry A.W., 332
O'Sullivan
  E.L., 369
Ottey
  B.L., 441
  L.L., 441
Oughton
  Iyler, 87
  Mrs. Thomas, 86
  Rev. Samuel, 87
  T.B., 265
Owen
  Helena Louise, 492
  Mr. and Mrs. L.E.,
    492
  Olive, 458
  Rev. Canon, 310
  Rev.Edward, 63

P

Packer
  A.H.C., 439
Page
  H.T., 435
  Henry T., 216, 256

Rev. Henry T., 215
Paine
  B.F., 218
Palache
  Eliza. *See* Isaacs
    Solomon
  Hon. J.T., 264
  J.T., 209, 384
  John T., 14
Palmer
  A.E., 465
  E.E., 440
  Mr. S.J., 380
  Rev. Edwin, 94
Panama Canal, 301,
  310, 311, 436, 442,
  458, 469
  Trip to, 388
Panama Disease, 470
Pankhurst
  Mrs., 419
  Mrs. Emmeline,
    425
  Sylvia, 425
Panter, 150
Panton
  Annie, 423
  Archdeacon, 201
  Charlotte, 201
  Ella, 126
  Lilian Daughtry,
    100
  Rev. D.B., 75, 100
  Rev. David Brooke,
    125, 126
  Richard Brook
    Morrison, 75
Panton. Jnr
  Geo.B., 349
Parcells
  Arthur, 45
  Miss, 323
Parker
  Fred., 436
  Mrs., 152
  P.T., 441, 466, 467,
    488
  Rev.M., 337
  V.E., 369, 489
Parkin
  Dr., 315
Parkins

552

Index

Dr., 67, 184
E.C., 198
Emma, 67
Hon. Dr., 170
Hon. Dr.J.C., 175
Hon. J.C., 102,
   174, 178
James Cecil, 161
Lieut J., 478
Mr. E., 478
Phillipps
   John H., 99
   Joselin L., 401
   Lucia Maria
      Frederica, 401
   Rudolph, 364
   William H., 364
   Zipporah, 99
Phillips
   Amy, 202
   August Leach
      DeLeon, 353
   C., 239
   C.B.H., 243
   C.L., 382, 434,
      465, 466
   Catherine, 353
   D.D., 431
   Dr. Charles M., 235
   E.L., 474
   Elizabeth
      Catherine, 358
   Emma, 104
   Emma Leslie, 235
   F.L., 104
   George, 358
   Hon. George L., 92
   Joseph, 353
   Mr. and Mrs., 373
   Mr. and Mrs. A.S.,
      437
   Mr. C. L., 428
   R.O., 439
   Rev. J.K., 431
   Rev. T.J.R., 430
   W.F.B., 430
Phillmore
   Mr. Justice, 418
Phillpots
   Mrs., 261
Phillpotts
   Mrs., 465

Phillps
   Joseph, 37
Philpotts
   Mrs., 415
Pickwick
   Mr. W.S., 421
Picot
   Charles Henry, 346
   Miss J.B.C., 214
   Mr., 255
   Rev. T., 215
   Thomas R., 216,
      256
Pierce
   Major Robert, 479
   Rev. Edward., 479
Pike
   Rev., 386
   Rev. E.V., 397
Pinnock
   Col., 264
   Thomas Ricker, 89
Pinto
   Julia, 79
   Moses, 79
Piper
   Jospeh Allen, 81
Pitt
   Edward A., 436
Plant
   H.A., 441, 446, 489
   William Henry,
      275
Plunkett
   John Isaac, 54
Plymouth Brethren,
   220
Pneumatic typewriter,
   189
Polack
   Jonas, 111
   Mary, 401
   Myer, 111
   Myre, 401
Pomier
   Mrs., 381
Ponsonby
   Inspector, 144
Poole
   Charles B., 63
   Charles Baker, 349

Charles Frederick,
   268
Charles P., 63
Mary Louisa, 349
Mr. C.A., 386
Mr. E.A., 269
Sarah, 386
Popham
   Arhur Ewart Hugh,
      387
Port Maria, 154
Porter
   Hon. N., 161
   Hon. Neal, 166
   James T., 386
   Margaret Ann, 386
   Miss E.M., 198
   Rev. Thomas, 58,
      69
   Wm. Coloridge,
      258
Post Cards, 313
Post Office, 131
Potter
   Major, 388
Powell
   F.C., 259
   I.L., 440
   K.H., 218
   Kathleen, 177, 192
   Miss H.L., 454
   Miss K.H., 198,
      214
Power
   Ambrose, 346
   Mrs., 305
Pratt
   Edward, 115
   Edwd., 139
   F.W.D., 479
   G., 139
   Mr., 229
   Mr. E., 479
   Mrs., 116, 260
   Rev. W., 207, 221,
      277, 379, 429
   Rev. William, 113
   Victor, 139
Prawl
   William B., 330
   Zipporah Beatrice
      Maud, 330

Index

Randall
  Marguerite, 379
  Rev. J., 379
Randell
  Miss, 437
Rankin
  George, 75
  Georgie, 75
Ratigan
  Luke, 71
  Mary Elizabeth, 71
Rattigan
  Ann, 307
  Jessie Ann, 379
  L.A., 307, 415
  Luke, 66, 341
  Luke Augustus,
    341
  M., 258
  M.A., 260, 378
  Miriam, 417
  Miss M., 418
  Mr. L.A., 307, 432
  Mrs., 307
  Winifred, 378, 418
Rattray
  J.L., 305
Raw
  Robert, 11
Rebeiro
  Mrs., 258, 421
  Rebecca Nunes,
    126
  T.Nunes, 257
Redcam
  Tom, 166, 169,
    195, 444
Redmond
  John, 468
Redock
  Rev. Father, 333,
    338
Redpath
  C.W., 344, 352
  Jospehine, 344
Reece
  Anne, 330
  C.L., 205, 496
  Charles, 330
  Elizabeth Mary,
    372
  I. Richard, 371, 397

I.R., 205
Isaac, 372
Isaac Richard, 99,
  372
J.R., 148
J.Richard, 491
L., 411
Master, 330
Mr., 176
Mr. and Mrs. I.R.,
  260
Mr. and Mrs.I.R.,
  330
Mr. I.R., 330
Mr. Justice, 165
Mrs., 116
R.H., 330
Vanda, 330
Vanda Moore, 397
Reed
  F.E., 445
Reeves
  Rev. John, 39
  Rev. W., 8
  W., 9
Regg
  F.E., 164
Reid
  Ann E., 165
  B. DeC., 428, 437
  C.C.A., 260
  Cecil Alexander,
    269
  F.L., 440, 490
  G.L., 449
  G.Lowe, 80
  George, 269
  Gladys, 417, 457
  H.D.A., 90
  H.L., 369
  Helen, 379
  Henry D.A., 80
  Ivy Ethlin, 371
  J.Bolton, 371
  James Hally, 111
  W.O., 218
Renado
  Ruby, 458
Rennalls
  Agnes Eliza, 85
  Samuel, 85
Rennie

A.B., 439
Report of Jamaica
  Schools
  Commission, 387
Rerrie. See Townend,
  Mrs Arthur
  A.B., 139, 147,
    230, 243, 306,
    411
  A.W., 409
  Eliza, 499
  Errol S.E., 479
  Hon. Alex., 479
  Hon. Alexander,
    499
  Leslie, 479
  Mr. A.B., 116, 198
  Mr. C.A., 479
  Mr. R.P., 479
  Mr. W.H., 421
Rest Pen, 47, 59
Retreat
  Brown's Town, 176
Reuben
  S.R., 324
Reynado
  Angele, 457
Reynolds
  Caleb, 135, 160,
    190, 216, 255,
    435
  Charles R.S., 480
  D., 382
  Mary Annie, 485
  Misses, 468
  Rev., 185, 187
  Rev. C., 430, 463
  Rev. Caleb, 154,
    159, 192, 205,
    216, 254, 260,
    268, 470, 485
  Rev. D.J., 93
Rhodes
  Cecil John, 315
Rhodes Scholarship,
  294
Rhodon
  F.L., 148
Richards
  Boy, 107
  Mr. W., 365
  T., 382

Index

Findlater, 192, 199
Frank, 345
Harold, 444
Harold L., 485
Hon. Findlater,
    199, 272
Joseph, 395
L.L., 400
Leicester L., 360
Lena Maude
    Forbes, 345
Mr. Justice, 38
Mr. L., 227
Rosada
    F.A., 172
Rosado
    T.A., 163
Rose
    J.P.M., 262
    Lucy, 57
    William Bromley,
        57
Ross
    Ann Eliza, 127
    Richard, 10
    William, 62
Rothenberg
    Hilda, 375
    Mrs. Rachel, 375
Rothnie
    Rev. D.A., 430
Rouse
    Mabel, 379
Rowbotham
    Corporal, 116
Rowbottom
    J.W., 9
Rowe
    C.D., 448
    Ven. Arch., 84
Rowle
    Rev. Father, 491
Roxburgh
    Adam, 108, 293,
        306, 407, 496
    Archibald, 31, 51
    Catherine Gibson,
        297
    E.M., 369
    Florence, 187
    Francis Thomas,
        297

Hon. T.L., 496
Julia C.Mais, 63
K.L., 496
Katherine Julia,
    293
Kenneth Laurence,
    293
Mr., 402, 405
Mr. A., 411
Mr. T.A., 497
T. Laurence, 293
T.F., 114
Thomas, 11
Thomas Francis,
    286
Royal Academy of
    Music, 456, 493
    Exam Results, 417
Royal College of
    Music, 456, 493
Royal Drawing
    Society's
    Examination, 468
Royes
    Charles John, 313
    Hon. Chas. John,
        496
    Margaret Taylor,
        496
    Wesley, 248
Rubie
    H.P., 356
    M.P., 439
Ruble
    H.P., 496
Ruggles
    Rev. Vernon, 492
Rundall
    Rev.J.E., 495
Russel
    Edna, 464
Russell
    James, 145
    Julia, 121
    Logan, 121
    Rev. J.P., 45
    Rev. Thos. P., 254
    Robert, 121
    T.P., 139
    Thomas Fraser, 400
    Thomas P., 135,
        216, 256

Thomas Porter, 400
Russian Japanese War,
    292
Rutty
    E., 418
    Ellie, 457
    Ernest W., 322
    F.S., 320
    Frank, 337
    Frank S., 378
    Frank Swire, 275
    Joseph W., 340
    Joseph Waterhouse,
        1
    Mr., 227
    Mr. W. H., 21
    Rev.W.H., 222
    W.H., 5
    Willard Dorian,
        322
    Winifred, 322
Ruttys
    Misses, 227
Ryan
    Rev.J., 58
Ryley
    Mr. and Mrs, 420
    Mr. and Mrs., 421

S

Sachell
    Elizabeth, 81
Sadler
    Edward John, 74
    Ella Jane, 74
    Mr. E.J., 264
Sailman
    J.M., 51
    Jane, 51
    M., 258
Sainson
    Paul C., 85
Saint Ann High
    School, 387
Sale
    A.M.B., 441
Salmon
    Chas. S, 496
    Dr.A.J., 496
    Elizabeth Frances,
        19

Index

S.L., 440, 449
T.B., 251, 285, 444
Thomas B., 355
Thomas Beecher, 139
Scudamore
  Beryl, 417
  C.E., 114
  C.G., 501
  Florence, 417
  Mary, 418
  Master R., 422
  Misses, 422
  Mr. and Mrs G.E., 422
  Mr. S., 422
  W.S.K., 488
  William Edward, 492
Scurfield
  Rev., 216, 243
Seaton
  Mr., 119
Segre
  John Swaby, 219
  L.E., 369
  M.A., 439
  Mary Laura, 219
  Mr. B.H., 422
  Ralph, 33
Segree
  A., 500
Seidelin
  Dr., 399
  Dr. Harold, 426
Seivright
  W.McK., 490
Seligman
  Jesse, 361
Seller
  Alice Maud, 334
  Mr. and Mrs. Peter, 334
Senior
  B.M., 18
  Bernard M., 31, 45
  Margaret, 45
  Mary Louisa, 18
Sergeant
  Revd. George, 19
Sewell
  Capt. H., 478

Hon Henry, 219, 320
Hon. H., 478
Hon. Henry, 305
Mr., 303
Mr. A., 298
William, 5
Sewright
  E.McK., 441
Sfassiah
  Rev. J., 277
Shakespeare, 188
Sharp
  Edward, 28
  F.G., 163, 172
  Frances Maria, 28
  James Henry, 397
  L.C., 260
  Lieut. C., 478
  Miss F., 437
  Mr. and Mrs., 421
  Mr. H.S., 184
  Mr. T., 420
  Mr. T.H., 478
  W.L. Thornton, 437
Sharpe
  Aimee Isabelle, 99
  Caroline Isabella, 292
  E.S., 496
  F.G., 217
  H.F., 496
  Herbert F.R., 235
  J.C., 430
  Mrs. F.J., 293
  Rev. F.H., 34, 86, 99, 235, 292
  Rev. H., 348
  Rev. Herbert, 346
  Rev.F.A., 179
  Rev.H.F., 499
  Ven. Archdeacon, 346
Shaw
  Bernard, 351
  J.A., 441
  L., 258
  Samuel Augustus, 31
  T.A.D., 356
  Wm., 139

Shearer
  Alexander, 109
  Margaret Ann, 109
Shelton
  F.O., 441
Sherlock
  A.M., 434
  C.M., 206, 268, 432, 469
  Capt. J.E., 355
  Charles, 58
  Charles M, 135
  Charles McClelland, 320
  Dr., 434
  F.H., 499
  Frances, 426
  Frances Reid, 499
  H.T., 358
  Hannah, 355
  J.E., 358
  J.T., 355
  Mary, 358
  Mary Ann, 432
  Mrs. C.M., 432
  P.M., 490
  Rev. R.M., 430
  Rev. T.M., 431, 499
  Sydney Matilda, 268
  T.M., 255
  Terence M., 215, 435
  Theodore, 499
  Thos., 426
  W.M., 434
Shield
  Professor, 261
Shin San
  Mr., 365
Ships Sailing, 101
Shirland
  Edith, 359
  Gertrude, 359
Shirley
  A.E.B., 380
  Helen, 456, 457
Shore
  J., 430
Shrimpton

Index

Index

Index

John Noel, 415
Miss, 420
Monica, 452
Mr., 210
Mr. and Mrs. J.A.,
452
Mr. F.S., 422
Mr. J.A., 367
Mr.C.R., 452
Mrs. and Miss, 359
Mrs. J.A., 363
Rev. A.N., 430,
445
Rev. Adam, 37
Revd. R.A., 25
Viola, 494
Thomson & Co
J.B., 262
Thornton
E.Leslie, 261
Thourens
Rev. St., 120
Thwaites
Helen, 464
W.A., 333
Tibbals
Rev. C.A., 62
Tice
Christopher H., 436
Tie Ten Quee
Mr. and Mrs., 365
Tilley
Amy, 202
Tillman
Mr. J., 379
Tingle
Amanda, 353
James Randolph,
353
Titanic
Passenger
Survivors, 375
Terrible Diaster,
373
Todd
Alexander Evans,
63
Amy Louisa, 25
Ann Elizabeth, 63
Arthur Rochfort,
499
David, 61

Dr., 236
Eliza (Cissie), 204
Frederick Lamont,
272
Louisa, 99
Marguerite, 457
Mary Annette, 350
Mr., 227
Richard, 312
Richard Utten, 378
U.T., 204, 499
Utten T., 25, 99,
378, 423
Utten Thomas, 22,
24, 272, 287,
350
W.P., 96
William, 312
Todd, Jnr
U.T., 46, 47
Utten T., 28
Todd.
Utten, 347
Tomlinson
A.E., 163, 354
A.E.O., 439
Toone
Mr., 157
Mr. J.W., 120
Topper
Frederick Timothy
Sanftleben, 497
Touzalin
Stephen, 17
Townend
A., 243
Arthur, 248, 409,
499
Arthur E., 446
Mary Alice
Stewart, 285
MaryArthur, 285
Miss, 420
Mr. Arthur, 399
Mrs. Arthur nee
Rerrie, 399
Stephanie Maud,
499
W.Vincent, 494
Townend Jr.
Vincent William,
350

Townsend
A.M., 377
Alice, 201
Alice M., 198
Arthur, 357, 411
Beatrice, 357
E., 339
Miss, 227, 304,
373, 457
W., 339
Trafford
Mrs., 198
Train, 119
Trelawny Girl's
School. *See*
Westwood High
School
Trelawny Girls'
School, 201
Trench
C. Lepoer, 320
Charles Lepaer,
278
Daniel Power, 351
Dutton, 275, 351,
423
Frances Charlotte,
351
Gladys, 423
J., 375
J.S., 115, 278, 297
Josephine
Elizabeth, 375
L.A., 377
Lizzie Louise, 297
Maxwell D., 350
Miss L., 456
Mr., 119
Mr. J..S., 116
Mrs., 116
Trewick
R.L., 496
W.E.L., 415, 465
Trinity College
Musical
Examination, 204
Tucker, 439
David Alexander,
243
Eileen, 359, 454
Mr., 220
Mr. D.A., 167, 236

Index

Index

Whittingham
Elmos Japhat, 297
J.W., 297
Wigan
A.E., 431
Wightman
Jane Elizabeth, 70
Wildams
Rev. Joseph, 58
Wilde
Rev. F.P., 431
Wilkie
Louise Matilda,
292
Robert, 292
Wilkins
Mr. E., 319
Wilkinson
Ann Eliza, 4
William
G.L., 449
James Rowland,
416
Rev. W.J., 276
Rev.P., 81
Rev.W.J., 397
Williams
A.N., 431
Alice Augustus
Swinhoe, 283
B.W., 478
C.L.G., 441
Charles H.P., 28
Edith, 464
Elizabeth, 103
G.E., 377
Henry, 103
Hon. J.R., 379, 478
J.H., 430
John, 105, 305
L.G., 441
M.E., 441
Mary, 103
Miss, 275
Mr., 437
Mrs., 437
R.C., 440
R.G., 380
Rev. E.P., 370
Rev. Jos., 63
Rev. Joseph, 63
Rev. W., 215

Rev. W.H., 485
Rev. W.J., 255,
342, 432, 495
Rev.J.W., 155
Rev.S.F., 100
V.G., 440
William J., 135,
216, 256, 435
Wm Rowe, 283
Willis
Alex., 42
Alexander, 32
Mary Cathleen, 358
Milborgh, 32
Robert, 358
Willky
M., 218
Wilmot
H.J., 386, 407
Wilson
Dr., 356, 364, 452
Dr. W.E., 176, 420,
452, 498
Edna, 437
Ernest, 437
Herbert Joseph,
125
Ismay, 464
John, 114
Lena, 457
Mr. and Mrs. H.C.,
157
Mr. W.E., 162
Nathaniel, 125
Olive, 437
R.E., 488
Wilbert Edward,
421
Wingate
Mrs. and 3
children, 116
Winn
C.A., 436
Charlotte, 338
Margaret F.R., 61
Rev. C.A., 61, 283
Rev. Charles
Augustus, 356
Rev.Chas
Augustus, 338
Zipporah Fryer,
436

Winsor
R.J., 104
Wint
D.T., 474
D.Theo, 380, 402
Mr., 376, 380, 386,
394
Winter
Mrs., 157
Wolfe
Bollvar, 157
David, 57, 277
Ellis, 57, 67, 146,
262, 277, 291
Ellis Bollivar, 63
Emily, 291
James B., 61
Louisa, 67
Mr. and Mrs. Ellis,
157
Mrs. Ellis, 263
Wollett
Rev.J.S., 82
Wolmer's, 93
Wolmer's Girls
School, 438
Wolmer's Girls'
School, 267
Wolmers, 4
Wolmer's Free School,
54
Wolmer's School, 464
Prize Giving, 379
Wolverston
Mr., 444
Wong San Kook
Mr., 365
Wongeam
Mr. E., 365
Wood
G.W., 71
J.J., 71
John Jarrett, 79
Judith Ophelia, 71
Revd. W.J., 25
Wookey
A.J., 217
Rev., 221
Rev. C.A., 163
Wooler
Edmund Upton,
476

Index

ABOUT THE AUTHOR

The compiler was born in Brown's Town, St. Ann, Jamaica. She went to St. Hilda's in Brown's Town and St. Andrew's High School for Girls in Kingston until she left for Canada where she attended Macdonald College of McGill University, 1959-1963. She studied nutrition at Cornell University attaining a Masters in 1965 and a Ph.D. in 1968. She became a U.S. citizen in 1974. After teaching and researching in human nutrition at Washington State University, Pullman, Washington for thirty-five years, she retired to Dunnellon, Florida where she now resides. Her hobby has been genealogy for twenty-three years and besides the books she has compiled, "Jamaican Ancestry: How to Find Out More" and "Index to Early Wills of Jamaica" she maintains the World Gen Web Jamaica site at http://www.rootsweb.com/~jamwgw/index.htm

9 780788 444975